MAJOR FIGURES OF
NINETEENTH-CENTURY
AUSTRIAN LITERATURE

Studies in Austrian Literature, Culture and Thought

MAJOR FIGURES
OF
NINETEENTH-CENTURY
AUSTRIAN LITERATURE

Edited and with an Introduction

by

Donald G. Daviau

ARIADNE PRESS
Riverside, California

Ariadne Press would like to express its appreciation to the Austrian Cultural Institute, New York and the Bundeskanzleramt – Sektion Kunst, Vienna for their assistance in publishing this book.

Library of Congress Cataloging-in-Publication Data

Major figures of nineteenth-century Austrian literature / edited and with an introduction by Doanld G. Daviau.
       p.   cm. -- (Studies in Austrian literature, culture, and thought)
    Includes bibliographical references and index.
    ISBN 1-57241-047-7
    1. Austrian literature--19th century--History and criticism. 2. Authors, Austrian--19th century--Biography. I. Daviau, Donald G. II. Series
PT3817.M345   1998
830.9'9436--dc21
[b]   97-43722
                                  CIP

Art Director and Designer: George McGinnis

Contents

Preface

Major Figures of Nineteenth-Century Austrian Literature is the fifth volume in the planned seven-volume series which is intended to present an overview of nineteenth- and twentieth-century Austrian literature through portrayals of the most representative authors. Each volume contains essays on fifteen authors from a particular time period, each written by a specialist and including bibliographies of primary works in German, of translations into English, and of secondary works in English and German. An Introduction provides an overview of the political and cultural situation to serve as a general background for the individual contributions. The previous volumes which have been published to date include: *Major Figures of Contemporary Austrian Literature, Major Figures of Modern Austrian Literature, Major Figures of Austrian Literature—The Interwar Years 1918-1938,* and *Major Figures of Austrian Turn-of-the-Century Literature.*

The nineteenth century offers a rich, complex panorama, which traces the decline of Austria from a multinational Monarchy of some fifty million people around 1800 to a small Republic of approximately eight million in 1918. The reasons for this drastic transformation are discussed in the Introduction, which details the policies of the Habsburg emperors from Joseph II to Franz Joseph I, who ascended the throne in 1848 and served until his death in 1916, a term longer than that of any other monarch. Franz II (after 1806 Franz I) and his Chancellor Metternich engaged in a concerted effort to stifle progress in Austria and restore an absolutist government, a benevolent despotism— today we would say dictatorship— based on feudal principles of strict order and hierarchy. Serving the state became the highest good, given a higher priority than the welfare of the citizens. To carry out Habsburg policies and to enforce the principle of absolutism became the mission of Metternich, who was charged with maintaining the status quo and preventing any possibility of radical change or revolution as had been witnessed in France in 1789. This repressive regime, which used strict censorship and police-state methods to suppress free speech and to stifle the possibility of any uprisings, retarded progress in Austria, causing the country to fall behind the development of Germany and the rest of Europe.

Austria's relationship to Germany remained problematical throughout these two centuries, and the Introduction traces the manner in which the two countries began to develop differently and to diverge politically, culturally, and economically. At the beginning of the nineteenth century Austria was politically stronger than fragmented Germany, and Franz II wore the crown of the Holy Roman Empire, which loosely bound the two countries together. Metternich, possibly the most astute politician and diplomat of his time, served as Chairman of the Deutscher Bund, a position which gave him considerable presence in German affairs. But Germany, while strict enough in retarding efforts to gain a constitutional government and greater freedom of expression, was not as politically regressive as Austria. Germany was much more progressive, looking forward, not back, more receptive to economic growth, to the rise of industrialization, and to the expansion of scientific development than Austria, which Franz would have preferred to keep an agricultural society. Germany embraced the new ideas of the time and advanced, while the Habsburg emperors, one after the other fearing change, tried to turn back the clock of history or at least to halt its progress. Consequently Germany rapidly grew stronger, while the Habsburgs, trying to maintain an outmoded form of government, weakened Austria. Ironically, the very measures employed to guarantee the longevity of Habsburg rule caused its demise.

The revolution of 1848 brought the constitutional reforms that the intelligentsia had been clamoring for in Germany, while in Austria the new young emperor Franz Joseph I, acting on the bad advice of his backward-looking advisors, embarked on a course that repeated the same failed policies of his predecessors. The second half of the nineteenth century in Germany made a radical break with the past, while in Austria it virtually mirrored the first half, until the forces at the end of the century combined to overcome the opposition of the government and the Catholic Church and moved the country forward into the twentieth century. While Bismarck created a unified German state, spurring Germany's economic growth and creating a sense of national consciousness, Franz Joseph frittered away his power and resources in the vain attempt to maintain the

status quo. The country did grow, but slowly and against heavy opposition, while the sense of dissatisfaction escalated both at home and in the
member states of the monarchy which clamored for a greater voice in
running their own countries. The differences grew to the point that
Bismarck severed all political connections with Austria in 1867 to keep
Austria from having any further say in German affairs. The culmination
came for Austria after World War I, when at the peace negotiations in
1918 the decision was made to end the multinational Habsburg Monarchy
and grant all of the member states self-determination.

Against this historical background the attempt has been made to put
the relationship of Austrian and German literature into a new and hopefully more accurate perspective. This relationship has long been problematized by Austrian as well as German literary historians, who refuse to
accept the idea of an autonomous Austrian literature and continue to insist
that everything written in German is German literature. It is my stand-
point that the national identification of an author is not solely a matter of
the language used, but depends first and foremost on the subject matter.
A writer who mirrors the life of a specific nation belongs to the literary
tradition of that country. For that reason American, Australian, Canadian,
and Irish literatures are all universally recognized as being independent of
English literature. Absolutely no scholar would make the claim that everything written in English is English literature. Only in the unique case of
Austria do literary historians steadfastly ignore the evidence and persist in
falsely presenting Austrian literature as part of the German tradition.
Austrian literature can be rightly called a German-language literature, but
it cannot justifiably be characterized simply as German literature. The fact
of being a literature written in German does not preclude the Austrian
literary tradition from having its own independent identity.

The Introduction traces the literary development of Austria to show
how it proceeded on its own course, cognizant of conditions and circumstances in Germany but focused on subject matter portraying the conditions and circumstances of life in Austria. A number of writers felt
strongly that they were Austrian, not German writers. Yet, curiously, even
when Austria was so much more powerful than Germany politically up to
1848, it failed to assert itself culturally and has never really done so in an
organized way and with conviction because Austria has never yet developed
a strong sense of national consciousness.

Because of the importance of this issue of national identity—"Is there
an Austrian literature?" and "What is Austrian literature?" remain the

"prize questions" of Austrian literary history—the authors of the individual essays were asked to address the issue of how strongly their particular writer felt about his or her Austrian identity. The prime case is Grillparzer, who emphatically proclaimed that he was an Austrian and not a German author.

The contributors were also asked to feature the role of women both in terms of their own literary careers, as in the case of Karoline Pichler and Betty Paoli, and also in the manner in which they are portrayed in the literature. It may prove surprising to see how many strong, independent women are to be found in the predominantly male literature written in the context of the paternalistic system of the time.

One complex matter that is touched upon without being resolved, because it goes far beyond the scope of this book, concerns the relationship of Austria—primarily Vienna—to the member states of the monarchy. Austrian literary history has always been concerned almost exclusively with the literature written in German in Vienna or in Austria proper, not with literatures in the languages of other member states of the monarchy. If little or no national consciousness existed within Austria, there was also none throughout the various lands and territories, at least none for the Austrian Monarchy. While the Germans in Austria were willing to go to war in 1867 to preserve their affiliation with Germany, the member states, which were required to use German as the language of officialdom, lacked the same sense of urgency to maintain such ties, much preferring to gain their own independence, including the use of their own language in the army, in the courts, in schools, and in government. Because of the language problem, no sense of unity was ever established in terms of a common literature or culture. Those writers who were oriented toward German-speaking culture, most of them Jews from German-speaking cities in their own lands, moved to Vienna for their education and literary career. The majority, however, remained at home, where, inspired by Austrian and German culture, they worked to develop something similar in their own language in their own countries. For this reason, even without the Austrian bureaucratic mismanagement, the monarchy would have foundered at some point in time, even if Woodrow Wilson had not insisted on dismantling it at the peace negotiations following World War I.

The Austrian nineteenth century is a rich, complex, and fascinating literary and cultural period. It is not only important in its own terms, but it is also crucially important for understanding the developments of the twentieth century leading up to World War II. It is hoped that the following Introduction and the individual essays will make clear the course that steered Austria toward disaster but that ultimately helped not only the country, but also the literature and culture to emerge stronger than ever.

Donald G. Daviau

Acknowledgments

First and foremost I wish to express my appreciation to my colleagues who contributed the individual essays to this book. In addition, I am grateful to the Austrian Cultural Institute, New York, to Ministerialrat Dr. Wolfgang Unger of the Bundeskanzleramt—Sektion Kunst, Vienna, and to the Research Committee of the University of California, Riverside for their support of this volume. Finally, my sincere thanks go, as always, to my colleagues Beth Bjorklund, Harvey I. Dunkle, Jorun B. Johns, and Richard H. Lawson for reading the manuscript and for their valuable suggestions.

Introduction

Historical Background from 1789 to 1848

Austria has been referred to as a laboratory in miniature for world history, and the events of the nineteenth century serve as a good example of this saying. As a powerful, influential, multinational realm (*Vielvölkerstaat*) strategically situated between east and west, north and south, Austria was well positioned geographically to act as a bridge between countries, as it still does today, and was strong enough to play a leadership role in Europe. Its failure to achieve its full potential serves as a political parable for governments that refuse to respect the basic law of life: change. The natural world remains in a constant state of flux, and accordingly states as well as people must continuously develop with it—or have time pass them by. Under the Habsburgs Austria enjoyed growth and expansion and flourished up to the late eighteenth century. The change of fortune began with Empress Maria Theresia (1717-1780), who was forced to cede Silesia to Germany after the Seven Years' War (1756-1763), and continued under Joseph II (1741-1790), who ruled from 1765 to 1777, first as co-regent with his mother and then alone until his death in 1790. The problems continued throughout the entire nineteenth century until the end of the Monarchy in 1918. Joseph II and the following Habsburg rulers turned reactionary and, ignoring the many signals for change in all other European countries, tried to cling to the past rather than continuing to move forward. Ironically, the attempt to preserve Habsburg rule by maintaining the feudal system of absolute despotism that prevailed prior to the French Revolution of 1789 produced the opposite result of hastening its demise. The course of the House of Habsburg, which had successfully ruled Austria since 1273, proceeded in a straight line from the high point of power and influence under Joseph II, to its lowest point, the abolition of the Monarchy and the establishment of the First Austrian Republic in November 1918.

In historical terms the nineteenth century must be considered a longer than normal period, a continuum stretching from the French Revolution of 1789 to the end of World War I. This time span is divided by the revolution of 1848 into two unequal parts that essentially repeat the same political scenario with only slight variations. Awakened by the ideas of the Enlightenment and spurred on by the success of the French Revolution, the people throughout Europe sought freedom of expression and the introduction of democratic principles through more representative government. At the same time the member nations of the Monarchy—never comfortable with or reconciled to Habsburg rule—sought the same ideals in the form of greater self-determination.

The parallellism of the two halves of the nineteenth century reflects the intransigence of the ruling house, which totally opposed change, locked in struggle with the equally unbending, unstoppable forces of progress. Consider these virtually identical developments:

(1) the radical transformation of human and political values by the Enlightenment and the French Revolution at the end of the eighteenth century; the transformation of all values by industrialization, scientific developments, and cultural innovations at the end of the nineteenth century.

(2) The struggle of the intellectuals and writers for freedom of expression and for the abolition of censorship under Franz II(I) and Metternich; the same struggle under Franz Joseph I.

(3) The demand of the people for greater representation in government under Franz II(I); the same demand under Emperor Franz Joseph I, who is forced into making some concessions such as granting voting rights to more citizens.

(4) The use of Metternich's diplomatic skills to maintain Austria's role in Germany; Franz Joseph I goes to war against Germany in 1866 to prevent the severance of political ties but is defeated, resulting in the complete loss of further Austrian influence.

(5) The pressure brought by member nations of the multinational realm for greater political autonomy, including the right to use their own language instead of German in official agencies like schools, courts, and bureaucratic offices; increased pressure on Franz Joseph as the nationalistic impulse grows in intensity and strength until he is forced to concede these autonomous rights to Hungary in 1867 with the establishment of the Dual Monarchy, which the Emperor of Austria also rules as the King of Hungary. The other lands and territories

clamor for equal treatment with respect to language and right of self-determination.

(6) The general dissatisfaction in Austria leads to the revolution of 1848, the driving out of Metternich, and the installation of a new emperor—Franz Joseph I—on the throne; the end of World War I in 1918 leads to the dissolution of the Monarchy and the founding of the First Republic.

At the beginning of the reign of Joseph II matters looked promising, for this ambitious, intelligent, and well-intentioned monarch desired the creation of a state that would guarantee peace for his realm and well-being for all citizens. However, the good intentions of this enlightened ruler were undermined by his distinctly unenlightened insistence on preserving a feudal government system of absolute despotism. His uncompromising requirement that he rule as a benevolent dictator put him out of phase with a world caught up in the process of radical transformation under the impact of the liberal thinking of the Enlightenment and the irrevocable changes—particularly ideas of freedom, equality, and human rights—brought about by the Pandora's box of the French Revolution in 1789. Once the lower classes had experienced even the smallest taste of freedom and equality, there was no possibility of ever returning the world to its previous system of absolutism. The Enlightenment had brought not only a new understanding of human potential, but also a heightened regard for the value of all human beings and the desirability of allowing the full development of each individual. With time, the gulf between Joseph's reactionary form of government and the new, liberal ideas embraced by the intellectuals and writers could only widen, arousing a spirit of dissatisfaction that grew eventually into outspoken protest in the charged post-revolution atmosphere. The continuation of this same misguided ruling policy of absolutism by Joseph's successors—each having this principle handed down as a legacy—culminated ultimately in the March revolution of 1848 in Austria.

Joseph II serves as a classic example of one who wants only the good and who for the most part achieves the opposite effect. He worked for the benefit of his people, but he adamantly rejected the idea of their participating in deciding their own fate. He wanted only their gratitude which they could express by their loyalty. He had chafed under the control of his mother, Maria Theresia, with whose cautious policies he had often disagreed, and when he became sole regent in 1777, he introduced ambitious reforms of government, of the judicial and tax systems, and of social hygiene. One of his important measures with long-lasting effects not only abolished serfdom (*Leibeigenschaft*), a practice whereby a poor person could remain a virtual slave on a farm for life, but also—significantly—included a provision prohibiting nobles from buying back the land granted to the peasants. Another, perhaps his greatest achievement judged in humanistic and humane terms, was his measure on behalf of religious tolerance, the "tolerance edict" (*Toleranzpatent*) of 1781, which proclaimed all religions equal and released Jews from the ghettos. Although not granted full equality, Jews were allowed to work and, most importantly, go to school. While he accepted the notion of religious equality and the right of freedom of worship, at the same time Joseph worked to keep the Catholic Church subordinate to the state, among other things secularizing education. During Joseph's reign Austria reached its greatest geographical expansion since the time of Charles V when Spain belonged to the empire, stretching from the Atlantic (today's Belgium) to Poland (Galicia), to northern Italy (Lombardy, including Venice and Trieste), and in the southeast to Siebenbürgen. The country grew to a population of 28 million people, consisting of 41% Slavs (11 million), 17% Italians (5 million), 14% Hungarians (4 million), and 17% (4.8 million) German-speaking Austrians.

Joseph's ambition to reform his country often outstripped his patience, and his hasty, autocratic methods kept him embroiled in political difficulties, for, unlike his mother, he lacked tact in dealing with people and the necessary diplomacy in negotiating with the member nations of the Monarchy. His brusque, dictatorial manner as well as his radical policies led to conflicts with Belgium, with Hungary (which he offended by declining to accept the Crown of St. Stephen), with the Catholic Church (he closed more than four hundred monasteries and disbanded the Jesuit order in 1773), and with the ultraconservative aristocracy, which disagreed with many of his views. Often he pushed his ideas too rapidly, rushing reforms into policy before they had been totally thought through. Also the manner in which the new programs were introduced by his representatives was often not the most tactful. As a result Joseph's efforts to improve his country met with resistance that prevented his forward-looking ideas from having the positive effect that was intended. Indeed, his policies aroused such strong resentment that he was forced to rescind a number of them in his last years. Because of his inability to implement his program, Joseph died an embittered man in 1790. Most of the remainder of what he had accomplished was undone in subsequent years by his successors, who returned the country to slower, more conservative development.

One of Joseph's rulings with far-reaching impact that no one at the time could possibly foresee involved the requirement promulgated in 1784 that German henceforth become the standard language throughout the lands and territories of the Monarchy. This eminently sensible attempt to install a common language so that all parts of the realm could communicate and by this means achieve a greater sense of unity—equivalent to what Martin Luther had accomplished for Germany by providing a standardized language—proved to be a two-edged sword which—again ironically—actually led to the severing of the ties it was intended to strengthen. No other issue contributed more to the dissolution of the Monarchy than the matter of language and the national pride which it symbolizes.

Joseph's immediate successor on the throne, Leopold II (1747-1792), the third son of Maria Theresia and Franz I (1708-1765), continued the enlightened ideas of his older brother. However, he differed radically in his basic concept of governance, which diametrically opposed that of Joseph. Leopold believed in greater self-determination for the individual member states of the Monarchy rather than in centralism with everything controlled from Vienna. He discerned that the French Revolution had resulted from a failure to heed the necessity for social change, and to head off any possibility of popular uprisings in Austria, he set about introducing new policies. Leopold was a capable, practical politician and a skilled diplomat who understood the role of compromise in negotiations. He could soothe Hungary by not insisting, as Joseph had done, that German be the official language of the courts and the bureaucracy. He could end the anti-Prussian policy of Joseph and come to an agreement with the German neighbors to the north. His program included economic reforms and the introduction of principles of constitutional law. He wished to develop a state based on law and democratic ideals rather than on imperial edict. Among other humane measures, he abolished torture and the death penalty. Leopold, who enjoyed the reputation of a consummate negotiator, seemed to be exactly the right man in the right place at the right time. His intelligent leadership preserved Austria at a time of crisis. Unfortunately, his reign of less than two years, from 1790 to his death in 1792, did not grant him enough time to complete a new constitution or put many of his plans into practice.

Emperor Franz II (1768-1835), who succeeded Leopold in 1792, found himself beleaguered throughout his reign, partly from the external circumstances of the Napoleonic Wars, over which he had no control, and largely from his total misreading of the spirit of the time and his attempt to turn back the clock of history, a situation well within his power to determine. Initially he had to withstand the pressures of the hard-fought and costly war with Napoleon which ended in Austria's defeat in 1809. Subsequently Franz lived and ruled in fear of revolution by the lower classes, a specter that motivated many of his repressive measures, which in turn retarded the growth and prosperity of the country. Franz was aware of the enthusiasm in intellectual circles in Austria and Hungary for the ideas of the French Revolution, while he himself regarded with suspicion this new thinking with its emphasis on freedom and democratic representation by the people in the governance of the country.

The Jacobin Conspiracy in 1794, led by his former mathematics teacher Andreas von Riedel (1748-1837), who had once served as an advisor to Leopold, and the philosopher and publicist Franz Hebenstreit (1747-1795), to protest the end of Leopold's reforms, only reinforced Franz's mistrust of the masses and his sense of guardedness against the revolutionary spirit. He stamped out the Jacobins mercilessly as a deterrent to others. Riedel was able to escape to Paris, but Hebenstreit along with others was executed.

The Habsburgs never seemed to have had any larger goal or plan for their country beyond maintaining their control. Franz's major goal continued to be the preservation of Habsburg rule. To this end he reverted to the same system of absolutism initiated by Joseph II, canceling out the liberal progress made by Leopold. Franz rigidly opposed any thought of citizen participation in government and any right of self-determination for the nations constituting the Monarchy. He ruled under the principles of order, hierarchy, and the belief that individual interest must be subordinated to that of the state, by which he meant himself. Like the feudal lords before him and the dictators of the twentieth century after him, he wanted the fealty of his subjects not to the country but to him personally.

Franz's ideas brought with them the return of rule by decree, enforced by strict police oversight. He halted the progressive, liberal spirit that had begun with such promise and had produced such favorable results under Leopold. Yet, despite his tyrannical reign, Franz so successfully persuaded the citizens that he was not responsible for the system of government they disliked, that his public image was totally favorable and he came to be known as "the good emperor Franz." For example, when an author once asked him to lend support for his manuscript that he could not get past the censors, Franz claimed that he would have no better chance of success than the writer himself.

Rather than Franz, who actually set the policy, the man who bore the brunt of the people's hatred was Klemens Lothar Prince Metternich (1773-1859), one of the most loyal and dutiful subjects any monarch ever employed to carry out his program. It is Metternich whose name has become attached to this era from 1815 to 1848, and not the emperor's. Franz was intelligent and interested in culture, but he was neither creative nor enterprising. Yet in his own way he was interested in the welfare of his citizens; in 1811 he approved a general reform of the legal system to guarantee all citizens equal treatment before the court. This document is considered the greatest legislative accomplishment of the period.

Franz II showed that he could engage in political maneuvering when circumstances required it. When Napoleon became Emperor of France in 1804 he insisted that Franz relinquish the crown as Emperor of the Holy Roman Empire, because he thought it unseemly that Franz should hold a higher title than he. Furthermore, Napoleon was thinking about assuming that crown himself. This condition was made part of the Treaty of Pressburg in 1805. On 6 August 1806 the Holy Roman Empire, which had existed since 962, beginning with Otto I, and whose crown had been in Austrian hands with one break of five years since 1483, came to an end. In actual fact it had long been only an empty title, and a number of German princes had been urging Franz to surrender it. After the final defeat of Napoleon in 1814, the Holy Roman Empire could have been revived, as Austria suggested, but the Germans had no interest in restoring their ties to Austria by doing so. This decision not to reunite held implications for Austria and Germany that extend all the way to 1938.

While Franz was forced to comply with Napoleon's demand, he astutely combined the move with a political maneuver favorable to himself. He had grown worried about the reliability of the German electors, who traditionally selected the heads of ruling houses, for there was now a Protestant majority. To insure the future continuity of Habsburg rule, Franz II on 11 August 1804 renamed himself Franz I and proclaimed himself Emperor of Austria with the right of inheritance, in order to insure that the house of Habsburg would keep parity with the imperial families in the other countries of Europe. Although this unilateral proclamation of Habsburg legitimacy was not strictly legal, the German electors did not protest and the Habsburg right of determining its own line of succession became established practice.

A low point for Austria was the presence of Napoleon in the summer palace of Schönbrunn in 1809. In the hope of gaining concessions from him during the peace negotiations, the Archduchess Marie Luise entered into an arranged marriage with Napoleon, an example of the Austrian adage: "Let others wage wars, you, lucky Austria, marry." The hoped-for benefits never materialized, and Austria had to pay France costly reparations in money and land. The destitute government was forced into printing paper money, resulting in bankruptcy in 1811 until monetary reform could restore financial stability. The most severe loss was the surrender of Belgium, thus ending the visionary plan to trade Belgium to Germany for Bavaria, so that Austria would gain greater influence in central Europe.

Following the final defeat of Napoleon in 1814, the Austrian Foreign Minister Klemens von Metternich called a meeting of European leaders in Vienna. The resulting Congress of Vienna lasted for six months, beginning in December 1814 and ending in June 1815. Metternich, who completely shared Franz's restorative ideas of ruling, was not only a brilliant political theorist, but also a peerless tactitian and diplomat. He was the strongest and perhaps ablest figure at the Congress, rivaled only by Talleyrand from France. Metternich was elected president of the Congress on 27 December 1814. Because of the relaxed atmosphere of dances and parties, the Congress has always been renowned for its celebrations and balls. At the time the saying went that "The Congress dances, but it doesn't move ahead." In actuality, through Metternich's masterful direction as well as his clear vision for European harmony, important results were achieved for Austria and for Europe in general. By establishing parity between nations, the Vienna Congress set a peaceful course for Europe for the next thirty years.

The French Revolution and the Napoleonic wars had significantly altered the balance of powers essential to peace in Europe. Metternich's goal was to protect national interests by restoring European equilibrium. The spirit of freedom introduced into European thinking at all levels by the revolution still frightened all of the European monarchs, who, as seen in the case of Franz, feared their own people as much as threats from the outside. Under Metternich's persuasion, it was agreed that a new Europe would be formed in terms of restoration, that is, by returning to the principle of absolutism that prevailed before 1789. In addition to ratifying the governing principle desired by Franz, the Congress, as a means of insuring equality of influence, also decreed the return of most of the Austrian territories lost to Napoleon. Talleyrand wisely acceded to the idea of restoring the borders of 1792, for by doing so France escaped from paying any war reparations for Napoleon's conquests. Austria thus regained Lombardy and Venice, Galicia, and the territories in Vorarlberg, the Tyrol, Upper Austria, and Salzburg. However, the territories of Breisgau and Belgium remained lost. To oversee the peace and preserve the balance of powers, a Holy Alliance, consisting of representatives from all European countries, was formed. In addition, Metternich headed a German Union (*Deutscher Bund*) to oversee relations between Austria and Germany. Metternich's important role and leadership skills were acknowledged by all others with whom he negotiated, as can be seen in the appellation he was given as "the coachman of Europe" (*Der Kutscher Europas*).

Once he had established peace and removed any external threat to Austria, Metternich, who had been appointed Chancellor in 1821, could turn his attention to internal matters, namely, to carry out Franz's desire for a state based on a system of order and hierarchy. To implement this program, Metternich was ably supported by his "shadow" Friedrich von Gentz, who, like Metternich, came from Germany. Gentz (1764-1832), who rivaled Metternich as a suave and intelligent politician, completely shared his superior's political ideas and emulated his fanatical service to the state. Gentz's translation of the English philospher Burke had attracted notice, and on that basis he had been called into Austrian service in 1802. In 1806 he wrote what is generally reputed to be his best book, *Fragmente aus der neuesten Geschichte des politischen Gleichgewichtes von Europa* (Fragments from the Most Recent History of the Political Balance of Power in Europe). This work resulted in his entrance into the State Chancellery in 1809 and eventually to his close association with Metternich. These two men, working in tandem, inaugurated one of the most regressive and repressive governments in Austrian history and of any European country at that time. They were committed to Franz's idea of restoring the royal house to the position of dominance it had held before the French Revolution. While Franz and Metternich claimed to believe in freedom, they insisted that it could only exist in a climate of order (*Ordnung*), by which was meant a hierarchical system in which everyone knew his or her place and stayed in it. Franz's fear of revolution required that the demand for freedom must remain secondary to the preservation of security and the maintenance of the established hierarchy. The policy of absolutism was bad enough, but the execution of it was worse. The diplomatic skill that Metternich had displayed at the Congress of Vienna and in negotiating with other countries was conspicuously absent in his implementation of internal policy and in his dealings with the member states and territories of the multinational Monarchy.

To enforce the government's program, Metternich appointed Joseph Count von Sedlnitzky (1778-1855), who zealously carried out his duties as Police Chief and created an early version of a police state. He introduced a tight system of censorship and employed an army of spies, who, like the conservative government censors, pursued and stamped out any criticism of the government, any rebellious idea or attempt at free speech. The police chief was not considered a bad human being per se, only a misguided one in the sense that he committed himself totally to carrying out his designated task of guaranteeing the success of the hated Metternich system. Not surprisingly, the government's highly unpopular policies aroused bitterness and a spirit of opposition among artists, professional men, intellectuals, and students as well as among some liberal aristocrats.

Like all dictatorships, Metternich attempted to invoke thought control by preventing the flow of information into Austria as well as by restraining the spread of ideas within the country by denying freedom of expression and controlling all publications. His system of censorship, which monitored all written materials coming into the country, including private letters, severely inhibited all political, cultural, and social life and impacted the development of Austria in ways that left lasting negative consequences for the rest of the nineteenth century. The apolitical nature of literature and art, the adoption of the Biedermeier lifestyle, the fear of publicly revealing one's true nature, the feeling of inner dividedness (*Zerrissenheit*), the role of education and the church, the slow industrial and scientific progress were all affected by Franz's policies; without freedom of expression all areas of life as well as the people themselves were prevented from developing naturally. The entire society suffered from the constraint of having to conform to a repressive government system which anticipated the methods of twentieth-century fascism.

Industrial growth could not be impacted to the same degree as the cultural area, for, as Metternich recognized, the government needed the money it generated. Nevertheless, Franz attempted to slow the growth of industrialization in the country, and what development did take place was, at his insistence, restricted to the suburbs to keep the workers outside of Vienna. Despite these cautious measures, the unregulated factories with their exploitative sweatshop practices created the conditions to produce exactly the revolution that Franz so feared. The government's attempt at suppressing free speech achieved the opposite of its intention in the cultural area as well. Salons of wealthy women along with other clubs, organized groups, and the coffeehouses provided forums for a free exchange of ideas within Vienna, while a stream of political pamphlets decrying the lack of freedom and representation was published abroad—usually in Germany—and smuggled into Austria for distribution.

Vormärz and Biedermeier

The period of Metternich's control, extending from the Congress of Vienna in 1815 to the revolution of March 1848, has come to be known as the *Vormärz* (pre-March) era, a comprehensive term including all aspects of life, politics, and culture. As a subcategory within *Vormärz*, the term Biedermeier has been adopted as a description of the culture and lifestyle of the well-to-do bourgeoisie. This name was not used at the time but, as so often happens, was coined later and applied retroactively. It resulted from joining together the names of two German philistines, Biedermann and Bummelmeier, created by the German author Viktor von Scheffel for the humorous magazine *Fliegende Blätter* (literally Flying Pages) in Munich. The poet L. Eichrodt published a series of poems in 1850 under the title *Biedermeiers Liederlust* (Biedermeier's Desire for Songs), and the name caught on. Initially the term was applied to furniture, then extended to painting, and finally was used satirically to describe the Weltanschauung of the comfortable bourgeoisie willing to trade freedom of expression for a tranquil life in their own cozy nook, a lifestyle generally derided as "happiness in a corner" (*Glück im Winkel*). This segment of bourgeois society shared the ideas of the court and the aristocracy, which it tried to emulate. It was thus never a troublesome group for the ruling house or the police. Biedermeier connotes a striving for moderation, a need for order, an acceptance of authority, a search for contentment in private life, an emphasis on family and the attempt to create an idyllic family life, satisfaction in material possessions, and fondness for nature, which was expressed in well-kept gardens as well as in walks in the country and picnics.

Over time the term Biedermeier lost its satirical thrust, and today characterizes those who, having gained money through the rise of industrialization, could afford a lifestyle that corresponded to their financial position in life. Because they attained their status through money, they were imbued with a materialistic outlook, illustrated by the manner in which they lived: attractive, light, airy homes, decorated with handsome wood and upholstered furniture—Biedermeier furniture, solidly crafted and stylistically handsome, became a European success—lavish use of textiles, drapes, and wall tapestries, ornate glassware, flower arrangements, and porcelain decorations, including a fancy tiled stove (*Kachelofen*). Much of what is found in Biedermeier was paralleled later by the creation of the Wiener Werkstätte, founded in 1905, providing another similarity between the two halves of the century. In the 1830s Joseph Danhauser (1805-1845), whose firm was already a leading manufacturer of Biedermeier furniture, introduced lighter, simpler designs in more delicate forms resembling a second rococo movement.

Music played an important role in this family-oriented lifestyle, and a piano and other musical instruments were usually in evidence. Many of the paintings of the time portray an individual at the piano, often surrounded by his or her family, or a family group making music. It was a trend much encouraged and appreciated by the government because it kept people at home engaged in non-political activities instead of congregating with others. Various organizations were founded throughout Austria to cultivate musical activity, such as the Society for the Friends of Music (*Gesellschaft der Musikfreunde*) in 1812, an organization which still exists today. In 1841 the Mozarteum, which is more prominent than ever at present, was established in Salzburg in commemoration of its favorite son and one of Austria's great contributions to world music, Wolfgang Amadeus Mozart.

The world-famous Austrian musical tradition had begun its rise to prominence during the days of Maria Theresia through the composers Christian Willibald Gluck (1714-1787), the founder of German opera, Joseph Haydn (1737-1809), and Mozart (1756-1791), whose operas still form a staple of most repertoires in all opera houses. The line of development continued at the same high level with Ludwig van Beethoven (1770-1827) and Franz Schubert (1797-1828). Music could develop freely without the intrusion of censorship that restricted all written forms, whether scholarship, journalism, or literature. Although Beethoven was born in

Germany, he spent most of his life in Vienna and has been acclaimed for Austrian music, another prominent example of the idea that not birth but cultural orientation determines a person's national affiliation. Schubert, who belonged to the middle class and wrote for his peers, became known as the Prince of Song (*Liederfürst*). He continued the rich tradition of songs (*Lieder*) but surpassed all of his predecessors with the great variety of his melodies and his genial compositional skill. Joseph Lanner (1801-1843) and Johann Strauss, senior (1804-1849) became prominent for their development of the Viennese waltz.

Austria had become renowned as a land of music, and this reputation continued throughout the nineteenth century, represented by Johannes Brahms (1833-1897), Anton Bruckner (1824-1896), the Hungarian Franz Liszt (1811-1886), and two Czech composers Antonin Dvorak (1841-1904) and Friedrich Smetana (1824-1884). In the second half of the century Hugo Wolf (1860-1903) continued the song (*Lieder*) tradition. Johann Strauss, the son (1825-1899) surpassed his father and Lanner with his waltzes, and Gustav Mahler (1860-1911) gained international recognition for his symphonies as well as for his conducting.

One of the best sources of information about the Biedermeier era is to be found in the paintings of the time. Biedermeier families loved to decorate their houses with works of art and were partial to scenes that reflected their own life in realistic terms so that they could easily identify with them. In keeping with the modest aspirations of Biedermeier, the small genre picture featuring family life, room interiors, and still-lifes—flower or fruit arrangements—was a preferred form. A great similarity exists between Biedermeier art and seventeenth-century Dutch painting in terms of subject matter and use of light. Artists such as Moritz Michael Daffinger (1790-1849), Peter Fendi (1796-1842), Karl Schindler (1821-1842), known as soldier Schindler because he mainly painted portaits of military men, Friedrich Guermann (1807-1862), Josef Danhauser (1805-1845), son of the furniture designer and manufacturer, Franz Steinfeld (1787-1868), a landscape painter who was influenced by Dutch painting, and Johann Nepomuk Höchle (1790-1835), a genre painter and lithographer, represent the most popular artists who furnished the genre pictures, landscapes, and portraits that the Biedermeier public desired. Others who achieved great success and recognition were Joseph Kriehuber (1800-1876), who painted portraits of many of the members of Viennese society, Friedrich Amerling (1803-1887), and Moritz von Schwind (1804-1871), who spent the last part of his career in Germany and specialized in depicting German fairy tales and legends. Ferdinand Georg Waldmüller (1793-1865), who has come to be regarded as the most representative Biedermeier painter because of his many scenes portraying the life of the time, achieved recognition not only as one of the best artists of his time, but also as one of the most innovative. He anticipated the techniques of the French Impressionists by introducing the effect of natural light in his paintings in contrast to the standard classical style of disregarding outside lighting. In keeping with this development Waldmüller led the way in changing the artists' approach to nature by moving away from idealized landscapes to realistic portrayals of scenery and people. Through their meticulously accurate renditions of the people, the houses, and the life of the time, the Biedermeier painters created an enduring social as well as artistic legacy.

Those financially able to enjoy the Biedermeier lifestyle did not chafe under the restrictive Metternich system of government and did not suffer from the spirit of resignation and the division between their inner and outer lives which are inseparably associated in the literature about the *Vormärz*. Biedermeier is often erroneously considered a form of inner emigration, but the sense of contentment seems too genuine to regard these people as unhappy with their lot in life any more than their counter-parts in *fin-de-siècle* Vienna were. Actually with their financial means they were able to fulfill their own self-interests and achieve their goals within the prevailing political system and without arousing the reaction of the state.

Yet—and this point is often overlooked—while they maintained order and harbored no rebellious or revolutionary thoughts, in their own quiet way they subverted the government's notion of a God-ordained hierarchy, for they had learned on the basis of their own experience that through accomplishment and money it was possible to rise to a higher position in life. They created a new nobility through their financial success. This view differs from the interpretation of Roger Bauer, who sees a continuation of the Baroque tradition in Austria until the middle of the nineteenth century, basing his argument on the fact that the absolutist form of government remained constant until 1848.[1] Baroque literature celebrated the hero who strove for fame and honor in order to esteem his lord and master and through him the state. According to Bauer, this ideal con-tinued to exist in the form of the exemplary bourgeois who, like his Baroque predecessors was a model citizen of the state. This argument does not take into account the fact that the Biedermeier group was a financially privileged minority and thus not typical of the majority of the population which suffered under the repression of the time and wanted change. If the masses, whose poverty excluded them from the Biedermeier lifestyle, remained good citizens, it was not out of conviction or commitment to a Baroque courtly ideal, but only because they had no other choice. The intellectuals, writers, journalists, and even some liberal aristocrats likewise gave up the Baroque ideal because they no longer shared the same idea of government as the ruling house. Citizens were forced to become divided personalities in order to survive. They remained good citizens under duress, which is quite different than the Baroque ideal of serving out of devotion. In short, Austrian society was no longer monolithic as in the Baroque period. Bauer also does not take into consideration the fundamental changes that were occurring subtly and orderly enough not to arouse any political response from the government, but that were significant enough to cause the society to develop differently than the government's ideal of preserving the hierarchy. Finally, to see a continuation of the Baroque tradition until 1848 ignores the new themes and forms of the changing literature as well as the many political pamphlets that were being written at the time which document how out of phase the people were with the will of Emperor Franz.

The middle- and upper-middle-class bourgeois who comprised Biedermeier were indeed solid, obedient citizens, but they were also successful businessmen and upward-bound entrepreneurs. Even though they remained apolitical, they were energetic, intelligent people not content to stagnate in resignation. They did not openly contravene the state's ruling principle of order, but they operated quietly under a progressive Weltanschauung that subverted the hierarchical views of the state. They strove to emulate the nobility and recognized that through money they could improve their station in life and even be raised to the nobility or marry into the aristocracy.

This attitude had profound implications for literature. For just as the artists portrayed the Biedermeier world in their paintings, the writers, who normally mirror the time in which they live, likewise began to feature the middle class in literature, conveying the positive message that anyone could aspire to a better life based on achievement rather than on birth or inheritance. The developmental novel, an outgrowth of the Enlightenment, was intended to present this optimistic message about the benefits of education, travel, and experience. In the course of the century these novels began to feature bourgeois protagonists who outwit aristocrats, document-ing the major social change that was occurring: the declining importance and influence of the nobility and the commensurate rise to power of the bourgeoisie.[2] Alongside the novel, the writers developed a shorter narrative form, the novella, which better suited the reading habits of the bour-geoisie, and as a result became the dominant literary form of the nine-teenth century. These were no longer aristocratic forms of literature as found in the Baroque, but works written predominantly by middle-class authors for their peers, showing clearly the transition that was taking place.

The term Biedermeier refers to an elite group just as does the Vienna *fin-de-siècle* in the 1890s. It does not apply to the less fortunate working class in Austria, nor was it shared by intellectuals, writers, artists, journalists, and even some aristocrats, who wanted to promote the ad-vancement of their country by struggling to see freedom of expression introduced as well as political representation. Hermann Bahr, who devoted his life to analyzing Austrian conditions, described the goal of the Habsburg rulers as an attempt to create a nation of artificial people according to their own design. They did not want independent-thinking individuals but patriots for them personally. When a person was recom-mended to Emperor Franz as a patriot, he remarked: "You say he is a patriot for Austria. But is he also a patriot for me?"[3] In Bahr's view, the Habsburgs always harbored mistrust against anyone or anything that is real: "The Habsburgs regard real people as their enemy. They need arti-ficial citizens. Those are Emperor Franz's 'patriots for me.' To create such patriots, to form a Habsburg nation of such artificial people has always been the problem of every Austrian regime."[4]

Bahr regarded this fear of being real as the source of Austrians' suffering from a sense of isolation and as the cause of the role playing so prevalent in the *fin de siècle*. In all of his writings Bahr always praised those he considered real people (*wirkliche Menschen*), men like Joseph von Hormayr (1781-1848) at the beginning of the century and Franz Stelzhamer (1802-1874) at the end, who refused to bow to the government's will and to follow any guide other than their own conscience. The desire to help his countrymen break through their shell of isolation and find their way to a real, independent life motivated his decision in 1905 to publish his diaries weekly in the *Neues Wiener Journal* to provide a point of view on major issues around which others could unite. He intended his ideas to act as a catalyst; it did not matter whether others agreed or disagreed with them. In either case they served their purpose of giving people a point of view to help them form their own ideas.[5] To illustrate how patterns have repeated themselves in Austrian literary history, after 1945 Hans Weigel in his book *Flucht vor der Größe (Flight from Greatness)* similarly described what Bahr had called the "Austrian Fate," namely, that anyone talented or progressive would be harassed until silenced.[6]

Having to conceal one's true opinions, the necessity of leaving one's real self at home when leaving the house,[7] caused many people to suffer from a divided personality, a common psychological state known at the time as *Zerrissenheit*. As one contemporary writer described it: *"Zerrissenheit* is nothing feigned. It is the illness of our time. We are inwardly divided in belief, in writing, in philosophy, in morality. The old-world unity of antiquity and of the Middle Ages is gone. We know that freedom must come, yet we are chained and held like schoolboys; that hurts, that tears one apart."[8]

Government officials found themselves under particular stress at having to act against their principles. The toll on nerves can be seen in the case of Johann Mayrhofer (1787-1836), poet and friend of Schubert. His official duty as a state censor of imported books caused him such distress that he committed suicide.[9] On the larger scene this same lack of basic freedoms caused widespread discontent among the member nations of the Monarchy.

The people who suffered the most, as is always the case, were the workers lured off the farms to find employment in the factories sprouting up around Vienna, mainly to the south. Franz would have preferred to maintain Austria as an agrarian society, and his backward policy caused Austria to lag far behind Germany in industrial development despite the progress that was being made by the initiative of the entrepreneurs who ignored the Emperor's will. Metternich knew what was happening but was pragmatic enough to recognize that some liberalization had to be allowed in order to attract foreign capital for the building of railroads and ships to carry on trade. The government needed the taxes, for without money it was powerless.

The bourgeois employers felt no sympathy for the workers and generally exploited them. Housing was in short supply, and so factory towns were built. In them the life of the employees was highly controlled. Fourteen-hour workdays were not uncommon, often in unhealthy conditions and for minimal wages. Women and children also formed part of the labor force. As industrial methods improved in efficiency and more machinery was introduced, unemployment resulted, stranding workers who could now not return to the farm. The frustrations of such treatment led to some futile attacks on machines, but, as in other countries, the workers, lacking any concern or involvement on the part of the government and without any leaders to organize them, were powerless to effect any improvement in their lot. These circumstances caused a widening gulf between the proletariat and the bourgeoisie which became a major reason for the failure of the Revolution of 1848; for the proletariat without leaders, organization, and unity could not alone mount the effective resistance needed to force the substantial social changes that were desired and necessary.

The reactionary thinking of the ruling house can be seen clearly in the attitude toward education. Despite the Enlightenment, which taught the benefits of learning and knowledge, and despite the example of Joseph II, who opened the schools to everyone, Franz II (I) demanded that the education system be restricted to producing loyal servants of the state and faithful subjects to the throne. He limited the role of the universities solely to teaching; research, which might lead to the introduction of new ideas, was forbidden. What scholarly work was done, took place privately. Under these restrictions the prominent German Romantic writer Friedrich Schlegel, who settled in Vienna and entered into government service, could not give his lectures "Über die neuere Geschichte" (1810, On Recent History) and "Geschichte der alten und neuen Literatur" (1812, The History of Ancient and Contemporary Literature) at the University but had to deliver them in private quarters. In an address to a group of professors the Emperor made clear his position: "Hold to the old, for it is good; I do not need scholars, but good loyal citizens. To educate the students so that they fulfill this goal is your responsibility."[10] This credo of clinging on to the past is the same ideal that Metternich and other European leaders had endorsed at the Congress of Vienna in their attempt to return Europe to its configuration prior to the French Revolution. How this policy retarded the development of Austria can be seen in the comparison to Germany which, while repressive enough, at the same time remained more attuned to the changing times.

One important difference can be seen by comparing the approach of the two countries to general education. In Prussia approximately 60% to 80% of the children attended public school (*Volksschule*) between 1816 and 1848. In Austria half that number were enrolled in school, meaning that every second inhabitant of the Danube Monarchy was unable to read a book or a newspaper.[11]

The Reign of Ferdinand I

Upon the death of Franz II(I) on 2 March 1835, he was succeeded by his eldest son Ferdinand I (1793-1875). Although Ferdinand did not possess the qualities physically or mentally to rule the country, Franz insisted on his appointment in keeping with the principle of legitimacy he had established in 1804. He left a testament to Ferdinand directing him to hold to the past: "Do not disturb anything in the basic structure of the state; rule, and do not make changes."[12] Because of Ferdinand's physical and mental incapacity, a "secret state committee" (*Geheime Staatskonferenz*) was established to govern the country. Metternich found himself opposed in political outlook by Franz Anton Count von Kolowrat-Liebsteinsky (1771-1861) and no longer able to direct government policy single-handedly. The two differed radically in political outlook, and Metternich was increasingly relegated to his earlier role of handling foreign affairs. Thus to label this period the age of Metternich and make him solely responsible for the failed policies of the years 1835-1848 is not accurate. The disputes between these two powerful men had a negative effect on the smooth running of the government. Ferdinand, whom people charitably called "der Gütige" (the kind-hearted), simply rubber-stamped the documents that were put before him but had no responsibility for the decisions that were made. Under these circumstances the situation in the country grew steadily worse, culminating in the revolution of March 1848, when Ferdinand was forced to abdicate in favor of his nephew Franz Joseph I.

During the 1840s pressures continued to mount below the seemingly serene surface. Just as the ideas of freedom and brotherhood stemming from the French Revolution could not be halted, so too Metternich, despite his best efforts, proved unable to insulate Austria from outside influences. Although books and plays coming into the country could be censored and adapted by the book examiners (*Bücherrevisoren*), it was not possible to keep the progressive thinkers and activists from traveling to Germany and France to meet with their liberal counterparts and become informed about the revolutionary ideas and plans in those countries. It also proved impossible to control the stream of political pamphlets criticizing the intolerable conditions within Austria. These were usually printed in

Germany either anonymously or under a pseudonym and smuggled into Austria for distribution. This situation resulted in a new law prohibiting the publication of material outside the country without prior permission. Traveling abroad to publish materials or to voice protest involved considerable risk. Individuals who ventured the trip were often pursued by Metternich's spies, and those who were identified often did not dare to return.

One who burned his bridges to Austria, not necessarily for political reasons alone, was Charles Sealsfield (pseudonym for Karl Postl, 1793-1864), whose revealing book *Austria as It Is,* published in England in 1828, provided a comprehensive overview of life in Austria, including a candid and unsparing denunciation of the Metternich system of government. Among other things Sealsfield predicted that Franz's—he placed the responsibility on the emperor, not on Metternich who was only the agent of his master's will—"crusades against human liberty and understanding will, doubtless, have the same results [as the Crusades], and undermine what they are intended to strengthen—the foundation of Despotism."[13] He also foresaw that the member states, led by Hungary, would revolt: "The ties of honor and good faith which bound the Austrian subjects to their Emperor are entirely broken, and the death of Francis will disclose scenes of which we never dreamed."[14] Except for the scenes of carnage Sealsfield envisioned, his predictions proved accurate. But the time was not yet ripe for action; conditions had to worsen considerably before the people would grow desperate enough to resort to open rebellion.

Even the revolution of 1830 in France produced no significant reaction in Austria. Because of the tight police control no unified organization could be developed to lead an opposition movement. In Germany there was a loose-knit association of writers and intellectuals called Young Germany which spearheaded the drive for freedom there, but the vigilant spy network in Austria made it impossible for any parallel group to emerge. Madeleine Rietra has entitled her book *Young Austria* in an attempt to create the impression of an analogous organization in Austria. However, the similarity remains an artificial construct, because in Austria the protests resulted from individual efforts and not from unified action.

This does not mean that there were no open discussions within Austria, only that the censorship ban had to be circumvented with discretion. Private clubs were founded, and the Freemasons had their lodges. The coffeehouses, a legacy of the Turkish wars, flourished—by 1837 there were

eighty of them in Vienna alone. However one of the best means of bringing together people of different professions and callings was in the salons
provided by cultivated, intelligent, wealthy women like Karoline Pichler
and Johanna Anna Baroness Cranstown. The latter, a Scottish woman
married to Gottfried Wenzel Count von Purgstall, had known and influenced Sir Walter Scott. The Baroness von Purgstall showed her independence of mind by using her home as a meeting place for followers of
Kant, whose philosophy was anathema to the government to the point
that it could not be taught at the university. After the early death of her
husband and son, the Baroness adopted the writer and prominent orientalist Joseph Baron von Hammer, who added the name Purgstall to his own.

Other prominent salons affording writers, intellectuals, government
officials, and military officers the opportunity to meet and exchange
views—the tradition, which began in the eighteenth century, continued
throughout the nineteenth and into the twentieth century—included those
of Princess Marianne von Schwarzenberg, the mother of the poet Friedrich
von Schwarzenberg, who lived the adventurous life of a mercenary soldier,
of the Metternichs, of Fanny Arnstein, Henriette Pereira, Eleonora Fliess,
Henriette Wertheimer, Franziska Wertheimstein, and Bertha Zuckerkandl.

A salon of particular note was that of Charlotte and Hofrat Franz von
Greiner, the parents of the writer Karoline Pichler (1769-1844), who met
all of the literary greats of the time there: the Collins brothers, Heinrich
Joseph and Matthäus, Joseph von Hammer-Purgstall, Joseph von Hormayr, who was known as the Austrian Plutarch, Franz Grillparzer, Nikolaus Lenau, as well as the German writers Zacharias Werner, August
Wilhelm, Friedrich and Dorothea Schlegel, Clemens Brentano, Ludwig
Tieck, Theodor Körner, and the French author Germaine de Staël. At the
height of Pichler's career, it was said that there were two main sights not
to be missed in Vienna: St. Stephen's Cathedral and Karoline Pichler.
Later, as the wife of an official named Andreas Pichler, Karoline established her own salon. Equally important in the literary and salon life of
the time was Babette Elisabeth Glück (1814-1894), who wrote under the
pseudonym Betty Paoli. She served as a companion to Princess Schwarzenberg and thus played a role in her salon, one of the most fashionable
meeting places of the time.

Because of the lack of press freedom, no political newspapers existed in
Austria. The *Austrian Observer,* founded in 1810, served as the official
paper of the ruling house. The only newspaper with any freedom at all was

the *Journal of the Austrian Lloyd*, which began appearing in German and Italian in 1836 in Trieste. All foreign publications were censored before they could enter Austria. Within the country censors operated with total disregard of authors and artists. Their duty was solely to insure that the literature conformed to the wishes of the the emperor, who set the guidelines and insisted on their being strictly followed. The writers often had to wait for months or longer before their manuscripts were returned, and the system provided no possibility of challenging a censor's decision. Censorship provides yet another parallel with the later turn of the century, when, as Arthur Schnitzler experienced, submitted manuscripts could be held at the Burgtheater for years without a decision, and a sign of disapproval by an aristocrat could cause a play to be banished from the repertoire.

All theater performances were monitored to control extemporaneous commentary, an important feature of folk plays. All foreign plays had to be carefully revised to eliminate any material that might prove offensive to the emperor. Newspaper editors made a unified appeal for greater freedom of expression in 1842, the book dealers followed in 1845, and a petition signed by ninety-nine authors was also submitted in the same year. The popular Burgtheater playwright Eduard von Bauernfeld, one of the most outspoken liberals, published an essay against censorship entitled "Denkschrift über die gegenwärtigen Zustände der Zensur in Österreich" (1845, Reflections on the Current State of Censorship in Austria). The same year, after visiting Paris and London, he also submitted a formal petition requesting that the government abolish the practice of censoring literature. All of these appeals were summarily rejected. Censorship was stricter in Austria than in Germany, and so the writers argued that since Austria belonged to the German Union, the same rules should apply. This plea was also ignored.

Another significant document of the time that ranks alongside Sealsfield's book in importance was Baron Viktor von Andrian-Werburg's (1813-1858) discerning analysis of contemporary conditions, *Österreich und dessen Zukunft* (1843, Austria and Its Future), which created a sensation when it appeared anonymously. The police soon identified the author but, given his status, took no measures against him. Andrian belonged to the small group of liberal aristocrats who broke ranks with the ruling house to try to change the policies stifling Austria. He identified the bureaucracy as the major problem of the government system, calling it an unprecedentedly complicated government machine, without any intelligence, without any direction other than the preservation to the greatest degree possible of the status quo, a situation which stifles all independent development of public life and of communities, and binds the slightest of its activities in a thousand formal requirements, documents, and harassments. The bureaucracy has suffocated all progressiveness in the state and watches over the slightest, most insignificant activity of the citizens in every possible way, controls people, and draws them into the orbit of their spying.[15]

Other complaints advanced by Andrian concerned the costly pensions of the army of officials, the constant deficits in the budget that made new loans necessary, and the system of nepotism (*Protektion*), whereby officials made appointments to jobs based on personal relationships rather than on merit. He also spoke out on behalf of the downtrodden workers and correctly predicted revolutionary consequences if conditions were not improved:

Thousands of people are in the middle of a rich, growing civilization, forgotten and sacrificed to nameless misery, people who do not know from one day to the next where they will put their head, where they will find a piece of miserable bread so that they can continue their sorrowful life. Because of these circumstances the proletariat, which has nothing and is without a home, whose number grows with every day, is preparing an upheaval, the dimensions and consequences of which we cannot conceive—and all this while material interests are praised, idolized, placed on altars.[16]

By the middle of the 1840s the liberal opposition was flooding Austria with so many brochures and pamphlets against the government that it became impossible to stem the tide any longer; the censors spent so much time trying to control the pamphlets that they did not have sufficient time for the literature. There were many calls for the writers to politicize literature and, if necessary, to go into voluntary exile in order to be able to speak out as Sealsfield had done. By 1847 public opinion had grown into such a spirit of opposition that even loyal high-ranking government officials were coming to accept the ideas of the enlightened liberals concerning freedom of expression.

Political-minded Austrians developed close connections with the Young German writers, with whom they shared similar interests about such matters as reforming Catholicism, the struggle against the nobility, the clergy, and the bureaucracy, the separation of church and state, the removal of class privileges, open court proceedings, freedom of association, of the press, of religion, of teaching and learning, and democratic participation in the governance of the state through the vote. The feeling was widespread that the traditional ideas of religion, philosophy, morality, and art had lost their validity, just as it occurred again in the "revaluation of all values" that took place at the end of the nineteenth century. The former unity found in feudalism had been irretrievably lost. Now the division between what they were expected to believe and accept and what they knew had widened into an unbridgeable gulf.

As will be seen, the literature of the major writers lagged considerably behind the political pamphleteers in attacking the conditions of the time. They shared the same views, but the authors could not hide behind anonymity or pseudonyms like the pamphleteers. Julius Seidlitz called for writers to put their art in the service of the time:

> Destroy the old, give the age we live in its cues, create something contemporary, that is, modern literature. Such literature does not grieve over the past, the present is the god to whom it builds altars, and its eye flirts with the future . . . Modern literature is less a daughter of fantasy than a child of reason, less idealized and more realistic. For that reason the poet must actually identify with what he writes, must become totally modern in thought and action.[17]

The call of Seidlitz for a literature that faithfully reflects its own time represents another parallel with the coming turn of the century, when Bahr in 1891 made an equally impassioned plea for the reunification of art and life in his seminal programmatic essay "Die Moderne" (1981, Modernity).[18] The Secessionist building designed by Joseph Olbrich in 1898 features a motto which enunciates Bahr's concept of art: "To every age its art, to art its freedom." It is noteworthy that in 1945, immediately following World War II, Edwin Rollett made the identical plea once again for restoring the union of art and life.[19]

Along the same lines as Seidlitz the critic Joseph Tuvora pointed out that the Greek dramatists had become great because they had dared to criticize the leaders of their country and even the gods. But Austrian writers, he laments, cannot even venture to name the social problems openly, not to mention criticize and try to eliminate them.[20] In the tightly controlled political climate of the time, authors embedded social and political criticism, if at all, into their works in the effort to pass the censors. None of the leading authors undertook to attack overtly the policies and repressive measures that needed correcting, because all recognized how unavailing the effort would be. Three of the politically oriented writers, Anastasius Grün, Friedrich Halm, and Nikolaus Niembsch von Lenau, were members of the nobility sympathetic to the activist efforts of other authors and intellectuals who were willing to incorporate ideas of freedom into their works, always masked by settings other than contemporary Austria. Bourgeois authors, like Grillparzer, who earned their living primarily as state employees—then as now most writers found it impossible to live from the proceeds of their writings—remained dutifully conservative and loyal subjects despite the inner conflict that this caused within them. They introduced some criticism, but for the most part their sense of loyalty outweighed all other considerations.

Two other critics were Ferdinand Raimund and Johann Nestroy, whose plays, performed in the suburban theaters, contained ideas critical of contemporary conditions. Nestroy particularly tried to deliver relevant commentary by means of satirical extemporaneous speeches or songs introduced into his performances. He had to be cautious, for a censor usually sat in the audience to monitor the presentations. At times he was caught, the performance was interrupted, and he was fined and occasionally even imprisoned. Even when successful, his remarks reached only limited audiences. Nevertheless he carried on the struggle despite the risk to himself.

One means of defense the government employed against the swelling tide of liberal opposition in the country was to restore ties to the Catholic Church in order to enlist its aid as a conservative force. The Catholic Church and the Habsburg Monarchy had long engaged in a struggle for supremacy, and since the time of Joseph II the church had been subordinated to the state. Now Metternich thought to hold up the shield of religion as the defender of absolutism. This new alliance resulted in several concessions to the church and accommodations such as the restoration of the Jesuit order and the evacuation of Protestants out of the Tyrol in 1837. Most importantly the church regained control of the schools, the methods of teaching, and the curriculum.

The Revolution of March 1848

The revolution of March 1848 should have come as no surprise to the ruling house, for there were numerous foreshadowings. Galicia had been in a state of turmoil since 1846, and the flood of pamphlets protesting the lack of freedom of expression as well as the February revolution in Paris offered unmistakable signs of the widespread anger and discontent not only throughout the Monarchy, but also throughout Europe. On 3 March 1848 Lajos Kossuth delivered a revolutionary speech before the Hungarian Parliament, and on 11 March the Czechs likewise began to make political demands for greater self-determination. While many of these situations had occurred previously and had been successfully defused, the Austrian government this time failed to recognize that a unique combination of circumstances had resulted in social and economic conditions that had grown so intolerable, not just for one segment of society but for all levels and classes, that the people were forced to act, simply for the sake of survival.

With the accession of Ferdinand I to the throne in 1835, censorship had been intensified to combat the increased political activity within the country. This step served only to heighten the dissatisfaction among the intellectuals and writers. At the same time the workers, who had patiently endured their lot in life, were being pushed beyond all limits. An economic downturn in the 1840s resulted in widespread unemployment, and for those still working wages were cut. Housing, always a problem, grew worse, and a bad harvest in 1847 caused increased prices which the poor could not afford. A hard winter further exacerbated the situation. The workers felt they had nothing to lose because their plight could hardly grow worse. The government mounted a few public work projects in the Prater along with a few other stopgap measures, but it was a case of too little too late. Beginning on 13 March 1848, the workers stormed the factories in the suburbs, and in the ensuing general uprising the Emperor and his court prudently left Vienna.

Writers and intellectuals supported the revolution as did the petty officials. So too did the students, who held a rally at the University of Vienna. All groups demanded the abolishing of censorship, freedom of expression, freedom of teaching and learning, the equality of all religious faiths, individual representation through the vote, and a constitution. Bauernfeld particularly distinguished himself by collaborating with the politician Alexander Bach (1813-1893) on a petition submitted on 11 March 1848 requesting an end to autocratic rule. On 15 March Bauernfeld went with Anastasius Grün to negotiate a constitution with the government. For his active role Bauernfeld was asked to serve as a representative in the parliament in Frankfurt, but the experience of serving as a leader had so unnerved him that he pleaded illness and declined the honor. Kossuth valued his participation so much that he came to Vienna to consult with him, but Bauernfeld had had enough of activist politics and refused even to see the revolutionary leader for fear he would be persuaded to do something he did not feel suited for.

The government had quickly conceded to the demands for a constitution on 15 March after two days of fighting. The hated trio of Metternich, Gentz, and Sedlnitzky had to flee, and the *Geheime Staatskonferenz* was replaced by a provisional government under Count Franz Anton Kolowrat-Liebsteinsky, who on 3 April resigned in favor of Count Karl Ludwig von Ficquelmont. He in turn was replaced on 4 May by Baron Franz von Pillersdorf (1786-1862). On 25 April 1848 the first draft of a constitution was rejected and further fighting ensued, continuing sporadically throughout the summer. On 1 October major battles occurred in Vienna, which was placed under siege by Imperial troops. On 27 October the center of Vienna being held by the revolutionaries was stormed, and the Hungarian relief force which attempted to rescue the besieged students and workers was defeated in the suburbs. The city was retaken, and the leading representatives of the revolution were shot. A number of the participants were able to escape to Germany. On 2 December 1848 eighteen-year-old Franz Joseph I assumed the throne, restoring order by promising a constitution. However, the state of emergency remained in effect until 1853.

Young and inexperienced as he was, the eighteen-year-old Franz Joseph could only follow the recommendations of his advisors, who perpetuated the same backward-looking philosophy that had determined the policy of the Habsburg rulers since Joseph II with such disastrous results. After a year of delay Franz Joseph dissolved the first Austrian Parliament without producing the promised constitution. The concessions from the imperial house, gained so expensively in terms of life and suffering in the revolution, were slow in coming from a most reluctant ruler, so intent on restoring the earlier political and social conditions that he brought the hated

Metternich back from his exile in 1851 to serve as an advisor. Like his
forebears, Franz Joseph still considered the state the highest good and
himself the first citizen. Throughout his sixty-eight-year tenure—the
longest reigning monarch ever—he never wavered in his defense of the
status quo and in his fight against all progressive tendencies. As a result of
this attitude, as noted, the second half of the nineteenth century became
a virtual replay of the first half. Although it proved impossible for Franz
Joseph to maintain the same degree of absolutism—Robert Kann labels his
reign neo-absolutism[21]—he devoted his energies under the urging of his
mother, one of his most influential advisors, to the closest policy possible,
a system dedicated to clinging to the past and discouraging progressiveness
in every way he could achieve. Consequently the young emperor found
himself forced to cope with the same problems as his predecessors: the
constant pressure of the people for greater freedom of expression and
representative government internally, and increasingly vocal agitation for
self-determination by the member nations of the Monarchy externally. As
will be seen, these issues continued to plague the royal house until the end
of the Monarchy in 1918.

Ironically, the class that gained the most from the revolution was the
one that did not participate: the bourgeoisie, another indication that those
who enjoyed the Biedermeier lifestyle were neither resigned nor discon-
tented. They always emulated the aristocracy and did so now, standing by
passively while the government put down the uprising. The well-to-do
bourgeoisie feared the masses and revolution as much as the nobility did.

It was evident that the revolution changed the basis of Austrian society
and established conditions that should have enabled it to catch up with
the progressive tendencies evident throughout the rest of Europe. The age
of absolute despotism was irretrievably over, despite Franz Joseph's stalwart
efforts to maintain it. The materialistic bourgeois era quickly developed,
changing the country fundamentally. While the upper middle class should
have been grateful for the sacrifice that opened its path to dominance, they
felt no sympathy toward the workers or the liberals, only distrust and
wariness. When the workers in August 1848 were driven to rise up against
the factories again because of the imposition of harsher working conditions
for lower pay, the owners called in the Viennese Guard to quell the
disturbance in a bloody confrontation. It was clear that the struggle was
now between the bourgeoisie and the proletariat. The soil for Karl Marx
had been prepared.

The Literature to 1848

In viewing the Austrian literature of the nineteenth century, a curious situation emerges. Namely, the fact that although Austria dominated the German-speaking area politically up to 1848, it never asserted itself culturally, never insisted on the autonomy of its literature. Austrian writers, with few exceptions, seemed always to be content to accept a subordinate role to Germany even at the time when Metternich attempted to isolate the state politically and culturally, in order to insulate Austria from German thinking and influence and preserve it independently as an absolute monarchy. The two literatures and cultures clearly developed in separate ways, as the contemporary French writer Germaine de Staël observed as early as 1808 in her book *De l'Allemagne*. She commented that Austrian literature was provincial, that Austrians were different from Germans and, indeed, that they suffered from not being German enough.[22]

Part of the reason that Austria never made any strong, organized attempt to assert its literary autonomy stems from the lack of any strong nationalistic feeling or national consciousness in Austria as developed in the course of the nineteenth century in Germany beginning with the Romantic writers around 1800. National consciousness has always been strong in France and England. Madame de Staël, influenced by the thinking of her companion and mentor August Wilhelm Schlegel, one of the leaders of the first German Romantic school, attributed the lack of a significant literature in Austria at the beginning of the nineteenth century directly to this deficiency of national spirit.[23] As a multinational and multicultural monarchy, Austria maintained a supranational stance, even though the pluralism is usually ignored in literary-historical accounts, which concentrate almost exclusively on Vienna and often ignore even the provinces of Austria, not to mention the other lands and territories of the Monarchy. In contrast to Austria, which still does not possess a strong national feeling, these other states were encouraged to develop an Austrian national consciousness and to assimilate or at least to acculturate by being required to learn German. The imposition of this linguistic mandate eventually did result in the creation of a national spirit in the lands and territories by the second half of the nineteenth century. However, ironically, when it developed, it was for their own ethnic identification and their own nationality and country, not for the Austrian Monarchy.

Even the war with Napoleon at the beginning of the century failed to generate strong nationalistic feelings within the Monarchy. The threat of invasion spurred some patriotic poetry in Austria in 1809, such as the poems of Joseph von Collin, one of the most patriotic poets of the time. His volume of poems, *Lieder österreichischer Wehrmänner* (1809, Songs of Austrian Soldiers), celebrated the indestructability of Habsburg rule— "Habsburg's throne shall last forever, Austria shall not go under"—and summoning his countrymen to meet the Napoleonic threat by forming armies. However, such works were isolated phenomena, and no widespread outburst of patriotic literature occurred as in Germany.

The nature of the cultural relationship to Germany, however, cannot be explained solely by the supranational feeling in Austria deriving from the multinational composition of the Monarchy and the commensurate lack of any specific national feeling. Since Austria was stronger than Germany politically during the *Vormärz*—Germany was still fragmented into many small, independent states—this failure to assert literary autonomy also did not derive from any sense of inferiority, even though there were far fewer important authors and the literature was not as varied as in Germany. A more compelling reason for Austria's acceptance of the subordinate role can be seen in the desire of the Germans in Austria, who, although at that time only a small minority, dictated the political course of the country, to maintain their ties to their northern neighbor—but for their own advantage, not for that of Germany. Metternich's presidency of the German Union, for example, gave Austria a strong voice in German affairs. The practical desire to preserve this political attachment partly motivated the requirement of using German as the common language throughout the lands of the Monarchy. Primarily, the imposition of German served the important function of enabling the different ethnic populations to communicate with each other and with Vienna. German was the language of Austrian officialdom throughout the Monarchy and under Franz Joseph came to be used even by the Emperor's court, which, cosmopolitan and supranational, had traditionally spoken French or Italian rather than German. Similarly the use of German replaced Latin in science.

Further, the Austrian bureaucracy was educated in German and was brought up reading German literature and usually given a German orientation as well. Many of these officials also became the Austrian writers of the time—Franz Grillparzer may serve as a case in point. However, although authors wrote in German—and this is the salient point—their subject matter always concerned Austria and not Germany. Because of the censorship Austrian writers could not have emulated German themes even if they had so desired. Thus Austrian authors, while employing the German language, dealt with matters and conditions in their own country, as writers normally mirror the age in which they live. Viewed in these terms, the claim that everything written in German belongs to German literature, as is frequently made, is clearly erroneous. Austrian writing can correctly be called German-language literature but never simply German literature, a term which conveys a completely different and false connotation. By comparing the course of the two literatures throughout the nineteenth century and continuing to the present day, it can be seen beyond any doubt that Austrian literature has followed its own path in terms of themes and forms independent of Germany. Yet, despite this fact, in the view of German and even some Austrian literary historians, Austria has been and continues to be treated as a literary province of Germany.[24]

Austria has remained tied to Germany through the commonality of early history, heritage, and above all language, and this linguistic union has influenced the way in which the cultural relationship between the two countries has developed. German as well as some Austrian scholars have presented and often still do present the literary history of the German-speaking countries from the point of view of German dominance, with Austria—without objection—along with Switzerland annexed in a subordinate position, as cultural provinces of Germany despite the abundance of evidence to the contrary. Today, in addition to the persuasive evidence of separate thematic emphasis, a case can even be made for sufficient differences in language usage in Germany and Austria to view the latter in its own terms on linguistic grounds alone. Yet no amount of evidence seemingly can alter the German refusal to recognize Austrian literature in its own right or cause Austrian scholars to present a unifed front to defend literary autonomy.

The history of Austrian literature from the early nineteenth century to the present documents such a different manner of development in the two countries that it is difficult to understand how the idea of an autonomous Austrian culture and literature could have ever been, not to mention can still be, a matter of serious scholarly debate. Among other things the history can be cited to bear out the differences. Since the major union between the two countries, the Holy Roman Empire had been abolished in 1806, at Napoleon's insistence, and since the Germans declined to renew this bond after the threat of Napoleon had passed, Austria remained formally linked with Germany only through agreements such as the Holy Alliance and the Deutscher Bund, both organizations created at the Congress of Vienna to maintain the balance of powers. With Metternich serving as Head of the Deutscher Bund, Austria enjoyed a direct and strong voice in Germany which it wanted to maintain. When Bismarck, intent on building Germany into a strong, unified nationalistic state, wanted to sever all ties with Austria and remove all Austrian presence and influence in Germany, Austria was prepared to go to the extreme measure of declaring war to maintain the connection and to protect its representation in central Europe, not out of any feeling that it could not survive without Germany. The matter was decided against Austria at the battle of Königgrätz on 3 July 1866.

Austria then, against its will, existed politically as an independent country without any formal ties to Germany, just as it was to emerge again in 1918 with the establishment of the First Republic, and once more in 1955 with the founding of the Second Republic. Since the country clearly now exists as an internationally sanctioned and recognized independent nation, it would seem logical to regard it also as culturally autonomous. But this has never been and is still not the case, even though it should be self-evident that a politically independent nation could properly claim to have its own autonomous literature and culture. Austria remains a unique situation, for the matter of the independence of Austrian literature continues to be debated and problematized to the present day. The secondary literature dealing with this problem up to 1974 numbers more than four hundred books and articles devoted to the subject without making any impression on the continuing debate or reaching any resolution.[25] More articles and books on the same subject continue to appear each year, and the topic remains a lively one for debate at literary conferences.

Why can scholarship not resolve this matter? One can only conclude that the persistence of this problem and the impossibility of finding any agreement means that it has less to do with the rational facts of language, literary history, and logic in Austria than with the emotional desire of the Germans to maintain a dominant position in Austria and of the Germans in Austria to remain attached to Germany, even at the price of accepting a subordinate position. This deeply rooted feeling can be seen in several factors: the feeling of the Habsburgs that they were German emperors; the willingness of Austrians to go to the extreme of waging war in 1866 in order to maintain their connection with Germany; in the teaching in schools up to World War II that a good Austrian is a good German; in the initial attempt to call the First Republic a German-Austrian Republic, an idea that the Allies vetoed because of the wish to keep the two countries separate; in the undermining of Austria to achieve Anschluss, including the refusal of Chancellor Schuschnigg to defend the country and firing his Defense Minister Rüdiger von Starhemberg in 1936 when he proposed such a course of action; and in the unwillingness of most Austrian scholars and writers even today to insist on literary autonomy. One pragmatic reason often cited involves the Austrian dependence on the German book market. However, most Austrian writers have German publishers and all Austrian publishers have branches or connections in Germany, making it doubtful that sales would be affected since the authors are clearly identified on the book covers as Austrian. German readers are well aware of what they are purchasing. To explain this Austrian attitude of voluntary acquiescence fully would carry us far beyond the confines of this Introduction for it is a fundamental matter with ramifications that extend far beyond literature. This thinking and this relationship with Germany influenced and guided Austrian political policy throughout the 1920s and 1930s, leading to the Anschluss in 1938 and World War II.[26]

The question of the identity of Austrian literature first surfaced as early as the middle of the eighteenth century, when Johann Baptist Marek (1728-1810) and Franz Sartori (1782-1832) began to assemble the first bibliographies of Austrian writings.[27] Other efforts followed. The characteristics of Austrian literature have been traced back to the most celebrated medieval poet Walter von der Vogelweide in the twelfth century, who was conscious of his identity and importance as an Austrian writer. If one accepts Nadler's claim that the anonymous national epic, *Das Nibelungenlied* (ca. 1200) was written by an Austrian and belongs to Austrian literature, then it becomes older than German literature. Nadler also makes the remarkable and startling assertion that Joseph II could have put an Austrian imprint on German literature in the late eighteenth century while the latter was still in the process of development. However, he claims the opportunity was lost out of inaction and never returned; German literature developed its own structure and direction and could no longer be changed.[28] This is a provocative notion, but unfortunately Nadler provides no explanation of how and why this possibility existed, gives no evidence that Joseph II ever really thought about Austrian cultural superiority, and, if so, why it was not acted upon. In fact, it appears highly dubious that

Joseph II ever devoted attention to this matter. Not even many scholars or writers were thinking about an autonomous Austrian literature at this time, and even those who did were certainly not considering the possibility of dominating German literature, although Blumauer raised the suggestion privately that Austrian literature might be ahead of German writing.

A prominent eighteenth-century voice, the writer Aloys Blumauer (1755-1798) strongly defended the idea of an independent Austrian literature. He began as a Jesuit, worked for a time as a government censor, narrowly escaped conviction for his involvement in the Jacobin Conspiracy, and ended his life running a bookstore. In his most notable literary work *Vergils Aeneis travestiert* (1784, A Travesty of Virgil's Aeneid), one of the first Austrian monuments of the eighteenth century, he satirizes the conflict between the Catholic Church and the Imperial House caused by the reforms of Joseph II. His strong support for the idea of an independent Austrian literature found its clearest expression not in a public document but in a letter to the writer Friedrich Nicolai in Berlin:

> The Austrian state, which is usually represented everywhere in terms of masculine strength, is still regarded with respect to literature as not yet of age and therefore must continue to content itself with accepting valuable advice from unwanted foreign intellectual mentors. . . . Is not Vienna the center around which Germany's smaller and larger planets revolve? Isn't it—at least now—the focal point of all Europe?, . . . Doesn't everyone look at us and haven't even foreign writers acknowledged that if German literature, as it stands at present, declines any further, it will have to be led from Vienna.[29]

It is one of the common errors of literary criticism to extract a quotation from a letter, a document written in the mood of the moment, and to then regard such an opinion as representing a lifelong conviction. The problem with a letter like this is how to weight it. Was the satirist Blumauer being serious or whimsical? If one compares the two literatures in 1784, one has serious grounds to wonder, although his essay "Beobachtungen über Österreichische Aufklärung und Literatur" (1782, Observations on Austrian Enlightenment and Literature) leaves no doubt about his sincere concern for the Austrian literary scene. Here he discusses the freedom of the press granted by Joseph II on 11 July 1781 and laments the subsequent flood of brochures devoted to current events, a literary trend that ended only after 1790. Zeman suggests that all the attention devoted to political questions precluded the possibility of producing literary works as found in Weimar.[30] However, it is more likely that the absence of talented authors rather than involvement in politics produced the situation that kept any major Austrian writers or works from emerging in the eighteenth century. While the Germans experienced the "Storm and Stress" period of the 1770s and 1780s as a prelude to flowering of literature in the nineteenth century, the Austrian authors used their newly granted freedom of expression to produce a flood of brochures dealing with the politics of the time. There was no influence in Austria of the German "Genie" period, and a work like Goethe's *Die Leiden des jungen Werthers,* which made such an impact in Europe, had no effect in Austria. Other writers, like Heinrich Joseph von Collin (1771-1811) and Josef Baron von Hormayr (1781-1848), both dedicated patriots who had played active roles in the fight against Napoleon, stressed the idea of Austrian literature. Notably, both attempted to involve all of the lands of the Monarchy in this concept. Collin believed that Austria should stand as the first state among equals and that Austrian culture in the German language should lead but not control the education and culture of the other states.

Hormayr, a historian from the Tyrol, represented a similar approach. He saw the strongest connection between the states of the Monarchy in the hundreds of years of common history. Hormayr stood out as one of the most outspoken participants among those trying to awaken a sense of patriotism against Napoleon, and his activism was not limited to his writings. He helped organize the Tyrolean uprising led by Andreas Hofer against Napoleon in 1809, and in so doing aroused the enmity of the French general. In 1813 Hormayr tried to arrange an Alpine Union, which was to include Switzerland and Southern Germany. For this political involvement he was dismissed from the government position he had held since 1808 as Director of the State Archives and imprisoned. After his release in 1816, he could not return to his former post. Embittered, he moved to Germany, where he held a variety of government jobs. Bahr considered Hormayr another case of the "Austrian Fate," one of the "real people" not tolerated in Austria.

In his journal *Österreichischer Plutarch* (1807-1812, The Austrian Plutarch), Hormayr published literature from all of the lands of the Monarchy, each selection in its own language, as a means of creating a sense of community and a feeling of national consciousness. Theoretically the concept sounds ideal, but without a common language no bond can be created. This was true then and it remains true now, where different languages within the same country continue to divide people. Other notable contributions by this prolific author include *Wiens Geschichte und seine Denkwürdigkeiten* (1823-1825, Vienna's History and Memorable Events) and *Taschenbuch für die vaterländische Geschichte* (A Short History of Our Austrian Homeland). Grillparzer received ideas for his national drama *König Ottokars Glück und Ende* (*King Ottokar's Rise and Fall*) from Hormayr's historical writings. Like Nadler later, Hormayr advocated the idea that the action of the *Nibelungenlied* took place in the area around Vienna, signifying that Austrian literature was older than German.

The most prominent author who insisted that he was an Austrian not a German writer was Franz Grillparzer. His contemporaries, Ferdinand Raimund and Johann Nestroy, the major representatives of the uniquely Austrian institution of the Folk Theater (*Altwiener Volkstheater*), for which there is no parallel in Germany, were also conscious of their Austrian identity. However, the author who is held up today as the representative par excellence of Austrian literature in the nineteenth century, Adalbert Stifter, never discussed the question of his being an Austrian writer. He took his Austrian identity for granted and saw no need to proclaim or defend it. He simply embodied it, lived it, and expressed it in his works. Ulrich Greiner, who states that Austria is definably separate from Germany historically and politically, that it has a different past, different traditions, a different present, and different literature, regards Stifter's *Nachsommer* (Indian Summer) as the incarnation of Austrian literature.[31]

In these views he echoes Bahr, one of Stifter's greatest admirers, who devoted the year 1918 to reading his works and the rest of his life to publicizing the importance of Stifter to Austria: "No one had a purer image of the Austrian spirit, no one protected and cherished this image in creative hands with gentler and more fervent reverence than Stifter. He created the human type, which one day will make a true Austria possible."[32] It is important to note Bahr's emphasis on the idealistic nature of Stifter's writings: his Austria did not yet exist but still lay in the future. When it is realized, then his countrymen will know what they had in Stifter.

The sense of Austrian patriotism that developed at the beginning of the nineteenth century in response to the threat of Napoleon deteriorated over time in reaction to the oppressive government policies. In the second half of the nineteenth century, when Franz Joseph continued to maintain the status quo while Germany grew rapidly into a modern industrial state, Austrian writers looked longingly and enviously at German growth as opposed to Austrian stagnation. Politically, scientifically, educationally, and economically Germany surged ahead, while in Austria progress was stifled. With Bismarck's strong leadership creating a powerful, unified state that demonstrated its strength in the Franco-Prussian War of 1870-1871, Germany developed into the most powerful country in Europe. Some Austrian writers felt so strongly about the discrepancy between the two countries that they moved to the Reich to experience the vitality, to share in the vibrant growth and exciting changes. Hermann Bahr, Karl Emil Franzos, Jakob Julius David, and later Robert Musil, among others, all lamenting that nothing was happening in Austria, studied and worked in Germany.

Through his writings from 1889 to 1906 Bahr, who wanted to work on the European scene, made Austrians aware of the cultural movements not only in Germany, but also in France and Spain.[33] However, upon discovering a generation of young talented writers during a visit to Vienna in 1891, he remained in Austria to play a major role in leading Austrian culture into the twentieth century on a par with the literature and art in other European countries.[34] Neither before nor after Bahr has Austria ever had such a forceful, energetic, deeply committed cultural advocate to proclaim and promote Austria's place in the literary and cultural hierarchy of Europe.

For Bahr, a cosmopolitan and supranationalist, no doubt ever existed about the existence and autonomy of Austrian literature:

> Yes, there absolutely and unqualifiedly is an Austrian literature, as Grillparzer, Feuchtersleben, and Stifter knew and never doubted. However, liberalism gradually blurred and erased this concept. The idea of an Austrian literature has long existed and could be recognized everywhere in Austria, a literature that is not merely an appendage tucked away in some corner or other of the German literary tradition, but a literature *sui juris*, indigenous, autonomous, unique, and independent from time immemorial. To be sure, it took my courage, my boldness, my

> delight in paradoxes, especially those that are only the shell of
> a platitude, to proclaim it boldly.[35]

When the first volume of the four-volume *Deutsch-Österreichische Literatur-geschichte* (1900-1937, German-Austrian Literary History), still the most detailed and useful Austrian literary history for the time it covers, appeared in 1900, Bahr criticized the editors Nagl and Zeidler for including the word German in the title.[36] He insisted that Austria had a literature separate from German and urged literary scholars to document this idea. He did not recognize then what became evident later, namely, that the editors were oriented toward Germany and became National Socialists, as did other prominent Austrian literary historians, such as Josef Nadler, Wilhelm Scherer,[37] Adalbert Schmidt, Herbert Cysarz, and Heinz Kindermann.[38]

The matter of Austrian identity was also never in doubt for Hofmannsthal, who defended the idea of Austrian literature with a passion equal to Bahr's:

> My own attempt to give form to this intellectual manner, the
> unique blend of self-consciousness and modesty, sure instinct
> and occasional naiveté, natural balance and minimal capability
> for dialect, all of these elements that comprise the Austrian
> essence speak just as clearly in my comedies such as *Der
> Rosenkavalier* (1908, The Cavalier of the Rose), *Der Schwierige*
> (1918, *The Difficult Man*), which are nothing if they are not
> documents of the Austrian type (*Wesensart*), as they do in
> more precise formulation in numerous essays and speeches
> such as "Maria Theresia," "Prince Eugen," and "Austria in the
> Mirror of Its Literature."[39]

Both Bahr and Hofmannsthal, influenced by Nadler, saw the uniqueness of the Austrian literary tradition in the Baroque.[40] One can assess all of the reasons, detail all of the evidence, as has been done repeatedly, but it still does not bring consensus or end the debate. Following World War II there was a burst of patriotism and national feeling as a reaction against Nazi Germany and as a means of dissociating Austria from its former ally. All efforts were made to reestablish the connection with the Austrian tradition that had been halted by the Anschluss in 1938.[41] This enthusiasm for an independent Austrian literature culminated with the establishment of the Second Republic in 1955 and then slowly deteriorated, with the issue becoming problematized again in the absence of any strong commitment to this concept by scholars and writers.

As the many publications and synopses devoted to this topic show, providing the evidence to document the existence of an autonomous Austrian literature has not proved sufficient to establish a consensus. The resistance comes from within Austria, from Germany, and from German-born professors in the United States. Other countries have no difficulty in accepting Austria and Austrian literature in their own right, independent of Germany. When one addresses the question of why this self-evident matter continues to be problematized, the answer can only be that it is not treated in a logical matter. The issue of the autonomy of Austrian literature will continue to be debated, for, like such matters as religious faith and predestination, it is a question of feeling and attitude, not of reason. There can be no resolution of this problem, despite the overwhelming abundance of evidence, because emotion rather than rationality and scholarly logic continues to fuel the controversy. Because of this approach, this question will remain unresolved until Austrians, in concert, insist on their literary autonomy and assert and defend the idea internally and externally.

Such, however, is far from the case. Recently, a leading Austrian scholar has argued that that question of Austrian identity should be laid to rest because it no longer matters: "In terms of literary theory this question [of Austrian identity] can very probably be regarded as obsolete . . . Why should one separate Austrian from German literature, why should we speak of 'autonomy,' why should Austrian literature be discussed as an Austrian literature at all?"[42]   One can only answer that the reason the question should continue to be discussed is because it exists. For scholarly inquiry no other reason is needed. Universities teach Austrian literature as they do many other national literatures. Why should literature written in Austria by Austrian writers and dealing with Austrian conditions not be called Austrian literature? Every other literature is named according to its national origin. Why should one employ the formulation German-language literature from Austria instead of Austrian literature? American, Australian, Canadian, and Irish literatures are referred to in terms of their national origin, not as English-language literatures from these respective countries.

Why should Austrian literature be treated differently, establishing it as a unique case in literary history?

To consider the issue irrelevant—the equivalent of quietly accepting the notion of literary Anschluss—is simply not a viable scholarly solution because it ignores an existing factual situation. Silence is a way of finessing the problem and allowing the existing situation of Austrian literature subordinated to German literature to continue. A better approach would be to resolve the problem, which could be accomplished if Austrian scholars and writers would insist on literary autonomy, if the new literary histories that are being written would feature the idea of an independent literature, and finally if the designation of the language that Austrians speak were changed from German to Austrian. Then the common language issue, which is the major source of the difficulty, would be eliminated as a continuing source of confusion. This suggestion is not as radical as it may sound at first, for there is a precedent. This change would be analogous to the solution used in the United States, where authors write American, not English, literature, just as Australian, Canadian, and Irish writers, among others, all use English but are presented under their own independent national designation. Just as these countries are separated from England by the same language, so too is Austria from Germany.

In addition to the failure to insist upon its literary independence Austria faced a political and cultural issue of profound importance: the integration of the member states into the Monarchy, a problem that still persists today in the attitude toward the minority ethnic groups within Austria such as the Slovenians and Croatians. The imposition of the German language on other ethnic groups in the eighteenth and nineteenth centuries, while logical and necessary to enable the Monarchy to function, never achieved its goal of creating a unified national consciousness, not to mention any sense of common cultural identity except in the German-speaking enclaves in those countries. Viktor von Andrian-Werburg perceptively noted this failure in 1843:

> There are Italians, Germans, Slavs, and Hungarians, who together constitute the Austrian imperial state, but Austria, an Austrian nationality does not exist and has never existed. . . . Therefore, a national feeling, a national pride, a strong, uplifting consciousness of one's own strength is and must be foreign to the Austrian as such—for he considers and feels himself isolated, beyond all intellectual and sympathetic union

with his fellow citizens of a different ethnic group which he neither wants to nor can recognize as his countrymen—and his narrow patriotism does not extend beyond his village or at most his province.[43]

If the monarchy was not a unified nation politically, it was even less so in literary terms. For the language problem posed an insuperable barrier for writers in the various lands and territories. Only those authors who wrote in German about Austrian life and conditions were ever accepted into the Austrian literary tradition. Even those in the Prague circle around Max Brod, who preferred initially to establish ties to Berlin rather than to Vienna,[44] have been incorporated into Austrian, not German, literary history. If, however, authors like Rainer Maria Rilke, Franz Kafka, Ernst Weiss, and Franz Werfel had written in Czech or Elias Canetti in Bulgarian, they would not be recognized as belonging to Austrian literature, and there is every likelihood that they would not be known in the western world today. Authors who wrote in languages other than German have never been absorbed into the Austrian literary tradition to any degree even in translation, despite the multicultural makeup of Austria. Thus one can see that the incorporation of a writer into a literary tradition is not simply a matter of birth and language but results primarily from the choice of subjects and themes. Just as the great authors in every literature discuss the world around them that they know, the writers from the various lands addressed issues of their own countries, just as Austrian writers discussed conditions within Austria. Beyond language the factors of subject matter, theme, form, and style determine the literary tradition to which an author belongs and serve as the criteria that distinguish the writers of one nation from those of another. This measure is just as valid in defining the individuality of Austrian literature vis-à-vis German writing as well as that of other nations.

The matter of language became one of the thorniest issues to resolve in attempting to forge the Monarchy into a unity. The issue still exists in terms of Slovenian and Croatian literature which is ignored by the mainstream Austrian literary tradition, even though these ethnic groups form part of Austria. Only those authors, like Janko Ferk, whose works become available in translations or dual language editions have any hope of recognition outside their own ethnic community. For this reason a comprehensive history of Austrian literature incorporating all of the lands and territories will probably never be written.

The language question, a critical problem throughout history, remains a central issue in many countries of the world at the present time. As in the past, the question remains a matter of whether different ethnic groups will assimilate or acculturate and thereby accept the language and culture of the majority, or whether they will attempt to preserve their own language and customs and live as a separate minority within the larger society with all the problems that this situation entails. In nineteenth-century Austria those who moved to Vienna from other lands usually wanted either to assimilate, which involved converting to Catholicism in the case of Jews, or at least to acculturate, which meant to join the mainstream in every way except changing religion. One notable exception was the group of Galician Jews who came to Vienna where they preferred to maintain their own dress and customs. In doing so they drew the ire of other assimilated Jews for calling attention to themselves and for arousing anti-Semitism. Jewish anti-Semitism was not unfamiliar at this time.

The history of Austrian literature in the nineteenth century—actually already in the eighteenth, as seen—reveals more differences than similarities with German literature. The literary course clearly shows itself to be indigenous, not borrowed from Germany. The two dominating tendencies in German literature around 1800 were the opposing movements of Classicism and Romanticism. Classicism, represented by Goethe and Schiller in Weimar after a decade of "Storm and Stress" in the 1780s, followed the idealistic aims of the Enlightenment, with writings serving the ideal of moral guidance, in order to develop a sense of moderation within the individual and a feeling of harmony between human beings and the world about them. The writings of Goethe in particular became the measure of all German literature in the nineteenth and well into the twentieth century—but not of Austrian writing, although some influence existed.[45] Goethe's influence faded in Austria after his death until in 1896 he was rediscovered by Bahr and others of his generation, who from then on kept his name before the public eye. Goethe's developmental or educational novel *Wilhelm Meisters Lehrjahre* (1795, *Wilhelm Meister's Apprenticeship*), with its sequel *Wilhelm Meisters Wanderjahre* (1821, *Wilhelm Meister's Travels*) became the model for many other works of this type, including Gustav Freytag's *Soll und Haben* (1855, *Debit and Credit*), showing the triumph of the bourgeoisie over the aristocracy, and the most famous representative from Austria, Adalbert Stifter's classic work *Der Nachsommer* (1857, *Indian Summer*). Goethe's *Faust*, also in two parts, and completed only in the year of his death (1832), demonstrated that the greatest good for human beings lay in service to others. Through striving to benefit society, one could overcome any missteps along the way and earn redemption. Similarly Schiller viewed the stage as a moral institution for the edification of the public. Both writers abhorred revolution and defended the principles of order and moderation. Bahr, who had consistently held Goethe up as a model for writers and public alike,[46] felt that these values were needed in Austria after World War I, and as director of the Burgtheater in 1918 he staged Goethe's *Die natürliche Tochter* (1803, *The Natural Daughter*) as a warning against revolution.

In terms of form, Classicism (the Apollonian) aimed at presenting a sense of completeness. Writings were rounded off to portray a total situation and draw a moral conclusion rather than being left ambiguously open-ended. This closure represents a major difference from Romanticism (the Dionysian), which eschewed any sense of finiteness. Romanticism was anti-rational and resembled life in remaining in a constant state of progressive development, pursuing a goal symbolized by a blue flower, that is, a goal that can never be reached. The writers of the first Romantic school—Friedrich Schlegel, August W. Schlegel, Ludwig Tieck, and Novalis (pseudonym for Friedrich von Hardenberg)—believed that people should be free to develop to the full extent of their potential without outside restrictions and limitations. Whereas the watchword for the Classical writers was moderation, the Romantics preached individual freedom to the limits of license. They opposed any sense of order or hierarchy that restrained personal development.

Unlike the Classical writers, the Romantics, particularly those of the Second Romantic School—Achim von Arnim (1781-1831), Clemens Brentano (1778-1842), Joseph von Eichendorff (1788-1857), and E.T.A. Hoffmann (1776-1822), were not defenders of the aristocracy but sought the strength of the nation in the ordinary people. This idea led them to foster the folk spirit of the nation by reviving fairy tales, myths, and legends, as in Tieck's *Volksmärchen* (1797, Folk Fairy Tales), Arnim and Brentano's *Des Knaben Wunderhorn: Alte deutsche Lieder* (1806 and 1808, The Boy's Magic Horn), Joseph Görres (1776-1848), *Die Teutschen Volksbücher* (1807, German Folk Books). The trend of reviving folk literature of the past led to the philological studies of the Grimm brothers, the classical volumes of Grimm's fairy tales which children around the world grew up reading, and Grimm's definitive dictionary, begun in 1852 and completed a century later. Classicism ended with the death of Goethe in 1832, while Romanticism lingered on until 1848, although without the intellectual impact or influence of the original Schlegel-Tieck circle, which had provided the theoretical basis of Romanticism.

In the 1830s a political literary movement developed in Germany to protest against the repressive political and social conditions there. Such writers as Georg Büchner, Heinrich Heine, Karl Gutzkow, and Ludwig Börne, among others, were grouped together under the name Young Germany by the police. The group had to disperse when it was discovered that one member had become a police informer who was betraying the others whenever he needed money. Heine was forced to flee to Paris and Büchner to Switzerland. Both died in exile.

Other literary currents in Germany included the Fate Drama (*Schicksalstragödie*), an offshoot of Romanticism and the supernatural literature prevalent at the time, represented by Adolf Müllner and Zacharias Werner, provincial literature (Berthold Auerbach), patriotic lyrics (Theodor Körner), poetic realism (Theodor Storm, Wilhelm Raabe, and the two Swiss writers Gottfried Keller and Conrad Ferdinand Meyer), the Munich art-for-art's-sake group (Paul Heyse, Emanuel Geibel), historical novels written by professors (Felix Dahn, Georg Ebers, Viktor Scheffel), and realism (Theodor Fontane), leading in the 1880s into naturalism (Arno Holz).

Standing alone is one of the greatest writers of his time, Heinrich von Kleist, a Romantic who was driven to early suicide in 1811 because he found no place in the literature or the society of his time. Like a number of German writers, Kleist visited Vienna but could establish no footing there any more than he could anywhere else. Later his plays—in adaptation—were performed at the Court Theater. In the middle of the century German drama was represented by Friedrich Hebbel and Otto Ludwig. Hebbel lived for many years in Vienna but without playing any role there and without absorbing any Austrian influence on the pan-tragic outlook of his dramas. Otto Ludwig's dramas were influenced by Shakespeare, while as a representative of poetic realism he helped introduce the working class into literature in the novel *Zwischen Himmel und Erde* (1856, *Between Heaven and Earth*).

By contrast Austrian literature does not reveal this variety and complexity of overlapping literary currents and trends but develops in a relatively smooth line of progression. To be sure one always finds the two conflicting trends of continuity and change, innovation and tradition, occurring concurrently in Austrian as in every literature, but the transition to the new phase is always orderly rather than represented by any sharp break. Regard for the past and respect for earlier writers and artists has always been strong. To characterize the Austrian literary tradition as consisting of "a series of rebellions and radical protests against tradition," as Claudio Magris has claimed, is a misrepresentation.[47] Andrian's perceptive, more accurate description has held true throughout Austrian history: "More even than nature in terms of its immutable laws, Austria hates all jumps—it is the true, classical land of routine, of habit, of the everyday—this is the way things are today, because this is the way they were yesterday."[48]

Literature was not allowed to develop freely in Austria up to 1848 because of tight government control and censorship. Joseph von Collin wrote some patriotic poetry during the Napoleonic wars, but no trend of pronouncedly nationalistic literature developed. There was no fate drama despite the fact that Zacharias Werner moved to Vienna shortly after the great success of his play *Der vierundzwanzigste Februar* (1810, *The Twenty-fourth of February*). On the contrary, he repudiated this drama, turned his back on literature, and lived out his life as a successful preacher in Austria. There was neither a Classical nor a Romantic movement despite the presence of the Schlegel brothers, Friedrich and August Wilhelm, along with many other German Romantic writers such as Ludwig and Dorothea Tieck, Theodor Körner, and Clemens Brentano. No movement equivalent to Young Germany was formed within Austria. Rietra attempts to label the political activists and pamphleteers "Young Austria,"[49] but in the absence of any formal organization in Vienna, the two groups cannot be considered parallel. The protesters within Austria remained individuals and were never recognized as being unified. Because of censorship and the police network of spies, political protest was confined to books and pamphlets usually published anonymously outside Austria.

Austrian literature developed independently of German writing and offers a much less complicated line of development. Grillparzer combines within himself aspects of a number of the German trends: Classicism, Romanticism, fate tragedy, historical drama, and the baroque. Lyric poetry was represented by Grillparzer, Anastasius Grün, Nikolaus von Lenau, and Betty Paoli, historical plays by the Collin brothers, Karoline Pichler, and Friedrich Halm, dialect poetry by Franz Stelzhamer (1802-1874) and Ignaz Franz Castelli (1781-1862), drawing-room comedies and conversation dramas by Eduard von Bauernfeld, and oriental studies and translations from the Persian by Hammer-Purgstall. Ferdinand Raimund and Johann Nestroy brought a flowering of the uniquely Austrian folk theater, for which no parallel exists in German literature. Literature about America is represented by Nikolaus Lenau and Charles Sealsfield.

The major analogous tendency to Germany is to be found in the works of poetic realism, represented by Adalbert Stifter, Friedrich Halm, Ferdinand Kürnberger, Karl Emil Franzos, Leopold von Sacher-Masoch, Ferdinand von Saar, and Marie von Ebner-Eschenbach. Naturalism, which never took root in Austria just as Impressionism was never practiced in Germany, was represented solely by Jakob Julius David, one of the authors who moved to Germany to work and write. Anzengruber, who is often mistakenly considered a naturalist writer, remains a realist in both his prose and dramas because they do not contain the element of determinism essential to naturalism. The same is true of the Tyrolean Karl Schönherr (1867-1943), who is essentially a realist but who also experimented with Expressionism.[50]

The Theater to 1848

The theater served as an important institution in nineteenth-century Vienna, functioning with governmental blessing as a means of occupying the people's attention and hopefully distracting them from concern with social and political problems and with their lack of freedom. In addition to its entertainment function, the theater also fulfilled a moral and an educational purpose as well, serving as both pulpit and university. The theater-going public received moral instruction, proper guidance in how to behave as good loyal citizens, and through the idolized performers even models of social behavior, manners, and dress.

Vienna, which was still a walled city at the beginning of the nineteenth century, had two court theaters within the inner city: the Burgtheater, which was attached to the Hofburg palace, and the Kärntnertortheater. The Burgtheater presented a literary repertoire of European plays, which before the performance first had to be adapted to conform to the guidelines of the ruling house. The most frequently performed author by far was August Friedrich Kotzebue, the prolific German creator of sentimental, moral melodramas. He not only dominated the Burgtheater repertoire, but he was also the most performed author in the other lands of the Monarchy, where actors from the Court Theater traveled to put on performances. Following Kotzebue in popularity came Schiller, Shakespeare, Goethe, and Kleist. For the most part, however, the repertoire consisted of minor playwrights who have all faded into literary oblivion. Well-known authors from other countries were performed in translated and adapted versions of their plays: Molière, Scribe, and Voltaire from France, Gozzi and Goldoni from Italy, and Calderón from Spain.

The censors and the book adapters were instructed to insure "public entertainment without danger to the mind, heart, customs, and mood of the public."[51] At this time the Burgtheater was considered a court, not a national theater—it received the designation only later—and the strict censors always used the criterion of what would please the emperor and the court. Under this stricture the Burgtheater could not earn any reputation for its repertoire but rather became celebrated for the quality of the acting—its luster attracted the best performers of the time and gave the theater a European-wide reputation for its ensemble of star performers—not for its literary, directorial, or stage-design innovations. Nevertheless the theater became renowned under the two outstanding early directors, both from Germany, Josef Schreyvogel (1768-1832) and Heinrich Laube (1806-1884), who produced these results while working under the severe constraints of censorship, on the one hand, and the supervision of conservative aristocrats who actually controlled the policy and budget of the theater, on the other.

The Kärntnertortheater operated quite differently in terms of management and repertoire. Up to 1848 the theater was usually leased to private individuals, often Italian entrepreneurs, who featured Italian operas and ballets among other entertainments. It also presented a broad range of plays, since it appealed to a wider audience than the Burgtheater, which remained the exclusive domain of the aristocracy, but its specialty remained musical performances.

Outside the walls of Vienna three theaters operated for the broader public: the Theater in der Josefstadt, Theater an der Wien, and Theater in der Leopoldstadt, which was refurbished and renamed the Carltheater in 1847 and was brought to prominence under the entrepreneurial director Carl Karl. These theaters were the homes of what has come to be known as the Old Vienna Folk Theater (*Altwiener Volkstheater*). The term "Volk" causes some confusion because not everyone understands the word in the same way. As used in the *Vormärz,* it means people from the lower classes, not the nation per se, as it came to signify in the twentieth century in the attempt to create a national unity. The two most prominent representatives of the Folk Theater were Ferdinand Raimund (1790-1836) and Johann Nepomuk Nestroy (1801-1862), who along with Grillparzer constitute the major and most enduring contribution of Austrian theater in the first half of the nineteenth century.[52] It is a mistake, however, to reduce the Folk Theater to these two names, for in addition to the plays they offered the three theaters played an important social role by providing a rich diversity of popular entertainment, ranging from local comedies to foreign attractions, from pure spectacles to melodramas and musicals, from plays involving magic and the supernatural to operas.

Other notable popular playwrights were Alois Gleich (1772-1841), who was also a director and for a time the father-in-law of Raimund, Karl Meisl (1775-1853), and Adolph Bäuerle (1786-1859), who achieved great popularity with the character Staberl that he created. Between them these writers produced hundreds of farcical plays (*Possen*) intended purely for light entertainment. None had literary pretentions, and none lasted beyond their own time.

Another playwright, Emanuel Schikaneder (1751-1812), who distinguished himself as an actor, director, and theater entrepreneur, is remembered for writing the libretto for Mozart's opera *Die Zauberflöte* (1790, *The Magic Flute*), which has become a virtual cultural icon and is still performed frequently. Schikaneder's subsequent plays, all written according to the tastes of the time, have been forgotten. More important than his works was his contribution to the theater life of the time through his enterprise in finding wealthy backers to fund the construction of the Theater an der Wien. Initially he successfully directed lavish productions, but after 1807 his luck changed and his fortunes declined.

Like most folk theater authors, Raimund and Nestroy began their careers as actors who turned to writing their own plays as vehicles for showcasing their unique talents. Both were celebrated performers, but in addition they were also serious writers not content merely to amuse their audiences. Like the painters, who mirrored their time, they too made their plays socially relevant by introducing themes and commentaries that addressed contemporary issues and problems. In doing so they elevated the folk play to a literary level and invested this form with a significance that it had not previously held. The form of the critical folk play was born. Of all the writers for the Folk Theater, they are the only two whose works have survived as part of the literary tradition and are still performed today.

As so often happens in literature, the term folk play and the category of the Old Vienna Folk Theater were established by later critics. The classification seemed logical, since these works were performed in the popular theaters for the ordinary people and could not be staged in the aristocratic Burgtheater. The writers themselves never designated any of their works Folk Plays. The importance of the movement was discerned only belatedly. In its own day, when Lessing's strict literary classification and rigid separation of forms and genres was still observed, the folk play, which was often not printed or even written down formally, was regarded as popular or trivial literature. This designation was deserved in the latter part of the nineteenth century when the form deteriorated to the point that the folk play came to be held in such disrepute that it fell completely out of favor.

Writers in the 1920s and 1930s, like Veza Canetti, Marieluise Fleisser, Ödön von Horváth, and Jura Soyfer, rediscovered the form and revived it as a useful vehicle for social satire and criticism. One might have expected Bertolt Brecht to use this form because of his preference for a folk quality in his plays, but he rejected it because of what he regarded as its formulaic construction and melodramatic features. The Folk Play has experienced another revival in recent years and continues to be used as a major form by such contemporary authors as Wolfgang Bauer, Elfriede Jelinek, Felix Mitterer, and Peter Turrini.[53]

Although he began writing in the tradition of the supernatural and magical plays that attracted and dazzled eager audiences with remarkable stage effects such as a stagecoach and other vehicles traveling through the air, Raimund aspired to recognition as a serious dramatist. He wanted his plays to be regarded as literary works and performed in the Burgtheater. It became the tragedy of his later life that his contemporaries refused to accept his writings as anything but entertainment. He had been typecast in the eyes of his audiences, and when he became too serious they reacted negatively.

If his plays might at first sight look like escapism from the harsh conditions of the time, a closer reading illustrates how Raimund took issue with contemporary social problems, but in a discreet manner to avoid trouble with the censors. However, the public and the critics also seemed to miss his intention. Raimund was no revolutionary who brought an overtly political message to the theater, which would have been censored in any case, no satirist, whose characters were created to arouse anger and protest, and no cynic who regarded things as hopeless. He was not resigned, as is frequently alleged, but a believer in moderation. The two may appear similar but they are not the same. Raimund maintained a positive attitude, not the negative one that resignation represents.

Raimund was a gifted writer who could capture genuine human emotions without pathos. He portrayed the reality of his time albeit with the extravagant stage effects expected of a folk playwright and left it to the audiences to interpret his works as they wished. In keeping with his public's expectations, his plays always ended harmoniously and thus seemed to uphold the Biedermeier idea that happiness came from accepting one's place in life and staying in it. Yet what Raimund was really saying was quite different, in fact the reverse. Reinhard Urbach illustrates by his interpretation of *Moisasurs Zauberfluch* (1827, *Moisasur's Curse*) how Raimund criticized the Biedermeier ideal by presenting it in mirror image. Urbach demonstrates persuasively that the play conveys a political message, presenting effective theatrical scenes which turned Biedermeier reality into *Vormärz* political literature.[54] To read the play as advocating resignation is to miss the author's intention. Raimund wished to show the reality of his time, which was anything but ideal for the lower level of society. Just as Hugo von Hofmannsthal and Arthur Schnitzler were unjustly criticized for advocating aestheticism in the 1890s, when in fact they were condemning this lifestyle, Raimund has long been presented as defending the Biedermeier social order when he was actually exposing its negative side by simply presenting it truthfully without commentary. Only belatedly did scholars recognize that Raimund's achievement matched his ambition and finally accord him his earned place in the literary tradition. Today his plays are considered classics and are performed in the Burgtheater.

When Raimund saw Nestroy's play *Lumpazivagabundus* at the Theater an der Wien in 1833, he recognized immediately that it was a portent of the future direction of the theater. Nestroy stood in sharp contrast to Raimund. He was daring, brash, and gifted, qualities that made him into the social critic and satirist that the time needed. Nestroy's biting sarcasm, sharp wit, and caustic cynicism which he lavished on contemporary writers, suited the harsher, rebellious climate of the *Vormärz* better than Raimund's warmer humor and sentimentality, which accorded better with the gentler Biedermeier public that wanted to be entertained without having its peace of mind disturbed. Nestroy always flirted with the limits of tolerance allowed by the censors, who monitored all theater performances and were particularly watchful of the extemporaneous monologues he added to each presentation to comment on current affairs. Sometimes he overstepped the boundaries, the performance was halted, and he was fined or imprisoned. Nestroy spared no one, for he harbored no illusions about the nature of human beings: "I believe the worst of every person, even of myself, and I have seldom ever been disappointed."

In this vein, he criticized rich and poor alike without partiality, as seen in *Zu ebener Erde und erster Stock* (1835, *On the First and on the Second Floor*). He also criticized prominent figures of his day such as Friedrich Hebbel and the well-known composer Richard Wagner. In general his writings in a variety of forms—magic plays, parodies, farces, folk plays, and political comedies—hold up a critical mirror to his age. As was customary among folk play authors he borrowed his plots freely, usually from French or English sources, but he adapted them to Viennese conditions. For that reason his works provide an overview of his time. His extraordinary popularity made him the outstanding author of the suburban theaters. Much of the effectiveness of his plays derives from Nestroy's brilliant use of language. In this respect he may be regarded as a forerunner of Karl Kraus, who regarded him highly. Because of the language and the universality of his themes these works have retained their power and appeal and have kept Nestroy a perennial favorite to the present day. His plays are still performed regularly in the major theaters, including the Burgtheater, and also have become a staple of summer theaters in Austria.

Like all other aspects of life in the *Vormärz,* the development of the theater was retarded by the strict censorship. The situation provides an excellent example of the negative effect caused by the absolutist system, which was carried out by dedicated officials who followed orders with great zeal. Since the theater was one of the few places where large numbers of people came together, it was held under tight surveillance. The censors took their responsibility very seriously and insured that not only performances, but also the literature remained within the government's guidelines. Once authors submitted a manuscript, they lost all control. There was no way to speed up the approval process, and works that displeased a censor or aroused his suspicion could be buried for years without any means of recourse. There was also no means of challenging a decision. Unless the required changes were made, the work would not be approved. In his perceptive analysis of Austrian conditions, *Austria as It Is* (1828), Sealsfield asked rhetorically: "What would have become of Shakespeare had he been doomed to live or write in Austria?"[55] Grillparzer echoed these sentiments in similar terms: "An Austrian poet should be held in higher esteem than all others. Anyone who does not lose heart under such circumstances is truly a hero."[56]

One example of how the repressive system worked will serve for many. In his play *Ein treuer Diener seines Herrn* (1828, *A Faithful Servant of His Master*), Grillparzer portrayed the way in which a master can abuse the loyalty of a devoted retainer who willingly and trustingly serves him. The play, which was successfully performed in the Burgtheater, aroused the concern of Emperor Franz, who believed that people might interpret the play as reflecting upon him personally as well as upon the nobility in general. Since the matter involved such a prominent figure as Grillparzer, he decided to proceed with tact rather than by simply invoking the normal censorship process. Franz tried to flatter his leading author by offering to purchase all copies of the play for himself, a move that would have allowed him to withhold it from further performances. Grillparzer, however, who easily saw through the scheme, declined the offer with the excuse that he could not guarantee that he would be able to recover and submit all outstanding copies. His refusal resulted in the play's disappearance from the repertoire of the Burgtheater until 1851.[57]

Before Grillparzer arrived on the theater scene with *Die Ahnfrau* (1817, The Ancestress), serious drama was represented by Heinrich Joseph von Collin (1771-1811), whose plays combined sentimentality with the moral enthusiasm of Schiller. Collin, who was trained as a lawyer, serves as an example of how a member of the bourgeoisie could on the basis of accomplishment be ennobled, as he was in 1803. In addition to his ballads and his lyric poems written to arouse patriotism during the Napoleonic war, Collin produced a series of dramas which were performed in the Burgtheater. One of the most noteworthy is *Regulus* (1801), one of the few Austrian dramas on a Roman theme. Collin treats the theme of patriotic loyalty to the state, whose interests are held higher than the life of the individual. Regulus is captured by the Romans and offered for ransom: his release in exchange for returning a large number of Roman prisoners. As a loyal soldier he feels that the bargain is not in the best interests of the state and urges that it be rejected, even though this decision will mean his death. As a recent article shows, this theme of whether or not to bargain for hostages gives the play new relevance in the current climate of terrorist kidnappings.[58] The same cannot be said of *Coriolan* (1807), which is remembered, if at all, only because Beethoven wrote an overture for this opera. None of Collin's works, including his *Ideen zur Verbesserung der Wiener Bühne* (1806, Ideas for Improving the Viennese Stage) have survived their own time. Neither have the writings of his younger brother Matthäus von Collin (1779-1824), who displayed a better sense of the theater in his dramas based on Austrian history and thus can be seen as a precursor of Grillparzer's historical dramas.

Grillparzer was discovered for the Burgtheater by Joseph Schreyvogel (1768-1832), an admirer of Joseph II and the Enlightenment. A German from Königsberg, he was a follower of the German philosopher Kant, which shows his independence of mind, for the Austrian Court considered Kant's ideas anathema. Two professors were dismissed from the university for teaching his ideas. Schreyvogel lived for a time in Jena, where he contributed to literary periodicals such as Friedrich Schlegel's *Allgemeine Literaturzeitung* (General Literary Newspaper) and carefully studied Goethe's theater practices in Weimar. In 1802 he was appointed Court Theater Secretary at the Burgtheater—a position equivalent to dramaturge today—but because of the restrictive censorship he resigned in 1804.

Schreyvogel was better suited to criticism than to writing plays, as shown by his editorship of the *Wiener Zeitung* (Vienna Newspaper) and the *Wiener Sonntagsblatt* (1807-1808, Vienna Sunday Paper). He considered himself a writer who was drawn to the theater as a means of spreading enlightenment. He was recalled to the Burgtheater in 1814 and brought its reputation to new heights, even though he was never the director but served under the supervision of appointed aristocrats who kept tight rein over the budget and the repertoire. In addition to supporting and protecting Grillparzer, he was one of the few at the time who understood and appreciated the literary importance of Heinrich von Kleist, whose talent even Goethe failed to recognize. He worked untiringly to broaden and enrich the Burgtheater repertoire with plays by the most important authors of other European countries. He carried on correspondences with numerous writers, helped revise their plays, fought the censors for approvals, and helped with casting and hiring of new performers. Under his guidance the Burgtheater grew into European prominence.

All the while Schreyvogel continued to produce his own works—dramas, prose, and lyrics—all of which are forgotten. In the *Wiener Sonntagsblatt* he fought against the concept of Romanticism developed by Friedrich Schlegel, his brother August Wilhelm Schlegel, and Adam Müller. Schreyvogel defended the Enlightenment, Lessing, Aristotle, Goethe, and Schiller. He opposed the "new school" of narrowly conceived German Romanticism, in his view a cult of genius and mysticism, infused with the piety of the new converts to Catholicism such as Friedrich Schlegel, who opportunistically entered the church so that he could be accepted into Austrian government service. By means of a political career he hoped to have his title of nobility restored. Ultimately Schreyvogel, like all strong-willed, independent-minded individuals in Austria, suffered the "Austrian fate." His enemies harrassed him out of the Burgtheater shortly after he commemorated Goethe's death in 1832. He died shortly thereafter in a cholera epidemic.

Schreyvogel rejected Grillparzer's first play *Die Ahnfrau,* but advised him on how to revise it, for with his keen theatrical sense he could appreciate its potential. In the following years he became Grillparzer's great admirer and gave him his full support. Grillparzer, who developed into Austria's greatest writer, contributed works in all the major forms in use at that time— Classicism (*Sappho, Des Meeres und der Liebe Wellen* [*Hero and Leander*]), Romanticism bordering on the Fate Tragedy (*Die Ahnfrau* [*The Ancestress*]), Baroque (*Der Traum, Ein Leben* [*The Dream, a Life*]), comedy (*Weh dem, der lügt* [*Woe to Him Who Lies*]), national historical dramas (*Ein Bruderzwist in Habsburg* [*Struggle in the House of Habsburg*]), *König Ottokars Glück und Ende* ([*King Ottokar's Rise and Fall*], *Libussa*), and tragedy (*Das goldene Vliess* [*The Golden Fleece*]), *Die Jüdin von Toledo* [*The Jewess of Toledo*]). He also represents the status of many writers during the *Vormärz* who were authors as well as officials of the state. To a degree he suffered from a divided personality, on the one side loyal to his position as a government official, and on the other repressed by the lack of freedom of expression. Yet he was neither a rebel nor a revolutionary but exhibited the mentality of a typical official in performing only what his duty required and nothing more. On one occasion, while visiting the zoo with Raimund, the latter excitedly pointed out the gyrations of the monkeys and exclaimed that he could not possibly duplicate those feats. Grillparzer responded sarcastically: "Who asked you to?"[59]

While Grillparzer suffered from the conditions in which he lived, as his poems and particularly his diaries document,[60] and as contemporary accounts by others confirm, his problems derived in large part from his peculiar nature rather than from official repression. His personal life provides a clear indication of his difficulty in finding the inner harmony and happiness that he held up in his plays as the highest good: "One thing only is happiness in this world: inner contentment and a guilt-free conscience!" In his view, everything else that one aspires to—greatness or fame—is vanity, illusory, and empty.

Grillparzer suffered largely from his inability to take action. He considered renunciation the lot of human beings, but he himself did not accept this self-imposed attitude gracefully. He became an irascible, difficult person, who insulated himself against the outer world. Accounts mention him as wandering around Vienna alone and without attracting any attention. He could never decide to marry. Nothing shows his stubborn, unyielding nature better than his decision to withhold all further writings from the stage after the failed production of his comedy *Weh dem, der lügt,* which audiences booed in 1838. He did not succumb to the system but continued to write some of his greatest successes; he simply refused to share these dramas with an ungrateful public. In a sense his withdrawal from the public view benefited him and his work, for he could write as he felt without fear of censorship. While his last three plays *König Ottokars Glück und Ende, Die Jüdin von Toledo,* and *Libussa* still defend the idea of order, their purpose is viewed as making possible the happiness and equality of all people. He remained opposed to nationalism, which he felt led to bestiality, but he defended humaneness, equality of the sexes, and moral balance in the conflict between duty and inclination, commitment and freedom.

Actually Grillparzer received favorable treatment in his position as an official, even though the censors became suspicious of his loyalty early on because of his critical poem "Campo Vaccino" (written in 1819 on a trip to Italy to recover from the death of his mother). To show the Burgtheater management's appreciation after the success of *Sappho,* Grillparzer was granted a five-year contract. Even more important than Schreyvogel's good will was the support of the Finance Minister Count Johann Phillip von Stadion (1763-1824), who controlled the repertoire and the purse strings. Grillparzer received special benefits such as extra vacation time and additional stipends. He was promoted to the position of Director of the

Court Archives in 1832. His financial situation enabled him to travel to Italy, to Germany, where he visited Goethe but without achieving any meeting of the minds, as well as to France, England, and Greece. Probably the most productive trip was the one in 1836 to Paris, where he witnessed how far the Burgtheater lagged behind French theater, particularly in the area of stage design. In Paris realism had been brought into the theater and was reflected in the stage settings: a room was presented in complete detail and not simply suggested by back-drops and side wings as in Vienna. In spite of his enthusiasm for this new technique, it was not introduced into Vienna until the end of the century. Although indecisive in many ways, in one matter Grillparzer took a definite position which he maintained throughout his lifetime: he insisted that he was an Austrian and not a German writer. His diaries provide the best evidence of how strongly he felt about this identity.

Austria did not abound in great dramatists, even though Vienna was known as early as the *Vormärz* as a city of theater enthusiasts. Huttner suggests that this reputation may be somewhat exaggerated, for despite the considerable growth of population, the number of theaters remained at five until the 1860s.[61]

At some remove from Grillparzer, who stands alone as the pinnacle of Austrian writing to date, was Friedrich Halm, pseudonym for Franz Joseph von Munch-Bellinghausen (1806-1871), who was educated in the *Gymnasium* at Melk. Halm became and remained a protégé of his favorite teacher, the monk Michael Enks (1788-1843), who devoted his life to writing and was well known and highly respected in the *Vormärz*. Halm became Director of the Court Library and also Supervisor (*Generalintendant*) of the Court Theater. His friends included Nikolaus Lenau and Eduard von Bauernfeld.

Halm became one of the most popular dramatists of his time, and his series of plays—*Griseldis* (1835), *Der Sohn der Wildnis* (1842, The Son of the Wilderness), *Der Fechter von Ravenna* (1854, The Fencer of Ravenna), and *Wildfeuer* (1863, Wild Fire), dealing with Spanish and classical as well as romantic and contemporary themes—were all performed at the Burgtheater as well as throughout Europe. He was not a naturally gifted dramatist, and his works, in which reason predominates over emotion, are developed with strict logic along a single line and without subplots. Yet he knew how to blend elements to appeal to audiences. A favorite theme was the clash of two cultures. In this choice of topic he resembles Hebbel, as does his poetic credo: "I seek to represent the moral world order, how an individual fights against it, and, because he frequently places himself above it, must necessarily end tragically."[62]

Halm did not have the temperament for humor, and his comedies were generally unsuccessful with the exception of the comedy of errors *Verbot und Befehl* (1857, Prohibition and Command). His drama *Griseldis* is set in the time of King Arthur's court, but Halm modernized the attitude of the protagonist. Although Griseldis devotedly carries out all the tests of her fidelity that Percival demands of her, she rebels when he uses her as a bet in gambling and chastises him in emancipated terms foreshadowing Ibsen's *The Doll's House:* "O Percival, you have wagered my happiness! / This faithful heart was a plaything for you!" In *Der Fechter von Ravenna,* set in the time of the Roman emperor Caligula and involving a confrontation between Thusnelda and her son Arminius, Halm combines romantic decadence with German nationalistic feelings. This play with its lurid effects found great success until the German schoolmaster Franz Bacherl accused Halm of plagiarizing his drama *Die Cherusker in Rom.* However, the claim is exaggerated. Apart from some overlap in historical details, the two plays in essence display little similarity. On the whole, Halm stands as a representative of the turn to historicism that dominated the cultural scene after 1848 and that was exhibited in monuments as well as in celebrations glorifying the past. In 1859 Halm participated in the Schiller Centennial by writing a festival play entitled *Vor hundert Jahren* (1859, A Hundred Years Ago).

As a lyric poet Halm was an epigone, but his prose works, modeled on Kleist are lasting achievements, even though they are no longer read. Like Kleist, Halm explores the dark side of life, and like twentieth-century authors, he leads his characters to the abyss open before them, before he reaches a moral resolution, as in *Die Marzipanliese* (1854, Marzipan Liese), the tale of the decline of a murderer. *Die Freundinnen* (The Girl Friends) and *Das Haus an der Veronabrücke* (The House by the Verona Bridge) appeared postumously in 1872, and both show his masterful manner of creating and then resolving complications. The latter novella deals with the tragedy of an aging man who can no longer produce an heir to his fortune but who desperately wants one. He arranges a friendship of his young wife with a cavalier in the hope that she will become pregnant. Her sense of fidelity thwarts his plan, however, and he, feeling cheated out of his life's aim, surrenders to death as a way out of an existence that has become senseless.

Another writer, whose specialty of drawing-room comedies earned him great popularity with audiences, was Eduard von Bauernfeld (1802-1890), who remained one of the house authors of the Burgtheater until his death. Forty-three of his plays were presented in numerous performances. Bauernfeld lived through the entire nineteenth century and attempted to create a rounded portrayal of the social life of his time. As has been shown, he was well-informed about the political and social conditions of his day which he presented in balanced fashion in his works. In the years before the revolution he refused to accede to his critics who pressed him to drop his objectivity in favor of a more critical view of society. However, he remained the spokesman for the open-minded bourgeois characters who in his plays discussed the matters of the day. His enormous popularity derived from his ability, unmatched by any other writer of his day, to capture the essence of Viennese society which formed his audiences. Just as the Biedermeier painters had found favor by producing genre portraits of Biedermeier life, so Bauernfeld earned approbation from the society he was portraying. His early works reveal his roots in the popular plays of Raimund and Nestroy which Bauernfeld elevated to acceptability for the Burgtheater. The godfather of his dramas could have been Kotzebue.

Bauernfeld took traditional figures and relocated them into drawing rooms and salons, and let them converse. His plots were usually unimportant, for he was not possessed of great inventiveness. Like Noel Coward, his plays are more for the ear than for the eye. In contrast to Halm, who featured plot over character, Bauernfeld offers unpretentious plays in which the well-drawn characters, the clever dialogue, and the charming conversational tone stand central in importance.

Bauernfeld is the master of the genteel, witty, entertaining play which gave audiences what they wanted to see—the manners, the social behavior, and the ideas of their own time. As a result, all of his plays were bound to his own day and lost their relevance in the social changes at the turn of the century. He was forgotten, but his legacy was continued by Hermann Bahr, who felt that he carried on the tradition of Bauernfeld in his plays. He cited the Preface that Bauernfeld wrote for his comedy *Leichtsinn aus Liebe* (Frivolousness Caused by Love) to characterize his intention as a playwright:

This comedy initiates a series of lighthearted dramatic productions that make it their task to mirror on the stage the relatively harmless society of earlier days. By means of pleasing dialogue, cheerful atmosphere, and good characterization, a play based on real life, offering actors rewarding roles, came into being on the stage—thus audiences pardoned or overlooked the lack of a truly significant plot and the loose conception.[63]

Bauernfeld's light-hearted society milieu and sparkling dialogue were continued well into the twentieth century in the comedies of Alexander Lernet-Holenia (1897-1976), written between 1926 and 1970.

Others who tried to contribute to the theater without finding much success were Nikolaus Lenau, Karoline Pichler, Ferdinand von Saar, and Marie von Ebner-Eschenbach. Both Lenau and Pichler came to recognize that their primary gift lay in the lyric, while Saar and Ebner-Eschenbach discovered that their real talent was to be found in narrative prose.

Lyric

The foremost lyric poets of the *Vormärz* were Grillparzer and Nikolaus Franz Niembsch Edler von Strehlenau or more simply Nikolaus Lenau (1802-1850). Like Grillparzer, Lenau was a melancholy individual, who suffered from pessimism, religious doubt, and an inability to find his niche in life. He was psychologically incapable of adapting to the Biedermeier lifestyle of finding "happiness in a corner," but was driven by an inner restlessness that made it impossible for him to find a satisfying existence or even the kind of resigned acceptance of his lot in life that Grillparzer adopted for himself.

Lenau moved to Vienna in 1823 and studied philosophy and then medicine at the University of Vienna without completing either course of study. He associated with the leading liberal writers in Vienna such as Anastasius Grün and also with the Swabian poets Ludwig Uhland, Gustav Schwab, and Justinus Kerner. Lenau's *Polenlieder* (1830, *Songs of Poland*) and *Die Albigenser* (1842, The Albigensians) show his hatred of tyranny and his yearning for freedom.

Lenau ventured to America in 1832 in search of freedom, prosperity, and himself, but grew bitterly disappointed when he could fulfill none of his ambitions in "the land of unlimited opportunity," as America was known in Europe at this time. He returned to Europe in 1833 but never managed to establish a satisfactory existence there either.

As was the case with Grillparzer, Lenau's sense of uprootedness which caused his pessimistic outlook and unhappiness derived not from the politics, although the oppressive system weighed on him as on his contemporaries, but from his own nature. He found himself unable to resolve the dichotomy between life and art, between spirit and nature, a problem that affected almost all of the leading Austrian and German writers from the 1880s until World War I. Like Kafka later, Lenau could not separate art from life. His inability to find inner peace caused periods of depression. During his later years his mental instability increased until he lapsed into madness and made attempts at suicide. He spent his final years in a mental institution, where he died in 1850.

Lenau foreshadowed the problems of turn-of-the-century writers. He was not only an individual, but also an outsider who tragically could not find his place in life or establish a philosophical rationale that could alleviate his pessimistic view of life and change it at least into viable acceptance of nature and the world, as Grillparzer managed to accomplish. Neither could he find solace in the positive outlook of Goethe and Schiller. One point of comparison is illustrative: while Goethe's Faust survives all of the errors and tribulations of his questing life to find redemption at the end, Lenau's nihilistic Faust in *Faust. Ein Gedicht* (1835, Faust. A Poem) commits suicide out of complete frustration with life.

In his poems Lenau gave voice to the wave of Byronian *Weltschmerz* which swept over Europe, to the suffering and hopelessness of life, unrelieved by any positive vision. His verses of despair, in which he captures the feelings of many contemporaries, and particularly his exquisite nature lyrics raised him to the forefront of lyric poets. Because of the unfortunate events in his life, Lenau viewed the world as pan-tragic. In contrast to Adalbert Stifter, he saw no harmonious system in nature, which, largely on the basis of his negative experience in America, he found hostile—not friendly—to human beings. For that reason he liked to portray downtrodden and oppressed people such as the Native Americans and society's outcasts. In this sense his poetry takes on a political dimension as a protest against social inequities and restrictions. His pure nature poetry often features the fall season, although he has also created beautiful positive images in his *Schilflieder* (1832, Songs of the Marsh) and *Waldlieder* (1843, Songs of the Forest).

Other poets who were prominent at this time included Joseph Christian Baron von Zedlitz (1790-1862), Anastasius Grün (1806-1876), and Betty Paoli. Zedlitz served as an officer in the military and fought in the campaign against Napoleon in 1809. He wrote patriotic lyrics before he resigned from the army in 1811. His attempt to find acceptance in the Burgtheater for his many fairy-tale dramas, plays written on Spanish themes, and fate dramas such as *Herr und Sklave* (1831, Master and Slave) remained without success. Nadler claims that the play *Waldfräulein* (1843, Young Woman of the Forest) was accepted and performed,[64] but the drama is not recorded in Alth's listing of performances.[65] Zedlitz shows in his *Gedichte* (1832, Poems) that he had absorbed Romanticism from the same group of Swabian poets with whom Lenau had associated. He was a personal friend of Eichendorff. Zedlitz, like so many poets of the time, was also greatly influenced by Byron, whose works he translated into German. He used Romance forms such as the canzone, which he employed in his most highly regarded work, *Totenkränze* (1828, Funeral Wreaths), a series of eulogies composed for delivery at the graves of famous people: great leaders such as Wallenstein and Napoleon, outstanding poets, and renowned couples like Tristan and Isolde.

An equally important literary figure was Betty Paoli, pseudonym for Elisabeth Glück (1814-1894) whose eventful life, like that of Bauernfeld, spanned most of the nineteenth century. Paoli, the natural daughter of an Austrian nobleman, had inherited money, but her mother could not manage it properly, and so it became necessary for the young woman to earn her own living. She obtained a position as a companion to Princess Schwarzenberg, and this post provided a great opportunity for her literary development. In the Schwarzenberg salon Paoli met all of the leading authors in Vienna and developed a close friendship with Adalbert Stifter in the years 1840-1842, when he also served as a reader to the Princess. She expressed her admiration in the poem "An Adalbert Stifter" (1848, To Adalbert Stifter). Paoli, whom Grillparzer praised as Austria's greatest lyric poet, developed into the most important woman writer between Karoline Pichler and Marie von Ebner-Eschenbach at the end of the century.[66] Ebner-Eschenbach sent her first works to Paoli for her opinion. The variety of her works enables one to understand why she was regarded as the most talented woman in the Vienna of her day. She anticipates not only Ebner-Eschenbach, but also Rosa Mayreder (1858-1938).[67]

Paoli's intelligence, educational background, travels, and struggles in life made her into an independent-minded, self-supporting individual, who served as a model for early feminists. She translated literature from French, English, Italian, and Russian, and worked as a theater critic for the newspaper *Wiener Lloyd.* Her three volumes of novellas under the title *Die Welt und mein Auge* (1844, The World and My Eye), written in a realistic manner reflecting the influence of Turgenev, all concern the fates of women in terms of the thinking of the time; no one can escape his or her destiny—but the manner in which one meets it is the important factor, for this sense of personal responsibility demonstrates the character of the individual. Paoli was well informed about the life of her time as few others and set her narratives against a realistic background of the social and political conditions.

Paoli's crowning achievement, however, lies in her volumes of lyric poetry: *Gedichte* (1841, Poems), dedicated to Lenau, whom she greatly esteemed, *Nach dem Gewitter* (1843, After the Storm), *Neue Gedichte* (1850, New Poems), and *Neueste Gedichte* (1870, Newest Poems). Like Ebner-Eschenbach later, Paoli displays both intellect and genuine emotion, and her verses reveal her originality of expression as well as a freedom from sentimentality. In these terms her writings already reflect the transition toward Realism in literature that continued to the end of the century. However, Paoli halted before the extreme realism represented by the Berlin Naturalism of Arno Holz and Gerhart Hauptmann. She voiced her criticism of the approach of Naturalist writers in the poem "Die naturalistische Schule" (The School of Naturalism), noting that art consists of more than reproducing the surface reality of the world as it is; it requires a creative element to become poetry.

In her earliest poems such as "An die Männer unserer Zeit" (To the Men of Our Day) and "Die Dichterin" (The Poetess) she showed her support of the women's movement. Like Pichler before her and Mayreder after her, Paoli advocated equal education and employment for women. She confronted the prevailing patriarchal system (which still exists in Austria) and spoke out against the misogyny she had experienced both in terms of her own life and in the reactions to her writing. When the honest emotions of her *Gedichte* (Poems), which were based on her personal experiences, brought negative reviews by male critics who considered them unwomanly because of their candidness, she responded that the mind had nothing to do with gender. Her response anticipated the aphorism of Ebner-Eschenbach: "An intelligent woman has millions of born enemies— all the stupid men."[68] Ebner-Eschenbach published a collected edition of Paoli's poems in 1895.

Paoli grew discouraged with the negative critical response to her novellas and gave up creating narrative prose, including the novel Stifter had encouraged her to write. She supported herself by producing contributions for a variety of newspapers and literary periodicals and earned regard as a notable essayist. In the 1860s and 1870s she was especially active as a theater reviewer for several newspapers, including the *Neue Freie Presse*. She approached the task seriously and in the process earned the hostility of male authors like Friedrich Hebbel, the dominant German dramatist until his death in 1863, whose work she dared to criticize. Paoli was particularly sympathetic to Ferdinand von Saar,[69] whose writings she admired as among the best of the time and whose sympathy for the working class she shared. In social terms she, like many others, had been enthusiastic about the revolution of 1848, but she was greatly disappointed by the results that were achieved. She was also distressed by witnessing the tragedy that such an uprising invoked. The experience caused her to urge greater support of the lower classes to prevent any repetition of the class struggle.

Anastasius Grün, the pseudonym for Count Anton Alexander von Auersperg (1806-1876), was one of the liberal aristocrats who believed in freedom and progress, and thus felt that he had to oppose the stifling Metternich system. He was one of the few aristocrats who had a strong commitment to personal freedom and showed a willingness to take an activist political stance even if it meant breaking solidarity with his own class. He had worked with Bauernfeld in attempting to negotiate the new constitution in 1848 and served as a representative in the Frankfurt Parliament. After 1861 he was a member of the Austrian House of Lords (*Herrenhaus*).

Grün's early collection of lyrics *Blätter der Liebe* (1830, Pages of Love) and *Der letzte Ritter* (1830, The Last Knight), a romance in verse about Maximilian I), were epigonal. However, his volume of satirical poems, *Spaziergänge eines Wiener Poeten* (1831, Walks of a Viennese Poet), in which he addressed problems of the time such as the need for freedom of expression and greater political representation, the July revolution in

France in 1830, and America as a model of freedom, showed the strength of his character as well as his poetic talent. The book was widely read. The poems in *Schutt* (1835, Rubble) again hold America up as a model of progressive thinking; Grün argues that the past must not be glorified for its own sake but should be employed as a means of stimulating the present. In this view he anticipates the approach of Hofmannsthal in his *Österreichische Bibliothek* (1915-1918, Austrian Library), among other writings.

Grün's final works turned to different, lighter themes, revealing his humor and his interest in other peoples of the Monarchy. The humorous epic *Die Nibelungen im Frack* (1843, The Nibelungs in Tuxedo) was followed by another epic, *Der Pfaff vom Kahlenberg* (1851, The Priest of Kahlenberg), which amusingly describes Austrian foibles and satirizes the church along with portraying the landscapes of the countryside. In *Volkslieder aus Krain* (1850, Folksongs from Krain) Grün retells a number of Slovenian folk songs. While he continues to be recognized as a gifted lyric poet, he is generally remembered today for his political poetry and his outspoken role in attempting to change the political and social conditions in Austria.[70]

Another representative writer from outside Vienna is Karl Isidor Beck (1817-1879), who was born in Hungary as the son of a merchant. He began learning German at age eight and later studied medicine in Vienna and philosophy in Leipzig before pursuing his ambition to become a poet writing in German. The political conditions in Vienna and the meetings with members of Young Germany aroused revolutionary tendencies within him, and he showed a sense of social engagement not common at the time. He was considered both a literary and political hope, for he seemed to combine the lyric qualities of Lenau with the political acumen and essayistic skill of Ludwig Börne, the German political essayist and member of Young Germany. Beck's first poems, collected in the volume *Nächte. Gepanzerte Lieder* (1838, Night. Songs in Armor) appealed to the emotions of the time and were designed to arouse political feelings against the government. In his *Lieder vom armen Mann* (1846, Songs of a Poor Man) he continued his efforts to fuel agitation by portraying the economic and social distress of the proletariat as well as the class distinctions that had built up and were soon to explode. This book received a negative review by the Marxist theoretician Friedrich Engels, who did not consider such a work useful for the revolution. Beck further lost favor among the political agitators and activists for withdrawing from the revolution after the defeat of the Hungarian relief force which was attempting to rescue the students and others trapped in the center of Vienna. He went so far as to beg Franz Joseph for mercy in his poems. This capitulation from the revolutionary goals earned him contempt from his earlier supporters. He lived a hard life always marred by difficulties and lack of money.

Beck was not only a political writer. Like his countryman Lenau, Beck brought descriptions of the Hungarian people and the landscapes of the *pusztas* into Austrian literature in additional collections of poems as *Der fahrende Poet* (1838, The Traveling Poet), *Stille Lieder* (1840, Quiet Poems), *Aus der Heimat* (1852, Poems of My Homeland), *Jadwiga* (1852), *Mater dolorosa* (1853), the elegy *Täubchen im Nest* (1860, Baby Doves in the Nest), and *Still und bewegt* (1870, Quiet and Animated). The realism of his novel in verse *Janko, der ungarische Roßhirt* (1844, Janko, the Hungarian Horse Groom) makes it into a document of the life of the time in Hungary.

Another political poet who played a role in the *Vormärz* was the Tyrolean Hermann von Gilm (1812-1864), who worked as a government official. His poems include aggressive *Jesuitenlieder* (Songs about Jesuits) as well as love poems that Richard Strauss set to music. Other works include sensitive, melancholy *Gedichte* (1853, Poems), *Schützenleben* (1863, Life of a Marksman), and *Lieder eines Verschollenen* (1864, Songs of a Missing Person).

Prose to 1848

While drama and poetry were well represented in Austria during the *Vormärz*, prose was less prominent. The Metternich system of censorship made it impossible to mirror the conditions of the time, and as in the case of the theater, writers had to avoid contemporary politics or any criticism of current social circumstances.

Karoline Pichler (1769-1843), well-educated and widely read and, as seen earlier, prominent in the salon life of the time, became the first of a long line of important women writers in Austria that extends to the present day. At the urging of Hormayr she began as an author by writing patriotic historical novels in the manner of Sir Walter Scott and also tragic dramas emulating Schiller. Critical response rejected her works primarily on the basis of her subject matter: serious historical themes were deemed the province of men, and it was considered unseemly for a woman to be dealing with them. She also wrote novellas, ballads, and lyric poems which, like her novels and plays, were translated into several languages. Despite her personal prominence, her works were relegated to the category of women's, that is, trivial, literature. Her memoirs, *Denkwürdigkeiten aus meinem Leben* (1844, Memorable Events from My Life), which covers her life up to 1837, have proved to be her most lasting contribution because of the fund of information that they provide about people and events of this period.

Pichler played an important role as a model for other women, for she was truly a liberated spirit of high intelligence who addressed many of the social problems of the time. Like the champion of the Enlightenment Joseph Sonnenfels, she advocated in "Über die Bildung des weiblichen Geschlechts" (1840, On the Education of the Female Sex) the educating of women of all classes to make them self-supporting and more useful to the state. Her ideas were echoed in the writings of succeeding women writers such as Ada Christen, Marie von Ebner-Eschenbach, Rosa Mayreder, Betty Paoli, and Bertha von Suttner.

Grillparzer wrote only two novellas in his career, because he regarded the narrative form as less poetic than drama. In *Das Kloster bei Sendomir* (1828, *The Cloister at Sendomir*), he created a powerful tale of love, passion, infidelity, murder, and penance that reveals its debt to the German Romantic tradition as represented by Ludwig Tieck and E.T.A. Hoffmann. The psychological turning point in this tale told in flashback is the willingness of an unfaithful wife to kill the child born as the result of an affair in order to save her own life. The betrayed Count, who is finally revealed as the narrator of this tale, kills her because of her selfishness and callousness. Then, to do penance for his crime, he spends the rest of his life as a monk in the cloister he has had built next to the murder site.

By contrast, Grillparzer's novella *Der arme Spielmann* (1847, *The Poor Musician*), transpires as quietly and unassumingly as if it had been created according to Stifter's "gentle law." Although written during the hectic period of the pre-revolutionary ferment in Vienna, this portrayal of an eccentric musician who lives on the fringes of society in an imagined world of his own creation reflects nothing of the turbulent conditions around him. Even though he lives as an outsider, he is no selfish aesthete who is indifferent to the people around him, as he proves by sacrificing his life to rescue a drowning person.

With this tale that continues to fascinate readers and critics alike,[71] Grillparzer has presented a genre portrait of the type so favored in the Biedermeier era. Of particular interest is the character Barbara, who loves the musician but accepts the reality that she cannot marry him because he cannot support her. Instead, she marries the owner of a small store, harboring her true love in her heart as a source of satisfaction. She is but one example of the strong-minded working-class women found in nineteenth-century Austrian literature. They are uneducated women to be sure, but they are women blessed with common sense that enables them to make their own decisions based on practicality and a firm grasp on reality rather than on emotion. These women are shown to have greater intellectual potential than they are allowed to develop and utilize in the restrictive patriarchal society. However, although circumstances force them to compromise outwardly, they do not capitulate inwardly.

Like Grillparzer, Adalbert Stifter (1805-1868) avoided politics and social criticism, but out of artistic principle, not out of a spirit of resignation. He began his artistic career as a landscape painter until he accepted his limitations and brought his keen descriptive eye to his narrative writings. Like so many of his contemporaries, including Grillparzer and Lenau, Stifter was a divided personality: a solid citizen, dutiful functionary, contented and secure on the surface, but a demonically driven, anxious, uncertain individual within, one finally driven to suicide in 1868 to escape from the torment of chronic illness.

As in the case of Grillparzer and Lenau, Stifter's problems were rooted in his own psyche. Hermann Bahr, a fellow Upper Austrian, who, as shown, greatly admired Stifter and devoted himself to publicizing his importance, considered him a case of an individual who fled into literature to escape from life, which he could not master. Perhaps one can see this characterization as a key to the orderly world Stifter created in his writings, a decent, moral, and harmonious world (*heile Welt*), inhabited by people who, however quirky or misguided they might be or have been, find the possibility, like Faust, of achieving harmony within themselves, with those about them, and with nature. As a moralist Stifter ranks alongside Schiller, Goethe, and Grillparzer.

Like the miniature genre painters, Stifter in his collections of novellas such as *Studien* (1844-1850, *Studies*) and *Bunte Steine* (1852, *Colorful Stones*), celebrated nature in its most modest manifestations in a way unique in literature. As a preface to *Bunte Steine*, Stifter wrote a programmatical statement to make clear his approach to literature. By means of this "gentle law" (*sanftes Gesetz*), his works represent the diametrical opposite of those of Friedrich Hebbel, who always used the strongest effects possible, and who poked fun at Stifter's quiet literary style. By contrast, Stifter taught people to understand that the often unnoticed commonplace phenomena of nature were evidence of a physical power as great as that of such cataclysmic occurrences as volcanos, floods, and storms. His major work, *Der Nachsommer* (1857, *Indian Summer*), an idealized developmental novel which celebrates humanity and a moral, harmonious world, was detested by Hebbel but acclaimed by Nietzsche (1844-1900) as one of the great prose works of the nineteenth century. In our own day it is generally recognized as an idealistic representation of the Austrian essence.

The long historical novel *Witiko* (1865-1867), which deals with the problem of royal succession in Bohemia in the twelfth century, is written in Stifter's usual slow, tranquil manner, emphasizing the small, the simple, the unexceptional, avoiding the violence contained in a subject dealing with warring armies. The excessive length, combined with the slow pace and the lack of action, have always deterred readers. Yet the theme was highly relevant to Austrian circumstances, dealing as it did with the question of royal succession: who should inherit the crown, the legitimate heir regardless of suitability, or the person who would make the best leader for the country? Whether Stifter might have been thinking about the succession from Franz II(I) to his son Ferdinand, who he knew was incapable of ruling, has never been established, but it does not make the parallel less valid.

Bahr also felt that the theme of doing what was right made the book relevant for the post-World-War-I era.

> Today this book seems as though it had been written for us, as though it would lift us out of our confusion and need and lack of counsel. For everything which to us all our lives long has seemed "legitimate" is now broken up, and yet we feel that this destruction alone means nothing, that strength can destroy an enfeebled right but thereby does not become right itself, that in order for might to become right it must first legitimize itself by good deeds! And now it may be imagined with what wonder and eagerness the German falls on this old forgotten

book, in which a voice from the grave instructs the living generation on the problems of its fate![72]

Unfortunately, Bahr's enthusiasm for *Witiko* has never found an echo among readers, and this misunderstood novel remains one of the great unread classics of Austrian literature. Stifter has not only remained a perennial favorite with the reading public while Hebbel has been forgotten, but he has also always exerted a strong influence on Austrian literature and continues to do so among contemporary writers.[73] With Stifter, Grillparzer, and Lenau, among others, Austrian literature, which around 1800 could not match German literature, could by mid-century compare favorably in the quality of the writing as well as in the variety of forms.

Ernst Freiherr von Feuchtersleben (1806-1849) was a Viennese psychiatrist who served as Dean of the medical faculty at the University of Vienna and also as undersecretary in the Education Ministry. In this latter position he contributed importantly to school reforms, which he outlined in the essay "Über die Frage von Humanismus und Realismus als Bildungsprinzip" (1848, On the Question of Humanism and Realism as Educational Principles). Among other recommendations, he advocated freedom of teaching and learning, the use of German rather than Latin in instruction, the equality of religions, and better training for teachers. Just prior to the revolution of 1848 the educational system began to emerge from the tight imperial control mandated since the days of Joseph II. Feuchtersleben stood in the forefront of those who helped reshape the curriculum and also supported the need to end the ban which the emperor imposed on research in the universities.

Feuchtersleben was a follower of Kant, from whom he learned not philosophy per se but how to philosophize. He was guided by the belief that the ethical principle supersedes the intellectual and the practical the theoretical. Like Grillparzer and Stifter as well as Schiller and Goethe, Feuchtersleben placed morality at the center of life. As an enlightened liberal he regarded education, character, and enthusiasm for something higher than oneself as the keys to life, for they bring self-awareness. In turn, this understanding provides a guide to the limits one should observe to achieve the ideal of a harmonious, healthy life. Like all of the major writers of the time, Feuchtersleben was a moralist.

Feuchtersleben wrote lyric poetry and aphorisms, but he was not possessed of great literary talent. His great achievement lay in blending his philosophical and medical background into a practical discussion about life entitled *Zur Diätetik der Seele* (1838, Concerning a Spiritual Diet). Here, anticipating Mary Baker Eddy and the teachings of Christian Science, he stressed the relationship of mind and body and demonstrated the primacy and the power of the mind over the body. He showed what every teacher knows—an educated mind can free people from their fears and help them rise above the concerns of daily existence. Feuchtersleben's book, which consists of an instructive essay as a guide to proper living, followed by numerous, often witty and humorous aphorisms to illustrate his points, became extremely popular and went through fifty printings. Its practical teachings remain relevant, and this work can still be read with profit and pleasure.

As a member of the nobility who was outspoken against the absolutist regime, Feuchtersleben welcomed the revolution as a means of improving conditions. However, like many others who had held high hopes for long-sought relief from the repressive system, he grew disillusioned when it became apparent that it did not produce the changes that had been anticipated. When he recognized that he could not realize the teaching reforms that were needed (and that were carried out later by others), he resigned his position in the Education Ministry. He died less than a year later, another victim of the "Austrian fate."

Like Feuchtersleben, another aristocratic author, Freiherr Josef von Hammer–Purgstall (1774-1856), also contributed to the development of scholarship in Austria. He was an outstanding orientalist whose reputation extended beyond the borders of Austria. Maria Theresia had established an academy for eastern languages as early as 1754, and oriental studies flourished as one of the strong educational fields. With this background Hammer served as a diplomat in Constantinople (Istanbul) from 1799 to 1801 and again from 1802 to 1806. From 1811 to 1839 he held the position of court translator for oriental languages. He also established the journal *Fundgrube des Orients* (1809-1818, Treasury of the Orient). From the Countess Purgstall, who had adopted him after the loss of her husband and son, he inherited Castle Hainfeld, and there he spent his summers from 1825 to 1835 writing his ten-volume *Geschichte des osmanischen Reiches* (History of the Ottoman Empire). Beyond the wealth of information it contained, this extensive history of the development of the Orient introduced scholarly methodology to the field of oriental studies. This work along with Hammer-Purgstall's translations and literary-historical articles spread beyond Austria and created a greater awareness of the eastern world throughout Europe.

While he himself did not write poetry, Hammer-Purgstall created a three-volume novel, *Die Galerie auf der Riegersburg* (1845, The Gallery on the Riegersburg), set at the time of the Turkish invasion of Styria. He was a better translator than novelist and in this former capacity he made an impact on other authors. His translation of the *Diwan* by the Persian poet Hafiz (1326-1389) served as the basis for Goethe's *Westöstlicher Diwan* and also influenced the oriental poems of the German poet Friedrich Rückert (1788-1866), *Die Weisheit des Brahmanen* (1836-1839, The Wisdom of the Brahmans) and of August von Platen 1796-1835), *Ghaselen* (1821-1824). Hammer-Purgstall's final important contribution was his ability to persuade Metternich to establish an Akademie der Wissenschaften (1847, Academy of Sciences), of which he served as first president. This academy still exists today.

The fermenting mood of discontent expanded and intensified throughout the course of the 1840s, arousing reactions and protests not only in Vienna, but also in other parts of the Monarchy, climaxing in the revolution of 1848. Politically active writers from the German-speaking areas of the other lands of the Monarchy, usually influenced by the ideas of the Young Germany movement, came to Vienna both for greater employment opportunity and to be closer to the source of political power. A number of these authors were Jewish, and with them began three important trends that accelerated when the restrictions prohibiting Jews from residing in Vienna were lifted after the revolution: an increase in the number of newspapers, since many of these writers had a background in journalism in their own lands; a rise in anti-Semitism because of the greater visibility of the Jewish presence in the professional and intellectual life of Vienna; and a greater recognition of the works produced in the other lands, showing that Austrian literature consisted of writings from throughout the Monarchy and not simply from Vienna or Austria proper.

The journalist and author, Alfred Meissner (1822-1885), born in Teplitz, added a further note from another land of the Monarchy, in this case advocating the national cause of the Czechs. His lyric poems, *Gedichte* (1845, Poems), *Im Jahr des Heils* (1848, In the Year of Our Lord), *Der Sohn des Atta Troll* (1870, The Son of Atta Troll), and *Zeitklänge* (1870, Sounds of the Time), reflect the influence of Lenau, Byron, and Heine, not unusual at the time. His poems portraying the proletarian workers and the outcasts of society make him one of the first authors to describe the conditions of the urban underprivileged. Meissner's main passion was for the theater, but in vain. His plays such as *Das Weib Urias* (1851, Urias's Wife) and *Der Prätendent von York* (1855, The Pretender of York) failed on the stage.

Meissner's political novels attracted readers more for their revolutionary fervor, which abounded at this time, than for their gifted writing. The epic *Ziska* (1846), dealing with the Hussite uprising (1425-1431) in the historical past of Bohemia, served as his contribution to the Czech struggle for independence. Meissner made his intention clear in his Preface, stating explicitly that his book was addressed to German hearts to show the suffering the Czech people were enduring in their struggle for freedom and justice. Like so many others, who had held such high hopes for the revolution, he was extremely disappointed by the results. But rather than join the new Pan-Slavic movement, he traveled to France, where he wrote his *Revolutionäre Studien* (1849, Revolutionary Studies), which showed how closely his thinking paralleled that of Heinrich Heine and the Young Germany movement. Meissner met Heine in Paris, where he was living in political exile at the time, and in a curious twist of fate the two men shared a passion for the same woman. Meissner paid tribute to Heine in the book *Heinrich Heine* (1856).

Over the years Meissner wrote many novels—his collected works appeared in 1872 in eighteen volumes—most of them of inferior literary quality. *Schwarzgelb* (1862, Black and Gold), which deals with Austrian conditions, stands out. Meissner also wrote numerous novellas and tales such as *Lemberger und Sohn* (1865, Lemberger and Son), *Die Sirene* (1868, The Siren), *Die Kinder Roms* (1870, The Children of Rome), and *Feindliche Pole* (1878, Hostile Poles). None of his prose works have survived their time.

A stranger ending to a life than befell Meissner can scarcely be imagined. A writer whom he had befriended claimed that he had written Meissner's novels. In what must be considered a reflection of an unstable personality, Meissner committed suicide rather than defend himself.

The Jewish writer, Moritz Hartmann (1821-1872), born in Bohemia, began his career writing political verse advocating Czech nationalism. He also published poems in the prominent journal *Ost und West* (*East and West*), edited by Rudolf Glaser in Prague. This literary publication served an important role in its efforts to create understanding in the west for the cultural activities of the east by means of translations and critical essays.

Hartmann's first book of poems, *Kelch und Schwert* (1845, Chalice and Sword) laments the treatment of Bohemia by Austria and portrays the rich history of Bohemia which he desires to make known in the west to support the country's efforts to achieve freedom. His book is intended to use poetry as a sword in the fight for independence. Because of all the suffering that Austria has inflicted on Bohemia, Hartmann hopes for assistance from Germany. However, he became as disappointed by the German treatment of Bohemia as he was by the results of the revolution. Hartmann had played an active role in the revolution in Vienna and had escaped capture only by fleeing to Germany. There he served as a delegate to the Frankfurt Parliament, until he again had to avoid arrest by going into exile in London and then in France. He vented his bitterness over the political activities in Frankfurt in the *Reimchronik des Pfaffen Maurizius* (1849, Rhymed Chronicle of the Priest Maurizius), a satire on the Frankfurt Parliament of 1848, which shattered his hopes for the annexation of Bohemia by Germany. Instead, Austria was allowed to absorb the country. Hartmann was particularly sarcastic in describing the declining power of the Habsburgs, whom he blamed for preventing Bohemian freedom.

While in exile Hartmann made a name as a journalist by publishing articles in many European newspapers and journals. He also recorded his life in France in *Tagebuch aus Languedoc und Provence* (1852, Diary from Languedoc and Provence). In 1868 he was granted a pardon in Austria for his earlier political activities and returned to Vienna to play a role in the growing world of journalism. He worked first as a feuilletonist and then until his death in 1872 as one of the editors of the *Neue Freie Presse,* which had been founded in 1864 by Max Friedländer and Michael Etienne (1827-1879). Under Moritz Benedikt (1849-1920), who employed such leading critics as Ludwig Speidel (1830-1906), Hugo Wittmann (1829-1872), and Eduard Hanslick (1825-1904), as well as such prominent feuilletonists as Theodor Herzl (1860-1904) and Raoul Auernheimer (1876-1948), this newspaper grew into an influential voice not only in Austria, but also throughout Europe. Anecdotes abound attesting to the paper's powerful influence. For example, a person asked about his opinion on a given issue, replied that he did not know what he thought because he had not yet read the *Neue Freie Presse.* Another measure of the paper's continuing central position in the life of the time may be seen later at the turn of the century in the vehemence of Karl Kraus's unrelenting attacks, satirizing and criticizing everything from the editorial policy and the politics to the cultural reporting and use (in his view, misuse) of language.[74]

Many more names could be added to this list of German-speaking authors from other lands of the Monarchy, but let us conclude with Fritz Mauthner (1849-1923), an important figure who provides an understanding of the linguistic situation faced by Jews in the German-speaking cities of the Monarchy.

> Indeed, I do not understand how a Jew who was born in one of the Slavonic lands of the Austrian Empire could avoid being drawn to the study of language. In those days he learned to understand three languages all at once: German as the language of the civil service, of culture, poetry, and polite society; Czech as the language of peasants and service girls, and as the historical language of the glorious kingdom of Bohemia; a little Hebrew as the holy language of the Old Testament and as the basis of Jewish-German jargon which he heard not only from the Jewish hawkers, but occasionally also from quite well-dressed Jewish businessmen of his society, and even from his relatives. . . . Moreover, the mixture of quite dissimilar languages in the common Czech-German jargon was bound to draw a child's attention to certain linguistic laws.[75]

Because of this background Mauthner devoted his life to creating a philosophy of language. His writings such as the *Beiträge zu einer Kritik der Sprache* (1901-1902, Contributions toward a Critique of Language) played a significant role at the turn of the century when language had come to be considered problematic. Mauthner believed that his book paralleled Hofmannsthal's seminal "Ein Brief" (1902, "A Letter"), better known as the Chandos Letter, to such a degree that he wrote to the young author and asked him to acknowledge that he had used his book. Such a testimonial would have greatly benefited Mauthner's reputation. Hofmannsthal, however, declined to oblige him, insisting that he had arrived at his conclusions independently.[76]

Mauthner belonged to those authors from the Monarchy who were drawn to Bismarck because he was a practical man of action, not given to useless talk. Although Mauthner came from Prague, he considered himself a German, not an Austrian or Czech. He moved to Berlin in 1876 and lived there for twenty-five years, working as a feuilletonist and drama critic for several newspapers and journals, while continuing his language investigations. He contributed other important studies to the analysis and understanding of language: *Die Sprache* (1907, Language), *Wörterbuch der Philosophie. Neue Beiträge zu einer Kritik der Sprache* (1910, Dictionary of Philosophy. New Contributions to a Critique of Language), *Der Atheismus und seine Geschichte im Abendlande* (four volumes, 1920-1923, Atheism and Its History in the Western World), and *Die drei Bilder der Welt. Ein sprachkritischer Versuch* (1925, Three Pictures of the World. A Linguistic Critical Essay). Mauthner is often considered a forerunner of the philosopher Ludwig Wittgenstein (1889-1951).

The Reign of Franz Joseph I

The rule of Franz Joseph I, who was appointed emperor on 5 December 1848 to restore order to the country, meant that the conservative forces had triumphed in Austria once again. Like his predecessors, the young emperor, guided primarily by his mother, believed in the traditional Habsburg concept of absolutism. He set about establishing a strong bureaucracy and military force that could ensure the preservation of the status quo throughout the monarchy. He himself symbolized this reliance on the army, for he always dressed in the uniform of a general. The soldierly appearance was not just show; Franz Joseph actually led his troops at the battle of Solferino in 1859, but with disastrous results, putting an end to his personal military ambitions. He recalled Metternich from exile in 1851 to act as an advisor, confirming his tendency to continue the thinking of the past. His leading statesman, however, was Prince Felix Schwarzenberg (1800-1852), who, like the emperor, was a strong conservative.

This reestablishment of an absolutist government is only one of the many parallels of the second half of the nineteenth century with the first half. Thus the two halves of the century stand almost as mirror images of each other, with only a change of key or of tone to differentiate them. Franz Joseph stood at the head of a Monarchy that still suffered from the same two major problems that had plagued his illustrious forebears: a demand by the people for greater freedom of expression and political representation, and a steadily growing pressure by the member states and lands of the Monarchy for greater self-determination, including the use of their own language in schools, officialdom, and the army.

While these pressing problems of the Monarchy and of the Emperor continued unaltered and unresolved, the rest of the western world had changed considerably from what it had been in the first half of the nine-teenth century. People both within Austria proper and within the other lands of the Monarchy were no longer content to suffer a repressive government. The development of Austria from an agrarian into an indus-trial state, carried out despite the ruling house and not because of it, brought with it the same change witnessed in other European countries: the preeminence of the nobility gave way to the dominance of the new wealthy bourgeois class, which had supplanted the upper class, not in governing the country, which remained in the hands of the ruling house and the aristocracy, but in controlling the economic affairs of the country. As a result, the tone of the nation shifted from the conservatism of the ruling house and the aristocrats to a new liberalism of the wealthy bourgeoisie. While the aristocrats often became impoverished, businesses expanded, creating an affluent Vienna which grew rapidly into a world capital of grandeur and beauty. The prosperity was, as always, not equally shared. The living conditions of the lower classes remained as miserable under the new conditions as under the old.[77]

The long-awaited constitution, which was finally presented on 21 De-cember 1867, contained provisions that revealed its origin in the prevailing liberal thinking. Citizens were granted equality before the law, freedom of religion and expression, and the protection of private property. Most im-portantly the vote was extended to more people, and the formation of political parties was allowed. As a gesture toward resolving the problems with the member states, each ethnic group was granted the right to the preservation and use of its own language. Another positive move of the regime was the reform of the education system and the concordance with the church in 1855, granting it greater independence and removing it from the control of the Emperor. In 1869 a new school law was passed that introduced an interconfessional, eight-year, state-required school plan. This move, demanded as a condition for gaining the support of the church in the effort to restrain liberalism, restored obligatory Catholic education, thus granting this religion preference over others. One of the major bene-fits of the constitution was the provision extending the vote, as will be seen.

Perhaps the major casualty of the revolution and the fall of Metternich was Austria's inability to maintain the strong political role in Germany that it had played during the first half of the century. Then there was no unified Germany to contend with; the country consisted of thirty-nine separate states, each ruled independently. Hence Austria, as one of the largest and strongest countries in Europe, could maintain considerable influence over German affairs, since Metternich sat as head of the German Union. In 1850 Schwarzenberg could still humiliate Prussia by forcing it to back down from its plans for a German Union. At the same time Austrian influence was not strong enough to gain acceptance of the entire Monarchy into the German Bund. Matters changed dramatically with Bismarck's creation of a unified German state, which threatened Austria's very ties to Germany. The "Iron Chancellor" wanted to eliminate any further Austrian involvement in German affairs and consequently mandated the exclusion of Austria from any connection with the new Germany. He no longer wanted an Austrian serving as the head of the Deutscher Bund. In a desperate attempt to prevent this unilateral severance of all political ties, to which it attached enormous importance, Austria went to war with Germany, only to suffer defeat at the battle of Königgrätz on 3 July 1866. Bismarck achieved his goal and the new Germany was launched without any further participation by Austria. The reason for losing the battle is instructive about the different directions the two countries were taking. Germany had purchased breech-loading rifles, which gave its troops six times the firepower of the Austrians still using the old muzzleloaders. The inventor of the new gun had first offered it to the Austrian military, only to be rejected. This episode serves as a metaphor for the conservative status-quo attitude of an Austria held in bondage to the past, as opposed to the progressiveness of Bismarck's Germany looking to the future.

The severance of connections by Germany represented only one of the setbacks experienced by Austria in the second half of the nineteenth century. Austria took sides against Russia in the Crimean war (1853-1856), thus worsening relations with that country without at the same time gaining trust from the western powers. When Austria wanted to establish closer ties with the Danube principalities, the western powers would allow this move only on the condition that Austria give up Lombardy and Venice. To defend its interests in Italy against the Italian unification movement, Austria declared war in 1859, with Franz Joseph himself leading the troops at Magenta and Solferino. Both battles were lost at great cost in lives and material. The Emperor was downcast by the defeat and had the feeling that the Austrian Empire was crumbling in his hands. He was fored to cede Lombardy to Napoleon III, who then returned it to Sardinia.

In 1867 the Hungarians, recognizing the weakness of Austria, raised the matter of independence once again and finally gained major concessions. Franz Joseph was forced to declare a Dual Monarchy, which became known as the Imperial and Royal (*Kaiserlich und Königlich*) Austrian-Hungarian Monarchy. The Emperor of Austria served also as the King of Hungary, but to all intents and purposes Hungary could henceforth manage its own affairs as a constitutional monarchy, with its own parliament, laws, and above all with the right to use its own language instead of German. The president was Gyula Andrassy. The creation of the Dual Monarchy marked the beginnings of Pan-Slavism, which grew into a strong movement, for Hungary's example reverberated through the other countries of the Monarchy, contributing further to the unrest that had long prevailed. The creation of the Dual Monarchy served only as a makeshift solution to resolve the problem with Hungary, while leaving the major difficulty of how to handle all of the other lands unresolved. The rise of Slavic prestige caused the Germans in Austria to worry about a possible Slavic invasion during the 1880s.

The widespread dissatisfaction of the various lands makes it appear almost certain that the Monarchy would have ended at some point, for various ethnic groups—the Poles, Czechs, Bohemians, Moravians, Croats, Slovenians, Ruthenians, Slovaks, and Italians who together constituted a majority of the Monarchy—had never developed any Austrian national feeling and, with the exception of individuals who had grown up in German-speaking cities, had never acculturated or assimilated. However, the Monarchy did not have to end after World War I and would not have been dissolved at that time if the American President Woodrow Wilson had not stipulated that the peace treaty of St. Germaine contain a provision granting all of the lands and territories the right of self-determination. The end of the Monarchy was dictated from without; shaky as it might have been, it did not collapse from within in 1918.[78]

Politically the period after 1848 up to World War I was a continuous checkerboard of secret treaties uniting emerging nations in a variety of ways as a means of trying to maintain a balance of powers. Germany, recognizing that Austria was its best partner in holding France and Russia in check, formed an agreement called the *Zweierbund* (two-nation union), then a three-emperor agreement (*Dreierbund* or three-nation union), including Russia, to ward off France as well as a second three-country treaty with France to protect against any aggression from Russia. In 1878 Austria gained control over Bosnia and Herzegovina; Serbia attached itself to Austria in 1881. In 1883 Austria made a pact with Romania, with Germany and Italy joining in 1888. In 1887 Austria signed an agreement with Italy and England to ensure the status quo in the Mediterranean and to guarantee the independence of Turkey as well as its rights over Bulgaria.

The establishment of the German Reich in 1870 brought the realization that Austria would never again play a role in Germany, not to mention exert any influence or control over the country. The Germans in Austria, as distressed by Franz Joseph's conservative rule and the circumstances in Austria as they were impressed by Bismarck and the progressive developments in Germany, founded their own German National Party under the lead\ership of Georg von Schönerer, with the sole object of restoring the union with Germany. This goal of reuniting with Germany, pursued singlemindedly by the German National Party in the 1880s, by many individuals from the provinces as well as by professors and writers through the turn of the century up to World War I, and by the National Socialists in Austria in the 1920s and 1930s, stands out as the dominant political idea, which led the country directly from Königgrätz in 1866 to the Anschluss in 1938.

As Germany rapidly grew into a major power, Austria remained beleaguered by the nationality problem with its eight nations, fifteen crownlands, and seventeen parliaments to deal with. In 1910 the Monarchy consisted of approximately 33% Germans, 22% Czechs, 12% Poles, 5% Ukrainians, 3% Slovenians, 3% Italians, 3% Serbo-Croatians, and 7% other nationalities. At the same time Hungary had a population of 11% Germans.

In Vienna's parliament the Slavs possessed a majority, as they did in Hungary. Franz Joseph, whose responsibility it was to hold all these forces and tendencies together, simply was not equal to the task. Among other things he was plagued by personal problems. His brother Maximilian had been executed in Mexico in 1867, his son, crown prince Rudolf, committed suicide in 1889 in Mayerling,[79] and his unhappy wife Elisabeth, who was never suited for the role of queen and spent her life aimlessly wandering from country to country, had been killed by a political dissident in 1898 in Switzerland, and finally the heir apparent Franz Ferdinand and his wife were assassinated in Sarajevo in 1914. The beleaguered Emperor, with the aid of one minister after the other, tried to perpetuate the Monarchy by muddling through the multitude of problems with the tried and true tactic of the Metternich regime, namely, police-state methods. After 1879 the short period of liberalism ended in Austria, and Edward Taaffe (1833-1895), together with the "Iron Ring," a Catholic-Conservative-Slavic coalition, restored repressive rule. However, these measures could no longer work as effectively as in Metternich's era, because now Austria had political parties and a parliament.

The Founding Years (*Gründerjahre*) and the Ringstrasse

While Franz Joseph lived his life under a cloud of military defeats and reversals in foreign policy as well as a series of personal tragedies, the country itself enjoyed one of its greatest periods of prosperity. So serene and pleasant was the latter part of the nineteenth century that Stefan Zweig called it "the golden age of security." Just as in the Biedermeier period, the wealthy bourgeoisie at the end of the century again took refuge from political reality in materialism and the good life. Industry continued to grow, the sciences developed, the railroads expanded, there were record crops in the 1850s and 1860s, businesses flourished, and the Vienna stock exchange, which, after the French defeat by Germany in 1871, had become the leading market in Europe, reached an all-time high—until the crash of 1873. The period witnessed a continuous triumph of the bourgeoisie, which aspired to no other ideal than its own well-being. It was, as one commentator noted, a "prosaic, calculating time without ideals."[80]

Just as a major division between the ruling house and the people had existed in the *Vormärz,* so it continued in the second half of the century. The government attempted to preserve the status quo, while the bourgeoisie was interested solely in progress to increase its ability to make money and take pleasure in life. On the day of the battle of Königgrätz, which was so fateful in the history of Austria in terms of the connection with Germany, the concert halls, restaurants, and *Heurige* (wine houses featuring new wine) were full. Life seemed so casual and carefree that the American Ambassador Motley, who served in Vienna from 1861 to 1867, once asked whether there were no artists and scientists in Vienna. If there were, he stated, he had never met them.[81]

The German physician, Theodor Billroth (1829-1894), whom the Emperor had appointed professor of the first surgical clinic in Vienna on 12 May 1867, was struck on his arrival by the lack of larger goals, of interest in politics, of real people, and of personalities. In 1869 he commented: "Here everything is comfortable! The city's art treasures are inexhaustible, and anyone who takes pleasure in music can go into raptures here. We sing and make music, we go to the theater and to Strauss concerts, and hide our heads in the sand of our cozy geniality."[82]

The greatest positive achievement during Franz Joseph's reign was the creation of the Ringstrasse, although not everyone at the time greeted this innovative development with enthusiasm.[83] Many critics lamented the emperor's decision to tear down the wall surrounding the inner city of Vienna and replace it with a broad boulevard, which would be lined with a number of stately buildings. The removal of the wall would permit the expansion of the center of Vienna, a change that had become necessary because of the influx of people into the city. From 1870 to 1900 400,000 people came from Bohemia and Moravia, 90,000 from Hungary, 11,000 from south Slavic areas, 37,000 Poles and Ukrainians, and almost 180,000 Jews.[84] Franz Joseph signed the proclamation authorizing the construction of the Ringstrasse on 20 December 1857, and the work was completed on 4 December 1874. The emperor personally commissioned one of the buildings, the Votivkirche (1856-1858), designed and built by the architect Heinrich Ferstel in Neo-Gothic style, to fulfill the vow he had made after he survived an assassination attempt. The recognition that the wall could serve the purpose of assassins and dissidents played a part in motivating the Emperor's decision to order its removal.

The meaning of the Ringstrasse for Austria can be seen in the comment of Alexander Witeschnik:

> The Ringstrasse was not only the symbol, but also the source of the new feeling of life. The city, which had spun itself into an idyllic cocoon in the *Vormärz*, now received another push into cosmopolitanism, resembling the days of the Baroque emperors. Only the feeling of worldliness grew this time not from within, not from the consciousness of a worldly political mission, but was literally forced upon the Viennese from the outside by the buildings of a decorative street. This situation gave the entire period an inner division. In losing the closeness

and compactness of the *Vormärz*, the city also lost its stability and spiritual solidity. The history of the Ringstrasse is a continuous chain of divisions. The optimism of a new, not yet solidified entrepreneurial spirit lives in it just as the fascinating façade of a truly decorative period. The festive atmosphere created by its ornamental appearance formed the accompanying music to the steady decline of the Monarchy.[85]

Just as the rising stock market caused investors to get carried away and to lose all sense of reality, so too the desire of the wealthy elite to reside along the Ring or in the inner city ran rampant. While the government was building the new Burgtheater, the City Hall, the University, the Palace of Justice, the Art and Natural History Museums, and the Opera House, the wealthy were commissioning their palaces, all of which had spacious rooms to be lavishly decorated, giving profitable commissions to architects, painters, and sculptors. Just as the salon had flourished in the first half of the nineteenth century as an open meeting place, it continued to play this important role in the salons of the wealthy financial families such as the Wertheimsteins, the Todescos, and the Laudenburgs. One of the largest salons was that of the Metternichs, who had returned to Vienna in 1872 after he had served as Austrian Ambassador in Paris for fourteen years. Perhaps the last salon of note was that of Bertha Zuckerkandl-Szeps (1864-1945), a prominent author and journalist, whose home provided a meeting place for all of the famous personalities in the fields of art and culture at the turn of the century.[86]

The man who more than any other stamped his imprimatur on the growth years from 1866 to 1873, was the flamboyant painter Franz Makart (1840-1884). After being rejected by the art school in Vienna, he went on to become the most celebrated painter of his time. Whether one admired his paintings or not—and most professed dislike because of their gaudiness—no one could avoid being aware of him from the time he emerged on the cultural scene with his painting "The Seven Deadly Sins," which was later named "Plague in Florence." His presence enlivened Vienna in the 1870s as no other personality of the time. His atelier, which can still be seen in the painting he made of it, became one of the major sights of Vienna. The gala procession that he prepared to celebrate the silver wedding anniversary of the royal couple on 27 April 1879 was acknowledged as a major event of the time.

Along with the new buildings, the Ringstrasse was further decorated with statues of famous personalities, military leaders, musicians, and writers. Since there were no new triumphs to celebrate, the purpose was to call attention to the glories of the past. The statues further contributed to the spirit of historicism which the Ringstrasse celebrates. It serves as a metaphor for the usual Austrian dichotomy of innovation and tradition: remove the wall and permit expansion of the city, but at the same time adhere to the past by creating the new buildings in terms of older styles. The Ringstrasse also epitomizes the struggle between liberalism and conservatism (*Kulturkampf*). The triumph of historicism demonstrated clearly that the short era of liberalism had ended and that the balance of power had shifted back to the conservatives.

In its own day the Ringstrasse was derided for the architects' decision to build the monumental structures in historical styles, each building in a historical style appropriate to its purpose, for example, the University of Vienna in Renaissance style and the City hall in Gothic. This decision accorded with the backward-looking policy of the ruling house and was interpreted by liberals as another sign of the lack of progressive spirit in the country. The conflict between the younger, innovative artists who were looking forward and the conservative Künstlerhaus painters, who dominated the art scene, and who promoted historicism, continued through the end of the century. In 1897 the Secessionist painters, voices for the new contemporary spirit, led by Gustav Klimt and with the movement publicized by Bahr, triumphed. The principle of modern art prevailed and celebrated its victory in Vienna in 1898 with the construction of the Secession building, designed by the architect Joseph Olbrich and bearing the motto: "To every time its art, to art its freedom."

The Ringstrasse was maligned and ridiculed, but time has proved the naysayers wrong. This street survived all of the controversy surrounding its construction and has become Vienna's major tourist attraction, giving the city an opportunity to show off its new cultural and cosmopolitan face to the world. It remains the best investment in tourism that Austria has ever made, for it continues to draw people from all over the world to Vienna to see the very buildings that were once so suspect. Even Hermann Bahr, the pioneer of modernity who had been one of the more outspoken critics of the Ringstrasse, came finally to appreciate the fact that it had ultimately established its own integrity and, historicism notwithstanding, had become a major artistic triumph.[87] The new Opera House, in Italian Renaissance style, opened on 25 May 1869 with a performance of Mozart's *Don Giovanni*. Building went on apace, and Vienna became a glittering metropolis of wealthy, often titled, people who could afford to support the arts. Culture and the arts flourished through the turn of the century in a manner unmatched in Austrian history.[88]

The euphoria of the founding years came to a temporary halt in 1873 with the crash of the stock market. This setback followed by only one week the opening of the World Exhibition on 1 May 1873, which failed to achieve its anticipated success, for it suffered the misfortune of taking place at a time which witnessed an outbreak of cholera as well as the stock market debacle. The Exhibition closed with a deficit of almost fifteen million Gulden. These were truly disastrous events, but through it all the theaters and concert halls performed to full houses and life went on as usual. Many businesses and banks were forced into bankruptcy. Properties were sold at a fraction of their value. Not everyone was unhappy, however. The journalist and writer Ferdinand Kürnberger, who served as the conscience of society in those days, wrote in an open letter of 10 May 1873: "The stock exchange collapsed under the weight of its crimes. Since yesterday honorable people can walk on the street again, and people who work will no longer be called fools. Since yesterday a thief can be called a thief again and no longer a baron. Never has a more beautiful storm cleansed a more pestilent air."[89]

In retrospect the seeming setbacks of Solferino (1859), Königgrätz (1866), and the establishment of the Dual Monarchy (1867) could all be viewed as positives. Solferino relieved Austria of the problem of defending the Italian provinces. Königgrätz released Austria from its rivalry with Prussia, and the Dual Monarchy removed the pressure for greater autonomy that the Hungarians had kept up for more than twenty years. Austria could and did turn its attention to its own internal matters and became a large, successful capital through the growth of businesses, the expansion of Vienna, and the greater freedom of trade. However, the stock market crash in 1873, the effects of which lasted into the 1890s, slowed the energy and drive of the liberal founding years considerably and produced the period of lethargy and indecision, during which Franz Joseph's philosophy of the status quo could dominate once again. The age of liberalism ended along with this spirit of growth, at least temporarily. This hiatus in the 1870s and 1880s between the founding years and the ebullient, youthful spirit at the turn of the century, when liberalism, the entrepreneurial spirit, and cultural eminence returned, created the feeling in a number of writers and artists that nothing was happening in Austria, while Germany was vibrant with growth and development. The Germans in Austria had never ceased looking longingly to Germany ever since the battle of Königgrätz, and now they had more reason than ever to feel unhappy with their own country.

A major development in the second half of the nineteenth century was the extension of the vote granted by the new constituion in 1867. Many citizens remained disenfranchised, a situation that Count Eduard Taaffe (1883-1895) tried to rectify by lowering the income level for voting from ten to five Gulden in 1882. In 1893 he attempted to extend the vote to all males over twenty-four years of age, but on that issue his government fell. He paid the price of being ahead of his time: the universal franchise that he wanted to institute was approved in 1896 under the leadership of Count Kasimir Badeni (1846-1909), who had been appointed to replace Taafe in 1895 and served until 1897. In May 1907 the parliament was elected for the first time by a general vote. Women finally received the right to vote after World War I.

Along with the right to vote came the privilege of forming political parties: the Christian Socials, the German Nationals, and the Social Democrats. The Christian Socials, the party of the middle class, joined together with the conservatives to form a major anti-liberal force. The most noteworthy of the Christian Social leaders was Karl Lueger (1844-1910),[90] a notorious demagogue, who used the virulent anti-Semitism of his time for his political purposes.[91] He continued the trend which was begun by Schönerer and which led to Hitler, who admired Lueger and felt that he understood mass psychology better than Schönerer. Lueger's party was religious as well as political, for he traded on both the loyalty of his constituents to the Catholic Church as well as on the church's anti-Semitism which helped to legitimize his own use of this prejudice. The Emperor regarded him with suspicion and three times declined to approve his election as mayor before he finally relented. Despite his dubious political methods, "handsome Karl," as Lueger was known, served Vienna well. He turned the gas and electric companies as well as the streetcar system into municipal companies, had a new water delivery system constructed, and worked for the improvement of the public health plan.

The German National party, founded by the radical Georg von Schönerer, built its constituency from the university fraternities (*Burschen-*

schaften) and the farmers.[92] Schönerer's program advocated overthrowing the Austrian Monarchy and annexing Austria to Germany under the leadership of the party's idol, Bismarck. The German Nationals were anti-Catholic and launched a program at the turn of the century called the Separation-from-Rome (*Los von Rom*) movement, but it achieved little, as did the party in general. Had it not been for its use of anti-Semitism to accomplish its political purposes, the German Nationals would have come and gone without a trace, like so many extremist political parties. As it was, however, in 1885 Schönerer added to the Linz program of 1882 a resolution that became the basis for racial anti-Semitism. Up to this time anti-Semitism, which has a long history in Austria as in other countries, had been primarily based on economic arguments. Now Schönerer declared that anyone with a single drop of Jewish blood was Jewish, and also that a Jew could never change his identity even through assimilation. In consequence of this policy all Jewish members of the party were ejected, including Theodor Herzl, who later founded Zionism.

The Social Democrats, the party of the workers, under Viktor Adler (1852-1918) shifted from the ideas of Ferdinand Lassalle to those of Karl Marx. Adler established a Socialist weekly called *Gleichheit* (1886, Equality), and the *Arbeiterzeitung* (1889, Workers' Newspaper). As a delegate to parliament, he worked for universal voting rights, primarily out of self-interest. He needed to make it possible for more of the poorer workers to vote, in order to expand his party. The Marxist party was banned in 1888 and had to go underground, but this did not affect Adler and the Social Democrats. In 1918 he held the position of State Secretary of the Exterior in the First Republic, headed by the Social Democrat Karl Renner (1870-1950), and in this capacity worked to implement the Anschluss of Austria with Germany.

After his success in introducing universal voting rights, Badeni, who attempted to bring a strong hand to the government, tried to reduce the constant friction with the lands and territories of the Monarchy by ordering that all officials had to know the language of the country in which they were serving. The reaction against this requirement was so strong that it led to demonstrations in Vienna and other cities as well as to violent scenes in parliament. The dispute continued to be so passionate and violent that any agreement on the language question, a troublesome issue even in the days of Joseph II, was hopeless. To restore calm, the Emperor finally had to dissolve parliament and dismiss Badeni.

Since Austria had been forced to relinquish its positions in Germany and Italy, it turned its attention to the Balkan area. It moved troops to occupy Bosnia and Herzegovina, until under the new foreign minister Alois Aehrenthal (1854-1912) the decision was made to change the occupation into annexation, causing the Serbs to threaten war. They sought support from Russia and Turkey, but neither country would risk a war over this matter. Since France was indifferent and Germany supported Austria, peace was preserved. These final years before World War I were marked by constant problems with Hungary and Czechoslovakia. A Balkan war broke out in 1912, but Austria did not participate directly. Many people saw hope for Austria's future in the heir apparent Franz Ferdinand, who they believed could achieve a reconciliation with Russia and peace in the Balkans. He was also regarded as the leader who would transform the Monarchy into a federation of states with greater self-determination. However, Serbian Nationalists considered Franz Ferdinand an enemy and assassinated him on 28 June 1914 during a state visit to Sarajevo, leading to the outbreak of World War I.

There was no necessity for the First World War, but Franz Joseph with great misgivings allowed himself to be persuaded by his generals that a war would help the prestige of the country and bring him personal glory. As it turned out, it led directly to the dissolution of the Monarchy. Franz Joseph did not live to see this final humiliation; he died in 1916. His great-nephew Karl I (1887-1922), who ascended to the throne, never had an opportunity to show his ruling capabilities. In 1918, when the treaty of St. Germaine declared the end of the Monarchy, a decision was made internally to transform Austria into a republic. It is noteworthy that the name of the new republic would have been the First German-Austrian Republic. The Allies would not permit the use of the term German, since they did not want to see the union of the two countries continued after the war. However, the choice of name shows that the desire to rejoin Germany, a wish that had remained alive in Austria since the battle of Königgrätz, continued as strong as ever.

Austrian Literature after 1848

While the Austrian ruling house with a procession of ministers muddled through one crisis after another to keep Austria on a peaceful political course, the literature proceeded along its own path. The major writers of the second half of the nineteenth century began to pay increasing attention to the social circumstances around them but of necessity they avoided political developments. As in the first half of the century, censorship still controlled what could be published, although for the most part it was not as strict under Franz Joseph as in the *Vormärz*. Even after Austria changed from a Monarchy to the First Republic in 1918, writers generally ignored the fact that the country's government had radically transformed and continued to write about the Habsburg era.[93] This trend continued with few exceptions until 1955.

The period from 1848 to 1890 was dominated by Realism, not unexpected at a time when society itself had adopted a materialistic outlook. Although censorship barriers no longer isolated Austrian writers from those of other countries, as in the first half of the century, Austrian literature still proceeded on its own course without particular influence from the outside beyond the impact of individual writers such as the Russian realist Ivan Turgenev and the Norwegian dramatist Henrik Ibsen, who served as the godfather of the Young Vienna movement at the turn of the century. Austrian and German literature ran to some degree along parallel lines, but each essentially developed and remained within its own tradition. Germany displayed a number of movements that found no counterpart in Austria: the Munich group of art-for-art's-sake poets around Paul Heyse and Emanuel Geibel, the novels by professors (*Professorenromane*) of Felix Dahn and Georg Ebers, and the historical novels of Gustav Freytag and Viktor Scheffel, stimulated by the nationalistic spirit resulting from the founding of the new German Reich in 1870, and the pan-tragic dramas of Friedrich Hebbel.

The difference between the two literatures became most pronounced at the end of the century, when Realism in German literature, represented by Theodor Fontane, led directly into Naturalism, an attempt to make literature more scientific. Naturalism utilized the scientific findings of Charles Darwin with their stress on the importance of heredity and environment in determining human behavior. Other influences on the German Naturalist movement, which consisted mainly of Gerhart Hauptmann and Arno Holz, were Henrik Ibsen, who was a major factor in the development of the movement, the French writers Emile Zola and Hippolyte Taine, and the major Russian writers Turgenev, Dostoyevsky, and Tolstoy. The pessimistic philosophy of Arthur Schopenhauer and the atheism of Ludwig Feuerbach and Ludwig Büchner (*Kraft und Stoff* [1855, *Power and Substance*]) were also influential. Even though the ideas of Marx and Engels found little echo in the literature, they strongly influenced the thinking of the time in general, as Bahr and Kralik showed,[94] as well as of Viktor Adler and the development of the Social Democratic party specifically. Naturalism held no appeal for Austrian writers, with one major exception: Jakob Julius David, who was German oriented and who spent the last years of his life in Germany. Austrian writers in the nineteenth century remained within the framework of Realism until the major writers at the turn of the century—Andrian, Bahr, Beer-Hofmann, Hofmannsthal, and Schnitzler—turned to Impressionism.

The revolution of 1848 caused no break in the literary tradition, which essentially continued its straight line of development until the 1880s when the fundamental shift in thinking occurred that ushered Austria into the twentieth century. The leading writers spanning the middle of the century were the same authors who had begun their careers before 1848, namely, Grillparzer, Stifter, and Nestroy, although Grillparzer played little role in the second half of the century, since he no longer released any of his new plays for performance. Each of these writers stands as a uniquely Austrian phenomenon; each wrote from within himself with little regard for outside influences, with the exception of Nestroy, who freely borrowed plots from French literature but always adapted them to Austrian circumstances. They continued along the same lines with which they had begun until the end of their careers: Nestroy died in 1862, Stifter in 1868, and Grillparzer in 1872.

The major writers of the second half of the nineteenth century include Ludwig Anzengruber, Ada Christen, Jakob Julius David, Marie von Ebner-Eschenbach, Karl Emil Franzos, Robert Hamerling, Ferdinand Kürnberger, Betty Paoli, Peter Rosegger, Ferdinand von Saar, Leopold von Sacher-Masoch, and Franz Stelzhamer.

Ada Christen (pseudonym for Christiane Friderike-Breden, 1839-1901), has still not received the attention her writings merit as examples of outspoken feminism before any idea of an organized movement had been formulated. She herself did not think in programmatic terms, and she never regarded herself as a pioneer. She was an honest, outspoken woman, who wanted to express her views candidly and openly without the facade of discretion behind which women of her day were expected to conceal their true feelings and thoughts. Docile housewives, who adopted the passive role of wives and mothers expected, indeed commanded, of them by the patriarchal society, only aroused her scorn. She believed in equal opportunity, equal education, and equal freedom of expression. She did not subscribe to the male division of women into two groups, femmes fragiles and femmes fatales, madonnas and vamps. In her view young girls start out with unlimited potential. How they turn out results from the influences to which they are subjected. These views make her an unusual representative for women early in the nineteenth century.

Ada Christen's life was also atypical, for she grew up poor and had to earn her own living and make her own way early in life. She gained her education not so much from school as from life directly, for she became an actress with a traveling theater group. As was the case for performers in such troupes and in theaters in garrison towns, they were expected to entertain the patrons both on and off the stage. Schnitzler described this situation later in *Das Märchen* (1993, The Fairytale) and *Freiwild* (1896, Free Game). Christen described her life as a prostitute in frank terms in her first book of lyric poems, *Lieder einer Verlorenen* (1868, Songs of a Lost Woman), which brought strong, negative reaction from male critics. Ferdinand von Saar, who greatly admired Christen as she did him, had helped her to find a publisher while at the same time urging her to tone down what he considered the overly candid, confessional aspects of her poems. She displayed the same frankness in the scandalous autobiographical novel *Ella* (1869), which created more negative backlash after first appearing serialized in a newspaper and then in book form. She herself had worked as a journalist and theater critic for two newspapers to help earn her living.

The improvement in her life came with her two marriages, both with well-to-do men, bringing her not only financial security, but also social respectability. She portrays this change in status with her usual honesty in her subsequent volume of poetry *Aus der Asche* (1870, Up from the Ashes), in which she reveals how differently people treat her now that she is relatively successful. The same theme is continued in *Aus der Tiefe* (1878, Up from the Depths), in which she describes how, to her own surprise, she had become totally socially acceptable. Because of her new status and because she now had the money to do so, she bought up all of the copies of her novel *Ella* in 1873 and removed it from the market.

Her collections of novellas, *Aus dem Leben* (1876, From Life), *Unsere Nachbarn* 1884, Our Neighbors), and *Jungfrau Mutter* (1892, Virgin Mother), represent Christen's major literary contribution, for in these works she shows greater artistic restraint and more controlled form.

Usually she wrote about social problems of the poor, and in this choice of theme she may be seen as a forerunner of Naturalism. However, she herself tended toward Impressionism in her later works. Through Saar she became a friend of Ebner-Eschenbach, and in 1879 she associated with Anzengruber, with whose anti-clerical views she agreed. She had converted from Catholicism to Protestantism in 1869. In the novella *Im Armenhaus* (In the Poorhouse) she portrays an old woman who questions the existence of God because her son was killed during the revolution of 1848 right in front of their church.

Strangely, Christen, despite her social acceptance, was never accorded any great measure of literary recognition. For example, her works were rarely included in literary anthologies of her own time. Even today, when women writers are being searched out for special treatment, Christen has not yet received the attention that her works, on the basis of the feminist as well as universal ideas they contain, would seem to merit.

Ludwig Anzengruber (1839-1889), like many of his literary forebears, was a government official; he worked for the Vienna police while attempting to establish himself as a writer. The uproar caused by his first play *Der Pfarrer von Kirchfeld* (1870, The Pastor of Kirchfeld), forced him to resign from his position. The play was written in reaction to the Papal Letter (Concordat) published by Pope Pius IX in 1870, declaring the doctrine of papal infallability. This document initiated the *Kulturkampf* (Cultural Struggle) that took place during the 1870s in Austria and Germany. Anzengruber, a dedicated liberal, felt strongly that there had to be a response. Since no one else seemed inclined to use the stage to address this question, he took the matter upon himself. Like this drama, all of his subsequent writings deal with real issues of the time that affected people's lives, for he was determined to serve as an educator and moral guide for the people. With his first play Anzengruber picked up the mantle of drama left vacant by the death of Grillparzer in 1872 and became the major Austrian dramatist of the period 1870 to 1890. He was also one of the most hated by the Catholic Church, not only for his first play, but because he continued to be one of the church's most outspoken critics. When his folk play, *Das vierte Gebot* (*The Fourth Commandment*), was performed in Vienna in the fall of 1890, after it had been staged by the *Freie Bühne* (Free Theater) in Berlin, it was denounced in a sermon at St. Stephen's cathedral.

Although Anzengruber was born in Vienna, he usually set his works in the provinces, basing his plots on his reading of country tales and on observations that he had made as a touring actor. He continued the folk play in the manner of Nestroy and Raimund, and his comedies ranked as some of the finest in German. All of his plays deal with ethical and materialistic concerns, and usually end by resolving the problem favorably in a moral context. Literary historians often consider Anzengruber a Naturalist, but he never carries his realism that far. The elements of determinism, heredity, and environment as the controlling factors of existence are lacking in his writings. So too is the exemption from guilt. He was extremely popular in his day but is forgotten now except as a historical figure, even though the themes of many of his plays are universal in nature. Even specialists of the nineteenth century have come to ignore his works at present, although they belong to the major contributions of Austrian Realism and the trend toward Naturalism toward the end of the century.

All of Anzengruber's plays and novels, like the works of Karl Emil Franzos and Marie von Ebner-Eschenbach, were intended as enlightenment for the broad public. His dramas continued the idea of the early nine-teenth-century improvement play (*Verbesserungsstück*), that is, a drama in which a character learns a moral lesson and reforms into a better person. They are ethical plays in that justice always triumphs over evil. His humorous plays are comedies in the true sense, often touching on tragedy before ending with humaneness and morality triumphant.

In addition to writing plays dealing with themes of money, the church, human values, and interpersonal relationships, Anzengruber was one of the few male writers of his day who defended the rights of women. In 1875, for example, in the comedy *Doppelselbstmord* (Double Suicide), he presents a reversed village Romeo and Juliet. Because their fathers are feuding, the young man and woman run off with each other, but not to consummate their love and then die, as in Gottfried Keller's novella *Romeo und Juliet auf dem Dorfe* (1856, *A Village Romeo and Juliet*), but to celebrate the all-powerful call of nature and to live. Their sensible approach to life, which the atheist Keller would have approved, causes the fathers to settle their quarrel and restore their friendship.

Strong women are found also in *Der ledige Hof* (1876, Celibacy Farm), in which a young woman is being pressured to remain single so that she will leave her inherited farm to the church when she dies. She finally comes to the realization that she should use her own intelligence and make her own decisions. She takes charge of her own life, withstanding the persuasion of the priest and the falseness of her would-be fiancé Leonard. Agnes becomes almost too strong, for she can send Leonard, the man she is supposed to love, to almost certain death because he lied to her out of fear that he would lose her and all that he had gained. Even when he returns after having almost died, she refuses to accept him back and sends him away. She does show her inner goodness by adopting his son so that he, instead of the church, will inherit the farm and have an advantage in later life.

Anzengruber further displays his support of women in *Die Trutzige* (1878, The Shrew) in which a young, independent woman defends herself against the attempts of other villagers to humiliate her. The ensuing events show a Hofmannsthal-like mutual transformation, for not only does she change a man who had only pretended to court her into a serious suitor, but she herself, now confident in her love, can also change into a gentler person without sacrificing any of her self-confidence or moral integrity. Through these plays, Anzengruber, in his own way, presented enlightened messages on important issues to his audiences, carrying out the Schillerian injunction to use the stage as a moral institution.

Ferdinand Kürnberger (1821-1879), born in Vienna, is a transitional figure to the modern era in a number of ways. Even Karl Kraus recognized him as one of the most important writers of the nineteenth century, and he is clearly a forerunner of Kraus in his language criticism and in the fearless outspokenness of his social commentary and literary judgments. Hermann Bahr also greatly admired Kürnberger as an independent thinker, not afraid to take an unpopular stance, just as he himself frequently did.

Kürnberger, a liberal journalist and enlightened author, had to leave Austria during the revolutionary days of 1848 and take refuge in Germany. However, even there he ran afoul of the law for his political activism and had to spend nine months in jail in 1849. He remained in Germany and did not return to Austria until 1856. While in Germany he wrote his most recognized work, *Der Amerikamüde* (1855, *The Man Tired of America*), a novel written on the basis of Nikolaus Lenau's diaries dealing with the latter's experiences in America. The book was intended as a reply to the novel by the German writer Ernst Willkomm, entitled *Die Europamüden* (1838, The People Tired of Europe), glorifying life in America as the land of unlimited opportunity, a view widely accepted at that time. Kürnberger wished to counteract Willkomm's praise of the freedom to be found in the new country as opposed to the repression in Austria and Germany. Kürnberger's ideas were gained second hand, for he never visited America personally. Critics today generally agree that his real purpose in writing the novel was to present a critical view of American capitalism in an attempt to prevent its adoption in Europe.

Because of the centrality of the theater in Austrian life and culture, almost all writers tried to write plays, hoping for success in the theater and above all in the Vienna Burgtheater. Like Karoline Pichler, Marie von Ebner-Eschenbach, and Ferdinand von Saar, Kürnberger began his career with dramas and tragedies. However, as was the case with these other writers, none of his six plays such as *Catalina* (1854), *Firdusi* (1902), or *Das Pfand der Treue* (1902, The Pledge of Fidelity) brought any success. Indeed, a combination of censorship and plain bad luck kept all of them from ever being performed.

Kürnberger found his real forte as a journalist. Newspapers began to proliferate and gain in importance after the revolution, when greater freedom of speech was permitted. In his feuilletons later collected in the volumes *Literarische Herzenssachen* (1877, Literary Matters of the Heart) and *Siegelringe* (1874, Signet Rings), Kürnberger performed the function of a public conscience in addressing the major issues of his day, for example, what he called the "Austrian tragedy," namely, the promises made by the royal house in 1848 that were never kept, the political events which redounded negatively to Austria such as the war with Germany in 1866, and the compromise resulting in the Dual Monarchy with Hungary in 1867. He commented on the stock market, to which he was opposed, and on labor unions, which he favored. He was an early environmentalist who criticized the cutting down of the forests in the hills around Vienna. As a strong liberal and advocate of Enlightenment, he viewed negatively the ultraconservatism of the Catholic Church as well as the Jesuits' proselytizing of native peoples around the world. His criticism of the language usage found in newspapers marks him as a forerunner of Karl Kraus, who carried on a lifelong vendetta against the stylistic lapses of the *Neue Freie Presse.*

Kürnberger anticipated Freud and Schnitzler by introducing psychology into writings such as the novella *Die Last des Schweigens* (1869, The Burden of Silence) and the novel *Schloss der Frevel* (1904, The Castle of Blasphemy). Because of its provocative theme—the problems of Catholicism in dealing with eroticism—the novel could not be published in his lifetime. Kürnberger also argued against the idea of the fixed ego, making him a forerunner of the physicist and philosopher Ernst Mach (1838-1916), who became the philosopher of Impressionism by proclaiming in his seminal book *Die Analyse der Empfindungen* (1888, The Analysis of Perceptions), that the idea of a fixed ego was a fiction and that the human ego remained in a state of constant flux. In his writings and thinking Kürnberger clearly anticipates many of the attitudes that became accepted by the generation at the turn of the century, and it is apparent why he was so admired by those who received his legacy. He was a dedicated Austrian despite his criticism of conditions that needed to be improved. It was one of his ambitions to see Austria raised culturally to the level of other European countries, an idea that was brought to fruition by writers and artists of the turn-of-the-century generation, led by Bahr and Klimt. So too did they adopt Kürnberger's advocacy of international reciprocity and of openness and receptiveness to other cultures. Among other contributions, he publicized the writings of Ivan Turgenev and helped spread his reputation as a masterful prose writer. Turgenev became a major influence on Austrian prose writers of this time such as Ebner-Eschenbach and Sacher-Masoch. Although he played an influential and important role in his own time and despite the fact that his novellas, all written in the style of realism, were critically acclaimed, Kürnberger has been forgotten today. However, anyone with a serious interest in understanding the nineteenth century cannot ignore him.

Such is also the case with Karl Emil Franzos (1848-1904), who follows the line of those Jewish authors from outside Austria proper who brought the life of their own country—in this case Galicia—to the attention of Austrian and German readers. It is noteworthy that his family was oriented toward Germany, not Austria. Franzos' grandfather was so taken with the ideals of the German Enlightenment that at age forty he traveled to Germany to study. He and Franzos' father passed on to the boy their love of the Enlightenment and of German culture. As a law student, first in Vienna and then in Graz, Franzos joined a German National fraternity, and at one point was indicted for treason for his speeches advocating the Anschluss of Austria with Germany. In this regard he resembles young Hermann Bahr, who followed Franzos by a decade in the same direction of German Nationalism. Bahr also advocated Austrian Anschluss with Bismarck's Germany. Bahr, a follower of Schönerer, could have been arrested for treason, but instead he was punished by being dismissed from the University of Vienna, at which point he too enrolled at the University of

Graz. Both young men, like many others, took their position for the same reason: they saw everything happening in Germany and nothing transpiring in Austria except that it continued to decline in influence and progress because of the stifling policies of the regime intent on maintaining the status quo.

Franzos ranks alongside of Kürnberger as one of the important writers of his time, not only through his tales of Eastern European life and his novels dealing with moral and legal questions, particularly with the importance of upholding the law, but also because of his literary journal in which all of the major writers of the time appeared. The volume *Deutsches Dichterbuch aus Österreich* (1883, Book of German Literature from Austria) shows his orientation toward Germany which never abated, indeed, only grew stronger with time. He moved to Germany in 1887 out of disillusionment, believing that the idealism brought to Austrian public life by Joseph II was dead and that there was no hope on the horizon for improvement.

Not only the hope for greater opportunity, but also the anti-Semitism in Vienna motivated Franzos' move to Berlin. Jews had been granted equality again in Austria in 1867, but they were still not free from the anti-Semitism that grew in direct proportion to the greater visibility of the Jewish population. For they used the opportunity that had been granted to them and devoted themselves to study—the number of Jewish students in the Gymnasium far exceeded their proportion in the population— entered into the professions and assumed a major place in the arts. As individuals became more and more successful as journalists and writers as well as in professional and business life, the more intense the reaction became, spreading even to the provinces, where there were few Jews. Franzos claims to have been the only Jew in Graz at the time he was there, but he still felt an atmosphere of anti-Semitism. His view shows that the phenomenon of anti-Semitism without Jews existed then as it still does. Yet through money and/or accomplishment Jews could find acceptance among the highest levels of society. One of the most prominent families was the Rothschilds, the banking family, which made itself indispensable to the Emperor and to the government. Franzos himself enjoyed a personal friendship with Crown Prince Rudolf, but he kept it private and never commented about it to other people either during the friendship or after the Crown Prince's suicide at Mayerling in 1889.

Joseph II had tried to abolish anti-Semitism by releasing Jews from the ghettos in 1782, so that they could study and work. With the payment of a fee they could even live in Vienna. Before 1848 only 179 Jewish families were allowed to reside in the capital. There did not seem to be any significant discrimination prior to the revolution of 1848, even though Franz II did not subscribe to the tolerant attitude of Joseph II. The Jewish petition for equal treatment and the number of Jewish activists, who had come to Vienna from other lands of the Monarchy to take part in the revolution, aroused resentment and reaction. On 3 April 1849 Franz Joseph I permitted the establishment of a Jewish Cultural Community in Vienna. In 1851 the law granting Jews equality was canceled, and the restriction against owning property was not lifted again until 1867, when the government restored their equality. On 21 December 1867 Jews received freedom of religion along with all other citizens. The relaxation in the control of housing in Vienna brought a significant increase in the Jewish population. In 1857 there were 6,217 Jews in Vienna (1.3% of the population), while in 1869 there were 40,227 (6.6%).[94]

The growth of the Jewish population brought a number of writers who had begun their careers in journalism in the various lands and territories. In Vienna they not only continued as journalists causing an increase in the number of newspapers, but they also became authors. In the *Vormärz* there had been no Jewish authors, and Jews also do not form the subject of any plays in the folk theaters. Rossbacher reports that of three hundred plays during the period 1853 to 1887, only twenty used Jewish themes and/or characters.[95] One of the most prominent plays is Friedrich Kaiser's (1814-1874) *Neue Jerusalem* (1867-1868, New Jerusalem), an attempt to present all of the prejudices of Christians and Jews. Kaiser was a liberal who held strong views about fairness toward Jews, and his drama is a plea for tolerance analogous to Lessing's *Nathan der Weise* (1779, *Nathan the Wise*).

Franzos serves as a good example of an assimilated Jew, the path he believed Jews should follow in order to become fully integrated into their society. The government's granting of equality was based on the idea of the benefits to the country from assimilation, the idea that Joseph II had proposed a century earlier. At the turn of the century Franzos opposed the idea of Zionism proposed by the journalist and writer Theodor Herzl (1860-1904), a stance which brought him the enmity of many of his fellow Jews. Franzos, who wanted fervently to be German, could see no rationale for returning to a home in Palestine, the topic of one of the great debates of the time among Jews.

Franzos was a prolific and widely recognized author in his day—his works were translated into sixteen languages. In his novels such as *Die Juden von Barnow* (1877, The Jews of Barnow), *Moschko von Parma* (1880), *Ein Kampf um Recht* (1882, A Struggle for Justice), *Der Wahrheitssucher* (1894, The Truth Seeker), and *Der Pojaz* (1905, The Clown), he took clear stands on major issues of the time. For example, he made a plea to raise the educational level of the eastern provinces and to grant greater freedom and self-determination to the various ethnic groups, showing an awareness of how the government could head off the rebellious spirit that was developing there. In *Ein Kampf um Recht* Franzos depicts an uprising of a small group of eastern European mountain people against the Austrians. As a liberal and representative of the Enlightenment, Franzos believed that reason and education could solve most of the problems of society. He also extended this need for education to women, whose rights he defended in his writings.

Franzos' works often deal with Jewish-Christian relationships and present many instances of intermarriage, usually with bad results, as in *Leib Weihnachtskuchen* (1896). He wrote as a realist and avoided idealizing or romanticizing the harsh conditions of life. We owe to him accurate portrayals of the hard life in the shtetls or small villages in the eastern territories of the Monarchy. Franzos remains significant because he is one of the first major writers to bring a non-Viennese perspective into literature along with insights into life in the east that are not found even in other writers of that period. His reputation has faded because time has passed the world of Franzos by, and most of the conditions and problems that were burning issues of his day no longer exist. Nevertheless, his eminently readable writings remain important for those who would like to understand the nineteenth century in its contemporaneous terms.

Franzos had wide-ranging interests, and two additional contributions with long-lasting influence merit attention. Franzos published the first full edition of Georg Büchner's writings (1876-1879) and is credited with beginning the renaissance that soon elevated Büchner to the status of a major German author. He also published an important literary anthology entitled *Deutsches Dichterbuch aus Österreich* (1883, German Book of Poets from Austria). With this volume Franzos ranks alongside Schönerer as a leading voice for Anschluss. It served as a rallying call for the writers in

Austria who considered themselves Germans and provided them with an opportunity to voice their allegiance to Germany. In this sense Franzos' book anticipates the notorious *Bekenntnisbuch* (1938, Book of Allegiance), in which Austrian authors tried to outdo each other in demonstrating their adulation of Hitler and their enthusiasm for the return of Austria to the German Reich.

In his Preface to the anthology *Deutches Dichterbuch aus Österreich*, Franzos clearly announces his intention to show that Austrian literature belongs to the German tradition. He plans to feature the German idea "because we Germans in Austria are again experiencing days which make it twice as much our duty to permit no mistake about the way we think and feel."[96] The writings of the Germans in Austria had become too cosmopolitan, he felt, and did not reflect German themes, style, form, or viewpoint. Some, like Grillparzer, even offended Germany. People preferred to speak of an Austrian literature in the German language rather than of a German literature in Austria.[97] Those opposed to a German spirit in Austria thought they would see a genuine Austrian literature after 1866, but it did not happen. The Germans can be satisfied with their representation. German-Austria used to be a German province politically, but intellectually it was a closely related, albeit independent neighboring empire. Today it still continues this latter relationship, while, as far as its intellectual life is concerned, it appears to be integrated as a province into the great Reich of the German spirit, and to be sure as a province of which the Reich does not need to be ashamed. The anthology plans to show that the Germans in Austria are conscious of their task and are carrying it out in worthy fashion.[98]

Franzos reports enthusiastically about the tremendous response that his call for contributions received—2500 poems from 304 poets in addition to prose and dramatic entries.[99] Of these he selected fifty-five authors, including such leading writers as Anzengruber, Bauernfeld, Karl Beck, J. J. David, Ebner-Eschenbach, Franzos, Grillparzer, Grün, Halm, Hamerling, Hebbel, Kralik, Rosegger, and Saar. Two aspects of this anthology raise questions. It appeared at the height of the German National movement, and it is surprising that, as a Jew, Franzos would not have been repelled by Schönerer's anti-Semitic program, which caused all Jews to be ejected from his party. One can only presume, on the one hand, that Franzos, who was the third generation of his family to be totally German oriented, could not change his attitude at this point in his life, and, on the other hand, that he was not well informed about Schönerer's campaign at the time he produced his book. One also wonders why such Austrian conservatives as Anzengruber, Bauernfeld, Ebner-Eschenbach, and Saar would desire to be represented in this volume celebrating Austria as a cultural province of Germany and promoting a nationalistic concept of greater Germany (*Grossdeutschland*).

Robert Hamerling (Rupert Johann Hamerling, 1830-1889) stands as an eclectic figure representing the tendencies of the founding years (*Gründerzeit*) in his monumental epics, his penchant for epigonal historicism, his advocacy of Austrian union with Germany, and his cultural pessimism influenced by Schopenhauer. Hamerling had a hard life, growing up poor and suffering often from ill health. He became a teacher in a *Gymnasium* but was able to take early retirement in 1866 because of the enormous success of his epic *Ahasverus in Rom* (1865) and henceforth devote himself totally to writing.

In a sense Hamerling's works resemble the paintings of Makart: he strove to create big effects with his sensual, emotional plots that often ranged to the decadent. It was his ambition to create new myths for his time like Wagner, but for the most part he did not get beyond bombastic rhetoric. Yet, while he inclines to aestheticism, he also adds an ethical dimension. The conflict between aestheticism and ethics, eros and spirit, which became such a prominent theme at the turn of the century, is central to his lyric poetry such as *Ein Sangesgruss vom Strande der Adria* (1857, A Greeting in Song from the Adriatic Beach), *Venus im Exil* (1858, Venus in Exile), *Amor und Psyche* (1882), and *Blätter im Winde* (1883, Leaves in the Wind), and in fact runs through most of his writings.

As a dramatist Hamerling remained unsuccessful because he lacked the ability to create believable, rounded characters. His knowledge of history enabled him to present detailed portrayals of earlier periods, but he could not populate them with figures that would bring them to life. In *Der Germanenzug* (1862, The Advance of the Germans) he shows his belief in the coming dominance of the Germans, while in *Danton und Robespierre* (1871) he celebrates the founding of the German Reich under Bismarck, whom he idolizes. Like Franzos, Hamerling advocates the union of all German-speaking peoples. *Teut* (1872) is a satirical play on the idea of Greater Germany. *Lord Lucifer* (1880) depicts the struggle of light and darkness that is also found in the cantata *Die sieben Todsünden* (1872), written for the composer Adalbert Goldschmidt. Here Hamerling voices his anti-Semitic feelings so characteristic of the time, but he also criticizes Christians for their hypocrisy, saying that the more Christians themselves turn away from religion, the more they encourage Jews to assimilate. In Hamerling's view, Jews cannot assimilate, and for this reason he recommended their return to Palestine even before Herzl proposed this course of action in the Zionist program *Der Judenstaat* (1896, The Jewish State).

Der König von Sion (1869, The King of Zion), about Johannes von Leyden, contains the same blend of history, moral allegory, and contemporary politics found in most of Hamerling's works. In *Homunculus* (1888) he presents a satire on the founding years (*Gründerzeit*). As Homunculus travels, he appraises the world he encounters with new eyes and enables readers to see their lives from a different perspective. He observes and comments on the materialism of the time, the stock market, capitalism, the exporting business, and rapacious greed for money and gold. Like Kürnberger, Hamerling criticizes America for idolizing money and turning people into commodities. He fears that these values will lead the world to ruin. At the end of his career Hamerling wrote his autobiography, *Stationen meiner Lebenspilgerfahrt* (1889), Stations of My Life's Pilgrimage).

As in the cases of Franzos and Kürnberger, Leopold von Sacher-Masoch (1836-1895) has been largely forgotten today, although his writings seem to be experiencing something of a renaissance at the present time.[100] He has been remembered primarily not for what he accomplished as a literary figure, but for the use of his name in the term masochism, coined by the psychologist Richard von Kraft-Ebbing (1840-1902) in his work *Psychopathia Sexualis* (1886). Because of being stigmatized for what was then considered aberrational sexual behavior, his book *Venus im Pelz* (1879, *Venus in Fur*) has come to be regarded as a standard pornographic work and for that reason has until recently been his only book to remain in print.

Sacher-Masoch, despite an encouraging beginning to his literary career, is generally ignored by histories of literature. Most of the more recent accounts, as is also the case with Franzos and Kürnberger, failed to include him at all, or if so only briefly. Yet Sacher-Masoch is another of those authors from the east (Galicia) who have much to offer in terms of understanding the time in which he lived. His writings in fact anticipate the idea of the aesthete and the dilettante made popular by writers at the turn of the century. It did not help Sacher-Masoch's reputation that his constant financial difficulties caused him to turn out his works faster and faster with a commensurate sacrifice of literary quality. From 1858 to his death in 1895 he produced a collection of novellas and tales every year along with novels.

Because of his tales depicting eastern European Jews, whom he knew well from growing up in Lemberg, the capital of Austrian Galicia in southern Poland (now Lvov in Ukraine) and from being raised by a Ruthenian peasant woman who related many accounts from the local lore to him, Sacher-Masoch is sometimes assumed to be a Jewish writer. However, he was the son of an Austrian nobleman and a Ruthenian woman, and it is claimed that he spoke Polish and Ruthenian before he learned German. He described himself as a Galician Russian, and his wife described him as a Slav to the last drop of his blood. He devoted himself to the problems of Eastern European ethnic groups but recognized that any hope of achieving unity was made impossible by the infighting and lack of cooperation of the various lands and territories.

Sacher-Masoch took his degree in German History at the University of Graz and taught there for ten years before he devoted himself solely to writing. His first novel *Eine galizische Geschichte: 1846* (1858, *A Galician Story: 1846*) dealt with the Polish uprising of 1846 which he remembered from his youth in Lemberg. The novel becomes more important than just a study dealing with this revolt because Sacher-Masoch set the action against a large-scale portrayal of the conditions at the time. He described the social order in Austrian Galicia, how the Austrian bureaucracy and the military functioned there, along with portraying the customs and manners of the Ruthenians and Jews. The novel was related in a realistic manner and without idealizing the characters. All of his works belong to Realism, and none developed into Naturalism based on determinism. Sacher-Masoch attempted other historical novels, but none of them proved as successful as his first effort.

Sacher-Masoch received his start as a writer with the assistance of Ferdinand Kürnberger who helped him produce manuscripts about his native Galicia that he could publish in his literary journal. Indeed, Kürnberger was so impressed with the tale "Don Juan von Kolomea," describing the Polish uprising in 1863, that he wrote a preface in which he compared Sacher-Masoch to Goethe and Turgenev and hailed him as "the dawn of a new literature."

Sacher-Masoch's modernity can be seen in his belief in the equality of men and women. He illustrates this idea in his works, supporting the beginnings of women's emancipation that were developing at the time. In his view, the only reason that the two sexes cannot coexist in a spirit of true equality is because women have not been educated to the same level as men. In his works he frequently depicts the difficulties of achieving and maintaining a sense of equality in any relationship. The inability to do so usually produces the conflicts and problems that his characters experience. In those cases where equality prevails, the man and woman are shown to enjoy a happy marriage or relationship. When women are denied the possibility of achieving equality through education, Sacher-Masoch reasons that they are forced to use their sexuality to achieve a balance in their association with men. At times the situation goes beyond balance and leads to relationships in which men willingly serve a chosen woman in varying degrees of attachment from adoring admirer from afar in the manner of the medieval knights and troubadours to virtual voluntary slaves.

Sacher-Masoch attempted to portray this idea of equality between the sexes in a series of works published under the overall title *Das Vermächtnis Kains* (1870 and 1879, Cain's Legacy). The first two volumes, entitled *Die Liebe* (1879, Love), contained six novellas which explore six kinds of relationships, including the bondage depicted in *Venus im Pelz* (Venus in Fur), as well as homoeroticism in *Die Liebe des Plato* (Plato's Love). Seen in this context of the general title, these works are appropriate to the serious purpose that Sacher-Masoch was attempting to achieve, namely, to describe the different kinds of relationships that people may encounter in life. However, the novella *Venus im Pelz*, published separately and thus taken out of its original context, distorted his intention and harmed his reputation as a writer.

The second volume of novellas entitled *Das Eigentum* (1877, Possessions) treated additional social relationships that form a part of Cain's legacy, such as ownership of property, the operation of the state, and the necessity of war. In each case he feels that the problem lies in materialism, and in the willingness of entrepreneurs to exploit the work of others.

Sacher-Masoch anticipates the turn-of-the-century aesthete in this cycle of novellas. The protagonist of *Venus im Pelz* describes himself as a dilettante, as an amateur in life. He lives a passive existence devoted to the appreciation of art, not to its creation. The cult of the ego depicted here emulates the writings of the French authors such as Maurice Barrès and especially of Joris Karl Huysmans, who created the textbook case of the aestheticism in his novel *A Rebours* (*Against the Grain*). In short, Sacher-Masoch was by no means alone in his decadent approach to the sexuality of the time, only more outspoken, not only out of inclination, but also to sell books. For authors to use sex to sell books is not a new tradition, and the nineteenth century discreetly produced considerable pornographic material. Only in the present day has pornography entered mainstream literature. Around 1900 there were only minor instances such as the mild tales of perversion in Hermann Bahr's attempt at decadence, *Fin de Siècle* (1892, End of the Century), and Felix Salten's *Josephine Mutzenbacher* (1903). Today these works seem mild and inoffensive compared to such explicit mainstream writings as Peter Turrini's *Tod und Teufel* (*Death and the Devil*), and Elfriede Jelinek's *Lust* (*Lust*).

As a follower of Schopenhauer, Sacher-Masoch believes that life is misery and that death as the final release should be welcomed rather than feared. He sees work as the only way that human beings can free themselves from the burden of existence. Turn-of-the-century Viennese writers expounded this same message in their writings to illustrate the bankruptcy of the aesthetic life. This demonstrates that Sacher-Masoch, far from being a pornographer, which means to describe sexual activities for their own sake without redeeming purpose, was a moral writer ultimately, just as the young Vienna writers, who were likewise falsely understood to be advocating rather than criticizing the aesthetic life. Sacher-Masoch is a good example of how literary judgments formed early in a writer's career, just as in the case of the Jung Wien writers, can stand for long periods of time without revision. It took literary critics more than fifty years to correct this misconception about turn-of-the-century authors and finally recognize that they were criticizing, not endorsing, the aesthetic life. After a century, a reappraisal is beginning now in the case of Sacher-Masoch.

In terms of this new evaluation, John K. Noyes has persuasively argued a new perspective from which to view Sacher-Masoch's writings to achieve a more accurate understanding of their importance:

> Sacher-Masoch's literary work may be read as an extension of his historical studies. Here he was concerned not only with political power, but with the way political power was always coextensive with private, and more particularly, sexual power relations. Throughout his literary career, Sacher-Masoch was

careful to portray himself as siding with the socially and politically disadvantaged peoples of Eastern Europe, much in the same way he unabashedly derived sexual pleasure by staging situations of powerlessness. In this way he was able to see his erotic writing as compatible with his political sympathies.[101]

In addition to championing women's rights, Sacher-Masoch created a series of works dealing with life and the ghetto: *Galizische Geschichten* (1876, Galician Stories), *Galizische Geschichten, Neue Reihe* (Galician Stories, New Series), *Polnische Ghettogeschichten* (1896, Polish Ghetto Stories). These tales, full of warmth and humor, are related from a sympathetic but not idealizing point of view. He also wrote about the peasants in Galicia, considering them a "primitive people" like the American Indians in the western United States.

Like Franzos, who set many of his works in the same Galician ghettos, Sacher-Masoch was in favor of assimilation as the appropriate course for Jews to follow. As the enlightened liberal that he was, he assumed that education and work would transform the Jews' position in society to a positive one, just as he expected the same elements to improve life for women and assist them to gain equal status. He portrayed the Galician Jews coming to Vienna in positive terms. In this stance he differed from Franzos, who, like most of the assimilated and acculturated Jews in Vienna, resented the orthodox Jews from the shtetl and from the ghettos of eastern Europe because they stood out prominently. The assimilated Jews of Vienna did not want the Austrians reminded of the Jewish element in their midst by the sight of these poor orthodox Jews coming from the east. Fear of arousing anti-Semitism made assimilated Jews into some of the fiercest anti-Semites of their time.

Sacher-Masoch found the opportunity in 1893 to put into practice his belief that education was the means to a better future for all individuals. In the German town of Lindheim he founded an organization to promote the establishment of public libraries, as well as to organize concerts, plays, and lectures for the peasants of the surrounding area. He also provided financial support for young men and women to attend school. The organization, however, died with Sacher-Masoch in 1895.

Marie von Ebner-Eschenbach (1830-1916),[102] like Sacher-Masoch, also believed in the central importance of education as a means of improving society and, like him, extended that idea to include women. Like other aristocratic authors, even those of prerevolutionary days such as Grün and Lenau, her social criticism did not stand in conflict with her status as a member of the nobility (she was the Countess Dubsky). Her sense of fair-mindedness overcame her own self-interest as a member of the aristocracy, just as had been the case for Anastasius Grün and Nikolaus Lenau. Ebner was less concerned about preserving her own prerogatives than in improving society as a whole. She turned to social questions early in her career and engagement for the lower classes—the poor, the oppressed, the outsiders—became the program of her works. She intended her writings not as confrontation but as a bridge between the aristocratic estates and the villages, between the haves and the have-nots.

As Karoline Pichler and Betty Paoli had discovered before her, the dramatic form was considered a male prerogative and unsuitable for women. Thus, even though Grillparzer, who had befriended her at a young age—she later paid homage to this friendship in her book *Meine Erinnerungen an Grillparzer* (1916, My Memories of Grillparzer)—and praised her plays, success as a dramatist eluded her.

The novel *Ein Spätgeborener* (1875, *A Late Born Boy*) showed that her real talent lay in narrative writing and was followed by a series of prose works which soon brought her name into prominence. Her background in Moravia added another ethnic dimension to Austrian literature. The settings on rural estates or in villages, as in the two volumes of *Dorf- und Schlossgesichten* (1883, *Village and Castle Stories*) and *Neue Dorf- und Schlossgeschichten* (1886, *New Village and Castle Stories*), placed her in the line of provincial literature along with Franzos, Sacher-Masoch, and the Styrian author Peter Rosegger. Her novel *Unsühnbar* (1890, *Beyond Atonement*) can compare favorably to *Effi Briest* (1895) by the German realist Theodor Fontane. Both novels treat the theme of young women who have children as the result of an affair and who are then treated as outcasts by society and even by their own parents. Her *Aphorismen* (*Aphorisms*), which show the clarity of her mind, her range of interests, and her ability to use language, contain a wealth of valuable insights into the social mores of the time.

As a prose writer Ebner-Eschenbach, influenced by Turgenev, remained in the sphere of realism, describing life on the basis of her own experience, her observations of human nature, and her strong Catholic faith. She presents a rich portait of social life among the aristocrats on their estates and in their dealings with the villagers as well as of the villagers themselves. She always proceeds from her belief in the best in human beings. She showed in her novel *Das Gemeindekind* (1887, The Ward) the capacity of human beings to transform into better people through being treated with love and kindness. Consequently like Betty Paoli, she rejected Berlin Naturalism with its emphasis on scientific determinism and belief in Darwinian ideas of heredity and environment.

Although she lived through the end of the century, which witnessed the fundamental transformation of Austrian literature as well as of Austria itself in the transition from the nineteenth to the twentieth century, for the most part Ebner-Eschenbach remained thematically rooted in the past. Her plays and prose are modern in the sense that she recognized the limitations of words. She does not try to describe the psychology of her characters, but presents actions that allow the reader to contemplate the thinking that produced them. In the use of this technique she parallels the turn-of-the-century writers.

Ferdinand von Saar[103] (1833-1906) was a good friend of Ebner-Eschenbach, and in many ways his literary career paralleled that of Ebner except with far less success. For unexplained reasons Saar has never been accorded the appreciation that he deserves as a transitional figure to the modern period, and he still has not found the readership that his works merit. Although he was born in Vienna, he lived in many of the other lands of the Monarchy during his career as a military officer and described life in these outlying areas in his *Novellen aus Österreich* (1877, expanded edition 1897, Novellas from Austria). Like Ebner, he wrote in a realistic manner about the conditions and circumstances that he had witnessed, but without her positive spirit of optimism and religious faith in the inherent goodness of people. Instead, influenced by Schopenhauer's pessimism and his own hard life—he had to live in his later years on support from benefactors like Josephine von Wertheimstein as well as with severe pain that caused him to take his own life in 1906—he saw life with a harder eye and a more melancholy cast than Ebner. Because of his pessimism he generally treats characters for whom life ends tragically. The dominant theme in his works is the universal idea of the transitoriness of life. As is the case for his contemporary Arthur Schnitzler, the themes of Eros and Thanatos form the twin motifs of Saar's collected works. Also, like Schnitzler, whether happy or sad, life is lived in the constant awareness of death. An atmosphere of resignation suffuses his writings. Saar's novellas reflect his belief that the Monarchy had lost its glitter and was beginning to decline.

Originally, Saar had wanted to write classical tragedies such as he attempted in *Heinrich IV* (1865-1867 in two parts), but he never achieved success on the stage. He found more favorable response to his lyric poetry and elegies, particularly *Wiener Elegien* (1893, Vienna Elegies), which clearly reveals his attitude of resignation and renunciation.

Although Saar was recognized and admired by the Young Vienna writers such as Schnitzler, Hofmannsthal, and Bahr, he never became a member of their circle and made no attempt to embrace the new style of Impressionism. He remained within his own sphere as a chronicler of the late nineteenth century through which he had lived. In a sense he plays the same role in Austrian literature as a transitional figure to modernity that Theodor Fontane played in Berlin. When Bahr established his newspaper *Die Zeit* in Vienna in 1894, he requested permission to publish Saar's novella *Herr Fridolin und sein Glück* (Mr. Fridolin and His Happiness) in the first issue to make the programmatic statement that he intended to blend innovation with tradition.

Although thematically Saar looked backward, like Schnitzler, he explored the subconscious life of his characters, particularly the problems of unsatisfied, unhappy, lonely women whom he excelled in portraying. In *Schloss Kostenitz* (1892, *Kostenitz Castle*) he utilized the modern literary technique of the inner monologue before Schnitzler brought this method to prominence in *Leutnant Gustl* (1900), which is usually considered the first use of the form.

Like Ebner-Eschenbach, Saar's works remained focused on the nineteenth century, and also like her he never accepted Naturalism. A recent article by Jean Charue attempts to make a case for considering at least some of Saar's stories as Naturalistic writings by seeing fate, which is present in Saar's writings, as equivalent to determinism caused by the effects of heredity and environment. Charue claims that Saar's preference for the past determines not only his choice of subject and characters, but also his prose technique. Saar's method of recalling the past, Charue says, fits together well with determinism. He concludes that "determinism was never utilized as consistently and as radically as in the works of Ferdinand von Saar."[104] Joseph Nadler agrees with this opinion, stating that "Saar's art is exactly what was meant by Naturalism long before this movement existed in Berlin."[105] Actually, Saar's view parallels that of Naturalism, for human beings are helplessly delivered into the hands of fate, which may be considered analogous to Darwinian determinism. The one factor that keeps Saar from being a pure Naturalist, if one accepts this interpretation of fate as determinism, is the fact that Berlin writers disregarded the issue of guilt. If the characters were truly determined by their heredity and environment, they could not be held accountable for their actions. By contrast, Saar, a moral writer, like all of the Viennese authors at the turn of the century, always invokes the question of guilt. His characters must always expiate any crimes or errors of conduct that they commit. Saar's works also differ radically from Berlin Naturalism in terms of setting and choice of characters. He almost always deals with the middle and upper classes, while the Berlin Naturalists preferred to concentrate on the lower classes.

The Austrian writer who followed the precepts of Darwin in terms of the influence of both heredity and environment on an individual's life was Jakob Julius David (1859-1906), the purest Naturalist writer in Austrian literature. Like Ebner-Eschenbach he was born in Moravia but after spending his youth there moved to Vienna. He came from a poor family and lived apart from his parents from an early age. His hard life continued throughout his university years in Vienna, where he studied German and History. In the second half of the nineteenth century it had become standard for authors to support themselves by working as journalists, and David followed this path as well. Journalism took the place of employment as government officials, which had been the normal mode of livelihood for authors in the first half of the nineteenth century. The numerous positions for journalists attest to the growth in the number of newspapers in the second half of the century when the censorship laws were no longer as stringent. Franzos employed David on the *Neue Wiener Illustrierte Zeitung* where he worked until 1887. In 1889 he finally completed his degree, and in 1894 he went to work for the *Neues Wiener Journal.*

Like many Jews of the time, David felt comfortable in Vienna and made every effort to assimilate, converting to Catholicism in 1894. Despite his attachment to life in the capital, he wrote about the life he had witnessed in Moravia, further bringing this ethnic group into mainstream Austrian literature. It is noteworthy how many of the major writers after 1848 came from areas outside of Vienna.

As in the case of Saar, David's works are infused with an air of pessimism. His first novel *Das Höferecht* (1896, The Right of Inheritance) shows him to be a follower of Anzengruber whom he greatly admired. His work is very similar to Anzengruber's drama *Das vierte Gebot,* but they differ in the fact that Anzengruber's play is resolved at the end, while David leaves the ending open, showing the rise of the new generation along with the decline of the old one.

Throughout the nineteenth century Vienna had been known as a theater city, and the attraction of the stage grew even stronger towards the end of the century. David was not immune to this lure of achieving fame in the theater, and wrote several plays. After *Hagars Sohn* (1891, Hagar's Son) was performed in the Volkstheater in 1894 without success and two additional plays also failed, he gave up drama to return to narrative prose, where his talent really lay.

From the beginning David was a determinist who believed in the power of the environment to shape his characters' lives. He showed this influence in the novel *Am Wege sterben* (1900, To Die along the Way), the story of five students from Moravia, four of whom are destroyed by life in Vienna. This novel was first serialized in the *Neue Freie Presse* in 1897. David provides a rich tapestry of life in Vienna in the second half of the nineteenth century, while describing the experiences of students from the provinces studying at the university, which plays the role of fate in their lives. Only the Jewish medical student survives because he becomes resigned to his hard life and decides to become a doctor for poor people. David creates a negative picture of how students from the provinces were treated at the University of Vienna, and in this view parallels the opinion of Bahr, who attributed to this hostile treatment the lasting negative attitude of the provinces toward Vienna.

David's novel *Der Übergang* (1903, The Transition), which portrays the decline of a silk manufacturing family over several generations, resembles the idea of Zola's series of novels comprising *Les Rougon Macquart.* David was also quite likely familiar with Thomas Mann's generational novel *Buddenbrooks* (1900), which also depicted the decline of a family, although in a totally different technique and with a completely different emphasis. In David's novel, Vienna itself is subject to an outside fate, namely, the process of transformation that took place in the second half of the nineteenth century, when the upper classes were losing their strength and declining, and the country was finding fresh strength in the people coming into Vienna from the provinces and from the other lands and territories. This work belongs to the tradition of novels portraying Viennese social behavior (*Sittenbilder*), which had become a recognized form in the later nineteenth century. Usually these novels were designed to show the ills and problems of the big city. Even Anzengruber had planned a Vienna novel to be entitled "Sumpf" (Swamp), depicting the decline of a family and of a generation, but he failed to complete it.

In addition to his two provincial novels, David wrote historical novellas set in the Renaissance, emulating the German *Professorenroman*. His main contribution, however, remains his works set in Moravia. He produced three collections of novellas: *Probleme* (1892, Problems), *Vier Geschichten* (1897, Four Stories), and *Die Troika* (1901), The Triumvirate). Although the artistry of his landscape descriptions and characterizations raises his novels above the level of provincial art (*Heimatkunst*), nevertheless his works never went beyond Naturalism which passed from the literary scene very quickly. He remained consistent in terms of form and style, and his final works, the novellas *Die Hanna* (1904), *Filippinas Kind* (1905, Filippina's Child), and *Das Ungeborene* (1905, The Unborn) continue this same technique.

While David's prose tales are his most important works, he also contributed a volume of poems (*Gedichte,* 1881) as well as a book of *Essays* (1905). These feuilletons, written between 1885 and 1905 resemble Ferdinand Kürnberger's *Herzenssachen.* They contain portraits of authors and artists such as Grillparzer, Halm, Heyse, Ibsen, Saar, and Tolstoy. David also included portraits of actors and musicians. His aim in each case was to identify the basic character of the artist and present it, as one would expect in a feuilleton, in a colorful word picture written in elegant fashion. The accounts of his experiences while traveling in Naples and Pompeii, among other places, remain vivid even today.

Literature about Vienna became featured in the 1870s and thereafter to the point that some critics talk of a genre called the Vienna novel (*Wiener Roman*). Representative examples include Friedrich Schlögl's sketches entitled *Wiener Blut* (1873, Vienna Blood), Eduard Pötzl's (1851-1914) *Wiener Skizzen aus dem Gerichtssaal* (1884, Viennese Sketches from the Courtroom) and *Rund um den Stephansdom* (1888, Around St. Stephen's), and Daniel Spitzer's (1825- 1893) *Wiener Spaziergänge* (1869-1894). These works met with great success not only at home, but also in Germany. Vincenz Chiavacci (1847-1916), editor of the *Österreichische Volkszeitung* and the weekly *Wiener Bilder* (Vienna Pictures), was accorded great acclaim for his sketches of life in Vienna which featured two characters he created: "Frau Sopherl vom Naschmarkt" and "Herr Adabei," who became much-quoted figures in their day in the same way Helmut Qualtinger's "Herr Karl" did in the post-World-War-II era. One also finds this trend of featuring Vienna in operettas such as Johann Strauss's *Wiener Blut* (Vienna Blood) and Franz von Suppé's (1819-1895) *Die Fiakermilli*. Bahr considered his own novels *Theater* (1897, Theater) and *Die Rahl* (1906, Rahl) Viennese novels.

The development of a literature featuring Vienna was matched by the increasing presence of literature from the other Austrian provinces. While the *Volksstück* began to deteriorate after the death of Nestroy until it became a travesty of itself and lost its following, provincial literature (*Heimatkunst*), sometimes in dialect, began to grow in importance with the writings of Peter Rosegger[106] (1843-1918) from Graz (Carinthia), followed later by the authors from the Tyrol Hugo Greinz (1873-1946), Franz Kranewitter, and Karl Schönherr, the dramatic successor to Anzengruber.

Rosegger had begun publishing the journal *Der Heimgarten* (The Home Garden) in 1876 (it continued until 1935), in which he pursued a cultural program he called "Los von Wien" (Freedom from Vienna). The idea was modeled on the rallying call *Los von Berlin* (Freedom from Berlin), of the German provincial writer Friedrich Lienhard (1865-1929). There was also a *Los von Rom* movement in Germany in reaction to the increasing Catholic influence in the second part of the nineteenth century.

It was not uncommon at the turn of the century to find Hermann Bahr, who seemed omnipresent on the literary scene, heralding every new artistic phenomenon and trend to reenforce his cultural program. The idea of a broad-based Austrian literature fit perfectly into the overall cultural program that Bahr methodically pursued in Vienna from 1891 to 1906, a comprehensive plan that included not only literature representative of the entire country, but that was also receptive to interaction with writers and the arts from other European nations. In this case his publicistic efforts were directed to calling attention to the growing importance of literature from the provinces. Bahr reported enthusiasticaly about Hugo Greinz's anthology *Jung-Tyrol* (1899) in an essay entitled "Die Entdeckung der Provinz" (1899, The Discovery of the Provinces).[107] The article included a questionnaire to which Rosegger responded (*Die Zeit,* 15 March 1899) somewhat sarcastically, noting that literature from the provinces would be a considerable enrichment to intellectual life in Vienna and also show that the intellectual elite lived not only in the big cities. Rosegger not only represented *Heimatkunst,* but also the use of dialect in literature in such works as *Zither und Hackbrett* (1870, Zither and Dulcimer). Other important dialect authors were Johann Gabriel Seidl (1804-1875), *Gedichte in niederösterreichischer Mundart* (1844, Poems in Lower Austrian Dialect), and Franz Stelzhamer (1802-1874), *Gedichte in obderenns'scher Volksmundart* (four volumes, 1844-1868, Poems in above-the-Enns-River Dialect). Bahr was particularly enthusiastic about Stelzhamer, a fellow Upper Austrian whom he constantly praised as one of the "wirkliche Menschen" in Austria. In 1900 he wrote a biographical dramatic tribute to Stelzhamer entitled *Der Franzl,* a work that he considered one of his best.[108]

Rosegger was not only influential in bringing provincial literature to prominence, but he also played a role in the turn of provincial writers as early as the 1870s to the endorsement of National Socialism. Rudolf Hans Bartsch (1873-1953), Karl Schönherr, and Franz Kranewitter represented this trend in the early twentieth century. In pursuing this aim of Anschluss, the writers from the provinces anticipated and reenforced the activities of Adler, Siegfried Lipiner (1856-1911), and Schönerer in Vienna. Lipiner, the Wagner follower—Wagner ranked second only to Bismarck in importance for the German nationalists in Austria—united such revolutionary Marxists as Viktor Adler, the Schönerer follower and later Social Democrat, Engelbert Pernerstorfer, and Richard Kralik (1852-1934), the prolific author and founder of the Gralbund, an organization dedicated to renewing life and art on the basis of classical antiquity, folk culture, and Catholicism. Adler and Pernerstorfer were both associated with Schönerer, until Adler was ejected from the German National party as a result of the anti-Jewish plank of the Linz Program. He then began his own Social Democratic party, to which Bahr, also coming from the German National movement of Schönerer, belonged until he decided to give up politics in favor of literature in 1887. Adler and Pernerstorfer had planned a political future for Bahr, but he disappointed them for reasons explained in his early realistic play *Die große Sünde* (1887, The Big Sin). Here Bahr portrays his disenchantment with politics because he discovered that the Social Democrats and Marxists only intended to talk about revolution without ever really planning to act. His "big sin" was in ever believing them.

Toward the end of the century a strong Catholic presence reasserted itself in literature, led first by the Leo Gesellschaft, an organization established by Catholic intellectuals for the purpose of staging religious theater productions. This group sponsored a series of performances between 1893 and 1898. Their efforts were reenforced and continued by Richard von Kralik (1852-1934), who became the leading figure of the Austrian Catholic scene for more than thirty years. On the one hand, Kralik, although without any direct ties, supported Lueger's ties to the Catholic Church, which shared his anti-liberal ideology, his dynastic loyalty, and his anti-Semitism. On the other hand, Kralik's work to re-vitalize Catholic literature and a Catholic folk or festival theater found independent support from Bahr, who in 1903 already envisioned the development of outdoor performances for everyone in the manner of earlier Baroque theater, and from Hofmannsthal, Max Reinhardt (1873-1943), and Richard Strauss, who founded the Salzburg Festival in 1920 following Bahr's ideas. Hofmannsthal contributed his own festival dramas, *Jedermann* (1911, *Everyman*), which is still a standard offering at the Salzburg Festival, and *Das Salzburger grosse Welttheater* (1922, *The Salzburg Great World Theater*), based on Calderón, who was a major influence on Kralik as well. The conception of folk and festival theater contained a blend of culture, politics, and religion. Bahr, Hofmannsthal, Kralik, Max Mell (1882-1971), Richard von Schaukal (1874-1942), and Anton Wildgans (1881-1932) all thought along similar lines in seeking strength for the present in the literature and culture of the past and in promoting Catholic conservative values through Baroque folk theater to help unify the country. All of these men were "old Austrians," dedicated to the Austrian idea, that is, the principle of an independent Austria.

Kralik grew up in Linz, and his formative years there imbued him with a strong, lasting sense of the importance of *Heimat,* that place where one feels completely at home as opposed to the sense of estrangement and coldness that he, like so many others from the provinces, felt in Vienna. Other influences forming his intellectual and artistic makeup derived from ancient Greek culture, Shakespeare, Calderón, German Romanticism, Wagner and Bayreuth, and the Oberammergau passion play. He came to believe that literature was not a matter of individual authors writing for their own interests but that it was a part of a nation's culture and thus belonged to everyone and must be accessible to all. These views motivated his prolific writings, which ranged from collections of German sagas and legends such as *Deutsches Götter- und Heldenbuch* (1900, Book of German Gods and Heroes) and *Nordgermanische Sagengeschichte* (1906, History of North German Sagas) to his many historical and religious dramas, festival plays, collections of novellas, and essays, including *Die Türken vor Wien* (1883, The Turks before Vienna), *Osterfestspiel* (1894, Easter Festival Play), *Die Erwartung des Weltgerichtes* (1898, Awaiting the Last Judgment), *Der 12jährige Jesu* (The Twelve-Year-Old Jesus), *Jesu Leben und Werk* (1904, The Life and Work of Jesus), and *Die Legende der heiligen Einsiedler in der Wüste* (1920, The Legend of the Holy Hermits in the Desert). Kralik particularly liked to put on cycles of dramas in the manner of Calderón and Shakespeare.

Kralik's view of culture as something by and for the people caused him to ignore the question of literary quality. For him, the message was more important than the craft. He carried this idea over to the staging of plays, preferring amateur actors to professionals, as he had observed at Oberammergau. This indifference to aesthetic values involved him in a dispute in 1907 with Karl Muth, editor of the Catholic journal *Hochland,* the official organ of the Gralbund in Germany. While both men pursued the same goal of promoting Catholic literature, Muth insisted that to really achieve its purpose of attaining prominence the quality of the Catholic writings had to equal that of non-Catholic authors. This dispute was finally resolved in 1911 by the intervention of the Pope.

Kralik's Austrian views can be seen in such representative narrative prose writings as *Heimaterzählungen* (1901, Tales of Home) and *Neue Heimaterzählungen* (1910, New Tales of Home), *Das unbekannte Österreich* (1916, Unknown Austria), *Das Buch von unserem Kaiser Karl* (1917, The Book of Our Emperor Karl), *Die Gründung Wiens* (1925, The Founding of Vienna), and *Der letzte Nibelung in Wien* (1925, The Last Nibelung in Vienna). Through his writings and the many theater productions that he staged, Kralik created a strong Catholic presence in the later nineteenth century and in the years up to the Anschluss in 1938.

*

In surveying the nineteenth century as a whole, it can be seen that, while the revolution of 1848 neatly divides this time period chronologically, it does not serve to divide the two halves either politically or culturally. The history is one political continuum of absolutism realized and then attempted from the rule of Franz II (I) to the forced abdication of Karl I in 1918 and the founding of the First Austrian Republic. In terms of the literature the nineteenth century begins with Grillparzer in 1817 and with the

Vienna Volkstheater of Raimund and Nestroy, the lyrics of Lenau, the realistic narrative prose of Sealsfield and Stifter, and continues to the end of the century, concluding with Ebner-Eschenbach and Saar who continued to look backward. Beginning in the 1870s, Austrian literature reveals a variety of tendencies, a richness and diversity not seen earlier: the classical epics of Robert Hamerling, the mythological writings of Lipiner, and the German nationalism of Franzos and Rosegger, the focus on Vienna as a theme, the provincial writers, the Catholic movement of Kralik and the Gralbund, and the growing importance of women writers as represented by Ada Christen, Ebner-Eschenbach, Betty Paoli, Rosa Mayreder, and Bertha von Suttner. The unprecedented flowering of literature and culture at the turn of the century begins in the European-wide cultural ferment of the 1880s and comes to dominance in the 1890s under the Nietzschean injunction to "revaluate all values," creating the greatest period to date in Austrian literary history. For a detailed examination of this era the reader is referred to the volume *Major Figures of Turn-of-the-Century Austrian Literature.*[109]

Notes

1. Roger Bauer, *Die Welt des Reich Gottes* (Vienna: Europa, 1974), p.19.

2. One of the earliest and best examples is Gustav Freytag's developmental novel *Soll und Haben* (1855, Debit and Credit).

3. Hermann Bahr, *Wien* (Stuttgart: Carl Krabbe Verlag, 1906), p. 30.

4. Ibid., p.31.

5. Cf. Donald G. Daviau, "Hermann Bahrs veröffentlichte und unveröffentlichte Tagebücher," in: D.G.D, ed. *Österreichische Tagebuchschriftsteller* (Vienna: Atelier Verlag, 1994), pp. 21-64.

6. Hans Weigel, *Flucht vor der Größe* (Vienna: Morawa, 1960).

7. Hermann Bahr, *Wien*, p. 72.

8. Madeleine Rietra, *Jung-Österreich* (Amsterdam: Rodopi, 1980), p. 12.

9. Peter Csendes, ed. *Österreich 1790-1848* (Vienna: Christian Brandstätter, 1987), p. 237.

10. Ibid., p. 12.

11. Rietra, p. 32.

12. Csendes, p. 236.

13. Charles Sealsfield, *Austria as It Is*, ed. Primus-Heinz Kucher (Vienna: Böhlau Verlag, 1994), p. 69.
14. Ibid.
15. Viktor Andrian-Werburg, *Österreich und dessen Zukunft* (Hamburg: Hoffmann und Campe, 1843), p. 52. Unless otherwise attributed, all translations of quotations are my own. D.G.D.
16. Ibid., p. 24.
17. Rietra, p. 12.
18. Hermann Bahr, "Die Moderne," in: *Die Überwindung des Naturalismus* (Dresden: Pierson, 1891), pp. 1-6.
19. Edwin Rollett, *Österreichische Gegenwartsliteratur. Aufgabe, Lage, Forderung* (1945, Austrian Contemporary Literature. Task, Situation, Challenge) (Vienna: Neues Österreich, 1946).
20. Rietra, p. 15.
21. Robert Kann, *A History of the Habsburg Empire 1526-1918* (Berkeley: University of California Press, 1980), pp. 318-326.
22. Roger Bauer, *Laßt sie koaxen, die kritischen Frösch' in Preußen und Sachsen!* (Vienna: Europa, 1977), p. 11.
23. Ibid.
24. Paul Twaroch, "Deutsche 'Kulturprovinz?'" in: *Morgen*, vol. 19, no. 104 (December 1995), p. 10f.
25. Donald. G. Daviau and Jorun B. Johns, "On the Question of Austrian Literature—A Bibliography," in: *Modern Austrian Literature*, vol. 17, nos. 3/4 (1984), 219-258.
26. Cf. Donald G. Daviau, ed. *Austrian Writers and the Anschluss* (Riverside: Ariadne Press, 1991).
27. Cf. Herbert Zeman, "Die österreichische Literatur und ihre literaturgeschichtliche Darstellung vom ausgehenden 18. bis zum frühen 19. Jahrhundert," in: Herbert Zeman, ed. *Die österreichische Literatur. Ihr Profil an der Wende vom 18. zum 19. Jahrhundert*, Teil 2 (Graz: Akademische Druck- und Verlagsanstalt, 1979), pp. 563-586.
28. Josef Nadler, *Literaturgeschichte Österreichs* (Salzburg: Otto Müller, 1951) p. 238.
29. Aloys Blumauer, *Werke*, vol. 4 (Vienna, 1884), pp. 261-263.
30. Herbert Zeman, ed. *Literaturgeschichte Österreichs* (Graz: Akademische Druck- und Verlagsanstalt, 1996), p. 293.
31. Ulrich Greiner, *Der Tod des Nachsommers* (Munich: Carl Hanser Verlag, 1979), pp. 11f. and 15.

32. Hermann Bahr, "Adalbert Stifter. Eine Entdeckung." In: Heinz Kindermann, *Hermann Bahr. Essays* (Vienna: H. Bauer, 1965), p. 94. Also in: *Österreichischer Genius* (Vienna: H. Bauer, 1946), pp. 15-68.

33. Hermann Bahr, *Zur Kritik der Moderne* (Zurich: Schäbelitz, 1890), 2 volumes and *Studien zur Kritik der Moderne* (Frankfurt: Rütten und Loening, 1894).

34. Cf. Donald G. Daviau, "Hermann Bahr. Catalyst of Modernity and Cultural Mediator," in: Hermann Bahr (Boston: Twayne, 1985), pp. 35-55.

35. Hermann Bahr, *Selbstbildnis* (Berlin: S. Fischer, 1923), p. 277.

36. Hermann Bahr, *Bildung* (Berlin: Schuster und Loeffler, 1900), pp. 114-115.

37. Karl Müller, "Vaterland Preussen—Heimat Österreich: Wilhelm Scherers Beitrag zur österreichischen Literaturgeschichtsschreibung," in: Hanna Schnedl-Bubenicek ed. *Vormärz: Wendepunkt und Herausforderung* (Vienna: Geyer-Edition, 1983), pp. 121-144.

38. Hans H. Hiebel, "Der Anschluss der Ostmark an das Reich. Zur präfaschistischen Germanistik in Österreich," in: Donald G. Daviau, *Austrian Writers and the Anschluss. Understanding the Past—Overcoming the Past* (Riverside: Ariadne Press, 1991), pp. 70-104.

39. Hugo von Hofmannsthal, "Österreich im Spiegel seiner Dichtung, in: *Prosa III* (Frankfurt am Main: S. Fischer, 1952), pp. 333-334.

40. Donald G. Daviau, "Hermann Bahr, Josef Nadler und das Barock," in: *Vierteljahresschrift des Adalbert-Stifter-Institutes*, vol. 35, nos. 3/4 (1986), 171-190, and George C. Schoolfield, "Nadler, Hofmannsthal und 'Barock,'" ibid., pp. 157-170.

41. Joseph McVeigh, *Kontinuität und Vergangenheitsbewältigung in der österreichischen Literatur nach 1945* (Vienna: Braumüller, 1988), pp. 45-107. Cf. also Donald G. Daviau, "The Postwar Revival of the Austrian Literary Tradition," in: *Deutsche Exilliteratur. Literatur der Nachkriegszeit* (Zurich: Peter Lang, 1981) pp. 73-87.

42. Wendelin Schmidt-Dengler, *Bruchlinien. Vorlesungen zur österreichischen Literatur 1945 bis 1990* (Salzburg: Residenz, 1995), p. 11.

43. Viktor Andrian-Werburg, p. 7f.

44. Donald G. Daviau, "Max Brod and Berlin," in: Margareta Pazi/-Hans Dieter Zimmermann, *Berlin und der Prager Kreis* (Würzburg: Königshausen und Neumann, 1991), pp. 145-158.

45. Cf. Herbert Seidler, *Österreichischer Vormärz und Goethezeit* (Vienna: Verlag der österreichischen Akademie der Wissenschaften, 1982).

46. Hermann Bahr, *Um Goethe. Essays* (Munich: Urania, 1917).

47. Claudio Magris, *Der unauffindbare Sinn. Zur österreichischen Literatur des zwanzigsten Jahrhunderts* (Klagenfurt, 1978), p. 10.

48. Viktor Andrian-Werburg, p. 37.

49. Madeleine Rietra, *Jung-Österreich*. See note 8.

50. Susan C. Anderson, "Karl Schönherr," in: Donald G. Daviau, ed. *Major Figures of Austrian Literature. The Interwar Years 1918-1938* (Riverside: Ariadne Press, 1995), pp. 393-420.

51. Johann Hüttner, "Zum Wiener Theater, 1815-1848," in: *Bürgersinn und Aufbegehren. Biedermeier und Vormärz in Wien 1815-1848* (Vienna: Jugend und Volk, 1988), p. 413.

52. For the most detailed account of the Folk Theater see Otto Rommel, *Die Alt-Wiener Volkskomödie* (Vienna, 1952).

53. Cf. "The Contemporary Austrian Volksstück." Special issue, *Modern Austrian Literature*, vol. 26, nos. 3/4 (1993) and Ursula Hassel und Herbert Herzmann, eds. *Das zeitgenössische deutschsprachige Volksstück* (Tübingen: Stauffenburg, 1992).

54. Reinhard Urbach, "Ferdinand Raimund", in: *Bürgersinn und Aufbegehren*, p. 418.

55. Charles Sealsfield, *Austria as It Is*, p. 102.

56. *Bürgersinn und Aufbegehren*, p. 413.

57. Ibid.

58. Peter Skrine, "Collin's *Regulus* Reconsidered," in: *Bristol Austrian Studies*, ed. Brian Keith-Smith (Bristol, 1990), pp. 49-72.

59. Quoted in: Hermann Bahr, *Wiener Theater (1892-1998)* (Berlin: S. Fischer, 1899), p. 289.

60. Cf. Hinrich Seeba, "'Arznei meines Übels.' Zur Therapie des Schreibens in Grillparzers Tagebüchern," in: Donald G. Daviau, ed. *Österreichische Tagebuchschriftsteller* (Vienna: Edition Atelier, 1994), pp.109-149.

61. *Bürgersinn und Aufbegehren*, p. 412.

62. Quoted in Ernst Alker, *Die deutsche Literatur im 19. Jahrhundert 1832-1914* (Stuttgart: Kröner, 1969), p. 163.

63. Hermann Bahr, *Selbstbildnis* (Berlin: S. Fischer, 1923), p. 287.

64. Josef Nadler, *Literaturgeschichte Österreichs*, p. 248.

65. Minna von Alth, *Burgtheater 1776-1976* (Vienna: Ueberreuter, n.d.).

66. Cf. Danuta S. Lloyd, "Marie von Ebner-Eschenbach," in: Donald G. Daviau, ed. *Major Figures of Turn-of-the-Century Austrian Literature* (Riverside: Ariadne Press, 1991), pp. 109-134.

67. Cf. Harriet Anderson, "Rosa Mayreder," in: Ibid., pp. 259-290.

68. Marie von Ebner-Eschenbach, *Aphorisms*, translated by David Scrase and Wolfgang Mieder (Riverside: Ariadne Press, 1994), p. 36.

69. Cf. Kurt Bergel, "Ferdinand von Saar," in: Donald G. Daviau, ed. *Major Figures of Turn-of-the-Century Austrian Literature*, pp. 369-406.

70. Anton Janko and Anton Schwab, eds. *Anastasius Grün und die politische Dichtung im Vormärz* (Munich: Verlag Süddeutsches Kulturwerk, 1995).

71. For a variety of recent interpretations of this oft-analyzed novella, see Clifford Bernd, *Grillparzer's Der arme Spielmann* (Columbia, SC: Camden House, 1988). See also Christopher R. Clason "Grillparzer's Spielmann in Light of E.T.A. Hoffmann's Kreisler," in: Special Franz Grillparzer Issue, *Modern Austrian Literature*, vol. 28, nos. 3/4 (1995), 65-78.

72. Hermann Bahr, "A Letter from Germany," in: *The London Mercury*, vol. 6 (May-October 1922), p. 87.

73. Cf. Norbert Gabriel, *Peter Handke und Österreich* (Bonn: Bouvier Verlag Herbert Grundmann, 1983), pp. 231ff.

74. Cf. Harry Zohn, "Karl Kraus," in: Donald G. Daviau, ed. *Major Figures of Turn-of-the-Century Austrian Literature*, pp. 187-210.

75. Cf. Elisabeth Bredeck, "Fritz Mauthner," in: Ibid. pp. 233-258.

76. Cf. Martin Stern, ed. "Der Briefwechsel Hofmannsthal—Fritz Mauthner," in: *Hofmannsthalblätter*, vol. 19/20 (1978), 22-32.

77. For a description of life among the poor see Hubert Ch. Ehalt et al., eds. *Glücklich ist, wer vergißt. . .? Das andere Wien um 1900* (Vienna: Böhlau, 1986) and J. Robert Wegs, *Growing up Working Class. Continuity and Change among Viennese Youth 1890-1938* (University Park: The Pennsylvania State University Press, 1989).

78. Joachim Remak, "How Doomed the Habsburg Empire?" in: *The Journal of Modern History*, vol. 41 (1969), 142ff.

79. For a good portrait of Vienna in 1889 and a detailed account of Mayerling, see Frederic Morton, *A Nervous Splendor. Vienna 1888/1889* (Boston: Little, Brown and Company, 1979). For the latest revelation on how the prince and his consort died, based on forensic

evidence, see Georg Markus, *Crime at Mayerling* (Riverside: Ariadne Press, 1995).

80. Quoted in Fred Hennings, *Die Ringstrasse* (Vienna: Amalthea, 1977), p. 21.
81. Ibid., p. 84.
82. Ibid., p. 85.
83. Cf. Elisabeth Springer, *Geschichte und Kulturleben der Wiener Ringstrasse* (Wiesbaden: Franz Steiner Verlag, 1979).
84. Gertraud Marinelli-König and Nina Pavlova, eds. *Wien als Magnet. Schriftsteller aus Ost-, Ostmittel- und Südosteuropa über die Stadt* (Vienna: Verlag der österreichischen Akademie der Wissenschaft, 1996), p. 3.
85. Quoted in: Hennings, pp. 152-153.
86. Cf. Lucian O. Meysels, *In meinem Salon lebt Österreich: Bertha Zuckerkandl und ihre Zeit* (Vienna: Herold, 1984) and *Österreich intim. Erinnerungen 1892-1942*, ed. Reinhard Federmann (Frankfurt am Main/Vienna: Propyläen, 1970).
87. Hermann Bahr, *Selbstbildnis*, pp. 104-105.
88. Cf. Robert Waissenberger et al., *Traum und Wirklichkeit. Wien 1870-1930* (Vienna: Eigenverlag der Museen der Stadt Wien, n.d.).
89. Quoted in: Hennings, *Die Ringstrasse*, p. 160.
90. Cf. Richard S. Geehr, *Karl Lueger: Mayor of Fin-de-Siècle Vienna* (Detroit: Wayne State University Press, 1990). See also Carl E. Schorske, "Politics in a New Key," in: *Fin-de-Siècle Vienna: Politics and Culture* (Cambridge University Press, 1981), pp. 133-146.
91. Cf. Bruce F. Pauley, *From Prejudice to Persecution. A History of Austrian Anti-Semitism* (Chapel Hill: University of North Carolina Press, 1992). On the anti-Semitism of Lueger and Schönerer see pp. 35-44.
92. Cf. Andrew G. Whiteside, *The Socialism of Fools: Georg von Schönerer and Austrian Pan-Germanism* (Berkeley: University of California Press, 1975).
93. Cf. Claudio Magris, *Der habsburgische Mythos in der österreichischen Literatur* (Salzburg: Otto Müller, 1966).
94. Karlheinz Rossbacher, *Literatur und Liberalismus. Zur Kultur der Ringstrassenzeit in Wien* (Vienna: Jugend & Volk, 1992), p. 379.
95. Ibid.

96. Karl Emil Franzos, ed. *Deutsches Dichterbuch aus Österreich* (Leipzig: Breitkopf und Härtel, 1883), p. V.

97. Ibid., p. VI.

98. Ibid., p. VIII.

99. Ibid., p. XI.

100. Cf. John K. Noyes, "The Importance of the Historical Perspective in the Works of Leopold von Sacher-Masoch," in: *Modern Austrian Literature,* vol. 27, no. 2 (June 1994), notes 2 and 3, 17. Also Michael T. O'Pecko, "Comedy and Didactic in Leopold von Sacher-Masoch's 'Venus im Pelz,'" in: *Modern Austrian Literature,* vol. 25, no. 2 (June 1992), pp. 1-14. See also Leopold von Sacher-Masoch, *A Light for Others and Other Jewish Tales from Galicia,* translated by Michael T. O'Pecko (Riverside: Ariadne Press, 1994).

101. Noyes, p. 16.

102. Cf. Danuta S. Lloyd, "Marie von Ebner-Eschenbach," in: Donald G. Daviau, ed. *Major Figures of Turn-of-the-Century Austrian Literature*, pp. 109-134.

103. Cf. Kurt Bergel, "Ferdinand von Saar," in Ibid., pp. 369-406.

104. Jean Charue, "Sein und Schein in Saars Novelle *Leutnant Burda*," in: Kurt Bergel, *Ferdinand von Saar. Zehn Studien* (Riverside: Ariadne Press, 1995), p. 263.

105. Josef Nadler, *Literaturgeschichte Österreichs*, p. 357.

106. Cf. Dean G. Stroud, "Peter Rosegger," in: Donald G. Daviau, ed. *Major Figures of Turn-of-the-Century Austrian Literature* (Riverside: Ariadne Press, 1991), pp. 335-368.

107. Hermann Bahr, "Die Entdeckung der Provinz," in: *Bildung* (Berlin: Schuster und Loeffler, 1900), pp. 184-192.

108. Hermann Bahr, *Der Franzl. Fünf Bilder eines guten Mannes* (Vienna: Wiener Verlag, 1900).

109. Donald G. Daviau, ed. *Major Figures of Turn-of-the-Century Vienna* (Riverside: Ariadne Press, 1991).

Bibliography

Works in English

Daviau, Donald G. *Österreichische Tagebuchschriftsteller.* Vienna: Edition Atelier, 1994.

_____. *Austrian Writers and the Anschluss.* Riverside: Ariadne Press, 1991.

_____. *Major Figures of Turn-of-the-Century Austrian Literature.* Riverside: Ariadne Press, 1991.

_____. and James Hardin, eds. *Austrian Fiction Writers, 1875-1913. Dictionary of Literary Biography,* vol. 81. Detroit: Gale Research, 1989.

Good, David F. et al., eds. *Austrian Women in the Nineteenth and Twentieth Centuries.* Providence: Berghahn, 1969.

Himka, John-Paul. *Galician Villagers and the Ukrainian National Movement in the Nineteenth Century.* Edmonton: University of Alberta, 1988.

Johnston, William M. *The Austrian Mind.* Berkeley: University of California Press, 1972.

Kann, Robert A. *A History of the Habsburg Empire 1526-1918.* Berkeley: University of California Press, 1974.

Keith-Smith, Brian, ed. *Bristol Austrian Studies.* Bristol: Department of German, 1990.

Klostermaier, Doris M. *Marie von Ebner-Eschenbach: The Victory of a Tenacious Will.* Riverside: Ariadne Press, 1997.

Kucher, Primus-Heinz, ed. Charles Sealsfield—Karl Postl, *Austria as It Is.* Vienna: Böhlau, 1994.

Levy, Miriam J. *Governance and Grievance: Habsburg Policy and Italian Tyrol in the Eighteenth Century.* West Lafayette, Indiana: Purdue University Press, 1988.

May, Arthur J. *Vienna in the Age of Franz Joseph.* Norman: University of Oklahoma Press, 1966.

Modern Austrian Literature. Special Issue on Austrian Women Writers, ed. Donald G. Daviau. Vol, 12, nos. 3/4 (1979).

Natan, Alex, ed. *German Men of Letters,* vol. 5. London: Oswald Wolff, 1969.

Pauley, Bruce F. *From Prejudice to Persecution: A History of Austrian Anti-Semitism.* Chapel Hill: University of North Carolina Press, 1992.

Robertson, Ritchie and Edward Timms, eds. *The Habsburg Legacy.* Edinburgh: Edinburgh University Press, 1994.

_____. *The Austrian Enlightenment and its Aftermath.* Edinburgh: Edinburgh University Press, 1991.

Rozenblit, Marsha L. *The Jews of Vienna, 1867-1914: Assimilation and Identity.* Albany: State University of New York Press, 1983.

Steiner, Carl. *Of Reason and Love: The Life and Works of Marie von Ebner-Eschenbach.* Riverside: Ariadne Press, 1994.

Ungar, Frederick, ed. *Austria in Poetry and History.* New York: Frederick Ungar, 1984.

Waissenberger, Robert, ed. *Vienna in the Biedermeier Era 1815-1848.* New York: Rizzoli, 1986.

Wistrich, Robert S. *The Jews of Vienna in the Age of Franz Joseph.* Oxford: Oxford University Press, 1990.

Works in German

Adel, Kurt. *Vom Wesen der österreichischen Dichtung.* Vienna: Bergland, 1964.

_____, ed. *Heinrich Joseph von Collin. Auswahl aus dem Werk.* Vienna: Bergland, 1967.

_____. *Österreichs erste Literaturgeschichte aus der 2. Hälfte des 18. Jahrhunderts (Johann Baptist Gabriel Marek).* Vienna: Schendl, 1972.

Alker, Ernst. *Die deutsche Literatur im 19. Jahrhundert.* Stuttgart: Kröner, 1969.

Andrian-Werburg, Viktor. *Österreich und dessen Zukunft.* Hamburg: Hoffmann und Campe, 1843.

Aust, Hugo, Peter Haida and Jurgen Hein, eds. *Volksstück. Vom Hanswurstspiel zum sozialen Drama der Gegenwart.* Munich: C. H. Beck, 1989.

Bahr, Hermann. *Bildung, Essays.* Berlin: Schuster und Loeffler, 1900. Vienna/Stuttgart: Carl Krabbe Verlag, 1906.

_____. *Selbstbildnis.* Berlin: S. Fischer, 1923.

Bartsch, Kurt, Dietmar Goltschnigg, Gerhard Melzer, eds. *Für und wider eine österreichische Literatur.* Königstein/Ts: Athenaum, 1982.

Bauer, Anton. *150 Jahre Theater an der Wien.* Vienna: Amalthea, 1952.

Bauer, Roger. *Die Welt als Reich Gottes. Grundlagen und Wandlungen einer österreichischen Lebensform.* Vienna: Europa, 1974.

Bauer, Roger. *Laßt sie koaxen, die kritischen Frösch' in Preußen und Sachsen! Zwei Jahrhunderte Literatur in Österreich.* Vienna: Europa, 1977.

Benda, Oskar. *Die österreichische Kulturidee in Staat und Erziehung.* Vienna: Saturn Verlag, 1936.

Berg, Erich Alban. *Als der Adler noch zwei Köpfe hatte.* Graz: Styria, 1980.

Bergel, Kurt. *Ferdinand von Saar: Zehn Studien.* Riverside: Ariadne Press, 1995.

Bernhard, Marianne. *Zeitenwende im Kaiserreich. Die Wiener Ringstrasse. Architektur und Gesellschaft 1858-1906.* Regensburg: Friedrich Pustet, 1992.

Beutner, Eduard, Josef Donnenberg, Adolf Haslinger, Hans Holler, et al., eds. *Dialog der Epochen. Studien zur Literatur des 19. und 20. Jahrhunderts. Walter Weiss zum 60. Geburtstag.* Vienna: Österreichischer Bundesverlag, 1987.

Bodi, Leslie and Philipp Thomson, eds. *Das Problem Österreich. Arbeitspapiere.* Melbourne: Monash University Germanistisches Institut, 1980.

_____. *Tauwetter in Wien. Zur Prosa der österreichischen Aufklärung 1781-1795.* Vienna: Böhlau, 1995.

Breuss, Susanne, et al. *Inszenierungen. Stichwörter zu Österreich.* Vienna: Sonderzahl, 1995.

Bruckmüller, Ernst. *Nation Österreich.* Vienna: Böhlau, 1996.

Csaky, Moritz. *Ideologie der Operette und Wiener Moderne.* Vienna: Böhlau, 1996.

Csendes, Peter, ed. *Österreich 1790-1848.* Vienna: Christian Brandstätter, 1987.

_____. *Das Zeitalter Kaiser Franz Joseph I. Österreich 1848-1918.* Vienna: Christian Brandstätter, 1989.

Drabek, Anna, et al., eds. *Das österreichische Judentum. Voraussetzungen und Geschichte.* Vienna; Jugend und Volk, 1988.

Endler, Franz. *Österreich zwischen den Zeilen.* Vienna: Molden, 1973.

_____. *Das k. und k. Wien.* Vienna: Ueberreuter, 1977.

_____. *Wien im Biedermeier.* Vienna: Ueberreuter, 1978.

Erdelyi, Ilona T., ed. *Literatur und Literaturgeschichte in Österreich. Helikon, Sondernummer.* Vienna: Verlag der österreichischen Akademie der Wissenschaften, 1979.

Fejto, François. *Requiem für eine Monarchie. Die Zerschlagung Österreich-Ungarns.* Vienna: Österreichischer Bundesverlag, 1991.

Feuchtersleben, Ernst Freiherr von. *Dietätik der Seele.* Halle: Hermann Gesenius, 1879.

Frodl, Gerbert and Klaus Albrecht Schröder. *Wiener Biedermeier. Malerei zwischen Wiener Kongress und Revolution.* Munich: Prestel Verlag, 1992.

Greiner, Ulrich. *Der Tod des Nachsommers.* Munich: Hanser, 1979.

Haeusserman, Ernst. *Das Wiener Burgtheater.* Vienna: Fritz Molden, 1975.

Hahnl, Hans Heinz. *Vergessene Literaten.* Vienna: Österreichischer Bundesverlag, 1984.

Hawlik, Johannes. *Der Bürgerkaiser.* Vienna: Herold, 1985.

Heer, Friedrich. *Der Kampf um die österreichische Identität.* Graz: Böhlau, 1981.

Hennings, Fred. *Die Ringstrasse.* Vienna: Amalthea, 1977.

Holzner, Johann, et al., eds. *Studien zur Literatur des 19. und 20. Jahrhunderts in Österreich.* Innsbruck: Institut für Germanistik, 1981.

Ivask, Ivar. *Das grosse Erbe.* Graz: Stiasny Verlag, 1962.

Kapner, Gerhardt. *Die Denkmäler der Wiener Ringstrasse.* Vienna: Jugend und Volk, 1969.

Kaszynski, Stefan H. von. *Galizien—eine literarische Heimat.* Poznan University Press, 1987.

Kindermann, Heinz and Margret Dietrich, et al., eds. *Dichtung aus Österreich. Versepik und Lyrik.*
     1. Teilband. Vienna: Österreichischer Bundesverlag, 1974.
     2. Teilband. Lyrik. Vienna: Österreichischer Bundesverlag, 1976.

Klauser, Herbert. *Ein Poet aus Österreich. Ferdinand von Saar—Leben und Werk.* Vienna: Literas, 1990.

Kralik, Richard von. *Tage und Werke. Lebernserinnerungen.* Vienna: Vogelsang-Verlag, 1922.

Kudszus, Winfried and Hinrich C. Seeba, eds. *Austriaca. Beiträge zur österreichischen Literatur. Festschrift für Heinz Politzer.* Tübingen: Max Niemeyer, 1975.

Lang, Attila E. *Das Theater an der Wien. Vom Singspiel zum Musical.* Vienna: Jugend und Volk, 1977.

Lyon, Dirk, et al., eds. *>bewusst< sein—bewusst Österreicher sein? Materialien zum Österreichbewusstsein seit 1945.* Vienna: Bundesverlag 1985.

Madl, Antal and Hans-Werner Gottschalk, eds. *Jahrbuch der ungarischen Germanistik.* Budapest: Gesellschaft Ungarischer Germanisten. Bonn: Deutscher Akademischer Austauschdienst. 1993.

Marinelli-König, Gertraud and Nina Pawlowa, eds. *Wien als Magnet?* Vienna: Verlag der österrreichischen Akademie der Wissenschaften, 1996.

Martini, Fritz. *Deutsche Literatur im bürgerlichen Realismus 1848-1898.* Stuttgart: Metzler, 1962.

Mayerhofer, Josef, ed. *Wiener Theater des Biedermeier und Vormärz.* Ausstellungskatalog. Österreichisches Theatermuseum. Vienna, 1978.

McVeigh, Joseph. *Kontinuität und Vergangenheitsbewältigung in der österreichischen Literatur nach 1945.* Vienna: Braumüller, 1988.

Mraz, Gottfried. *Österreich und das Reich 1804-1806.* Vienna: Schendl, 1993.

Mühlher, Robert. *Österreichische Dichter seit Grillparzer.* Vienna: Braumüller, 1973.

Nadler, Josef. *Literaturgeschichte Österreichs.* Salzburg: Otto Müller, 1951.

Nagl, J.W., Jakob Zeidler, Eduard Castle. *Deutsch-Österreichische Literaturgeschichte,* vol. 2. Vienna: Carl Fromme, 1914; vol. 3 Vienna: Carl Fromme, 1937.

Polheim, Karl Konrad, ed. *Literatur aus Österreich. Österreichische Literatur.* Bonn: Bouvier, 1981.

_____. *Ferdinand von Saar. Ein Wegbereiter der literarischen Moderne.* Bonn: Bouvier, 1985.

Rossbacher, Karlheinz. *Literatur und Liberalismus. Zur Kultur der Ringstrassenzeit in Wien.* Vienna: Jugend und Volk, 1992.

Rumpler, Helmut. *Österreichische Geschichte 1804-1914.* Vienna: Ueberreuter, 1997.

Sacher-Masoch, Leopold von. *Dunkel ist dein Herz, Europa.* Graz: Stiasny, 1957.

Schmidt, Adalbert. *Dichtung und Dichter Österreichs im 19. und 20. Jahrhundert.* 2 Bde. Salzburg: Verlag das Bergland-Buch, 1964.

Schmidt-Dengler, Wendelin. *Bruchlinien. Vorlesungen zur österreichischen Literatur 1945 bis 1990.* Salzburg: Residenz, 1995.

Seidler, Herbert. *Österreichischer Vormärz und Goethezeit.* Vienna: Verlag der österreichischen Akademie der Wissenschaften, 1982.

Schondorff, Joachim, ed. *Zeit und Ewigkeit. Tausend Jahre österreichische Lyrik.* Düsseldorf: Claassen, 1978.

Springer, Elisabeth. *Geschichte und Kulturleben der Wiener Ringstrasse.* Wiesbaden: Franz Steiner Verlag, 1979.

Strelka, Joseph. P. *Zwischen Wirklichkeit und Traum. Das Wesen des Österreichischen in der Literatur.* Tübingen: A. Francke, 1994.

Thurnherr, Eugen. *Katholischer Geist in Österreich.* Bregenz: Eugen Russ, 1953.

Tietze, Hans. *Die Juden Wiens.* Vienna: Atelier, 1987.

Urbach, Reinhard. *Die Wiener Komödie und ihr Publikum. Stranitzky und die Folgen.* Vienna: Jugend und Volk, 1973.

Zeman, Herman, ed. *Die österreichische Literatur. Ihr Profil an der Wende vom 18. zum 19. Jahrhundert (1750-1830).* 2 vols. Graz: Akademische Druck- und Verlagsanstalt, 1982.

————, ed. *Die Österreichische Literatur. Ihr Profil im 19. Jahrhundert (1830-1880).* Graz: Akademische Druck- und Verlagsanstalt, 1982.

————. *Geschichte der deutschen Literatur vom 18. Jahrhundert bis zur Gegenwart (1918-1980).* Vol. 3. Königstein/Ts.: Athenäum, 1984.

————. *Literaturgeschichte Österreichs.* Graz: Akademische Druck- und Verlagsanstalt, 1996.

Zmegac, Viktor. *Tradition und Innovation. Studien zur deutschsprachigen Literatur seit der Jahrhundertwende.* Vienna: Böhlau, 1993.

Zöllner, Erich, and Therese Schüssel. *Das Werden Österreichs.* Vienna: Österreichischer Bundesverlag, 1990.

Ludwig Anzengruber

Kenneth Segar

Peter Rosegger, the Styrian writer of rural tales, was astonished at his friend Anzengruber's understanding of peasant psychology and the manifestations of village life: Surely he had, like Jacob in the service of Laban, served thrice seven years laboring on an Upper Bavarian farmstead.[1] How did Anzengruber, born in Vienna on 29 November 1839 and in fact living almost his entire life in various parts of that city, acquire his knowledge? His father, although the son of a farmer, had married into the Viennese bourgeoisie, worked in the imperial tax department, and written poetry and drama in his spare time. Anzengruber was five years old when his father died, and although he was later proud of his father's poetic skills, these had given birth to Schillerian drama and sententious verse rather than peasant tales. Was it, then, in his years with a troupe of itinerant actors (1860-1865), when he trailed the Austrian provinces with his devoted mother, that he discovered rural mores? It would appear so, since he writes of "hundreds of meetings and observations."[2] Nonetheless, he told Rosegger that he had never had any close relationship with a rural community, that he needed only to catch a glimpse of farming folk and hear them say a few inconsequential words to know them inside out.[3] He claims that his "reserved nature" forced him into the role of "listener, watcher, observer" (to Duboc, 30 October 1876), but it is clear that much of his awareness came from voracious reading. He found realist psychology in the village- tale (*Dorfgeschichte*), the prose narrative which was much in vogue in the second half of the century. We know that Anzengruber admired tales by the Black Forest writer Berthold Auerbach, whose narrative works attest his understanding of peasant mentality. In all probability Anzengruber came upon these in the five years preceding his own first successful rural drama in 1870.[4] Hermann Schmid's circle of Upper Bavarian writers provided Anzengruber with even more realistically conceived rural characters than those of the artistically superior Auerbach.[5]

This will bear on our discussion of Anzengruber's realism.

Anzengruber knew he lacked first-rate histrionic talent, but he stayed in the theater to earn desperately needed money and because he hoped for success as a dramatist. By mid-1864 he had written thirteen plays, one of which had been performed, and he had thirty-two notebooks full of ideas. Dismissed from his troupe in September 1865, he returned to Vienna, where he acted in suburban theaters and inns. Meanwhile he continued to write. In the years 1866 to 1868, he had a play torn apart by the critics, shared failure with the then unknown conductor/composer Karl Millöcker, for whom he wrote three libretti, and served up the requisite romance and excitement in trivial narratives for popular magazines. He later called these years his "pre-historic period," but they clearly gave him his training in both the business of theater and creative writing.

In 1869 Anzengruber took up employment as a clerical trainee with the Vienna Police and burned most of his earlier work. But in 1870 he made his name—still his stage-name Ludwig Gruber—with a serious popular drama *Volksstück* set in a rural community, *Der Pfarrer von Kirchfeld* (The Parish Priest of Kirchfeld). With Leopold Rosner now his publisher and the director of the Theater an der Wien agreeing to pay him 1200 gulden a year for two plays per season, there quickly followed three more successes: *Der Meineidbauer* (1871, *The Farmer Forsworn*), *Die Kreuzelschreiber* (1872, They Signed with Three Crosses), *Der G'wissenswurm* (1874, The Worm of Conscience). All four plays, in a stage dialect intended to suggest the rural world but comprehensible to all,[6] deal with figures and problems of peasant life. His attempts to write in the higher style or with Vienna as his setting, never—excepting perhaps *Das vierte Gebot* (1877, The Fourth Commandment)—reached the level of his best rural dramas.

After the success of 1870 Anzengruber acquired a host of friends, who were to be a solace in his misfortunes and a stimulus in his artistic and intellectual life. There were his most benevolent critics, Rosegger in Graz and Professor Wilhelm Bolin in Helsingfors, the latter translating him into Swedish and Finnish and sending him his studies of Shakespeare and Feuerbach. In Vienna Anzengruber frequented two weekly gatherings, the circles around the writer Friedrich Schlögl and the poet Ada Christen. These two, the writer Vinzenz Chiavacci, and the editor of the magazine section of *Die Presse,* Anton Bettelheim, could all offer serious opinions on his work; and, like Rosegger and Bolin, his young followers Bettelheim and Chiavacci sought to promote him publicly. Surrounded by artists, intellectuals, academics, journalists and politicians Anzengruber gave vent to his love of life, his fondness for (excessive) eating and drinking, his wit, and his critiques of the social and literary world. Yet, clearly, this was the extent of his contact with Viennese society. Should it surprise us that, as with the essentially literary sources for his rural works, he drew on many a Viennese popular drama and his friend Friedrich Schlögl's descriptive pieces for his Viennese types?[7]

The erstwhile out-of-work actor was not only achieving his dream of becoming a successful playwright but, together with royalties from various magazines for his stories, this provided the material basis for his marriage in 1873 to the sixteen-year-old Adelinde Lipka. By all accounts she remained a rather immature person and there was never any meeting of minds. She also displeased Anzengruber's mother, who was on his own admission "a piece of his heart and soul" (to Rosegger, 25 September 1875). Anzengruber also appears to have loathed the sexual appetite as something degrading where love and friendship are absent, and he describes the purely sensual in the most strongly censorious terms. He even wrote verses *Wider das Fleisch* (Against the Flesh). How could he have taken this partner? His wife eventually confessed to infidelity, and their divorce was sanctioned shortly before his death in 1889. The theme of sexual degradation is important in his work, but his intelligent, self-confident women characters are clearly the wishful obverse of his marriage partner.

The death of Anzengruber's mother in March 1875 occurred between two consecutive theatrical failures: *Hand und Herz* (Hand and Heart) had been dropped after three performances in January 1875, and *Doppelselbstmord* (A Suicide Pact) was given a lukewarm reception in February 1876. There had been a still-born child and another had died only hours after birth; his wife was sickly and he too was ill; there was nagging financial insecurity. Artistic failure was harder to bear in these circumstances, and in any case Anzengruber viewed the theatrical scene bleakly. In 1876 he writes sadly that there were no longer audiences for a serious popular theater: "To what end, or indeed for whom, should anyone actually write serious popular plays [*Volksstücke*]? Theater directors want box-office success and people here want nothing to do with these dramas of ordinary life—isn't it simply labor lost?" (to Rosegger, 12 February 1876). Economic conditions were worsening and ticket prices increasing; the new moneyed class sought the shallower fare of light farce and the poorer sort of operetta; massive immigration was depriving dramatists of their traditional popular audience, and they were abandoning Vienna as a setting for their works; theater managers were introducing a foreign repertoire, driving the centers of popular Austrian drama into liquidation, and dispersing the actors of talent in the genre.[8] Chance added to this progressive debacle with fires that destroyed the Ringtheater in November 1881 and the Stadttheater in May 1884.

During this entire period Anzengruber was suffering great inhibitions about the theater: Apart from several failures, he constantly feared mutilation of his dramas by the censor, and the thought of having been merely fashionable and now dispensable made him lose heart (to Ada Christen, 9 August 1881). After his brief period of glory, things seemed to be on the wane. The need to earn money forced him to desert the theater, which was proving so intractable, and concentrate on narrative works. "I can manage to tell a story, and that doesn't produce the usual frustration" (to Ada Christen, 12 August 1880). And indeed, he had done this from his earliest days, publishing thirty-three stories of village life between 1868 and 1889, and two novels in his last decade.

The period from 1877 to his death is a curious seesaw of failure and recognition. Following his disappointments, he wrote no dramas between 1881 and 1884; yet he became dramaturge at no fewer than four Viennese theaters between 1877 and 1889. There was a renaissance of his theatrical fortunes towards the end of 1883, when the director of the Vienna Stadttheater, Karl von Bukovicz, began an Anzengruber cycle of seventy-four evenings, until fire destroyed the theater on 16 May 1884. Graz applauded his work, Wittmann wrote in *Die Neue Freie Presse* of a "modern exponent of our folk muse,"[9] Rosegger and Bettelheim carried the writer's fame into Germany, where after his death he was taken up by Otto Brahm and the Berlin *Freie Bühne* (Free Stage). The man who thought he had finished with theater came to believe, after all, in a contemporary public for his work and was ready to start writing plays again. *Heimgfunden* (The Return Home) appeared in 1885 but was not a success. However, the Burgtheater performed *Stahl und Stein* (Steel and Stone) to acclaim in 1887, the year in which he received the Grillparzer Prize; and an outstanding production of his last play *Der Fleck auf der Ehr'* (Dishonored) in 1889, written to open Bettelheim's Deutsches Volkstheater, was given an ovation. Even so, he spent much of the decade earning much-needed money from journalism. From 1882 to 1885, he edited the magazine *Heimat,* from 1884 *Figaro,* and from 1888 *Wiener Bote.* It was while he was correcting proofs for *Figaro* that he died in the early morning of 10 December 1889.

The Rural Drama (*Bauernstück*): *The Essential Mode*

Anzengruber's rural world, as we know, owes its concreteness largely to the village-tale. Of the many dramas in the popular theater following Nestroy, who was one formal influence on Anzengruber,[10] it was the moralizing intrigues and social criticism of Friedrich Kaiser's plays in which Anzengruber found both "truly dramatic life" (to Duboc, 30 October 1876) and realist matter.[11] But whereas Kaiser's plays tie his social criticism so closely to topical issues that the works have lost their interest, Anzengruber's early rural dramas find a poetic vein in which village life, social relations and human concerns coalesce into general paradigms. *Der Pfarrer von Kirchfeld,* designated a "popular drama with songs," exhibits a mode that he would successfully rework: psychologically individualized characters, an essentially comic structure with scenes of high pathos, and a moral theme. The main plot and artfully connected sub-plot are set within a frame, making for rich substance. The priest at Kirchfeld, Hell, takes Anna Birkmaier, a young orphan from a distant village, into his service, and an illicit love blossoms without their awareness, threatening the priest's ruin. Anna takes the decisive step of attempting to salvage the priest's reputation by accepting marriage with the peasant Michel and asking Hell to perform the marriage ceremony. In the sub-plot a village outcast, Wurzelsepp (Joe the root-gatherer), who had once been denied marriage to a Lutheran girl and had come to hate the cassock, spreads the rumor about Hell and Anna. When his mother commits suicide and he discovers that the priest has no intention of denying the old woman an honorable burial, he renounces his misanthropy and returns to the community, thereby attesting to Hell's moral power. These two interlocking plots are set in a political frame: Hell's liberal and humane faith does not please the local aristocrat, Count Finsterberg, who incites the Consistory Court to remove him from his priesthood, news that comes just as Hell has to perform the marriage ceremony of Anna and Michel.

The issues in the play belong to a precise historical moment, the move to end the 1855 Concordat between Austria and the Papacy, and the events surrounding the "culture struggle" (*Kulturkampf*), which had in fact been raging in Austria throughout the liberalizing 1860s. Anzengruber's realism displays the reactionary spirit of the higher clergy and the simple caring faith of the parish priest; the problem of celibacy of the priesthood; the effects of prohibiting marriage between Catholics and Protestants; and the distress caused by denying a suicide Christian burial. If the political maneuvering of Finsterberg remains marginal to the fabric of the work, this is partly the censor's hand, and perhaps partly the theatrical craftsman knowing that plot and sub-plot are sufficient focuses for one play. Yet there is also satirical effect in employing a caricature mouthpiece for inhumanity, akin to Lessing's Patriarch in *Nathan the Wise*. The social and political realities are, in any case, occasion for a morality play in the tradition of Viennese popular drama, with the speaking names of Hell (light) and Finsterberg (dark hill) symbolizing humane beneficence and bigotry. Likewise the action involving Wurzelsepp—the outcast's reintegration into the community—is the traditional comic form of "regenerative drama" (*Besserungsstück*).

The same double focus holds for Anzengruber's realist characterization. Hell himself is not a sub-Schillerian idealist but a genuine naif. For him Anna was to replace the lost sister with whom he had hoped to live in love and companionship; his giving her his mother's gold crucifix, which fuels the rumor of impropriety, symbolizes his capacity for selfless love. In Michel's wooing of Anna, Anzengruber depicts Anna's naturalness and integrity as well as Michel's gritty peasant mentality—here even the songs and comic material of the Viennese popular theater are turned to realist account. The psychology of Wurzelsepp, a brilliant invention, is made real by his pre-history, his moral indignation creating a vengeful bitterness to be finally assuaged by goodwill from the most unexpected quarter. Yet these four characters have a function beyond realist portraiture, namely to embody Anzengruber's humane vision of natural joy, selfless love, and moral strength. Hell, Anna, Michel and Wurzelsepp all act, in Anna's phrase (repeated by Hell), "uprightly and honestly" (III, iv). The suggestion that no more is required, with its implied assault on all dogma and bigotry, points to what makes Anzengruber's works, for all their topicality or realism, symbolic vehicles of his rational, secular, and progressive ethic. In the final version Hell does not leave the Church, and Wurzelsepp, the first of Anzengruber's "outsiders," is not yet the humanist rebel; yet the play does constitute Anzengruber's initial ideological attack "in the good cause of popular enlightenment" (to Duboc, 30 October 1876).

If *Der Meineidbauer*(1871), which Anzengruber again called a "popular drama with songs," takes the form of tragic analysis, it would be wrong to view it as a tragedy.[12] This work, too, is a morality play deepened by psychological realism and given comic structure. The pre-history—always the prerequisite of psychological understanding in Anzengruber—is that Matthias Ferner, the owner of Crossroads Farm, has destroyed the will by which his brother had left the farm to his illegitimate children, Jakob and Vroni, thus dispossessing Matthias' own legitimate children, Franz and Crescenz. Having perjured himself in declaring that there was no will, Ferner has sent Franz to Vienna to study for the priesthood so that he can one day absolve his father of the sin. Anzengruber convincingly portrays the mental dualism of Matthias, who can read signs from God that the perjury is his duty to his family and equally suffer guilt feelings for taking a false oath. These past events come into the open when Vroni discovers in her father's bible Matthias' letter of protest that his own children receive nothing. Matthias' crime is palpable and she intends to seek her rights. Three scenes advance the dramatic action: Matthias attempts to get the letter back from Vroni, who, warned by the upright Franz, quick-wittedly claims that he has the letter; Matthias pursues and shoots his son, whom he leaves for drowned with the incriminating document; Matthias stumbles upon the dwelling of the old Baumahm, a sibylline figure, who tells him an allegory of his own life in which the sinner's hand is paralyzed as he tries to cross himself to escape the devil, at which moment Matthias' own hand is paralyzed and he dies of a stroke.

What makes this poetic justice that of a morality play rather than a tragedy is the nature of the plot. Not only does Matthias find himself forced by events to engage in ever more drastic dealings to protect himself, but there is comic proliferation of failure and disaster: Franz will not become the absolving priest, Vroni will beat Matthias at his own game, Matthias' threat succumbs to Vroni's ruse, Franz does not drown, the evidence is not destroyed, seeking refuge from a storm is Matthias' undoing. This sheer exaggeration makes Ferner's stroke in the sibyl's hut very akin to Don Giovanni's descent to hell in Mozart's opera, an equally moralizing not tragic denouement. Critics have wanted to see its protagonist as a Macbeth, but this can surely be only as travesty? Even so, the use of this traditional genre of the Viennese popular theater in no way prevents a fine delineation of Matthias' complex peasant mind in action: Its naive ability to embrace simultaneously concern for his children, material self-interest, brutal manipulation, and genuine piety constitutes an inbred, barely conscious hypocrisy. It is this that gives the play its power. However, Matthias' "damnation" is not the resolution of the work. Anzengruber's essential optimism redresses the balance again, as a rich study of peasant mores compels the action towards comic resolution. The chief farmhand of Adam Farm warns Vroni not to heed the attentions of the farmer's son, who is promised to a rich farmer's daughter, and he reminds her that her own mother had suffered from such gullibility. This paves the way for Vroni's brave stand, her marriage to Franz, and inheritance of Crossroads Farm. Her self-reliant character, her peasant guile and resilience, but also her warmth and hopefulness (captured precisely in her songs), all this points away from a tragic outcome into the realm of comedy. Music, indeed, concludes the drama in such a way that the deaths of Jakob and Matthias are transcended by the brightness of a humane vision: "A better breed is coming, the world is just beginning" (III, vi).

Within this morality play and comic structure, of course, lie patterns of profound ideological importance. Matthias becomes a symbol of religious confusion: In the absence of incontrovertible evidence, how can he know whether signs come from God or the Devil? Anzengruber here reveals his distrust of theistic beliefs by showing how they so easily collapse into their demonic complement. Matthias' metaphysics cannot offer the path to Vroni's and Franz's sane and fruitful existences. Finally, if in *Der Pfarrer von Kirchfeld* a humane faith remains within the Church, here Franz's decision to desert the ministry, marry, and enter into his inheritance symbolizes a humanist redemption and, as the final stage direction tells us, a new dawn.

Die Kreuzelschreiber (1872) is one of the great comedies in the German language. That we should be back in an ecclesiastical conflict is because an issue has suddenly become immensely topical—the attempt by Pope Pius IX to counter increasing liberalism in the Church with his declaration of papal infallibility, and the intensified *Kulturkampf* undertaken by the liberal political class in Austria. "A pious and learned old gentleman in the city" (I, iv), namely, Ignaz von Döllinger, has stood manfully against the new dogma, and the wealthiest farmer of Grundldorf wants all the men in Zwentdorf to sign a letter of support. Led by the newly wedded Toni, the farmer of Yellow Croft, the married men, understanding nothing of the matter but caught up in the situation, all sign with the three crosses used by the non-literate. The bachelor Hanns the Stonebreaker is mocking: He is not going to add to their "graveyard of crosses" (I, iv); they have accepted the whole pound of dogma up to now, what difference will a couple of ounces more make? If the support were for material improvements and social justice he would sign (I, vi).

The comic action begins with the call from the cloth for the women to deny their husbands conjugal rights until the menfolk have pilgrimaged to Rome in penitence. This drastic demand (probably based on events in a Bavarian village reported in the press in 1871) clearly draws on Aristophanes' *Lysistrata,* a favored model for the clergy. Again Anzengruber can exploit the comic form of travesty. Toni and his wife Sepherl become the central characters in the sexual war, and the trials of their young love in the face of religious pressure, male pride, and female jealousy are the core of the comedy. But it is not only the imperiousness of young love that suffers the intrusion of the clergy into domestic intimacy: Old Brenninger has lived with his Annemirl for fifty years, and when she too heeds the priestly call, banishing him from bed and board, he loses his "sense of order" (II, viii) that has become second nature, and drowns himself. This calamity prompts Hanns into energetic action: He organizes a Band of Pious Virgins to accompany the men on their pilgrimage of repentance, works on the concern of the wives, who already fear the wiles of dark Italian women, and most of all he fuels Sepherl's jealousy. The priestly stratagem fails before it has begun in the face of Hanns's resolute defense of nature against cult—in Toni's angry words: "What right do they think they have to come between man and wife?" (II, v).

Hanns's intervention results from a hard-won philosophy, which proves capable of promoting a personal optimism of value to the community. He tells Toni how he had all his life been rejected by the villagers of Zwentdorf because he was a bastard child, and how one day in his isolated hut by the stone-quarry he had lain desperately ill and sensed that he was going to die. He dragged himself out into the open air, and there "beneath two towering pines" he received his "Special Revelation":

> There around me was the whole wide world, moving,
> humming, alive through and through. And as the sun went
> down and the stars came out . . . this feeling welled up in
> me: Nothing can happen to you! The most terrible torture
> can't hurt you when it's over! Whether you're already six feet

under the earth or you're going to see what lies before you a thousand times more—nothing can happen to you!— You're part of all there is and it's part of you! Nothing can happen to you!—And the idea was so merry that I shouted it joyfully to everything around me: Nothing can happen to you!—Hurrah!—For the first time in my life I was happy and have been ever since, and I can't bear others to be miserable and destroy my merry world. (III, i)

This experience and its lasting effect—the foundation of his moral vision that the good life rests on recognizing the interdependence of everyone and everything—give Hanns strength to help the ill-deserving villagers of Zwentdorf. He uses "natural" means against "unnatural" ones in his counter-stratagem to restore the natural order. As his songs (to music by Adolf Müller) tell, he is the voice of nature. If Hanns's language appears to recall Spinoza's "Deus sive natura," we soon realize that his "revelation" remains sturdily worldly—that mysticism is foreign to Anzengruber himself emerges from his claim to be nothing but "a joyful pair of eyes" (to Rosegger, 28 May 1884). At all events, Hanns is interested only in practical consequences, especially freedom from anxieties that obstruct the business of living. Deprived of divine agency, his natural world as the source of an ethic is, in fact, Feuerbachian.[13] As he sees the various couples again in each other's arms, he concludes the play as chorus, with the knowing humor of one who rejects all forms of conventional morality: "And in the big city they're going to call this a triumph for freedom of conscience" (III, iv). Grounded in a realist portrayal of rural life (of sexual and marital matters, village politics, and moral rigidity, but also natural energy and warmth), the play moves in the orbits of social satire, pathos, farce, and the high comedy provided by a substantial character.

Der G'wissenswurm (1874) takes us from Lysistrata to Tartuffe. Grillhofer, who had deserted a serving-maid and their child, is consumed with a remorse constantly intensified by his artful brother-in-law, Dusterer, who sees a way of getting Grillhofer to sign over his farm to him as an act of contrition. If by turns Grillhofer can take Dusterer desperately seriously and yet slap him down when his game becomes too gross, this is the naive mentality of one who is both credulous and canny, but it also shows realism at the mercy of comic effect. Even so, in Grillhofer we have a study of pathological proportions, which makes for far more human interest than that offered by most of the gulls who serve as victims to the cozeners of comic literature. Dusterer is also a fully drawn character: A schemer and self-seeker, but a former army chaplain with powerful religious eloquence—for Grillhofer even a bad priest is God's mouthpiece. Dusterer's image of conscience as the worm eating away at Grillhofer's vitals—the metaphor of the play's title— is taken literally by the victim in the manner of naive Catholicism, and his health fails before our very eyes. However, Dusterer is constantly forced to revise his images of damnation: His vision of the betrayed maid suffering in purgatory and awaiting Grillhofer's redemptive act (handing over the farm) will not serve when the maid is discovered to be in splendid health, mother of twelve children and owner of a sizeable farmstead. So, it must have been not the mother but the dead child he saw in his vision. Alas, the child, too, reappears! It is none other than Horlacher-Lies, brought up by a distant relative of Grillhofer's, and arriving at his farm to see if she can charm "a bit of inheritance" (II, iv) out of the old man.

Here we are in the realm of broad comedy, our villain becoming a Jonsonian temporizer frantically trying to keep intact the structure he is building. Liesel's honesty in admitting her legacy hunting is part of a realist portrayal of a natural, headstrong, witty young girl, but of course also has a comic forebear in Grillparzer's *Weh dem, der lügt!* (*Thou Shalt Not Lie!*), where the scullion Leon tells only the truth and wins out because no one believes him. She is abetted by Wastl, Grillhofer's sturdy head farmhand and suitor to Liesel, another character who is half realist portrayal, half typical figure from the Viennese comic tradition, the "Trusty Servant of his Master." Wastl counters Dusterer's verbal assaults on Grillhofer's frail psyche with down-to-earth, destructive ripostes, fighting the battle his master cannot or will not. When Liesel is revealed as Grillhofer's child, it is a fitting comic denouement that she should have her inheritance, that Wastl should have her hand, and that Dusterer (as Tartuffe/Mephistopheles) should have nothing for his pains.

At the heart of the drama stands Anzengruber's serious moral intent. Not simply hypocrisy, but also the false religious ambience that provides its breeding ground are the butts of his deflating tactics. Yet, the comic form is not exhausted by satire. The denouement reminds us that we have also been watching a comic morality play, suggested from the outset by the speaking-names, "Grille"= depression, "Duster"= dismal. The father has found his child and overcome his mental torment; the worthy lovers are united; the useful inheritance is honestly gained; a bright future awaits uncorrupted nature. In Liesel's final song Dusterer's God of torment and judgment is replaced by a God who intends human life to be "joyful" so that "What we get wrong / He makes come right" (III, vii). Her naive deification of Anzengruber's optimistic and secular ethic conjures again Hanns the Stonebreaker's "merry" world.

With *Hand und Herz* (1874, Hand and Heart) we are in a rural world, but a long way from the felt life of the previous works. Presciently Anzengruber had written: "I'm working on a tragedy for the Burgtheater, but I'm afraid it's going to show more craft than heart" (to Gürtler, 20 August 1873). The language is rather stilted, a dialectally colored High German satisfying neither the realist nor the would-be Burgtheater tragedian. Strangely, even the rural location lacks Anzengruber's much-praised verisimilitude. It has been suggested that need to make the setting the Swiss canton of Wallis and Berne—the plot required a Catholic land in which divorce was an impossibility, and the censor would scarcely have permitted the perpetration of bigamy in Austria—did not strike an artistic chord in Anzengruber.[14] Yet perhaps the real culprit of this woodenness is the intrusive social theme, which undermines characterization and makes this work not only a weak tragedy, but also too much a *pièce à thèse*. We learn that Käthe's brutish husband Görg Friedner wasted her substance, abandoned her, and then disappeared. She left the village to seek employment as a servant and after terrible heart-searching married her kind and noble-minded employer, Paul Weller, without revealing her past and the consequent bigamy. Görg, following imprisonment, has now discovered his wife's whereabouts and situation, and decides to blackmail her into providing for his material comfort, even contemplating demanding his conjugal rights. This is intended as the tragic situation. However, Käthe's profound love for a man worthy of her is dramatically diminished by Weller's idealized goodness, and his murdering Görg for announcing designs on Käthe is Anzengruber's unconvincing attempt at tragic effect. Equally, Käthe's accidental rather than premeditated death on her panicky flight (a bigamist and suicide would be asking too much of the audience's sympathy?) also undermines tragedy. The monk Augustin, the honest but subservient priest who has been unable to advise Käthe against the dictates of Church dogma, is clearly introduced to underline the social theme: the crudity of the laws of Church and State faced with the moral turpitude of a husband and the rights of an injured wife. The successful element of this work is undoubtedly the characterization of Görg. In his total cynicism, traced in part to the early experience of seeing his poor family gratefully accepting compensation from his sister's aristocratic seducer, he is at once appalling, powerful, and witty. We owe this memorable portrait not to any false tragic mode but to the writer's psychological realism, which in this case would be better placed in comedy.

Such a combination makes the succeeding work, *Doppelselbstmord* (1875) a very fine piece. Anzengruber called it a "farce" (*Posse*), but that will do only if one considers the antics of the lovers, thwarted by their fathers' twenty-year enmity. The naive Agerl and her puppy-like swain Poldl leave a note to tell their fathers they have "gone to where they can be eternally united" (II, ix), and the fathers believe the two intend suicide; in fact the youngsters have followed nature's imperious call and run off into the hills to fulfil their sexual longings. A village hunt is organized, but instead of finding two corpses the fathers are confronted with a living couple, Poldl defiant, Agerl shamefaced, and both indescribably happy. This farcical inversion of *Romeo and Juliet* is abetted by the nature of the minor characters: the landlord of the tavern who speaks only in rhyme, the village grocer stirring trouble, his crudely inquisitive wife, the old gaffer who joins the hunt believing it is a pilgrimage (as, indeed, it turns out to be: a pilgrimage to the shrine of nature and life). At the level of farce, the (in fact topical) newspaper article on a rash of suicides is an appropriate technical device to give Poldl his good idea and the fathers the wrong one.

However, behind all this lighthearted, if psychologically apt, foreground stands the profounder study of the two fathers. Rather than with the future of our largely inarticulate lovers we are concerned with the past and present of these two former bosom friends, whose paths have parted. Sentner, the rich farmer, had once courted a poor local girl; Hauderer, the poor farmer, a rich one. Sentner, always the taker, persuades Hauderer, always the giver, into an exchange of partners since "like and like go together" (I, viii). The latter, tormented by his now envious wife, realizes he has been duped, while the former cannot even bear to go past the house of the man he has swindled. Following the deaths of their wives in an epidemic, each decides to make peace with his erstwhile friend, but they unknowingly pass each other by on their separate missions, and the attempt is never repeated. The scene in the tavern in which the two men find themselves rehearsing this tale moves convincingly from comic antagonism through pathos to reconciliation (I, viii). But the possibility of the

young lovers' union encounters a "block" in Sentner's religious scruples—
he is, of course, a pillar of the Church!—since Hauderer and Agerl are not
churchgoers. The hunt for the two children and finding them alive is all
that is needed finally to reconcile the two men, who have clearly always
been drawn to one another. This prehistory and its happy outcome are the
real crux of the play. While Poldl has only his love games with Agerl and
his purposefulness to suggest burgeoning nature, and Agerl her characteristic songs to expand on her naive presence, Hauderer's complexity is
demonstrated by a range of utterances: From his catch phrase "it's all
nonsense" to powerful monologue, his words reveal the extent of his hurt,
his self-defensive nihilism and yet his longing for reconciliation and
acceptance of life. All this deepens the tale that is told. A farce has become
high comedy, tinged as always in Anzengruber with the pathos of loss and
pain, but "coming right" in its restoration of what is natural and life-
enhancing. Village life refracted through the traditions of comic theater
turns Shakespearean tragedy into an appeal for optimism without sentimentality or camouflage.

It is tempting to be disparaging about *Der ledige Hof* (1876, Celibacy
Farm), where the simple rural setting is seriously at odds with both non-
dialect language and tone. Yet several contemporary critics (like Julius Bab,
R. M. Meyer, and Anton Bettelheim) were won over by the character of
its heroine Agnes, trained to celibacy by her priest and devout housekeeper
so her farmstead can be left to the Church. The plot is constructed out of
four self-willed acts by which Agnes achieves self-realization as a woman,
the theme of Ibsen's later work *A Doll's House*. Her love for her new head
farmhand, Leonhardt, is her first act of will, indirectly opposing her to
priest and housekeeper, who quickly insure that she learns of Leonhardt's
desertion of Therese and their bastard child. Agnes' second such act is to
discover for herself (by seeking Therese out) that there is substance in the
accusation made by those to whom she has until now given total trust.
When confronted, Leonhardt cannot admit his abject behavior for fear of
losing all he has striven for in his humble life. In her third act of self-will,
Agnes prepares to punish Leonhardt for the lie that has betrayed love she
has so long withheld and finally so fully given. Her murderous intent in
sending Leonhardt across the lake with a storm imminent is clearly intended to give tragic dimension to the heroine's rage at betrayal. When
Leonhardt unexpectedly returns after nearly drowning, tragic emotion is
replaced by moral argument: Leonhardt is dismissed on the grounds that

he might become a better man in other circumstances, but that here he could only continue the deceit he has begun. The denouement shows Agnes, in her final self-willed act, taking in Leonhardt's little son, who will inherit the farm and so destroy the last vestige of her subservience to the Church.

The structure of the work does, then, show the startling possibility of a young woman's casting off social fetters and determining her own role in the world. She can repudiate a priesthood that denies nature and a male world that plays fast and loose with womanhood. The problem is that the character is overblown. Are we given grounds to believe that Agnes, who has shown such docile attitudes until now, who falls gently and deeply in love, whose conscience is pricked by a schoolmaster's disquisition on moral lapses, would really try to kill Leonhardt for his dishonesty? Or that she could then so singlemindedly and coolly send away the man for whom she still feels love? There is also a discrepancy between the realist setting and Agnes' heroic aura: Love between employer and employee, a man deserting his family, a rural dinner party with schoolmaster and priest, the inheritance of a farmstead are on a different plane from the demonic murderess and implacable judge. The female protagonist is here asked to take on all the dramatic dimensions available to male characters. It is an exciting feminist direction to strike out in, but the hybrid genre undermines the psychological coherence of the character.

Anzengruber manages his liberal vision of womanhood more convincingly in *Die Trutzige* (1878, The Shrew), where a witty and humane peasant comedy fairly turns Shakespeare's theme on its head. Liesel Hübner has been orphaned early in life and by sheer hard work has paid off the debts on the family farmstead. Her independent spirit and refusal to lower herself to the duplicities of the nearby village have earned her the nickname of the play's title. After a drinking bout some of the young villagers decide to play a vicious prank on Liesel in order to humiliate her. Martin Wegmacher, a handsome and rich young farmer, is to be the vehicle of their malice. He must pretend to woo Liesel and "bring shame on her" (I, vi) so that she can be mocked. The encounter between the two shows Liesel at her combative best. She has seen through Martin's hollow words of love and recognized a village plot, but considers Martin the worst scoundrel of them all for telling the worst lie a man can tell a woman. She sends him packing. When the village youth mount a second assault on Liesel, arriving in a mock procession to dismantle the roof of her hard-won dwelling, Martin, who has warmed to her spirit, fights them off. He seeks her love in earnest, and the self-willed woman in her own free-spirited way accepts her now genuine suitor. Critics have accused Anzengruber of decking out a very slight plot to make an evening's entertainment, with incidents like Liesel's giving shelter to a one-armed soldier, whom we at the close discover to be her erstwhile rescuer. Yet this episode incites the villagers to a further attack and gives Martin cause for jealousy. Clearly, we are dealing with a basic procedure of comic drama, again that of a "block," a retarding effect, to create confusion and hold off resolution.

The strength of this comedy lies, however, not so much in lively rustic doings as in the character of Liesel which shapes the work. A character study given vibrant life by one of several actors schooled in the Viennese tradition was what carried a play with contemporary audiences,[15] and we might try to imagine a performance by the actress "Pepi" Gallmeyer for whom Anzengruber wrote this *bravura* role. Liesel shows naturalness, honesty, warmth, wit, and fire, but also courage in demanding the same consideration—and, in working for her material independence, why not the same rights?—as any man. This gives the play a modern thrust, and the comedy of twofold regeneration also makes the play anything but traditional. For not only does the woman wrest the man's essential goodness from his weak acquiescence in the frivolity and malice of others, but she also undertakes her own self-transformation. When Martin asks her to put aside her "defiance and act more like a woman," she agrees, if she can find a man who "acts like a man" (II, viii). Her decision is finally her own: "Father had a quick tongue, mother was sociable—it's time to stop my father talking and give my mother a turn!" (II, x). Here Liesel, choosing her mother's role, in no way undermines our sense of her verve, self-confidence, or moral integrity, and she remains a thoroughly "modern" woman.

Der Fleck auf der Ehr' (1889) is stylistically flawed by being too insistent a piece of social criticism, and this then having to fight with comic improbabilities. Franzl, unjustly accused of stealing by her employer, has been released from prison when the piece of jewelry is found. Franzl returns from the city to her village aware that to have "done time" is a stain on her honor. (Why should she know that she might ask for an attestation of her innocence?) She marries and keeps her secret, that is, until Hubmayr, a petty criminal who knows of her past, arrives in the village and drunkenly reveals all. Her husband, also in a drunken state, brutally throws her past in her face, but she refuses to defend herself. Constrained by a miscarriage of justice and the mores of the village, she sets off to drown herself in the lake. There she is saved by the arrival of a funeral cortège: Her former accuser has died on the very spot, and the priest will announce her dying regret to the community. The coincidences of the plot—Hubmayr's chance arrival, the death on site of the former employer—together with Franzl's history and the righting of wrongs at the lakeside attempt to combine comic form with the substance of a *pièce à thèse:* a demonstration that people more easily assume guilt than innocence, and that the law is quicker to condemn than make honorable amends. The play's strength resides in two characters: Franzl, pert, heart-warming, initially strong in self-esteem and resolve; and Hubmayr, reminiscent of (and with the same structural function as) Görg in *Hand und Herz,* but lacking Görg's malice he belongs to the world of pure comedy, his essential goodness of heart at odds with his overpowering need to steal. The scene at the lakeside making all come right is a sentimental *coup de théâtre,* and there is no sense of a new order of things, only that luck would have it so. The forced denouement of Anzengruber's last play suggests public taste for a happy ending rather than the joyful affirmation which had given his early rural dramas their coherence.

The Viennese Dramas: A Problem of Genre

We have seen how Anzengruber successfully integrates pathos, psychological depth, and a serious issue into an essentially comic vision, and how he falters when he attempts the tragic mode or when social criticism is too intrusive. There are doubtless several explanations for his trying his hand at dramatic genres other than that of the rural comedy. In 1872 the Vienna Burgtheater wanted something from the dramatist famed for *Der Pfarrer von Kirchfeld,* and it got *Elfriede,* a high-style work on bourgeois marriage; then, Anzengruber was also worried about not tackling social problems head on—an interest attested by his memoirs, letters, journalistic pieces and *Kalendergeschichten* (Almanac Tales); finally, there was the box-office need to give the Viennese public the sordid urban realities, criminal doings, and melodramatic incidents which had become its prevailing tastes. Mostly this led him to write less than convincingly, giving social circumstances and issues greater weight than the fates of individual characters, and the compassionate humanist appears to foist his moral and optimistic denouement on the work.

Anzengruber called *Elfriede* (1872) simply a "drama" (*Schauspiel*). Set in a well-to-do milieu—mention of the Ringstraße reveals that we are in Vienna—it tells how Elfriede has been forced to abandon a loved suitor because of his social status and finds herself in a respectable marriage, where she is treated with gallantry and charm by her husband but never as a serious partner. The crisis is brought about when a friend of her former love, who has since died in the Far East, returns with a portrait of the man and a letter for her. She discovers that she feels free and authentic in the presence of the portrait, but her husband wrenches her secret from her and reacts brutally, until he suddenly appreciates the value of his wife's new-found individuality and changes heart accordingly. They are both now capable of a real marriage. Sadly, the author is too taken up with his thesis, and Elfriede's tirade (II, iii) shows a character debating a problem rather than living it. Anzengruber's gift for characterization is given scope only with Dr. Knorr, the quirky scholar friend of Elfriede's former love: his witty, often caustic comments on the absurdities of modern European life (another "outsider") give him a role akin to that of the *raisonneurs* of traditional Viennese comic theater, whose function includes communicating across the footlights. The happy ending to this tense and melancholy drama was no doubt to public taste, but it lacks *vraisemblance:* the husband's complete change of character takes place during a brief solitary walk. Yet it is Anzengruber's moral perspective which is partly responsible. Significantly, when he came to review Ibsen's *A Doll's House* in 1880,[16] he disapproved of Nora's ability to abandon husband and children. Ibsen may be relentless in his treatment of the theme of woman's subjugation in marriage, but Anzengruber's pace, his social and psychological realism permits of no sentimental escape from the dictates of the genre.

The problem of genre is even more apparent in *Die Tochter des Wucherers* (1873, The Moneylender's Daughter), whose strident effects and wooden characterization undermine the morbid realism of the conception. The moneylender—and money was headline news with the crash of the Vienna stock exchange in May 1873—forces his daughter to ensnare young men and then refuse marriage at the last moment when the suitor is financially in her father's grip. The immorality of capitalism, marriage as prostitution, and the undeserving parent's hypocrisy in invoking the fourth commandment could not be more grotesquely portrayed than with the unintentionally comic repetition of the amorous trap. When this grim ruse is combined with a sentimental ending, Anzengruber's problem with genre is all too evident. He himself wrote: "Looking for tragic effects in the Viennese milieu was an error of judgment. Rough-and-ready types have to be treated comically or at least humoristically—that was my mistake" (to Schlögl, 20 October 1873).

Yet when he used the same themes in his powerful social drama *Das vierte Gebot* (1877, The Fourth Commandment), he came closer to the fusion of character studies with milieu so successfully achieved in his best rural dramas. Three family stories constitute the interlocking strands of a rich portrayal of Viennese society. Hedwig Hutterer is denied the love of her piano teacher, whose genteel poverty her parents reject in favor of the wealthy good-for-nothing August Stolzenthaler. Hedwig bears him a sickly child—the implied cause, as later in Ibsen's *Ghosts,* being her husband's earlier dissolute life—and she finally returns, broken in body and spirit, to her parental home. Connecting with the second strand of the work, Hedwig's fate is laid partly at the door of the priest Eduard Schön, only son of the Hutterers' gardener. Blessed himself with loving and supportive parents, he tells Hedwig that obeying her parents and putting her trust in God is the proper course, only subsequently recognizing the—subservient priest's—folly in demanding obedience to bad parents. The third strand of the play, the doings of the Schalanters, neighbors of the Hutterers, powerfully reinforces the theme of the fourth commandment. The family, with the exception of the old grandmother, Herwig, has degenerated: The mother attempts to seduce her honest manservant Johann; the father, a master cabinetmaker, is drunken and malicious; the children, Martin and Josepha, are aimless. The play ends with Martin facing execution for murder, and in a moving final scene his infirm grandmother comes to offer him solace before death. Put baldly, the theatrical effects appear cruder than the delineation of characters in social interaction actually warrants, and there is a convincingly realist depiction of a changing society, the values of an earlier time (grandmother Herwig, the Schön parents) losing ground to a brutally grasping, self-gratifying generation (the Hutterer and Schalanter parents, August Stolzenthaler). However, if the mode is already a pre-Naturalist treatment of milieu, characters are made to show an insight into their condition which runs counter to Naturalistic theory.[17] The Schalanter children recognize the import of their grandmother's warnings: so the ostensibly "depraved" Johanna sacrifices her happiness by telling her suitor Johann to find a better woman than herself; and in his death cell Martin sends for his school friend Eduard

Schön to give him a chorus-like summation of the social hypocrisy which has ruined him: "When you tell schoolchildren to honor father and mother, you should also preach to parents that they must prove worthy" (IV, v). This self-consciousness of characters is, of course, the ethical voice of the absent narrator—another genre problem—crying against dogmatic morality and hypocrisy. Yet if this ethical "voice" and the dramaturgical need for comic-plot coincidences, to intertwine the lives of three families, force the play's realism into a certain artificiality—Ödön von Horváth's later montage technique is not yet a possibility—the spirited pace and the life given to such a range of characters, especially the Schalanter household, give this piece a special place among Anzengruber's Viennese dramas.

Anzengruber's ethical vision is seen in two other plays, relying not on authorial intrusion but on the agency of comic protagonists, who use their traditional right to embody the dramatist's voice. *Alte Wiener* (1878, Viennese of the Old School) documents the doings of Martin Kernhofer, who gives financial assistance to a ne'er-do-well, saves a marriage between an old friend and his young wife, and secures the agreement of two sets of parents to the (necessary) marriage of their children. From the moment we see the hidden Kernhofer's fishing rod as the curtain rises to the final line—"I just have to, I just have to"—when he hears of a further need for charitable doing, it is his spirit that lurks in wait for the stupidity, thoughtlessness, arrogance, or malice of the other characters. And it is this Hanns the Stonebreaker *redivivus* who gives these comic portraits of Viennese life a dramatic thread and gently corrective vision.

A similar figure is Thomas Hammer, the toy seller in *Heimgfunden* (1885, Home at Last), who acts as the conscience of his ruined and criminal lawyer brother, bringing him back from the brink of death to family and the moral order. In restoring faith to a lost soul and persuading his brother's wife to join her formerly rich socialite husband in his more lowly estate, Thomas duplicates the strength and purposefulness of Kernhofer; but in this later play the good-hearted pedagogue is the bumpkin (*Kasperl*) of Viennese farce, falling over his words and bumbling in situations but coming out naively right. The denouement reunites the family around the Christmas tree. Is this Christmas comedy, a genre popular with Viennese audiences, merely a world of toys and tinsel? The family reunion cannot quite eradicate the melancholy atmosphere of embezzlement, ruin, family shame, and attempted suicide, and leaves us with a sense of Thomas Hammer's barely surviving value system, of a threatened idyll. The social realism to be found in Friedrich Kaiser's "portraits of real life" (*Lebensbilder*) is combined with Anzengruber's own brand of sentimental and moral comedy, in which the spotlight falls, somewhat incongruously, on a character from traditional farce. If this is finally a regenerative comedy in the manner of Raimund, evil yields here (as in *Alte Wiener*) not to a higher power but to a lone human figure standing above the fray, mindless of his own advantage, and directing selfish or unseeing characters to good ends. It is Anzengruber's ill-fated attempt to adapt the Viennese comic and moralizing theater to the needs of a new, economically harsher urban world.

Prose Narrative: The Realist Tale as Exemplum

Writing in 1882 of his collection of *Kalendergeschichten* (edifying tales published on a calendar), Anzengruber states an aesthetic necessity: since the calendar hangs the whole year round, the tales must be such as to be worth frequent rereading, and hence, "the last words of the story must give food for thought and leave their imprint on the reader's feelings."[18] Of course, we also have here a liberal attitude to the educative function of art. Morally edifying stories were traditionally the domain of Church and Establishment, and these writings were ideologically normative. Anzengruber's open-ended structures—the reader has to supplement and augment their import by relating them to the business of living—are an enlightened thrust against such propaganda. This meant that the language had to be accessible, drawing on the register, idioms, proverbs, folk tales and customs of the lower orders who bought the calendars. Yet at the same time the familiar had to be examined, reflected upon and recast. If Anzengruber is a successor to the Austrian "folk teacher" Adalbert Stifter, the act of bringing the Enlightenment and a dying liberal tradition to bear upon the realities of the modern world gives his moral voice a different ring.

Such is the tenor of the best of his calendar stories, *Die Märchen des Steinklopferhanns* (1875/1879, Tales told by Hanns the Stonebreaker). We know Hanns from *Die Kreuzelschreiber,* and these tales give him the chance to put into further practice his humane affirmation of life, his view that it is a "merry" world for those who handle it aright. He comes to the rescue of humble rural folk who, like himself, are marginalized by the social structure and narrow-mindedness of the world they inhabit. They do not have either his freethinking capacity to destroy the imprisoning

walls of convention or his objection to a hereafter which impedes fruitful-
ness in the world of here and now. Thus, Hanns can offer a vision of lost
opportunity to two young people so that they reject the common view
that you cannot marry if you are poor (*Vom Hanns und der Gretl,* Hans
and Gretel). Or he convinces a poor villager that God will not mind if he
sleeps through Judgment Day because he has worked so hard on earth, i.e.
that he should not neglect this world for exclusive concern with the
afterlife (*Die G'schicht vom Jüngsten Tag,* The Tale of the Last Judgment).
He prevents angry peasants from destroying a new type of harvesting
machine by conjuring a picture of the humane possibilities inherent in
progress (*Die G'schicht von der Maschin',* The Tale of the Machine). He
creates sympathy for a criminal by revealing how easily any of us can step
into crime, and thereby educates the reader out of unimaginative self-
righteousness (*Die Versuchung,* Temptation). He persuades a poor widow
not to listen to a religious bigot but turn her energies fruitfully to the daily
round (*Dö G'schicht von dö alten Himmeln,* The Tale of Heavens of the
Past). Finally, the Devil himself asks Hanns to give a drubbing to the old
"sinner" Lehner-Franzl, who was quick to consign Hanns to the Devil for
taking the old widow's part in the previous tale (*Eins vom Teufel,* One
from the Devil)! In these tales Anzengruber achieves what he cannot offer
in his gnomic verse and aphorisms: a form in which his philosophizing is,
thanks to his narrator, at one with images of the natural world and the life
of ordinary people. Here he enacts his enlightenment and liberalism
through a character with no claim to authorial omniscience or authority:
The message is presented as persuasive but not doctrinaire through an
"outsider" questioning the norms of society, a perspective not unlike that
of Lucianic satire.[19]

In another collection of short narrative works, *Dorfgänge* (Sketches and
Tales of Village Life), Anzengruber similarly combines a "psychology of the
peasant world"[20] with his moral vision. In *Der Einsam* (1881, The Hermit)—to take perhaps the best of these tales—a small-minded rural community acquiesces in the persecution of an unmarried but contented young
couple and in the attempt to expel an outsider living as a hermit in the
hills. The priest brings about the death of the outsider, who unbeknown
to him is his own bastard child. The psychology of both is finely drawn.
The former's stringent moralism springs from his own misspent youth,
causing him to project guilt feelings onto the hapless hermit; the latter's
unintended crime and subsequent Godless but harmless existence result

from griefs and maltreatment in early life. Beyond a realist depiction of village life, the work is a humane plea for empathy and charity. It seeks understanding for simple folk who are easily led, for those who live in "sin," for those who are guilty of a crime, and even for bigots whose attempts to come to terms with their own unruly natures have distorted their perceptions.[21]

Anzengruber's two novels both have realist substance, but *Der Schandfleck* (revised version, 1884, The Stain on the Family), is the more traditional. In its original form, with its second part set in Vienna, it failed to satisfy even benevolent critics. However, as a reworked two-part tale of peasant life it achieves a coherent structure. The story is for a great stretch taken up with the love between Leni and Flori, childhood sweethearts who are unaware that through the lapse of Leni's mother he is her half-brother. When Leni learns the truth, she leaves home, becomes the companion to the small epileptic daughter of Kaspar, a rich farmer in a distant village, and ends up marrying him. While the reader is quickly aware of the impediment to marriage between Leni and Flori, so that prolonging the situation beyond novella length produces a continual irony that is too heavy, Leni's long-drawn unawareness of burgeoning love between herself and Kaspar is appropriate to a novel that reveals fruitful emotional and moral life to be in harmony with the tempo and rhythm of the natural order.

There is a corresponding organic development in the treatment of Leni's relationship with her stepfather, Joseph Reindorfer. He begins by doing no more than his Christian duty in educating his wife's illegitimate daughter. Only gradually does his natural inclination overcome the moral affront of her birth and let him show any affection for the loyal, loving girl; but not until the end of the novel, when the Lear-like Reindorfer has been turned out by his own children, can Leni receive him in reciprocal love as she helps him to a peaceful end. The rhythm of nature also underlies the vision of life and death as part of the great chain of being, a point made by the opening and closing sections of the work: Leni is born as the old miller, Flori's grandfather, is dying in the village, and Leni's stepdaughter, Burgerl, visits the grave of old Reindorfer to tell "grandpa" that his daughter has produced a handsome little boy, who is going to be called Joseph. Nature is not squeamish and asks only that life continue. It is Hanns the Stonebreaker's "special revelation," that all manner of things are made well when seen from the perspective of an all-encompassing and perpetually self-renewing natural order.

This is not to say that the rural world does not also offer a darker vision—Reindorfer's harsh treatment of his erring wife, Leni's curt farewell to the author of her woe (who has spent her life atoning with goodness for her fault, and whom Leni will never again see), Flori's despair and resulting dissolute life, immediate causes of his untimely death. Against the optimistic final vision of good is set the double funeral of Leni's mother and Flori, the son of her mother's seducer. All this is the dark ground of potential renewal, the realist showing that the natural order also has its victims. Nonetheless, it is for human agency to promote a moral order within the natural one. We see how Leni's "natural" father yields his place to the father who shapes a life: human nature is not merely the life force expressed in procreation but even more the act of caring, nurturing, and loving. It is for Leni and Kaspar to effect the final transformation of the "stain on the family" into its blessing—even Burgerl's epilepsy appears to have been cured by Leni's love for the girl. Out of undirected natural forces and human potential Anzengruber creates a moral idyll as exemplum. His realist village tale in fact stands close to the earlier nineteenth-century novel of self-development and to Stifter's portrayal of the rhythm of nature as a model for moral growth.

Der Sternsteinhof (1885, Starstone Farm), Anzengruber's other novel and most powerful narrative, is by far the more modern work. It is tautly developed, one might almost say with dramatic skill, from the first moment when the beautiful Helene Zinshofer raises her eyes from her humble dwelling in the village to the Sternsteinhof on the hillside and vows that she will one day be the wife of the wealthy farmer's son. If she then allows the woodcarver Muckerl Kleebinder, her neighbor, to woo her, it is because his religious statuettes bring in enough money for him to be able to buy her gifts and she can exploit him. Toni, the Sternsteinhof farmer's son, soon discovers the attraction of Helene, who allows herself to be seduced and then extracts a written promise of marriage from him. But the old farmer wants a rich bride, Sali, for his son, and when Helene confronts him with the written promise he laughingly tears it up. Individual scenes and set-piece confrontations, the essential structural components of this novel, have taken us to a climax. With the humbling of Helene, we enter upon the peripeteia, as she turns her thoughts back to village life, hard work and Muckerl as husband and father for Toni's child. That she has not given up her ambition may be guessed from her decision to bring the child up as a stranger in the home she has been forced to make. Against his will Toni marries the sickly Sali, who bears him a daughter, but his passion for Helene remains, and he pursues her again. When Sali and Muckerl both die (events carefully prepared by the narrative), Toni and Helene marry. This is the essential resolution of the drama of poverty-driven ambition. But there is a coda, giving a new dimension to Helene's natural energies. After Toni is killed in one of the Empire's many wars, the feud with her father-in-law abates as he gains respect for her honest industry, and as she devotes herself to her own son, to Sali's daughter, and to good works which gain her public esteem. Personal ambition does not vanish but finds a fruitful social outlet. The realist's constant refusal to judge his heroine's natural struggle—quashing her rivals, betraying Muckerl, trampling on filial piety—is softened by a moral vision of ends rather than means. With Helene's desire to count for something and win the respect of the community Anzengruber again wrests human good from the play of natural forces. We are, though, a long way from the idealism of *Der Schandfleck:* moral potential is realized through a distinctly amoral natural energy and material success.

Throughout the novel, motifs of the natural world (seasons, the river) become metaphors of human energy and purposefulness. The self-interest of Helene, Toni, and the old Sternsteinhof farmer is allowed to triumph over the sickness and resignation—the "Nazarene" mode—of Muckerl, of Sepherl, the girl devoted to him, and Sali. This Nietzschean study of "will to power" in the strong, though Nietzsche would scarcely have approved of a woman as his "predator," is depicted with earthiness and pitilessness. Yet Helene's power struggle with men is viewed optimistically on two counts. The good with which the story closes shows that Anzengruber's horror at the havoc wrought by sexuality (so pessimistically treated in *Das vierte Gebot*) is turned from a judgment on moral turpitude into objective contemplation of "something capable of being quite honorable in the economy of nature."[22] Secondly, the heroine taking her place in the male world, running the farmstead, and contributing to the building of roads, bridges, and schools diverts the study of power into a forward-looking, larger view of woman's nature and social potential.

Finally, the novel represents Anzengruber's most explicit use of the village as metonymy for the great stage of life. The rural world is, it is true, depicted with the realist's eye for its social conditions (land, marriage, mores), but the author leaves us in no doubt that with this study of sexual and material appetites he is writing nothing less than a myth of human activity. In his epilogue, he asserts that the narrow limits of the rural world have "less effect on the primal life of the instincts," and that "passions coming to the fore in an unrestrained manner, or at most clumsily camouflaged, are more easily understood"; and, alluding to Homer—our sexually triumphant heroine is called Helene—he notes that "in our oldest, simplest and most effective tales the heroes and princes were cattle breeders and estate owners, while their ministers and treasurers were swineherds."[23] Later the writer is even clearer that the realities he sought in the rural world had never been essentially social issues: "I am no longer interested in the rural scene. . . . Sections of the rural population are becoming alive to political, or more accurately social, problems, and poetry has no part to play in solving these" (to Bolin, 26 March 1886). He had always known that his was a symbolic realism: "I first take a human being and clothe him in the dress of his condition, and then I place him in as much everyday local ambience as I need for my artistic intention" (to Duboc, 30 October 1876). This intention was ultimately always the human condition: "There is not much to learn from the peasant world, whose types are quickly drawn. I am interested in what is human!"[24] In this sense *Der Sternsteinhof* is a key to the poetics of his rural dramas and stories; in substance and formal quality the novel embodies what is best in Anzengruber.

Anzengruber was the last in the line of dramatists seeking to preserve the Viennese popular theater. He transformed the increasingly empty farce set in a local "milieu" (*Lokalposse*) into a socially committed popular drama (*Volksstück*). Yet, with few exceptions, he combines his modern depiction of social tensions with an optimistic moral vision harking back to an older comic dramaturgy of ultimate harmony. This subordination of his social theme to an over-arching pattern of regenerative or sentimental comedy has mostly been seen as leaving "an unresolved discordance between . . . modern intent to be critical of society and . . . dependence on traditional moral and aesthetic ideas."[25] But although Anzengruber shares in the general "stylistic confusion"[26] of an age of radical social change, his experiments often create a successful hybrid form for the needs of his day. His early rural dramas are a happy fusion of realist milieu, social issue, comic mode shot through with pathos and moral point. Tragic effects are outside the compass of his humanistic optimism, and elsewhere his modern social concerns—e.g. the institution of marriage, women's status, Church dogma, capitalism—can distort his aesthetic construction, with the result that effects become melodramatic and the work less cohesive. His prose narratives of village life—which are in no sense the kind of "regional literature" (*Heimatkunst*) which led balefully to "Blood and Soil" writing—are also part of the contemporary shift into realism, away from sentimental love stories to depiction of environmental forces and social conflicts. Yet here, too, his narratorial voice confronts natural and social determinism with moral idealism. While it was his realism, showing the instinctive self-interest of rural folk or crude materialism as the driving force of city life, that appealed to the budding Naturalist movement, our own response should perhaps privilege his most frequent—conservative—poetic structure, the dissolution of powerfully delineated conflicts into moral idyll. Here, after all, we have the essence of his humane art.

Notes

1. Cited in Sigismund Friedmann, *Ludwig Anzengruber* (Leipzig: Hermann Seemann, 1902), p. 7.

2. To Julius Duboc, 10 October 1876. Letters are hereafter cited in the text by date and can be found in *Ludwig Anzengruber. Briefe,* ed. Anton Bettelheim (Stuttgart/Berlin: J.G. Cotta, 1902), vol. 1 1859-1877, vol. 2 1878-1889.

3. Reported by Peter Rosegger, "Aus einer Zwiesprach," *Jugend* (1905), Heft 22. Cited by Otto Rommel, "Ludwig Anzengruber als Dramatiker," in *Ludwig Anzengruber. Sämtliche Werke,* eds. Rudolf Latzke and Otto Rommel (Vienna: Anton Schroll, 1922), vol. 2, p. 391. This edition is hereafter referred to as *SW.*

4. *SW,* ibid., p. 401.

5. *SW,* ibid., p. 402.

6. See Ludwig Anzengruber, "Eine Plauderei als Vorrede, Dorfgänge II," *SW,* vol. 15, 1, p. 294.

7. Otto Rommel, *SW,* vol. 2, p. 533.

8. See Otto Rommel, *Die Alt-Wiener Volkskomödie. Ihre Geschichte vom barocken Welttheater bis zum Tode Nestroys* (Vienna: Anton Schroll, 1952), pp. 973-975.

9. Alfred Kleinberg, *Ludwig Anzengruber. Ein Lebensbild* (Stuttgart/Berlin: J.G. Cotta, 1921), p. 256.

10. See W.E. Yates, *Nestroy. Satire and Parody in Viennese Popular*

Comedy (Cambridge: University Press, 1972), pp. 185-189.

11.   See Jürgen Hein, *Das Wiener Volkstheater* (Darmstadt: Wissenschaftliche Buchgesellschaft, 1978), pp. 153-155.

12.   For this view, see Edward McInnes, "Ludwig Anzengruber and the Popular Dramatic Tradition," *Maske and Kothurn* 21 (1975), especially pp. 149-152.

13.   See Otto Rommel, "Ludwig Anzengrubers Leben und Werk," *SW*, vol. 15, 3, especially pp. 427-436. It was Wilhelm Bolin and Julius Duboc, both intimates of Feuerbach, who directed Anzengruber's attention to the philosopher's ideas. In a letter of 21 October 1876 Anzengruber thanks Duboc for his "substantial piece on the ethical content of atheism." Bolin's letters, among Anzengruber's posthumous papers in the Vienna Stadtbibliothek, refer frequently to Feuerbach, of whose ideas Anzengruber clearly approves (to Bolin, 14 May 1877). According to Rommel, Anzengruber "has treated with almost encyclopaedic thoroughness all the problems arising from the confrontation of theism and atheism" (*SW*, ibid., p. 436). Although we lack evidence of Anzengruber's *direct* experience of Feuerbach, the aphorisms in *SW*, vol. 8 deal in large measure with the atheistic way of life. See Karlheinz Rossbacher, "Ludwig Anzengruber: 'Die Märchen des Steinklopferhanns' (1875/1879). Poesie der Dissonanz als Weg zur Volksaufklärung." In *Romane und Erzählungen des Bürgerlichen Realismus,* ed. Horst Denkler (Stuttgart: Reclam, 1980), pp. 243-244, note 22.

14.   Alfred Kleinberg, p. 222.

15.   This partly explains triviality and incoherence in a play like *s' Jungferngift* (1878, Mandragora), where Anzengruber is writing roles for no fewer than three comic actors in the Carl Theater ensemble.

16.   Quoted by Kleinberg, p. 212.

17.   See Roy C. Cowen, *Das deutsche Drama im 19. Jahrhundert* (Stuttgart: Metzler, 1988), p. 188.

18.   "Eine Kleine Plauderei als Vorrede, Kalender-Geschichten," *SW*, vol. 15, 1, p. 302.

19.   The Enlightenment technique of using the "outsider" to satirize norms taken by society as natural or self-evident (e.g. Montesquieu's *Lettres persanes* and Voltaire's *Candide*) hark back to Lucian's *ingénu* satire. In Anzengruber's *Elfriede* the traveler Dr. Knorr, a visitor from abroad seeing with "foreign" eyes, is precisely in this mode.

20. This was Anzengruber's own title for a volume with four of these stories, but Kleinberg notes (p. 418, note 1) that it is appropriate to a good half of the village tales.

21. Anzengruber's dramatization of this story, *Stahl und Stein* (1887, Steel and Stone), with its drawn out depiction of the mores of an Alpine village, its characterizing stage directions, and ill-placed reminiscence of the criminal hero's early life are all too obviously trying to fill in the detail of the narrative work. The thrust against zealous dogmatism is weakened by the priest's transformation (the censor!) into the village mayor. Not least, the need to give the hermit figure stage presence requires a girl's amorous pursuit of him, reducing the pathos of his isolation.

22. From a generalizing note in the posthumous papers, cited by Kleinberg, p. 407, note 13.

23. *SW,* vol. 10, pp. 369-370.

24. A verbal communication to Chiavacci, cited by Kleinberg, p. 145.

25. Roy C. Cowen, p. 186.

26. See Hein, pp. 145-147.

Bibliography

I. Works by Ludwig Anzengruber in German

1871   *Der Pfarrer von Kirchfeld*
1872   *Der Meineidbauer; Die Kreuzelschreiber*
1873   *Elfriede; Die Tochter des Wucherers*
1874   *Der G'wissenswurm*
1875   *Hand und Herz*
1876   *Doppelselbstmord*
1877   *Der ledige Hof; Der Schandfleck* (2nd version, 1884)
1878   *Das vierte Gebot; 's Jungferngift*
1879   *Alte Wiener; Die Trutzige; Die umkehrte Freit; Dorfgänge*
1880   *Aus 'm gewohnten Gleis*
1881   *Bekannte von der Straße; Der Einsam*
1885   *Heimgfunden* (Printed theater ms; book 1889); *Der Sternsteinhof*
1887   *Stahl und Stein* 1889 *Der Fleck auf der Ehr'* 1892   *Brave Leut'
        vom Grund* (completed 1880).
Briefe. Ed. Anton Bettelheim, vols. 1-2. Stuttgart/Berlin: J.G.
        Cotta, 1902.
Gesammelte Werke, critical edition. Eds. Rudolf Latzkte and Otto
        Rommel. Vienna: Anton Schroll, 1920-1922.

II. Anzengruber's Works in English

"The Farmer Forsworn." Translated by Adolf Busse in *German Classics
        of the Nineteenth and Twentieth Centuries,* vol. 16. Eds. Kuno
        Francke and W.G. Howard. New York, 1914.

III. Secondary Works in English

Howe, Patricia. "End of a Line: Anzengruber and the Viennese Stage."
        In *Viennese Popular Theater: A Symposium,* Eds. W.E. Yates
        and John R.P. McKenzie. University of Exeter, 1985.
McInnes, Edward. "Ludwig Anzengruber and the Popular Dramatic
        Tradition." In *Maske und Kothurn* 21 (1975).
Yates, W.E. "An Example of Nestroy's Influence: Anzengruber's 'Ausm
        gewohnten Gleis.'" In *Nestroy, Satire and Parody in Viennese
        Popular Comedy.* Cambridge: University Press, 1972.

IV.   Major Studies in German

Baasner, Rainer. "Anzengrubers 'Sternsteinhof.'" *Zeitschrift für deutsche Philologie* 102 (1983), pp. 564-583.

Baumer, Franz. *Ludwig Anzengruber. Volksdichter und Aufklärer.* Ein Lebensbild. Weilheim: Stöppel, 1989.

Kleinberg, Alfred. *Ludwig Anzengruber. Ein Lebensbild.* Stuttgart/Berlin: J.G. Cotta, 1921.

Latzke, Rudolf. "Ludwig Anzengruber als Erzähler." In *Sämtliche Werke.* Eds. R. Latzke and O. Rommel. Vienna: Anton Schroll, 1920-1922, vol. 15, p. 1.

Rommel, Otto "Ludwig Anzengruber als Dramatiker." In Ibid., vol. 15, p. 2.

_____. "Ludwig Anzengrubers Leben und Werk." VI: "Ludwig Anzengrubers Weltanschauung." In Ibid., vol. 15, p. 3.

Rossbacher, Karlheinz. "Ludwig Anzengruber. Die Märchen des Steinklopferhanns (1875/1879). Poesie der Dissonanz als Weg zur Aufklärung." In Horst Denkler, ed. *Romane und Erzählungen des bürgerlichen Realismus.* Stuttgart: Reclam (1980), pp. 231-245.

Schmidt-Dengler, Wendelin. "Die Unbedeutenden werden bedeutend. Anmerkungen zum Volksstück nach Nestroys Tod: Kaiser, Anzengruber, Morre." In *Die andere Welt. Festschrift für Hellmuth Himmel.* Ed. Kurt Bartsch. Berne/Munich: Francke (1979), pp. 133-146.

Eduard von Bauernfeld

Carl Steiner

Eduard von Bauernfeld, who is virtually unknown outside of Austria today and who even in his native city of Vienna is primarily remembered only because of a street and a city square named after him, was one of the most popular Austrian writers of lighthearted comedy throughout much of the nineteenth century. For a number of decades, in fact, he vied for popularity as a playwright of lighter fare with the likes of Raimund and Nestroy. Time itself, this most crucial judge of artistic endurance, if not excellence, it seems, has consigned him to literary oblivion.

Even the facts surrounding his birth and origin are shrouded in some mystery. Whereas there is little doubt that he was an illegitimate child—with all the social disapproval, prejudice, and even derision attached to such status in those days—the details of this affair that gave rise to his birth and the period of his early nurture and upbringing are subject to much speculation. From all accounts it appears that he was born in Vienna on 13 January 1802, as the illegitimate son of Laurenz Cajetan Novag, at the time a student of medicine at the University of Vienna, and the widowed Elisabeth Feichtinger. His father, who was later to become a prominent physician at the St. Mary Hospital and a professor of physical education at the University of Vienna, had come to Austria's capital city from the Prussian part of Silesia to study there. Eduard's mother, a native Viennese, had lost her husband Joseph Feichtinger, who was a court attorney by profession, in 1791. She was the daughter of Johann Anton Hofbauer, an imperial food commissioner, and of Anna Barbara von Teibler. Her father had been elevated to nobility when Empress Maria Theresa bestowed on him the title Von Bauernfeld in 1763. His illegitimate grandson Eduard was to assume this name as well as the title on maturity.

As if the circumstances surrounding Eduard von Bauernfeld's origin and name were not complicated enough, the relationship between his parents added to further complications of his upbringing. His mother (1770-1831) was four years older than his father (1774-1849). This difference in age seems to have been the principal cause of Novag's failure to legitimize their relationship, marrying instead the widow's daughter, who also went by the name of Elisabeth. This young woman, who bore Novag five children, was Eduard's half sister.[1]

Yet Dr. Novag was not a man devoid of morality and honor, nor did he lack a sense of parental compassion and responsibility. Consequently, he not only raised the boy, but also took an active interest in the education of his first-born son, obtaining stipends which made it possible for Eduard to finish the gymnasium. Later he attended the university, where he studied philosophy and law.[2] These were the turbulent years of the war of liberation from French domination under Napoleon and the early years of political restoration to the *status quo ante* under Metternich's strict regimen. Bauernfeld was a thirteen-year-old student at the Vienna Schottengymnasium when the glittering Congress of Vienna was staged to legitimize the return of Europe to the days of the *ancien regime.* He attended this college preparatory school from 1813 to 1818. When the *Karlsbader Beschlüsse* (Resolutions of Karlsbad) doused the last glimmer of political liberalism in Austria for decades to come, he had just begun to study philosophy at the University of Vienna.

In those years Bauernfeld was not smitten with political fervor, nor did he appear to have been an overly enthusiastic student of jurisprudence, which he studied from 1821 to 1825. Following in his father's footsteps, he was at that time enamored of women, wine, and song. In later years he related his formative experiences in his memoirs, largely collected under the title *Aus Alt- und Neu-Wien* (From the Old and the New Vienna). Rather than immerse himself in the study of law, to which he looked as a means of ensuring a livelihood in later years, he engaged in the pursuit of art, music, and literature, thereby sharing the taste and enthusiasm of the offspring of the well-to-do burghers and aristocrats of Austria's capital city. He inclined to be a man about town, if not a man of the world. Thus he frequented social soirées and hobnobbed through Vienna's social scene with such prominent artistic friends as the painter Moritz von Schwind, the composer Franz Schubert, and the dramatist Franz Grillparzer. He soon expanded this close and inner circle of friends by establishing personal relationships with other young notables in town such as the playwright Ferdinand Raimund and the poets Nikolaus Lenau and Anastasius Grün. The latter actually used bourgeois pseudonyms to disguise their aristocratic origins. Lenau's given name was Niembsch Edler von Strehlenau. The progressive thinking Grün, in effect, belonged to the highest level of Austrian aristocracy, being born a Count von Auersperg. Bauernfeld in detail referred to these notables in his recollections: "In the gymnasium, Mortiz von Schwind and I shared the same school bench. Since then more than half a century has passed. Yet we classmates had remained close friends till one of us had to depart forever. A third friend had joined up with us, Franz Schubert—regrettably, only for a few years."[3]

In such stimulating company it was easy for Bauernfeld in his formative years to develop a permanent love for the arts and for literature and to contemplate a career in the Austrian civil service only with the greatest reluctance. When he was forced by sheer necessity to enter the civil service in 1826, he was most despondent and deeply unhappy. On being offered the post of a civil service trainee in the governing body of Lower Austria, he entered in his diary the disparaging remark: "I feel as if I am about to be hanged" (*Ausgewählte Werke:* 1:10). Fortunately for him, he was able to endure this—to him—most unpleasant, indeed unbearable, assignment, which he also likened to slavery, inasmuch as he found an understanding and sympathetic supervisor in Josef von Spaun, who—like himself—was among Schubert's closest friends and admirers.[4]

Of all the arts, however, it was the theater which proved to be most irresistible to young Bauernfeld. His early fascination with the stage played a crucial role in his artistic development. Yet he soon became aware that his dramatic talent did not lie in the area of the iambic meter and in the field of classical tragedy but in the lighter sphere of elevated social comedy. He was especially encouraged to develop along these lines by Josef Schreyvogel, the gifted, indeed ingenious director of the Burgtheater, Vienna's most prestigious stage. In later years Bauernfeld captured the youthful enthusiasm of those early years in verse:

> We young folk were enraptured
> By Goethe and by Schiller;
> Egmont had us fully captured;
> We cried with Luise Miller.

But our favors in the public forum
Also found *dii gentium minorum!*
Thus without hesitation or ado,
We took to Iffland and Kotzebue.
(*Ausgewählte Werke,* 1:XVII)[5]

There seems to be little doubt, however, that regarding all these intellectual stimuli and influences, Bauernfeld's initially close friendship with the older and successful Franz Grillparzer was most instrumental in his own attempt to establish himself as a successful playwright. He met Grillparzer through Josef von Spaun in December 1826. There was an immediate kinship between them. Although they were by their very nature quite different, their literary path to success progressed along similar lines. They both shared an intense love for Goethe and a pronounced dislike of Romanticism. They met often in Grillparzer's apartment and discovered that they favored similar literary themes and also shared their political convictions. Grillparzer was extremely knowledgeable about the historical and contemporary development of the comedy and was able to advise Bauernfeld. In some instances he even directed the fledgling author in this genre. Bauernfeld's dramas profited immensely. For his part the young man was able to imbue the older dramatist with new enthusiasm and youthful fervor. He wrote spirited homages to Grillparzer in which he encouraged the acknowledged master to engage his genius in new and productive ways. Grillparzer responded in kind, albeit much more philosophically: "The world exists because of what we see. / Without our views and insights, it could never truly be." In subsequent years they took many excursions together and even joined forces against the imperious and influential theater critic Moritz Saphir.[6] Only in later years did Grillparzer turn against Bauernfeld and criticize not only his political activism, but also his literary talent.[7] Thus he wrote about him in his autobiographical essay *Meine Erinnerungen aus dem Revolutionsjahr 1848* (My Recollections of the Revolutionary Year 1848):

> Bauernfeld, the author of the polemical treatise against Baron Hügel, had begun for quite some time to play a political role. . . . He came into literature partly as an adherent of Goethe, partly as an admirer of Tieck. His incomparable talent for details was very much curtailed by the lack of

steadfastness of his nature vis-à-vis the total picture. . . .
Bauernfeld had enough intelligence and literary honesty to
work against this weakness of his talent. However, it soon
turned out that whenever he dealt with a major idea, the
details turned out to be stiff and cold, while he permitted
himself to write on merrily in order to have all parts sparkle
with life and interest.[8]

To be sure, Bauernfeld began his writings for the theater in the manner
of Kotzebue but soon found his true talent in the light comedy of
manners of French origin. The first play of this type, the comedy *Der
Brautwerber* (The Marriage Broker) was performed in the Burgtheater on
5 September 1828. The reception was unfavorable. Critics considered this
comedy too slow moving and too stiff and stilted because of the Alexan-
drine verse after the French model. Bauernfeld was understandably discouraged at the failure of his play. It took special encouragement by
Grillparzer and Schreyvogel to restore his confidence. His prose comedy
Leichtsinn aus Liebe (Imprudence for Love's Sake), which premiered in the
Burgtheater on 12 January 1831, the evening of his twenty-ninth birthday,
was a rousing success. In this play he gave the public what many comedy
aficionados enjoyed in those days, a play based on clever conversation in
the French manner, yet without the stiffness of the foreign form. The
audience became absorbed by the lively dialogue and overlooked the
comedy's lack of a coherent and meaningful plot and action. The play's
locale, a country spa, and its chief characters, members of the lower
nobility and the upper strata of bourgeois society, increased its overall
appeal to the kind of theater goers for which it was intended. It mattered
little to them that the plot of the comedy was as simple as its action was
shallow. The protagonist, Heinrich Frank, is a studious physician with
high moral and professional principles. Although seemingly attracted to the
orphaned Friederike von Minden, the bright and beautiful ward of his
father, he has serious reservations about her, thinking her much too im-
prudent for his taste. She in turn has been in love with him for a long
time and therefore rejects prospective suitors for her heart and hand.
Predictably, Heinrich and Friederike overcome their differences and join
for life, as does the second couple of young lovers in the play, Hans von
Bonstetten and Marie. In both instances, though in reversed order, a
person of the nobility will marry a member of the bourgeoisie.

With this play Bauernfeld discovered the proper vehicle to launch a successful career as a writer of light comedy. Dozens of plays patterned on this first successful comedy were to follow. Slowly he was able to overcome his lack of imagination and inventive genius by perfecting the psychological profiles of his *dramatis personae*. In this manner he was able to make the clichéd character of his plots less obvious and increase the overall appeal of his comedies. After spinning out such stereotypical clones and slight variants of his first successful play—like *Das Liebesprotokoll* (The Protocol of Love) and *Die ewige Liebe* (Eternal Love) in 1831, *Das letzte Abenteuer* (The Last Adventure) in 1832, and *Die Zusammenkunft am Brunnen* (The Get-Together at the Fountain) in 1833— he reached a higher level of dramatic artistry with Grillparzer's assistance in the three-act comedy *Bekenntnisse* (Confessions), first performed in the Burgtheater on 8 February 1834.

After the dismissal of Schreyvogel as director of the Burgtheater, Bauernfeld was able to establish even friendlier and closer relations with the new and succeeding director Deinhardstein. However, Bauernfeld's success over the years in this prestigious establishment was in no small measure the result of the gifted actor Karl Fichtner, who, beginning with the role of Doctor Frank in *Leichtsinn aus Liebe,* played, indeed personified, Bauernfeld's leading characters to rave reviews in no less than twenty-nine of the forty-five of his plays performed in the Burgtheater. Fichtner's acting range was amazingly broad, extending from lovers and bons vivants to social lions and men of the world. He played these many roles of Bauernfeld types for no less than thirty-four years.[9]

In the comedy *Bekenntnisse* the helpfulness of Grillparzer, who at the time took an especially active interest in both the author and this particular play, produced its success on the stage, not the acting or the plot with its happy union of Bauernfeld's stereotypical couples at the end after the resolution of the usual misunderstanding between them. While the rich Baron von Zinnburg attempts to win the hand of the beautiful widow Anna von Linden for his nephew Adolf, the latter marries Julie, the daughter of the well-to-do entrepreneur Herrmann, although he has learned from his prospective father-in-law that his bride to be may still be infatuated with an earlier love. In order not to make his uncle angry, Adolf keeps his marriage a secret from him and pretends to court the widow. In so doing, however, he arouses the jealousy of a former school-mate of his, the Assessor Bitter, who, as it turns out, not only pursues the widow himself, but was also Julie's former great love. She, on the other hand, follows her husband in the disguise of a lieutenant. Yet in so doing, she arouses the interest of Anna von Linden, who seemingly forgets all about Bitter, who is obviously jealous of the supposed rival. Julie, however, incensed by the infidelity of her former beau, is permanently cured of her youthful infatuation and now gives her full love to her husband Adolf, who in turn can secure the blessing of his uncle for his liaison with Julie, since the older baron had become angry at Anna because of her seemingly choosing the lieutenant over his own choice.

Bauernfeld owed both the psychological refinements of the action and the tightening of its structure to Grillparzer, as he acknowledged:

> The third act of this comedy was partly reworked in accordance with Grillparzer's staging concepts. Thus I owe the author of "Sappho" many beneficial changes, many subtle psychological features, such as in the scene between Julie and Bitter (3rd act, scene nine), in which the latter praises the current flame of his heart in front of the supposed brother of his former love without any regards to Julie's feelings, who—incensed by such deviousness and completely freed from the aftereffects of her first innocent infatuation—rejects the man of her youthful passion now and opens her heart fully to her husband and protector.
>
> I myself drafted the play in three acts but reduced them to two while writing on it rapidly for no longer than a week, as I feared tediousness. Grillparzer, who had taken a friendly interest in me—a young author—for years and to whom I was in the habit of showing all I wrote (especially since Schreyvogel's departure), recognized the poor organization of my comedy. Thus following his advice and incorporating his suggestions and changes, I pretty much restored the third act. (*Ausgewählte Werke,* 2:172)

While *Bekenntnisse* was successfully staged for years, Bauernfeld's next dramatic effort, *Fortunat,* a fairy tale in five acts, failed to meet with the approval of the theater-going public. As the author revealed later, it was based on a romantic sketch which he penned in the 1820s and expanded in the mid-thirties into a full-fledged play. Its fantastic plot, conceived in the vein of Raimund's dramatic fairy tales, was praised by Grillparzer, Tieck, Raupach, and Zedlitz, to whom the author turned for critical appraisal. They all felt that this play was superior to Bauernfeld's previous dramatic efforts, although Grillparzer—ever so prophetic—doubted that it would amount to more than a *succés d'estime.* Deinhardstein, an assistant director of the Burgtheater at the time, tried in vain to have *Fortunat* performed there, but his request was denied by the theater's overseer, Count Czernin, who felt that such "magic shows" ought to be performed in the suburban Theater of the Leopoldstadt.

Bauernfeld, encouraged by the largely favorable reactions his play had received among professionals and close friends, was unwilling to give in. He sought to gain an audience with the emperor himself in order to obtain his personal approval for the performance of *Fortunat* at the court theater. Although these efforts came to naught, Bauernfeld eventually succeeded in having his fairy tale staged at the Theater in the Josefstadt on 24 March 1835, before a well-attended house. Bauernfeld comments about this event:

> It was at the time of my fight with Saphir. His adherents, my enemies, had occupied half the orchestra seats. But my friends were there, too—in short, in those still nonpolitical days, a theatrical faction fight was in the offing, which, in effect, ensued and which, more or less, also encompassed the audience. Nobody seemed basically interested in the play itself.—I sat next to Grillparzer and Zedlitz in a box seat to the end of the third act, at which time all was still relatively peaceful— later we left the comedy to its fate and to the unpredictable public. . . . The play turned out to be a flop and was performed only one more time. Saphir wrote a gloating review laden with jokes. Zedlitz undertook the thankless task of writing a long and serious rebuttal, which offered the "humorist" the opportunity to reply with new jokes.
>
> I myself came recently to the realization that the German theater public will neither now nor in the future accept any such play of fantasy on the stage unless it were presented in the form of a parody. (*Ausgewählte Werke,* 2:216)

The author, obviously disappointed and hurt, was in error here with his negative appraisal of future public taste. Be this as it may, however, his disappointment did not keep him—as was to be the case later with his friend Grillparzer—from continuing to write for the stage. He completed *Bürgerlich und romantisch* (Bourgeois and Romantic), a four-act comedy, a couple of months after the dismal failure of *Fortunat*. This new play, which premiered in the Burgtheater on 7 September 1835, became his most popular and successful work, as he described:

> *Fortunat* had met with failure in March 1835 and I felt initially as though someone had shot me through the heart. But in May I looked at the final script of *Bürgerlich und romantisch*—perhaps my most popular comedy. Saphir, who felt that I poked fun at him in the character of the "paid lackey Unruh (Restless)," threw as much venom at the play and its author as he was capable of doing, and that was no small amount. The public, however, acted in this instance in a highly nonpartisan fashion—that is to say, the people read with great pleasure how I was put down but took their assigned seats in the orchestra and in the boxes with the same amount of delight to enjoy the lampooned play. (*Ausgewählte Werke*, 2:289)

Bauernfeld normally preferred to avoid such negative confrontations, and directed his criticism toward generally positive ends. He also shied away from extremes, especially in his literary opus. As a man of practical views, his philosophy of life aimed for the middle ground. Consequently, the underlying message of *Bürgerlich und romantisch* is as much directed against the eccentricities of Romanticism as it aims to expose the life-killing inhumanity of ossified philistinism.[10]

The plot of this four-act comedy is as typical of Bauernfeld's dramatic ingenuity as its outcome is predictable. In a fashionable spa a Baron Ringelstern meets an unaccompanied woman. Fascinated with her beauty and thinking she is a dancer, he takes liberties with her that one would not venture with a lady of social standing, The woman, Katharine von Rosen, the daughter of a general, is incensed by Ringelstern's behavior and she outrightly rejects his advances. After learning her identity he tries a different approach to capture her heart. He pretends to be a government official, but again he is rejected. His friend, the bathing commissioner

Sittig, who is eager to marry Cäcilie, the daughter of the philistine Councillor Zadern, is pressed by Katharine to take a ride with her. Her plan to get even in this way with Ringelstern backfires, however, for Sittig's morals are suddenly subjected to public gossip and scorn. Now Ringelstern, who turns out to be upright and good-natured after all, explains the situation to his uncle, the council president. As a result, Sittig is promoted and events begin to move in the right direction for all the principal characters. Sittig can now marry Cäcilie, and Ringelstern gains Katharine's hand in marriage after his uncle has informed him that she was his intended bride from the beginning. The play closes with Sittig's conciliatory comment: "Congratulation! (points at knitting frame and stocking) You romantics, as you can see now, don't do things much differently than we commoners." To which Baron Ringelstern replies: "In front of God Amor, we are all equals. But let us pledge never to become philistines!" (*Ausgewählte Werke*. 2:349) Although these recognizably coded lines cannot be taken as outright social and political criticism, they were bold enough, considering the times and the strictness of Metternich's censors, to add to the play's public appeal and to explain its great popularity.

Das Tagebuch (The Diary), a comedy in two acts completed soon after *Bürgerlich und romantisch* and first performed a year later in 1836, was much less bold in social and political terms but psychologically more adept in its story line. The young army captain Wiese married Lucie for her money in order to use her considerable dowry to buy back the old country estate and family seat Fridau and to secure it for his progeny after it seemed lost for lack of funds. When Lucie learns the truth about his original intention to marry her merely for her money without really attempting to get to know her, she resolves to seek revenge by feigning simple-mindedness. As a result, her disappointed husband finds more of a cook in his wife than the soulmate for whom he innately longs. It takes his friend to open his eyes to the ruse and to make him aware what a true jewel his wife really is. However, instead of being happy now, Wiese is overcome by jealousy. This in turn causes Lucie to see that he has at last fallen in love with her. Since she has been in love with him from the very beginning, which she can document by showing him her diary, all obstacles to their marriage have been removed.

From 1836 to 1844 Bauernfeld, more prolific than ever, wrote over a dozen plays, none of which, however, deserves much recognition or exposure. Among them were such run-of-the-mill comedies as *Die Kunst-*

fänger (1836, The Art Catchers), *Der literarische Salon* (1836, The Literary Salon), *Der Vater* (1837, The Father), *Der Selbstquäler* (1837, The Man Who Tortures Himself), *Die Geschwister von Nürnberg* (1840, The Siblings of Nuremberg), *Die Gebesserten* (1840, The Improved Ones), *Ernst und Humor* (1842, Seriousness and Humor), and *Industrie und Herz* (1842, Industry and Heart), which were multiple replicas with different characters, sceneries, and plot variants of his early theme of lovers gone astray or apart and invariably finding ultimate happiness in one another's arms.

More successful was his three-act play *Ein deutscher Krieger* (1844, A German Warrior), which was significant for two reasons. Firstly, according to the author's own statement, it suited its time, sharing the prevailing pro-German nationalistic sentiments of the public. The historic action of the play takes place in the electorate of Saxony in 1648, at the end of the Thirty-Years' War, and addresses national concerns. Secondly, the play expanded on the earlier, ever so subordinated theme of political discussion in *Bürgerlich und romantisch,* leading now to severe censorship restrictions. *Ein deutscher Krieger* ran into such difficulties well into the 1870s. Bauernfeld referred to this work in later years as "a kind of political barometer in Austria" (*Ausgewählte Werke,* 3:3).

What makes this play especially interesting is the fact that it is not one of his perennial comedies but a drama. It contains comic characters and funny scenes, but by and large the overall tenor of *Ein deutscher Krieger* is serious, at times even philosophical in a political sense. It deals not only with the theme of war and peace, but also with the relationship between the French and the Germans in their historic roles of antagonists and enemies in their ongoing struggle for hegemony in Europe. Hand in hand with this historic and political focus goes the theme of nationalism, a still novel and very potent force on the Austro-German stage in these pre-revolutionary years. Its contemporary impact can be gleaned from the words of Büttner, who—although a minor character in the play—addresses them to the protagonist Colonel von Götze, the prototypical upright, brave, and aggressive German soldier: "Well now, Sir, I maintain that there was one Germany and that it will rise again. . . . I maintain that our conquerors are not foreign soldiers, but foreign cooks and foreign tailors (*Ausgewählte Werke,* 3:26).

These words of strong nationalistic convictions are seconded and even enhanced later by the colonel, who at this point is engaged in a heated political discussion with Frau von La Roche, his female French counterpart, representing the national interest of France:

> Above all, it [Germany] is a country, which generates its language
> From within and its spirit in a unique fashion.
> And like the language are the people: a marvelous people. . . .
> And this country and these people are chosen
> By the all-powerful, all-wise deity
> To rejuvenate the aged planet earth,
> To fill this world with a new content,
> And to inject fresh blood into the arteries
> Of a sick, a withering, and an ailing Europe— . . .
> To play the mediator and the peace-maker. . . .
> To divide Germany means not only to weaken Germany,
> But it also means to weaken yourselves. . . .
> The heart of the world—Europe—tumbles with Germany.
>
> (*Ausgewählte Werke,* 3:33)

As the colonel represents Germany's best and bravest, Frau von La Roche is the embodiment of the beauty, courage, nobility, and brilliance of France. Although unyielding enemies at first, while their two nations are still at war, their hearts meet at long last in symbolic union after peace is declared. Frau von La Roche finds the true words of peace while uttering the drama's ultimate message: "Then one moves closer and closer—till at last / They sink into each other's arms as friends. / This is the beautiful era of eternal peace" (*Ausgewählte Werke,* 3:59).

With the blessing of the Elector of Saxony, whose role is somewhat reminiscent of Heinrich von Kleist's elector figure in *Prinz Friedrich von Homburg* (*Prince Frederick of Homburg*)—although less central, not as pronounced, and, above all, less imperious— Colonel von Götze and Frau von La Roche will find each other, as the play ends, in a both symbolic and utopian union, representing their two once inimical countries and nations.

Bauernfeld's interest in politics grew noticeably during the years after he visited Paris and London in 1845. Already in 1842 he had written his first political paper *Pia desideria eines österreichischen Schriftstellers* (Pia Desideria of an Austrian Writer), in which he inveighed against the strictures of censorship. His growing commitment to liberal causes was further strengthened by his preoccupation with Charles Dickens's socio-critical works, leading to Bauernfeld's translation of four of this author's novels in 1844: *Die hinterlassenen Papiere des Pickwick-Club* (*Posthumous Papers of the Pickwick Club*), *Oliver Twist, Leben und Abenteuer Nicholas Nickelbys* (*Life and Adventures of Nicholas Nickelby*), and *Barnaby Rudge.* These translations were followed in 1845 by another politically provocative essay entitled "Denkschrift über die gegenwärtigen Zustände der Zensur in Österreich" (Reflections on the Current State of Affairs of Censorship in Austria). With these activities Bauernfeld became one of the leading liberals who dared to speak up publicly on the Metternich regime's restrictive and backward-looking political practices. In 1845, the year of his visit to Paris and London, he went still one step further in his attack on the repressive rules of the Metternich government and its attempt to stifle liberalism by drafting a petition for the repeal and abolition of all censorship on matters of literary expression.

In 1846, *Großjährig* (Coming of Age), his second play with political undertones to slip through the restrictions of censorship, saw its premiere in the Burgtheater. The author commented himself on this matter with feigned detachment: "I will eventually relate in my "memoirs" how it happened that a comedy in which I poked fun at a "system" prevailing in Austria and its representatives was able nonetheless to get on the politically innocent stage of the Burgtheater" (*Ausgewählte Werke,* 3:61).

The play is a thinly disguised political satire which levels its humorous criticism at the anti-intellectual and artistically stultifying practices of the Metternich system. However, although Bauernfeld frequently throws caution to the wind in this comedy and directs hefty verbal salvos at the regime's excesses, he nevertheless retains balance by depicting both liberals and conservatives as ridiculous, self-centered, bumbling, and therefore comic types. The comedy's youthful male protagonist, Hermann, a miniscule reborn Cherusci prince, represents Germany in this non-historical political farce. His symbolic coming of age, leading to self-determination, is the inner serious message of this otherwise free-wheeling and frolicking comedy. The story line is vintage Bauernfeld. The greedy political conservative Blase welcomes his niece Auguste to his house. He has been her guardian ever since her father passed away. He has also been the guardian of Hermann, the scion of a wealthy aristocratic family. Now that Hermann is coming of age and about to be fully in charge of the family fortune, Blase plots to keep his wealth permanently in his own family. To achieve these ends, he wants to see Hermann marry his niece Auguste. However, the latter thinks Hermann is too passive and immature for her taste and gives him the brush-off. Blase's antagonist in this comedy is the bachelor Schmerl, a forty-five-year-old liberal who not only wants to marry Auguste himself, but who also believes in progress. His favorite expression is "opposition." Blase, on the other hand, only believes in very limited and restricted freedom of thought.

> Thoughts are altogether permitted commodities only as long as they are generated on home ground, namely, in our brain. As soon, however, as they pass the boundary threshold in spoken or written form and are to be smuggled abroad—that is to say, into the heads of other people, the custom officials step in and treat them as contraband.
>
> (*Ausgewählte Werke*, 3:61-62)

Blase's plot to have Schmerl marry Auguste's mother is successful, but his plans for Hermann appear to fail. On being informed of his new status of legal maturity, the latter suddenly becomes bold and independent-minded. Over Blase's objections he proposes reforms in the governance of his land holdings and of the simple people living on this land as his subjects. There is no holding him back now: "The time of my childhood is over—I want to become now what I have promised other people as well as myself: a man, a new man!" (*Ausgewählte Werke*, 3:93).

His transformation is so complete and so convincing that Auguste changes her mind about him and truly falls in love with him. In the end we see the two compatible couples happily united. They all have compromised and they all can now reap their well-balanced rewards. Even Blase's original wish comes true. He and Schmerl acknowledge and accept the change in Hermann's life: "What good is freedom if one has no ideas?. . . What good are ideas if one has no freedom?" (*Ausgewählte Werke*, 3:95).

At this time in his life, it looked as though Bauernfeld would commit himself as a fighter for individual and collective freedoms of thoughts, ideas, and actions. In 1847 he published a treatise, the title of which reveals its content, "Schreiben eines Privilegierten aus Österreich zur Beleuchtung der merkwürdigen Broschüre: über Denk-, Rede-, Schrift-, und Preßfreiheit" (Paper of a Privileged Austrian to Clarify the Remarkable Brochure: On Freedom of Thought, Speech, Written Expressions, and the

Press). Although his paper did not call for a complete repeal of censorship, it was still significant in that it proposed a return to earlier, more relaxed standards of speech and press control. In addition, Bauernfeld castigated the ideas and practices of the archconservative Baron Clemens von Hügel. But even in this political treatise, Bauernfeld displayed his innate sense of humor:

> The pious hypocrites, the censors, the police, will say no—and if they had their way, nothing of the great ideas of . . . [the] great minds would have been passed on to us. . . . Those great men have now and then made mistakes—who denies that? . . . But are we to destroy the single work because of some weakness, or even prevent it from being conceived? . . . Are we to expunge a work, the destiny of which it is perhaps to influence the development of mankind, simply because some immature people could be angered by it?—Heavens! If one of these men, let us say Spinoza, were to live today, were to live in Austria and were to hand over his *Principia* or his *Cogitata metaphysica* to Austrian censorship, and the latter were to express its ever so popular "damnatur" about the one or the other item, but were to give the author out of a certain sense of national and jovial respect the advice from the brochure: to write in accordance with the censorship instructions of 1810 and perhaps to occupy a chair in the philological faculty of the academy—imagine what kind of expression poor Spinoza would have on his face![11]

Bauernfeld followed this, by all contemporary measures, remarkable paper at the beginning of the revolutionary year of 1848 with increased political activities, which led to further journalistic exploits. These undertakings catapulted him into the forefront of politically active Austrian writers and intellectuals. Liberal circles in Vienna embraced him now as a comrade-in-arms and increasingly implored him to become a major outlet and spokesman for their political and civic grievances. Buoyed by this public acclaim, he fashioned in collaboration with the prominent politician Alexander Bach a short but strongly worded petition demanding a constitution and freedom of the press. Persistently and bravely, he pressured the authorities to loosen their stranglehold on individual liberties and to give the people a voice in public affairs. The petition reads in part:

> For a number of years, every true supporter of our country has felt the strong desire and many a one vociferously has expressed in speech and in writing the necessity of wanting to see our beautiful and powerful Austria enter upon the path of peaceful and genuine progress. . . . If Austria's citizens feel above all compelled to express their unshakable love and devotion to the illustrious imperial family, they consider it at the same time their sacred obligation to state those measures openly and freely which, in their opinion, are solely and uniquely qualified to provide the dynasty as well as our whole country with renewed strength and a new foundation in these threatening times.
>
> These measures are: Immediate publication of the government budget;—periodical summoning of a diet representing all the lands of the monarchy as well as the classes and interests of the people with the right of approval of taxes and of budget control as well as of participation in legislation;—creation of protective covenants for the press by introducing a statute of obstruction;—implementation of the maxim of public participation in the administration of justice and in all administration;—the granting of an up-to-date municipal and community constitution and, based upon it, representation in the areas of agriculture, industry, commerce, and human services, which is not at all or only partially implemented in the current . . . constitution.[12]

This petition was passed on to the proper authorities on 11 March 1848. Two days later, on 13 March, Bauernfeld, accompanied at the time by the writer Anastasius Grün, looked from his window at an exalted crowd pushing into the courtyard of the parliament building, and on 15 March, after two more exciting days had passed, he rushed with Anastasius Grün to the emperor's residence and secured the immediate acceptance of the proposed constitution.

On this momentous day of political triumph, Bauernfeld and Anastasius Grün also partook in events of a less personal nature. They witnessed the arrival of a delegation of Hungarian deputies led by the charismatic revolutionary Kossuth himself. The author described this event in later years in his book of reminiscences *Aus Alt- und Neu-Wien:*

> We came to Michaels Square. It was just about noon. A speaker had mounted a barrel and harangued the people in full view of the military, the canon. The ideas of social democracy, never before heard in politically innocent Vienna, reverberated in our ears and found credulous, indeed enraptured, listeners in the naive populace. I don't deny that I was amazed, indeed frightened. Who can ascertain how these utopian ideals of the abolition of private property, of the sharing of possessions and other such ideas would affect an already overly excited, uneducated mob! In short, anarchy was clearly visible to me at Michaels Square—to my sensibilities the ugliest monster one could conceive of!
>
> (*Ausgewählte Werke,* 4:173)[13]

On the next day, 16 March, Kossuth attempted to visit Bauernfeld personally but did not find him at home. Bauernfeld felt obliged the following day to seek out Kossuth in his hotel. Yet, by his own admission, he failed to meet the revolutionary firebrand because he lacked the courage to go through with it. In retrospect, it seems obvious that the revolutionary events, the concomitant excitement, and his own unaccustomed political prominence—he was on the verge of being appointed a minister of the new post-Metternich Austrian government and was also chosen, again together with his friend Anastasius Grün, to go as a representative to the all-German Frankfurt Parliament—were too much for him. When on the following morning of 18 March, a delegation of the new diet visited him at home, among them Alexander Bach and other political friends whom he had invited for breakfast, Bauernfeld, on being offered the minister post, lost—in his own words—his "strength and conscience and had to be carried to bed. A severe case of encephalitis had set in" (*Ausgewählte Werke,* 4:179). He stayed in bed for over a week and upon his alleged recovery withdrew from all further political activities.

At this point, one feels compelled to speculate that Bauernfeld, realizing that he was politically over his head and unwilling to go any further in this area, feigned, at least in part, his illness as the only way out of his unwelcome status of political prominence and fame. It seems that—skeptical by nature and sensing that the revolution would fail—he lacked the courage to continue in this role of a political radical and revolutionary, into which his honest liberal convictions and fate itself had pushed him earlier. Illness, as can be surmised, remained the only safe refuge for him, the only honorable way out of the political morass in which he found himself and which threatened to envelop and submerge him. To be sure, these days and weeks in the political limelight had not only caused him agony, but had also opened his eyes and led to a sobering process in him. He suddenly recognized that the political world could not be seen in the stark contrast of black and white. There were many areas in which shades of gray prevailed. Radicalism, excesses, abuse of power, and violence could be seen on both sides of the political conflict in this revolutionary year.

Much of what Bauernfeld had seen and many of the political lessons he had learned are reflected in his next play, the satirical drama *Die Republik der Tiere* (1848, The Republic of Animals). Following the tradition of the Viennese popular stage and also that of the Greek comedy of Aristophanes, the author employed the ancient model of the animal fable to make his political point. By these means he portrays some of the actual happenings of the revolution in allegorical form. As a subterfuge he shows supposed events and episodes of the French Revolution.

The play is loosely organized. Bauernfeld is less interested in the step by step development of a coherent plot in this play as he is inclined to depict the outer and inner forces of the revolutionary process. Nor is he about to glorify the revolution as such. The negative and seamy sides of the revolutionary struggle are depicted, and the action, like its true historic model, ends with the failure of the revolution. Real life and actual historic happenings are portrayed on the stage. After the revolution collapses, the political and historic clocks are turned back to the *status quo ante.*

While with public approval Nachtigall (Nightingale), the idealistic protagonist and freedom fighter, is to be guillotined, the General of the Eisbären (Polar Bears) and Walrosse (Walruses) moves in with his forces and puts the Drachen (Dragon) back in power. The other animals are less ingeniously chosen. The author follows popular clichés in their selection. The minister who restores the ancient regime through clever tactics and political manipulations is represented by a fox. The imperial aristocracy is depicted in the guise of such animals as the hyena, leopard, tiger, and panther, while fierce dogs prepare their howling appeal to the people in the office of a newspaper. Even more satirical is the figure of the chief of police, portrayed as an ox and addressed as his "Oxcellenz." The well-to-do burgher, enthusiastically praising law and order while chewing on a big cigar, is the appropriately fat Hamster. His complacency and happiness are much subdued, however, when the tax collectors Kellerratte (Cellar Rat) and an army of spiders take his fortune away. A major exception in this satirically castigated animal kingdom is the king himself. He is presented in human form and surrounded by *Melancholie* (Melancholy) and *Sentimentalität* (Sentimentality). His moving words of departure and his lonely death add a measure of sobriety to the otherwise comic action. Yet the play as a whole still lacks a central focus, a moral, or even a political message beyond the obvious happenings. As it unfolds, it becomes more and more diffused and ends in a cryptic and nearly utopian vein with an epilogue in which vague references to the dawning of a new age are uttered.

This play clearly reflected Bauernfeld's own innermost thoughts after his own withdrawal from political activity and the revolution in October 1848, which had begun so hopefully and auspiciously in March. He was now about to enter a period of rude awakening, even contemplating for a while to leave his native Austria altogether. As his political ambitions fizzled out and the bitter taste of withdrawal entered his subconscience, a welcome turn of events gave him new buoyancy. He was elected to the *Wiener Akademie der Wissenschaften* (Vienna Academy of Sciences and Humanities). Now that the old monarchy returned for the most part to its old ways of rule, he felt obliged to go back to his earlier vocation of being just a playwright and would voice any commentary on past and present happenings in his society in a strictly nonpartisan and rather apolitical fashion.

Yet he soon discovered that time and the world did not stand still. While, as in past years, he intermingled his standard fare of comedies with occasional dramas, it soon became apparent to him that his time as a major player on the drama stage of the Austrian theater had passed. All the plays he wrote after 1848 met with little success. Not that he had become devoid of ideas. He continued to write with indefatigable zeal and sizable productivity. Among the near score of plays he wrote after 1848 was *Der kategorische Imperativ* (The Categorical Imperative), which was produced with little success in 1851. The public showed little taste for its sophistication, nor did it appreciate the comedy's allusions to Kant's famous theorem. Grillparzer, who had in the previous year denounced Bauernfeld's political attitude in his *Erinnerungen aus dem Revolutionsjahr 1848* (Recollections of the Revolutionary Year 1848), also criticized the play, accusing him of political naiveté and lust for popularity, thereby also signaling the end of their friendship. Yet, Grillparzer served as one of five judges who had recommended this comedy as the winning entry in a competition which Laube, the Burgtheater director at that time, sponsored for new comedies. Bauernfeld's four-act drama *Krisen* (Crisis), performed at the Burgtheater in November 1852 and initially inspired by Voltaire's *Memnon ou la sagesse humaine* (*Ausgewählte Werke*, 3:103), was less successful, as were his later plays *Aus der Gesellschaft* (From Society) and *Moderne Jugend* (Modern Youth), performed in 1867 and 1869 respectively.

In *Aus der Gesellschaft* the author had tried his best to present a play with a social message that he felt strongly about, the idea that all those who strive and prove themselves to be competent and efficient deserve fullest recognition and must be looked upon as true equals, even if they are of a lower social status. Following this forward-looking theme, Bauernfeld returned to his older theme of misalliance in the three-act comedy *Moderne Jugend*. Count Rietberg, who, as his symbolic name implies, is a bachelor past his prime, intends to marry the beautiful widow Julie Braun. But when her daughter Else returns from boarding school, he falls in love with her, and she accepts his proposal. Bauernfeld presents this theme in a punitive manner. It is perhaps noteworthy that the author himself never married.

As entertaining as this dramatic fare was, the great success of his earlier plays eluded him in these social comedies. This remains true also of his later comic plays *Die reiche Erbin* (1876, The Rich Heiress) and *Die Verlassenen* (1878, The Abandoned). His verse comedy *Der Landfrieden: Deutsche Komödie in drei Akten* (Public Peace: A German Comedy in Three Acts)—written in 1869 and performed in the Burgtheater in 1870—with which Bauernfeld hoped in vain to have created the apotheosis of his poetic endeavors, must also be looked upon as an outright failure. The public, in fact, reacted cooly to the semi-historical plot concerning the abduction of Katharina Menzinger, the beautiful daughter of an Augsburg patrician, by squire Robert, who had fallen in love with her. Although Katharina returns his feelings, Robert is still guilty of having broken the law. However, since he is Emperor Maximilian's natural son, he escapes prosecution and is allowed to unite permanently and legally with Katharina.

This plot makes it clear why Bauernfeld's plays after 1848 failed to meet with the same level of public approval that his earlier plays had achieved. His stance as *Altliberaler* (old-fashioned liberal), which he proudly and happily assumed in the socio-political arena after 1848 was also reflected in his writings. Even in more forward-looking plays, such as *Aus der Gesellschaft*, his light-hearted conversational style was considered outdated. The public and the critics were ready for the dawn of a new era in the theater which was to come soon with the approaching age of literary Naturalism. Moreover, the ever broader masses of theater goers wanted to see plays that suited their less sophisticated taste in theme and message as well as style. This may explain why Raimund's and Nestroy's folksier plays continued to pass the test of time in later years and remained perennial public favorites on the stage while Bauernfeld's output progressively disappeared from the repertory altogether. His themes, pitting the old nobility against the upwardly mobile bourgeoisie, lost much of their earlier appeal toward the end of the century, when Social Democrats and Christian Socialists were catapulted into growing public and political prominence with their messages of social equality.[14]

To be sure, there is evidence that the author sensed this decline in his dramatic popularity. He broadened his literary output after 1848, attempting to achieve success with essays, narrative prose, and poetry. Two factors helped him in his endeavors: he gained more time and freedom by achieving the possibility of leaving his hated government post with a pension in 1849 at the relatively early age of forty-seven; and his financial security was further buttressed by generous royalties from the performances of his plays. At the age of eighty he received the handsome sum of 3,500 guilders for life from the Burgtheater. In his later years he was generally admired as a representative and even a symbol of old Vienna. Venerated and much celebrated on his seventieth and eightieth birthdays, he was made an honorary citizen of Vienna in 1872 and he received the meritorious Franz Joseph Medal from the emperor himself. In addition, his government pension was tripled. In 1883 the University of Vienna honored him with an honorary degree. Shortly thereafter, the Burgtheater performed his tragedy *Des Alkibiades Ausgang* (The Exit of Alcibiades) as a further tribute.

In the last two decades of his long life Bauernfeld polished his prose, principally collected in his autobiographical and culturally enriched collection of essays entitled *Aus Alt- und Neu-Wien,* which was published in 1873. Many of these essays had previously appeared in the *Neue Freie Presse* (New Free Press), in the *Konkordiakalender* (Concordia Calendar) in Vienna, in the Berlin *Gegenwart* (Our Time), and the *Berliner Salon.* The broad range of topics extends from recollections of early formative years to his friendships with leading contemporary literary and artistic personalities and from the prerevolutionary fervor of Old Vienna, via the promising days of March 1848, to the postrevolutionary and reactionary political debacle of the later years. They end on a prophetically sounding note of admonition and exhortation:

> Political and religious freedoms are beautiful gifts. But they do not fall into our laps from one day to the next. Only education leads to the beautiful goal, ongoing, incessant education. The question of [better] schools is a question of basic existence for Austria-Hungary. Regrettably, the unholy "system" has postponed a solution for over half a century and big children and old nations do not want to learn anything anymore.
>
> Surely, only what is good, beautiful, and true
> Is of everlasting value—. . .
> Truth will not come your way,
> Unless you strive for it every day. . . .
> Religious doctrine you may decry
> And shy away from preaching fools,
> But if your level of knowledge is not high,
> Only one thing helps: Go to schools!
> (*Ausgewählte Werke,* 4:222)

His novel *Die Freigelassenen: Bildungsgeschichte aus Österreich* (The People Who Have Been Freed: A Developmental Tale from Austria), published in 1875, is of fleeting interest today if we approach it merely as an example of Bauernfeld's skill as a novelist or for its status of being his longest work of fiction. The chief quality of this lengthy prose work in two volumes does not lie in its, to a great extent, unimaginative plot or its dated style but in the fact that it is a significant document of his age. Bauernfeld's descriptions of local color and background combined with his personal memoirs—which are only partially contained in *Aus Alt- und*

Neu-Wien—invest the work with lasting cultural and historic value. The author chose Goethe's dictum, "We all draw life from our past and perish of our past,"[15] as the novel's motto. The story line bears out this rather pessimistic view.

The two-part novel deals with lives and events leading up to and following the Revolution of 1848. Part one, entitled "Friedliche Zeiten" (Peaceful Times), ends with the ides of March 1848. Part two, appropriately called "Stürme" (Storms), focuses on the revolutionary happenings themselves, leading to the revolution's collapse and to the reactionary times following it. This segment concludes chronologically with the financial crash of 1873. Within this historical background Bauernfeld sets a typical love affair, as found in his comedies, the socially still not condoned misalliance between a commoner and a member of the aristocracy. The fact, however, that the commoner Karl Günter and the Countess Weissenstein leave Austria after their wedding and found a colony in Texas adds a measure of novelty to Bauernfeld's usual plots. Yet, after twenty years in America, the still happily united couple returns to Austria in order to settle there again permanently. The very last lines of the novel, however, already stated at the beginning, "We all draw life from our past and perish of our past," add, via the technique of a completed circle, a measure of nostalgia, but also some unmistakable sarcasm to the ultimate message of the novel: Return to your roots. There appears to be no better solution. This advice is, in Bauernfeld's view, also applicable to Austria itself. As the couple's friend Chalybeus states in the work's epilogue: The sea attracts the rivers. We return to where we came from. The real Germany has not emerged yet, but it must come, and the wave, German-Austria, must flow back to its original source."[16]

In the final analysis, however, both the title *Die Freigelassenen* as well as the subtitle *Bildungsgeschichte aus Österreich* add a touch of irony to the serious admonition of the novel to return to one's roots. The couple was never completely free to follow its inclinations in the Goethean sense to begin with; the two were only set free to end up ultimately where they started. Thus the novel cannot be called a *Bildungsroman* (developmental novel), nor should it be so named in Bauernfeld's eyes, but at most, and not without sarcasm, a developmental "tale from Austria." Seen from this vantage point, the novel, though far from being a masterpiece, is Bauernfeld's subtle way of paying the Austrian authorities back for the many years of political frustration that he suffered. The novel also makes clear his pro-

German, if not pan-German, nationalistic sentiments.

When Bauernfeld died in Vienna on 9 August 1890, he left a voluminous work behind that had failed to survive him. He was both intellectually and stylistically out of touch with the mindset of the ensuing 1890s, which saw the rise to prominence of such writers as Arthur Schnitzler, Hugo von Hofmannsthal, and Hermann Bahr. Today Bauernfeld's importance lies chiefly in his autobiographical writings and his commentaries on the changing cultural, social, and political scene of the "Old Vienna" he knew and witnessed. As a playwright, poet, and novelist, he achieved nothing of lasting value. His biographer Emil Horner pointed to his flair for combining his writings with self-promotion and publicity. He calls this tendency a necessary byproduct of the epoch in which Bauernfeld wrote. It should be added that for most of his life the author needed the income from his works and achieved financial security only during his last years. He had to fend for himself to the best of his ability, learning from his early youth onward literally to "stretch with the blanket." (*Ausgewählte Werke,* 1:LV). His social ideals of treading the middle ground and of seeking balance and restraint, leading to intellectual resignation, reflect this lifelong struggle for subsistence and existence. Yet he never fully forsook his ever so subtle critique of social prejudice on the part of the upper classes and of the regimentation and the patronizing attitude of the political establishment.

One of his major limitations was the restrictive atmosphere and scope of his portrayal of society, in which he failed to stress the vast differences between the social classes.[17] He was a "moralist" in the French sense, focusing on the *mores* of his day and age rather that on the *morals.* Some of his contemporaries such as Karl Gutzkow took him to task for that, calling him a "spoiler." Julian Schmidt, another contemporary critic, says of Bauernfeld: "His language is nobler than that of Benedix; his vocabulary is that of the educated; his remarks are to some extent very refined. On the other hand, his imagination is not very great, and the good mood, which he, in fact, displays, is not as rollicking as one might expect in a comedy [writer] of a higher class."[18]

It was a peculiar trademark of Bauernfeld's not to draw his characters sharply. The author was aware of this deficiency and counted on the actors to round out his characters in their own image or in line with their own moods and sensibilities.[19] Grillparzer had slightly different ideas about Bauernfeld's approach to characterization: "Bauernfeld is very good in the characterization of his minor characters, since he can depict them in a negative light and needs to introduce them only intermittently by leaps and bounds. The characterization of his protagonists is insignificant and very general."[20]

Bauernfeld realized some of these shortcomings himself and remained humble about his literary importance. He could look at himself with humorous detachment, as seen in his *Poetisches Tagebuch,* his last major literary work published three years before his death:

> When I was young, I was ashamed
> To show my enthusiasm galore,
> Now that I'm getting old, I can't
> Be enthusiastic anymore.
> (*Ausgewählte Werke,* 1:99)

His advice to anyone seeking public recognition is contained in a another of his humorous aphorisms:

> How to create a lasting public image?
> Don't ask!
> From youth to ripe old age
> Always wear the same old mask.
> (*Ausgewählte Werke,* 1:99)

Notes

1. See the Preface in *Bauernfelds Ausgewählte Werke in vier Bänden*, ed. Emil Horner (Leipzig: Max Hesse, n.d.), vol. 1, p. ix. Subsequent references to these volumes will be incorporated into the text.
2. Compare Dolores Hornbach Whelan, *Gesellschaft im Wandel. Der Engel mausert sich: Das Bild der Frau in den Komödien Eduard von Bauernfelds 1830-1870* (Frankfurt am Main: Peter Lang, 1978), p. 14.
3. Eduard von Bauernfeld, "Aus Alt- und Neu-Wien," in *Dichtung aus Österreich,* ed. Robert Mühlher and Schmitz-Mayr-Harting (Vienna: Österreichischer Bundesverlag, 1969), vol. 1, p. 184.
4. Eduard von Bauernfeld, *Bilder und Persönlichkeiten aus Alt-Wien,* ed. Wilhelm Zentner (Altötting: Hans Geiselberg, 1948), p. 10.

5. This translation as well as all other renderings of original German quotations and materials into English are my own.

6. Compare Josef Nadler, *Franz Grillparzer* (Vienna: Bergland, 1952), pp. 100-101.

7. See Joachim Müller, *Franz Grillparzer* (Stuttgart: Metzler, 1966), p. 41.

8. Franz Grillparzer, *Sämtliche Werke: Ausgewählte Briefe, Gespräche, Berichte* (Munich: Hanser, 1965), vol. 4, pp. 211-212.

9. *Dichtung aus Österreich: Drama.* eds. Heinz Kindermann and Margaret Dietrich (Vienna: Österreichischer Bundesverlag, 1966), p. 57.

10. Compare Zentner, p. 9.

11. *Eduard von Bauernfelds gesammelte Aufsätze*, ed. Stefan Hock (Vienna: Verlag des Literarischen Vereins in Wien, 1905), pp. 44-45.

12. Ibid., pp. 54-55.

13. See W.E. Yates, *Grillparzer* (Cambridge: University Press, pp. 31-32.

14. Compare Whelan, p. 15.

15. Eduard von Bauernfeld, *Die Freigelassenen: Bildungsgeschichte aus Österreich* (Berlin: Otto Janke, 1875), vol. 1, p. 1; vol. 2, p. 267.

16. Ibid., vol. 2, p. 266.

17. See Friedrich Sengle, *Biedermeierzeit,* vol. 2, *Die Formenwelt* (Stuttgart: Metzler, 1972), p. 423.

18. Julian Smith, *Geschichte der deutschen Literatur im neunzehnten Jahrhundert* (Leipzig: Herbig, 1855), vol. 3. p. 213.

19. Kinderman and Dietrich, p. 58.

20. Franz Grillparzer, *Samtliche Werke,* vol 1, p. 817.

Bibliography

I. Major Works by Eduard von Bauernfeld in German

Ausgewählte Werke in vier Bänden. Ed. Emil Horner. Leipzig: Max Hesse, no date.

1. Einleitung—Reime und Rhythmen
2. Das Liebesprotokoll—Die ewige Liebe—Helene—DieBekenntnisse—Fortunat—Bürgerlich und romantisch
3. Ein deutscher Krieger—Großjährig—Krisen—Aus der Gesellschaft—Landfrieden
4. Aus Alt- und Neu-Wien

Bilder und Persönlichkeiten aus Alt-Wien. Ed. Wilhelm Zentner. Altötting: Hans Geiselberg, 1948.

Die Freigelassenen: Bildungsgeschichte aus Österreich. Berlin: Otto Janke, 1875.

Gesammelte Aufsätze. Ed. Stephan Hock. Vienna: Literarischer Verein, 1905.

Wiener Biedermeier: Begegnungen und Erlebnisse. Ed. Karl Jordak. Vienna: Bergland, 1960.

II. Works in English Translation
None

III. Secondary Works in English
None

IV. Major Studies in German

Horner, Emil. *Bauernfeld.* Leipzig: E.A. Seemann, 1900.

Nathansky, Alfred. *Bauernfeld und Schubert.* Vienna: R. Fromme, 1906.

Steiner, Carl. "Eduard von Bauernfeld (1802-1890). Eine vergessene Größe," in: Carl Steiner, *Aus alter und neuer Welt. Essays und Gedichte.* Vienna: Braumüller, 1995.

Whelan, Dolores Hornbach. *Gesellschaft im Wandel. Der Engel mausert sich: Das Bild der Frau in den Komödien Eduard von Bauernfeld 1830-1870.* Bern/Las Vegas: Peter Lang, 1978.

Jakob Julius David

Florian Krobb

The few published letters of Jakob Julius David (1859-1906) display one striking feature: David seems to have been constantly at odds with his fate. He comes across as ceaselessly complaining about his living conditions, his ability to work and to earn his livelihood, the recognition his work received, and not least his health. His friend and mentor Erich Schmidt, in the foreword to his edition of David's *Gesammelte Werke* (1908/1909, Collected Works), relates a farewell letter with one last plea for recognition: "I compare [my work] with what others have achieved [and] I think I pass the test; I think it would be unjust if I were to be totally forgotten."[1]

Erich Schmidt understood this as a request to look after David's literary legacy and preserve it for posterity. A large number of subscribers—the list at the end of volume six reads like a "Who's Who" of turn-of-the-century Vienna[2]—ensured the appearance of the *Gesammelte Werke* in 1908. In an obituary for the *Österreichische Rundschau* Stefan Zweig reiterated David's resentment, at the same time voicing the contemporaries' shame at having ignored and neglected this major protagonist of Austrian letters: "And then his bitterness: . . . What he said to us must now be said publicly: how a poet, one of the best in Austria, has been treated with disdain. One must point the finger at a German-reading public and its leaders, who begrudged him the opportunity to read the words 'second edition' on the most perfect works.[3] In spite of such high esteem from his contemporaries,[4] it seems as if David's last wish fell on deaf ears: today he is an almost forgotton author and, some critics believe, rightly so. In a brief entry in a recent collection of portraits of unknown Austrian authors, Hans Heinz Hahnl reaches the verdict: "I am afraid his work cannot be salvaged."[5] However, contrary to his own belief his contemporaries perceived him as very much an integral part of the Viennese literary scene of the 1890s: his *Lieder von der Straße* (Songs from the Street) were recited at the first meeting of the Neue Freie Bühne; and his two small collections of occasional works *Wunderliche Heilige* (1906, Wondrous Saints) and *Stromabwärts* (1903, Downstream) were published in a series of the *Wiener Verlag* alongside collections by many important representatives of modern tendencies in German and Austrian literature: Arthur Schnitzler, Hugo von Hofmannsthal, Felix Salten, Felix Dörmann, Otto Julius Bierbaum, Johannes Schlaf, and Heinrich Mann, to name but a few of the authors in the *Bibliothek moderner deutscher Autoren* (Library of Modern German Authors). Both of David's volumes feature fashionable *Jugendstil* graphic ornamentation which seems quite inappropriate as none of the stories contained in the volumes vindicates such an association.[6]

David cannot easily be counted as a representative of one particular school. The first critical appreciations emphasized his vivid and colorful portraits of Moravian rural life ("A profound exploration of the peasant soul seemed to be David's vocation in life").[7] This fact was quickly seized on by German nationalist critics: "To the highest degree he combines qualities which the German is used to considering with pride to be specifically his own."[8] In the 1930s, "völkisch" ideologists labeled him a *Heimatkünstler* (provincial writer) "in the full, unhackneyed, original meaning of the word," and his writings "*Heimatkunst* with a genuinely national effect,"[8]—thus making the Jewish-born Moravian who lived in Vienna all his adult life a literary pioneer of Nazism. In spite of this misuse the stories set in Moravia are still widely regarded as his most important and mature efforts, which introduced this region into the realm of German literature. David's beginnings clearly lie in Realism and sometimes seem slightly epigonal; yet recent scholarship has stressed that this author should be seen as the only main representative of Naturalism in Austrian literature, and that many themes and features in his writings display more resemblances to other literary movements of the time than has previously been recognized. His posthumous works even reveal the influence of the innovative tendencies of contemporary literature, namely, a subjective, impressionistic style.[10] Generally speaking, David's contribution to turn-of-the-century Austrian literature has not yet been fully appreciated. Many of his texts might not appeal to the taste of the late twentieth-century reader, and whether his works are actually read in the German-speaking countries today must be very doubtful. Yet not only his position in the context of his time, but the diversity and nature of his *oeuvre* itself make him more than just an interesting, but a major figure in Austrian literature.

I. David's Life

Very little is actually known about David's life. The source of almost all information remains Ella Spiero's biography of 1920. Only one rather short autobiographical account by David himself is known; his contribution to the column *Im Spiegel* (In the Mirror) in the January 1902 issue of *Das Literarische Echo*. In this article he frames the story of his life with the two features he always regarded most positively: his rural Moravian origin and his late but happy family life: "I was born on the 6th of February 1859 in Weißkirchen in Moravia. My childhood was spent in Fulnek, the main town of the so-called Kuhländchen." He closes his report with the laconic but deceptively joyous statement: "I am married and the father of one single child, a daughter who gives me a lot of joy."[11]

Indeed, the bulk of his life—his later youth, the first two decades in Vienna, and the last few years before his death in 1906—was marked by hardship, illness, and the absence of literary success. At least this is the way the author saw it himself: a hint of self-pity is evident in most of his remarks. In letters to Marie von Ebner-Eschenbach he complains: "My voice is not loud enough and I have no luck" and: "I am like Moses, clumsy in conversation, both spoken and written."[12] Several years later his colleague Adolf Pichler is the recipient of another of David's laments: "I am approaching my fortieth year. There remains little prospect any more of fruitful production for someone who has had to slave and struggle so much."[13] As an epitaph he chose the words "Er starb am Wege—he died en route," with reference to the title of one of his novels *Am Wege sterben* (1900, Dying en route), indicating how he wanted to be remembered by posterity: as somebody who was not allowed to mature. In another letter to Ebner-Eschenbach he comments on an imminent excursion to Moravia: "One of the next week [sic] I will start my travels. . . . Honestly—it is a last desperate attempt to become master of myself."[14]

David's life can be understood as one great unsuccessful attempt to master his fate; a constant fight against the odds. He hails from the periphery of the Habsburg Empire, a region between the Czech and Hungarian parts of the Danube Monarchy, close to Prussian Silesia, Russian Podolia, and Austrian Galicia, yet through the river March oriented towards the Empire's center, Vienna. David's father came from a privileged Jewish family; as a fairly well-off tobacco merchant he was integrated into the social order of this agrarian country with its numerous market towns in which the first signs of industrialization were starting to become apparent. The problems of immigration and ethnic tensions were only just emerging.

During the nineteenth century, middle-class Jews became a Germanizing factor in Moravia; in David's family German was the first language, and naturally it was expected that Jakob should go to the German Grammar School. Cholera, following the armies in the Austro-Prussian war of 1866, killed David's sister and father. Deprived of its breadwinner, the family became quickly impoverished, and David was put into the care of various friends and distant relatives. From 1869 he attended the Grammar Schools in Kremsier, Teschen, and Troppau. David seems to have been a very bad student: he was expelled from one school and had to repeat a class. A bout of typhoid he contracted as a teenager left him shortsighted and partially deaf. Still, the multicultural market towns of the region, steeped in history, and impressions from the Slovak farming communities in the fertile farmland between the river March and its tributary, the river Hanna, left deep imprints on his imagination.

In 1877 David entered the University of Vienna to study education, history, and German literature, thus joining the steady stream of migrants into the melting-pot center of the Empire. During his first years there the living conditions must have been dreadful for the penniless young man, and hunger an all-too-frequent guest; he had to earn his living as a copyist. Some of the despair and misery he experienced found its way into his novel *Am Wege sterben* and into several of his novellas. As his disability prevented him from pursuing a career in teaching (his preferred profession) he had to seek other sources of income. The mid-1880s brought about a slight improvement in David's situation. After passing parts of his examinations he was able to find work as a private tutor, his acquaintance with Karl Emil Franzos led to the publication of two poems in the *Deutsches Dichterbuch aus Österreich* (1883, German Poetry Book from Austria) and eventually to a job at the *Wiener Neue Illustrierte Zeitung* (Vienna New Illustrated Newspaper). In 1889 he completed his doctorate with a thesis entitled *Zur Psychologie Heinrich Pestalozzis* (On Heinrich Pestalozzi's Psychology). The second half of the 1880s saw David's romance with the witty and urbane writer Baroness Hermance de Potiers, a relationship doomed to failure not least because of David's insecure social position and his apparent lack of all social graces.

On 28 May 1891 David converted to Roman Catholicism.[15] From the available documents on his life, it appears that David never mentioned or explained this move. The Jewish figures in his work reveal very little about his self-assessment as a Jew, and the problem of anti-Semitism, increasingly pronounced in the last decades of the nineteenth century, does not feature at all in his writings.[16] The conversion might simply have been meant as a conclusion of his integration into non-Jewish society; the step facilitated his marriage to a Catholic, Juliane Christine Ostruszka, three days later. David never denied his Jewish origins, and he did not replace his original first name Jakob, but added the non-Hebrew 'Christian' name Julius to form the double name under which he became known as an author.

David had married Christiane Ostruszka after his first moderate successes as a writer. Their only child Marlene was born soon after. To support his family David had to take up journalistic work again, an obligation from which he continually suffered as he saw it distracting from his literary vocation and sapping the energy he would have liked to devote to his art. But the insights into the media business which he gained on this treadmill were used in his essays *Die Zeitung* and *Von der Zeitung* (The Newspaper and On the Newspaper, both 1906), his sharpest and politically most outspoken nonfictional pieces. For a long time he toiled freelance for several Viennese papers like *Wiener Mode, Zeit, Waage*, and *Montagsrevue*; he held an editorship at the *Neues Wiener Journal*. From 1894 until 1903, when a broken leg that failed to heal forced him to retire from this secure post. Only two years later a bronchial cancer turned dangerous and confined David to his bed. His last concern was to ensure the subsistence of his family. Membership in the writers' insurance association *Concordia* and a stipend from the Bauernfeld trust saw to that. Jakob Julius David died on 20 November 1906 at the age of only forty-seven.

David's active life as a writer lasted less than twenty years—his first book, *Das Höferecht* (The Farm Law) was published in 1890, his major essays appeared in the year of his death 1906. David's *oeuvre* comprises poems, four plays, three novels, twenty-six major novellas und several minor ones published in his lifetime, three fragments of novellas from his unpublished literary legacy, and countless essays, sketches, newspaper and magazine articles. David himself felt very strongly that he did not achieve as much as he would have liked, and especially that he was prevented from realizing his full potential. In his farewell letter to Erich Schmidt he sums up: "I look back over my work: of course it remained and will remain fragmentary, as is natural for somebody who first and foremost had to earn his bread."[17] Whether David could have achieved more had he lived longer is of course a matter for speculation. In which direction he would have liked to develop in order to reach his goal, he did not say. What David left to posterity is evidently not the inspired work of a literary genius, but rather the result of a lifelong struggle and wearying effort.

II. The Poetry

During his lifetime David's poems appeared in one volume simply entitled *Gedichte* (1892, Poems). A quarrel over a new, extended edition of his poems led to the breach with his long-standing publisher and friend Heinrich Minden in 1899. A second edition of poems never appeared.

"Und meine Muse heißt sich Not—And my Muse is deprivation"—this last line of the poem *Meine Muse* (My Muse) could be considered a motto for David's entire work. *Meine Muse* is the first piece in the series of poems entitled *Lieder von der Straße* (Songs from the Street), in which a lyric "I" relates his observations of urban life. The "I" of these "songs," most probably David himself, portrays himself as someone who does not analyze but intuitively senses what he puts into words. The things he notices in his environment are more often unpleasant than cheery:

> I am no poet, just a scout
> I hear what boils beneath the ground
> The Plebeian hammering with calloused fists
> On the portals of the palaces.[18]

The street thus appears as the locus of social conflict, even of class struggle. But what seems like the vocabulary of class conflict in this stanza functions metonically: the starving plebeian stands for the suffering creature in general, helplessly calling for justice. The location of David's street impressions is Vienna. He writes about Burgmusik and other festivities where innocent girls lose their honor: "Eternity for a garment, Honor for a dance!"[19] The poem *Sonntag* (Sunday) starts off as a pleasant impression of a day in the Prater, only to take a sudden turn towards at once pessimistic and compassionate sentiments:

The suffering of the poor, the ruined,
Rose up before me plaintively—
While the hate of the disinherited
Swelled within my soul.[20]

This dark and gloomy tone is a feature of most of David's poems. The cycle *Visionen* (Visions), for instance, contains the three-part poem *Gefangene* (Prisoners), painting the fearful picture of a horrible prison, *Turm der Schrecken* (The Keep of Horrors), and of a slave galley, locations which again are not described for their own sake, but to illustrate the human condition of isolation and of futile longing.

The poems of the cycle *Ein Winternachtstraum* (A Midwinter Night's Dream) are believed to have been inspired by his relationship with Hermance de Potiers.[21] They express deeply felt emotions of love and yearning; yet, like almost all the other poems, they are not unequivocally positive in tone but speak of sacrifice and loss or give comfort to a hurt lyric "I." An example is the last stanza of the first poem in this cycle, entitled *Ein Sehnen* (A Longing):

—And gradually I gained hard-won rest . . .
Now a burning desire rouses me—
I spread out my arms. Whereto? Wherefore?
Unhappy heart, when will you learn to part![22]

Some features of this stanza point to undeniable aesthetic weaknesses in David's poetry and can be taken as representative of others which cannot be discussed in detail: inversions to fit the meter, exalted rhetorical questions, apostrophes, exclamations, excessive use of punctuation, and the hollow rhymes like "Begehren/entbehren." David attempted different poetic genres and forms. We find long narrative poems, ballads of love's labors and tragedy. The "I" perspectives prevail, either the "I" of a lover or suitor speaking, or the "I" of role poems. Many of the poems try to imitate the simple tone of folk songs, almost all of his verses show a traditional regular meter and rhyme scheme.

The *Hussiten-Lied* (Hussite Hymn) and the *Bauerngebet* (Peasants' Prayer) treat historical subjects similar to those of David's historical novellas. They take the perspective of the oppressed in times of religious upheaval and convey strongly the feeling of fanaticism and furor as well as an earnest struggle for liberation. Two short excerpts can serve to illustrate this:

Peasants' Prayer
Now pray you each and all—
A prayer that is an oath:
"Lord, save us from the priests' spell,
And the lords' bonds!
Let us gain freedom—"[23]

Hussite Hymn
Ours is the battle, the constant fight
To inherit the heaven of the blessed—
Behind us may loneliness fall silent,
Before us may destruction rage.[24]

Some of David's subjects are quite original: the poem *Ein Judenkind* (A Jewish Child), for instance, a sad recollection of Jewish history in the image of a young girl, Ahasvera, has no parallel in German or Austrian poetry. The execution, though, remains mostly quite conventional. All in all David's poetic *oeuvre*, though not particularly extensive, is quite disparate, and definitely does not reflect the strong side of his talent.

III. The Plays
David wrote four plays: *Hagars Sohn* (1891, Hagar's Son), *Ein Regentag* (1896, A Rainy Day), *Neigung* (1898, Affinity), and *Der getreue Eckart* (1902, Faithful Eckart). His first play, *Hagars Sohn*, transposes the eponymous biblical story into the time of the Thirty Years' War. The plot centers on the illegitimate son of a wealthy farmer and the tragedy that develops in the relationship between these two people on a secluded homestead high up in the Alps. The historical background is an uprising of the Calvinist population of Upper Austria against the Catholic authorities in the early 1620s. The father, a leader of the rebels, has let his son grow up unaware of his position as his son and heir to the estate. Subjected to the pressures of prejudice against illegitimate children, Christian becomes a hard-bitten and misogynistic outcast. After his dying mother has revealed to him the identity of his father, the young man's hour of revenge arrives when he is given charge of a contingent of rebels in their final battle for religious self-determination: the disturbed son betrays his men to the

Catholic forces and thereby the Protestant cause. The drama reaches its climax in a confrontation between father and son, in which the old man accuses his son of having failed the test of proving himself worthy of inheriting the farm. The drama ends with the rebels sentencing and executing the traitor. His life in shambles and the Protestant cause lost, the old man sets fire to his house.

The play suffers from its evident lack of integration between the historical background and the actions of the individuals. The agitation of the times remains purely atmospheric. The old man's treatment of his son, for instance, is never linked to his religious persuasion, thus the notion that the turmoil in this particular historical constellation might have driven people to the extreme behavior portrayed, remains merely peripheral. For an historical drama in the tradition of Hebbel or Grillparzer, the figures in *Hagars Sohn* are not representative enough, either of human behavior in general, or of the historical moment the play reflects. The year in which the drama is set, 1620, may have been crucial for the shaping of the Austrian nation, but the author fails to show in what way.

With *Ein Regentag* David turned to figures and issues in current Austrian society. The play shows two spheres of society, rural and urban, strong and weak, waning and waxing. The head of a formerly landed family has to work as an insurance broker to support his two granddaughters. Baroness Kitty, the elder, a flighty and vivacious Viennese child, has the chance to win the estate back for the family by marrying its present owner, fittingly named von Bauer (i.e. an ennobled farmer). The confrontation between Kitty and the present owner's mother, the simple farmer's wife who had helped to win the noble estate by honesty and hard labor, forms the heart of the dramatic action. One rainy day, when the autumn countryside fails to provide any entertainment for the young visitor from Vienna, she realizes that her place cannot be among these bigoted but hard-working people, not even as mistress of her ancestral home. Even though the old lady, with her strong principles and rigid moral stands, represents the simple and healthy, unspoiled rural way of life, the black and white pattern is contradicted by the figure of Kitty, who wins the spectator's sympathy and becomes the tragic heroine of the play with her clear-sighted awareness of her incongruency and brave resignation to the inevitable, the breaking off of the engagement.

Baroness Kitty is a strong, well-portrayed character, obviously reminiscent of David's friend Hermance de Potiers (originally David wanted to call this play *Hermance*).[25] Helene von Bauer's portrayal relies rather heavily on constant references to her honest and busy daily routine, and on platitudes like the following, intended to illustrate her moral strength: "I have lived long, but as far as I could see nothing happens in the world that does not have to happen."[26] Though some of the dialogues between Kitty and members of the Bauer household genuinely convey the notion of two incompatible spheres clashing, on the whole the play lacks color and the wit the dramatic situation might otherwise have allowed. The minor characters, especially Kitty's grandfather, and her sister Lizzi, who is introduced in the first act and does not appear again, remain fairly pale. And to let the gardener preface a turning point in relations between Kitty and the Bauers with the words: "Cover the flower beds! The weather is going to change," is a rather awkward dramatic device.[27]

Neigung is a convincingly realistic story of the disintegration of a formerly respectable Viennese family, a theme related to David's last novel *Der Übergang* (1902, The Transition). Von Köster, a cashier in a large company, is a dreamer who fails to provide his family with the requisite bourgeois standard of living, and instead spends his time and money in the coffeehouse dreaming of future fame and wealth. The eldest daughter, a schoolmistress like Lizzi in *Ein Regentag*, is wooed by a colleague, but her hardened and disillusioned mother warns her against marrying a poor man. The moment of truth arrives when von Köstler realizes that his constant embezzlement will soon be discovered by his company, and he kills himself. While the younger children, pleasure-seeking and irresponsible products of the city, turn their backs on their family's misfortune, the schoolmistress and her colleague seal their renewed engagement with an oath to devote all their meager savings to paying back von Köstler's debt and restoring the family honor. The contrasting sub-plot about the egotistical son Felix who tries to get rid of his beloved to pursue a more advantageous match is insufficiently integrated into the main story; and climactic moments like the mother's advice to Lizzi to sacrifice what she thinks is futile love, lack dramatic intensity—in this case, because the figure of the mother remains too colorless throughout. The strength of the play, though, lies in the characterization of von Köstler.

Both Viennese plays provide insights into certain layers of metropolitan society. The contrast between an old community in decline and a new generation taking over, better equipped for the challenges of the times, characterizes *Ein Regentag* as well as *Neigung*. Both plays are analyses of the deficiencies of modern urban life in a period of transition. It is striking, though, that David bestows on the members of the strong new group the old-fashioned virtues of modesty, honesty, and the work ethos. As alternatives to the ills of urbanization and the loss of strong bonds in an anonymous society these recipes seem rather weak.

For his last dramatic effort, *Der getreue Eckart,* David chooses another genre, something of a mixture between fairy tale and political drama. The title figure, a king's chief advisor in an unidentified historical time and place, struggles against the despotism of his liege as well as the whims of the subjects to reconcile the hostile parties of the country and bring about harmony. The Eckart figure is a monument to prudence and leniency in political dealings, and a clear plea for the power of education in perfecting man and the political organization of his affairs. In concrete terms the reference to Bismarck is apparent, and this fairy-tale play, with all the required ingredients of old gothic props, works better as a comment on the contemporary situation than the author's previous more realistic attempts.

All of David's plays found their way onto the stage during his lifetime, but none of them had any lasting success. To David's great joy, *Hagars Sohn* was staged at the Prague Stadttheater in May 1891 and was well received, but it took the play three years to be staged in Vienna, with its première on 10 May 1894 at the Deutsches Volkstheater. *Ein Regentag* was also produced by the Deutsches Volkstheater (12 October 1895), and *Neigung* even made it to the Burgtheater but was given only five performances (première on 24 March 1898, then 30 and 31 March, 24 April, and 4 October of the same year). *Der getreue Eckart* was staged in Graz in 1905, and for this last of his plays David received the highly prestigious Bauernfeld prize. But even the success of this piece lasted only a very short while. David's poetic and dramatic efforts must be considered a mere episode in the history of his creativity; not a complete failure but of rather minor significance. His narrative works—the novels and novellas—undoubtedly deserve more attention.

IV. The Novels

David's four novels are set in the contemporary period. His last two novels, *Am Wege sterben* (1900, Dying en route) and *Der Übergang* (1902, The Transition), introduce the reader to different classes of metropolitan society, the latter following the decline of a bourgeois family from respectability to social and moral degradation, with resemblances to the play *Neigung* in this respect; the former taking the reader into the suburbs with their drifting, impoverished student population. *Das Blut* (1892, The Blood), David's second novel, is set in rural Moravia, and the first, *Das Höferecht* (1890, Farm Law), takes the reader from the countryside into the big city. All these longer narrative works reveal connections with David's own experience, still one should not overemphasize their autobiographical character. These novels do not reflect concrete facts or events of his own life but rather the author's general familiarity with the circumstances he depicts, and his understanding for the underdog characters whose fate David shared during his teens and twenties distinguish these books. This holds true particularly for those figures from the fringes of the Austrian Empire described in *Das Höferecht* and *Am Wege sterben*, for whom the big city became their fate, disillusioning them and thwarting all their aspirations.

David's first prose work, *Das Höferecht*, in fact bears the subtitle *Eine Erzählung* (A Story), though it does exceed the genre. The title actually refers to the "Majoratsverfassung," the common law prohibiting the division of a farming estate by leaving it to the eldest son only—a traditional regulation which was meant to preserve the integrity and hence the viability of the independent farm. In this story the law leads to the tragedy of fratricide. The issue of inheritance and the common law of the farming community is in fact interlinked with a plot about the brothers' attraction to the daughter of the poor Jewish toll collector living on the edge of the village, Fanny Bermann, whose ambition and hunger for advancement in life draws the brothers into a ruinous spiral of envy and rivalry. Fanny's scrupulousness is explained as a function of the miserable living conditions of the marginalized Jewish family: "And the barb of poverty drove deep into her heart, with the resolution to get rid of it—at any cost."[28]

Characteristically, the place where this ambition with all its negative consequences manifests itself, is the big city Vienna, where Gustav, the non-inheriting but gifted younger brother goes to pursue his university studies and be with Fanny. While Fanny becomes a success with dubious members of the demimonde, Gustav throws away what fortune he has trying to win her attention. The idea that Fanny becomes another's mistress, though never explicitly mentioned, is strongly suggested. Her lover is the image of morbid decadence, a consumptive aristocrat and rake. His sweetheart's affair drives Gustav home where he serves as a farmhand under his older brother. At one Thanksgiving dance the situation erupts, Gustav cannot bear the humiliation and injustice any more, and, provoked by his brother into a fight, kills him.

Das Höferecht was entitled *Fanny* in the magazine serialization, and the renaming indicates that it was not primarily intended to be a story about the Jewess, indeed, it definitely cannot be regarded as an expression of anti-Semitism or Jewish self-hatred. On the contrary, Fanny's rootlessness is not conceived as a feature of her "race." The Jewish girl's actions are explained as determined by the social situation of her parents, for which in turn the Christian community is to blame.

One remarkable feature of this first longer narrative of David's is the inevitability with which the events unfold. There is a strong sense of ineluctable, yet undefinable forces which govern man's life. They can be identified as social or historical, as immanent and environmental influences combined. They are still conceived as leaving the individual powerless and unable to change, as the inevitable route to the catastrophe represented by the clash between the farming family's and the Jewesses' incompatible concepts or spheres of existence illustrates. A tragic momentum is added through the fact that it is the brothers' mother Marianne, a strong and impressive character, who unwittingly becomes responsible for the disastrous turn the events take, by attempting to ease the Jewish girl's lot and introducing Fanny into her house. The basic question underlying this book is what drives and motivates man's actions, and the answer given in *Das Höferecht* is by no means the only one David has to offer.

The concept of social and environmental determinism is counterbalanced in David's second novel, with the symptomatic title *Das Blut*. Here he tries to identify a person's nature and fate as determined by inherited biological factors. The protagonist of *Das Blut* Gabriele Wagner, the illegitimate daughter of a runaway who becomes a member of a traveling actors' company, comes to live in the morally strict and constricting household of her Calvinist aunt and uncle after her mother's death. The novel mainly explores the upbringing of the teenage girl on her foster parents' farm, and her suffering until finally her spirit of independence awakens—characteristically raised by her only friend, a Jewish orphan boy, who tells her about his plans to break free from the restrictions of his situation and advance in life.[29] The young girl escapes from her oppressive environment to follow what is glossed as the voice of her blood, i.e. to do as her mother had done: break free and become a circus rider. And like her mother she dies in undignified circumstances; only eighteen years old, she is fished out of the river Oder. Whether she drowned by accident or took her own life is left unexplained by David.

Besides the strong and vivid images of life in a small rural Moravian community, both of David's first longer narratives have another common feature: their object is to illuminate a thesis, an idea he formed from his own experience, namely, the power of invincible forces over the individual, whether environmental or ingrained.

Am Wege sterben concentrates mainly on the fate of a Moravian, Karl Stara, and his career in Vienna, descending from a lazy student life to the point beneath which it is impossible to sink, even unable to carry out the only honorable course of action left in his life and himself. Assumed dead by all who knew him, he leads the lonely and despised life of a police informer. Among other things his trail of corruption, ambition, selfishness, and degeneration caused the death of a young girl dishonored by him. Again, it is not only the story of one particular character which gives the book life and makes it a significant portrayal of Vienna in the 1880s; it is the wealth of atmosphere, authentically capturing the desperate and meaningless existence on the social and geographical edges of the big city. In the story *Ein wunderlicher Heiliger* David gives a short description of a similar milieu: "They lived on the edge of the city, where the suburbs began. And they banded together in numbers. The core was a group of lazy medics who were likely to reach quite an advanced age and were more attached to the neighborhood than their studies, loafing about between coffee-house and public house."[30]

Sometimes David finds quite gory images to illustrate the dark side of Viennese life. In one scene of *Am Wege sterben* the oldest regular of the students' pub, Delirium Tremens, kills the owner because he had contemplated closing his establishment—which would have made the murderer's existence even more meaningless than it already was. However, in this novel a ray of hope shines from the figure of Simon Siebenschein, who actually finishes his studies to become a doctor. But having witnessed too many of his comrades go under chasing after the temptations of the good life beyond their reach, Siebenschein does not pursue a glittering career, but instead devotes his life to the care of the poor in Ottakring. After all the social analysis the book provides, describing accurately and in exemplary detail the misery society inflicts on the individual, David's alternative presents itself as individualistic. It does not embrace a change of the political system responsible for the desperate conditions but is solely concerned with the integrity and survival of the individual. The last scene of the book, where Siebenschein is invited to join a workers' demonstration, illustrates this point very clearly:

> A formal procession appeared. . . . They kept a straight back, and the red blouses of the women and the red carnations in the men's lapels were shining. . . . He watched them as they came down from the hillsides into the first poor alleyways with their scattered houses, into the dark side of the city and of life, in which they all spent all their days. To work for them, to be associated with them, but not tied to them. To be one with them in their goals but not on their pathways, that seemed to him to be a worthy task with which he could be content. But to satisfy it, he had to be in every sense alone. And engrossed in such thoughts the doctor to the Ottakring poor walked home through the noisy and animated summer streets.[31]

Obviously David recognizes the necessity for political change and that an organized working class is the force to bring it about. Still a deep mistrust of any form of community seems to prevail, and hence the resigned and melancholy note of this novel.

Der Übergang, finally, presents the story of the decline of a bourgeois family by means of a relatively unsophisticated plot. The different members of the Meyer family follow their own paths toward deterioration: whether crime or eros. Occasionally, when describing how old Franz Meyer tries to keep up appearances, the author comes close to satire, as he finds typical images to capture the milieu of crumbling respectability. Again, the book ends on an optimistic prospect. The two younger daughters of the family regain their self esteem and manage to pull themselves out of the downward spiral: one by pursuing educational studies (yet again) to become a schoolmistress, the other by marrying a carpenter, previously despised by her family and dismissed as a suitor. Education and honest manual work—two key elements David emphasizes as crucial for the integrity and survival of society. In this novel these elements appear only at the very end; he had, however, planned to follow up his two basically gloomy Viennese novels with a third, entitled *Der Sieger* (The

Winner). But the book presenting the goal of this "transition," showing the way to coping with the modern urban world, was never written.[32]

David's last two novels remain interesting as realistic pictures of Viennese society. Their focus on the dark and problematic side of the urban community relate them to the literature of the Naturalist movement. Several motifs: illegitimate childbirth, suicide, crime, and prostitution, governed by an overall deterministic outlook, appear as the signs of David's times; most of these motifs recur in his novellas.

V. The Novellas

David's stories undoubtedly form the core of his *oeuvre*. His twenty-six major novellas were published in the volumes *Die Wiedergeborenen* (1891, The Reborn), *Probleme* (1892, Problems), *Frühschein* (1896, Early Light), *Vier Geschichten* (1899, Four Stories), *Die Troika* (1901, The Troika), and *Die Hanna* (1904, The Hanna). The volumes *Stromabwärts* (1903, Downstream) and *Wunderliche Heilige* (1906, Wondrous Saints) contain a number of rather insignificant occasional works, small sketches, character studies, and stories about rural life on the brink of industrialization which were not included in the *Gesammelte Werke*. The three stories *Filippinas Kind* (Filippina's Child), *Das Ungeborene* (The Unborn), and *Halluzinationen* (Hallucinations), which David did not publish during his lifetime, must be considered among his major works. Very roughly one can distinguish three different groups of stories: historical novellas, the Moravian novellas, and the stories dealing with contemporary urban subjects. Most of the various volumes of stories contain examples of more than one of these sub-genres.

His first work in the novella genre, though, *Die Wiedergeborenen*, is a collection of solely historical narratives, which clearly betray Conrad Ferdinand Meyer as a model. Stories like *Die Tochter Fortunats* (Fortunat's Daughter) and *Olivenholz* (Olive Wood), set against a rather artificial Italian background and striving almost too hard for proportion and timelessness, remain epigonal and hence unconvincing. The other stories in this first collection are played out on David's home soil: they are set during the Hussite Rebellion or other periods of religious turmoil in Bohemia and Moravia. These stories describe the erotic aberrations of a young Benedictine monk (*Petre, quo vadis*), or tell the tale of a mother and her illegitimate daughter who save their home town from marauding hordes after their expulsion from the city (*Ruth*). The outcome of this latter story and David's obvious sympathy for a character who in the eyes of the world has sinned and has to be punished suggests a superior, more humane morality above the petty quarrels and bigotry of man.

The best of these early stories show characteristics of the later, more mature historical narratives by David: the major players of world history do not figure in his stories; only very rarely are they mentioned by the narrator so as to allow the events depicted to be located in time in order to keep his readers aware that it is they who are pulling the strings. In the collections *Probleme* and *Frühschein* David's sympathy lies increasingly with the victims of the historical forces—the ordinary people and their sufferings. Hunger and hardship are always understood as accompanying the events depicted. The author's attention, though, is not directed primarily towards the physical deprivation; he focuses rather on the spiritual, intellectual, or moral suffering. No grandiose gestures, no notable decisions are reflected in David's stories, but the daily despair, the trail of emptiness and neglect, of loss of purpose and values in ordinary peoples' hearts and minds is what his stories are about. He shows the inevitability with which the dammed-up and maltreated emotions erupt and lead to catastrophe. He shows, too, how inexorably the turmoil of the times produces disturbed, tormented people and actions.

"Das Totenlied" (The Song of the Dead), for instance, presents a displaced and isolated Burgundian countess, forced to live worlds apart from her home with an unloved man, a warlord of the Thirty Years' War who treats her like a piece of booty from one of his campaigns. "Der Letzte" (The Last Monk) is the old Benedictine father who, as a result of the tide of the time sweeping through the formerly impenetrable walls of the monastery, loses his last confrère to what the narrator calls the voice of his blood—sexual love and marriage. A passage from the dedication of his collection *Frühschein. Geschichten vom Ausgang des großen Krieges* (i.e. the close of the Thirty Years' War) casts an illuminating light on David's experience of history. All the four *Frühschein* stories deal with the impact of the epoch-making war on individuals. "Verstörte Zeit" ("Troubled Times" —a very programmatic title) tells of a young man who, after having spent all his life from early youth in the trains of the warlords, comes home to his family's farm where he starts a relationship with the half sister he had never known. This drives their father mad, and he burns their homestead, which had just started to flourish again—brutalization and degeneration are the result of a complete loss of orientation in a violated world:

> To portray war itself was not at all my aim. I am not strong enough for that. In any case you tell the power of a fire by its reflection, and the fury of a battle perhaps even better if you cross the field over which it has raged. . . . I myself remember a story from my youth, I do not know whether I read it or heard it. A lonely hunter lives in a vast forest, and a girl who has got lost finds her way to him, a girl in whom the light of reason had been extinguished by the terrors she has seen in the town that has been overrun. They keep each other company, and with a wild smile the progenitrix of the line sees the wood cleared and a new settlement rise up in the middle of the wilderness.[33]

A woman driven to insanity by the War as ancestress of the human race is David's emblem of an incomprehensible, cruel world, the course of history, and the individual's exposed and powerless position in it. All these stories have a strong sense of inevitability, and they show people at the mercy of forces beyond their reach; thus the tone of many of David's historical novellas is rather sad, and those fatalistic, resigned subjects actually leave the most powerful impact on the reader. In fact, when David tries to end his tales on a more optimistic note his art is in danger of becoming shallow and sentimental. The sunrise metaphor in the story "Frühschein" (similar to the ending of "Sonnenaufgang" [Sunrise] from the *Probleme* collection) strikes one as both very conventional and very strained: "But at the front, on the bow, stood the judge, staring into the gold of the morning and the unknown which seemed to us all to be happiness."[34]

David, unlike some of his contemporaries in this period of rising Czech nationalism, does not revert to history to make a political point. For him, Bohemia and Moravia in the periods of religious unrest during the sixteenth and seventeenth centuries are an exemplary historical landscape, the epitome of human obsession and upheaval, and of the human condition in the world per se. And this condition is suffering—often self-inflicted by passions and rage, but always futile. Thus these historical narratives prelude themes and motifs which recur in his contemporary stories with Viennese or Moravian settings.

In his portrayal of contemporary Viennese society David does not intend to present the reader with a comprehensive insight into the diversity of groups and classes in the capital's population. In marked contrast to his plays, he is not concerned in his stories with the rich bourgeoisie and nobility. His Viennese stories, like his Moravian ones, in fact have a fairly limited repertoire of figures, themes, and motifs. He deals with outcasts and underdogs, people overcome by the big city, people from the fringes of the Habsburg Empire like himself and the students in the novel *Am Wege sterben.*

In his novellas, industrialization and urbanization are held responsible for all the consequences of social change, like the rootlessness and impoverishment of large portions of the population at the end of the nineteenth century. In the tragic title story of the volume "Stromabwärts" David refers to both these developments when he describes a village which "lay snuggled up so closely to factories, from whose chimneys a foul smoke poured incessantly."[35] This, and "a reflection of the metropolis, beckoning from afar,"[36] become the hallmarks of the contemporary agitation, the impact of which is still felt disadvantageously in the rural setting of this story, away down the Danube, because it overshadows what could be an ideal community and lures their members away into the vice and anonymity of the metropolis.

Three of the *Vier Geschichten* (1899, Four Stories) are about different types of people in Vienna, from outcast to well-to-do shopkeeper. "Das königliche Spiel" (The Royal Game) relates the fate of a stranded Rumanian chess player in an impersonal and incomprehensible metropolis, where traditional values have ceased to count and the security of the ties within smaller communities is replaced by anonymity. The words with which the protagonist and first-person narrator explains his move to the capital reflect the hopes of thousands at the time: "So we sold everything and moved to Vienna. Where else should we have gone otherwise? It was a big city, and perhaps one could get ahead in it."[37] The novella "Der Talismann" (The Token) from the volume *Die Troika* (1901) is set against a similar background and shows even more clearly that these kinds of circumstances were instrumental in destroying a person's physical, mental, and social well-being.

But even where on the surface the appearance of respectability is maintained, there are deep problems beneath. "Schuß in der Nacht" (Shot in the Night) pursues the motif of suicide out of desperation. This story is a bitter attack against hypocrisy and petty-bourgeois morality in the Viennese lower middle class. The tragic incident opens up deep cracks in the façade of decency. Suicide, too, ends the life of the protagonist of the story

"Ein Poet?" (A Poet?) from *Probleme* (1892, Problems), a writer who has
to support his family by toiling as a journalist but is a failure in his job
because his "poetic" imagination produces news stories which are too lyrical for publication. Ironically, only his last article—about his own death—
meets his superiors' requirements for a catchy piece of news. The autobiographical allusions are obvious; possibly this intimate knowledge of his
locale allowed David to substantiate his bitter criticism of the inhuman
media business with sharp and explicit observations: "In newspaper parlance there is no 'was,' there is only an 'is!' . . . It means we live for the
moment, and we only let live with us one who can serve the moment well:
he is our man, only him! . . . The newspaper is a machine, and the correspondents are machines."[38]

For David, his native Moravia in later life seemed like a *Segensland*[39]
(land of bliss). Such a euphemistically positive assessment appears as a
sharp contrast to the social realism of the Viennese stories. The Moravian
novels *Das Höferecht* and *Das Blut*, though, contradict this impression, as
do the Moravian novellas "Die Mühle von Wranowitz" (The Wranowitz
Mill) from *Die Troika* and the three stories of *Hanna* (1904) which paint
an increasingly ambivalent picture of this "land of bliss." In the eyes of
most critics David reached his peak of maturity with his Moravian stories.
This native countryside remained his dominant theme until his death, and
two of his three posthumous novellas are also set there.

The protagonist Hanka in *Die Mühle von Wranowitz* appears self-
assured and at ease with herself, firm and confident in her judgments and
moral positions. Hence, when she bears the consumptive nobleman's illegitimate child, this is not a sign of social and moral degradation but
instead marks a victory for somebody who trusted and stood by her feelings and remained true to herself. The revaluation of David's much-used
motif of pregnancy out of wedlock is apparent; it becomes a sign of a
natural morality. David symbolically named her after the region which
produced her: Hanka means Hanna.

The later stories of the *Hanna* cycle express greater doubts in human
nature and the social stability of the rural community. Both the stories
"Cyrill Wallenta" and "Ruzena Capek" deal with displaced people, the failure of relationships, and the arbitrary administration of justice. The title
story "Hanna" is the recollection of a painter who, after an education in
Vienna, returns to his native village, where he finds what seems to be a
genial and congenial environment for his art, in the person of the girl by

the name of Hanna. After she has become his wife and he has painted her in the nude, the incompatibility of their sense of dignity brings about the catastrophic conclusion: Hanna cannot cope with the fact that her husband intends to exhibit her intimate portrait in front of strangers in Vienna, and even get paid for it. In taking her own life, she manages to protect her integrity and prevent herself from being prostituted. With this story David not only reconfirms the notion of a natural morality superior to man's laws, but at the same time he expresses the fact that for those who have knowledge, the artists, this higher state of blessed simplicity and innocence is irretrievably lost. The first person narrator calls himself a *verwunschener Landschafter*, (an enchanted landscapist). The spell is the recognition that the landscape, the native soil and all the good it stands for, has become unreal, a phantom of the past.

The posthumous stories "Das Ungeborene" (1908, The Unborn) and "Filippinas Kind" (1908, Filippina's Child) belong to the group of Moravian novellas, too; but they clearly mark a new stage in David's aesthetic development. Particularly in "Filippinas Kind" there is hardly any plot left: a group of Moravian girls and women are shown about to emigrate to America from a deserted provincial railway station. One of them tries to locate a former neighbor in the nearby market town to return the illegitimate child this neighbor had left in her care a few years previously. The novella remained unfinished, so the outcome of this search is not related. Yet the fragmentary character highlights the modernity of this story. David, for the first time in his career, employs almost impressionistic means, showing highly subjective excerpts of reality by "painting" images of "dust" and "Erntedürre" (harvest drought) in the surrounding countryside. The trees, for example, display "narrow and frightened leaves."[40] The references to mass emigration, poverty, alcoholism, and the women's melancholy songs create an atmosphere a far cry from the healthy affirmative tone of his earlier Moravian stories. In his last literary effort *Halluzinationen* (1908, Hallucinations), David relates the dreams, visions, recollections, and inner monologues of a hallucinating patient on his deathbed; a fragmentary piece without plot or any characters in the traditional sense. Here David truly crossed the threshold into Modernism.

The Moravian stories prove very clearly something that holds true for the majority of David's work: they portray strong, willful heroines—sometimes brave, always struggling or fighting, often suffering and losing. These heroines are frequently embodiments of a natural morality that transcends the narrow mores of the nineteenth century. However, these female figures do not highlight women's issues in a particularly modern way: the aspect of sexuality is treated without reference to the psychological theories of the time, and there does not seem to be any concrete political or social message connected with their portrayal. They are designed to command the reader's respect and sympathy, but they are not able to illustrate the complexities of modern existence like, for instance, Schnitzler's women do.

Several motifs recur in many of David's novellas: incestuous relationships, suicide, pregnancies out of wedlock, capital crimes. In addition, the notion of man's obsessiveness, the way he is driven by passions and urges figures prominently in his stories. As these characteristics can be witnessed in his historical figures as well as in his contemporary ones, it seems as if they represented David's understanding of human nature as such: social and genetic determination deprive the individual of the chance to steer his own fate. Only occasionally does David allow his characters to assume control of their lives actively and courageously and thus achieve a reconciliation between their destiny and their individuality. David's understanding of the individual's apparent confinement as the hallmark of any time—the agitated past and the troubled present alike—does not merely express personal feelings but also reflects the general perception of being homeless and alienated in the modern world.

Several of David's novellas—especially the contemporary ones ("Die Troika," "Das königliche Spiel," "Woran starb Sionida" [What Sionida Died of, from *Probleme*], *Der Talismann*, *Die Hanna* to name but a few) are frame stories ("Rahmenerzählungen"): set in a characteristic locality, the recollections of the first-person narrator come across as vivid and genuine. The tone of the frame and the story proper have an enhancing effect on one another, and the reader quite often finds himself sharing the sentiments of the narrator in the frame: commiseration or pity, anticipation or suspense. This is one of the ways David manages to create a complete image of a person or capture the spirit of a certain situation. Often he needs only a few sketches; a technique used particularly impressively in the narratives of the *Hanna*-cycle: "It was a very sultry summer's day. Such a bright sun that even the sky seemed lead-gray, and it was as if dust was flitting across it, a dust which lay thickly on the country road and moved with the slightest breeze."[41] On the other hand, his metaphors and images can sometimes strike the reader as too deliberately constructed and unoriginal.

But generally David's style is at its best in the novellas. If one sets aside the obvious diversity—from the slightly epigonal tone of the early historical novellas to the tentative experiments of "Filippinas Kind" and *Halluzinationen*—David's language shows some distinctive features and an unmistakable personal note. The characteristics of his use of language are quite hard to pinpoint: it has, rather generally, been described as coarse and cumbersome, the means employed seem scarce and occasionally even crude. The true splendor, especially in his later narratives, stems from his ability to recreate the rhythm and breathlessness of a distinctive spoken language, for instance, by concatenating staccato phrases and using punctuation to underline the intonation rather than just to separate the syntactic units.[42] In this respect David's narrative techniques are quite innovative, anticipating *Sekundenstil* or other aspects of later stream-of-consciousness literature, yet without the mediating voice of the traditional narrator ever being entirely abandoned.

VI. The Essays

To the various papers and magazines David worked for in Vienna, he contributed countless articles, sketches, theater and book reviews, obituaries, and travel writings. These latter include some impressions from Moravia: in "Montsalvatsch—in Mähren" (Montsalvat—in Moravia) the onlooker, a Viennese student, imagines the old seat of the Przimislid family as a grail castle from medieval epic literature. Learned associations overshadow the immediacy of his reaction; a sentimental notion of loss is the consequence: The "feeling that something precious had been lost forever."[43] "Jugendland (Land of Youth) is the recollection of the author's own visit to Moravia, his only, very late return to the region that had shaped him and his work so much; a search for his own roots as a person and a writer: "We went over the land of our youth [the article ends], in other words we greeted the land again and blessed it in our heart, for it was so much more generous than we could know at the time, and we looked around for our own traces and marks, to see if they had not all been obliterated."[44]

More important than these valedictions to times past and places lost in reality but alive in the writer's imagination are his essays on contemporary actors, painters, and writers. The names of the fellow authors to whom David devoted essays reveal something about the nature of his writings, and as he did not make any theoretical comments on his works, these articles provide the only information about his literary concepts and self-assessment as a writer. When, for instance, in the introduction to his essay on Ferdinand von Saar he laments about how the German writers are met with "dislike" and "noble disdain" in Austria,[45] this betrays not only his own perception of being undervalued, but similarly his self-assessment as a decidedly German writer.

The essays collected in Volume VII of the *Gesammelte Werke* include articles on Ibsen, Tolstoy, Zola, Herzl, and on the German Realists Fontane, Heyse, Meyer, and Raabe. It is particularly telling that none of these essays deals with authors of his own generation, or with the younger protagonists of Viennese Modernism, like Arthur Schnitzler, Hugo von Hofmannsthal, Richard Beer-Hofmann, or Felix Salten, who represented the 1890s for posterity far more than the writers David admires, such as Hermann von Gilm or Ferdinand von Saar. Obviously David felt greater kinship with these representatives of the nineteenth-century realist tradition.

In most of his literary essays David praises the respective authors' deep feelings for their characters and their ability to give an idea of human misery and suffering. Quite illuminating, for example, is his essay on Emile Zola. Almost in passing he recognizes that the French author introduced new registers into the literature in his native language: "He was unconcerned in reaching for provincialisms, and from the Parisian gutter he fetched rude, foul-smelling, strong slang expressions"[46]—thus achieving a genuineness and power David himself tried to create by turning to the people and themes of his native Moravia. Equally important and equally significant for the understanding of David's own work is his reference to Darwin's impact on Zola and his emphasis on the "influence of heredity."[47] As complementary to this, as "the second, modern destiny alongside heredity" he recognizes "environment" and "general conditions,"[48] that is the environment, upbringing, and all the social conditions of human life. An awareness of both is essential for the author to enable him to understand a person and portray a convincing and genuine literary character. David's understanding of Zolas's novels thus enables us to appreciate what David himself was trying to express in his work: the inevitability of man's actions, the lack of real options owing to the absence of free will. In contrast to optimistic anthropologies of the autonomous individual, David stresses the dominant forces of genetic and social conditioning and the artist's awareness of these limitations as the prime characteristics of modern existence.

In the essay on Zola David indicates that for him the description of the social forces is crucial; in Zola's case this means the living conditions of the lower classes. Here David seems quite outspoken (in contrast to his usual abstention from politically explicit views) in naming capitalism as the reason for misery and suffering. With reference to Zola's *Germinal* he states that "Modern capitalism weighs more heavily than the weight of the mountains on the heads of the wretched, the disinherited of the mining quarter."[49]

Compassion with the oppressed seems to be his criterion for praising Wilhelm Raabe.[50] The author's intention when dealing with the misery of the lower classes should be a compassionate view to evoke a strong feeling of distress and to make an emotional impact on the reader. This kind of subjective approach that distinguishes Raabe and David alike separates the real poetic spirit from the new movement of coldblooded social vivisection. This is how he understands the contemporary Naturalist movement, and even though many of his stories exploit Naturalist personae and motifs (like suicide or infanticide), the review illustrates why David himself wanted to think of himself and his literature differently:

> Long before the invention of the modern keyword "Natur-
> alism," which is actually only justified by wanting to be the
> interpreter of the mute, the lawyer of the weak, Raabe in his
> own way contributed to a true and truthful poetry. He de-
> scended to the quarters of the poor and needy and cast light
> into their caves. He did not do so with the calm which a
> modern tendency demands of such tasks. . . . He did it with
> a deep inner dread and did not conceal when he was shaken
> by what he saw. . . . But the fact that such a man should tell
> such sad stories about everyday folk and should commemorate
> such misery . . . , lies as strong an accusation as any accuser
> of modern society and its shortcomings can level.[51]

Evidently David is talking as much about himself as about Wilhelm Raabe. There are no hints as to whether David drew any political consequences from his strong convictions about the deficiencies and cruelties of modern, capitalist society. Peter Goldammer, in his excellent essay on David, con-cludes: "He never counted himself among the exploited and the oppressed, but he only ever conceived of his fate personally: as the fate of one who had been cheated and swindled of his happiness and prosperity."[52] The same holds true for the characters he portrays in his work. David's essay on the press, *Die Zeitung* (1906, The Newspaper) is his most radical political statement. Here he reiterates the criticism of "Ein Poet?" in socially explicit terms. Like the story, the essays are deeply rooted in his own experience of what he saw as an oppressive service to various Viennese papers which distracted him from his true literary vocation. His main concern was the impact of economical necessities on the creative individual inside the trade: "The majority of those in its service get polished plain and flat;"[53] and the "space in which attitudes and talents can be expressed and engaged," becomes "more and more restricted." On the other hand, the virtues of the responsible journalist, "conviction" and "altruism," which enable the reader to distinguish the important from the irrelevant, are about to be irretrievably lost.[54]

His analysis of the reasons for such an undesirable development are very clear and still relevant to the present day. Financial pressures dictate the rules of the trade: high circulation is aimed at to please the advertisers, and sensationalism helps to sell the product: "So the newspapers become more and more the instrument and the creature of interest groups, who above all want to see themselves and their plans represented."[55] David illustrates the wider political implications of this approach with the role of the so-called "yellow press" in an American election campaign, which proved that "The alliance of financial and verbal power, which was leaping into action here for the first time, is by no means so entirely harmless."[56]

The sources and motivations of the writer's creative abilities were outlined in various other extensive essays, collected under the title *Vom Schaffen* (1906, On Creating). Apart from a kind of productive uniqueness, a mysterious fertility, the true writer is distinguished by humility and respect for creation: "What is more, to a certain extent the creator must have a great interior humility despite his pride in the mysteries which take place in him."[57] David reiterates this point about the writer's modesty by introducing the metaphor of a Philistine, indicating the fact that everyone is tied to the restrictions of the ordinary and the unspectacular. The real choice is between complacency and compassion:

> Joys and pains are alike to everyone under the sun. They are simply perceived differently according to the personality which they enlighten or obscure. And especially the effect of

suffering, and the receptivity to it, determines the difference between the philistine, who is nothing else, and him who has to pay tribute to philistinism, but still remains his own strong self.[58]

Clearly David saw himself as one of the Philistines who had remained a strong and upright person by staying receptive to suffering. In his work he was able to mold the awareness of his own misery into universally applicable images of man exposed to the injustice of his times and social situation.

The ambivalence of contemporaneity and outsiderhood is surely the prime feature of David's position in nineteenth-century Austrian literary history. As far as we can tell, his contemporaries perceived him as a rather insignificant part of the 1890s literary scene in Vienna. Too much separated him from the dominant group of young writers and their circles; and though he was only two years older than Arthur Schnitzler, he appears much more a figure of the nineteenth century. A certain amount of epigonality is undeniable in David's work; and in his beginnings he must surely be considered a successor of the Realist generation of writers. Later he became an innovator in different respects: his social concern, and several symptomatic themes and motifs have led to the claim that he is the only noteworthy representative of Austrian Naturalism. And his Moravian stories definitely represent a unique contribution to German letters in the last decades of the Habsburg Monarchy.

David's *oeuvre* can be regarded as one great autobiographical confession, as he so frequently stated himself:

What did I want, what did I give?
What pours from my heart,
Perhaps a whole sum of life,
Easily just a symbol and an image;
Yet so much I did not invent,
Just desperately wanted, and thus experienced,
I spun it into my stories,
Weaving it in with its threads.[59]

Some of the weaknesses of David's writings have been pointed out in the foregoing. In spite of such evident deficiencies, which have prevented

David from being counted among the very best of Austrian writers, his life and work are distinguished by his compassionate sense for the human fate (*menschliches Fatum*), by his perceptiveness for suffering (*Empfänglichkeit fürs Leid*).

Notes

1. Jakob Julius David, *Gesammelte Werke,* ed. Ernst Heilborn and Erich Schmidt (Munich/Leipzig: Piper, 1908), vol. 1. p. vi. Henceforth this edition is quoted as *GW* followed by volume (Roman) and page numbers. The writer wishes to express his gratitude to Professor Mary Howard, University College Cork, and Dr. Duncan Lorpe, University of Wales, Swansea, for their help in translating all the texts by David used in this essay.
2. *GW,* vol. VI, pp. 350-364.
3. Quoted in Peter Goldammer, "Jakob Julius David—Ein vergessener Dichter," in: *Weimarer Beiträge,* vol. III, p. 323.
4. Karl Kraus called him "einen der wenigen anständigen Menschen der hiesigen Literatur"; *Die Fackel,* 561-567 (1921), 47, quoted in Konrad Paul Liessmann, "An Schönheit sterben. Zur Verfahrensweise des poetischen Geistes im Wiener Fin de Siècle. With notes to Hugo von Hofmannsthal and Jakob Julius David, in: *Glücklich ist wer vergißt . . . Das andere Wien um 1900,* eds. Hubert Ch. Eholt, Gernot Heiß, and Hannes Stakl (Vienna/Cologne/Graz, 1866), p. 354.
5. Hans Heinz Hahnl, "Jakob Julius David," in: H.H.H., *Vergessene Literaten.* (Vienna: Österreichischer Bundesverlag, 1980), p. 104.
6. The ornamentation was actually by Richard Lux (*Wunderliche) Heilige*) and Otto Friedrich (*Stromabwärts*), two very well-known graphic artists of the time. Compare Florian Krobb, *Graz vertraut und fremd. Jakob Julius David über Wilhelm Raabe, Jahrbuch der Raabe Gesellschaft* (1991), p. 123.
7. Arturo Farinelli, "J.J. Davids Kunst," in: *Jahrbuch der Grillparzer-Gesellschaft,* vol. XVI (1906), p. 229.
8. Anna Caspari, *In Memoriam: Jakob Julius David* (Cologne: Paul Neubner, 1908), p. 3.
9. Hans Kloos, *Jakob Julius David als Novellist* (Freiburg im Breisgau [Ph.D. dissertation] 1930), p. 141.

10. Rudolf Latzke's entry in Eduard Castle's *Geschichte der deutschen Literatur in Österreich-Ungarn* under the heading "Die Realisten" can be regarded as the first objective scholarly account of David's *oeuvre*. It is still a useful and readable introduction. In a major article Peter Goldammer ("Jakob Julius David—Ein vergessener Dichter") tried to illustrate the social-historical context of David's writing. The Naturalistic aspect of it is pointed out by Joachim Schondorff ("Auf der Rutschen"). For additional interpretation approaches and focus on more modern aspects of David's *oeuvre* see Konrad Paul Liessmann, "An Schönheit sterben," and Florian Krobb, "Nachwort," in: J.J. David, *Verstörte Zeit,* pp. 306-328.

11. Jakob Julius David, "Im Spiegel. Autobiographische Skizze," in *Das Literarische Echo,* 4 Jg., Heft 4 (January 1902), 523ff, reprinted in the "Nachwort" to J.J. David, ibid., pp. 306-309.

12. Letters printed in Jiri Vesely, "Marie von Ebner-Eschenbach, Ferdinand von Saar, Jakob Julius David. Wechselseitige Beziehungen. Beitrag zur Biographie dreier mährischer Dichter," p. 127f. These undated letters must have been written before 1891.

13. Jiri Vesely, "Jakob Julius Davids Brief an Adolf Pichler," p. 153f (11 December 1896).

14. Jiri Vesely, "Marie von Ebner-Eschenbach, Ferdinand von Saar, Jakob Julius David," p. 128 (undated). For David's sentimental recollection of this nostalgic visit of *Jugendland* see Herman Groeneweg, *J.J. David in seinem Verhältnis zur Heimat. Geschichte, Gesellschaft und Literatur,* pp. 209-212.

15. Compare Florian Krobb, "*Jeder prügelt mich, wer gerade Lust hat.* Zur jüdischen Problematik bei Jakob Julius David," in: *Bulletin des Leo Baeck Instituts,* vol. 85 (1990 [recte 1991]), 5-14.

16. The most comprehensive bibliography of David's *oeuvre* is given in Groeneweg, *J.J. David in seinem Verhältnis zur Heimat. Geschichte, Gesellschaft und Literatur,* pp. 213-219.

17. *GW* I, p. vi.

18. Ibid., p. 29.

19. Ibid., p. 33.

20. Ibid., p. 31.

21. Ella Spiero, *Jakob Julius David,* pp. 38ff.

22. *GW* I, p. 42.

23. Ibid., p. 77.

24. Ibid., p. 64.
25. Ella Spiero, *Jakob Julius David*, p. 98.
26. *GW* III, p. 231.
27. Ibid., p. 251.
28. *GW* I, p. 118
29. Compare Florian Kobb, *Jeder prügelt mich, wer gerade Lust hat*, pp. 10ff.
30. Jakob Julius David, *Wunderliche Heilige*, p. 10.
31. *GW* IV, pp. 314ff.
32, Compare Ella Spiero, *Jakob Julius David*, p. 135.
33. *GW* III, p. 279f.
34. Ibid., p. 420.
35. Jakob Julius David, *Stromabwärts*, p. 13.
36. Ibid., p. 20.
37. *GW* IV, p. 11.
38. *GW* III, pp, 157, 166.
39. Jakob Julius David, *Jugendland*, reprinted in Groeneweg, *J.J. David in seinem Verhältnis zur Heimat, Geschichte, Gesellschaft und Literatur*, p. 209.
40. *GW* IV, p. 231.
41. *Ruzena Capek, GW* IV, p. 112.
42. Unfortunately the editors of the *Gesammelte Werke*, compared with the first editions of David's novels and novellas, have interfered with the text rather too much, normalizing punctuation and spelling according to the standardized use of German but losing some of the unique character of David's style (cf. the "Editorische Notiz" in: Jakob Julius David, *Verstörte Zeit*, pp. 328f.)
43. *GW* VII, p. 336.
44. *Jugendland*, in: Groeneweg, *J.J. David in seinem Verhältnis zur Heimat, Geschichte, Gesellschaft und Literatur*, p. 212.
45. *GW* VII, p. 117.
46. Ibid., p. 49.
47. Ibid.
48. Ibid.
49. Ibid., p. 53.
50. Florian Krobb, *Ganz vertraut und fremd*, p. 126.
51. *GW* VII, pp. 102f.

52. Peter Goldammer, *Jakob Julius David—ein vergessener Dichter*, p. 331.

53. Jakob Julius David, *Die Zeitung*, p. 18.

54. Ibid., pp. 9f.

55. Ibid., p. 12.

56. Ibid., pp. 72f.

57. Jakob Julius David, Vom Schaffen und seinen Bedingungen," in: *Vom Schaffen*, p. 131.

58. Jakob Julius David, "Von den großen Philistern," in: *Vom Schaffen*, pp. 104f.

59. *GW* I, p. 103.

Selected Bibliography

I. Works by Jakob Julius David in German

Das Höfe-Recht. Eine Erzählung. Dresden/Leipzig: Heinrich Minden, 1890.

Die Wiedergeborenen. Erzählungen. Dresden/Leipzig: Heinrich Minden, 1891 (*Petre, quo vadis?, Ruth, Der neue Glaube, Gold, Olivenholz, Die Tochter Fortunats.*)

Hagars Sohn. Schauspiel in vier Akten. Vienna, 1891.

Das Blut. Roman. Dresden/Leipzig: Heinrich Minden, 1891.

Gedichte. Dresden/Leipzig: Heinrich Minden, 1891.

Probleme. Erzählungen. Dresden/Leipzig: Heinrich Minden, 1892 (*Woran starb Sionida?, Die Schwachen, Der Letzte, Sonnen-Aufgang, Die stille Margareth, Ein Poet?*).

Ein Regentag. Drama in drei Aufzügen. Dresden/Leipzig: Heinrich Minden, 1896.

Frühschein. Geschichten vom Ausgang des großen Krieges. Leipzig/Berlin: G.H. Meyer 1896 (*Verstörte Zeit, Der Bettelvogt, Das Totenlied, Frühschein*).

Neigung. Schauspiel in vier Aufzügen. Berlin/Leipzig: G.H. Meyer, 1898.

Vier Geschichten. Leipzig/Berlin: G.H. Meyer, 1899 (*Das königliche Spiel, Digitalis, Schuß in der Nacht, Das Wunder des heiligen Liberius*).

Am Wege sterben. Roman. Berlin/Leipzig: Schuster & Loeffler, 1900.

Die Troika. Erzählungen. Berlin/Leipzig: Schuster & Loeffler, 1901 (*Die Troika, Der Talismann, Die Mühle von Wranowitz*).

Der Übergang. Roman. Berlin/Leipzig: Schuster & Loeffler, 1902.

Der getreue Eckart. Ein Schauspiel in fünf Aufzügen. Berlin/Leipzig: G.H. Meyer, 1902.

Stromabwärts. [Erzählungen] (= Bibliothek berühmter Autoren, vol. 6). Vienna/Leipzig: Wiener Verlag, 1903 (*Stromabwärts, Petri Hahn, Stimmen in der Dämmerung, Der Herr Regierungsrat, Der Jubilar*).

Die Hanna. Erzählungen aus Mähren. Berlin/Leipzig: Schuster & Loeffler 1904 (*Cyrill Wallenta, Ruzena Capek, Die Hanna*).

Ludwig Anzengruber (= Die Dichtung, vol. 9). Berlin/Leipzig: Schuster & Loeffler, 1904.

Friedrich Mitterwurzer (= Das Theater, vol. 13). Berlin/Leipzig: Schuster & Loeffler 1905.

Wunderliche Heilige. [Erzählungen] (= Bibliothek moderner deutscher

Autoren, vol. 17). Vienna/Leipzig: Wiener Verlag, 1906. (*Ein wunderlicher Heiliger, Stimmen der Dämmerung, Die Weltreise des kleinen Tyrnauer, Parabel, Prolog*).

Vom Schaffen. Essays. Jena: Eugen Diederichs, 1906.

Die Zeitung. [Essay] (= Die Gesellschaft. Ed., Martin Buber, vol. 5. Frankfurt am Main: Rütten and Loening, 1906.

Hellborn, Ernst and Erich Schmidt, eds. *Gesammelte Werke.* Munich/ Leipzig: Piper, 1908/1909.

    Vol. 1: *Gedichte, Das Höferecht*

    Vol. 2: *Die Wiedergeborenen, Hagars Sohn, Blut*

    Vol. 3: *Probleme, Ein Regentag, Frühschein*

    Vol. 4: *Vier Geschichten, Am Wege sterben*

    Vol. 5: *Die Troika, Der Übergang*

    Vol. 6: *Die Hanna, Filippinas Kind, Das Ungeborene, Halluzinationen*

    Vol. 7: *Essays*

Die Hanna. Erzählungen edited by Ernst Heilborn und Erich Schmidt. Berlin: Aufbau, 1960. (*Der neue Glaube, Der Letzte, Die stille Margareth, Frühschein, Die Mühle von Wranowitz, Cyrill Wallenta, Ruzena Capek, Die Hanna*).

Verstörte Zeit. Erzählungen edited and with an Afterword by Florian Krobb. Göttingen: Wallstein, 1990. (*Der Letzte, Verstörte Zeit, Der Bettelvogt, Die Mühle von Wranowitz, Die Hanna, Filippinas Kind, Ein Poet?*).

Erzählungen aus Mähren, edited by Jiří Veselý. Berlin: Nicolai, 1993. (*Die Schwachen, Ruzena Capek, Die Hanna, Die Weltreise des kleinen Tyrnauer*).

II. Works in English Translation
None

III. Major Studies in German
Caspari, Anna. *In Memoriam J.J. David.* Cologne: Paul Neubner, 1908.

Farinelli, Arturo. "J.J. Davids Kunst." *Jahrbuch der Grillparzer Gesellschaft* 18 (1908).

Goldammer, Peter. "Jakob Julius David—Ein vergessener Dichter." *Weimarer Beiträge.* Vol. 3 (1959).

Groeneweg, Herman. *J.J. David in seinem Verhältnis zur Heimat, Ge-*

schichte, Gesellschaft und Literatur. PhD dissertation. Graz, 1929.

Hahnl, Hans Heinz. "Jakob Julius David," in Hans Heinz Hahnl, *Vergessene Literaten. Fünfzig österreichische Lebensschicksale.* Vienna: Österreichischer Bundesverlag, 1980.

Kloos, Hans. *Jakob Julius David als Novellist.* PhD dissertation. Freiburg im Breisgau, 1930.

Krobb, Florian. "*Ganz vertraut und fremd.* Jakob Julius David über Wilhelm Raabe." *Jahrbuch der Raabe-Gesellschaft,* 1991.

———. "*Jeder prügelt mich, wer gerade Lust hat.* Zur jüdischen Problematik bei Jakob Julius David," in: *Bulletin des Leo Baeck Instituts,* 85. 1990 [recte 1991].

Latzke, Rudolf. "Jakob Julius David." *Geschichte der deutschen Literatur in Österreich-Ungarn im Zeitalter Franz Josephs I.* Ed. Eduard Castle. Vol. I: 1848-1890. Vienna: Carl Fromme, 1935.

Liessmann, Konrad Paul. "An Schönheit sterben. Zur Verfahrensweise des poetischen Geistes im Wiener Fin de Siècle. With notes to Hugo von Hofmannsthal und Jakob Julius David," in: Glücklich ist, wer vergißt . . . Das andere Wien um 1900. Eds. Hubert Ch. Eholt, Gernot Heiß, and Hannes Stekl. Vienna/Cologne/Graz, 1986.

Rocek, Roman. "Jakob Julius David oder die vorweggenommene Moderne," in: R.R., *Neue Akzente. Essays für Liebhaber der Literatur.* Vienna/Munich: Herold, 1984.

Schondorff, Joachim. "Auf der Rutschen. Jakob Julius David oder Wiener Naturalismus," in: *Ein Bündel Modellfälle. Streifzüge durch Literatur und Geschichte.* Vienna/Munich/Zurich, 1981.

Spiero, Ella. *Jakob Julius David.* Leipzig: Heinrich Finck, 1920.

Veselý, Jiří. "Ebner-Eschenbach—Saar—David. Tschechische Elemente in ihrem Werk und Leben," in: *Lenau-Forum* I, 3/4, 1969.

———. "Eine unveröffentlichte Erzählung Jakob Julius Davids." *Philologia Pragensia,* 12, 1969.

———. "Jakob Julius Davids Brief an Adolf Pichler," in: *Philologia Pragensia*, 1917.

———. "Marie von Ebner-Eschenbach—Ferdinand von Saar—Jakob Julius David Wechselseitige Beziehungen. Ein Beitrag zur Biographie dreier mährischer Dichter. *Germanistike Pragensia* VII, 1976.

Karl Emil Franzos

Carl Steiner

Among Austrian writers of the second half of the nineteenth century and the beginning of our own era, none is more unusual than Karl Emil Franzos. Even though he was an Austrian citizen all his life—living there from 1848 to 1904—and staunchly refused to give up his national affiliation, he was nonetheless above everything else a Germanophile at heart whose love for German as a language and as a culture caused him to leave his native Austria at a time when, in his estimation, the influence of the country seemed to be declining. He spent the last two decades of his life as a writer and editor of international reputation in Berlin. He was also very much out of the ordinary among contemporary Austrian writers for another reason. He was a self-assured, though nonpracticing Jew from Galicia, one of Austria's easternmost provinces.

Even the circumstances of his origin and birth are most unusual. His forebears were Sephardic Jews who had first settled in Holland after their enforced departure from Spain and then in eastern France, where they made their living as candlestick makers and acquired the name of Levert. Being nontraditionalists, however, they soon made enemies among their fellow Jews. When the opportunity arose for them to reestablish themselves in Poland, they moved there not just for economic reasons alone. In the new country the author's grandfather continued the family line of business and opened a candlestick factory in Tarnopol. There, as in all of Galicia, Jews had to acquire new names after the province became an official crownland of Austria by edict of Emperor Joseph II. Since the family members were readily distinguishable from their Jewish neighbors by their French accents and customs, they were given the name of Franzos. Karl Emil's grandfather soon developed a great liking for the ideals of the

German Enlightenment and as a consequence embraced German culture enthusiastically. The author himself referred to his grandfather's resolve in an autobiographical essay in later years: "Around 1790, the forty-year-old husband and father entrusted his factories to his managers and went to Lemberg in order to study at the German university . . . what he liked best: German and history, law and aesthetics."[1]

When a son, Heinrich, was born to him in later years, who became the author's father, he was subsequently sent to institutes of higher learning in the Austrian and German heartlands. Although he was especially interested in the humanities, the law of the land in the first half of the nineteenth century would have made it impossible for him to obtain a teaching post after graduation. Consequently he had no other choice but to pursue the study of medicine—the traditional academic field that was fully open to Jews at that time. Soon after graduation Heinrich fell in love with a highly talented woman of Jewish extraction, Karoline Klarfeld, daughter of a Jewish businessman of moderate means living in the southern Russian port city of Odessa. He married her after a brief but passionate courtship. Although his own father wanted him to settle in Germany, he could obtain her father's consent only after agreeing, by way of a compromise, to establish his medical practice in Galicia. The latter wanted his daughter to live as close to him as possible. Moreover, he shared the fear of many eastern European Jews that he would lose both his daughter and his prospective son-in-law through conversion to Christianity, a practice that many German Jews were following. The young couple chose to settle in the small Galician town of Czortkow, in which, together with the majority population of Ukrainians and Poles, a Jewish ghettoized minority and even fewer upper-crust Austrian officials resided. In this ethnically mixed milieu, not altogether atypical for the multi-ethnic Austrian Empire, Karl Emil Franzos spent his early childhood.

The story of his birth on October 25 of the revolutionary year of 1848 is so unusual in the annals of literary history that it deserves some special attention. When Heinrich Franzos's wife Karoline was preparing to give birth to her—as it turned out—youngest and last child, a second son as fate would have it, revolution was raging in France and in the German heartlands. The doctor, a liberal-minded, emancipated Jew who had little in common with his fellow Jews in the Czortkow ghetto or *shtetl,* was beside himself with joy. Finally, a liberal and liberating revolution would come to these backward regions of the Austrian empire and free Jews and

Gentiles alike from the age-old yoke of political and cultural backwardness. But conditions in Galicia ever since the Polish nationalistic uprising of 1846 were rather tenuous. Polish nationalists felt superior to both Ukrainians and Jews, despising the latter and suppressing the former. When violent unrest did spread to the province again, the doctor, who had treated poor Ukrainian peasants free of charge and was admired and loved by them, made matters worse in the eyes of the Poles by saving the lives of some endangered Austrian officials. Fearing for the welfare of both his pregnant wife and his yet unborn child, he arranged for Karoline to seek temporary refuge on the other side of the nearby Russian border at the house of a devoted and indebted forester of Westphalian extraction. There, a true child of revolutionary circumstances, Karl Emil was born.

The exciting happenings surrounding and leading to his birth were to be a mere preamble to the high adventure of his later life, which was to take him from the backward region of eastern Galicia to the two cultural citadels of the German-speaking world, Vienna and Berlin. To be sure, his physician father tried to get him the best possible education in Czortkow by taking a personal interest in him, by sending him—for lack of any better school—as the only Jew to a local Dominican monastery for training, and by hiring a religious and Hebrew tutor to provide balance. He himself, though, instilled in the growing child highly unorthodox religious beliefs, conveyed to him by his own father: "There is One God above us all. All religions are equally benevolent, because all of them obligate their followers to be humane. Ceremonial practices are unnecessary. Having been born a Jew, you are obligated to remain a Jew, because this is God's will and because your coreligionists, who are still seen in an unfavorable light, are in need of good and educated men who ennoble and defend them."[2] In addition, his father never missed an opportunity to imbue him with a deep and abiding love for the German language and culture as well as for the German-speaking countries and peoples. Thus he grew up with admonitions like: "You are also the son of a German and will live in Germany one day" (222). Many years later, Karl Emil Franzos, reflecting on his early childhood experiences in Czortkow, was able to say: "Thus both, being German and being Jewish, coalesced in me into a unified whole. I heard only the most praiseworthy commentary about both, which fact could only greatly enhance my enthusiasm" (225).

A third influence in those years was exerted by his early familiarity with a love for the Ukrainian language and its native speakers. It came about as a result of the close contacts he had as a small child with his nurse Magdusia, a Ukrainian peasant woman who began to take care of him soon after birth, and his nearly daily dealings with house servants, carriage drivers, and peasants from nearby Ukrainian villages. Consequently, his familiarity with German and Jewish stories and historical happenings—such as the cunning and bravery of Arminius, chief of the Teutonic Cherusci, the German wars of liberation from the yoke of Napoleon as well as the struggle of the Maccabees for religious freedom, and the plight of the Jewish martyrs of Worms—was accompanied in his boyhood years by an early acquaintance with Ukrainian fairy tales, folk songs, and popular narratives. At the age of nine he read his first book, a German text by Gustav Nieritz with the exciting title *The Trumpet Player of Dresden*. It related the romantic tale of the adventures of a poor German boy during the end phase of the Napoleonic era. One year later, in the spring of 1858, he saw his first play, Salomo Hermann Mosenthal's *Deborah*. Unintentionally, the dramatic climax of the play occurred at the end of the second act when one of the principal characters exclaimed: "We don't need any Jews in this country." This anti-Semitic remark led the Poles in the audience to applaud in approval. When Karl's German schoolmate, the son of the town's apothecary—whose father had taken both boys to the theater—joined in the applause, Karl became so incensed that he slapped the boy's face. This incident, which nearly led to a riot in the theater, was young Franzos's first encounter with anti-Semitism.

Soon enough, however, real tragedy was to befall Karl. His father died after a short but severe illness a few months later, leaving his family almost destitute. Still, Karl's mother, who moved with her children after her husband's death to Czernowitz in the neighboring Austrian province of the Bukovina, could find the means to send the boy to the local *Gymnasium*. Karl studied very intensely there and was also able to help the family income by earning needed money tutoring less gifted students. He was fortunate in having excellent teachers. Under the tutelage of the school's director Stefan Wolf, Karl, in fact, excelled in his studies of classical philology. These were also the days when he began to write poems and highly imaginative stories. Two of his earliest novellas, later purged from his acknowledged *oeuvre*, "He Will Certainly Come"—a romantic tale— and "Menia"—a love story from the days of the Roman Empire—were even published locally in 1867.

In August of the same year Karl not only passed his final examination with distinction, but also graduated as the valedictorian of his class. Director Wolf encouraged him to apply for a government stipend to pursue university studies in classical philology, in which he had shown such great promise during the years in the *Gymnasium.* To his great disappointment, his application was rejected because of his Jewishness. Had he received the stipend, however, it most likely would not have served him well. Jews were still not permitted in those days to secure an academic appointment after graduation. As he was able to observe later: "A poor boy like myself who had to take care of his mother and sisters could not afford to choose a profession that offered no chance of financial security" (229).

Although his second public encounter with his Jewishness proved to be costly, both in terms of personal disappointment as well as missed opportunity, he had no intention of converting to Christianity. Now, as never before, he felt a special bond with his poor and disadvantaged coreligionists of the Czernowitz ghetto. Determined to succeed in this world no matter what it would take, he enrolled at the University of Vienna and later—to save money—at the provincial University of Graz to study law, a profession that had been open to Jews since the days of the enlightened Emperor Joseph II. While studying law in those cities, he did not neglect his family obligations. He continued to support his mother and sisters with money he earned from tutoring. During his visits home, he could also increase his earnings by editing a supplement to volume one of the *Bukowiner Volkskalender* (Bukovina Calender for House and Home). Even more significant in terms of prestige and experience gained was his later edition of the second volume of the Czernowitz magazine *Buchenblätter* (Beech Press) as a *Jahrbuch für deutsche Literaturbestrebungen in der Bukowina* (Annual for German Literary Endeavors in Bukovina).

Franzos's university years in Graz proved to be unusual for a number of reasons. Not only was he by his own account the only Jew in this provincial capital. He also immersed himself, as he had done in Vienna, in student affairs, as a result of which he was soon elected president of the local Orion Student Fraternity. Throwing all caution to the wind, he would engage in fiery pan-German rhetoric in public. These talks would soon get him into difficulty, however, with the conservative Austrian government. Yet unabated, his German nationalistic fervor rose to a fever pitch during the Franco-Prussian war of 1870-1871. On the occasion of being elected to the post of recording secretary of *Das deutsche Sieges- und Friedensfest* (The German Victory and Peace Festival) of the *Verein der*

Deutsch-Nationalen (Association of German Nationalists), he gave a highly emotional political speech on behalf of pan-Germanism, in which he criticized the government of the anti-German Austrian minister Hohenwart. This address went beyond what the irate Austrian authorities were willing to tolerate. As a result he was indicted for high treason. Even though these severe charges were later dropped and Franzos was merely assessed a modest fine for disturbing the peace, the legal career that he had contemplated for himself in government service appeared in jeopardy. Having been forced to give up all aspirations to become a philologist and an academician earlier in life because of his Jewishness, his espousal of radical pan-German causes forced him now to contemplate still another pursuit that would ensure him of a livelihood. To make matters worse, Franzos had also fallen unhappily in love with a young Christian woman in Graz. When he contemplated becoming engaged to her and divulged his espousal of Judaism, she rejected his proposal. Notwithstanding the fact that he was a nonpracticing Jew, he remained firm in his unwillingness to leave the faith. A so-called mixed marriage would have also been unthinkable in Graz, where, in spite of an absence of Jews, Judeophobia had always been a strong social, if not religious, undercurrent.

Happily, though, for Franzos's future development as a writer, there was a silver lining in this—for him—frustrating and painful experience. By his own statement he was driven within three days—"in a feverish state"[3]—to write his first novella about life in the ghetto. The main theme of the narrative was the socially nonpermissible and emotionally unrealizable love between a Christian woman and a Jewish man from an eastern ghetto. Franzos called this literary outgrowth of his own bitter experience "Das Christusbild" (The Picture of Christ). The story essentially confirmed his own inner feelings. Religious prejudice proved to be stronger than romantic love. This novella, which he was to incorporate a few years later into his first novella collection, *Die Juden von Barnow* (The Jews of Barnow) proved to be important to him for still another reason. It afforded him an emotional and psychological catharsis. Ultimately, his unhappy love for a Christian woman provided the spark that was to kindle the desire in him to write about Jewish ghetto life in Eastern Europe for the benefit not only of his western fellow Jews, but also of the general reading public.

Yet the path to success in these endeavors proved to be arduous and slow. First and foremost, he had to support himself and to provide some financial assistance to his mother and sisters in Czernowitz. To these ends, he turned toward journalism as a career. Although he worked very hard at it and wrote a number of articles about political and social events for a succession of newspapers and periodicals—principally the Viennese *Neue Freie Presse* (New Free Press) and the *Ungarischer Lloyd* (Hungarian Lloyd) as well as the *Pester Lloyd* in Budapest—there were diminishing results. Success stubbornly eluded him. When, despite perseverance and heroic efforts, he bungled an assignment for the *Neue Freie Presse*—his coverage of the sensational trial of the journeyman tub maker Wilhelm Kullmann, Bismarck's would-be assassin, was less comprehensive than that of his more experienced colleagues—it seemed that his dreams for a successful career in journalism had also come to naught.

At this point in his life, when all appeared hopeless and hunger began to gnaw at his viscera, a near miracle occurred. Stories and articles which he had written in the intervening years for various publications were printed as a book in 1876 entitled *Aus Halb-Asien* (From Half-Asia). Dealing with conditions in Eastern Europe, they caught the public's fancy and made Franzos a literary celebrity virtually overnight. Now his collection about life in the Jewish ghettos of these parts, which he had completed earlier and to which he had given the title *Die Juden von Barnow*, was also published and met with similar approval. These works were eventually translated into sixteen languages and gave the author an international reputation that reached as far as the United States. Now the floodgate of success opened up for him. Not only was the *Neue Freie Presse* eager now to have him on its staff, if not as a reporter, then as a permanent contributor. Other leading papers and weeklies opened their pages to him just as eagerly. In 1878 more cultural vignettes of his about life in Eastern Europe appeared as a book under the title *Vom Don zur Donau* (From the Don to the Danube), and ten years later, in 1888, he was able to complete his trilogy about the people and places of these parts with the volume *Aus der großen Ebene* (From the Large Plain). Even though the two sequels did not equal the success of *Aus Halb-Asien*, they were well-received and contributed to his reputation as one of the leading experts on Eastern European conditions.

Twelve years earlier, in 1876—the year which brought him early recognition and fame as a writer—he met Ottilie Benedikt, a young assimilated Jewess of considerable beauty and intellect. He fell in love with her and this time Aphrodite nodded benignly. There were no social or religious barriers to overcome. After a brief but ardent courtship—reminiscent of his father's courtship of his mother—Ottilie, who was eight years younger than he, consented to become his wife. The wedding, which took place on 28 January 1877, in the oldest Jewish synagogue in Vienna, became a true social event. Ottilie came from a prominent Viennese Jewish family. Her father Heinrich Benedikt was a respected businessman. Her mother, née Mauthner, daughter of a manufacturer in Prague, was known in Vienna as a gracious hostess. Their home was frequented by well-known liberal and Jewish writers, among whom Leopold Kompert, Moritz Hartmann, Karl Isidor Beck, and Ludwig August Frankl—who had introduced Franzos to Ottilie—were most prominent. Their marriage, although not blessed with children, proved to be a happy one. She was intellectually supportive of all his efforts in future years, accompanied him on many of his business trips and journeys throughout Europe, and even entered the world of writing herself. She authored a number of novellas, which were published in two collections: *Das Adoptivkind und andere Novellen* (The Adopted Child and Other Novellas) in 1896 and *Schweigen* (Silence) in 1902. Nearly a quarter of a century after her husband's death, she wrote in the low-key and modest fashion typical of her, about the relationship with Franzos and her own family background: ". . . my husband married me out of purest love. I was a poor girl. I did not receive a dowry, only furniture for our apartment and personal belongings. . . . On the other hand, however, I would say that I come from a good family. Still in his final moments of delirium, my husband said: 'I was really fortunate that I married this refined young woman from this distinguished family.'"[4]

The young couple settled in Vienna after their wedding and remained there for nearly a decade. Franzos earned his living for many years as a freelance writer. The last two and a half years of their stay in the Austrian capital, from 1 April 1884 to 1 October 1886, he was the chief editor of the *Neue Illustrierte Zeitung* (New Illustrated Newspaper) in Vienna. In all the intervening years he was also a most productive and prolific writer of fiction. He wrote and published three collections of novellas and four novels in these years in addition to completing the second volume of his *Halb-Asien* trilogy. In *Junge Liebe* (1879, Young Love) and in *Stille Geschichten* (1889, Quiet Stories) he broke away from narrations about Jewish ghetto life and Eastern Europe. His *Tragische Novellen* (1886, Tragic Novellas) however, returned to his initial theme of Jewish and Eastern European life again. His first novel, *Moschko von Parma* (1880, Moshko of Parma) dealt likewise with the life of a young Jew who attempted to break out of the confines of the ghetto but was forced to return in later years as a broken man. *Ein Kampf ums Recht*, which became his most successful and popular novel during his lifetime, was also well-liked abroad and translated into English in 1882 under the title *For the Right*. This historical novel portrayed the uprising of a small Eastern European mountain people against their Austrian overlords. Also Franzos's next two novels, *Der Präsident* (1884, The President) and *Die Reise nach dem Schicksal* (1885, The Journey to Fate) dealt with non-Jewish themes. The first of these relates the ultimately fatal consequences of the youthful transgressions of a highly respected Austrian judge. *Die Reise nach dem Schicksal* involves the theme of incest.

Franzos's most exciting experience in those years, however, was his chance meeting with the Austrian Crown Prince Rudolf in February of 1884 at the prestigious Concordia Ball of the *Wiener Journalisten- und Schriftstellerverein* (Society of Viennese Journalists and Writers). This remarkably gifted and versatile heir apparent to the Austro-Hungarian throne was keenly interested in the history, culture, and folklore of the eastern ranges of the Danube Empire and adjacent regions about which Franzos wrote as a journalist, social and cultural critic as well as a writer of fiction. A close relationship quickly developed between the liberal and astute crown prince and Franzos that can be said to have bordered on friendship. Franzos, however, remained tight-lipped about it especially after the untimely and sensational death of the prince through suicide in 1889, and he refrained from revealing confidences to which he had become privy in his professional and personal dealings with Rudolf of Habsburg.

Prior to his relationship with the prince, Franzos performed a most valuable service to his own and future generations by not only keeping Georg Büchner's name alive through a number of timely articles, but also by attempting and completing the momentous and difficult task of transcribing this writer's extant manuscripts and by publishing them in a first critical edition. Although Franzos's transcriptions of Büchner's collected works published under the title of *Georg Büchners Sämmtliche Werke und handschriftlicher Nachlaß: Erste kritische Gesammt-Ausgabe* (Georg Büchner's Complete Works and Literary Remains: First Critical and Complete Edition) in 1879 cannot be deemed satisfactory by modern standards of editorship since it contained many errors and misconceptions, they represented in the history of Büchner scholarship the first and most crucially necessary step toward canonization of this nineteenth-century literary genius, whose works—now internationally known—have inspired succeeding generations of writers to the present day. Even severe Franzos critics in this area, such as the Büchner specialist Fritz Bergemann, editor of later historical and critical Büchner editions dating from 1922 to 1966, gave Franzos full credit for his initial undertaking. Thus Bergemann states with convincing objectivity:

> Franzos, Karl Emil (1848-1904): edited and published Büchner's compl. works and literary remains in 1879 as "First Critical and Complete Edition." Even if this edition can no longer be considered to be "critical," Franzos deserves credit for Bü.'s recognit. and for the preser.'t. of h. lit. remains. We are also indebted to Franzos for the recollections of Bü. by Wilhelm Büchner. . . Luck . . . Zimmermann. . . . Franzos asked them for these contributions for h. biograph. introduct., which remained fragmentary, however.[5]

This outburst of editorial and literary activities was temporarily suspended when Franzos and his wife decided to leave Vienna in November 1887 in order to establish themselves permanently in Berlin, the glittering capital of the newly founded Second Reich. But their migration there was much more than a financial decision. It was—at least from Franzos's point of view—the fulfillment of a lifelong dream: a coming home, so to speak, to what appeared to be at the time the new heartland of his beloved German culture. In a negative sense it was also a clear-cut admission by him that his Josephinian idealism, which was to have imbued the Austrian lands with the fruits of philosophical enlightenment and political liberalism and was to have opened up the eastern parts of the empire to the brightness of German culture, was for all practical purposes dead. To this end he wrote in *Vom Don zur Donau*: "Until 1860 the Austrian government protected its Ukrainian subjects to a certain extent. . . . That changed with the advent of the October Diploma. Reactionary forces have pursued a political line in the east which keeps one ethnic minority in check by means of another—the constitution sacrifices one people for the sake of another."[6]

In later years he added to these critical remarks: "The fact that the influence of German acculturation in the east has experienced such considerable setbacks has had a most detrimental impact on the progress of Jews in Galicia and the Bukovina."[7]

This latter observation provides a clue for other reasons in addition to those already stated as to why Franzos left his native Austria permanently to settle in the new Germany: increasing dissatisfaction with conditions in Austria-Hungary for the Jewish subjects there in the eastern parts and the rising incidence of anti-Semitism in Austria proper. Although life in Berlin was by his own statement much more sedate than living conditions in Vienna had been, the facts do not seem to bear out this contention. For one thing, anti-Semitism in the eighties and nineties of the past century was also increasing in Germany, where the new term actually originated. True, as an acknowledged writer with international reputation and as the new editor of the literary magazine *Deutsche Dichtung* (German Literature) he no longer suffered economic hardships. But part of the reason why he also founded *Deutsche Verlags-Anstalt Concordia* (German Publishing House Concordia) had to do with the fact that he experienced difficulties in those days publishing his stories and novels that dealt with "Jewish" themes and backgrounds. His own publishing firm was a clever, if not necessary, way of getting around these difficulties. Still there were other problems brought about by the anti-Semitic groundswell in Germany. Paul Heinze, publisher and editor of the literary magazine *Deutsches Dichterheim* (German Writers Homeground), accused Franzos in a number of articles tinged with offensive anti-Semitic remarks, of shady practices in obtaining readers for his *Deutsche Dichtung*. Even though Franzos was vindicated after a two-year fight, he had to instigate a lawsuit that was to be costly to him both in time and psychic energy expended. Soon after this unpleasant affair, Franzos was accused by a certain Julius Grosse of refusing to publish some of his "patriotic" works because of "racial" bias. After much legal maneuvering the dispute was settled by arbitration before the *Deutsche Schriftstellerverband* (German Writers Association). This development was anything but pleasing to Franzos who felt very strongly that he was badly maligned and done an injustice.

Though this painful experience proved costly to the author and had a negative impact upon his creativity as a writer, his literary output in Berlin was still quite formidable. It consisted principally of the third volume of his *Halb-Asien* trilogy *Aus der großen Ebene,* three collections of novellas—*Ein Opfer* (1893, A Victim), *Ungeschickte Leute* (1894, Clumsy

People), *Allerlei Geister* (1897, All Kinds of Spirits)—and six novels: *Die Schatten* (The Shadows), *Der Gott des alten Doktors* (The God of the Old Physician), *Judith Trachtenberg*, *Der Wahrheitssucher* (The Seeker of Truth), *Der kleine Martin* (Little Martin), and *Leib Weihnachtskuchen und sein Kind* (Leib Weihnachtskuchen and His Child), which appeared in print from 1888 to 1896. Yet not a single one of these books achieved the popularity of his earlier works. They reiterated, with the exception of *Der Wahrheitssucher*, themes introduced and expounded earlier. From what we know about Franzos's intentions at the time, anti-Semitism had a great deal to do with his reluctance to publish his novel *Der Pojaz* (The Clown) during his lifetime in German. Only a Russian version of it—a kind of a trial balloon—came out in print before his death in 1904. This novel, which is acclaimed today as his masterpiece, was published posthumously in 1905 by his widow. Anti-Semitism in general and the pogroms of the eighties and nineties in Russia caused him to become an active member of the *Deutsches Zentralkomitee für die russischen Juden* (German Central Committee for Russian Jews). However, he did not agree with the aims of Zionism and rejected the idea of a national Jewish homeland in Palestine as unworkable.

All of this excitement and much of the bitterness it left behind, though largely unacknowledged by him, were detrimental to his health. In addition, just as his father had done, he paid little attention to his health and literally worked himself to death. His creative writing, the countless articles he wrote on literature, art, culture, minorities, and women's affairs, the strain as an editor and publisher—which forced him to stay up many a night, keeping himself awake with excessive amounts of coffee—were to exact their toll. Moreover, controversy continued to be a constant companion literally to the last year of his life. When the prominent contemporary writer Theodor Mommsen, who had become a close friend, passed away, Franzos took it upon himself to write a commemorative article about him. This very personal piece of writing, to which he gave the title *Erinnerungen an Mommsen* (Recollections of Mommsen), led to widespread protests in Czernowitz against him, where he was wrongly accused of having called the local university an academic penal colony. These words had actually been Mommsen's. Prior to this controversy, his health had already begun to fail. He developed heart and kidney problems. After a long and painful struggle and despite the best care that medical science of the day could offer, he died on 28 January 1904. Tragically, it was the day of his twenty-seventh wedding anniversary. His funeral on 31 January 1904, became a social event. His interment in the Jewish cemetery of Weissensee, a suburb of Berlin, was attended not merely by his widow and close friends, but also by prominent local writers and scholars. The Berlin rabbi Rosenzweig and the well-known Germanist Ludwig Geiger delivered funeral orations. Geiger's was later published in book form under the title of *Gedenkrede auf Karl Emil Franzos* (Commemorative Address on Karl Emil Franzos). Alfred Klaar, another prominent Germanist, wrote about him in a commemorative article:

> At a time when rekindled intolerance on the one hand and racial arrogance on the other attempt to bring about a re-kindled Jewish question and when a number of Jews . . . stress their own national identity, he represented by the type of his talent, through his work, thinking, and sensitivity the fusion of Jewishness and German nationalism. . . . Franzos was a German and a Jew. He was both not only by birth and through his rearing but . . . also by his innermost feelings, which he affirmed in his work.[8]

The fact that Franzos was also a socio-cultural and socio-critical writer, dealing with ethnic problems and frictions in Eastern Europe and the Balkans and committed to emancipation and assimilation of not only the Jewish ghetto inhabitants of these parts, but also all of the backward peoples of the region, is made clear in the initial volume of his *Halb-Asien* trilogy, which also established him as a prominent writer of the age. In this volume he coins the concept of *Halb-Asien* as a descriptive term for Eastern Europe. It met with immediate public acclaim. He explains its deeper meaning in the preface of volume one of the subsequent trilogy:

> The title with which I have prefaced this book may sound strange and striking. Yet I did not choose it for that reason, but because it seems to characterize pointedly and correctly the cultural conditions of those countries which I describe in it. For these countries have not been put between re-fined Europe and the desolate steppes just by geographic accident. . . . Also in the political and social conditions of these countries, European refinement and Asiatic barbar-

ism, European progressivity and Asiatic indolence, European humaneness and such fierce, such cruel struggle among nations and religious communities meet in a strange fashion. . . . The outer layer, the form, in those countries is in many instances borrowed from the West; the core, the spirit are largely autochthonous and barbaric.[9]

In the preface to the third volume, *Aus der großen Ebene*, he explains both his intention and his pedagogic message in still greater detail:

I decry the pressure which the Russians apply on the Ukrainians and the Poles. But when the Poles, as is the case in Galicia, do the same, I decry the pressure which they bring to bear on the Ukrainians, Jews, and German nationals. I stand up for the Jews because they are subjugated. But I attack the subjugation which the orthodox Jews themselves practice vis-à-vis their secular coreligionists. I am for the justifiable influence of German culture in the East. But when in its name forcible Germanizing is attempted, I condemn these disastrous endeavors. (*Aus der großen Ebene*, l:xii)

On reading the actual texts of these volumes, however, it becomes clear that the author by design or inadvertently also presents the reader with much more than outright social criticism and didacticism. The volumes are, in effect, comprised of spellbinding cultural vignettes, tales of adventure and intrigue, and genuine human interest stories that are in most instances as fascinating today—considering our renewed interest in this still highly volatile and backward region—as they were over a hundred years ago. In many instances—as the modern reader soon realizes—basic social, cultural, and even political conditions have not changed all that much in all of these intervening decades. The greatest exception is doubtless the mode of life and the fate of the Jews in those countries which the larger part of the trilogy investigates. Through the Holocaust, perpetrated by Hitler and the Third Reich, and simultaneous as well as subsequent Soviet persecution, Jewish life, so abundant and greatly increasing in Franzos's lifetime, has for all practical purposes ceased to exist. In "Markttag in Barnow" (Market Day in Barnow)—one of the most brilliantly written sketches of the entire trilogy, in which the author shows in a flowing and colorful style how the various ethnic groups of a typical Galician *shtetl* intermingled and interacted on the busiest day of their work week—Franzos states with almost uncanny vision: "Let us assume, Rothschild were to found a kingdom of Jerusalem and all the Jews of Galicia followed his call, we could experience great surprises in anti-Semitic Galicia. The whole territory would be in a state of despair. A Galicia without Jews would be an area devoid of life" (*Vom Don zur Donau*, 1:85).

Another vignette, "Tote Seelen" (Dead Souls) makes clear that the low moral stature which a Jew might project in these parts is but a reflection of the way he is treated there and is ultimately a mirror image of the respective host country and its people: "Alas, it is a sad question . . . who has to be more ashamed of Getzel, the Polish Jews or the Poles of Christian persuasion? . . . Every country has the Jews it deserves" (*Aus Halb-Asien*, 2:107-108).

The latter statement was frequently quoted worldwide as an adage and made Franzos famous during his lifetime. In "Schiller in Barnow" Franzos shows the beneficial influence that an old volume of Schiller's poems exerts on Jews and gentiles alike in these backward lands. The story culminates in the admonition: "Alas, little do you educated people in the big cities know how great under certain circumstances the value of a volume of Schiller's poems can be" (*Aus Halb-Asien*, 1:188).

The perhaps most thrilling and adventurous tale of the collection is "Der Aufstand von Wolowce" (The Uprising of Wolowce). It describes in semi-historical terms the brutal arrogance and inhumanity of the wealthy and propertied Polish aristocrats in their sordid dealings with the impoverished and culturally backward Ukrainian peasants of Galicia. Regrettably, justice did not prevail, and ultimately the authorities backed the dubious rights of the aristocratic land barons and oppressors and neglected the justified outcries of the oppressed. The author's portrayal of conditions in imperial Russia follows similar lines of exposure and condemnation.

But Franzos' approach to these matters and his socio-cultural discourse attempting to deal with them are not all negative. Essays interspersed throughout the trilogy also deal in a positive way with historical developments of the area. In his essay "Taras Szewczenko," for example, the author analyzes and shows the significance of the works of this Ukrainian poet laureate. In a related article, "Das Volkslied der Kleinrussen" (The Folk Song of the Ukrainians), he writes in an Herderian spirit: "The folk song of the Ukrainians is the best and most beautiful that a people's spirit has created . . ." (*Vom Don zur Donau*, 1:292).

The author's love of German culture manifests itself in three articles of the collection—"Von Wien nach Czernowitz" (From Vienna to Czernowitz), "Zwischen Dniester und Bistrizza" (Between Dniester and Bistrizza), and "Ein Kulturfest" (A Culture Festival). They are primarily positive accounts of the beneficial aspects of German culture at work in Eastern Europe. Franzos's attitude toward women is also of current interest. Whereas he cannot be called an advocate of women's liberation as it has become known today since he did not believe that women should serve in the military or as priests, he nonetheless was among the first of his generation to embrace the ideal of a genuine emancipation of women, stating categorically in this context: "The social position of women is the safest indicator of the level of culture that a people has attained and also the safest measuring device of the positive and negative sides of a people's spirit" (*Aus der großen Ebene*, 2:223). Most significant is the fact that in all the volumes of the trilogy he advocates the culture of an enlightened and classical German humanism as an ideal that all the peoples of Eastern Europe, including its Jewish inhabitants, should presently strive for and should ultimately embrace.

This very message provides also the inner core of his first and most important collection of novellas, to which Franzos gave the title *Die Juden von Barnow*. Although most of the stories, including its seminal work "Das Christusbild," were written before he was able to publish *Aus Halb-Asien*, they had to await the publication of the latter before a publisher was willing to risk bringing out a volume by an unknown and untested author. As it turned out, the book became almost instantaneously an international bestseller by today's standards, appearing soon in multiple editions in sixteen languages. Readers not only in German-speaking countries, but also abroad seemed ready and eager to learn about life in the Jewish ghettos of Eastern Europe. To be sure, however, there was no sugar coating provided by the author about living conditions there. The basic tone of his stories was grim, at times even bitter. Nor were the novellas in the collection based upon romantic fantasies and poetic fancy. They were written in the style which was to become Franzos's trademark: the same combination of socio-critical, didactic, and anecdotal writing which the public had already encountered and approved in *Aus Halb-Asien*.

Interestingly, though, as true to life as his tales seemed to be to contemporary readers, the name of Barnow itself was purely fictional. It is, in this sense, reminiscent of Gottfried Keller's Seldwyla, except that it does not carry any hidden symbolic or ironic meaning even remotely similar to Keller's tongue-in-cheek idea of referring to his fictitious Swiss town as "place of the blessed." By his own statement Franzos felt that his intended German readers might have difficulties with pronouncing and consequently reject his native Czortkow. Moreover, since the author had gained most of his personal experience with ghetto life in Czernowitz, the fictitious name was meant to be generic. To be sure, his Barnow stands for something rather specific. In its thematic and socio-critical impact it is the emblematic, prototypical Jewish *shtetl* of his native Podolia, an area desperately in need of emancipation and assimilation. Franzos himself called his book "a weapon in the struggle of enlightenment against the darkness" (*Die Geschichte des Erstlingswerks*, p. 240). From the author's point of view then, both the medium or locale of his stories and their thematic treatment are the message in the nine novellas that comprise the collection as stressed in the book's preface: "These novellas were written neither to ridicule nor to extol Eastern Jewry. They pursue . . . the aim of pointing out dark areas and to help illuminate them, as far as my voice can reach."[10] The tendentious fashion in which he pursues this intended goal becomes an inner self-propelling force of the various plots.

The very first novella, in fact, "Der Shylock von Barnow" (The Shylock of Barnow), sets the tone. The obvious reference that the title provides to Shakespeare's *Merchant of Venice* points to the inner theme of the plot, which is dramatic as well as tragic. What makes the narrative a novella in the traditional sense of the Goethean "unusual past event" is an orthodox Jewish father's unwillingness to forgive the trespasses of his daughter which caused her to leave her protected life at home and follow the romantic notions of her heart. He refuses to take her back after she has stumbled and fallen. He does not do this lightly, however, or on the spur of the moment, but under the dictate of strict Jewish orthodox law. The actual reference to the Shakespearean character is made by the town's unfeeling and anti-Semitic Christian gossips, who ascribe his actions wrongly to personal heartlessness and greed.

In the second selection, "Nach dem höheren Gesetz" (According to the Higher Law), the theme of Judeo-Christian relations is carried in a different direction. A poor Jewish girl has married a wealthy Jewish merchant. When she falls in love with a Christian town official and wants to leave her husband, the latter is overcome by rage and jealousy at first, but soon finds the strength of character not only to let her go, but also to forgive her. Yet neither Barnow's Jewish, nor the town's Christian community follows suit. They will not accept the mixed marriage and treat the couple and their children as social outcasts. The author's commentary is a combination of acerbic criticism and sardonic, tongue-in-cheek humor: "The small town of Barnow is tiny, indeed, a desolate, dirty place in a god-forsaken corner of the world, and the large current of life and culture brings rarely an atom of a ripple to its shores, but—it does have a 'casino.' To be sure, it is of very modest appearance" (68-69).

The novella "Zwei Retter" (Two Saviors) shows that the salvation of the Jewish community does not necessarily come from above. It has its humble origin in the courage and perseverance of some of its own members. Two examples of such heroic individuals are given in this tale, which also incorporates the Stifterian motif of greatness and smallness in human affairs and reflects Dostoevski's theme of crime and punishment. One is a married woman, the other a young man. The two culprits in the story, also a woman and a man from the Christian community who have endangered the security of the ghetto inhabitants, see their carefully crafted designs of covering up their own guilt come to naught.

The inner theme of *Aus Halb-Asien*, relating the underlying cruelty of all of the region's inhabitants, becomes also the leitmotif of "Der wilde Starost und die schöne Jütta" (The Wild Community Leader and Beautiful Jutta). In this tale of Christian arrogance and Jewish revenge, a young and willful local official, overcome by sexual desire for a young and beautiful Jewish woman whom he has observed on Corpus Christi day, forcibly abducts and rapes her the very same night. But instead of discarding her after attaining sexual gratification, he falls in love with her and decides to keep her as a permanent companion. She soon returns his love. After she bears him a child, they even make plans for her to convert to Christianity and to legitimize their relationship through marriage. They are unaware, however, that the Jewish community has made plans to free her while her lover is away and to bring her home. When in carrying out this mission the child is inadvertently killed, the distraught mother commits suicide. After he returns home and learns of the tragic events, the father of the dead child and husband to be is overcome with grief. He lives out his life in madness. Two old people symbolically represent the two hostile communities at the end, while the Corpus Christi procession again passes by on the outside: "An old woman sits . . . in a darkened room in the Jewish ghetto and utters, on hearing the commotion: 'Cursed be the Christians'—and an old man stands in the courtyard of the manor house, looks up to his mad master, who dances about for joy, and utters: 'Cursed be the Jews!'" (167).

This ultimate theme of mutual hatred fed by opposing and inimical religious sentiments and experiences is greatly altered in the novella "Das Kind der Sühne" (The Child of Atonement), which deals with the theme of pure maternal love. The novella also acquaints the reader with one of the greatest health scourges besetting the backward regions, in which ignorance, superstition, and resulting lax practices of sanitation are endemic: cholera. When one of the recurring cholera epidemics decimates an eastern Jewish community, the frightened inhabitants turn to a *Wunderrabbi* (a miracle-performing rabbi). After much experimentation he advises them to perform their wedding ceremonies in the local cemetery: "A sacrifice to our angry God" (183). In connection with this gruesome practice, a young Jewish man and a woman of poor background marry and beget two children, who die soon after birth, however. When, after a while, the woman is pregnant again, a new wave of cholera strikes the community. Her husband succumbs to the dreadful illness, but she and her newborn child survive. The *Wunderrabbi* proclaims that the child will live only in order to be the community's child of atonement and sacrifice some day. When still a third cholera epidemic threatens the region and her child falls ill, the mother resolves to make a pilgrimage to the far-away, very famous *Wunderrabbi* to plead with him for the life of her child. In order to do so, however, she has to leave her sick child in the care of neighbors. But halfway to the town of the *Wunderrabbi* she follows the dictates of her heart and returns home, where she is able to nurture her child back to health through loving care. Yet what is the reaction of the people of Barnow to this miracle? Franzos comments at the end of the story: "If they had only known that it was only love, the love of a mother, which had opposed the hatred here and exercised its healing and lifesaving powers, they would probably have been unceasing in their rancor against the widow and her child. But obviously, a simple 'heavenly miracle' had occurred here: And a miracle ascribable to God himself is singularly more powerful than a pronouncement of the *Wunderrabbi*" (202).

In the novella "Esterka Regina," on the other hand, Franzos intends to give yet another example of the impotence of romantic love in the face of orthodox rigidity and lack of enlightened education. A young and highly intelligent man who likes to think for himself moves away from the narrowness of Barnow to study medicine in Vienna. When he learns that the Jewish girl with whom he had fallen in love was forced by her father to marry a local Jew, he leaves Europe altogether filled with suffering to serve as a military physician in the far-off Dutch East Indies. He returns home only after an agonizing letter from the woman he still loves reaches him, begging him to help her in her struggle to overcome a grave illness. But he arrives too late. She has already died. Her life as well as their romantic love were evidently as fragile as the delicate name he had given her in their youth because of her dainty beauty.

"Baron Schmule" is a grim story of inhumanity on the part of power-ful outsiders breeding hatred and revenge within the Jewish ghetto. When the young aristocratic scion of a wealthy Polish landowner strikes a poor Jewish boy so hard that he loses an eye as a result, the latter swears to get even. He gets his revenge many years later when, after much hard work and self-denial, he has accumulated wealth and is able to buy the estate of the cruel Polish aristocrat who had come down in the world and lost most of his fortune because of addiction to alcohol. The novella ends on the same grim note on which it began. The "new baron" of the land and of the manor, who had even been willing to leave his Jewish faith to become a landowner—as required by law in those days, since Jews could not own land—gives a big party to celebrate the marriage of his daughter. The "old baron" is also invited and indulges in the freely flowing liquor to such excess that he dies as a result. Franzos combined in this tale the modern Naturalist theme of the scourges of alcoholism with the ancient biblical notion of an eye for an eye and a tooth for a tooth.

The novella "Das Christusbild" utilizes the theme of the depravity of the Polish aristocracy. An old count marries a young and beautiful Polish woman. When, because of alcoholic excesses, he is unable to consummate the marriage during the wedding night, he becomes so agitated that he shoots and kills himself. The life of the young widow takes on a new meaning when she meets the young and idealistic Jewish teacher of Barnow. She had met him, as it turns out, years ago, when he was a well-to-do society doctor. He gave up his lucrative practice to return to his humble roots. Now he serves his community, which is in need of commit-ted teachers. Although the two young people are inexorably attracted to one another, their love cannot be consummated because of religious barriers. When the countess returns to Barnow the following year, the Jewish teacher is no longer among the living, the victim of a fatal illness. She resolves to capture his countenance in a picture of Christ, which she intends to give to a nearby chapel. Relates the narrator: "And this painting showed indeed that she comprehended the nobility and the magnitude of the sacrifice which the Jew had made for her sake and for his own" (310).

The book's last entry, "Ohne Inschrift" (Without Inscription) is not a modern novella per se but a collection of anecdotes and reflections. These are held together by the central motif of death. Perhaps the most touching tale of the lot is the story of a young Jewish woman who has done the nearly unthinkable in Podolia. She married a widower not, as was customary, through arrangement but out of love. Unconventional as she is, she also offends the entire Jewish community by refusing to have her beautiful blond hair cut, as the tradition demands of a married woman. When belligerent members of the community force their way into her home to cut her hair over her objection, an altercation results, during which both she and her newborn child lose their lives. Yet the narrator refrains from indicting the perpetrators as true criminals. In his view, they were intellectually misguided and culturally stunted and deprived. Hence, he finds words of charity for them at the end: "Forgive them, don't be angry with them, for they know not what they do!" (348).

These words of forgiveness, which assume almost biblical proportions, notwithstanding, the basic tone of Franzos's ghetto stories debunked rather early the still widely held notion of any idyllic Jewish existence in the *shtetls* of Eastern Europe, ever so popular in many quarters today. His portrayal of *shtetl* life confirms his basic view that those Jewish ghettos were not secluded islands on which Jewish life could flourish and evolve. He saw them as rather primitive prisons, intellectually frozen in time and stultified, surrounded by inimical and threatening forces equally deprived and backward, but much larger in number and consequently much more powerful. In his *Juden von Barnow*, just as in his *Halb-Asien* volumes, he promulgated the idea of removing the walls of confinement. Both the backward peoples of Eastern Europe and the equally backward eastern Jewish communities were in dire need of emancipation and acculturation. They needed to absorb and practice the Western idea and ideals of Enlightenment. Although the author was able to write and publish seven more collections of novellas during his lifetime—two additional ones were printed posthumously—he was unable to emulate and surpass the popular-ity of *Die Juden von Barnow* in this genre. In later years, to be sure, he tried to get away from ghetto stories so that, all in all, nearly half of the novellas he wrote did not deal with *shtetl* conditions per se. His experi-ences in Austria and later in Germany induced him to write a number of novellas about life there in general and about the people in the big cities and in the countryside.

This duality in background and content applies to his novels as well. Only four of Franzos's eleven novels deal outrightly with Jewish themes. To be sure, his first biographer, Ludwig Geiger, called Franzos's very first novel *Moschko von Parma* his best novelistic achievement. It relates the story of an unusually strong and brazen Jewish fellow who, though leaving the confines of the Jewish ghetto and its traditions, is still unable to secure for himself a life of fulfillment and ultimate happiness. As in many of his previous shorter stories with Jewish content, here too, the roots of the problem lie in the area of Judeo-Christian relations. This area is precisely the seedbed out of which his second Jewish novel, *Judith Trachtenberg*, arises. It deals essentially with the ultimately unhappy marriage of a Jewess to a Polish aristocrat and the tragic consequences facing both. The actual cause of the debacle is not so much the disproportion of the principals' cultural background, but the opposition of outside forces to their attempt to break out of their religious and ethnic confines. This is also in only slight variation the underlying theme of *Leib Weihnachtskuchen und sein Kind*, the last of Franzos's novels still published during his lifetime. The poor, downtrodden, but basically kind and humane, Jewish tavern keeper cannot permit his obedient daughter to enter a legal or illicit relationship with the Ukrainian peasant pining for her because of religious con-ditioning beyond his rational grasp. As in previous stories, the outcome has to be tragic for all concerned.

This continuity of theme, however, is broken in the ghetto novel *Der Pojaz*, considered to be Franzos's novelistic masterpiece today. It is written in the vein of the German developmental and education novel, but has—as do most of Franzos's narrations—a tragic ending. The author combines here thematically the debacle of Jewish ghetto existence with the ill-fated drive of a young, naive, and intellectually pure ghetto boy to attain an appropriate education in the German classics in the deprived and spiritually ossified environment of Barnow. The novel's young Jewish protagonist, whom the author gave the symbolic name of Sender Glatteis, has to wither away and die. The manner in which his death occurs is almost immaterial. Incapable of breaking out of the confinement of the ghetto, he succumbs to the complications of pneumonia. He contracted this illness as a result of sitting for hours on end in the unheated library of a nearby monastery. Comments the author: "His crime is that he could not find German books in any other place but the unheated library of the Barnow monastery."[11]

Of the other seven novels which Franzos's wrote—narrations with non-Jewish themes—*Der Präsident* (The Chief Justice) and especially *Der Wahrheitssucher* (The Seeker of Truth) deserve special mention. The former tells the story of an Austrian provincial chief justice who is considered to be one of the best and most upright in the Empire. But there are skeletons in his closet. In his youth he had fathered an illegitimate child and deserted her mother. When many years later a young woman, who has murdered her baby born to her out of wedlock, is tried in his court, he recognizes her as his deserted daughter and saves her from certain execution by secretly freeing her and sending her abroad. Although his criminal behavior remains undetected, he divulges the truth to his startled superior, the minister of justice, and commits suicide afterwards, notwithstanding the fact that the latter is willing to hush up the whole affair for appearance's sake. *Der Wahrheitssucher* is a novelistic *tour de force* that takes the reader with breathtaking speed through the historic development and political life of Austria, Germany, and Italy in mid-nineteenth-century Europe. Georg Winter, the protagonist in this developmental novel, experiments with various life styles. After rejecting the monastic life, that of a communist revolutionary, and the sedate existence of a capitalist entrepreneur, he ultimately opts for an eclectic life style of the middle. He does this, however, not just for moral reasons, but also as a very practical solution to the complexities of modern life. It can be easily deduced that the author used his hero here to voice political and moral views of his own: "I hope that both can be avoided, the increasing wealth of some and the growing poverty of the masses. I am hopeful of it because millions of people recognize that this is the largest and the most pressing task we have to solve. . . . It is not merely brotherly love alone which pushes us in this direction, but also the anguish and selfishness of all those who have something to lose."[12]

However, it was not this politically astute and forward-looking novel that caught the public eye at the time it was published. Franzos's most popular novelistic narration was *Ein Kampf ums Recht*, which became known in the English-speaking world under the title *For the Right*. No less a public figure than the prominent English politician and statesman William Gladstone wrote the introduction to the work's first English edition. In it, he states:

> It is with some confidence that I commend to the notice of your readers a work of Karl Emil Franzos, entitled "For the Right." The work is a novel, of which the scene is laid in the Carpathian mountains. Among its secondary merits, it has that of laying open to the Western eye the manners of a Slavonic people, little known . . . even to their Austrian fellow subjects. . . . The story is of too much interest to allow of any marring it by a relation of the plot. Nor is such a relation needful . . . , because the commanding force and attraction of the plot itself is summed up in its central idea, which is that of a nature possessed and impelled by an enthusiasm for justice, alike passionate, persistent, and profound.[13]

It was the story's plot, in fact, which Gladstone left to the reader's own investigation, telling of a person's struggle against oppression, deceit, and disrespect for the law, which made the novel famous. German reviewers called its hero Taras Barabola, the Michael Kohlhaas of the East. Like his famous Kleistian predecessor, he is indeed a righteous and profoundly moral human being, who is also driven to open rebellion by his passion for the law and for justice. Unlike Kohlhaas, however, he does not fight for the purpose of rectifying an injustice done to him personally. He champions a wronged community and eventually pays the supreme price by martyring himself for both the cause and his personal ideals. Early on, the prominent contemporary Germanist Ernst Schultze summed up Franzos's personal beliefs in this regard:

> A passionate sense of justice lives in him. He looks at this stern sense of justice not only as an ideal toward which the cultural evolution of man has to advance, but also as the highest moral standard which every individual should make his own presently. Yet how that sense of justice can be-

come the driving force in a human life, cleansing and uplifting a human being, but causing his downfall when he
presumes to find the proper course in every instance not
just for himself but for all his fellow-creatures—he describes in his monumental, two-volume novel *A Struggle for
Justice.*[14]

Franzos's considerable fame as a writer began to diminish precipitously
after World War I. The principal causes for this development, preventing
his canonization as a literary figure and relegating him ultimately to the
large pool of nearly forgotten authors, are twofold. Both German-speaking
countries, his native Austria and Germany, his chosen second homeland,
lost the war of 1914-1918, and with it—because of their diminished
status—their previous interest in the eastern territories, about which
Franzos primarily wrote. The general reader shared and reflected these
national concerns. At the same time, the literary focus of the years after
the war was greatly influenced by the new Expressionist movement and
was, as were the main political and social trends of the epoch, turned
inward. Moreover, and in the third instance, Franzos's criticism and
concerns were anathema to many of the leading literary and cultural
opinion makers. His antisocialist stance on the one hand, and his rejection
of Zionism on the other, estranged him from many Jewish and Gentile
readers, who embraced socialist ideals or, as regards the former, the idea
of a Jewish homeland. The growing influence of a racially oriented
German nationalism hurt Franzos's image even more. When the National
Socialists came to power in Germany, his writings, together with those of
other Jewish authors, were blacklisted and burned. One of the leading
Franzos specialists after the Second World War, the Germanist Wolfgang
Marten, assessed the reception of the author's works from the 1920s to the
1960s this way:

The German book index of the 20s still shows a number
of entries of Franzos's books which were newly issued by
German publishers. This listing, however, ceases almost on
command in 1930, also in Austria: the verdict of the National Socialists regarding all Jewish authors goes into
effect. Only the Schocken Publishing House in Berlin receives permission in 1937 to publish a selection of 43 pages

in its *Jewish Readers.*—After 1945 a few works of Franzos
are printed in Vienna and Graz, above all, however, in
Leipzig and in East Berlin: novellas, a few selections from
his cultural vignettes *Aus Halb-Asien* and especially his
novels *Ein Kampf ums Recht* and *Der Pojaz.*[15]

Well into the 1970s, in fact, it was forgotten that Franzos was among the
most widely read and translated authors during his lifetime. Nor was it
remembered any longer that his *Deutsche Dichtung* was one of the leading
literary magazines in the era preceding and following the turn of the
century. Among the authors who published in this periodical were some
of the most prominent names of the period: Ludwig Anzengruber, Felix
Dahn, Marie von Ebner-Eschenbach, Theodor Fontane, Gustav Freytag,
Paul Heyse, Gottfried Keller, C. F. Meyer, Ferdinand von Saar, Viktor
von Scheffel, and Theodor Storm. Only in the 1980s did a renewed interest in Franzos's writings and contributions begin to surface.

Franzos's literary and socio-cultural legacy is considerable. Aside from
his literary and essayistic *oeuvre,* three areas of permanent significance
come into focus: his preoccupation with German writers of the past and
his own day and age, his extraordinary love of German culture, and his
strong interest in and commitment to Jewish affairs. Regarding the first of
these, his interest in German writers of the past originated in his youth
when he became an avid reader and devoté of the writings of especially
Börne, Heine, Lessing, and Schiller. As the editor and publisher of
Deutsche Dichtung he dealt with most of the principal authors of his own
age. Among the many articles he personally wrote for publication in these
and in preceding years, his commemorative contribution on C. F. Meyer
is—next to his essays about Georg Büchner—most notable, not just in
terms of timeliness, shortly after this author's death, but chiefly in terms
of insight into his craft and method of writing. Franzos was also in touch
with young and aspiring writers of his day. In many instances this contact
was close, personal, and extended over many years. The most notable
example here is young Stefan Zweig, who was both devoted to and felt
inspired by Franzos. He called the author "Meister" (maestro) in their
personal correspondence. Franzos's greatest and most lasting achievement
in all of these endeavors, however, was his painstaking transcription of
Georg Büchner's works, which he ultimately published in their entirety.

The importance he ascribed to German culture and its civilizing and humanizing influence in Eastern Europe can also be traced back to his early childhood and to the rearing and coaching he received from his father. Although he spoke out against forceful Germanization in the East, he favored politically and culturally a greater Austria as a "German cultural state" as well as a "German national state." In this sense he became a propagator of German refinement and culture in the vein of Lessing, Goethe, and Schiller and an emancipator and assimilationist championing Josephinian political enlightenment. Only by these means, he felt, could the East be delivered from its endemic state of backwardness and ossification and raised to a higher level of culture and civilization. His lifelong love of German culture found permanent imprints in two special books. The first of these, *Deutsches Dichterbuch aus Österreich* (Compendium of German Literature From Austria), an edition of lyric, epic, and dramatic selections from the works of living and deceased Austrian authors, was undertaken early in his career as a writer and editor in 1883. Of the second work, *Deutsche Fahrten* (German Travels), containing personal travel impressions of Germany and cultural vignettes, he was able to complete only the first of the two intended volumes.

Although never a practicing Jew in the religious sense, which is again ascribable to his early upbringing, he felt and remained Jewish all his life. Moreover, he fought in word and print against the superimposed backward conditions of the indigenous Jews of Eastern Europe, and against anti-Semitism wherever its hateful specter would raise its head. The internal battle, to which he devoted considerable energy as well, was the struggle against the entrenched and fanatical ultraorthodoxy of the eastern Jewish community. His rejection of Zionism can be ascribed to his belief that not ethnic separatism and the quest for a national homeland held the answer to the perennial dilemma of Jewish existence but genuine and beneficial cultural integration. In all of his endeavors he was more than just a writer, editor, and publisher. He was truly committed to the moral, social, and political assimilation of the disadvantaged, the downtrodden, and the persecuted, irrespective of their gender, race, or religion. Six years before his death, he summarized his *Weltanschauung* poetically and aphoristically:

> Improving the world is no dream.
> Thus let us not push this too far out.
> Doing it, that's what it's all about:
> Every one in his heart's own scheme.[16]

Notes

1. Karl Emil Franzos, "Familiengeschichte," *Im Deutschen Reich: Zeitschrift herausgegeben von dem Zentralverein deutscher Staatsbürger jüdischen Glaubens* (Berlin, 1895), 1, pp. 9-10. All translations from original sources are my own.

2. Karl Emil Franzos, "Mein Erstlingswerk: Die Juden von Barnow," *Die Geschichte des Erstlingswerks* (Leipzig: Adolf Titze, 1894), p. 217.

3. Karl Emil Franzos, "Vorwort," *Der Pojaz: Eine Geschichte aus dem Osten*, 2nd ed. (Stuttgart/Berlin: Cotta, 1905), p. 10.

4. Letter of Ottilie Franzos to Professor Julius Pée of 17 April 1928 (Inventory Number 187.553 of the Franzos Manuscript Collection of the *Wiener Stadt- und Landesbibliothek* (Vienna City and State Library).

5. Fritz Bergemann, ed. *Georg Büchner, Werke und Briefe: Gesamtausgabe* (Frankfurt am Main, 1966), p. 646.

6. Karl Emil Franzos, *Vom Don zur Donau* (Berlin: Rütten and Loening, 1970), 1, p. 200. The so-called October Diploma of 28 October 1860 promulgated a federalist constitution in the Habsburg monarchy but ran into political opposition. Ultimately, it failed to go into full effect.

7. Karl Emil Franzos, *Aus der großen Ebene: Neue Kulturbilder aus Halb-Asien* (Stuttgart: Bonz, 1888), 1, p. xxi.

8. "Franzos, Karl Emil," *Biographisches Jahrbuch und Deutscher Nekrolog*, ed. Anton Bettelheim (Berlin: Georg Reimer, 1907), 10, p. 344.

9. Karl Emil Franzos, *Aus Halb-Asien: Land und Leute des östlichen Europa*, 3rd ed. (Stuttgart: Adolf Bonz, 1889), 1, pp. iii-iv.

10. Karl Emil Franzos, "Vorwort," *Die Juden von Barnow*, 5th ed. (Stuttgart: Adolf Bonz, 1894), p. ix.

11. *Der Pojaz*, p. 482.

12. Karl Emil Franzos, *Der Wahrheitssucher* (Jena: Hermann Constenoble, 1893), 2, p. 336.

13. Karl Emil Franzos, *For the Right* (London: James Clark, 1889), pp. vi-vii.

14. "Karl Emil Franzos und sein 'Kampf ums Recht,'" *Blätter für Volksbibliotheken*, 9, Nos. 11 and 12 (1908), p. 205.

15. "Über Karl Emil Franzos," *Lenau-Forum*, 2, Nos. 3-4, p. 62.

16. *Das kleine Journal*, 1 (1 January 1898).

Bibliography

I. Works by Karl Emil Franzos in German

Allerlei Geister: Geschichten. Berlin: Concordia, 1897.

Der alte Damian und andere Geschichte. Stuttgart/Berlin: Cotta, n.d.

Aus Anhalt und Thüringen. Berlin: Rütten and Loening, n.d.

Aus den Vogesen. Reise- und Kulturbilder: Deutsche Fahrten. Stuttgart/ Berlin: Cotta, 1905.

Aus der großen Ebene: Neue Kulturbilder aus Halb-Asien. Stuttgart: Bonz, 1888.

Aus Halb-Asien: Culturbilder aus Galizien, der Bukowina, Südrußland und Rumänien. Leipzig: Duncker and Humblot, 1876.

Ein Kampf ums Recht. Berlin: Verlag Neues Leben, 1970.

Der Gott des alten Doktors. Berlin: Concordia, 1901.

Heines Geburtstag. Berlin: Concordia, 1900.

Die Juden von Barnow. Stuttgart: Bonz, 1887.

Judith Trachtenberg. Berlin: Concordia, n.d.

Der kleine Martin. Berlin: Concordia, 1896.

Konrad Ferdinand Meyer. Berlin: Concordia, 1899.

Leib Weihnachtskuchen und sein Kind. Vienna: Globus, 1988.

Mann und Weib: Novellen. Stuttgart/Berlin: Cotta, n.d.

Moschko von Parma: Geschichte eines jüdischen Soldaten. Leipzig: Duncker and Humblot, 1880.

Neue Novellen. Stuttgart/Berlin: Cotta, 1905.

Ein Opfer. Stuttgart: J. Engelhorn, 1893.

Der Pojaz: Eine Geschichte aus dem Osten. Stuttgart/Berlin: Cotta, 1905.

Der Präsident. Berlin: Concordia, 1896.

Die Reise nach dem Schicksal. Stuttgart: Bonz, 1885.

Die Schatten. Stuttgart: Bonz, 1889.

Stille Geschichten. Dresden/Leipzig: Heinrich Minden, 1881.

Tragische Novellen. Stuttgart: Bonz, 1886.

Ungeschickte Leute. Jena: Costenoble, 1894.

Vom Don zur Donau. Berlin: Rütten and Loening, 1970.

Der Wahrheitssucher. Jena: Costenoble, 1893.

Collections Edited by Karl Emil Franzos

Aus dem Neunzehnten Jahrundert: Briefe und Aufzeichnungen. Berlin: Concordia, 1897.

Buchenblätter. Czernowitz: J. Buckowski, 1870.
Deutsches Dichterbuch aus Oesterreich. Leipzig: Breitkopf and Härtel, 1883.
Die Geschichte des Erstlingswerks. Leipzig: Titze, 1894.
Die Suggestion und die Dichtung. Berlin: F. Fontane, 1892.

II. Works in English Translation

The Chief Justice. New York: John W. Lovell, 1890.
For the Right. London: James Clarke, 1889.
The Jews of Barnow. New York: Appleton, 1883.

III. Secondary Works in English

Gay, Ruth. "Inventing the Shtetl." *American Scholar* 53 (1984), 329-349.

Gelber, Mark H. "Ethnic Pluralism and Germanization in the Works of Karl Emil Franzos (1848-1904)." *German Quarterly* 56 (1983), 376-385.

Malycky, Alexander. *Jewish-Ukrainian Folk-Culture Interrelationships in the Works of Karl Emil Franzos*. New York: YIVO Institute for Jewish Research, 1974.

Sommer, Fred, *Halb-Asien: German Nationalism and the Eastern European Works of Karl Emil Franzos*. Stuttgart: Heinz, 1984.

Steiner, Carl. *Karl Emil Franzos, 1848-1904: Emancipator and Assimilationist*. New York/Bern/Frankfurt am Main/Paris: Peter Lang, 1990.

IV. Major Studies in German

Bickel, Martha, "Zum Werk von Karl Emil Franzos." *Juden in der deutschen Literatur*. Eds. Stéphane Moses and Albrecht Schöne. Frankfurt am Main: Suhrkamp, 1986.

Geiger, Ludwig. *Die deutsche Literatur und die Juden*. Berlin: Georg Reimer, 1910.

Hermand, Jost. "Nachwort." Karl Emil Franzos, *Der Pojaz*. Königstein/Ts: Athenäum, 1979.

Klaar, Alfred. "Franzos, Karl Emil." *Biographisches Jahrbuch und Deutscher Nekrolog*. Vol. 10. Ed. Anton Bettelheim. Berlin: Georg Reimer, 1907.

Poschmann, Henri. "Nachwort." Karl Emil Franzos, *Moschko von Parma*. Vienna: Globus, 1972.

Schwarz, Egon and Russel A. Berman. "Karl Emil Franzos, *Der Pojaz*

(1905): Aufklärung, Assimilation und ihre realistischen Grenzen." *Romane und Erzählungen des bürgerlichen Realismus.* Stuttgart: Reclam, 1980.

Steiner, Carl. "Deutscher und Jude: Das Leben und Werk des Karl Emil Franzos (1848-1904)." *Autoren damals und heute: Literaturgeschichtliche Beispiele veränderter Wirkungshorizonte.* Amsterdamer Beiträge zur neueren Germanistik. Vols. 31-33 (1990-1991). Amsterdam/Atlanta, GA: Edition Rodopi, 1991.

Strelka, Joseph Peter. "Nachwort." Karl Emil Franzos, *Erzählungen aus Galizien und der Bukowina.* Berlin: Nicolaische Verlagsbuchhandlung Beuermann, 1988.

Franz Grillparzer

Roy C. Cowen

Born in 1791 in an upper middle-class family, Grillparzer never felt that he could abandon his profession as a civil servant and devote himself totally to his creative efforts even though his first plays were well received. Nonetheless, he was destined to become the greatest Austrian dramatist of the nineteenth century and perhaps up to the present. Few critics would contest ranking him as the greatest playwright in the German language between Friedrich Schiller (1759-1805) and Gerhart Hauptmann (1862-1946); despite the relatively modest number of his works in other genres many historians consider him the outstanding Austrian writer of all times. All such evaluations, however, can neither find support in Grillparzer's personal aspirations to achieve these heights, nor can they—his long life notwithstanding—be based on the sheer quantity of his *oeuvre*. Although Grillparzer lived until 1872, he did not produce any new literary works after mid-century. Indeed, his public career as a playwright, which had begun in 1817, ended in 1838 without his ever achieving the high rate of "production" common to so many lesser contemporaries.

Only eight plays were produced on the stage during his life: *Die Ahnfrau* (1817, *The Ancestress*), *Sappho* (staged 1818, printed 1819, *Sappho*), *Das goldene Vließ* (1821-1822, *The Guest-Friend, The Argonauts,* and *Medea*). *König Ottokars Glück und Ende* (1825, *King Ottocar. His Rise and Fall*), *Ein treuer Diener seines Herrn* (1818-1830, *A Faithful Servant of His Master*), *Des Meeres und der Liebe Wellen* (1831-1841, *Hero and Leander*), *Der Traum ein Leben* (1834-1840, *A Dream is Life*), and *Weh dem, der lügt* (1838-1840, *Thou Shalt Not Lie*).[1] During this period he also wrote the libretto for an opera intended for Beethoven but eventually put to music by Conradin Kreutzer: *Melusina* (1833, *Melusine*). When his first comedy, *Weh dem, der lügt,* was badly received, Grillparzer abandoned the public stage forever. After the playwright's death, however, three more dramas were found in completed form: *Libussa* (1872, *Libussa*), *Die Jüdin von Toledo* (1872, *The Jewess of Toledo*), and *Ein Bruderzwist in Habsburg* (1872, *Family Strife in Hapsburg*). Since the last-named work is generally considered his masterpiece, one can scarcely speak of diminishing artistic powers as a reason for Grillparzer's withdrawal from the stage. He also even left several dramatic fragments, but from all indications he had already completed work on the finished plays at the latest shortly after 1848, and the fragments, the longest of which is "Esther" (*Esther,*) remained seemingly untouched for the last twenty years of his life.

Looking at other genres, we note that Grillparzer had published a novella, *Das Kloster bei Sendomir* (1827, The Cloister at Sendomir), which would later be dramatized by Gerhart Hauptmann under the title *Elga* (1905). Only once did Grillparzer break his self-imposed public silence with a major work, *Der arme Spielmann* (1847 but dated 1848, *The Poor Musician*), which has proven to be one of the most enduring novellas of that century and the stimulus for a large amount of Grillparzer scholarship in recent years.[2] Although praised by Adalbert Stifter upon its appearance and somewhat later by Paul Heyse and Gottfried Keller, this work suffered from critical and popular neglect till the end of the century. It is therefore not surprising that it did not encourage Grillparzer to write more prose narratives. Moreover, when he submitted it to the publisher, he stated his belief that he did not really have any great talent in this genre. Grillparzer also composed many poems and epigrams during his lifetime, many of which he published in journals, almanacs, and other places. But while several attempts were made by various publishers to bring out a collection of the poems in book form, Grillparzer steadfastly refused. As a consequence, his lyric and epigrammatic work appeared in its totality for the first time in his posthumously collected works.[3]

His chance to become the first great, if not greatest, serious dramatist in Austria can be explained by the long absence of an appropriate stage, for the Burgtheater as the Court and National Theater did not truly come into existence until 1756, just thirty-five years before Grillparzer's birth.[4] Until Grillparzer's emergence no Austrian showed any talent for serious drama. To be sure, Austria had already developed a distinct theatrical tradition dating back to the seventeenth century, but its roots lay to a large extent in the tradition of the Italian *commedia dell'arte*, and its productions, which appeared on the popular stage (Volkstheater) and were of limited use to Grillparzer in his later plays, presented no competition to him as a dramatist inclining toward tragedy even in his lighter works. In the eighteenth century and the first decade of the nineteenth Austria had not even produced a Johann Christoph Gottsched (1700-1766), let alone a dramatist of the stature of Lessing, Goethe, Schiller, or Heinrich von Kleist. Gottsched's reforms had not even been accepted in Vienna until the 1770s. By being forced to look to Germany for inspiration, Grillparzer could simultaneously feel himself a part of the general stream of German literature after Gottsched—for better or worse.

Lest one assume that Grillparzer accepted everything current in German literature, however, attention must be called to his frequently expressed antipathy toward Romanticism, which dominated the literary scene during his formative years and thereafter. The most enduring author among the Romantics was Ludwig Tieck, about whom Grillparzer comments in 1826: "With his talent for the comic he would have necessarily become a good author of comedies, if his undisciplined spirit had not moved in the direction of formlessness as his true element" (XVIII, 81). One of the most famous examples of romantic criticism can be found in August Wilhelm Schlegel's *Vorlesungen über dramatische Kunst und Literatur* (1809-1811, Lectures on Dramatic Art and Literature). About this work Grillparzer writes that it contains "not a single completely untrue sentence but also *not a single* completely true one" (XVIII, 80).

Furthermore, Grillparzer—and this belongs to the ironies of his public image and the contemporary reception of his work—never managed to outlive completely the reputation created by his initial stage production that he was a "fate-dramatist" (*Schicksalsdramatiker*). The so-called "fate-drama" or "fate-tragedy," albeit usually traced back to Schiller's *Die Braut von Messina* (1803, *The Bride of Messina*), soon came to be associated primarily with Romanticism. Practitioners of this popular dramatic form were, among others, Zacharias Werner, Adolf Müllner and Ernst von Houwald, and we even find elements of the fate-tragedies in novellas like Clemens Brentano's *Geschichte vom braven Kasperl und dem schönen Annerl* (1817, *The Story of the Honorable Caspar and Fair Annie*). The type of play involved usually begins with a curse or prediction, focuses on a fateful weapon as the ultimate instrument of retribution, and presents an intricate series of unexpected and inexplicable events and circumstances that culminate in the revelation of unsuspected family relationships.

Yet despite the ludicrous predictability of its supposed unpredictability the fate-drama prospered on German stages until the appearance of Count August von Platen-Hallermünde's parody *Die verhängnisvolle Gabel* (1826, The Fateful Fork). This popularity was at its zenith when the fledgling dramatist Grillparzer solicited the help of Joseph Schreyvogel to have his *Ahnfrau* performed in the Burgtheater. With an eye for the fashionable Schreyvogel suggested inclusion of several plot elements common to the fate-tragedies. His judgment proved correct inasfar as the play was a popular success, but the critical reception substantiated Grillparzer's reluctance to make the changes Schreyvogel wanted. In his autobiography Grillparzer points out how unnecessary these additions were: "The belief of the characters that they, as a result of a dark tale of an earlier guilt, are subject to a fateful curse—this belief no more produces a factual fate than a person's claim of innocence would make this person innocent" (XIX, 69).

The inspiration for this play supports Grillparzer's interpretation. In it he wants to combine two entirely different stories. He gives as one source an account of the capture of the French bandit Jules (= Louis) Mandrin, who, pursued by the authorities, has fled to a castle. There he has a love affair with a maid, "an upstanding girl who does not suspect to what kind of renegade she has opened her room and heart." Grillparzer claims that Mandrin's capture in her room and the maid's discovery of his true identity provided the "tragic seed" and made a "great impression" on him. In recasting this story he then changed the maid into a noblewoman who is unaware that she is the sister of the fleeing criminal. Obviously this alteration is intended to increase the psychological impact of the ultimate revelation, not its "fateful" implications. As his second source Grillparzer recounts a popular fairy tale. In it the resemblance of the last child of an old family to the wandering ghost of its founding mother gives rise to frightening confusions: her lover first mistakes the girl for the ghost and then elopes with the ghost instead of her. As with the first story Grillparzer seems to have been drawn to a situation illustrating man's inherent inability to transcend his immediate impression. This inference is borne out by another comment Grillparzer made immediately after the premiere: ". . . I must however only note that the *Ahnfrau* in its present form is not *my Ahnfrau*, the foreword—as good as it might be—not *my* foreword, and that in this piece in general, as far as its original intention is concerned, there can be no talk about the realization of an abstract universal idea" (XVIII, 172). What makes Grillparzer's instinctive reaction against the sub-genre of the fate-tragedy so revealing lies therefore not in the ludicrous particulars of its plot details but rather in his personal inability to accept their underlying premise regardless of whether it was truly "romantic." For the plot implies the presence of an all-embracing, supernatural "idea" or power behind events. A similar reluctance to accept religious or intellectual explanations of life and events will characterize all of his later works as well.

For Grillparzer's positive attitude toward contemporary German literature one should note that he wrote a short poem in 1846 on the later times but with a glance backwards: "Their feverish activity goes on and on / The country rings with their cry 'forward, forward,' / I would like, if possible, to remain there / Where Schiller and Goethe stood" (III, 83). Never a political or artistic revolutionary, Grillparzer saw himself and can still be viewed as the heir to Goethe and Schiller. Unlike most of the lesser playwrights of the nineteenth century, who idolized and imitated Goethe and especially Schiller, the Austrian recognized that his German predecessors' implied concept of drama had to be modified. For in his poem cited above, he says quite simply: "if possible" he would merely continue their efforts. Such a possibility, however, no longer existed (elsewhere he implies a similar attitude toward Lessing as well). Admittedly, during the nineteenth century audiences preferred the highly imitative plays by Friedrich Halm, Ernst Raupach and others, both in Germany and Austria. The natural result was that they not only ignored such "progressive" realistic playwrights as Grabbe and Büchner, but also condemned Hebbel because of his extreme "unclassical" characters and eventually drove Grillparzer into a premature retirement from the stage after it had become clear how far he had divorced himself from popular expectations. The chronology of Grillparzer's critical observations on his predecessors substantiates, however, that his deviations from "classical" German drama ensued with conscious intent and did not emerge through trial and error or through external influences.

In 1817 Grillparzer already recorded, albeit only for his own use, an incisive criticism of Goethe in which he implies the direction he must himself take. He calls Goethe's talent more narrative than dramatic, for while "drama ought to be a mirror in which live action is portrayed," Goethe's drama is a "painting." While conceding Goethe's greatness in everything else he does, Grillparzer finds him therefore "insignificant" as a dramatist. He continues:

The external form of drama exists, first of all, in the dialogue. But there is more to dramatic dialogue than different people speaking in turns. What they say must be the direct result of their immediate situation and present emotion. Moreover, every word must be unmistakably directed toward the meaning of the play or scene. This last aspect is usually not the case in Goethe's works. His characters customarily say everything great and beautiful that can be said about a subject. That is all well and good—I would not like, for anything in the world, to see any of the beautiful speeches taken out of *Tasso* and *Iphigenie*—but it is not dramatic. That is why Goethe's works are so beautiful to read and so bad to present as plays. (XVIII, 57)

And five years later he writes about Schiller: "If only one could eliminate the two monologues of Elizabeth and Leicester in *Maria Stuart*! Schiller's greatest mistake is undoubtedly that he is too often speaking instead of his characters" (XVIII, 73). From these negative comments we may infer that Grillparzer felt obligated to write plays with psychologically realistic dialogue that would portray man as unable to transcend the moment. Put simply: he rejected the "beautiful word" (*das schöne Wort*) for its own sake as the legitimate goal of any dramatist seeking to show life realistically. For human beings, unlike the playwright, lack the overview of their own lives and the events in which they participate.

Standing at the beginning of the nineteenth century, Grillparzer already foresees that drama must become realistic if it is to reflect not only life, but also the contemporary view of life. While the intellectual currents of the century will lead more and more away from a philosophical attempt to understand life and correspondingly more toward the answers provided by sociology and biology, Grillparzer restricts himself primarily to the psychological. The Romanticists had already manifested an intense desire to explore the subconscious and irrational in man, but their efforts were directed toward a revelation of the "night-side" (*Nachtseite*) of human existence. For his part, Grillparzer concludes his comments from 1828 on Novalis (Friedrich von Hardenberg) with the judgment: "I speak here, not as one unacquainted with this gloomy, dreamy condition, for it is my own. But I at least recognize that one must work oneself out of it if one wants to accomplish anything. Monks and hermits may sing, 'Hymns to the Night,' but for active people there is the light! (XVIII, 84).

By thus renouncing Novalis' most famous poem, Grillparzer makes clear his own attitude toward life. For a similar reason he rejects Jean Paul (= Johann Paul Friedrich Richter), whose "fancy, so glorious in reflecting inner circumstance, is almost totally unsuited for portrayal of external actions. For his works too are weakest where the dramatic element will dominate" (XVIII, 79). "Light" and "external actions" mean for Grillparzer understandability for the audience, if not for the characters. We viewers know how and why the characters act the way they do, even if they do not. In other words, speculative or mystical approaches to man must necessarily lack "drama." In turn Grillparzer will develop gesture and tangible stage symbols (*Dingsymbole*) as a means to make motivations and meanings comprehensible. In this direction he will have already progressed far beyond Friedrich Hebbel, whose first important premiere did not take place until 1840. His famous criticism of Hebbel, who lived in Vienna after 1845 till his death in 1863 but had little contact with Grillparzer, reinforces the older dramatist's rejection of intellectualism in drama: "In each poet there is a thinker and an artist. Hebbel is completely up to the intellectual task but not at all up to the artistic one. Or in other words: The thought does not make itself evident in the impression but rather in reflection" (XVIII, 104).

Grillparzer's ever-present rejection of reflection and rhetorical symbolism in art explains not only his lack of receptivity for romantic literature and even such a talented contemporary as Hebbel, but also the particular attraction of Spanish literature for him, especially that of the Golden Age. Moreover, what and whom he admired further distances him from Romanticism and German idealism in general. Pedro Calderón de la Barca (1600-1681) had already been popularized by the Romantics, and even Goethe had contributed to this popularity by staging the Spaniard's works in Weimar. As much as Grillparzer shared this admiration for Calderón, however, he chose Lope de Vega Carpio (1562-1635) as his more immediate model. Criticism in general and our understanding of Grillparzer's intentions in particular have been enriched greatly by his extensive and detailed comments on many of these Spaniards' plays. Frequently the Austrian plays them off against each other, for example, when he writes: "Calderón [is] the Schiller of Spanish Literature, Lope de Vega its Goethe. Calderón [is] a magnificent mannerist, Lope a natural painter"

(XVIII, 16). On another occasion: "Calderón and Lope de Vega speak in images. But Calderón is rich in images and Lope de Vega is graphic. Calderón decorates his dialogue with extended and brilliant comparisons. Lope de Vega does not compare, but rather each of his expressions has a sensual power, and the image is not a decoration but rather the thing itself" (XVII, 200). The very lack of intellectualism attracts Grillparzer to Lope de Vega, about whom he says: "It seems almost as if Lope de Vega with his great sense of nature in such pieces wanted to duplicate the capriciousness and chance of real life" (XVII, 53).

Furthermore, Grillparzer's contrast of Calderón and Lope de Vega illuminates his position in an even larger literary historical context. Throughout the nineteenth century theoreticians debated the relative merits of Schiller and Shakespeare. Grillparzer's most innovative contemporaries—for example Grabbe, Büchner, and Hebbel—inclined more strongly toward the Englishman. Grillparzer implies his agreement with them in such comments as the following on Shakespeare:

> What makes Shakespeare's spirit so individual and distinguishes him from all other writers is that the receiving or reproductive side of his nature outweighs the productive one by far; or, to put it in practical terms, that in him the actor is just as active as the poet. . . . Both sides really should be united in every writer, but the actor in him forced him to identify himself with the persons and situations and to write from within them and not into them. (XVI, 155)

In short: Grillparzer wants to follow the lead of the "naive" dramatists like Lope de Vega, Shakespeare and—with reservations—Goethe. For that reason he rejects the "sentimental" (*sentimentalische*) works of Calderón, Schiller, and the Romanticists.

In embracing his own form of realism, however, Grillparzer did not directly associate himself with contemporary, more radical efforts in that direction. He stops short of social realism as a criticism of specific contemporary conditions. None of his plays, which are all in verse, takes place in the nineteenth century. Only *Der arme Spielmann* has a contemporary setting, but the main thrust is not really sociopolitical. Although Grillparzer does let fly some sharply pointed arrows against contemporaries in his epigrams and makes some less than flattering remarks about political developments in Germany and Austria in his diaries, it should consequently come as no surprise that he had little in common with the authors of Young Germany, at least in his major works. This group, specifically Karl Gutzkow, Ludolf Wienbarg, Heinrich Heine, Heinrich Laube, and Theodor Mundt, was deemed socially disruptive, and after the publication of Gutzkow's novel *Wally, die Zweiflerin* (Wally, the Doubter) their works were forbidden by law in 1835. However, Grillparzer does not seem totally unreceptive to their efforts in his comment: "Admittedly, this young literature is nonsense, even an insanity. But through what other means should the old insanity be combatted? . . . Lacking a Lessing there remains nothing else for us to do but to curb one insanity by another one. The gibbering medieval, self-deceptively religious, formlessly foggy period of the incompetent Tiecks and [Wolfgang] Menzls has lasted long enough" (XVIII, 101).

In turn, a latent tendency toward social criticism, albeit in a broad general, not specific, sense has correctly been detected, for example, by Dagmar Lorenz.[5] The too active searcher for such criticism must nonetheless also heed what Grillparzer himself says about Gutzkow's early play *Nero* (1835). Among other things, the Austrian defends Goethe's critiques of the Romanticists. Goethe, he maintains, "knew that a form that lets itself be dominated by the material instead of dominating it necessarily carries the seed of a caricature; he knew that not the extension but rather the fulfillment determines the meaning; he knew that artists *make*, while suggesting and exciting remain the province of dabblers" (XVIII, 103). We can in general posit that in socially critical art the author's attitude toward the material and its real sociopolitical implications is indeed always in danger of permitting the material to take precedence over strictly aesthetic considerations of form that require irony and conflicts of values. To the extent that Grillparzer, despite his objections to Goethe's and Schiller's dialogue as unrealistic, places the demands of form over those of the subject, he must still be considered a true heir to classical drama.

Aside from his views on art, Grillparzer's reluctance to pursue a course of radically realistic social criticism stems on the one hand from his general historical situation and on the other from his implied view of the human condition. Paradoxically enough, both allow his work to be understood in the one larger context of the so-called *Weltschmerz*—poets like Grabbe, Büchner, Heine, and his Austrian contemporary Nikolaus Lenau (= Nikolaus Niembsch Edler von Strehlenau, 1802-1850), all of whom rejected the views of their idealistic predecessors, especially the Romanticists, yet frequently did so in romantic language and artistic forms. Despite all other often quite patent differences between their works and Grillparzer's they share with him a malaise of the time.

1815 marks the final defeat of Napoleon and the conclusion of the Vienna Congress under Prince Clemens von Metternich. The period from 1815 to the Revolution of 1848, which spread from France throughout Europe and drove Metternich from office but was ultimately crushed everywhere, goes variously under the names "Biedermeier," "Restoration," "Metternich-Era,"and "*Vormärz*"(that is, the period leading up to the March-Revolution). But regardless of the political or consciously apolitical implications of the individual designations, the entire period is now interpreted as one of superficial tranquility and normalcy accompanied by strong repressive measures and an undeniably strict censorship. While the largest segment of the population in Germany and Austria undoubtedly subscribed to the values promoted by the ruling class to keep law and order, a smaller but more insightful segment recognized the underlying brutal repression as such or at least the vacuousness of the society it produced. From the disappointing discovery that the idealism producing the wars of liberation against Napoleon's tyranny and the hope for a democratic society had been in vain—from this very tangible, demoralizing disappointment it was but a short step to the conviction that all idealism as such, be it political, moral or religious, cannot be justified or substantiated. The most radical expression of anti-idealism is *Weltschmerz*, which more often than not leads to absolute nihilism.

Regardless of his personal views Grillparzer would have had no chance of having his plays produced if he had been too critical of the prevailing system. This is substantiated not only by the ban on Young Germany and the difficulties his contemporary Johann Nestroy had with the censor but also by his own experience with *Ein treuer Diener seines Herrn* (1830, A Faithful Servant of His Master). Although—or because—the premiere on 28 February 1829 had been a success, Grillparzer was told by the police chief that the emperor wished to buy the play himself, the intent being to remove it from the public stage. However, Grillparzer cleverly extricated himself from the situation and saved the play.

While Grillparzer never falls victim to the nihilistic tendencies of several contemporaries, he nonetheless shares one conviction with proponents of *Weltschmerz*: one cannot depend on "the beautiful word" to explain life, and one cannot reconcile the *vita contemplativa* with the *vita activa*. As his criticism of Goethe and Schiller demonstrates, Grillparzer knows that most people are incapable of an overview of life and that, even if they were, they could not communicate it to others. Individuals who, like Sappho in his second play, begin with such an overview soon lose it when they attempt to participate in life. This work evoked the admiration of Lord Byron, the most famous proponent of *Weltschmerz* as a European phenomenon.

Sappho was the first work that Grillparzer could claim as completely his own. To be sure, he later asserted that he had "plowed with Goethe's calf," but his deviations coincide too consistently with his assessment of the genuinely dramatic approach lacking in *Iphigenie* to be considered anything but a truly independent work with all of the salient characteristics of his later stageworks. More significantly, Grillparzer undertook this play in response to what he perceived as the faults in *Die Ahnfrau*, faults that resemble the tendencies of Goethe and Schiller as playwrights. In his first work he found "subjective outbreaks" that he viewed as reflecting "almost more the feelings of the poet than those of the characters" (XVIII, 173). Basically, both Iphigenie and Goethe's treatment of her situation embody the "noble simplicity and quiet greatness" that J. J. Winckelmann ascribed to ancient Greek art and character. In keeping with his rejection of any play that is based on an author's overriding abstract "idea" or notion at the cost of individual psychological problems, Grillparzer describes his Sappho as the "gathering place for glowing passions, over which an *acquired* serenity, the beautiful fruit of a higher spiritual education, reigns until the fettered slaves [= her normal human emotions] break their chains and snort with rage" (XVIII, 173f.).

Such a breakthrough of emotions and with it the collapse of an acquired, not inherent, "noble simplicity and quiet greatness" ensues as a consequence of Sappho's decision to take the young naive Phaon as her mate. Using the laurel wreath just bestowed on her as a symbol, she expounds on her choice: "And after all, life's highest goal is living. The choir of muses did not choose in vain as its symbol the infertile laurel wreath, for, cold, fruitless, and scentless, it weighs on the head to which it promised replacement for many a sacrifice. It is even frightening to stand at the height of mankind, and eternal art is forced to beg life for its surplus" (IV, 148). She wishes to return to the "blossoming valleys of life"

(IV, 143), and she calls upon Phaon: "Let us then, my dear friend, set about weaving a wreath for each of our foreheads by drinking life from the intoxicating cup of art and art from the hand of life" (IV, 148).

Space prohibits a detailed discussion of Grillparzer's elaborate but clearly understandable use of stage symbols. It can be simply stated that they all serve, directly or indirectly, the basic situation and its necessary outcome: Sappho, who has been at the heights attained through stringent discipline, forsakes these heights and the serene overview from them in order to participate in the unexpected and unpredictable confusions of life. Unaware of what life really is, she quickly falls victim to the momentary feelings and momentary situations that could not be anticipated from her previous vantage point. Ultimately she says to Phaon in act 5: "I sought *you* and found *myself*" (IV, 224). She then releases Phaon, for she must stand "on more solid ground" (than life). After she has committed suicide, her servant Rhamnes closes the play with the verdict: "Her home was not on earth. She has returned to her own" (IV, 227). Yet after all we have seen unfold in this play, we perceive that his words express only another character's opinion, not necessarily Grillparzer's.

Many critics have tried to single out the dichotomy of art and life as the basic theme in *Sappho* despite the fact that Grillparzer agrees with the contemporary criticism that he has portrayed more the woman than the poetess. He even states that he has always been an opponent of dramas about artists and wanted to show Sappho as "the victim of a true passion, not of the confusion of her own imagination" (XIX, 74f.). While there exists indeed a basic dichotomy, it is a more universally human one. Elsewhere Grillparzer writes about this play: "In the catastrophe Sappho is a jealous woman who loves a younger man" (XVIII, 175f.). But the audience recognizes that Sappho shows her age less in years—nowhere is she called "old"—than in her superior education, experience, and ability. Her problem is that of anyone who has outgrown or thinks he has outgrown life and its necessary spontaneity. For her problem recurs in changed form but with a correspondingly unfortunate outcome in later plays. In *Das goldene Vließ* the situation is reversed; Medea lives on the wild island of Colchis and is seduced into accompanying Jason back to "civilized" Greece. Commenting on this trilogy, Grillparzer reveals how he has expanded a personal conflict to a cultural one: "In the case of the already mentioned combination of the romantic with the classic, I did not have in mind a superficial imitation of Shakespeare [especially *Anthony and*

Cleopatra] or any other poet but rather the greatest possible distinction between Colchis and Greece. This difference forms the basis of the tragedy in this work. For that reason I have used free verse and iambic pentameter wherever the different languages are called for" (XIX, 101). Here Medea proves incapable of attaining the "serenity" of classical Greece, but such a quality, if Jason is any measure, produces the same lack of sincere feeling of one for another as the heights described by Sappho. He cannot love Medea as she must be loved.

In his third and last play on a classical theme, *Des Meeres und der Liebe Wellen*, Grillparzer draws on a popular folksong and returns to the essentially individual psychological side of the incompatibility of life and higher spiritual attainments. At the same time he again casts doubt on such attainments as "higher." Hero becomes a priestess and accepts the vow of chastity because of her unhappy home life and without a previous understanding of the full implications of sexual abstinence. After meeting Leander she feels love and—almost without knowing it—becomes the vehicle of her repressed human feelings. In a statement on this play that almost echoes the one on Sappho's "fettered slaves," Grillparzer maintains: "Hero is never supposed to consider it important that the relationship is forbidden or even punishable. It is not so much that she fears an outside force; it is rather that her inner self did not feel love before and cannot submit without resistance" (VII, 107).

In other words, just as Sappho makes her catastrophic decision to join Phaon out of ignorance about herself and life, Hero initially resists the advances of an equally naive Leander because she does know herself. If these and other characters had had the necessary insight into the human condition, i.e. the unbridgeable gap between the *vita contemplativa* and the *vita activa*, they would, like Rudolf in *Ein Bruderzwist in Habsburg*, have recognized how lonely their life must remain: "Truth is in the stars, not in the stones, plants, animals, trees, and human beings. And whoever could learn how to be still like *them*, receptively pious, master of his own will, an open humble ear—he would perceive easily a word of truth, which goes through the world from God's mouth. . . . Up there lives order, there is its house; down here dwells only vain caprice and confusion" (IX, 25).

More than just a renunciation of romantic pantheism, his statements reflect the same situation as in *Sappho*. It sounds like an echo of that earlier play when Rudolf says in Act 4:

I have made many mistakes—I realize that—since I
climbed down from the clouds at the peak into that deep
valley in which the grave lies as the last step. I thought the
world to be intelligent, but it is not. Tortured by thoughts
of a threatening future, I imagined the time to be moved
by the same fear and only yearning for salvation in wise
delay. But man lives only for the moment, and only what
happens today worries him. There is no tomorrow. Thus
they all run into their mad work. (XIX, 107)

But even after he withdraws inwardly, he too must die. For mankind,
because of its basic shortcoming, prefers the lead of his brother Matthias,
a representative of the *vita activa*. At the conclusion Matthias says: "Mea
culpa, mea culpa, mea maxima culpa" (IX, 132). For our part we have to
ask whether there can be any guilt in the world as Grillparzer sees it. A
very similar problem confronts us in *Der arme Spielmann* (*The Poor
Musician*) in which we may feel compassion with another old man but also
ask ourselves whether the world and society can afford many such
characters. In this novella we face the question: To what extent do noble
motives outweigh bad results? And is the society in error when it
recognizes that without results its entire structure collapses?

Sappho is perhaps also Grillparzer's most personal play despite his
avowed attempt to remain completely objective. The only other work to
raise a like claim might be *Der arme Spielmann*. In both we sense his own
doubts about pursuing art as a career—once at the beginning, once at the
end of his career—and on a broader scale his doubts that art, regardless of
its motives, can ever do more than portray life. Art and the intellect in
general can never explain life or offer solutions for its problems. The latter
could in retrospect be attributed in part to the personal tragedies in
Grillparzer's private life.

No one acquainted with the details of his life could deny that Grillparzer suffered from unresolvable, deep-seated emotional problems, some—
like his tendency toward *Weltschmerz*—especially prevalent in his
generation, some—like those of Sappho and Rudolf—common to all sensitive intellectuals, and some caused by his heritage and early experiences
with family members. His life was correspondingly filled with paradoxes.
Although he never married, he held deep attachments to several women
who might have contributed to his often lauded portrayal of women in his

works. In view of his great sensitivity, one might expect him to have led an almost reclusive existence; in fact, he often experienced periods of melancholy and withdrawal. Personal insecurity almost made him miss the opportunity to meet his idol Goethe, who had in 1826 extended him an invitation to visit him in Weimar, where *Sappho* had been performed in 1818 and *Die Ahnfrau* in 1819. But Goethe remembered him as pleasant and likable. This impression seems, ironically enough, just as valid as Grillparzer's accounts of despair and depression, for he held many friendships—frequently interrupted by quarrels and disagreements—and was considered a good conversationalist and companion by many.

While we may find a similarly paradoxical combination of personality traits in other writers, we are in the case of Grillparzer not at loss for a quite clear explanation in terms of his heritage and family influences. His father was Wenzel Grillparzer, who had come from an old and respected family and had been educated in the spirit of "Josefinismus," the Austrian counterpart to the Enlightenment. Franz followed more or less in the footsteps of his father by taking up the study of law at the University of Vienna, which he completed in 1811. Wenzel Grillparzer had written a dissertation with patently antipapal implications, and along with his anticlerical attitude he undoubtedly communicated his own rationalistic approach to his son. Thus we can understand how both Franz's legal training and his early exposure to rationalistic thinking allowed him to earn his modest living in governmental service and ultimately made him eligible for a pension in 1856.

Diametrically opposed, however, was the influence from his mother, Anna Franziska Grillparzer, née Sonnleithner, to whom he felt an especially close attachment. Coming from a family noted for its activities in music and theater, she seemed almost by nature unhappy and masochistic. She fell victim to religious delusions after the suicide of Franz's young st brother Adolf and took her own life in January 1819. Franz Grillparzer, it could be claimed, always stood literally with one foot in the bourgeois world and the other in the artistic one, figuratively in that of rationality as the "light" and in that of unsuspected emotions as the "dark."

Recognizing this lighter, more social, side of Grillparzer, one cannot be surprised to learn that he wrote two works obviously indebted to the light fare of the contemporary popular theater in Vienna: *Der Traum ein Leben* (1840, *A Dream is Life*), and *Weh dem, der lügt* (1840, *Thou Shalt Not Lie*). While he did not commit any impressions of Johann Nestroy to paper, his comments on the other great exponent of popular comedy, Ferdinand Raimund, reveal his receptivity for the genre and for Raimund's talent in it (he even advised Raimund against writing serious dramas because his talent was comic). Yet even here he seems closer in tone and implication to the German tradition than to the popular Austrian one, for both of his works have their roots in a substratum that suggests a potentially tragic view of life. We need, for example, only think of Lessing's, Kleist's, and Büchner's comedies. Nonetheless, there are no truly tragicomic implications like those to be found in Grabbe's and Büchner's works, just as his tragedies have few, if any, comic scenes, let alone a pronounced tendency toward the bizarre and grotesque.

Der Traum ein Leben, Grillparzer's last notable success on the Viennese stage, cannot be called a comedy in the true sense of the times. Grillparzer subtitles it a "dramatic fairy tale." And while the German romantics were writing fairy tales, usually in the form of short prose narratives, so too were the authors of the Viennese popular theater, sometimes as "fairy tales," sometimes as "magic-plays" and the like. But Grillparzer's primary inspiration for this work, whose title echoes Calderón's *La vida es sueño* (Life is a Dream), was Voltaire's *Le blanc et le noir* (The White and the Black). In other words, this fairy tale was not inspired directly by the Romanticists or the writers for the popular theater. Lest it be assumed that Grillparzer did not begin writing lighter pieces until after his success with tragic ones had been established, it must be noted that he had begun *Der Traum ein Leben* immediately after completion of *Sappho* but had then abandoned it for several years. His later comedy, *Weh dem, der lügt*, was conceived in the winter of 1820/1821, long before Grillparzer's final work on it. Such early datings for his lighter works substantiates the ever-present dichotomy in his own personality between his lapses into melancholy and despair on the one hand and his ability to be witty and sociable on the other.

Regarding his entire *oeuvre,* one recognizes *Der Traum ein Leben* as one of his purest expressions of both his lasting admiration for the Spanish baroque of Calderón and Lope de Vega and the still present influence of the baroque in Austria through the medium of the popular theater. The continuing presence of baroque elements in Austrian cultural life can be readily explained by the close ties to Spain through the Habsburg dynasty and the Catholic Church. Grillparzer says about Raimund: "The baroque is his achievement, his great achievement" (XVIII, 134). The hero of *Der*

Traum ein Leben, Rustan, a simple man from the country, dreams of glory, which he attains in his dream but only through deception, intrigue, and murder. All the while he is egged on by his "Mephistopheles," the black slave Zanga, who also appears in the frame-plot. After awakening from his dream Rustan repents in his last important speech his grandiose, dark goals and says in praise of the new sun: "Spread the word with your rays, sink it into every breast: Happiness on earth means only one thing, and that is the quiet internal peace and a breast free of guilt. And greatness is dangerous, and fame only an empty game; what it gives is vain shadows, and what it takes is so much" (VII, 215). The baroque vanitas-motif underlies these lines. Moreover, the hero of this dream-play has occasionally been dubbed an "anti-Faust" and his thoughts as characteristic of the "unheroic" Biedermeier. Be that as it may, we recognize in the context of Grillparzer's more tragic plays that here we once again experience a character who, like Sappho, seeks something outside of himself but eventually comes to understand himself.

In its utilization of fairy-tale elements and its proximity to the *Besserungsstück* (reform piece) of the popular stage, *Weh dem, der lügt* bears some resemblance to the dream play, whose success might have induced Grillparzer to complete it as his only comedy. The fact that contemporaries even expressed some doubt about the second work as a comedy at all only substantiates the similarity between these two works with happy endings. Despite the wit and humor in the comedy's account of Leon, a kitchen boy, who cannot tell a lie in his efforts to rescue the nephew of a bishop from Frankish captivity, there is likewise a serious core, albeit one not directly comparable to that in *Der Traum ein Leben*.

Notwithstanding the repetition of elements from a previous success, the new piece was ill-received by the audience more accustomed to the farces of the popular theater. The public failure of *Weh dem, der lügt* can, however, be attributed primarily to the objections raised by the nobility to two of its features: the union at the conclusion between Leon and the princess of the Franks, and the portrayal of Galomir, a Frankish nobleman, who cannot utter a single entirely coherent sentence. As far as the violation of class distinctions is concerned, it can be simply pointed out that many fairy tales end with the marriage of a commoner to a princess (likewise from a foreign land). The second objection is more serious, not only because the portrayal in question could be interpreted as criticism of the ruling class, but also because it touches on the main theme of the comedy and thus strikes at the indispensable heart of the play. In the playwright's defense, one must note that Grillparzer, be it in his previously discussed tragedies, his criticism of other dramatists, or in his yet to be discussed historical dramas, seems preoccupied with the possibility of communication between human beings, the very lack of which, in his opinion, often produces drama in a situation. In the larger context of his time, especially that of *Weltschmerz*, we see how close Grillparzer stands to Grabbe and Büchner, whose works frequently express or imply skepticism about language and communication.

In *Weh dem, der lügt* the serious thrust in Leon's mission lies in the revelation of how the kitchen boy, i.e. someone with no formal education, can exploit people's misconceptions about what they hear in their search for "hidden" meanings. About Galomir, who cannot communicate at all, Grillparzer noted after the unfortunate premiere: "The actor who . . . played Galomir outdid himself in treating him as an idiot, as a cretin. Completely incorrectly so. Galomir is no more stupid than animals are stupid; they just do not think. Galomir cannot speak because he also does not think; that would, however, not hinder him, for example, from ascertaining quite well by instinct the right point to attack during a battle. He is animal-like but not stupid [*blödsinnig*]" (XVIII, 197).

Appropriately enough, Grillparzer sees less the nobleman in Galomir than the warrior, who as the extreme example of the *vita activa* lives only for the moment. Such people do not *need* rational communication. But Grillparzer implies in his comedy that the thinker is not to be viewed in an entirely positive light. Unable to use words the way his intelligence dictates, i.e. to lie, Leon can depend on his instincts and on his captors' thinking too much and ascribing more than a literal meaning to his words.

All the merits of *Die Ahnfrau*, the three tragedies on classical themes, and the two pieces with a happy end notwithstanding, Grillparzer is valued most highly as a playwright—at least in the eyes of many subsequent critics—as the author of historical dramas. Such, however, was to be expected, for this type of play dominated the stages of the nineteenth century, sometimes as tragedies in the manner of Schiller, sometimes as costumed comedies like those of Gutzkow, and sometimes simply as "plays" that owed much to the historicism and painting of the times. With the exception of Hebbel's middle-class tragedy *Maria Magdalene* and Büchner's *Woyzeck* the most important serious works until Naturalism have historical or classical settings. Even *Weh dem, der lügt* is based on a tale from a chronicle. Above all, however, it must be stressed that Grill-parzer selected his subjects from Austrian or Spanish history.

Grillparzer's first historical drama, *König Ottokars Glück und Ende* (1825, *King Ottokar, His Rise and Fall*), already reveals one possible reason for the general popularity of the past as a setting: the playwright could comment on historical events with less fear of censorship. Yet such expectations could take an unexpected turn: the opposition of Bohemian noblemen against Grillparzer's excursion into their past held up the performance for two years. There seemed to many to be another political implication that was certainly more contemporary but scarcely more objectionable: the negative parallels between the protagonist and Napoleon. Grillparzer admits in his autobiography:

> At that time Napoleon's fate was new and in everyone's memory. I had read everything that had been written by Napoleon and others about this extraordinary man. . . . While I was still filled with my impressions and considered my other historical recollections, a similarity, albeit a remote one, with the Bohemian King Ottokar [1230-1278] struck me. . . . The fact that the founding of the Habsburg dynasty grew out of Ottokar's downfall was an invaluable gift of God for the Austrian poet and crowned the whole work. Consequently, it was not Napoleon's fate that I wanted to portray in *Ottokar*, but a remote similarity already made me enthusiastic. (XIX, 107)

Quite aside from his use of the typically baroque theme of a "rise" and "fall" through personal arrogance, Grillparzer's comments on other historical dramas reveal that his primary intentions are never really political.

Historical dramas not used to exercise a veiled criticism of contemporary political ills (or, as later in Wilhelminian Germany, to praise contemporary politicians and institutions) often serve as vehicles for their authors' other personal views. Once again by reference to Tieck and the Romanticists' bad examples, Grillparzer rejects this approach as well:

> I found myself in the realm of historical tragedy even before Ludwig Tieck and his admirers dug up their absurdities [*Albernheiten*] about it. And absurdities they

were. The poet chooses historical subjects because in them he finds the seed of his own development. Above all, however, he does so in order to give his characters consistency and a center of gravity in reality, so that a portion from the realm of dreams also goes over into that of reality. Who could stand a fictional conqueror who has conquered a fictional country with fictional deeds of heroism?". . . As fictional characters Alexander the Great or Napoleon would be ridiculed by all reasonable people. (XIX, 108)

This criticism should not be interpreted as a call for slavish adherence to historical fact, for elsewhere Grillparzer asserts laconically: "Even if documents were found today that proved Wallenstein's complete guilt or innocence, Schiller's *Wallenstein* would not cease to be a masterpiece" (XIX, 108). And using Shakespeare's *Henry IV* as a paradigm, he concludes: "Is there any historical personage about whose character we can all agree? The historian knows only a little; the poet, however, must know everything" (XIX, 108).

This leads us ultimately to what we may consider as the lasting appeal of Grillparzer's historical dramas: his ability to recreate here, as in the classical dramas, characters who, although their original counterparts lived in times and places remote to our own, personify human types and conflicts without sacrificing their psychological individuality. We simply accept that Ottokar, Rudolf, and other historical characters must have had the personalities Grillparzer has given them, for all of their actions susceptible to historical documentation seem to stem directly and unavoidably from their personalities. This perspective results not only from Grillparzer's careful probings of human motivations in historical figures, but also from his patent refusal to interpret—as Schiller and Hebbel do—the historical process or man's role in it. At issue is always the human being in a distinctly human world.

Of all Grillparzer's plays, the one with the most contemporary sociopolitical implications is *Ein treuer Diener seines Herrn*, set in the thirteenth century. According to the individual interpreter, Bancbanus, the protagonist and "faithful servant," is either the personification of Biedermeier ideals and the properly obsequious attitude of a good subject or a vehicle to expose the author's doubts about the prevailing order in Metternich's Austria. Grillparzer's description does not resolve the controversy:

> This piece has been criticized as an apology for slavish sub-
> mission; I had in mind the heroism of loyalty to duty,
> which is a type of heroism that is as good as any other.
> . . . Bancbanus gave the king his word to keep peace in
> the country, and he keeps his word, in spite of everything
> that ought to sway and shake the human being in him. By
> the way, his attitudes cannot be considered those of the
> author, since Bancbanus, despite all of his strength of
> character, is, at the same time, a rather narrow-minded old
> man [*bornierter alter Mann*]. (XIX, 142)

Bancbanus' type of heroism does indeed conform to the expectations of
the ruling class at any time. (Brecht will later say that only bad generals
need good soldiers.) One could also point to similarities with the products
of an avowed revolutionary's pen: Büchner's Danton, who seems totally
passive, and St. Just and Robespierre, who likewise suppress their human
instincts for a "good cause." Grillparzer, it seems, has left us with as much
of a paradox as one would expect from a playwright who sees human existence in general and especially the individual as never completely fathom-
able.

In his last historical plays Grillparzer's inclination toward psychological
realism at the cost of any implied social criticism or an "idea" becomes
even more unmistakable. In *Die Jüdin von Toledo* Rahel, the heroine, is a
flighty, impetuous but trusting person who is destroyed by a cowardly self-
indulgent king's weakness and the machinations of his selfish, unscrupulous queen. Hebbel's Agnes Bernauer is the victim of historical developments; Grillparzer's Rahel that of other, less humane, individuals. In *Ein
Bruderzwist in Habsburg* all of the characters, regardless of their dramatic
functions, have equally distinct profiles as individuals. Only Rudolf, who
seems to be a spokesman for the unfulfillable idealism of a Sappho or of
the poor musician, might be interpreted as some sort of aloof yardstick by
which the others are to be measured. But even he remains passionately
human as a friend, father, and—failure: For in spite of his good intentions
the play ends with the beginning of the Thirty Years' War.

In all of his historical plays Grillparzer takes corresponding liberties
with his sources. But in *Libussa*, which in his testament he ordered
destroyed along with *Ein Bruderzwist*, the question of his fidelity to
historical fact is superfluous. In writing it he started with the legendary

love between the Amazon-like ruler and Primislaus, a clever peasant, who woos and wins her. He later also utilized the fairy tales of Johann Musäus to produce a work in the tradition of the romantic cultural-historical drama, e.g. Clemens Brentano's *Die Gründung Prags* (1815, The Founding of Prague). Subsequently, however, Grillparzer rejected attempts to interpret his play on a mythological and symbolic level. Because we see the progression from the old world personified by Libussa to the new one to be led by Primislaus, we have, if not a historical drama, at least a commentary on the value of progress. Yet this commentary stops short of presenting a binding interpretation of history, for example, in a philosophical or institutional sense. Only man's attitude toward man can be discerned. At the conclusion Libussa says to her people, who want to build a city (Prague) under Primislaus: "And you intend to build a city here, to leave your pious huts, where each was as a person, as a son and husband, a being sufficient unto himself. You no longer want to be a whole entity but only part of a greater whole that calls itself city, the state that swallows up the individuals, that weighs and values each of you, not according to good and evil, but use and advantage" (VIII, 213). Admittedly, Libussa subsequently rescinds this dark prophecy in favor of a time "of prophets and blessed ones" to come in a distant future. But the fact remains that such a time lies far beyond Grillparzer's. Until then, the world will be one in which a Sappho, Rudolf, Rahel, or poor musician has no place.

In 1850 Heinrich Laube, who had in the meantime tried to live down his Young German image by establishing himself as a very "unrevolutionary" playwright, assumed the direction of the Burgtheater. One of his first acts there was to reintroduce Grillparzer's plays. Laube's actions probably stemmed from his desire to gain acceptance in his new environment. In any case, Grillparzer remained unmoved by this epilogue to his career. Despite several public honors he lived out his life under the motto, "too late, too late." Nonetheless, his reputation had been reestablished, and many subsequent Austrian writers, e.g. Hugo von Hofmannsthal, were influenced by his works. In his autobiography Grillparzer named *Medea* as his last play to find its way onto the stages of Germany. His plays, even up to today, have, however, never won their rightful place in the repertoires of German theaters. This might be attributable to his Austrian themes and subjects and to his refusal to abandon Austrian idiom completely even after he had mastered the language of the classical German stage. Nonetheless, he will always occupy an incontestable place in every literary history of the German-speaking countries as a connecting link between the era of idealism and the subsequent one of increasing realism.

Notes

1. Plot summaries of these and other works, including the fragments, can be found in Bruce Thompson's excellent monograph of 1981 (vid. bibliography). All quotations from the texts are based on Franz Grillparzer: *Sämtliche Werke*. Fünfte Ausgabe in zwanzig Bänden, ed. August Sauer (Stuttgart: Cotta, [1892]). Translations from the German are my own.

2. See above all *Grillparzer's Der arme Spielmann: New Directions in Criticism*, ed. Clifford Albrecht Bernd (vid. bibliography). While Bernd makes a good case for the current critical interest in this novella and substantiates it effectively with statistics, trends in criticism are determined by many factors, only one of which is the aesthetic quality of the works themselves. In turn, Bernd's findings do not in any way invalidate the overwhelming recognition accorded Grillparzer as a dramatist and his historical role in this genre.

3. Most famous is the cycle "Tristia ex Ponto" (1835), a series of poems on episodes and people in Grillparzer's life.

4. On the larger historical context of Grillparzer's plays see Roy C. Cowen, *Das deutsche Drama im 19. Jahrhundert*. Sammlung Metzler, vol. 247 (Stuttgart: Metzler, 1988).

5. See the bibliography. Lorenz's monograph is also the most recent work to consider Grillparzer from a feminist viewpoint.

Bibliography

I. Works by Franz Grillparzer in German

Die Ahnfrau. Ein Trauerspiel in fünf Aufzügen. Vienna: Wallishausser, 1817.

Sappho. Trauerspiel in fünf Aufzügen. Vienna: Wallishausser, 1819.

Das goldene Vließ. Dramatisches Gedicht in drei Abtheilungen. *Der Gastfreund.* Trauerspiel in einem Aufzuge. *Die Argonauten.* Trauerspiel in vier Aufzügen. *Medea.* Trauerspiel in fünf Aufzügen. Vienna: Wallishausser, 1822.

Königs Ottokar's Glück und Ende. Trauerspiel in fünf Aufzügen. Vienna: Wallishausser, 1825.

Ein treuer Diener seines Herrn. Trauerspiel in fünf Aufzügen. Vienna: Wallishausser, 1830.

Melusina. Romantische Oper in drei Aufzügen. Music C. Kreutzer. Vienna: Wallishausser, 1833.

Der Traum ein Leben. Dramatisches Märchen in vier Aufzügen. Vienna: Wallishausser, 1840.

Weh' dem, der lügt! Lustspiel in fünf Aufzügen. Vienna: Wallishausser, 1840.

Des Meeres und der Liebe Wellen. Trauerspiel in fünf Aufzügen. Stuttgart: Cotta, 1872.

Ein Bruderzwist in Habsburg. Trauerspiel in fünf Aufzügen. Stuttgart: Cotta, 1872.

Gedichte. Stuttgart: Cotta, 1872.

Libussa. Trauerspiel in fünf Aufzügen. Stuttgart: Cotta, 1872.

Sämtliche Werke. 10 vols. Stuttgart: Cotta, 1872.

Die Jüdin von Toledo. Historisches Trauerspiel in fünf Aufzügen. Stuttgart: Cotta, 1873.

Sämtliche Werke. Historisch-kritische Gesamtusgabe. Ed. A. Sauer, fortgeführt von R. Backmann. 42 vols. Vienna: Gerlach & Wiedling, later Anton Schroll, 1909-1948.

II. Works in English

The Ancestress. Trans. H.L. Spahr. Hapeville, GA: Tyler, 1938.

A Dream is Life. Trans. Henry H. Stevens. Yarmouth Port, MA: Register, 1946.

A Faithful Servant of His Master. Trans. Arthur Burkhard. Yarmouth Port: Register, 1941.

Family Strife in Habsburg. Trans. Arthur Burkhard. Yarmouth Port: Register, 1940.

Franz Grillparzer: Plays on Classical Themes. Trans. Samuel Solomon. New York: Random House, 1969.

Franz Grillparzer: The Poor Musician. Trans. J.F. Hargreaves and J.G. Cumming. In *German Narrative Prose*. Ed. E.J. Engle. Vol. I. London: Wolff, 1965.

The Guest-Friend and the Argonauts. Trans. Arthur Burkhard. Yarmouth Port: Register, 1942.

Hero and Leander. Trans. Henry H. Stevens. Yarmouth Port: Register, 1962.

The Jewess of Toledo. Esther. Trans. Henry H. Stevens. Yarmouth Port: Register, 1953.

King Ottocar, His Rise and Fall. Trans. Henry H. Stevens. Yarmouth Port: Register, 1962.

Libussa. Trans. Henry H. Stevens. Yarmouth Port: Register, 1941.

Medea. Trans. Arthur Burkhard. 3rd revised edition. Yarmouth Port: Register, 1956.

Sappho. Trans. Arthur Burkhard. Yarmouth Port: Register, 1953.

Thou Shalt Not Lie. Trans. Henry H. Stevens. Yarmouth Port: Register, 1939.

III. Secondary Works in English

Bernd, Clifford Albrecht, ed. *Grillparzer's Der arme Spielmann: New Directions in Criticism*. Studies in German Literature, Linguistics, and Culture. Vol. 25. Columbia, SC: Camden House, 1988.

Daviau, Donald, ed. *Special Franz Grillparzer Issue, Modern Austrian Literature* 28, Nos. 3/4 (1995).

Obermayer, August, ed. "Was nützt der Glaube ohne Werke . . ." *Studien zu Franz Grillparzer anläßlich seines 200. Geburtstages*. Dumadin, New Zealand: University of Otago, 1992.

Roe, Ian F. *An Introduction to the Major Works of Franz Grillparzer*. Lewiston: Mellen, 1991.

_____. *Franz Grillparzer: A Century of Criticism*. Columbia, S.C.: Camden House, 1995.

Stein, Gisela. *The Inspiration Motif in the Works of Franz Grillparzer, with Special Consideration of "Libussa."* The Hague: Nijhoff, 1955.
Thompson, Bruce. *Franz Grillparzer.* Twayne World Authors Series, no. 637. Boston: Twayne, 1981.
_____. *A Sense of Irony: An Examination of the Tragedies of Franz Grillparzer.* Literaturwissenschaftliche Texte, Theorie und Kritik. No. 4. Frankfurt am Main: Lang, 1976.
_____, and Mark G. Ward, eds. *Essays on Grillparzer.* New German Studies Monographs. No. 5. Hull: New German Studies, 1978.
Wagner, Eva. *An Analysis of Franz Grillparzer's Dramas: Fate, Guilt, and Tragedy.* London: Mellen, 1992.
Yates, Douglas. *Franz Grillparzer: A Critical Biography.* Oxford: Blackwell, 1946, 1964.
Yates, W.E. *Grillparzer: A Critical Introduction.* Cambridge: University Press, 1972.

IV. Major Studies in German
Baumann, Gerhard. *Franz Grillparzer: Dichtung und österreichische Geistesverfassung.* 2nd revised edition. Frankfurt am Main: Athenäum, 1966.
Fülleborn, Ulrich. *Das dramatische Geschehen im Werk Franz Grillparzers.* Munich: Fink, 1966.
Kaiser, Joachim *Grillparzers dramatischer Stil.* Munich: Hanser, 1961.
Lorenz, Dagmar C.G. *Grillparzer: Dichter des sozialen Konflikts.* Vienna/Cologne: Böhlau, 1986.
Müller, Joachim. *Franz Grillparzer.* Sammlung Metzler. No. 31. 2nd. improved edition. Stuttgart: Metzler, 1961.
Naumann, Walter. *Grillparzer: Das dichterische* Werk. 2nd. revised edition. Stuttgart: Kohlhammer, 1967.
Pichl, Robert et al, ed. *Grillparzer und die europäische Tradition. Londoner Symposium 1986.* Vienna, 1987.
Politzer, Heinz. *Franz Grillparzer oder das abgründige Biedermeier.* Vienna: Molden, 1972.
Scheit, Gerhard. *Franz Grillparzer: mit Selbstzeugnissen und Bilddokumenten.* Reinbeck bei Hamburg: Rowohlt, 1989.
Skreb, Zdenko. *Grillparzer: Eine Einführung in das dramatische* Werk. Kronberg/Ts.: Scriptor, 1976.
Viviani, Annalisa. *Grillparzer Kommentar.* 2 vols. Munich: Winkler, 1972f.

Joseph von Hammer–Purgstall

Ingeborg H. Solbrig

In a little cemetery at Weidling near Vienna, next to the grave of the poet Nikolaus Lenau, stands a silver-gray granite monument of Oriental style. Carved inscriptions in the many languages mastered by the man buried there cover the memorial. Here lies one of the most prominent promoters of German-language literature in the early nineteenth century, the renowned Austrian man of letters, orientalist, and specialist for Islamic studies, consular agent, ambassador, historian, poet, author, and translator, Joseph von Hammer-Purgstall.[1] We may trace through Hammer-Purgstall a thread of public interest in the "exotic" Orient, woven unmistakably into the fabric of post-Renaissance German literature. It runs through the Baroque literature of the seventeenth century with its background of the Turkish Wars, through the flood of orientalizing dramas, song-plays, novels, operas, and stories of the eighteenth century, and continues unbroken in the oriental themes and imitative orientalizing literary works and mythical stories about a romanticized Orient of the nineteenth century.

"Orient" and "oriental"—what did Hammer's contemporaries associate with these terms? In general the word "Orient" meant the Islamic cultures of the Near East and the cultures of the Indian subcontinent. However, the word was used broadly and included a heterogeneous mixture of geographical areas and historical times. Orient meant marble sarcophagi and the lofty pyramids, the enigmatic Sphinx and majestic columns, dangerous deserts and caravan routes, lush oases and coastal strips of fields brimming with flowers, palm trees, and orange groves. The Homeric sea with its many islands also belonged to the unfathomable Orient, the ruins of Babylon and Nineveh, of Baalbek, Pergamum, and Ephesus, the presumed site of Troy, the highways of the great kings of Persia, the temple of King Solomon and the Black Stone in Mecca. "Orient" meant mysterious harems and lecherous Sultans, ancient places and names such as Elam, Ur, Chaldea, Canaan, Jericho, Tyre and Palestine, Babylon and Assyria, Arabia and Egypt, Carthage, Malta, the Greek holy temple of Delphi, India, and Constantinople. "Orient" indicated a fairy-tale world of unlimited riches or a place unbound by earthly time. The East was everything the West was not. All of these things might be conjured up for the reader during Hammer's lifetime. In German-speaking countries the Orient was also called *Morgenland*, a term coined by Martin Luther in his translation of the Bible of the Greek term *anatolé*, "land of the rising sun." In the German-speaking countries *Orientalistik* signified Asian studies, particularly the study of the languages and literatures of the pre-Islamic and Islamic cultures in the Near East and of the peoples in the Middle East. The spread of knowledge about these regions had begun, and Hammer was one of the most important forerunners opening the gates for the ensuing flood of new information about the East.[2]

Unless we know enough facts, names, and ideas we cannot read. Decoding words and sentences will not produce meaning unless the reader knows the variety of items to which the passage refers.[3] The basis of new approaches to non-western cultures and non-Christian religions during the later eighteenth and early nineteenth centuries were new reference works made available for the first time in the European languages. In the beginning German readers used mostly French and English sources, but toward the end of the eighteenth century there was an abundance of German translations of Near Eastern literatures including a few of the Koran and scholarly works about the Orient; Hammer's efforts were an important factor in these developments.

Joseph von Hammer was born on 9 June 1774 in Graz. His childhood memories include the clanging of the *Große Siebenglocke* bell in that city. Cast in 1587, its ringing had once announced the approaching Turks and later Napoleon's armies. The year 1787 signified the end of Hammer's carefree youth when he was sent to Vienna to continue his studies at the Barbarastift. At the same time he took preparatory courses at the K. K. Orientalische Akademie, which Maria Theresia had established according to the model of the Collège de Louis Grand in Paris to train linguistically gifted students for diplomatic service in the Levant. For the students the days passed with rigid uniformity according to a prescribed study plan.

After a one-year probationary period, Hammer was accepted into the academy. The curriculum included law, administration, Italian, French, English, Turkish, Persian, Arabic, Latin, Greek, music, mathematics, logic, physics, geography, and history. Later Hammer added Italian, Spanish, and Hebrew to his language studies. In addition the students received instruction in drawing, ballroom dancing, fencing, and riding. Gifted with the power of quick comprehension and a superior memory for words, Hammer rapidly acquired a good knowledge of the three most important Near Eastern languages: he spoke Turkish almost fluently, Arabic adequately, and mastered Persian to such a degree that he was soon able to negotiate in an official capacity with the Shah's intermediaries in their own language.

One of Hammer's most influential teachers, his professor of Persian and Turkish, Thomas von Chabert, loved Voltaire and was an ardent admirer of the French Revolution. The storming of the Bastille, which occurred during Hammer's student years, strongly influenced his intellectual development and political views. In retrospect he described himself as a "moderate liberal." But to young Hammer, who was destined for service in the Ottoman Empire, the campaign against the Turks was of even greater concern than the French Revolution. The student actively followed press reports of political events of the day in domestic and foreign gazettes.

In 1794, when Hammer had completed his formal education, no suitable position was immediately available for him, and therefore he was allowed to continue his scholarly activities at the Academy, serving as assistant to the renowned historian Johannes von Müller and to the later prefect of the Court Library, Baron von Jenisch. Hammer's first literary efforts date from these productive years, and Müller passed them on to the famous writer Christoph Martin Wieland in Weimar for publication in the *Neue Teutsche Merkur*. The *Merkur* was the first significant German-language literary periodical under its editors Wieland and Karl August Böttiger.[5] An editorial comment in the July issue for the year 1796 expresses the wish that a talent such as Hammer be strongly supported in his scholarly efforts, especially in the field of Islamic studies. This commendation was later echoed by Herder. Several flattering statements concerning young Hammer appeared in the *Merkur* over the next few years. With the Alcaic ode entitled *An die Freunde der Literatur* (To the Friends of Literature),[6] which was published in the *Merkur* during the same year, Hammer attempted to arouse public interest in the dissemination and transmission of everything that became known about Near Eastern literatures and cultures. Thus Wieland and Böttiger introduced the work of the young Viennese orientalist to the literary public; even Herder and Goethe took note of Hammer as early as the late 1790s. During the last stages of his student years Hammer concentrated more and more on the study of the Persian language and literature. At that time he began to translate various *ghazals* from the *Divan* of the Persian lyric poet Hāfiz (1320-1386). Hammer had also studied German literature and was especially interested in Goethe's literary works. In 1798, his last year at the Academy, he joined the literary and musical circles of the wealthy Viennese aristocrats who had distinguished themselves by generously supporting literature and the arts.

In May of 1799 the 25-year-old Hammer took up his first appointment as an assistant interpreter for the State Department at the Austrian Embassy in Constantinople. In his letters and memoirs he vividly describes his unforgettable impressions of the fairy-tale-like journey from Vienna to Constantinople, a trip that lasted about four weeks at that time. The view of the Imperial "City of Seven Hills" seemed like a tale from *A Thousand and One Nights* to him. He listened to the muezzin's call to prayer, witnessed the Sultan's magnificent excursion ships on the Golden Horn, and joined the cheering for the "Lord of Two Continents and Seas." But Hammer soon noticed that decay lurked behind the glamorous scene. At that time he was already convinced of the inevitable decline of the Ottoman Empire and the futility of attempts to remedy the situation with reforms; the course of history was to confirm his convictions. His work allowed him enough leisure to continue his studies of Arabic, Persian, and Turkish; he also took up modern Greek. When for the first time he heard a Persian dervish recite from the *Divan* of Hāfiz in his native language, Hammer decided to translate the complete collection into German. As often as he could, he searched the famous library of 'Abudu'l Hāmid in Constantinople and other collections there for sources regarding Ottoman history, literature, anthologies, and biographies. Finally he began to search out all the works available in Constantinople and to compile a bibliography. With such bibliographic projects here and elsewhere in the world Hammer-Purgstall provided invaluable material for Asian studies in the West.

In February of 1800 Hammer was commissioned to travel through the Levant and report on his impression of the situation in Egypt. In previous

years Bonaparte was entrusted by the government of France with conducting military operations against Austrian forces in northern Italy (1796-
1797). Subsequently he was made the leader of an expedition to conquer
Egypt as a base for future attack against the British possession of India.
Bonaparte's success against Austria in his northern Italian campaign of
1796-1797 had put an end to the First Coalition. During his absence in
Egypt a new alliance known as the Second Coalition was formed (December 1798); this alliance comprised Russia, Great Britain, Austria, the
Kingdom of Naples, Portugal, and the Ottoman Empire. By this time the
association of Napoleon not only with Alexander but also with Muhammad was becoming common in Europe; Napoleon had suggested such an
image himself.[7] Since his early youth he had been fascinated with Muhammad, and by 1798, instead of invading Britain, the leader of the coalition
opposing France, he attacked British colonial interests in the Near and
Middle East, using the Egyptian enmity toward the Mamelukes to his
political advantage. The French flagship anchored off the Egyptian coast
was called *Orient*. It was manned with a staff of experts in Islamic studies,
whom Napoleon used to conduct his business with the natives. He even
had his bulletins translated into Koranic Arabic. Napoleon had distributed
manifestos in Egypt, suggesting that the French were "true Muslims," and
that Napoleon was "like another Mahomet," acting only in the interest of
the Egyptians. In the summer of 1799 he defeated the Turkish forces at
Abukir, but saw that his position in Egypt was untenable. He slipped
through British lines, engineered a coup d'état in Paris, and replaced the
Directory by a Consulate, gradually centralizing the government. In December 1799 Napoleon became First Consul. This was the political situation when Hammer was sent to Egypt.

On the journey to the British warship *Tiger* Hammer saw the presumed sites of the Homeric epics. As eagerly as he may have searched for
ancient ruins and inscriptions, his attention was never directed solely to
antiquities; the people, their manners and customs, their dress and language, their stories and songs all captivated him even more. The political
developments in Egypt after the assassination of General Jean Baptiste
Kléber in Cairo and the presence of the British delayed the execution of
Hammer's commission. Spencer Smith, the brother of the ship's com-
mander, took Hammer into his service as a secretary and interpreter.
During the crossing on the *Tiger*, Hammer read a great deal in the Old
Testament and studied a Spanish-Arabic dictionary.

In 1801 Hammer participated in the British military expedition to Egypt. The Arabs, who continuously brought information concerning the movements of the French to the headquarters of Commodore Sidney Smith, called Napoleon "Pharaoh, the damned one." The untiring Hammer also searched for copies of the model for all Arabic chivalric romances, *'Antar*,[8] which comprises 500 years of Arabian history, and for fragments of more tales of *A Thousand and One Nights*.[9] He found twelve ancient Arabic works on veterinary science and fragments of a manuscript containing about one half of the collection of Arabic songs known as the *Kitab al-Aghani* (Book of Songs) by Abu'l Fradj al'Isfahani (b. 897). The *Kitab* had been commissioned by the famous Caliph Hārūn ar-Rashīd. At night Hammer often sat with the Englishmen outside the tents, listening to the tales of the Bedouins, observing with keen interest the effect of the stories on the listeners, and noting their reactions. We find those observations reflected in vivid colorful language in the prefaces to translations and in imitative, synoptic writings as well as in the numerous book reviews Hammer was to write throughout his long life. Some are also preserved in his memoirs. After a lengthy delay, Hammer was finally able to complete his report for the Austrian government.

After the completion of his commission he traveled to England without official approval. He spent nearly five months there from November 1801 to April 1802 and visited the Oriental collections at Oxford and London, especially the Bodleian library, the "Kaaba of the Orientalists." While in England Hammer established contact in Paris with the founder of modern Near Eastern studies, Silvestre de Sacy. The tone and content of de Sacy's numerous letters to Hammer, which are in part still preserved at Castle Hainfeld in Styria, bear witness to the cordial friendship of the two scholars. In March 1802 Hammer received a command from the Austrian State Department to return immediately to Vienna. The scholarly and literary harvest from this first journey into the Orient was abundant. The Münz- und Antiquitätenkabinett (Coin and Antiquities Museum) in Vienna was also indebted to Hammer for having sent the gravestone of Ibisnumin, which was covered with hieroglyphics, and the Hofbibliothek (Court Library) was indebted to him for a copy of the Arabic chivalric romance *'Antar* and other manuscripts. Hammer was the first to describe the marble from the temple of ancient Paphos.

Joseph von Hammer's second oriental sojourn lasted four years from 1802 to 1806. Once more in Constantinople, he continued to pursue his scholarly and literary interests and did not neglect his friends and social life. Hammer was a man of the world with a flair for generous hospitality. His voluminous correspondence, an exchange of ideas with prominent personalities of his time all over the world, not only provided him with a pleasant diversion, but also constituted an important part of his scholarly efforts and generous consulting *in orientalibus*. During these years Böttiger supported the publication of a romantic poem by Hammer entitled *Schirin, ein persisches romantisches Gedicht nach morgenländischen Quellen* (1809, Schirin, a Persian romantic poem based on oriental sources).[10] Goethe thought highly of this romantic work. He also had Hammer's two-volume work, *Enzyklopädische Übersicht der Wissenschaften des Orients, aus sieben arabischen, persischen und türkischen Werken übersetzt* (1804, Encyclopedic Survey, a Translation and Synopsis from Seven Arabic, Persian, and Turkish Works),[11] procured for the Weimar library. Other early works by Hammer include translated excerpts from a work about the Islamic conquests, published anonymously under the title *Die Posaune des Heiligen Krieges aus dem Munde Mohammed Sohns Abdallah des Propheten* (1806, The Trumpet of the Holy War, Sayings from the Mouth of Muhammad the Prophet, Son of Abdullah, with a preface by Johannes von Müller);[12] a creative retelling of a collection of tales from the *Suleiman Nameh*, later published under the title *Rosenöl oder Sagen und Kunden des Morgenlandes aus arabischen, persischen und türkischen Quellen gesammelt* (1813, Rose Oil, or Legends and Tales from the Orient from Arabic, Persian, and Turkish Sources);[13] and several works about his travels.

In May of 1806 Hammer was appointed Consul General in the district of Moldavia. Until his departure for Jassy, the provincial capital, and during his stay there Hammer worked intensively on a translation of Arabic tales. He left the Bosporus with great reluctance. From a political point of view he was leaving a sinking ship. Rebellion in many parts of the country and the weakness and corruption which Hammer observed in the government convinced him that the downfall of the Ottoman Empire was imminent and, in spite of Sultan Selim's military reforms would only be accelerated by the intervention of foreign powers, especially Russia. The maturing scholar-diplomat had become a keenly perceptive political observer. Hammer, the indefatigable writer, used the fourteen-day journey to Moldavia, an independent principality at that time, as another opportunity to make topographical observations. A dried-up fountain along the way, which according to legend had once been considered the source of life in paradise, appeared to him as a symbol of his time: "Of what use are the fountains of the nation," he wrote in his memoirs, "if the life-giving spirit of water is lacking."[14] The new consul general soon noticed that the increasing forces working against Turkey and Austria were becoming more and more apparent. Observations concerning the crumbling empires of that time form a substantial part of Hammer's reminiscences. In the prince's fortress at Jassy, Hammer noticed another fountain on which the inscription alluded to the source of eternal life, an image so important in the myths of the near East. Twenty-three distichs glorifying the sea adorned the marble fountain. The praise was actually intended for Sultan 'Abud'l Hāmid I, "who brought the Empire back to life with the life-giving spring of just government."[15]

In July of 1807 Hammer was called back to Vienna. Without knowing that he would never see the Levant again, he turned his back to it forever as a diplomat and traveler but not as an orientalist and man of letters. In Vienna he was assigned to the Chancellery. He composed a report in French on his observations in Turkey and the Principality of Moravia. Hammer's acquaintances included ladies and gentlemen from high society, many scholars and intellectuals, personalities such as Comte Antoine d'Andreossy, the Ambassador of France who was a competent Egyptologist, and many others. Had Hammer also spent his vacations in Karlsbad, like many high society people at the time, he would have met Goethe there. The Orientalist preferred to spend his holidays in the retreat home of the Orientalische Akademie located in Weidling, to dedicate himself to his scholarly work without interruption.

Hammer's frequent visits to the theater during the winter seasons of those years in Vienna prompted his first attempts at writing drama; *Dschafer, oder der Sturz der Barmegiden* (1813, Dshafer or the Fall of the Barmecides)[16] was a play which aroused Goethe's interest. In those years Vienna's men of letters and other friends of literature arranged public literary evenings on Himmelpfordt Street, from which women were excluded by police regulations. The guests at these gatherings included, among many others, the brothers August Wilhelm and Friedrich Schlegel, who were temporarily residing in Vienna. Hammer associated with both Schlegels, lent them books, discussed literary matters with them, and attended the salon of the poetess Caroline Pichler together with the Schlegels. The famous Baronesse Germaine de Staël-Holstein,[17] who was staying in Vienna in the company of August Wilhelm Schlegel, prevailed upon Hammer to write a drama about Muhammad or, as the founder of Islam was generally called in the eighteenth and early nineteenth centuries, Mahomet, the French form of his name. Madame de Staël asserted that prophets make most rewarding characters for tragedies, and the "true" Muhammad would have to evoke a reaction very different from Voltaire's "Mahomet" in his much debated tragedy *Le fanatisme ou Mahomet le prophète* (1741, *Fanaticism or Muhammad the Prophet*).[18]

As early as 1750 Voltaire's *Mahomet* had become a popular item in the German theater repertoire through a number of translations. In 1799 Goethe wrote a somewhat different adaptation of Voltaire's *Mahomet*.[19] Goethe's German version made other translations obsolete but more important was its impact on various theories of literature and drama in the following decades. History was now to replace in drama that which the Ancients had drawn from myth, namely, a reservoir of consequential actions. The presentation of drama as history, and of history as drama, found exemplary expression in Schiller's plays and Hegel's philosophy of history. Some critics and playwrights criticized Voltaire's presentation of Muhammed/Mahomet as "historically wrong," and Madame de Staël, conversing with Hammer during the 1807/1808 season in Vienna, called Voltaire's *Mahomet* figure a "tragic monster." She felt that Hammer, who knew the Islamic world, its literatures, thought, and languages at firsthand, should attempt to write an "historically true" Muhammad drama.

However, Hammer did not share her view that prophets make excellent protagonists for tragedy. As late as 1823 he published a five-act drama in rhymed iambic meter entitled *Mohammed oder die Eroberung von Mekka. Ein Historisches Schauspiel von dem Verfasser der Schirin und des Rosenöls* (1823, Muhammad or the Conquest of Mecca. An historical play by the author of "Schirin" and "Rose Oil.")[20] In an extensive historical introduction the orientalist states that he wanted to give a characterization of Muhammad and his time which corresponded to historical probability. Critics who maintain that Hammer simply produced a carbon copy of history are wrong. The drama did not make theater history but was to become an important link in the history of drama and the presentation of Muhammad in the nineteenth century.

In 1808 Hammer frequently visited the house of the Prince de Ligne, who was also one of Goethe's acquaintances from the Karlsbad circle. His mansion formed the focus for the intellectuals of Viennese society at that time; even the Schlegels and Madame de Staël visited there. At this point

Hammer had also been corresponding for a year with the publisher Cotta in Stuttgart concerning the publication of his translation of Hāfiz, which he was revising. In the palace of Prince Lobkowitz, where dilettantes performed Italian opera, he met the man who was to become one of his most important patrons and best friends, the Polish Count Wenzeslaus von Rzewuski. When the Pole expressed his wish to sponsor Near Eastern studies and publications, Hammer developed with him a proposal for an international periodical dedicated to the advancement of Islamic studies. This plan for the *Fundgruben des Orients* (1809-1818, Goldmines of the Orient, the last issue appearing in 1820) was promptly realized the following year.[21] On the occasion of the banquet to celebrate the establishment of the periodical, the editor Hammer proposed the first toast "to the Grand Master of Arabic Grammar, Silvestre de Sacy." Then another threat of war suddenly prevailed: Napoleonic troops were approaching the Imperial City of Vienna.

As the French army advanced toward Vienna, Hammer remained behind while the Court, state officials, and practically all of his friends left the city. This state of affairs resulted in Hammer's rendering an invaluable service to Austrian scholarship, which was not duly appreciated for some time. After losing his house in the bombardment he moved into Count Rzewuski's deserted home. During the French occupation Hammer remained active and tried to pursue his literary activities insofar as that was possible. The French began to plunder the galleries and libraries of Vienna: among other things they took several hundred valuable Arabic manuscripts from the Court Library and sent them to Paris. Since the responsible librarian could not handle the situation and failed to save the manuscripts, Hammer worked energetically to do so himself. The negotiations, which were carried on by Hammer in Vienna and in his behalf by de Sacy in Paris, lasted for several weeks, during which Hammer skillfully made good use of his personal and scholarly connections. Finally, the French returned some of the manuscripts.

After 1808 many newly converted Catholics were living in Vienna because there was a foundation for converts there. These "neophytes of Catholicism," whom Hammer regarded with some skepticism, as did Goethe, included two prominent figures from the blossoming school of Romanticism, Adam Müller and Friedrich Schlegel. Hammer relentlessly criticized Müller but considered Friedrich Schlegel a "thorough and perspicacious critic in spite of his religious conversion." Friedrich Schlegel read the manuscript of Hammer's Hāfiz translation, and his brother August Wilhelm read the completed manuscript of *Schirin* just before it was published.

In June of 1809, Hammer's revered friend Johannes von Müller died. In late autumn in negotiations with the Foreign Minister, Prince Klemens Wenzel Nepomuk Lothar von Metternich-Winneburg, Hammer asked to be sent to Paris in order to try to recover those oriental manuscripts which had not yet been returned. Metternich permitted him to travel only in his capacity as a scholar and editor-publisher of the *Fundgruben des Orients*, not as an Austrian official. At the beginning of December he arrived in the French capital for a sojourn of some five months. (A journey from Vienna to Paris took about one week at that time.) In Paris Hammer met the leading orientalists of his time and old acquaintances from his years in the Levant and in Vienna. Silvestre de Sacy kindly accepted him as a colleague, and helped him by word and deed. Among the Germans whom Hammer met in Paris during the first months of 1810 were Alexander and Wilhelm von Humboldt. At the beginning of the year conversations in the salons had turned to Napoleon's courtship of the Austrian Archduchess Marie Louise, and the marriage of the Corsican to the daughter of the Austrian Emperor, which took place in April, had a favorable effect on Hammer's errand. By May his mission was successfully completed, and he returned to Vienna.

In 1810 Hammer discussed a plan for the establishment of an Academy of Sciences and the Arts in Vienna with Josef Hormayr and Friedrich Schlegel. He spent more and more time in his native city of Graz in the home of Count Purgstall, a gathering place for the well-educated in Styria, and also became familiar with Castle Hainfeld, the residence of Count Purgstall near Feldbach. For the first time Hammer saw another important cultural monument of the area, which also belonged to the Purgstalls: the massive fortress of Riegersburg. This castle inspired him to write an ode and later a documentary novel entitled *Die Gallerinn auf der Rieggersburg. Historischer Roman mit Urkunden* (1845, The French Woman on the Riegersburg. An Historical Novel with a Documentary Appendix) in three volumes dealing with witch trials and a satanic cult in that area of Styria.[22]

In Vienna Hammer organized the Oriental collection of the Court Library for a catalog, a continuation of the voluminous bibliographical work he had started in Constantinople and continued throughout his life, which made Near Eastern literatures more readily available to interested scholars. In addition he corresponded a great deal with the theologian Johann Gottfried Eichhorn and with Böttiger, the managing editor of the *Neue Teutscher Merkur*, concerning Near and Middle Eastern historical and literary matters. In the spring of 1912 Eichhorn asked him to write the fifth volume of his *Allgemeine Geschichte der Kultur und Litteratur* (1799-1814, History of Comparative Cultures and World Literature), the "History of Ottoman literature." Hammer immediately began his preliminary studies of the subject, which he continued until he finally published a much more complete work, his own four-volume *Geschichte der Osmanischen Dichtkunst bis auf unsere Zeit. Mit einer Blüthenlese aus zweytausend zweyhundert Dichtern* (1836-1838, History of Ottoman Literature up to Our Time, Including a Collection from the Work of 2200 Turkish Poets).[23] This method is typical for Hammer; many of his works were written only after years of preparation, but when he wanted to bring them to completion he worked intensively and systematically to that end.

Hammer was finally appointed *Kanzleirat* with no particular duties. This sinecure enabled him to follow closely the latest literary publications along with his readings of Near Eastern and Greco-Roman classics. These articles are identified not only in his numerous extensive book reviews appearing in various periodicals, but also in his continuous orders from the Cotta publishing firm and in his correspondence with this important German publisher.

As always, Hammer spent the summer months of 1812 in the vacation home of the Orientalische Akademie in Weidling. He had begun preliminary studies for his *Geschichte der schönen Redekünste Persiens* (1818, History of Persian Literature, Rhetoric, and Poetology).[24] Among the few scholars from the early years of Near Eastern studies who were investigating the rhetorical art of Persian poetry and detailing it in the introductions to the editions and translations of these works, Hammer was the first to become especially interested in the matters of poetics. Whoever really wants to enjoy Persian poetry must master the whole complicated system of symbols and signs as well as be familiar with the roots of Islamic culture and history, for just as Western poets have gone back to the figures of Classical antiquity and have expressed the conflicts of their time with Oedipus, Iphigenia, or Orpheus, the Persian poets likewise possess a basic vocabulary that has remained the same for centuries but is continually refined. Hammer sent the manuscript to Friedrich L. Bouterwek, Professor of Aesthetics in Göttingen, who was just then working on portions of his *Geschichte der Poesie und Beredsamkeit* (1801-1819, History of Poetics and Rhetoric), and sought Hammer's advice on questions regarding the poetics of Near Eastern literatures. In a letter dated 13 February 1813, Bouterwek asked Hammer for permission to give a public lecture on the contents of the manuscript. From this lecture, which was published in the *Göttinger Gelehrten Anzeigen* (*Göttingen Intellectual News*), Goethe learned of the proposed work four years before its publication. The problem of inter-textuality between Hammer's texts and those of Goethe and subsequent nineteenth-century writers is well worth exploring. The *Geschichte der schönen Redekünste Persiens* became the basis of the most important portions of Goethe's *Noten und Abhandlungen zu besserem Verständnis des West-östlichen Divans* (1819, Notes and Commentary for the Better Understanding of West-Eastern Divan).[25] The *Redekünste* and the intro-ductions to Hammer's bilingual editions and translations of Arabic, Persian, and Turkish literature are still gold mines of information con-cerning aesthetic observations. He typically places these observations into the framework of their historical context, but without succumbing to com-plete relativism. He tries to show that literary works of art should be evaluated within their respective frames of reference. His interest in such matters, especially poetological problems, distinguishes Hammer from his more purely philologically oriented colleagues. With regard to Near East-ern literatures he was far ahead of his time and this may explain why Goethe took exception to Hammer's works and the introductory studies that preceded them.

In 1814 Hammer met with Cotta in Vienna after Cotta had published the two volumes of Hammer's translation of the Divan of Hāfiz (Tübin-gen: Cotta 1812 and 1813, actually published in 1814)[26] and took copies of the books some weeks later to Thuringia, where he gave them to Goethe. Cotta had chosen the beginning of the Congress of Vienna to time his business trip to Austria. Hammer experienced the weeks of this epochal congress only from the perspective of the social gatherings surrounding the political events. He also saw Duke Karl August of Saxe-Weimar, whom he viewed as the "driver of the triumphal team of German literature: the late men of letters, Johann Gottfried Herder, Christoph Martin Wieland, and Friedrich Schiller, and the last survivor of this quadriga of the mind, Johann Wolfgang von Goethe."[27] Even before the congress came to an end because of Napoleon's escape from the Island of

Elba, the host of the most glamorous *Salon* in Vienna died, namely Prince de Ligne, in whose palace the literary dignitaries of his day had met and who had coined the famous phrase: *Le congrès danse mais ne marche pas*, (The congress dances, but it does not move.) De Ligne's death marked the end of an era.

The first half of Hammer's life had been marked by the French Revolution, the collapse of great empires, the Turkish wars, the death of Joseph II, and the Coalition Wars. The Congress of Vienna and Hammer's marriage shortly thereafter formed precisely the middle of his long successful life.

At a soirée at the home of the ennobled financier Joseph von Henikstein, a converted Jew, while the forty-two-year-old Hammer played chess with Karoline von Henikstein, the beautiful and intelligent daughter of the house, he asked for her hand. The wedding took place on 9 June 1916, Hammer's birthday.[28] Soon afterward Hammer's superior, Metternich, invited the couple to dinner and stated in reply to the orientalist's request for a new appointment in the Near East: "As long as I am foreign minister, you won't go back to Constantinople. You, by virtue of your character, are not suited for diplomatic service. By God, no poets in business and politics! I shall take better care of you than you yourself do."[29] Thirteen years later, after the Treaty of Adrianople (1829), Hammer's perception of developments in the Near East certainly proved to be correct. In his partially published memoirs he wrote that Metternich's words called to mind Duke Karl August and the world-renowned Weimar Court of the Muses. Hammer was proud of being an *homme de lettres*. In German-speaking countries there was no intellectual and political center for the intelligentsia, as there was in France. The small principality of Weimar was an exception but was politically too unimportant and physically too small to offer the great minds of the time conditions similar to those Paris provided for her poets, writers, artists, and scholars. At that time Prince Metternich was involved in business correspondence with the prime minister of Weimar, Goethe, who repeatedly praised Hammer as a man of letters.

Hammer, who had become financially independent through marriage, organized literary evenings in his new home in Döbling near Vienna, to which he expressly invited "women and young ladies also."[30] At that time his scholarly interests were focused on Egyptology, the teachings of Zoroaster, the Gnosis, and the teachings of the Church Fathers in preparation for his Latin treatise entitled *Mysterium Baphometis relevatum s.*

fratres militiae templi, qua Gnostici et quidem ophiani apostasiae, idoloduliae, et impuritatis convicti sunt per ipsa eorum monumenta (1818, On the Legal Proceedings against the Order of the Knights Templars at the Beginning of the Fourteenth Century), which was to be included in the last volume of the *Fundgruben des Orients* and also published separately. Along with numerous book review essays he also completed several other projects, among which was a synoptic paraphrase, *Morgenländisches Kleeblatt, bestehend aus parsischen Hymnen, arabischen Elegien, türkischen Eklogen* (1819, Oriental Cloverleaf of Parsee Hymnic Poems, Arabic Elegies, Turkish Eclogues).[31] Before the work came to the market Hammer sent a copy of it to Goethe with the handwritten dedication "*Goeto Sphyra* (Written in Greek), *dem Zaubermeister das Werkzeug, Goethe'n, Hammer. Wien am 1. November 1818*" (To Goethe the hammer or tool, to the magician the working tool, to Goethe, Hammer. Vienna, 1 November 1818). The variations of the witty pun in the text of the dedication involving Hammer's name were of course intended. Goethe, whose *West-östlicher Divan* was already in press, was nevertheless able to include a remark of his appreciation of this work in the chapter "Von Hammer" of the *Noten und Abhandlungen.*

Although Hammer was not a university teacher, he was always willing to help young scholars who showed an interest in the Near Eastern languages. For instance, in 1818 Friedrich Rückert (1788-1866), returning to Germany from an extended stay in Italy, met Hammer in Vienna. Under his influence and tutorship Rückert began to devote himself successfully to Near Eastern languages. His impressive command of oriental philology and Hammer's recommendation led in 1826 to appointment as professor at the University of Erlangen.

In 1819 Goethe's *Divan* was published by Cotta. Hammer's translation of the Divan of Hāfiz and his *Geschichte der schönen Redekünste Persiens* had made a vitally important contribution to this work.

While making preparations for a state visit from Persia, an occasion during which Hammer was to act as interpreter, he thought of translating the reflections of the philosopher-Emperor Marcus Aurelius, *Ton Eis Heauton Biblia* (written between 170 and 178, *Meditations*), a compendium of twelve books of moral precepts written in Greek and an important formulation of the philosophy of Stoicism. Hammer translated this epochal work from Greek into modern Persian in order to bring some Western philosophy into the East; he published the bilingual edition under

the title *Markou antinou Autokrators ton eis heauton biblioi* (Vienna 1831).
After completing the work Hammer sent the book to the Shah of Persia,
who later awarded him the highest Persian distinction, the decoration of
the Sun Lion. In 1821 Hammer undertook a business trip to Berlin on
Metternich's behalf. He took part in a plenary session of the Akademie der
Wissenschaften, was impressed by personalities such as Schleiermacher and
Savigny, and also became acquainted with the composer Karl Maria von
Weber, whose romantic opera *Der Freischütz* had just enjoyed a very
successful premiere. On another business trip in 1925, this time to Prague
and Dresden, Hammer was inspired by the architectural magnificence of
the Dresden Library. In his autobiographical notes he wrote about this and
combined his memoirs of Dresden with those of other famous libraries in
which he had worked:

> This library, among the seven large ones in which I have
> worked, holds . . . one of my fondest memories. I can still
> see myself in the library near the tomb of Sultan Abdul
> Hāmid in Constantinople, sitting with crossed legs . . .
> quietly reading while the other readers are all responding to
> the call to the midday prayer from the minaret. In the Vat-
> ican Library, where the curtains on the high windows shut
> out the harsh sunlight, I can still hear the fountain on St.
> Peter's Square murmuring in the holy silence; in the Im-
> perial Court Library in Vienna I see myself sitting at one
> end of the long table while Prince de Ligne works at the
> other. From the bright windows of the library at Dresden
> I still look out on the river Elbe; from those at Naples I
> gaze out over the sea. At the Bodleian Library during the
> lunch hour I am locked in alone, sitting at my desk, and
> the chain which holds the manuscript rattles. In Paris I
> work in an uncomfortably cramped room in the harsh cold
> of winter with only a meager fire. . . . What joy seized me
> in Venice at the Library of San Marco, where news of the
> birth of my good son Max reached me.[32]

Since the death of Count Purgstall in 1812 his widow, a Scotswoman by
birth,[33] had grown closer and closer to Hammer, whose literary works she
held in high esteem. Later her affinity for Hammer extended to his wife

as well. With increasing frequency Hammer sought rest and relaxation at the estate of the Countess, Castle Hainfeld in Styria. Splendid leather-bound editions of all his works were made for the castle library.

In 1832 three men died who had made substantial contributions to the propagation of Eastern literatures in Europe: Goethe, Count Wenzeslaus Rzewuski, Hammer's sponsor who financed the publication of the *Fundgruben des Orients*, and Baron Johann Friedrich von Cotta, the publisher of Hammer's translation of Hāfiz and Goethe's *West-östlicher Divan*. In November of 1832 Hammer published a poem in commemoration of Goethe in the *Wiener Zeitschrift für Kunst, Literatur und Mode* (Periodical for Art, Literature, and Fashion);[34] this poem was long overlooked by Goethe scholars. It does not mention Goethe's name but appeared in the context of other poems commemorating him. The fourteen lines of the poem in trochaic pentameter, paint in an almost magical manner a fairy-tale image and create sounds of a sparkling mysterious world. Hammer's poem, a *ghazal* written in an elevated style, is a song in praise of Goethe. One may wonder why he did not choose the *qasida*, the traditional oriental form of panegyrical poetry, for his eulogy. The orientalist wished to combine the Western poet of the *Divan*, the German Goethe, with his Eastern model, the Persian Hāfiz. Nor was it by chance that Hammer wrote a *ghazal* in fourteen lines. Thus he combined the *ghazal*, the classical form of Near Eastern love poetry, with the oldest and most continuous form of Western love poetry, the Petrarchan sonnet. Hammer's poem praising and commemorating Goethe is written in the mood of an elegy and in the form of a love poem.

The translator of Hāfiz stood at the height of his fame: in the same year his treatise on the internal administration of the Caliphate received a prize by the Preußische Akademie der Wissenschaften (Prussian Academy of Sciences) in Berlin, and the Shah of Persia honored him with the highest decoration of his country for his translation of the *Meditations* of Marcus Aurelius into Persian. In 1833 Hammer obtained an audience with the Emperor in order to express to him his concerns for the Orientalische Akademie in Vienna. In 1834 he was still corresponding with numerous orientalists and other scholars from all over the world. He translated Shabistarī's *Gulshan-i-rāz* (fourteenth century, *Rose Garden of Mystery*)[35] into German and published it in Persian and German under the title of *Rosenflor des Geheimnisses* (1838).[36] This work deals with the idea of the Perfect Man, the stages of development, and mystical terminology. Its popularity in the East made it interesting to Western scholars, and Hammer's German translation was one of the first books on Sufism that was translated into Western languages. He did a comparable bilingual, Turkish-German edition of the romantic Turkish poem by Fazli, *Gül und Bülbül, das ist Rose und Nachtigal* (1833, The Rose and the Nightingale),[37] and gave it a motto from the divan of the Arab poet Mutanabbi:[38] "Mein Begehren ist nicht Gold, / Um des Klanges mich zu freuen, / Sondern Ruhm und Ehrensold, / Der mich immer soll erfreuen. (My desire is not for gold, / To please me with its clinking, / But rather for fame and honor, / Which will always give me pleasure.) In the course of his scholarly career Hammer saw this wish fulfilled. Through the years he became a member of numerous learned societies. In 1809 the Academy in Amsterdam nominated him as a member, and the Göttingen Academy did the same in 1811. In 1812 he was accepted into the Institut de France and the Asiatic Society of Calcutta. In 1817 the East Asiatic Society of Madras and Bombay chose him as a member, as did the Philosophical Society of Philadelphia in 1818, and both the Learned Society of Copenhagen and the Royal Society in London in 1825. That same year, Hammer took the place of the deceased Wilhelm von Humboldt in the Académie des Inscriptions in Paris, and in 1842 he was accepted by the Academy of Turin. Hammer-Purgstall was to serve as the very first President of the K. K. Österreichische Akademie der Wissenschaften (Royal Austrian Academy of the Humanities and Sciences) in Vienna in 1847. He held honorary doctoral degrees from the universities of Graz and Prague. In 1811 Hammer became *Wirklicher Kanzleirat* and *Hofdolmetscher*, and *Hofrat* in 1817.

In 1835 the 61-year-old Hammer faced the "peripeteia of his life." In March he received news of the serious illness of the Countess Purgstall. He hurried to Hainfeld but arrived there too late; his friend and sponsor of many years had died. Her will stipulated that the orientalist and his male descendants should be the heirs to the domain of Hainfeld and the name Purgstall, which otherwise would have died out. Hammer's succession to the property at first interrupted his usual activities. From then on he was called Joseph Freiherr von Hammer-Purgstall.

Even as the landlord of Castle Hainfeld, Hammer-Purgstall showed his varied talents; a total abstainer, he introduced the cultivation of hops and Rhenish grapevines there. While organizing the castle archives he came across the records of a witch trial and completed the *Rieggersburg* novel.

After the completion of this work he dedicated himself once more to his scholarly work. He employed two scribes, since his already poor hand-writing had become nearly illegible, and continued to work according to a rigorous plan. Between his sixtieth and eighty-second years Hammer completed numerous articles and long book-review essays as well as thirty larger projects, among them several books on the history of the Mongol dynasties, who in the thirteenth and fourteenth centuries united almost all of western and eastern Asia, thereby creating one of the largest land empires in history. Hammer's works on the history and culture of the Mongols constitute considerable contributions to little-known areas of Asian studies at that time. Another study on the Mongols was published in 1856, the year of Hammer's death. This work became an appendix to Hammer-Purgstall's main opus, the ten-volume *Geschichte des Osmanischen Reiches* (1834-1836, History of the Ottoman Empire). Hammer also prepared a shorter, four-volume edition of this work.[39] The *Geschichte der osmanischen Dichtkunst* and the *Gemäldesaal der Lebensbeschreibungen gro-ßer muslimischer Herrscher* (1837-1839, Biographical Portraits of Muslim Rulers)[40] were also completed and published along with seven mammoth volumes on the *Literaturgeschichte der Araber von ihrem Beginne bis zum Ende des zwölften Jahrhunderts der Hidschret* (1850-1856, A History of the Literature and Sciences of the Arabs, from the Beginnings to the Twelfth Century of the Higra).[41] During the same period appeared *Das arabische Hohe Lied der Liebe, das ist Ibnol Faridh's Taije in Text und Übersetzung zum ersten Male zur ersten Säkular-Feyer der K. K. Orientalischen Akademie herausgegeben* (1854, The Mystical Poems of Ibn al-Farid),[42] a beautifully printed and illuminated book published on the occasion of the centennial of the *Orientalische Akademie*, unfortunately a rather unsuccessful translation.

After he had become heir to the Hainfeld estate, the now financially independent Baron von Hammer-Purgstall had reached the pinnacle of his social standing. To his friends he remained unchanged, as is noted in the society pages of the Berlin *Figaro*. The series of Viennese writers treated in the essay begins with Hammer-Purgstall, about whom it says after a description of the casual atmosphere in Hammer-Purgstall's salon: "The elasticity of his mind is all the more amazing since he is overburdened with scholarly tasks, poetical productions, and business matters of every kind throughout the day; and yet this man, who never seems to age, still finds enough time to climb many flights of stairs with some frequency in order to surprise younger friends and scholars with his visits. . . . Baron von Hammer-Purgstall does not allow anything to dissuade him from his tireless devotion to friends or his unselfish hospitality, not even ingratitude."[43] The Baron-scholar's name and accomplishments were known not only in Europe and the Near East, but also in the United States. In his essay *Letters and Social Aims* Ralph Waldo Emerson (1803-1832), a younger contemporary of Hammer-Purgstall, praises Hammer-Purgstall's accomplishments.[44]

Soon after, Hammer-Purgstall began to work energetically for the establishment of an Academy of Sciences and the Arts in Vienna. By this time modern Asian studies based on philological work and on literary and cultural studies had made significant progress in the West; finally theological hermeneutics had been replaced by philological hermeneutics. During the first half of the nineteenth century the great European Asiatic societies were founded: the French *Société Asiatique* in 1822, the British *Royal Asiatic Society* in 1823, and the Deutsche Morgenländische Gesellschaft in 1845. The *American Oriental Society* was established in 1841, even earlier than its German counterpart.

In March of 1837 Hammer-Purgstall along with eleven other scholars and Court officials directed a petition to the Emperor, in which permission for the establishment of an academy was requested. Since the time of the founder of the Societas Litteraria Danubiana, Conrad Celtis (= Conrad Pickel, 1459-1508), and of Emperor Maximilian I scholarship had been on the decline in Austria. Gottfried Wilhelm Leibniz (1646-1716) and Gotthold Ephraim Lessing (1729-1781) had worked for the establishment of an academy for the arts and sciences in vain, but as Protestants they were unable to accomplish anything in Catholic Vienna. At first the plans of Hammer-Purgstall and his friends were also unsuccessful. Not until ten years later did they finally attain their goal. Metternich, who at first had deliberately delayed the foundation of an academy, ultimately promoted it for political reasons. The opening ceremony took place on 2 February 1848. In his inaugural address as the first president of the K. K. Akademie der Wissenschaften in Vienna Hammer-Purgstall expressed the idea of separating scholarship from teaching. The speech reflects ideas and principles which had been formulated in 1809-1810 by members of the founding committee (Johann Gottlieb Fichte, Friedrich Daniel Ernst Schleiermacher, and Wilhelm von Humboldt, all of whom Hammer-

Purgstall knew personally) during the establishment of Humboldt University, the new model university in Berlin.

The aging Hammer-Purgstall had grown lonely over the years. In 1844 he took Goethe's autobiography, *Dichtung und Wahrheit*, along on a journey to Bavaria, where he was given an audience with the artistically inclined Ludwig I. The orientalist gave a detailed description of his conversation with the King on 28 August in his memoirs, emphasizing that this date was Goethe's birthday. At this time Goethe had already been dead for twelve years. Hammer belonged to the younger generation, that of the early romanticists, who had gone in different directions during Goethe's lifetime. Later in 1844 Hammer-Purgstall's wife Karoline died. Hammer-Purgstall's thoughts turned inward more and more. He felt that death was an "entrance into eternal light and a return to eternal love," and he considered technological progress dangerous if it did not keep pace with moral progress. Another invitation with great honor arrived from Germany. His former academic rival, the Arabist Heinrich Leberecht Fleischer (1801-1888), invited Hammer-Purgstall to attend the foundation ceremony for the German oriental society, the Deutsche Morgenländische Gesellschaft, and to take over the chairmanship of the learned society. Hammer-Purgstall politely declined without mentioning the real reason for his refusal. To avoid postponing the long-planned educational journey with his ill seventeen-year-old son Max he preferred to forego the invitation. Two years later his son died.

On 12 March 1848 there were student uprisings in Vienna. Hammer-Purgstall's residence on Kärntnerstraße once again suffered damage from the bombardment as it had many years before when a French army took Vienna. Metternich was forced to abdicate. The world had changed greatly since Hammer-Prugstall had come to Vienna as a schoolboy. Among his correspondents there were now also numerous "Hebrews," as he states in his memoirs, for instance, the Rabbi at Wiesbaden, Abraham Geiger, whose prize essay *Was hat Mohammed aus dem Judentum aufgenommen?* (*1833*, What Did Muhammad Borrow from Judaism?) was made known by Hammer-Purgstall. He began to detect signs of the Empire's incipient decline. At the plenary session of the Akademie der Wissenschaften on 29 May 1852 he gave a speech in which he touched on the problems of the heterogeneous Habsburg Hegemony and offered some suggestions. The title of the lecture was *Vortrag über die Vielsprachigkeit* (1852, On

Multilingualism)[45]; it dealt with the problem of ethnic minorities and their languages within the Empire.

In 1855 Hammer-Purgstall once again traveled westward to visit the palaces and parks on Wilhelmshöhe in Kassel. He wrote a lengthy poem about the magnificent site and the structures which in the reddish light of sunset reminded him of the Alhambra in Granada, as described in Washington Irving's *The Alhambra* (1832). On the same trip he became acquainted with Goethe's friend of the *Divan* days, Marianne von Willemer. Hammer-Purgstall had also associated with Goethe's daughter-in-law Ottilie in Vienna, where her daughter, Goethe's granddaughter Alma, had died in 1844. But Goethe and Hammer-Purgstall never met in person.

Up to now Hammer-Purgstall's experiences and Islamic studies had been focused on regions in Eastern Europe and Western Asia. In connection with his Arabic studies his attention shifted to the Islamic influences on the other side of Europe, in Spain, where Christianity and Islam, Western civilization and Arabic culture had come into close contact with each other through the spread of Islam. During his last year Hammer-Purgstall read Cervante's *Don Quixote* in the original language "with great pleasure," since on every page so many traces of Arabic "in both word and deed" attracted his attention. For the old Joseph von Hammer-Purgstall Occident and Orient had merged into one. In November of 1856 he died in Vienna at the age of eighty-two. A ceremonial funeral took place in St. Stephan's Cathedral. The deceased was laid to rest in the small cemetery in Weidling. One of the verses which Hammer-Purgstall had engraved on his tombstone comes from Calderón's *El Príncipe Constante:*[46]

> A florecer las rosas madrugaron,
> y para envejecerse florecieron:
> cuña y sepulcro en un botón hallaron. Tales los hombres
> sus fortunas vieron:
> en un día nacieron y expiraron;
> que pasados los siglos, horas fueron.
> (11.1660-1665)

> (The roses woke up early to flower,
> and they flowered to grow old:

cradle and tomb they found in a bud.
Such were the fortunes men saw:
in a day they were born and expired;
once gone, the centuries were hours.)

Hammer-Purgstall's *oeuvre* resembles a *Musamara*, an evening entertainment in the Arabic style: he touches upon many areas of Near and Middle Eastern studies without treating them exhaustively, thus inviting the audience to use their imagination and further explore these cultures. Through his understanding of Arabic, Persian, and Turkish Hammer-Purgstall gained insights into the nature of Near Eastern poetry which reach far beyond what was known and recognized in his time. Non-specialists of Islamic studies have sometimes criticized Hammer-Purgstall's way of "teaching" the public, especially the poets of his day, so that they could in turn better understand the poetics of the poets of the East and enrich their own poetry with new treasures from the Orient. The introductions to his translations are masterpieces of cunning emulation. He could write quite differently though. The refined prose of his various works on travel such as the *Topographische Ansichten* and others was characteristic of the Austrian Restoration period; it stands out against the provincial language of the eighteenth century. It is true that this last Austrian polyhistorian "had many detractors because of his sometimes sloppy, though prolific, scholarship."[47] Yet this fact should not diminish Hammer's uncontestable merits as a pioneer of oriental studies or his stature in the social and intellectual circles of his time, nor should it obscure the enormous influence he had on many of his contemporaries. His contributions to Ottoman history remain useful to the specialists and quotable to this very day. Joseph von Hammer-Purgstall was one of the most important cultural mediators between Orient and Occident.

Notes

1. I owe special thanks to Timothy Parrott for aiding with translations and the formulation of the English text, and to Lawrence Rettig for reading and editing the final text. For a description of the monument, see Ingeborg Hildegard Solbrig, *Hammer-Purgstall und Goethe: Dem Zaubermeister das Werkzeug* (Bern: Herbert Lang, 1973), pp. 37-41, with photograph by the author in the appendix, iii. 9.

2. On this topic in general see Edward W. Said, *Orientalism* (New York: Pantheon Books, 1978). Sepp Reichl, *Hammer-Purgstall. Auf den romantischen Pfaden eines österreichischen Orientforschers* (Graz/Wien: Leykam, 1973). Also see my description in Ingeborg H. Solbrig, "Joseph von Hammer: Wieland-Verehrer und Beiträger zum *Neuen Teutschen Merkur.*" *Christoph Martin Wieland. Nordamerikanische Forschungsbeiträge,* ed. Hansjörg Schelle (Tübingen: Niemeyer, 1984), pp. 494-522 and 506f.

3. See Roger Shattuck, *Perplexing Dreams: Is there a Core Tradition in the Humanities?* Occasional Paper No. 2 (Washington, D.C.: American Conference of Learned Societies 1987), p. 4.

4. The following information is based partly on Hammer-Purgstall's autobiographical notes, a portion of which (about one-sixth) is published: Reinhart Bachofen von Echt, *Joseph Freiherr von Hammer-Purgstall. Erinnerungen aus meinem Leben 1774-1852.* Vol. 70 of *Fontes Rerum Austriacarum* (Wien/Leipzig: Hölder, Pichler, Tempsky, 1940). (Cited BE).

5. For more detail see Solbrig, "Joseph von Hammer: Wieland-Verehrer," note 2.

6. Hammer, "An die Freunde der Literatur." *Neuer Teutscher Merkur* (1796), p. 3, II, pp. 309-313. In Solbrig, *Hammer-Purgstall und Goethe*, note 1, pp. 192-194.

7. See Said, *Orientalism*, note 2.

8. The protagonist of *'Antar* is the Arab poet 'Antara ibn shaddad al-Absi (ca. 526-615). The slave 'Antar had been granted his freedom because of bravery in battle. The known of his Bedouin poems are the so-called *Muállaqa*. Hammer's translation of the *'Antar* fragments were posthumously published by M. Poujoulat (Paris: Amyot, 1868-1869). An English translation of *'Antar* was done by Terrik Hamilton, *'Antar, a Bedouin Romance* (London 1819), reviewed by Hammer in the *Jahrbücher der Literatur* (Vienna 1819) pp. 328ff.

9. Hammer, *Contes inédites des Mille et une Nuit, extrait de l'original arabe* (Paris 1828). German translations by E. Zinderling, *Der Tausend und einen Nacht noch nicht übersetzte Mährchen, Erzählungen und Anekdoten zum ersten Male aus dem Arabischen ins Französische übersetzt* (by Hammer), 3 vols. (Stuttgart/Tübingen: Cotta, 1823-1824). Hammer refers to the well-known collection *Les Mille et une nuits, contes arabes* (Paris 1704-1717), which A. Galland had

translated from Arabic into French; hence Hammer translated his supplement also into French.

10.   Hammer, *Schirin. Ein persisches romantisches Gedicht nach morgen-ländischen Quellen* (Leipzig: Fleischer, 1809), 2 parts.

11.   Hammer, *Enzyklopädische Übersicht der Wissenschaften des Orients, aus sieben arabischen, persischen und türkischen Werken übersetzt,* 2 vols. (Leipzig: Breitkopf and Härtel, 1804). French *Coup d'oeuil encyclopédique des sciences de l'orient* (Paris 1804).

12.   *Die Posaune des Heiligen Krieges aus dem Munde Mohammed Sohnes Abdallah des Propheten* (Leipzig: Gleditsch, 1806). Translator-author = Hammer, ed. Johannes von Müller. (Al-Dimyali, Ahmad ibn Ibrahim, d. 1411.)

13.   Hammer, *Rosenöl, oder Sagen und Kunden des Morgenlandes aus arabischen, persischen und türkischen Quellen gesammelt.* 2 parts (Stuttgart/Tübingen: Cotta, 1813; actually published in 1815). Reprinted Hildesheim: Olms, 1971. Partly reprinted in *Märchen und Geschichten aus dem Morgenland,* ed. C. Narciss (Stuttgart: Steingruber, 1961).

14.   See Solbrig, *Hammer-Purgstall und Goethe,* p. 60, note 1.

15.   See Ibid., p. 61.

16.   Hammer, *Dschafer oder der Sturz der Barmegiden. Ein historisches Schauspiel* (Vienna: Doll, 1813). See Katharina Mommsen, "Die Barmekiden im *Westöstlichen Divan.*" *Goethe* 14/15 (1952-1953), pp. 279-301 and Ursula Wertheim, "Noch einmal die Barmegiden im *West-östlichen Divan.*" *Goethe* 27 (1965) 45-79.

17.   Anne Louise Germaine de Staël-Holstein (1766-1817) spent the winter of 1807-1808 in Munich, Vienna, and Weimar. Critical edition of her famous controversial work *De l'Allemagne* (Paris: Hachette, 1958-1959).

18.   Voltaire, *Le fanatisme ou Mahomet le prophète. Tragédie en cinq actes* (1741/1742). *Oeuvres complètes,* ed. Lois Moland (Paris: Garnier, new edition 1877). There are several translations. *Voltaire. Mahomet the Prophet. A Tragedy in Five Acts* (New York: Ungar, 1964).

19.   Goethe's adaptation, *Mahomet,* was performed in Weimar in 1799 and 1800 and was first published together with *Tankred* (Stuttgart: Cotta, 1802).

20. Hammer, *Mohammed oder die Eroberung von Mekka. Ein historisches Schauspiel von dem Verfasser der "Schirin" und des "Rosenöls"* (Berlin: Schlesinger, 1823).

21. *Fundgruben des Orients, bearbeitet durch eine Gesellschaft von Liebhabern* (Vienna: Schmid, 1809-1818 and 1820). The *Fundgruben* are frequently quoted by specialists of Islamic studies and, of course, in studies on Goethe's *Divan*. Goethe had subscribed to the expensive periodical. See Solbrig, *Hammer-Purgstall und Goethe*, chapter V, p. 4, note 1.

22. Hammer, *Die Gallerinn auf der Rieggersburg. Historischer Roman mit Urkunden. Von einem Steiermärker.* 3 vols. (Vienna: Gerold, 1845).

23. Hammer, *Geschichte der osmanischen Dichtkunst bis auf unsere Zeit. Mit einer Blüthenlese aus zweytausend zweyhundert Dichtern.* 4 vols. (Pest: Hartleben, 1836-1838).

24. Hammer, *Geschichte der schönen Redekünste Persiens, mit einer Blüthenlese aus zweyhundert persischen Dichtern* (Vienna: Heubner und Volke, 1818). This epochal work contains the "Persian Parnassus," which Goethe consequently adopted in his *Noten und Abhandlungen zu besserem Verständnis des Westöstlichen Divans.* Annemarie Schimmel still based her new work, *Stern und Blume: Die Bilderwelt der persischen Poesie* (Wiesbaden: Harrassowitz, 1984) partly on Hammer's early analyses.

25. Goethe, *West-östlicher Divan* (Stuttgart: Cotta, 1819). In the first edition, 1819, the "notes" were published under the title *Besserem Verständnis.* In the *Ausgabe letzter Hand* of Goethe's works the poems and the prose part of the *West-östlichen Divans* were separated.

26. Joseph von Hammer, *Der Diwan des Mohammed Schemsed-Din Hafis.* From the Persian translated for the first time in its entirety. 2 vols. (Stuttgart/Tübingen: Cotta, 1812 and 1813; actually published in 1814). Hwaga Samsud'ddin Muhammad Hāfiz. Solbrig, "Entstehung und Drucklegung der Hafis-Übersetzung Joseph von Hammers." *Studi Germanici* (Rome), n.s., 10 (1972), 2, pp. 393-403. Solbrig, "Der Hammer-Hafis im Spiegel der Divan-Forschung." *Études Germaniques* (Paris) 26 (1971), 2, pp. 137-53. *Weltliteratur. Die Lust am Übersetzen im Jahrhundert Goethes,* ed. Reinhard Tgahrt et al. (Marbach-N.: Deutsches Literaturarchiv, 1982); exhibit catalogue no. 37, pp. 394-403.

27.   See Solbrig, *Hammer-Purgstall und Goethe,* p. 67.

28.   Ibid, pp. 68f. Five children were born of the marriage: Karl Josef (1817-1879), Isabella (1819-1872), Rosalie (1820-1824), Eveline (1824-1887), and Maximilian (1825-1846).

29.   See BE, p. 236.

30.   See Solbrig, *Hammer-Purgstall und Goethe,* p. 69.

31.   Ibid, vol. V, p. 5. Also Solbrig, "Über Hammer-Purgstalls ostwestliche Dichtung: Morgenländisches Kleeblatt und Duftkörner." *Jahrbuch des Wiener Goethe-Vereins* 78 (1978), 148-152.

32.   Hammer-Purgstall completed major bibliographical cataloguing projects of orientalia at a number of major libraries. In addition to those mentioned in the text above he worked also in Berlin and Bologna.

33.   Wenzeslaus Graf von Purgstall and Jane Anne Gräfin von Purgstall, née Cranstoun.

34.   *Wiener Zeitschrift für Kunst, Literatur und Mode* no. 141, 24 November 1832. See Solbrig, "Hammer's Ghazal in Commemoration of Goethe." *Modern Language Notes,* 92 (1977), 3, pp. 601-607.

35.   See Annemarie Schimmel, *Mystical Dimensions of Islam* (Chapel Hill: University of North Carolina Press, 1975). For the *Gulshan-i-rāz* see pp. 280-281.

36.   Hammer, *Mahmud Schebisteri's Rosenflor des Geheimnisses* (Pest: Hartleben, 1838), translated by Hammer and published in Persian and German. English translations: Mahmud Shabistari, *The Rose-Garden of Mysteries,* editor and translator. Edward Henry Whinfield (London 1880). Shabistari, *The Dialogue of the Gulshan-i-Rāz* (London 1887). Shabistarī, *The Secret Garden.* Translator Juraj Paska (New York/London 1969).

37.   Hammer, *Gül und Bülbül, das ist Rose und Nachtigall, von Fasli. Ein romantisches Gedicht* (Pest: Hartleben, 1833), in Turkish and German.

38.   Hammer, *Motenebbi, der größte arabische Dichter. Zum ersten Mahle ganz übersetzt* (Vienna: Heubner, 1824). Al-Mutanabbi. A detailed analysis of this translation was done by Baher Mohamed Elgohary, *Joseph Freiherr von Hammer-Purgstall (1774-1856). Ein Dichter und Vermittler orientalischer Literatur* (Stuttgart: Akademischer Verlag Heinz, 1979), pp. 59-167.

39. Hammer, *Geschichte des Osmanischen Reiches, großentheils aus bisher unbenützten Handschriften und Archiven,* 10 vols. (Pest: Hartleben, 1827-1835). 2nd. improved edition = 4 vols., 1834-1836. Translated into French by J.J. Hellert, *Histoire de l'Empire Ottoman* (Paris 1835-1843, 2nd. edition 1840-1842). Reprinted edition, Herbert W. Duda (Graz: Akademische Druck- und Verlagsanstalt, 1963).

40. Hammer, *Gemäldesaal der Lebensbeschreibungen großer muslimischer Herrscher der ersten sieben Jahrhunderte der Hidschret,* 6 vols. (Leipzig: Leske, 1837).

41. Hammer, *Literaturgeschichte der Araber. Von ihrem Beginne bis zu Ende des zwölften Jahrhunderts der Hidschret,* 7 vols. (Vienna: Staatsdruckerei, 1850-1856).

42. Hammer, *Das arabische Hohe Lied der Liebe, das ist Ibnol Faridh's Taije in Text und Übersetzung zum ersten Male zur ersten Säkular-Feyer der K.K. Orientalischen Akademie herausgegeben* (Vienna: Staatsdruckerei, 1854). Ibn al-Farid, 'Umar ibn 'Ali.

43. *Figaro,* no. 270 (1837).

44. See *Emerson's Complete Works,* vol. 8 (Boston: Houghton, Mifflin; Cambridge, Mass.: The Riverside Press, 1990), 223.51. Emerson refers to the *Geschichte der schönen Redekünste Persiens,* using Hammer's transcriptions of Persian proper names.

45. Hammer, "Über die Vielsprachigkeit." *Sitzungsberichte der kaiserlichen Akademie der Wissenschaften* (Vienna 1852).

46. Pedro Calderón de la Barca, *El Príncipe constante,* ed. Alberto Porqueras Mayo (Madrid: Espasa-Calpe, 1975). I thank Fidel Fajardo-Acosta for finding the source and for correcting and translating the text.

47. George Krotkoff, "Hammer-Purgstall, Hajji Baba, and the Moriers." *International Journal of Middle East Studies* 19 (1987), 103-108, note 11. The last sentence is a paraphrase of Krotkoff's assessment of Hammer-Purgstall's accomplishments. Other specialists such as Annemarie Schimmel agree with us.

Bibliography

I. Selected Works by Hammer-Purgstall

Fundgruben des Orients, bearbeitet durch eine Gesellschaft von Liebhabern.
6 vols. Vienna: Schmid, 1809-1818 (last issue 1820).

Schirin. Ein persisches romantisches Gedicht. 2 parts. Leipzig: Fleischer,
1809.

Der Divan von Mohammed Schemsed-Din Hafis. 2 parts. Tübingen: Cotta,
1812-1813 (actually published 1814). Translated.

Rosenöl, oder Sagen und Kunden des Morgenlandes. 2 vols. Stuttgart/Tübin-
gen: Cotta, 1813.

*Des Osmanischen Reiches Staatsverfassung und Staatsverwaltung, dargestellt
aus den Quellen seiner Grundgesetze.* 2 vols. Vienna: Camesina,
1815.

Die Geschichte der Asassinen, aus morgenländischen Quellen. Stuttgart/
Tübingen: Cotta, 1818.

*Geschichte der schönen Redekünste Persiens, mit einer Blüthenlese aus zwey-
hundert persischen Dichtern.* Vienna: Heubner und Volke, 1818.

*Morgenländisches Kleeblatt bestehend aus persischen Hymnen, arabischen
Elegien, türkischen Eklogen.* Vienna: Doll, 1819.

*Memnon's Dreiklang, nachgeklungen, in Dewajani, einem indischen Schäfer-
spiele, Anahid, einem persischen Singspiele, und Sophie, einem türkischen Lustspiele.* Vienna: Wallishauser, 1823.

Motenebbi, der größte arabische Dichter. Zum ersten Male ganz übersetzt.
Vienna: Heubner, 1824. Translated from Arabic.

*Baki's, des größten türkischen Lyrikers Diwan. Zum ersten Male ganz ver-
deutscht.* Vienna: Beck, 1825. Translated from Turkish.

*Geschichte des osmanischen Reiches, großentheils aus bisher unbenützten
Handschriften und Archiven.* 10 vols. Pesth: Hartleben, 1827-
1835.

*Wamik und Asra, das ist der Glühende und die Blühende. Das älteste per-
sische romantische Gedicht im Fünftelsaft abgezogen.* Vienna:
Wallishauser 1833. Translated from Persian.

*Gül und Bülbül, das ist: Rose und Nachtigall, von Fasli. Ein romantisches
Gedicht, türkisch herausgegeben und deutsch übersetzt.* Pesth/
Leipzig: Hartleben, 1834. Translated.

Über die Länderverwaltung unter dem Chalifate. Berlin: Dümmler, 1835.

*Geschichte der osmanischen Dichtkunst bis auf unsere Zeit. Mit einer Blü-
thenlese aus zweytausend zweyhundert Dichtern.* 4 vols. Pesth:
Hartleben, 1836-1838.

*O Kind! Die berühmte ethische Abhandlung Ghasali's. Arabisch und deutsch,
als Neujahrsgeschenk.* Pesth: Hartleben, Vienna: Strauß, 1838.
Translated from Arabic and German.

Geschichte Wassaf's. Persisch herausgegeben und deutsch übersetzt. Vienna:
Staatsdruckerei, 1856. Translated from Persian and German.

Erinnerungen aus meinem Leben 1774-1852. Ed. Reinhart Bachofen von
Echt. *Fontes Rerum Austriacarum,* part 2, vol. 70. Vienna:
Hölder-Pichler-Tempsky, 1940. *Nachträge* by A. Popek. 1942.

II. Works in English Translation

*Ancient Alphabets and Hieroglyphic Characters Explained with an Account of
the Egyptian Priests, their Classes, Initiations and Sacrifices in the
Arabic Language by Ahmad Bin Abubekr Washih.* Translated by
Hammer, ed. Wilkins. London: Bulmer, 1806. (Ibn-Washiyah,
Abu-Bakr Ahmad ibn 'Ali, 9th century).

*Evliya, Efendi. Narrative of Travels in Europe, Asia and Africa, in the 17th
Century.* Translated from the Turkish by Ritter J.V. Hammer.
London 1846-50. Printed for the oriental Translation Fund of
Great Britain and Ireland. Reprinted London and USA 1968.

Hammer. *History of the Assassins.* Translated by O.C. Wood. London:
1835, 1840. Reprinted New York: Burt Franklin, 1968.

III. Secondary Works in English

Krotkoff, George. "Hammer-Purgstall, Hajji Baba, and the Moriers."
International Journal of Middle East Studies 19, 1987.

Said, Edward W. *Orientalism.* New York: Pantheon Books, 1978.

Schimmel, Annemarie. "Hāfiz and His Critics." *Studies in Islam.* January
1979.

Solbrig, Ingeborg H. "Hammer's Ghazal in Commemoration of Goethe."
Modern Language Notes 92, April 1977. Abstracted in *LLBA* 13,
1979, 2:02619.

IV. Major Studies in German

Elgohary, Baher Mohamed. *Joseph Freiherr von Hammer-Purgstall 1774-1856: Ein Dichter und Vermittler orientalischer Literatur.* Stuttgart: Akademischer Verlag Heinz, 1979.

Fuchs-Sumiyoshi, Andrea. *Orientalismus in der deutschen Literatur.* Hildesheim/Zurich/New York: Olms, 1984.

Fück, Johann. "Josef von Hammer-Purgstall." *Die arabischen Studien in Europa.* Leipzig: Harrassowitz, 1955.

Goethe, Johann Wolfgang von. "Von Hammer." *Noten und Abhandlungen zu besserem Verständnis des West-östlichen Divans.* Stuttgart: Cotta, 1819.

Reichl, Sepp. *Hammer-Purgstall: Auf den romantischen Pfaden eines österreichischen Orientforschers.* Graz/Vienna: Leykam, 1973.

Schimmel, Annemarie. "Zum Problem der Übersetzung persischer Poesie." *Zeitschrift für Ästhetik und Allgemeine Kunstwissenschaft* 22, 1977.

_____. *Zwei Abhandlungen zur Mystik und Magie des Islams von Josef Hammer-Purgstall.* Introduction and commentary by A.S. Vienna: Akademieverlag, 1974. Reprinted.

Solbrig, Ingeborg H. *Hammer-Purgstall und Goethe.* Bern: Lang, 1973.

_____. "Die Inschrift von Heilsberg." *Jahrbuch des Wiener Goethe-Vereins* 75, 1971.

_____. "Joseph von Hammer: Wieland-Verehrer und Beiträger zum *neuen Teutschen Merkur.* Christoph Martin Wieland. *Nordamerikanische Forschungsbeiträge.* Ed. Hansjörg Schelle. Tübingen: Niemeyer, 1984.

_____. "Über Hammer-Purgstalls ost-westliche Dichtung: *Morgenländisches Kleeblatt* and *Duftkörner. Jahrbuch des Wiener Goethe-Vereins* 78, 1974.

Wertheim, Ursula. *Von Tasso zu Hafis.* Rütten and Loening, 1965. 2nd edition Berlin/Weimar: Aufbau-Verlag, 1983.

Ferdinand Kürnberger

Ingrid Spörk

One of the most important writers and feuilletonists of the Austro-Hungarian Monarchy in the nineteenth century, Ferdinand Kürnberger, has been unjustly forgotten. Today he is remembered only for his novel *Der Amerikamüde* (1855, Tired of America) and for preparing the way for the language criticism of Karl Kraus, who called him "the greatest political writer Austria ever had."[1] But this is only one part of Kürnberger's extensive production. In his novels and essays we find an abundance of reflections on the philosophy of language, the theory of literature, and on aesthetics, the reason Wittgenstein and Adorno expressed their high esteem for him.

But how did this famous yet "forgotten" thinker live and what were his writings and their significance?

Ferdinand Kürnberger's Life

Ferdinand Kürnberger was born in Vienna on 3 July 1821, the fourth of five children of penniless parents. His father was a gas lantern warden, and his mother sold vegetables and fruit at the Naschmarkt, the famous Viennese marketplace. Still his gifts were recognized early, and he was able to gain a university education. "A few friendly stars shone down on my educational career," he says in his autobiograpy, written for Konstantin von Wurzbach's *Österreichisches Lexikon.*[2] Very early he won the award of one hundred gulden for being the best pupil in his class, and later in the fifth grade of his school, the famous Schottengymnasium of the Piaristen, he wrote an epilogue for the annual graduation which not only received great praise but was even printed. But the young poet, who then wrote *Aphorismen*[3] (Aphorisms) and was highly interested in German literature—he adored Heine, Goethe, Schiller, and Hölty—also had problems. He had to repeat several classes, and when it came to the final examination at the Akademisches Gymnasium, he did very badly in mathematics, so he could not begin regular study at the university but was admitted only to a *studium irregulare*.[4] This fact led him to forge the year of his birth. In his autobiography he advances it to 1824 to hide the years he repeated classes.

At the university he studied philosophy for not very flattering reasons: "That faculty, however, which I chose, philosophy and humanistic sciences, was even more than the others an empty space."[5] We have to remember that Kürnberger's school years fell in the period of the *Vormärz* (pre-1848) when the Metternich regime censored any free discussion and suppressed free teaching at universities. Consequently he spent most of his time at the Belvedere Gallery and listening to the music of Mozart and Beethoven. He cultivated a "culture of instinct, the only culture permitted to Austrians in the period of the *Vormärz*,[6] a type of culture he was to develop later in his essays and prose works.

At this time he wrote his first novellas, *Des Volkes Stimme—Gottes Stimme* (The People's Voice—God's Voice), published in 1844 in Volume 22 of Ignaz Franz Castelli's (1781-1862) *Huldigung der Frauen, Taschenbuch für das Jahr 1844* (Homage to Women. Pocket Book for the Year 1844), and *Berthold* (written around 1845 but never published), both dealing with artists' lives. In 1846 another novel, *Eine Visionsgeschichte* (A Visionary Story), was published in Bäuerle's *Theaterzeitung* (Nos. 277-278), and he presented his play *Ein Trauerspiel im Böhmerwalde* (A Tragedy in the Bohemian Forest) to the Theater an der Wien, but the performance was prohibited by the censors. A second drama, *Quintin Messis,* was accepted by the Burgtheater in 1848 but was never performed. His experiences with the theater were a tragic chapter in Kürnberger's life. He wrote six plays (one is lost), but none of them was ever performed in Vienna, and his attempts to have them performed in Munich or Weimar were not any more successful. This failure is something he shares with most of the Austrian realist writers, including Marie von Ebner-Eschenbach and Ferdinand von Saar, both of whom became famous novelists but in their beginnings suffered very much from their lack of dramatic success.

But Ferdinand Kürnberger continued to write novellas, which could earn him the money he needed when published in literary journals. And so he wrote *Der Pact mit dem Teufel* (The Devil's Pact), *Ein Glücklicher* (A Happy Man), and *Otfried*. The latter two works remain lost to date.

Kürnberger dedicated himself also to another genre for which he demonstrated a genuine talent, namely, the feuilleton, combining the critique of language with philosophical reflections. Since 1841 he had written articles for *Der Humorist* (The Humorist), edited by Moritz Gottlieb Saphir (1795-1858), *Die Sonntagsblätter* (The Sunday Pages), edited by Ludwig August Frankl, *Die Presse* (The Press), *Der Freimütige* (The Candid Newspaper), *Die Wiener Zeitung* (The Vienna Newspaper), and *Die Constitutionelle Donauzeitung* (The Constitutional Danube Newspaper); some of these feuilletons devoted to literary subjects were included in Kürnberger's collection *Literarische Herzenssachen* (1877, Literary Matters of My Heart). In his essay *Ein Votum über die Literatur der Dorfgeschichten* (1848, A Vote on the Literature of the Village-Tale), Kürnberger expresses his original view of this genre; his rejection of it marks the beginning of the sharp and uncompromising literary criticism for which he was to become feared and appreciated.

The year 1848 brought another very important caesura in Kürnberger's life. The political developments leading up to the revolution of March 1848 influenced him deeply, and, "flushed with opposition," he fought in the front line of the "Revoluzzer," the revolutionaries. The police were very interested in getting hold of this "Grandartikelschreiber" (writer of inflammatory articles), and in November 1848 he was forced to leave Vienna for Dresden with a forged passport. He was arrested there in May 1849 when the uprising spread to Dresden—for wearing a wild beard and a low hat. Imprisoned for more than nine months, he was without any income. After he was released he stayed for periods in Bremen, Hamburg, and Frankfurt. During that time he had to support himself by journalism, but he also wrote his famous novel *Der Amerikamüde*, which he began writing in Hamburg, the drama *Catilina*, and the novella *Das Goldmärchen* (The Golden Fairy Tale), published in 1855. A selection from his large output of novellas was published in 1857 in Prague.[7] The novel *Der Amerikamüde* met with considerable success. In this work based on the biographical impressions of the famous Austrian poet Nikolaus Lenau (Niembsch Edler von Strehlenau), Kürnberger treats critically the American way of life.

After more than eight years in Germany, Kürnberger returned to Vienna in 1856 to visit his old and sick mother. He still had problems with his passport because he had been denounced; he also did not like the situation in Vienna generally. Therefore he tried to return to Germany. In

1860 he went to Munich, but the intervention of the Austrian authorities caused him to be expelled from Bavaria and so he moved to Coburg and Stuttgart. In 1862 he traveled via Munich and Salzburg to Graz, where his friend Isabella Wendelin lived. Kürnberger's friendship with this woman, who was married and the mother of two children, was the only constant relationship with a woman in his life. It started in the year of his mother's death and remained platonic until his death. Most of the time Kürnberger and his friend did not live in the same town, and this situation provides us with a large correspondence, containing many details about Kürnberger's life and thoughts. A selection of the letters was published in the posthumous edition *Briefe an eine Freundin 1850-1879*[8] (Letters to a Friend).

In Graz Kürnberger received a polite letter summoning him to an arrest of ten days, including two days of fasting, because of his illegal absence in foreign countries. He did not accept this "invitation" but traveled to Kallo-Semjen in Hungary, where his old friend Samuel Engländer lived. He stayed there for a year, writing his drama *Firdusi,* his important novel *Das Schloß der Frevel* (1904, The Castle of Blasphemy), and his novella *Die Last des Schweigens* (1869, The Burden of Silence). The two narrative works deal with psychological topics in masterly fashion, as will be discussed later to show how Kürnberger was a precurser of Sigmund Freud.

Kürnberger's sharp intellect and his deep psychological insight combined with a rough character did not allow him to make many friends during his lifetime, neither in his private nor in his professional life. His precarious situation as a freelance writer, his constant financial worries reinforced his tendency to be a lone wolf, and he cultivated this stance in his writings. Complementary to that bias towards isolation he developed a strong love for nature. Constantly roaming around and writing about his impressions, he is supposed to have been the first to call these activities "tourism."

At the end of 1863 Kürnberger returned to Munich and lived in the house of the famous draftsman Kaulbach, but he soon went back to Graz, where his drama *Catilina* was to be performed. But again he was unlucky, because the leading actor absconded and the performance did not take place. Later Kürnberger moved to Vienna, where he lived until 1877, then returned to Graz, where he lived with short interruptions until July 1879. That month he set out for a journey to Bregenz. It was to be his last one.

He was hospitalized in Munich, where he died on 14 October 1879. His body was transported to Mödling, where it was buried in a grave of honor.

Novels, Novellas, and the Tragedy of Drama

The biggest success in Ferdinand Kürnberger's productive life was the extraordinary reception of his novel *Der Amerikamüde*—in the first weeks after its publication in 1855, 10,000 copies were sold—a very great number at that time. One reason for this unusual success was certainly the great interest for the United States and for the literature about it at a time marked by a fever for emigration in reaction to the difficult political situation in Europe. But the most important reason for the novel's success was its excellent description of the American way of life and its criticism of both the American and the European situation. The title is a response to Ernst Willkomm's *Die Europamüden* (1838, The People Tired of Europe), a novel that paints a highly euphoric picture of the United States, expressing the enthusiasm of a large part of the progressive Austrian intelligentsia for America, which resulted from resignation and despair about Metternich's conservative, repressive policies.

Kürnberger's novel, by contrast, shows the disillusioning experiences of his protagonist within American reality, based on the journals of the Austrian poet Niembsch Edler von Strehlenau, better known as Nikolaus Lenau. When Dr. Moorfeld arrives in New York City in 1832, he is still enthusiastic: "The individual says: my better self; the globe says: America. What is impossible in Europe, is possible in America; what is impossible in America, is really impossible."[9] Moorfeld, the young artist, travels through the country with the highest of expectations: "Not how the people fight for freedom, but how they use their freedom, daily, hourly, at home, in church, in school—this must show me mankind at its highest level. This is why I went to America."[10] During Moorfeld's travels this idealistic conception of the United States is compared to personal experience, and Moorfeld has to realize that the American reality is influenced by "Yankeetum" (Yankeeism). In the beginning he thinks of it as cleverness and pragmatism, but during the course of events and talks with entrepreneurs, stock market speculators, brokers, and lawyers, he comes to regard "Yankeeism as a dollar fever that kills all human behavior. Instead of a country of reason and freedom he finds a nation of classes (*Klassenstaat*), which is structured by fraud, meanness, and profiteering, where man becomes a dollar-producing machine, "where man is nothing and goods everything."

Kürnberger shows this situation by an abundance of events, reports, and anecdotes from all social, cultural, and political spheres. During his journey from New York City to Ohio, to Lake Erie and back to New York City, Moorfeld not only loses his ideals about American reality, but also by the criticism of reality the ideals themselves lose their meaning because they are not able to change reality. This double disillusionment leads Moorfeld finally to return to Europe.

Knowing that Kürnberger never visited America and could not be seriously interested in criticizing a country he did not know, we have to ask what he really wanted to show with this picture of America and at what his criticism was really aimed. Rüdiger Steinlein suggests, in his epilogue to a new edition of Kürnberger's novel, that the "criticism of 'American' reality is ultimately a criticism of capitalism."[11] Using the United States as an example, Kürnberger's criticism of capitalism combines both a philosophical perspective like Hegel's and a literary perspective such as Heine's. Not least, however, the importance of this work is to be seen in Kürnberger's formal organization of his complex criticism of ideology and society.[12] In this respect Kürnberger may be seen as a forerunner of the great American socio-critical writers of the twentieth century from Upton Sinclair to John Steinbeck. Although his novel cannot provide more than a negation, this negation foresees also the general developments in Germany and in Europe. Hence his picture of the United States has to be seen as a metaphor which combines the criticism of American "reality" with the fear of European capitalism. In choosing a foreign country, Kürnberger employs a useful stylistic vehicle to evade censorship and at the same time to make things clearer.

When Moorfeld returns to Europe, he has no positive ideals left; his tragic Weltanschauung leads into resignation and a feeling of weakness and isolation. Thus at the end of the novel, the euphoric protagonist of the beginning has become a modern hero with all of the problems and fears of the modern human being. With this twist the novel extends far beyond the time of its production and can be seen as a penetrating description of future events in the philosophical, social, and political spheres.

Kürnberger's advanced thinking can also be seen in his other novels. For example, in his second novel *Der Haustyrann* (1875, The Bully), he discusses the role of the patriarch in the family and argues for the necessity of divorce if the character of the dominant person, is unalterable and hinders the other members of the family from enjoying a happy life.

Toward the end of his life Kürnberger worked for many years on another very interesting novel, *Das Schloß der Frevel* (The Castle of Blasphemy), published posthumously in 1904, which he considered the "treasure of his life." In this very impressive work he boldly discusses the pathos of Catholicism, including its problems with eroticism. The novel describes the homosexuality of Jesuits and analyzes the dogma of the Immaculate Conception as metaphor or symbol. The editor of the first edition of Kürnberger's works, Karl Rosner, writes in his preface: "Universally educated, a poet, philosopher, politician, a scholar of art and, at the same time, a man of the intense sensual life of powerful personalities, Kürnberger spreads out here before the eyes of the beholder a panorama radiant with rich and manifold colors."[13] Nevertheless he felt it necessary to make some cuts to evade censorship. The novel treats the development of a young man, Balm, who in the war of 1859 comes to Italy, where he is confronted with antiquity and Catholicism, sensualism and spiritualism. He makes the acquaintance of Marchese Santafiore, a spiritualist, and of the painter Zuppa, a sensualist. While viewing the antique frescoes in a castle he visits, Balm experiences a major shock. The reader does not know what he has seen, and so the novel becomes as thrilling as a whodunit. His marriage at the end reconciles Balm to life and reveals the shocking pictures of the frescoes—his bride in the nude—to have been a misunderstanding.

During his lifetime Kürnberger tried to have this novel published in a newspaper. He even sent a copy to the *New Yorker Staatszeitung* in New York, but it never reached its destination. Besides the tragedy of non-publication, we have to remember that Kürnberger, who was very poor, had to copy each work four or five times by hand if he wanted to present it to several publishers. And the *Schloß der Frevel* comprises 378 pages in print! Kürnberger did not live to see the publication of his most important novel, and even after his death it took nearly twenty-five years before it was first published in serial form in the Viennese newspaper *Die Zeit* (1902/1903) and then in 1903 as a book. Because of these difficulties in publishing his novels, his importance in the cultural life of his time does not derive primarily from his narrative prose but from his journalistic and critical writings in newspapers.

The Feuilleton Writer

Kürnberger's feuilletonistic writings include both political and social criticism as well as reflections on literature and the critique of language. Typically he was never employed by any newspaper but wrote his articles and essays as a freelance writer. Hence they truly reflect his personal opinion and point of view.

Kürnberger's political articles provided a running commentary on the "Austrian tragedy," as he termed it. His most important themes were the reemergence of "Pan-German politics," the war of 1866 with Germany, the compromise with Hungary, and the German Union. The "tragedy" resulted from the reactions to the events of 1848, from diverse political beginnings in Austria that were never realized. In addition to these topical themes, he criticized the general corruption, the venality of newspapers, and the intrigues of political parties. He warned against speculating in stocks and its fatal social consequences, and he understood the importance of the Labor movement.

In the preface to a selection of his feuilletons, *Siegelringe* (Signet Rings), which he published in 1874, Kürnberger describes the tenor of his essays as "reflection and passion."[14] Despite all his verve and commitment, he never attacked individuals in his writings but always argued in a distanced and objective way.

Kürnberger also intervened in activist fashion in practical social concerns. Arguing in a very modern ecological way, he fought against the cutting down of the *Wienerwald,* the forest on the hills west of Vienna, and he promoted the idea of building a hotel in the Semmering, which at the turn of the century became a famous tourist attraction.

Siegelringe contains a selection of his articles on the political and ecclesiastical situation.[15] In these articles Kürnberger is rather outspoken. Thus, for example, he writes about the Minister's reception of a delegation of workers in 1869: "If, for example, on the section of parquet floor, where, at the reception of the workers' delegation the Minister Count Taaffe was standing, a thinking man had by chance been present, the newspapers would have had a quite different dialogue to report."[16] Then he goes on to argue against Taaffe's statements rather than against Taaffe himself.

Despite being a liberal journalist, he clearly points out the problems of modern politics and media by using liberalism as an example: "Since bourgeois liberalism, either because of customary thoughtlessness or with deliberate cowardice, has agreed to establish the word of the press as a natural equivalent of the truth and to commit the holiest functions of speech into the custody of the machine, ever since then I have given up all hope for the liberty of Europe."[17] In another essay he explains the reason for his uncompromising criticism: "We are saying these harsh things about liberalism in its pseudoliberal role, so that it may better itself. One chastises that which one loves.[18]

Another situation he unremittingly fought against was the stupid and reactionary excesses of the Catholic church, especially of the Jesuits and their proclaimed intention of Catholicizing Protestants in "a street of blood."[19] In another article he deals with the European invasion of South America and the invaders' treatment of heresy:

> There can truly be a point of view, from which the philan-
> thropist must curse the day when Columbus sailed from
> the harbor of Palo, for his three ships were followed by the
> most poisonous pest ever brought forth on our globe; they
> were followed by those horrible creatures who carried the
> cross in one hand and the torch of fire in the other, with
> which they then, burning and pillaging, broke into the
> cabins of the innocents in Mexico, Lima, Chile and Peru
> in order to teach the so-called savages the most savage kind
> of human sacrifice. The Indian war dance to celebrate an
> orgy over the slaughtered and roasted enemy is a harmless
> ballet compared to the Roman invention of human
> slaughter, according to which the enemy was burned
> without first being killed—and without even being an
> enemy.[20]

The essays gathered in the second volume of feuilletons, *Literarische Herzenssachen. Reflexionen und Kritiken* (1877, Literary Matters of My Heart: Reflections and Reviews) include Kürnberger's discussions of literature, which have been compared to Lessing's *Literaturbriefe*,[21] (Letters about Literature), and his perceptive criticism of language, which shows him as a forerunner of Karl Kraus. Moreover, the collection contains reviews of Gottfried Keller's *Sieben Legenden* (Seven Legends), Shelley's *Prometheus Unbound,* and the translation of Michelangelo's *Rime,* as well as literary portraits of Turgenev, Claude Tillier, Bogumil Goltz, and Grill-parzer.

In his criticisms of language Kürnberger analyzes the phraseology of newspapers, to make clear the kind of imagery used—the newspaper style based on chivalry, for instance, using phrases such as "to throw down the gauntlet" or "to enter the lists"—and to reveal the unconscious irony of that style: "Having grown gray in jousting tournaments, the famous knight Aaron Mendel can now be seen breaking a lance for the duty-free import of yarns."[22]

Still he prefers this to the proletarian newspaper style, which uses images such as "to drag everything into the mud," "to fling something into someone's teeth," or "to get in each other's hair." His reflection about this language is very clear: "What has mud to do with the ideas of thinking people? What struggle of interests could in any sense lead to mud? Is mud a part of the economy of political parties? If not, why then does it belong to their language? If pigs could talk, it would most likely be important—in the language of pigs, but in the language of humans?"[23] By this kind of linguistic reflection, the critique of language departs from the normative or grammatical domain that was typical for the seventeenth, eighteenth, and nineteenth centuries and starts to investigate the social sphere and contents of language. His gift for powerful language makes Kürnberger also a much appreciated writer of aphorisms: Adorno quotes him in the motto of his *Minima moralia:* "Life doesn't live." Another aphorism—"Whatever there is, is visible"—has been compared to Wittgenstein.[24] Finally, this aphorism might be seen as motto for Kürnberger's commitment to writing as enlightenment: "It is that stupidity for its own sake, that pernicious, willful stupidity, which we are slapping in the face."[25]

Kürnberger and Psychology

In many of his works Kürnberger displays an excellent psychological description of character. One of the best novellas in this respect is *Die Last des Schweigens. Eine Seelenstudie*[26] (The Burden of Silence. A Psychological Study), a judgment shared by the contemporary reception. Immediately reprinted in twenty journals, this work brought Kürnberger the recognition he deserved. When it was published in 1869 under the title *Der Unentdeckte* (The Man Who Remained Undiscovered), it was compared with and even preferred to Victor Hugo's *Le dernier jour d'un condamné* and later was considered the equal of Dostoyevsky's *Raskolnikov.*

Kürnberger could not have known Dostoyevsky's work, and so his psychological study shows no outside influence. Together with Schnitzler's prose works *Leutnant Gustl* and *Fräulein Else,* it establishes an Austrian literary tradition of inner monologue that leads directly into psycho-analysis. In his work *The Austrian Mind: An Intellectual and Social History, 1848-1938,* William M. Johnston also points out this novella as a very surprising precursor of psychoanalysis.[27]

Die Last des Schweigens recounts the memory of a murderer, who recalls the genesis of his deed on the day before his execution. Yet, it is not for repentance that he writes his account, but to provide insight into his illness that became a mortal one—his passion for his wife Irma. His love for her drove him to kill the man she was going to marry so that he could marry her himself. The murder remained undiscovered for many years, until he felt impelled to confess it when alone out in nature, and in doing so is discovered one day. The murderer wants to explain his actions, because otherwise people might say it was his conscience that forced him to make the confession. "It wasn't my conscience. The reasons for it are deeper."[28]

Combining murder and illness, Kürnberger indicates that conscience has no part in the developments. The act of murdering is shown as a symptom of the illness "passion" rather than as a part of the ethical system. The murderer favors this illness as the best of all illnesses. "If passion is an illness, it is the only consequential one. No patient wants his illness, but the passionate person wants his passion."[29] He thinks that physical illness is an "injustice" because it can destroy the head and the heart. Passion, however, "is the only just measure for us."[30]

This separation of physical and mental illness does not seem to lead directly to psychoanalysis which tries to abolish precisely that division. But as the narrative continues, passion starts to trouble the murderer physically at the very moment when he passes from theoretical reflection to dramatic imagination. As he says, "I became as unhappy physically as I used to be intellectually."[31] However, he doesn't attribute these troubles to his conscience, but to a nervous shock, as experienced in the theater. Denying the force of conscience, he relativizes it by putting it in a historical and social context. "Morality affirms life; immorality denies it. . . . You shall not murder—you shall die for your homeland—it is the same. . . . Conscience is the instinct of life."[32]

In arguing for the relativity of conscience, Kürnberger comes close to Freud who defines the superego as the result of subordination to the laws of society, culture, and the family. But Kürnberger talks about the relation between the drive for self-preservation and ethics in a more radical and concise way. Freud argues more precisely that the function of the ego is to regulate the wishes of the pleasure principle so as to conform to the principle of reality; the superego has the function of formulating the norms and laws necessary to accomplish that.[33] For Freud as for Kürnberger the basis for the division of the psychological process into different agents derives from repulsing the primary functions of the "misery of life."[34] Freud first developed these ideas by referring to the physiology of the brain; Kürnberger provides a model that refers to social rather than to physiological systems. The moral demand not to kill arises from the interests of the clan and the individual's fear of the clan's revenge, an argument by the way which can also be found in Freud's writings. Again in accordance with Freud, Kürnberger relativizes conscience when he has his murderer argue that murder is not a crime in all societies but used to be a highly respected and recognized political instrument in antiquity. Thus he emphasizes again that the contents of conscience depend on society and that the question of guilt is a social one. As the murderer reasons: "Put me into a society where I may say: I murdered, where I may say it to men who have also murdered, then there would be no conscience, and my face could be free and open. Not his conscience but his secret makes a murderer a murderer.[35] By this, he describes exactly the function of the superego. Not the act as such, but the fact of being excluded from a society by the act causes the problem.

This discovery is so important for the murderer that he wishes to teach it from the "lecturing desk of his gallows,"[36] because it is a "theoretical perception on the same order of importance in ethics as the law of gravity is in physics."[37] The "murderer of culture" finds his confirmation in nature and therefore retires from men and human society. He acknowledges, similar to Freud, that "the god [of this society and order] is the colossal flattered ego."[38]

In the logic of the perpetrator, it is not the act which is the symptom of his illness but its inexpressibility. Quite straightforwardly he asks for the "talking cure" of psychoanalysis which permits the anamnesis of the repressed: "Language does not have the right to distinguish itself from animal sounds, *if it does not start at the point where innocence ends.*"[39]

When the murderer talks with his judge, he finds similarities: "You are a man to my taste. Your goal is your reputation, and my going to the gallows serves your goal. . . . I am happy to see an ego that is as intent on killing me as I was on killing [my rival]. Good company, my friend, good company!"[40] Beyond this attack on justice Kürnberger talks about a "law of opposition," a force of negation that leads Johnston to compare it with the destructive instinct in Freud.[41] The force of negation described by Kürnberger is "that strong because it is not known. There is nothing to oppose it. You cannot deny it, because it is negation itself."[42] Arguing like Derrida, Kürnberger thinks of a negation that is not itself an origin, that has always been a negation of something. He asserts in Freudian terms: "The wish rather than negation is the original voice of people."[43] For Kürnberger "the ego is a superstition"[44] that should be abandoned. People are like animals: merely a different form of nature's writing: "The typesetter sets this type sometimes and sometimes that one; sometimes he lays aside Cicero and takes up Borgis, but he always sets type. And every time he sets the same text. The text says: Live, feel, be there."[45]

With this image of writing Kürnberger goes far beyond Freud, who exemplified the rise of the psychical apparatus with an inscription on "the mystic writing pad" (*Wunderblock*)[46] Kürnberger directly pronounces what Derrida postulates in his *Grammatologie*[47]—the writing before the letter, the questioning of logicentrism, which is a "metaphysics of phenetic writing,"[48] a general metaphysics. In that way teleological thinking is questioned. Thus for the murderer in the novella there is no end and no purpose, and therefore he does not fear his death. The description of his development concludes with the words: "Be confident, dear moon, we shall see each other for many years to come. They cannot execute me any more than they can execute you."[49]

Kürnberger and Semiology

In his literary and feuilletonistic *oeuvre* Kürnberger displays an analytical sagacity and rhetorical elegance that earned him the flattering title "the Lessing of Austria." The aesthetic and semiotic reflections scattered throughout his work have not yet been systematized, and as we have seen from the manner of his literary production, he did not like to organize things. For example, he neglected to collect his novellas in books, so we may assume that this was simply a trait of his character. Also, since the early days of his study of philosophy, when he preferred the "empirical aesthetics" of the pictures in the Belvedere Gallery to the systems taught at the university, he inclined to be subjective rather than systematic. For this reason, we may find in his work some traces of Hegelian and post-Hegelian aesthetics and the theory of signs, but because of his uniqueness they become quasi little clouds with new, sometimes bizarre shapes.

The novella *Die Göttin* (1861, The Goddess),[50] for example, tells the story of the healing of a supposedly weak-minded man. He displays his deviant behavior during his boyhood, when he refuses to learn the names of the flowers. He thinks the signs of language are accidental and therefore not worth learning. Many years before Saussure, the child argues that the relation between the signifier and the signified is arbitrary, as his mother explains:

> A thousand times his mother would complain to me about the child's inability to remember the names of things. Hardly was he capable of properly naming horse and cow, sheep and dog; anything that went beyond that was all Greek to him. This peculiarity often drove his parents mad. This is saxifrage!, his father would often desperately shout, but Niels shouted back: *No, it is a flower, you just call it saxifrage!* . . . It was never more *fun* than when he was confronted with a whole bunch of flowers. What is it, dear Niels? Sage. No, it is rue. It is sage. Well, again, what is it that I have here? *It is rue or sage, or peppermint or daisy, or . . .* and so it went on and on. He poured out a bag of names and left it to the others to choose from them. In doing so, he did not even look at the objects but just laughed and lightheartedly pranced about. In his heart—which could be read on his brow—he considered the rest of us *crazy to sort out all those names.* He thought we were only pretending! *It seemed to him to be arbitrary, completely superfluous.*[51]

This formulation of the arbitrariness between the signifier and the signified is clearly not to be attributed to Kürnberger himself but to his knowledge of Hegelian aesthetics.[52] What can be attributed to him, however, is the choice and presentation of this theme, to which he dedicated a long passage of the novella, as well as the combination of this theme with a story based on the life of the Danish poet Oehlenschläger, which provides the plot, although Oehlenschläger did not recall this semiotic problem in his autobiography.[53]

Another novella, *Aug und Ohr* (Eye and Ear),[54] published posthumously, also deals with semiotic problems, by exploring, in accordance with a problem of body semiotics, the relation between face and voice. In this novella Kürnberger describes the discussion of two friendly professors, who debate whether it is possible to infer the face from the voice and the voice from the face, or whether both are truly symbolic.[55] They carry out an experiment in a girl's grammar school, where the professor of aesthetics tries to match the girls' voices to their faces in a photograph album. The experiment succeeds and the professor of aesthetics marries the girl with the most beautiful voice and the most interesting face. So, face and voice are symbolic, the relation between them is motivated, not arbitrary. As later in Saussure,[56] there is an opposition between the arbitrary sign and the motivated symbol, and in pointing this out Kürnberger again follows Hegel.[57] In this novella the theoretical problem is also reflected in the structure—the marriage is motivated by the mutual motivation from voice and face. But there is also an ironic element because the girl gives him a "sign" (flowers), following her intuition of the symbolic relation between physical appearance and character; she acts spontaneously without any theoretical reflection. Thus, the results of the professor's well-devised experiment are shown to be based merely on a feigned reaction.

In the novellas the theoretical problem is always shown in reflected form because, in terms of the plot, theory and practical life are mutually dependent for the protagonists. In his feuilletons Kürnberger cannot use such doubling. He explains this difference, again following Hegel: "The poetic idea strives to become a living image."[58] He distinguishes between language performance in a pragmatic and in a poetic sense: "[Everyday] words express the concepts of reason, but poetic words want to imitate sense impressions."[59] Despite following Hegel in many points, Kürnberger revaluates one of the important theorems of Hegelian aesthetics because he prefers symbolic polyvalent art to the monosemic classical art appreciated by Hegel. He argues against *Tendenzliteratur* (tendentious literature), which does not leave anything to the reader but "spells everything out,"[60] denying its value. Consequently, he declares himself against the use of illustration, which was then becoming more and more fashionable; poetic art should release the imagination, but illustrations bind it and make it monosemic.[61] Thus, Kürnberger is to be understood as a defender of the polymic in general, not only for aesthetic, but also for political reasons. For him the activity of the imagination in the reception of art should not be dominated by anyone else's imaginative activity. Thus, his argumentation is very modern; his valuation of the polysemic resembles the claims of the postmodern thinker Julia Kristeva for the semiotic practice of some of her French contemporaries.[62]

Kürnberger's modern thought, which was influenced by sensualism, also deals with the setting up of binary oppositions by language, its redistributive function, as Kristeva would put it.[63] In "Soll und Haben eines Naturgenies" (Debit and Credit of a Natural Genius) Kürnberger, following Friedrich Theodor Vischer, tries to link his definition of poetic language with the artist's specific mode of perception. Vischer describes the process as a subject taking on the form of an image inside the artist and being filled out later by the effort of his intellect,[64] Kürnberger enlarges this model by dividing the intellect organizing the matter into an intellect determined by nature and an intellect determined by culture. The nature intellect is the result of a sensual intuition, the sensual person (*Sinnenmensch*) has a power of conception, intuition, and sentiment that enables him to perceive mind in nature: "If one approaches sensual things in a linear way, one finally reaches the point where landscape changes and a thing is no longer a thing, but mind. We all know that mind and matter are one, and only language uses two words for this unity.[65]

This claim of the unity of matter and mind and their arbitrary division by language makes Hegel's and Vischer's distinctions between them a play on words, and their effort to describe the relations between them an effect of language, an effect of the symbolic order rather than a "given" reality. This situation takes us back to the beginning—the deviance of the so-called weak-minded in the novella *Die Göttin* becomes an element of Kürnberger's criticism of language. His literary work as presented here in a few examples, shows that the conception of language that sets up arbitrary differences and oppositions rather than motivated relations, puts forth the body as the last guarantee of a system of relations whose "imaginary" Kürnberger denies. For Kürnberger, the fiction of a subject identical with itself as well as signifying identities is still possible. His little theoretical clouds float toward Saussure, for Kürnberger, like Saussure, places the signified over the signifier, with the ellipse around them maintaining their unity.

Notes

1.   Karl Kraus, "Aus dem dunkelsten Österreich," in: *Die Fackel,* ed. Heinrich Fischer, vol. XII (1906-1907) (Munich: Kosel, 1968), p.

5. All translations are by Wilfried Prantner and the author.
2. Ferdinand Kürnberger, "Selbstbiographie," in: *Briefe an eine Freundin (1859-1870),* ed. Otto Erich Deutsch (Vienna: Verlag des Literarischen Vereins, 1907), p. XVL.
3. See Otto Erich Deutsch, "Gedanken des jungen Kürnberger," in: *Neues Wiener Tagblatt,* 10 April 1909, no. 100.
4. See W. A. Hammer, "Ferdinand Kürnbergers Studienjahre," in: *Zeitschrift für Österreichische Gymnasien,* vol. 6 (1910), pp. 175-182.
5. Kürnberger, "Selbstbiographie," p. XVI.
6. Ibid.
7. Kürnberger, *Ausgewählte Novellen* (Prague: Bellmann, 1857).
8. Kürnberger, *Briefe an eine Freundin* (1859-1879), ed. Otto Erich Deutsch (Vienna: Verlag des Literarischen Vereins, 1907).
9. Kürnberger, *Der Amerikamüde,* ed. Jan Kressin with an afterword by Rüdiger Steinlein (Berlin: Freitag, 1982), p. 7.
10. Ibid., p. 157.
11. Ibid., p. 372.
12. Cf. ibid.
13. Karl Rosner, ed. "Zur Einführung," in: Ferdinand Kürnberger, *Das Schloß der Frevel* (Berlin: Seemann, 1904), p. VII.
14. Kürnberger, *Siegelringe. Eine ausgewählte Sammlung politischer und kirchlicher Feuilletons* (Hamburg: Meißner, 1874), p. XIX.
15. Kürnberger, *Siegelringe,* p. 117.
16. Ibid., p. 430f.
17. Ibid., p. 135.
18. Ibid., p. 499.
19. Ibid., p. 484f.
20. Kürnberger, *Literarische Herzenssachen. Reflexionen und Kritiken,* ed. Otto Erich Deutsch (Munich/Leipzig: Müller, 1911).
21. See Adolf Watzke, ed. *Ferdinand Kürnberger, Aufsätze über Fragen der Kunst und des öffentlichen Lebens. Auswahl.* (Vienna/Leipzig: Tempsky, Freytag, 1920), p. 18.
22. Ferdinand Kürnberger "Die Blumen des Zeitungsstils," in: *Das denkende Herz.* Eine Auswahl (Klagenfurt: Kaiser, 1947), pp. 5-14.
23. Ibid., p. 10.
24. See Karl Riha, ed. "Zu Ferdinand Kürnbergers kritischen Positionen," in: *Ferdinand Kürnberger, Feuilletons* (Frankfurt am Main: Insel, 1967), p. 21.

25.   Kürnberger, "Eine hundertjährige vollkommne Ohrfeige," in: *Siegelringe. Eine ausgewählte Sammlung politischer und kirchlicher Feuilletons*, p. 171.

26.   Kürnberger, "Die Last des Schweigens. Eine Seelenstudie," in: *Brüder vom Trojanerberg. Drei Erzählungen*, ed. Otto Erich Deutsch (Vienna: Steyrermühl, 1826), pp. 24-42.

27.   See William M. Johnston, *The Austrian Mind. An Intellectual and Social History 1848-1938* (Berkeley: University of California Press, 1972), p. 249.

28.   See Kürnberger, *Die Last des Schweigens*, p. 25.

29.   Ibid., p. 24f.

30.   Ibid., p. 25.

31.   Ibid., p. 29.

32.   Ibid., p. 31.

33.   See Sigmund Freud, "Die Zerlegung der psychischen Persönlichkeit," in: *Studienausgabe*, vol. 1, *Vorlesungen zur Einführung in die Psychoanalyse. Neue Folge der Vorlesungen zur Einführung in die Psychoanalyse* (Frankfurt am Main: Fischer, 1980), p. 500f.

34.   Sigmund Freud, "Entwurf einer Psychologie," in: *Aus den Anfängen der Psychoanalyse. Briefe an Wilhelm Fliess, Abhandlungen und Notizen aus den Jahren 1887-1902*, eds. Marie Bonaparte, Anna Freud, Ernst Kris (London: Imago Publications, 1950), p. 381.

35.   Kürnberger, *Die Last des Schweigens*, p. 38.

36.   Ibid.

37.   Ibid.

38.   Ibid., p. 26.

39.   Ibid., p. 39. My emphasis.

40.   Ibid., p. 41.

41,   See Johnston, *The Austrian Mind*, p. 249.

42   Kürnberger, *Die Last des Schweigens*, p. 35.

43,   Ibid., p. 26.

44   Ibid., p. 42.

45.   Ibid.

46.   Cf. Sigmund Freud, "Notiz über den Wunderblock," in: *Studienausgabe*, vol. 3: *Psychologie des Unbewußten* (Frankfurt am Main: Fischer, 1982), pp. 363-369.

47.   Cf. Jacques Derrida, *Grammatologie* (Baltimore: Johns Hopkins University Press, 1976), especially "Writing before the Letter," pp.

1-93.
48. Ibid., p. 1.
49. Kürnberger, *Die Last des Schweigens,* p. 42.
50. Kürnberger, "Die Göttin," in: *Novellen,* vol. 1 (Munich: Fleischmann, 1861), pp. 269-347.
51. Ibid., p. 295. My emphasis.
52. Cf. Georg Wilhelm Friedrich Hegel, *Ästhetik,* vol. 1. Ed. F. Bassenge (Berlin/Weimar: Aufbau, 1976), p. 298. For Kürnberger's theoretical positions see: Wolf-Dieter Kühnel, *Ferdinand Kürnberger als Literaturtheoretiker im Zeitalter des Realismus* (Göppingen: Kümmerle, 1970).
53. Cf. Adam Oehlenschläger, *Meine Lebens-Erinnerungen. Ein Nachlaß* vol. 1 (Leipzig: Lorck, 1850), p. 143f.
54. Kürnberger, *Aug und Ohr.* Novella (Vienna: Daberkow, o.J.) (= Allgemeine National-Bibliothek. No. 264-265).
55. Cf. Ibid., p. 36.
56. Cf. Ferdinand de Saussure, *Grundfragen der Allgemeinen Sprachwissenschaft,* eds. Ch. Bally and A. Sechehaye (Berlin: de Gruyter, 1967), p. 80.
57. Cf. Hegel, *Ästhetik* vol. 1, p. 299. Concerning the theory of signs in Hegel see Dietrich Gutterer, "Ansätze einer Zeichentheorie bei Hegel, in: Achim Eschbach, Jürgen Trabant, eds. *History of Semiotics* (Amsterdam/Philadelphia: Benjamins, 1983), pp. 191-204 or Elisabeth Walther, *Allgemeine Zeichenlehre* (Stuttgart: dva, 1974).
58. Kürnberger, "Schillers und Goethes Briefwechsel," in: *Literarische Herzenssachen,* p. 142.
59. Ibid., p. 142f.
60. Kürnberger, "Der entfesselte Prometheus," in ibid., p. 136.
61. See Kürnberger, "Das Illustrationswesen," in ibid., p. 426.
62. See Julia Kristeva, *La révolution du langage poétique* (Paris: Seuil, 1974).
63. Cf. ibid., p. 53f.
64. See Friedrich Theodor Vischer, *Ästhetik oder Wissenschaft des Schönen,* vol. III (Munich: Deutsche Bibliothek, 1922), p. 17.
65. Kürnberger, "Soll und Haben eines Naturgenies," in: *Literarische Herzenssachen,* p. 90.

Bibliography

I. Works by Ferdinand Kürnberger in German

Der Amerika-Müde. Amerikanisches Kulturbild. 2 vols. Frankfurt am Main: Meidinger, 1855 (= Deutsche Bibliothek, 8).

Catilina. Drama in fünf Aufzügen. Hamburg: Hoffman und Campe, 1855.

Ausgewählte Novellen. Prague: Bellmann, 1857. Includes: *Das Kind mit dem Briefe; Die Versuchungen der Armen; Das große und das kleine Loos; Giovanna; Ein Brautpaar in Polen; Der Drache; Die Braut des Gelehrten; Der Windfall.*

Novellen. 3 vols. Munich: Fleischmann, 1861f.

Vol. 1 (1861): *Spieler und Bettler; Flucht und Fund; Die Opfer der Börse; Die Göttin.*

Vol. 2 (1861): *Drei Tage in Pyrmont; Der Dichter des Don Juan; Amor im Felde; Der Wildsenne; Auf einer Bergparthie; Der Kuß.*

Vol. 3 (1862): *Am Abend. Ein Idyll; Ein Abenteuer in Venedig.*

Novelleten. Munich: Fleischmann, 1864. *Eine Schlittschuh- Geschichte; Ein Orakel; Der letzte Taigherm; Der Mummelsee; Das Stiefkind; Das Räthsel in Erz; Witwentreue; Gideon Weise; Der Bildstock am Rain; Der Mann und die Kunst. Humoreske Charakterbilder: Der Phrenolog; Der Ammendoktor; Der Schachspieler; Der Schwinner. Aufruf für Schleswig-Holstein. Epistel an den Kaiser von Österreich.*

Die Last des Schweigens [under the title *Der Unentdeckte*]. In: *Ungarischer Lloyd.* Eds. Rothfeld and Weisskirchner, 1869.

Siegelringe. Eine ausgewählte Sammlung politischer und kirchlicher Feuilletons. Hamburg: Meißner, 1874.

Der Haustyrann. Vienna: Rosner, 1876.

Novellen. Berlin: Hertz, 1876.

Literarische Herzenssachen. Reflexionen und Kritiken. Vienna: Rosner, 1877.

Die Hexe von Riegersburg [Marie Maurer]. Drama in *Neue Illustrierte Zeitung.* Vienna (2 November 1879).

Das Schloß der Frevel. 2 vols. Ed. Karl Rosner. Berlin: Seemann, 1904.

Briefe an eine Freundin (1859-1879). Ed. Otto Erich Deutsch. Vienna: Verlag des Literarischen Vereins, 1907.

Gesammelte Werke. Ed, Otto Erich Deutsch.

Vol. 1: *Siegelringe.* Eine Sammlung politischer und kirchlicher Feuilletons. (Munich/Leipzig: Müller, 1910.

Vol. 2: *Literarische Herzenssachen. Reflexionen und Kritiken.* Munich/Leipzig: Müller, 1911.

Vol. 3 was not published.

Vol. 4: *Der Amerikamüde. Amerikanisches Kulturbild.* 3rd edition. Munich/Leipzig: Müller, 1910.

Vol. 5: *Das Schloß der Frevel. Löwenblut. Novelle.* Munich/Leipaig: Müller, 1914.

Aufsätze und Gutachtenberichte für die deutsche Schillerstiftung. Ed. Otto Erich Deutsch. Munich: Müller, 1911.

Briefe eines politischen Flüchtlings. Ed. Otto Erich Deutsch. Vienna/Leipzig: Tal, 1920.

Ferdinand Kürnberger und Emil Kuh. Briefwechsel. Ed. C. Höfer. In *Jahrbuch der deutschen bibliophilen Gesellschaft.* Vol. 19 (1932).

Other publications from the *Nachlaß* (literary estate) to be found in the Nationalbibliothek (Vienna) are:

No. 260/261: *Quintin Messis.* Lay.

No. 299/300: *Das Trauerspiel.* Comedy.

No. 301/302: *Firdusi.* Drama.

No. 303/304: *Das Pfand der Treue.* Drama.

II. Works in English
No translations found.

III. Secondary Works in English
Moltmann, G. "American-German Return Migration in the 19th and early 20th Centuries." In: *Central European History,* vol. 13 (1980), pp. 378-392.

Pache, W. "The Dilettante in Exile—Grove at the Centenary of His Birth. In: *Canadian Literature,* 90 (1981), pp. 187-191.

IV. Major Studies in German

Dissertations and Monographs
Arnold, Heinz. "Ästhetische Anschauungen und literaturkritische Urteile Ferdinand Kürnbergers." Dissertation, Leipzig, 1966.

Ederer, Charlotte. *Die literarische Mimesis entfremdeter Sprache. Zur sprach-*

kritischen Literatur von Heinrich Heine bis Karl Kraus. Cologne: Pahl-Rugensstein, 1979.

Halpern, Julius. "Ferdinand Kürnberger (1821-1879). Ein österreichisches Schicksal." Dissertation, Vienna, 1928.

Harrack, Paula Maria. "Ferdinand Kürnberger als Publicist." Dissertation Vienna, 1935.

Horner, Emil. "Produktive Kritik: Ferdinand Kürnberger." In: *Deutsch-Österreichische Literaturgeschichte.* Eds. Nagl, Zeidler, Castle. Vol. 3. Vienna: Fromme, 1930, pp. 152-162.

Immergut, Walter. "Ferdinand Kürnberger und Österreich." Dissertation, Vienna, 1952.

Jahl, Charlotte. "Weltanschauliche Probleme in Ferdinand Kürnbergers Novellen." Dissertation, Vienna, 1936.

Kritsch, Erna. "Ferdinand Kürnberger als Romanschriftseller." Dissertation, Vienna, 1946.

Kühnel, Wolf-Dieter. *Ferdinand Kürnberger als Literaturtheoretiker im Zeitalter des Realismus.* Goppingen: Kümmerle, 1970.

Meyer, Hildegard. *Nord-Amerika im Urteil des deutschen Schrifttums bis zur Mitte des 19. Jahrhunderts: eine Untersuchung über Kürnbergers "Amerikamüden,"mit einer Bibliographie.* Hamburg: de Gruyter, 1929.

Nachtigall, Gertrud. "Ferdinand Kürnberger als Novellist." Dissertation, Vienna, 1946.

Neuwirth, Curt. "Ferdinand Kürnberger als Dichter." Dissertation, Vienna, 1923.

Rehart, Herbert. "Ferdinand Kürnberger: Ein notwendiges Mißverstehen." Kritische Auseinandersetzung mit der Rezeptionsgeschichte. Dissertation, Vienna, 1982.

Wessely, Robert. "Ferdinand Kürnberger. Mensch und Kritiker." Dissertation, Vienna, 1948.

Wildhagen, Andreas. *Das politische Feuilleton Ferdinand Kürnbergers. Themen und Technik einer literarischen Kleinform im Zeitalter des deutschen Liberalismus in Österreich.* Frankfurt am Main/Bern/New York: Lang, 1985.

Wittibschlager, Hans. "Die Technik der Novellen Ferdinand Kürnbergers." Dissertation, Vienna, 1923.

Nikolaus Lenau

Julius M. Herz

Nikolaus Lenau, who was ranked by Gerhart Hauptmann and Stefan Zweig among the foremost German lyricists of the nineteenth century, was an individualist who belonged to no literary school. He cannot be assigned to any of the Romantic schools, although Romanticism had a strong impact on him. As a liberal fighting for civil liberties, he vigorously opposed censorship and repression, yet he was not a member of "das junge Deutschland," a German writers' group that shared some of his views but still attacked him. On the other hand, Swabian writers like Gustav Schwab, Gustav Pfizer, Karl Mayer, and Justinus Kerner were his friends. He also knew Ludwig Uhland, but the Austrian had no place in the Swabian School either. Although he lived during the age of rising German nationalism, the movement held no interest for him. Only one of his longer epic works, *Faust*, deals with a German topic. He did visit Germany frequently and liked to be identified as a Hungarian by his German friends;[1] he also emphasized his Hungarian birth when he did not obey Austrian censorship laws. Because he published his works in Germany, the Austrian authorities created difficulties for him. In his caustic "Gedanken und Einfälle" (Thoughts and Ideas) Heine referred to Lenau as "der arme Ungar Niembsch"[2] (the poor Hungarian Niembsch). After a brief visit to Hungary at age twenty-five in 1827, Lenau never returned and thus lost his ties with the land of his birth. It was Austria for which he felt an attachment despite his anger about repressive laws and censorship. Before leaving for America he was concerned about an Austrian law regarding emigrants. He did not want to lose his citizenship in Austria, which he identified as his home country; he thought there was no better place than Austria.[3] After his American tour he arrived in Upper

Austria, from where he wrote to his brother-in-law Anton X. Schurz: "At last I am back in our beloved Austria."[4]

Like his parents, Lenau was born in Hungary, but their language was German. Possibly of lower aristocratic background,[5] the Niembsch family traces its origins to the town of Strehlen in Silesia—Austrian until 1741—today's Strzelin, Poland; there Lenau's great-grandfather was born in 1717, became an Austrian officer and distinguished himself against the Prussians during the Seven-Years' War. His son, Joseph Niembsch, married in Hungary the daughter of an Austrian baron, rose to the rank of colonel in the Austrian Army, and towards the end of his life received the name "Strehlenau" as his title of nobility. These were times when members of the nobility took their titles seriously, no matter how recently bestowed nor how low the rank. Their sole surviving child of five was Lenau's father Franz (1777-1807), who attended Latin school, and at the age of twenty-one became a cadet in a dragoon regiment.

It was probably in Ó-Buda—today part of Budapest—that he met Maria Theresia Maigraber, Lenau's mother. Daughter of a respectable middle-class family, Theresia fell madly in love with the elegant, expansive, and handsome Franz Niembsch, a ladies' man who lived well beyond his means and had a reputation as a gambler. Theresia was a passionate and proud woman, willing to sacrifice everything for her love; she was known to sell her fur coat to pay his gambling debts. Not surprisingly, neither her mother, who must have had some knowledge of the reputation of the young man, nor Franz Niembsch's parents approved of the marriage. For his aristocratic and perhaps arrogant mother the Maigrabers were ordinary middle-class people. Theresia, who was more than six years older than Franz, became pregnant and threatened suicide if she were forced to become an unwed mother. The wedding took place in Pest; Franz Niembsch quit the military and received a government clerkship.

Their second child, Lenau, was born in the town of Csatád[6] on 13 August 1802 and, according to the records, was baptized in the Roman Catholic faith the same day. The area, which has belonged to Romania since 1919, was part of Hungary under the Habsburg dynasty at the time Lenau was born. From the sixteenth to the early eighteenth century it was part of the Turkish Empire, then for some time an Austrian province partly settled by peasants from the western regions of Germany, from Luxembourg and Lorraine. Ironically, since the middle of the twentieth century, when German place names all but disappeared from the maps of East Central Europe, Lenau's birthplace is now officially called Lenauheim, and the house where he was born is a memorial museum. He never returned to his place of birth and could not have any recollection of it because within the year the Niembsch family moved to Ó-Buda to be supported by Theresia's mother. Franz Niembsch squandered the little money they had, soon became ill, and died of consumption before his son Niki was five years of age. Lenau's mother worked as a seamstress to feed her three children—Niki and his two sisters. Her second marriage to a physician was not a happy one either and did not alleviate the poverty of the family, since her husband, Dr. Karl Vogel, earned little money, and two more daughters were born; Lenau, however, had no attachment to his half-sisters, nor was he fond of his stepfather. Lenau's mother loved her children—above all her son—considerably more than she loved her husband.

The story of Lenau's life and that of his parents has all the necessary ingredients of a novel. Full of emotions and passions, it deals with highly intelligent and proud people who knew how to love but who fell in love with the wrong persons. Restlessness, poverty, joblessness, and eccentricity point to more contemporary twentieth-century problems.

Lenau did not attend elementary school. At age ten he entered the Piarist[7] Gymnasium in Pest, where he learned some Hungarian, but the language of instruction was Latin. Despite their poverty, Lenau's mother managed to hire tutors for her gifted son. His studies were interrupted by a move to the town of Tokaj,[8] where Lenau came into contact with Hungarian country people, learning more of their language. He did not attend school for more than a year, enjoying the personal freedom, the landscape of the great plains (the "Puszta"), and the human contacts there. Buda, the next station in his life, brought the resumption of his schooling. Abject poverty finally forced his mother to let her beloved sixteen-year-old Niki go to his well-to-do paternal grandparents. Lenau loved his mother, who spoiled him terribly, usually letting him do what he wanted. Consequently he accepted preferential treatment as a matter of course but took criticism with a feeling of humiliation and anger. Clashes with his grandparents in Stockerau were inevitable. They wanted him to pursue a useful career, but he studied philosophy at the University of Vienna and Hungarian Law[9] in Preßburg,[10] then agronomy in Magyaróvár (Ungarisch-Altenburg)[11] at the College of Agriculture, again philosophy in Vienna; then he switched to Austrian law, and finally to medicine in Vienna and later in Heidelberg without ever earning a degree anywhere. His restless-

ness made him change schools and subjects despite his native intelligence
and initial bursts of enthusiasm and diligence.

Lenau belongs to the age of the Biedermeier, a period of solid middle-
class values often exemplified by modesty, contentment, and humility,
which we read about in the works of Franz Grillparzer or Adalbert Stifter
and hear in the melodies of Franz Schubert or Josef Lanner. Resignation
and melancholy are part of the picture together with a certain degree of
curiosity about the big wide world into which the somewhat narrow-
minded burgher or philistine did not often venture, and if he did, his
nostalgia for his native land usually got the better of him and he eventually
returned.

Lenau has almost always been associated with *Weltschmerz*, that sentimental pessimism which sometimes is reduced to a pose. Lenau stands
apart from this mode, although resignation and especially melancholy do
characterize much of his work. Still, he should not be simply labeled a
"poet of *Weltschmerz*;" for him art was like a religious commitment.

There are indications of Lenau's writing activity as early as 1820,[12]
when he lived in Vienna. By 1821 he informed his mother that he was
writing poetry and mentioned plans for a drama.[13] Some of his earliest
poems date from the years 1821-1822.

A tempestuous love affair with a very young girl, Bertha Hauer, who
bore him a daughter, and the death of his mother are milestones in his
life. A small inheritance from his grandmother Niembsch made him decide
despite warnings from friends to pursue a career in poetry, a rather bold
and highly unusual decision. Because of restrictive censorship laws in
Austria Lenau was eager to try his luck in Germany, where he was received
with open arms by members of the Swabian School of poets in and
around Stuttgart. The famous publisher Johann Georg von Cotta finally
accepted a collection of Lenau's poems which was published in 1832. His
new Swabian friends found the Hungarian nobleman fascinating, intriguing—a true poet. Most of these writers were deeply interested in
religion and philosophy, and Lenau had ample opportunity for lively
discussions, so much so that he spent part of his time studying Spinoza's
philosophy while enrolled at the University of Heidelberg. His courtship
of a niece of Gustav Schwab turned out to be a passing fancy. After one
of his mood swings he gave up his studies of medicine and prepared for
a voyage to America. Lenau did not intend to emigrate; he was simply an
impulsive, restless man looking for new experiences and investment oppor-

tunities. Despite all the pleas and warnings of his friends he went ahead with his travel plans and left Amsterdam on the vessel *Baron van der Kapellen*, a sailing ship that docked in Baltimore on 8 October 1832 after a difficult voyage of more than ten weeks.

Lenau never became an expert on America. He could not develop an understanding of this country. Full of too many expectations and not knowing its language, culture, literature, or intellectual class, he misjudged the new land quickly and rashly. Perhaps not deliberately looking for them, he did manage to find negative aspects of life everywhere in the USA, even criticizing the uniformity of nature and its lack of fantasy; of course, he never saw the Rocky Mountains! There are no references to Benjamin Franklin, Thomas Jefferson, Washington Irving, or James F. Cooper. The education of the Americans he considered to be "mercantile" and "technical"; he questioned their love for their country.[14] The ironic fact is that Lenau's visit to America was not totally idealistic but also "mercantile," since he intended to invest his money in land in the hope of a sixfold return.[15] Some of his negative impressions may have been exacerbated by a head injury suffered in an accident when his sled turned over. Lenau was seriously ill most of the winter and suffered from rheumatism. He spent much time in western Pennsylvania and visited there the Rappist religious settlement in Economy. He did notice that German immigrants were losing their attachment to their homeland, of which they often spoke disdainfully. He would not have made a good farmer or pioneer, and he was quite happy to return to Europe in the spring of 1833, although later he kept toying with the idea of returning to the United States. While he was in America, Lenau's first book *Gedichte* (1832, Poems), was published. It became a best-seller with seven editions during the next dozen years. Suddenly Lenau found himself to be a celebrity, a "hot commodity" in today's vernacular, the equivalent of a famous Hollywood star or rock singer. This was a time when poets enjoyed a kind of deification, with monuments dedicated to their memory after their death.

Lenau enjoyed the company of friends and acquaintances and spent a great deal of time in discussions with other writers and artists. In Vienna he usually spent part of the day in the Café Neuner, the meeting place of the Viennese intellectual élite. This café located in the Plankengasse was also known as "das silberne Kaffeehaus" (The Silver Café) because of the many silver items in the place. For a man like Lenau, who spent most of his life in rented rooms or guest rooms, the Viennese café was home. There the customers could read several newspapers and journals, eat and drink something, play billiards or cards, meet friends, gossip, discuss politics, philosophy, or any cultural event, conduct business, work (especially writers and composers), in any event feel at home and spend, depending on the mood, little time or many hours there. Lenau was an excellent billiard player and enjoyed smoking a pipe or cigars. It was always easy to find somebody who was eager to get involved in conversation. To the circle in the Café Neuner belonged Eduard Bauernfeld, Ferdinand Raimund, Johann Christian von Zedlitz, Josef Lanner, Johann Nepomuk Vogl, Ludwig August Frankl, Johann Strauß (senior), Franz Grillparzer, and Anastasius Grün (Count Auersperg). Grün was Lenau's close and devoted friend who dedicated his work *Der Pfaff vom Kahlenberg* (The Priest from the Kahlenberg) to him and became his biographer as well as editor of his posthumous and collected works. On the other hand, Lenau and Grillparzer never became real friends, partly because Lenau did not like Grillparzer's lyrical poems and thus did not consider him a great poet but rather a cold rationalist.[16]

Max Löwenthal (1799-1872), a well-to-do Austrian government official and a second-rate writer, poet, and dramatist, also was part of this Viennese circle of literati. It was a fateful year (1834) when Lenau met him, his young wife Sophie (1810-1889), and their three children. They became good friends and, possibly against his better judgment, Lenau managed to promote some of Löwenthal's works. Lenau was already aware of Sophie Löwenthal's reputation as a beauty and a socialite because he mentioned her reputed "irresistibility" in a letter to a lady-friend even before he met her.[17] Sophie, a highly intelligent, educated lady with strong religious principles and a mind of her own, was a good Catholic and a devoted mother. She was nevertheless flattered by the attention of this famous poet who was far more gifted and interesting than her husband. The friendship soon grew into mutual love and had its agonizing and tormenting ups and downs. Lenau loved her passionately, knowing that she had a fatal hold on him. She knew how to handle her husband, and Lenau had to agree never to sleep with her.[18] Sophie seemed to be satisfied with the role of a close friend and inspiring muse of the great poet whom she respected, loved, and controlled to a certain extent. In hundreds of notes ("Zettel") in his diary he expressed his passionate love:

Oh Sophie! . . . I have found more assurance of eternal life in communion with you than in all my study and observation of the world. . . . I saw in your lovely eyes today the full richness of the divine. . . . In such lovely eyes as yours is revealed, as in a prophetic hieroglyph, the material of which our eternal body will some day be made. When I die, I shall go from life a rich man, for I shall have beheld the loveliest of all things. Your farewell rose is as fragrant as a goodnight from you. Sleep well, dear heart. Keep the other rose as a keepsake. It was a lovely day. I love you beyond all bounds.[19]

In his letters to her he formally addressed her with "Sie," and no doubt most of them, if not all, were shared with her husband Max.[20] He also received his own personal letters from Lenau, who became what the Viennese sarcastically used to call a *Hausfreund*. The two men kept up their friendship and addressed each other with *du*—liberalism was on the rise—even though Sophie received many more letters (about three hundred) than Max. These letters, perhaps like Franz Kafka's *Letters to Felice* or *Letters to Milena*, constitute an integral and important part of the writer's work; we learn much from them about the personality and views of the correspondents. Lenau's friend, Anastasius Grün, called some of the letters "little works of art."[21] Sophie was able to help Lenau dissolve his engagement to the famous singer Karoline Unger. Yet he was much more determined to get married four years later after he met Marie Behrends in the summer of 1844. Was this a last attempt to free himself from the chains that tied him to Sophie? In the fall of 1844 he suffered a total mental collapse and spent the rest of his rapidly deteriorating life in mental institutions. He died in a suburb of Vienna on 22 August 1850.

Lenau, who enjoyed concerts and the opera, once wrote to Sophie that he had learned the best and the most from Beethoven, the sea, the Alps, and, of course, from her.[22] We could extend the mention of Beethoven to include music in general, as Lenau actually could be called a *Doppelbegabung* (dual talent). In his younger years he was an accomplished guitarist and later an exceptional and brilliant if somewhat undisciplined violinist who introduced to his Swabian friends the songs of Franz Schubert. With his musical talent his primary literary accomplishment was the lyrical verse, rather than his epic works, which often suffered from fragmentation. He called Beethoven's *Ninth Symphony* the greatest work in music at a time when most music critics disagreed. His poem, "Beet-hoven's Büste" (1842, Beethoven's Bust) is the expression of his deep admiration (C I, pp. 413-415). Incidentally, his sister Therese and her husband had an apartment in the Schwarzspanierhaus[23] where Beethoven had died in 1827, and with interruptions Lenau lived there with them for a fairly long time.

The musical quality and even the vocalism in his poems assure them their lasting value.[24] Their dynamic structure is comparable to pieces of music. The nineteenth century was the century of the "Lied." More than 800 composers, great ones as well as amateurs, set at least 160 of Lenau's poems to music. This underscores more than anything else Lenau's popu-larity and his impact; one poem alone, "Bitte" (1832, Prayer) was set to music at least 249 times. Winthrop H. Root aptly translated this short poem into English:

Prayer
Rest upon me, dark eyes, bind me
With your darkly magic might,
Earnest, mild, and deeply dreaming,
Inexplicably sweet night.

With your magic darkness rid me
Of the world of garish day,
That you over my life ever,
You alone, hold perfect sway.[25]

Today, most compositions of Lenau's poetry and their composers are forgotten, but some names still stand out such as Eugen d'Albert, Alban Berg, Carl Czerny, Leopold Damrosch, Friedrich von Flotow, Wilhelm Kienzl, Konradin Kreutzer, Franz Liszt, Karl Loewe, Felix Mendelssohn-Bartholdy, Adolf Müller, Max Reger, Anton G. Rubinstein, Robert Schu-mann, Richard Strauß, Felix von Weingartner, and Hugo Wolf.[26]

Lenau spoke Hungarian, although not perfectly, and in later years he must have forgotten a lot of it. He did not read Hungarian books. Yet Lenau had a very high respect and warm feeling for the Hungarian people and depicted Hungarian characters and the Hungarian landscape in a favorable light. During the nineteenth century most of the German-speaking population living in the Kingdom of Hungary had a positive relationship with the Hungarians, an attitude which eventually led to

voluntary assimilation. We can be certain that Lenau reflected his mother's
feelings toward their homeland; this special quality permeates a number of
poems with Hungarian memories and themes and goes beyond the description of an "exotic" land. The years of childhood and youth in Hungary left an indelible imprint upon his poetry over most of his productive
years. "Die Heideschenke" (1831, The Tavern on the Puszta), part of a
group of poems entitled *Heidebilder* (Pictures from the Heath), is full of
Hungarian memories and motifs: a herd of horses, riders with whips, a
thunderstorm on the plains, and outlaws dancing and singing in a tavern
while the gypsies are playing their violins. These outlaws had among many
Hungarians a reputation very much like Robin Hood. Lenau's romanticized picture of those men is a flashback to his youth. Far less romantic
is "Der Räuber im Bakony" (1842, The Highway Bandit in the Bakony
Forest), which conveys the social message that out of desperation the poor
may feel justified to kill. "Die Werbung" (1830, Recruiting) is probably
the first attempt in German literature to express the peculiarities of Hungarian gypsy music through poetry characterized by several changes in the
dynamics within the poem and underscored by an appropriate choice of
words.[27] The rhythm is the essential point. We can even speak of an
affinity of Lenau with the gypsies, their temperament, their lifestyle and
above all their music, primarily their violin playing. The dynamics of
many of Lenau's poems with soft quiet initial lines rising to a crescendo
and a loud wildness are strongly reminiscent of gypsy music. This is the
reason why poems with Hungarian motifs are often linked to gypsies. An
homage to Lenau's violin[28] is "Mischka,"[29] which consists of two parts:
"Mischka an der Theiß" and "Mischka an der Marosch" (1835, Mischka
on the Tisza,[30] 1842, Mischka on the Maros).[31] Here too we see the
Hungarian memories from Lenau's youth: the river Tisza, the town of
Tokaj with its famous grapes, hussars with their swords, the fisherman
dreaming of glorious battles, the tavern with black-haired gypsies playing
the violin and the cymbal, dancing Hungarians drinking wine, becoming
excited by an old battle song played by Mischka. They dream of the heroic
days of battles against the Turks to the point of losing their sense of
reality. The second part of this long poem written years later by a more
mature Lenau portrays a different and suffering gypsy who avenges his
daughter's death and in the end buries his violin at her grave. Lenau was
quite pleased with this poem.

His last Hungarian poem "Die Bauern am Tissastrande" (1844, The Peasants on the Banks of the Tisza) has obvious political and social undertones satirizing those who adhere to the old ways (and tunes) without recognizing their foolishness.

Music, especially Beethoven's music, was more important to Lenau than the works of such literary giants as Schiller and Goethe; he actually had a rather negative opinion of Goethe and in his youth was more influenced by Ludwig Hölty and Klopstock, much less famous poets.

The discovery of nature as a thing of beauty is not a new phenomenon of the nineteenth century, but Lenau was among the early travelers who did not spare any effort, exertion, or money to experience the marvels of nature first-hand, whether it was the Atlantic Ocean, the American virgin forests, Niagara Falls, or the Alpine beauty of Austria's mountains that he was raving about. An enthusiastic nature lover, he enjoyed climbing mountains and taking long hikes, and he was also a good rider; a great part of his travels in America was done on horseback. "An die Alpen" (1840, The Alps) is a good example for Lenau's attachment to his beloved mountains, but it is not merely a declaration of love to a beautiful landscape; for him nature is a symbol, a mirror image of human suffering, complaints, pain and love, longing and desire, and finally comfort and new courage. He wrote to Sophie Löwenthal: "For me nothing will ever be more beautiful than Aussee.[32] I will never forget the solitary walk I took yesterday."[33] The personification of nature or of inanimate things is nothing new in poetry, but perhaps no poet has carried this tendency as far as Lenau. Brooks whisper, complain, or jump up on trees, leaves are hanging down sleepy and tired, dewdrops are like tears of love, the wind and storm on the Hungarian plains resemble a large number of horses galloping full-speed ahead, rocks look defiantly, and in the fall trees drop their leaves as a sleepy child drops his toy. We can even detect an environmental and ecological side of Lenau, who criticized the hard-working people along the Rhine for using and taming every speck of soil.[34]

Lenau's is primarily a lyrical talent with frequent dramatic highlights and shifts in mood. Many of his poems have a song-like quality in their musical elements. Their range of subject matter is somewhat limited, the prevailing mood is nostalgic, melancholic, foreboding. "In Lenau's soul there gathered a sorrow and a sharing in the sorrow of nature" wrote Reinhold Schneider,[35] who called him the poet of earthly sadness. Lenau introduced into German literature not only the Hungarian landscape, the *puszta,* but also some of old Hungary's colorful characters such as the hussars in their striking uniforms, the horsemen of the steppes, the lively Hungarian peasants, the shepherds, the itinerant Jewish peddler, and the gypsies with their captivating music and their violins. One of Lenau's finest poems is "Die drei Zigeuner" (1838, The Three Gypsies),[36] which presents "an alternate lifestyle," while "Der Kürass" (1851, The Cuirass) pictures the brave if somewhat boisterous, cruel, and overly confident yet generous Hungarian cavalryman who refuses to buy armor from a Jewish peddler. In this poem the peddler is depicted according to the nineteenth-century stereotype: contrasted with the fearless Gentile soldier is the scared merchant who at the end, still shaking from fright, counts his money. "Der arme Jude"[37] (1842, The Poor Jew) shows a much more human and courageous side of a peddler who refuses to be baptized just to have an easier life.

Johann Gabriel Seidl published "Die Jugendträume" (1828, Dreams of Youth) in his almanac *Aurora,* "a small attempt," as Lenau called it, juxtaposing the paradisiac existence of a youngster with the "heavy iron step of reality" which leaves him in a state of disillusionment. Among his earlier poems *Schilflieder* (1832, The Sedge Songs) are among the note-worthy ones. They are associated with his love for Lotte Gmelin, whom he did not marry, probably because he was not ready to settle down to a middle-class existence and a regular job; he bemoans his suffering and thinks back to his beloved girl watching the sun go down and later the moon above the pond with the willow trees and the reeds. "Die Wurm-linger Kapelle" (1832, The Chapel at Wurmlingen) was written on the occasion of a visit to this chapel and cemetery on top of a hill not far from Tübingen in Württemberg. Lenau was there late in October, and his poem reflects the dying nature, the sadness accentuated by the graves and the birds of passage leaving for the south. Ludwig Uhland, Karl Mayer, and Gustav Schwab wrote poems describing the same beautiful spot. The fall season with its brisk wind and the leaves dropping from the trees seemed to captivate Lenau more than any other season. He feels sadness and autumn within himself. "Herbstgefühl" (1932, Autumn Mood), "Herbstklage" (1832, Lament for Autumn), "Herbstentschluß" (1834, Resolve for Autumn), "Herbstlied" (1838, Song for Autumn") are good examples of his prevailing mood.

The Polish uprising (November 1830-October 1831) against Russian rule left an indelible mark on Lenau who had a Polish friend, Nicolaus

Bołoz Antoniewicz. His ideological and pro-Polish sentiments for the freedom of Poland are expressed in the poems "In der Schenke: Am Jahrestag der unglücklichen Polenrevolution" (1832, In the Tavern: On the Anniversary Day of the Crushed Polish Revolution), "Der Maskenball" (1832, The Masked Ball), and "Der Polenflüchtling" (1834, The Polish Fugitive), which Lenau published under the subheading *Polenlieder* (Songs of Poland). Two later poems, "Zwei Polen" (1836, Two Men from Poland) and "Die nächtliche Fahrt" (1838, The Journey through the Night) also belong to his political poetry, in which he touches upon the political issues but concentrates on the human suffering and sadness caused by the historical events and the loss of one's native land. *Klara Hebert* (1832), a cycle of poems, also deals with a Polish subject and source.

Lenau's constant travels left him with a rich source of memories which sometimes bore fruit only years later. Several of these poems are grouped together under the heading *Reiseblätter* (Travel Notes). The main mode of transportation in his day was the stagecoach, and one of Lenau's best known and near perfect poems, "Der Postillion" (1833, The Postillion) immortalizes these coachmen. Cheerful tunes played by a coachman on a bugle echo through a mild night in spring in front of a cemetery where his friend lies buried.

Lenau's American experience is reflected in several poems, some fairly long, most of which do not completely betray his bitter impressions of the New World but rather concentrate on the virgin forest, Niagara Falls, and the American Indians. It is very likely that Lenau did see some members of Indian tribes, and he traveled along the Susquehanna River which he mentions. He lashes out against the white man's treatment and expulsion of America's natives and the destruction of the primeval forest by fire in "Der Indianerzug" (1834, Indians' Expulsion). Lenau was certainly not the first to bemoan the fate of the Indians, but he also emphasized the destruction of their culture and of their natural habitat, the forest; even the animals and birds were forced to flee or perish. This environmental concern is surprising. The poem "Die drei Indianer" (1834, The Three Indians) offers as the only solution voluntary death in the waters of Niagara Falls. Here Lenau gives us the idealized and romanticized picture of the noble savage. "Der Urwald" (1836, The Primeval Forest) shows some of the poet's negative feelings towards America, where even the dense forest crushes life and the birds have left, thus creating thoughts of death. Lenau was greatly impressed by both the sight and the sound of Niagara Falls, which inspired "Verschiedene Deutung" (1837, Different Interpretation) and "Niagara" (1837). "Das Blockhaus" (1838, The Log Cabin) describes a night spent in an American inn, whose innkeeper is reserved but honest and makes the traveler feel secure. Lenau pays tribute here to Ludwig Uhland, but the lonely poet cannot help but think of the transitoriness of life. The long ocean voyage to and from the USA and the impact of the sea are the source of the five poems under the heading *Atlantica*.

Lenau, who traveled thousands of miles in uncomfortable stagecoaches, lived to see the beginning of the revolution in traffic and transportation. In Austria the age of the railroad began in 1837 with the opening of the line from Floridsdorf to Deutsch-Wagram, and in the spring of 1838 this line, the Nordbahn, was extended closer to the center of Vienna. Lenau commemorates this occasion in his poem "An den Frühling 1838" (1838, The Spring of 1838), but instead of cheering technical progress he is rather skeptical about whether mankind will gain the hoped-for freedom from the greater speed. He is much more concerned with the trees and blossoms that have to be cut down to give way to the railroad. Lenau touches upon the same subject in "Am Rhein" (1838, On the Rhine).

It could be argued that *Waldlieder* (1844, *Forest Songs*), his last cycle of lyrical poems, belongs to his best achievements. These most personal nature poems owe their creation to Sophie Löwenthal and the Vienna Woods, where Lenau spent a fair amount of time, also taking long hikes from the suburbs of Vienna across the mountains to Weidling, where his sister Therese and her family were living. But there are other connections too, such as G.W.F. Hegel and his philosophy of nature. When Lenau stands at a cemetery, his thoughts soon turn toward the meaning of life and death, and nature as a symbol for both should be calmly accepted as such, even when a rainstorm is raging. The raindrops remind the poet of the tears shed by his ladylove, and it is nature's healing powers that he seeks. An image borrowed from Hegel describes nature as the bride who is wooed by the spirit, her suitor. Merlin, the magician and seer of Celtic sagas, is introduced in accordance with the Romantic taste of the time, and Lenau wants to be like Merlin, who hears in the forest what nobody else can hear, even the water flowing from a distant source and the creek bring back old memories full of sadness. The next (the seventh) stanza is a praise of sleep, which has miraculous powers, and the poet heard at times the sound of a flute in his sleep like primordial singing. The eighth stanza is a melancholy love poem describing the thirsty forest birds drinking from the source and expressing the poet's wish to drink just once from the source of love that his soul is longing for before death comes. The final stanza depicts an autumn scene full of quiet decay and dying, which may simply be a mysterious yet pleasant exchange.[38]

Lenau called his *Faust* (1836) a poem. It was not written for the stage[39] and is not related to Goethe's drama—there is no Gretchen, for example. However, Lenau did not escape the charge that his Faust, thirsty for knowledge and truth and aiming for the highest reaches of existence, is just another Goethe imitation, but Lenau, who after 1832 had been immediately recognized as a major poet, felt confident enough to find his own way and refused to accept the legend of Faust to be a monopoly of Goethe. Although Lenau used a number of different sources,[40] it is not difficult to find some similarities which prove that Lenau knew Goethe's tragedy well and was influenced by its language and imagery. However, personal elements such as his own religious doubts, symbolized by Faust's throwing the Bible into the fire, and memories of his mother and of his ocean trip to America are quite prominent. Mephistopheles promises Faust fame, power, and money, and assures him that he will learn the truth. The sea voyage, the ocean storm, and the forest dominate much of the imagery. Lenau's frustration with philosophy, which he studied and gave up, and the doubts about religion finally reach a critical point in his Faust, who vacillates between Christianity, mysticism, pantheism, atheism, and sensuality and finally kills himself, whereas Goethe's Faust is dissuaded from ending his life by the Easter bells. Lenau's *Faust* reflects some of the undercurrents of the nineteenth century from doubt and *Weltschmerz* all the way to nihilism and self-destruction;[41] as a literary work it lacks unity, but it contains many passages of great beauty.

Lenau comes to terms with philosophy in *Faust*, but with religion and the clergy in *Savonarola* (1837) and in *Die Albigenser* (1842, *The Albigenses*). The Roman Catholic Lenau turns here against the Catholic clergy and the Papacy by expressing what Hansgeorg Schmidt-Bergmann calls "a revolutionary philosophy of history."[42] *Savonarola* is the only completed part of a projected trilogy about Huss, Savonarola, and Hutten. When Lenau wrote this long poem, he had been thoroughly disillusioned by philosophy, including Hegel's; partly under the influence of the eminent Danish Protestant theologian Hans L. Martensen and even more so of Sophie Löwenthal he turned with fervor to religion. His special relationship to Sophie condemned him to an ascetic life, spiritual pain, and heartache which are expressed in this long poem named after the fanatical Florentine reformer Savonarola,[43] who was distressed by the moral decline and corruption in the Christian Church and in the general population. His growing religious and political power eventually pitted him against Pope Alexander VI and also against the political forces in Florence that brought about his excommunication, trial, and public execution (by hanging and burning)[44] on 23 May 1498. This poem, actually a verse epic of 3980 lines, attacks papal authority and is a product of Lenau's religious doubts.

In the "Tubal" episode of *Savonarola* Lenau depicts an old Jewish man whose three sons were murdered and who cannot overcome his hatred. The martyrdom of Savonarola, however, creates a miracle, and Tubal is converted to Christianity: an ancient recurring theme to solve "the Jewish question."

Die Albigenser,[45] which Lenau called "Freie Dichtungen" (Free Poetic Creations), is even more loosely structured than *Faust* or *Savonarola* and lacks a protagonist. The verse form varies, depicting various moods in a succession of scenes from the bloody religious wars in southern France in the early thirteenth century. In preparation Lenau studied various sources including French ones. He knew the history of Pope Innocent III (1198-1216), who decided to destroy the heretics. But Lenau took poetic liberties with historical events taking a stand against the Pope and government repression during the first half of the nineteenth century. *Die Albigenser* becomes the story of the destruction of a land, but the subject matter is so fragmentary that Lenau was unable to create a unified work, as he recognized. Some parts are of exquisite beauty, others dwell on gruesome scenes of violence and killings. It is to a large extent the triumph of hatred, but Lenau tried to glorify the freedom of thinking, the right to take a stand against rigid dogmas. He was not happy with his work. It dragged on for too long (1838-1842), and he became tired of the religious subject. Sophie Löwenthal predicted it would be unsuccessful. On the other hand, Lenau's friend Anastasius Grün considered it the "most powerful creation."[46] The work was published in 1842 and then reprinted in 1846 after Lenau had gone insane.

Don Juan, the last long work that Lenau attempted, also remained a fragment. However, enough text exists to prove these dramatic scenes are not a mere imitation of the old legend but a framework to express the poet's changing philosophy of life, the decision to turn away from celibacy and leap into the midst of life. Lenau was familiar with the old Spanish drama *El Burlador de Sevilla y Convidado de Piedra* (The Seducer of Seville and the Stone Visitor) attributed to Tirso de Molina. He also knew Lord Byron's *Don Juan* and Da Ponte's libretto for Mozart's *Don Giovanni*. Don Juan, who worships on the altar of Venus, finally becomes bored and disgusted by life and chooses death in a duel. Another short dramatic fragment entitled *Helena,* written in iambic pentameter and based on a medieval story from Bohemia, gave further proof that Lenau was no playwright.[47]

Lenau was a moody, rash, perhaps impatient and sometimes an undisciplined man, but he was not lazy. In 1835/1836 he worked hard as an editor to put out an almanac called *Frühlingsalmanach*.[48] He was one of a very few poets who made a living from his works. He belongs to a transitional age and is often torn between the preservation of the cultural and religious values of the past and the new ideas that led to the Revolution of 1848/1849. He was a bard of freedom, a liberal, yet in some ways a traditionalist staunchly opposed to the authoritarian bureaucracy of Metternich's Austrian government. He shared these ideas with many of his best friends who belonged to the upper classes; some were aristocrats. A seeker all his life, he regretted having lost the religious faith of his childhood. He belongs to the age of sentimentalism and *Weltschmerz* when a man was not ashamed to shed tears. Unhappy love is one of his favorite themes. At his best Lenau is able to create a synthesis between his own emotions and the objective images of nature. As a nature poet, especially with his poems containing Hungarian motifs, he contributed something new to German literature. He influenced a number of poets and writers, some of them second-rate. His impact in Europe, even outside the German-speaking countries, was greater than in England or the United States. The future of Lenau scholarship probably lies in Central-Eastern Europe where people slowly are rediscovering their common bonds.

Notes

1. Lenau referred to himself as a Hungarian to Justinus Kerner and to his brother-in-law Anton X. Schurz, but he lived in Austria most of his life. See *Lenaus sämtliche Werke*, ed. Eduard Castle, vol. III (Leipzig: Insel, 1911), pp. 75 and 306. This edition will be referred to as C.

2. *Heines Werke*, ed. Erwin Kalischer and Raimund Pissin, part 8 (Berlin: Deutsches Verlagshaus Bong, [n.d.]), p. 283.
3. C III, pp. 158f.
4. Ibid., p. 228.
5. The family did not have proof of the original title of nobility.
6. The town is located in the northern Banat region northwest of the city of Temesvár, today Timişoara, not far from the Serbian border. It belongs to the administrative district (Judeţul) Timiş.
7. A prominent Roman Catholic teaching order with seat in Rome.
8. Located in northeast Hungary on the river Tisza; center of a famous wine-growing region.
9. The languages of instruction, however, were German and Latin.
10. Today's Bratislava which is now the capital of Slovakia; its Hungarian name was Pozsony.
11. Today Mosonmagyaróvár, a city in northwest Hungary.
12. C III, p. 18.
13. Ibid., p. 23.
14. See letter to A. Schurz (Lisbon, OH, 8 March 1833), C VI, pp. 6-8.
15. C III, pp. 184f. He did buy 400 acres of land in Crawford County, Ohio.
16. Eduard Castle, *Lenau und die Familie Löwenthal* (Leipzig: Max Hesse, 1906), p. 79.
17. Letter to Emilie Reinbeck (C III, p. 283). Actually, Lenau had seen Sophie once when she was a 10-year-old girl; he was a close friend of one of her cousins.
18. Lenau, who was not a promiscuous man, became infected with syphilis on one of his travels. He obviously was not aware of his condition which eventually led to a complete loss of his mental powers. See G. Rosenstock, "Lenaus Krankheit." Dissertation, Jena, 1944.
19. *Poems and Letters of Nikolaus Lenau*. Translated by Winthrop H. Root (New York: Frederick Ungar, 1964), p. 180. In German: Eduard Castle, *Lenau und die Familie Löwenthal* (Leipzig: Max Hesse, 1906), p. 355.
20. Many of these letters close with "regards to Max and the children."
21. Nikolaus Lenau, *Sämmtliche Werke*, ed. Anastasius Grün. Vol. 1. (Stuttgart: J. G. Cotta, 1874), p. VI.
22. C IV, p. 379.

23. The building no longer exists; the address of the apartment house that replaced it is Vienna IX., Schwarzspanierstraße 15.

24. Søren Kierkegaard read Lenau, including his *Faust* and saw the connection there between sensuous genius and music. See also Othmar Dorazil, "Beobachtungen und Untersuchungen zur Musikalität von Lenaus Lyrik." Dissertation, University of Vienna, 1932.

25. *Poems and Letters of Nikolaus Lenau,* p. 85.

26. Ernst Hilmar, "Vertonungen von Nikolaus Lenaus Lyrik," *Lenau-Almanach* (1969/1975), pp. 51-124.

27. C VI, pp. 268ff. Lenau in his youth must have heard this kind of Hungarian recruiting song. In line with the stress pattern of the Hungarian language, Lenau's poem was written in the trochaic meter.

28. Lenau bought a valuable Guarneri violin in 1840.

29. Popular Hungarian form of "Michael."

30. River in Hungary.

31. River in Hungary, today mostly in Romania.

32. Located in northwest Styria surrounded by picturesque mountains.

33. C IV, p. 393. Quoted in English in Barbara Frischmuth, "Ausseerland—Water and Salt," *Austria Today* (1991), no. 4, p. 47.

34. C III, p. 173.

35. Reinhold Schneider, *Schwermut und Zuversicht. Lenau—Eichendorff.* 2nd ed. (Heidelberg: F. H. Kerle, 1948), p. 6.

36. Translated into English in Root, *Poems and Letters of Nikolaus Lenau,* pp. 144f.

37. Lenau's manuscript has the title "Der Pinkeljud"(C VI, p. 427).

38. For an interpretation of the *Waldlieder* see Hugo Schmidt, *Nikolaus Lenau* (New York: Twayne, 1971), pp. 56-67.

39. An adaptation for the stage was done long after Lenau's death, in 1869.

40. Such as Pfitzer's *Volksbuch,* and Maximilian Klinger, a puppet play. (See C VI, pp. 516ff.)

41. See Hansgeorg Schmidt-Bergmann, *Ästhetismus und Negativität: Studien zum Werk Nikolaus Lenaus* (Heidelberg: Carl Winter, 1984), pp. 114ff.

42. Ibid., p. 109.

43. Girolamo Savonarola (1452-1498), born in Ferrara, northern Italy, entered the Dominican Order. As prior of San Marco in Florence he became the most popular and captivating preacher and for a few years the most powerful man in Florence. He preached spiritual revival, asceticism, a kind of puritanism, and had some influence on Martin Luther.
44. Lenau omits the hanging.
45. The Albigenses were a Catharist religious group that adhered to a form of neo-Manichaeism. They believed the world belonged to the realm of the Devil. They rejected the Old Testament, the Christian Mass, and all material things from which the soul must free itself. They were quite numerous in southern France from the middle of the twelfth to the middle of the thirteenth century. Their power was broken by crusades led against them by Louis VIII of France and Simon de Montfort.
46. Nikolaus Lenau, *Sämtliche Werke—Briefe.* Ed. Hermann Engelhard (Stuttgart: J. G. Cotta, 1959), p. 1010.
47. Lenau may have written a comedy in his youth, entitled *Die Mariage in Ungarn,* and planned a tragedy *Barbara Radziwill* (See C VI, p. 36).
48. Published by the F. Brodhag'sche Buchhandlung in Stuttgart. Alas, it did not sell well.

Bibliography

I. Works By Lenau in German

Gedichte. Stuttgart and Tübingen: J.G. Cotta, 1832 (2nd expanded edition 1834; 3rd edition 1837; 4th edition 1840; 5th edition 1841; 6th edition 1843; 7th, revised and expanded edition 1844).

Faust. Ein Gedicht. In: *Deutscher Musenalmanach für das Jahr 1835.* Ed. A. von Chamisso and G. Schwab. Leipzig: Weidmann, 1834. Also in *Frühlingsalmanach.* Ed. Nicolaus Lenau. Stuttgart: F. Brodhag, 1835. Also in: Stuttgart and Tübingen: J. G. Cotta, 1836 (2nd enlarged edition 1840). Also in: *Gestaltungen des Faust: die bedeutendsten Werke der Faustdichtung seit 1587.* Ed. H.W. Geißler. Vol. 3. Munich: Parcus, [n.d.] pp. 243-349.

Savonarola. Ein Gedicht. In: *Morgenblatt für gebildete Stände,* 1837. Also in: Stuttgart/Tübingen: J.G. Cotta, 1837 (2nd edition 1844).

Neuere Gedichte. Stuttgart: Hallberger, 1838 (2nd expanded edition 1840; also 1843).

Die Albigenser. Freie Dichtungen. In: *Deutscher Musenalmanach für 1840.* Eds. Th. Echtermeyer and Arnold Ruge. Berlin. Also in: *Morgenblatt für gebildete Leser,* 1840. Also in: Stuttgart/Tübingen: J.G. Cotta, 1842 (new edition 1846).

Gedichte. Vol. 2. 3rd edition, Stuttgart/Tübingen, 1841 (4th expanded edition 1843; 7th expanded edition 1844).

Dichterischer Nachlaß (Posthumous Works). Ed. Anastasius Grün. Stuttgart/Tübingen: J.G. Cotta, 1851. Also Stuttgart/Augsburg: J.G. Cotta, 1858.

Sämmtliche Werke. Ed. Anastasius Grün. 2 vols. Stuttgart: J.G. Cotta, 1874. Also 1880 and 1881. 4 vols. 1882.

Werke. Ed. Carl Hepp. 2 vols. Leipzig/Vienna: Bibliographisches Institut, [n.d.].

Sämtliche Werke und Briefe. Ed. Eduard Castle. 6 vols. Leipzig: Insel, 1910/1923. This is by far the best and most thorough scholarly edition of Lenau's works.

Sämtliche Werke—Briefe. Ed. Hermann Engelhard. Stuttgart: J.G. Cotta, 1959.

Don Juan. Paris: Aubier, 1989 (collection bilingue). In German and French translations.

Werke und Briefe. Historisch-kritische Gesamtausgabe of the internationale
  Lenau-Gesellschaft. Eds. Helmut Brandt, Hartmut Steinecke,
  Norbert Otto Eke, et al.
  Vol. 1. *Gedichte bis 1834.* Vienna: Deuticke/Stuttgart: Klett-
  Cotta, 1995.
  Vol. 5, Part 1: *Briefe 1812-1837.*
  Vol. 5, Part 2: *Briefe 1812-1837. Kommentar.*
  Vol. 6, Part 1: *Briefe 1838-1847.*
  Vol. 6, Part 2: *Briefe 1838-1847. Kommentar.*
  Vol. 7. *Aufzeichnungen. Vermischte Schriften.* Vienna: Deuticke/
  Stuttgart: Klett-Cotta, 1993.

II. Works by Lenau in English
Poems and Letters of Nikolaus Lenau. Translated, with an Introduction, by
  Winthrop H. Root. With German poems and English versions
  on facing pages. New York: Frederick Ungar, 1964.

III. Secondary Works in English
Arndt, Karl J.R. "The Effect of America on Lenau's Life and Work."
  Germanic Review, 33 (1958), 125-142. Also in: *Deutschlands
  literarisches Amerikabild: Neuere Forschungen zur Amerika-
  rezeption der deutschen Literatur.* Ed. Alexander Ritter. Hildes-
  heim/New York: Georg Olms, 1977, pp. 254-271.
Daviau, Donald G. "Nicolaus Lenau." *European Authors 1000-1900; A
  Biographical Dictionary of European Literature.* Ed. Stanley J.
  Kunitz and Vineta Colby. New York: H.W. Wilson, 1967, pp.
  538-539.
Dickson, David Bruce. *Negative Spring: Crisis Imagery in the Works of
  Brentano, Lenau, Rilke, and T. S. Eliot.* New York: Peter Lang,
  1989. (Studies in Modern German Literature, vol. 24).
Dove, Richard. "The Rhetoric of Lament: A Reassessment of Nikolaus
  Lenau. *Orbis Litterarum ,* 39, no. 3 (1984), 230-265.
Palmer, Peter. "Some Musical Echoes of Lenau: An Article in Honour of
  Othmar Schoeck." *German Life and Letters,* 40, no. 4 (1987),
  265-286.
Rolleston, James: "The Society of the Dead: Allegory and Freedom in
  Lenau's Poetry." In: *Traditions of Experiment from the En-
  lightenment to the Present.* Essays in honor of Peter Demetz.

Eds. Nancy Kaiser, David Wellbery. Ann Arbor: University of Michigan Press, 1992.

Schmidt, Hugo. "Nikolaus Lenau's Imagery." Dissertation, Columbia University, 1959.

_____. *Nikolaus Lenau.* New York: Twayne, 1971. Twayne's World Authors Series (TWAS 135).

Vardy, Agnes Huszar. *A Study in Austrian Romanticism: Hungarian Influences in Lenau's Poetry.* Buffalo, NY: Hungarian Cultural Foundation, 1974.

IV. Major Studies in German

Auer, Gerhard Josef. "Die utopische Gemeinschaft der Harmonisten: ihr Einfluss auf das Amerikaerlebnis und das Werk Nikolaus Lenaus." PhD thesis, University of Illinois at Urbana-Champaign, 1989. Ann Arbor: University Microfilms, 1989.

Bischoff, Heinrich. *Nikolaus Lenaus Lyrik: Ihre Geschichte, Chronologie und Textkritik.* Berlin: Weidmannsche Buchhandlung, 1920.

Britz, Nikolaus. *Lenau in Niederösterreich.* Vienna: Wilhelm Braumüller, 1974.

Castle, Eduard. *Lenau und die Familie Löwenthal: Briefe und Gespräche, Gedichte und Entwürfe.* 2 vols. Leipzig: Max Hesse, 1906.

_____. "Die Urschrift der ersten Lenau-Biographie. Mit ungedruckten Briefen von Anastasius Grün." In: *Jahrbuch der Grillparzer-Gesellschaft,* 3. Serie, 2 (1956), 95-122.

Delfosse, Heinrich P., and Karl Jürgen Skrodzki. *Synoptische Konkordanz zu Nikolaus Lenaus Versepen.* Tübingen: Niemeyer, 1989. Indices zur deutschen Literatur 22.

Deliivanova, Boshidara. *Epos und Geschichte: Weltanschauliche, philosophische und gattungsästhetische Probleme in den Epen von Nikolaus Lenau.* Frankfurt am Main: Peter Lang.

Eke, Norbert Otto, Karl Jürgen Skrodski, eds. *Lenau-Chronik 1802-1851.* Vienna: Deuticke/Stuttgart: Klett-Cotta, 1992.

Errante, Vincenzo. *Lenau: Geschichte eines Märtyrers der Poesie.* Translated from Italian by Charlotte Rau. Preface by Stefan Zweig. Mengen (Württemberg): Heinrich Heine, 1966.

Gibson, Carl. *Lenau: Leben—Werk—Wirkung.* Heidelberg: Carl Winter, 1989.

Häntzschel, Günter. "Nikolaus Lenau." *Zur Literatur der Restaurations-epoche 1815-1848.* Eds. Jost Hermand, Manfred Windfuhr. Stuttgart: Metzler, 1970, pp. 62-107.

Lenau-Jahrbuch. Vienna: Internationale Lenau-Gesellschaft, 1996.

Mádl, Antal. "Lenau und der Vormärz." In: *Lenau Almanach* (1963/1964), 3-43.

_____. and Ferenc Szász. *Nikolaus Lenau in Ungarn. Bibliographie.* Budapest: 1979 (Budapester Beiträge zur Germanistik 5.).

Martens, Wolfgang. *Bild und Motiv im Weltschmerz: Studien zur Dichtung Lenaus.* Köln/Graz: Böhlau, 1957.

Neumann, Gerhard. "Das 'Vergänglich Bild': Untersuchungen zu Lenaus lyrischem Verfahren." In: *Zeitschrift für deutsche Philologie,* 86 (1967), 485-509.

Podlipny-Hehn, Annemarie. *Nikolaus Lenau in Rumänien: eine Bilddoku-mentation.* Bucharest: Kriterion, 1988.

Raducanu, Sevilla. "Lenaus Dichtung in Rumänien." In: *Lenau Forum,* pp. 9-10 (1977/1978), 12-48.

Scheffler, Walter. "Nikolaus Lenau." In: *Marbacher Magazin,* 5 (1977), 1-81.

Schmidt-Bergmann, Hansgeorg. *Ästhetismus und Negativität: Studien zum Werk Nikolaus Lenaus.* Heidelberg: Carl Winter, 1984.

Schneider, Edward, Stefan Sienerth, eds. *Nikolaus Lenau: "Ich bin ein unstäter Mensch auf Erden": Begleitbuch zur Ausstellung.* Munich: Verlag Südostdeutsches Kulturwerk, 1993. (Veröffentlichungen des Südostdeutschen Kulturwerks, Reihe A. Kultur und Dich-tung, vol. 34).

Schneider, Reinhold. *Schwermut und Zuversicht: Lenau—Eichendorff.* 2nd edition. Heidelberg: F.H. Kerle, 1948.

Schurz, Anton X. *Lenau's Leben.* 2 vols. Stuttgart/Augsburg: J.G. Cotta, 1855.

_____. *Lenaus Leben.* Revised and expanded by Eduard Castle. Vol. 1. 1798-1831. Wien: Literarischer Verein, 1913.

Stillmark, Alexander, Fred Wagner, eds. *Lenau zwischen Ost und West: Londoner Symposium.* Stuttgart: Heinz, 1992. (Stuttgarter Ar-beiten zur Germanistik, no. 268).

Turóczi-Trostler, József. *Lenau.* Translated from the Hungarian by Bruno Heilig. Berlin: Rütten & Loening, 1961.

Johann Nepomuk Nestroy

Maria Luise Caputo-Mayr

Johann Nestroy's personality and works underwent wide swings in evaluation and interpretation until scholarship started separating Nestroy the superb comic and principal actor in his own comedies from Nestroy the author of comedies in the Viennese folk-theater tradition in the first part of the nineteenth century. The controversy over his personality and his works started in his own lifetime. He elicited enthusiastic acclaim from his audiences while at the same time often receiving negative criticism from literary reviewers and the official imperial Austrian censors, particularly from the *Sittenpolizei* (morality police). His creativity and insight into human nature have induced more recent critics to compare Nestroy to Shakespeare, Molière, and Goldoni. The realistic language and social satire in his comedies show his affinity with his German contemporaries Christian Dietrich Grabbe, Heinrich Heine, and particularly Georg Büchner with whom he shares a distrust of eighteenth-century optimism. Nowadays Nestroy is considered one of the most radical critics of the Austrian Biedermeier and *Vormärz* (pre-1848) periods. He also has been associated with twentieth-century authors such as Bertolt Brecht, Ödön von Horváth, Jura Soyfer, Max Frisch, and Friedrich Dürrenmatt, as well as with Expressionism and the Theater of the Absurd. His reputation remains strong and he is considered an important influence on the contemporary sociocritical folk theater in Austria.

Until about 1914 general literary histories underestimated Nestroy's achievements as an artist and creator of language. His significant role as a social critic of his time and commentator on human nature also tended to be neglected. Generally the *Vormärz* references to his vulgarity, ambiguity, and cynicism were repeated, confusing the actor with the playwright, or his name was omitted altogether. Such was Nestroy's supreme imprint as the principal actor in his own plays, that after his death in 1862 his works were considered not performable, although they never disappeared completely from the stage. The favorite among them, *Lumpazivagabundus* (1833), was performed over one hundred times up to 1881. But for most of his works nearly two decades would pass after his death until his plays were brought back fully into the limelight again. This occurred in January 1881, on the occasion of the centennial anniversary of the Carl Theater (the former Leopoldstädter Theater) in Vienna, the stage of so many of Nestroy's triumphs.

Strangely enough, around this time the picture of a harmless, glorified, and even trivialized Nestroy also emerged, created by anecdotes and memories. During his lifetime only seventeen of his plays had been printed, partly because of the low esteem in which the folk-play genre was held, and partly to avoid their adoption by other theaters. However, the success of these posthumous performances revitalized the importance of the plays as independent literary works. The first published collection of his works followed in 1890-1891 (edited by Vincenz Chiavacci and Ludwig Ganghofer), and the first fifteen-volume critical-historical edition by Fritz Brukner and Otto Rommel appeared from 1924 to 1930 in Vienna (both editions contained monographs on Nestroy).

An essential part in the early literary rescue of Nestroy's works was played by Karl Kraus. In his well-known essay "Nestroy und die Nach-welt" (Nestroy and Posterity) the great Viennese turn-of-the-century satirist recognized in Nestroy a virtuoso of satiric language and the model for his own work.[1] Kraus had rented the large hall of the Musikverein in Vienna and read his accolade on the occasion of the fiftieth anniversary of Nestroys's death in 1912. He continued with his lectures on Nestroy and his readings of the plays until 1933, and also tried to raise the level of Nestroy performances.

But it took some time before Kraus's message was heard by scholars and literary critics; for although Nestroy's language had aroused admiration during his lifetime, its structure and creative ingenuity only began to be investigated by Franz H. Mautner in the 1930s, a goal he pursued into the sixties and seventies. Mautner was the first to single out Nestroy as the greatest German comedy writer and to identify the "satirical farce" as his most important contribution to literature.[2]

The first half of the twentieth century, for the most part, continued either to reject Nestroy as vulgar or to glorify him as harmless and entertaining. He was ultimately elevated to the status of a "popular classic," whereas the impulses given by Kraus, Brukner, Rommel, and Mautner defined a changed view of Nestroy only after 1945. On the stage Nestroy's "farces with songs" (*Possen mit Gesang* as he often had designated them) would steadily gain public favor in German-speaking theaters. The principal acting roles, which Nestroy had written for himself and his actor friends at the Carl Theater, would be among the most coveted parts sought by the greatest of German-speaking performers. By now his most successful comedies had moved from the popular stage to the prestigious Vienna Burgtheater (first in 1901 and then regularly from 1924 on) and other leading German stages.

A Nestroy boom followed World War II, starting out in Vienna and sweeping through all German-speaking countries in the 1960s and 1970s, parallel to the revival of the reactivated social-critical dramatists such as Ödön von Horváth, Marie Luise Fleisser, and Jura Soyfer who had received vital new incentives from the old master for their own satirical works. In time scholarly attention also increased dramatically.

Today Nestroy, formerly often considered a "trivial" author in the context of the Viennese popular dialect theater (1830-1860), has been fully rehabilitated. The political and social dimensions of his plays and their implications for our day are still being assessed.

After World War II numerous publications of his works testify to Nestroy's rise in literary and public esteem. Soon the need for a new critical edition became apparent, in order to deal with the complex problems of his literary estate (*Nachlaß*) and the authenticity of his texts (the few comedies published during his lifetime had been carelessly edited) resulting from his manner of writing as well as from the existence of multiple copies of his works (for the censor, the prompter, the individual actors, and others). Nestroy seems, moreover, to have been unconcerned about preserving his works for posterity, although he had kept his own manuscripts in good order.

The most recent critical-historical edition has been in preparation since 1977, crowning nearly one hundred years of effort. Jürgen Hein and Johann Hüttner, as general editors, assisted by Nestroy experts like Walter Obermaier, W. E. Yates, and Friedrich Walla, are using Nestroy's own original manuscripts whenever possible; the comedies are now arranged in chronological order to show Nestroy's artistic experimentation and development; a history of his reception is provided by reprinting the reviews. The editors presently envision an edition of forty volumes, of which seventeen have appeared to date at irregular intervals. A new edition of Nestroy's letters and a volume of iconography have already appeared.

In 1973 the International Nestroy Society was founded in Vienna and since 1974 has organized annual colloquia (*Nestroy Gespräche*) and a Nestroy periodical *Nestroyana*, which brings out information on all of these developments.[3] Scholarly efforts now are trying to place the playwright into the appropriate socio-cultural and political context of his time and attempt to clarify Nestroy's changing image, his relation to Baroque literature, to the Viennese folk-theater tradition, and to his presumed antagonist Ferdinand Raimund, as well as to the revival and change of the folk play in the 1960s.

Johann Nepomuk Nestroy was born in 1801 into a well-to-do bourgeois Viennese family. He was the son of a lawyer of Czech-Silesian origin and a Viennese mother, Magdalena Constantin, who died when her son was only thirteen years old. He went to the famous Theresianum, the finest secondary school in Vienna. He was soon stage-struck and had been acting in the popular private Viennese house-theaters for some time when he finally abandoned his law studies at the University of Vienna. He had a fine bass voice, great talent for music, and had performed on the piano as a child. Nestroy's professional Viennese stage debut occurred in 1822 with the role of Sarastro in Mozart's opera *The Magic Flute*. In 1823 he and his new wife Wilhelmine, herself an actress, moved to Amsterdam, where he performed at the Deutsches Theater, expanding his repertoire rapidly to fifty-two roles. In 1824 he and Wilhelmine had a son, Gustav, and in 1825 they moved to the Austrian provinces where he performed in Brünn. Between 1826 and 1830 Nestroy was seen in Graz, Pressburg, and in guest performances in Vienna. During this time he changed from the operatic genre to spoken roles, with more and more emphasis being shifted towards comic roles in the tradition of the Viennese folk theater; he appeared in many plays by his most immediate predecessor in Viennese folk comedy, Ferdinand Raimund (1790-1836), and performed his breakthrough comic role in 1827 as the one-eyed soldier Sansquartier in the French vaudeville *Zwölf Mädchen in Uniform* (Twelve Girls in Uniform).[4]

These were decisive years for him, both privately and on stage. When he permanently returned to theater-hungry Vienna in 1831, Nestroy had amassed an acting repertoire of nearly two hundred roles and had accumulated theatrical experiences that would have taken most actors a lifetime. These credentials would serve him well in his future as a playwright. During this time he had also come to know the disillusionment of life when his unfaithful wife abandoned him; indeed, marriage would forever remain a target for his most pessimistic and caustic remarks. However, he bounced back quickly and by 1828 he had found a lifelong and loyal companion in the young actress Marie Weiler in Graz. Although remarriage for Nestroy was impossible at that time in Catholic Austria, Marie (*die Frau* as he would later refer to her) would henceforth faithfully and efficiently take care of his home, children, and business affairs, with a devotion he did not always reciprocate. By the late 1820s Nestroy had established himself as a successful comic actor excelling in grotesque exaggeration; his gestures and intonation became the trademarks of his humor. But he had also been trying his hand at writing comedy himself: the genre had advanced to a major form of mass entertainment in Vienna, and there was a lack of good comedies available.

The waning popularity of Ferdinand Raimund, the master of the *Zauberstück* (the magic play where human beings were directed by superior powers), and the retirement of an entire generation of older comic actors, all combined to give Nestroy a tremendous opportunity to excel. The historic assumption of Nestroy as the antagonist of Raimund and as the destroyer of a more humorous and benign folk comedy is presently being reviewed; both Raimund and Nestroy belong to the same tradition of the Viennese folk theater, but they approached it in different ways. With his more realistic temperament Nestroy positioned humans as independent subjects in his plays and thereby touched the theatrical pulse of his time. In Raimund's allegorical plays, his *Zauberstücke* (magic plays), and also in his *Besserungsstücke* (improvement plays) order and harmony seem to be restored in the end, and the faith in the power of love and a supernatural dimension is never shaken, although parody begins to enter the genre. In Raimund's later works the powers of the supernatural world as well as the moral qualities they represented began losing their credibility, and the depiction of his characters' everyday life appears more realistic.

Nestroy, on the contrary, held a different world view: he believed in mankind's total dependence on a blind, uncaring destiny, a conviction that drove him to constant rebellion against this brutal world order and to ultimate resignation. Human nature was his most fascinating topic; he considered hypocrisy, wickedness, and love of money the driving forces of life and conveyed his belief in a grotesque-comical, often aggressive and cynical style. In spite of the happy endings, his plays, which formed a theater of disillusionment occasionally foreshadowing modern black comedy, negated every value. However, he was also able to create unforgettable characters who are good, pure, and simple at heart, among them several female characters such as the goose-girl Salome in *Der Talisman* (1848, *The Talisman*), or Kathi in *Der Zerrissene* (1844, *A Man Full of Nothing*).

His first one-act play *Zettelträger Papp* (1827, Papp Who Delivers the Theater Posters), an early parody on theater life, was presented in Graz, and Nestroy had his authorial debut in Vienna in 1829 with the comedy *Der Tod am Hochzeitstag* (1829, Death on the Wedding Day). A new period in his life began with a contract signed with the astute theater manager and showman, director Karl Carl, as an actor/playwright at the Theater an der Wien in 1832. A number of factors at this point in time come together to make Nestroy the star of the Viennese comic theater. These included Nestroy's early eagerness to perform popular comedic roles as well as his prodigious memory. In addition, Carl functioned as a catalyst for his work: without a contract and the pressures provided by this shrewd theatrical entrepreneur, well-known for his exploitation of actors and writers alike, Nestroy probably would not have been so productive. Furthermore, he had a family to support. Although Nestroy was privately a shy person, he had gone into the theater out of a passion for acting. A genuine showman who enjoyed amusing himself and his public, he exploded on stage in overwhelming satirical expressiveness. This passion for acting, together with a need for suitable roles, helped determine his turn to a career as a writer. He produced some eighty-three comedies in rapid succession, among them more than fifty major plays. Stylistically, these included magic plays, parodies, popular comedies, and realistic satirical farces with songs.

Today literary scholarship distinguishes essentially four developmental phases in his dramatic work. Between 1827 and 1835 he wrote magic plays and parodies. Gradually, however, he was turning to a more realistic type of farce, adding his own characteristic grotesque style, culminating in *Lumpazivagabundus* (1833). Already at that stage Nestroy appeared as the heir to the Viennese folk-theater tradition; but he anticipated modern, even absurd theater techniques by his use of parody and by ridiculing both the belief in a harmonious world as well as bourgeois ideals.

His second period, from 1836 to 1845, comprises his classical farces and experiments with the folk play (*Volksstück*). During this time he produced some of his greatest successes: *Die verhängnisvolle Faschingsnacht* (1839, The Fateful Night at the Carnival), *Das Haus der Temperamente* (1837, *The House of Humors*), *Der Talisman* (1840), *Einen Jux will er sich machen* (1842, He Wants to Have a Good Time), *Eisenbahnheiraten . . .* (1844, Weddings at Railroad Speed . . .), and *Der Zerrissene* (1844, *A Man Full of Nothing*). This phase shows Nestroy reacting to the changing times, to a changing public, and to his critics who preferred a more moral type of folk play. At times his theater public resented his overly caustic satirical attacks on their private lives and society, so Nestroy responded by changing the tone of his plays. Local farces alternated with aggressive social satires, parodies, and skillful adaptations from the French and English. Most of the plays of this time possess a closer relation to the contemporary reality of the *Vormärz* period, accentuating the social contrasts between rich and poor, exposing opportunism and narrow-mindedness, the influence of technical progress on society, and at times introducing a modern sense of alienation.

The plays and letters of his third period—1848 to 1850—show the "political" Nestroy reacting to the revolution of 1848 with plays such as *Freiheit in Krähwinkel* (1848, *Liberty Comes to Krähwinkel*), *Höllenangst* (1849, Hellish Fear), his criticism of the corrupt school system and the establishment in *Die schlimmen Buben in der Schule* (1847, The Naughty Schoolboys), and his concern for the rights as well as criticism of the cultural limitations of the bourgeois class in *Der Unbedeutende* (1846, A Man without Importance). Nestroy's crisis as a playwright at the beginning of the 1850s seems to be related to the internal and external circumstances of his life and to the drastically changing taste and composition of his audiences, which had lost interest in the farce; four of his comedies failed in 1850. Furthermore, his old enemy, censorship, had returned.

The plays from his appointment as theater manager to his death (1851-1862) deal with the new social realities and a stricter censorship; also a new genre, the operetta, had become popular. Nestroy, in tune with this new trend, adapted the French operetta *Orpheus in der Unterwelt* (Orpheus in the Underworld) by Jacques Offenbach and appeared in it in the role of Jupiter (1860). He also turned to the old formula of the magic play, and in other comedies emphasizes the new reality. His success returns with *Mein Freund* (1851, My Friend) and *Kampl* (1852) which continue the direction of the serious farce. His last two plays, *Frühere Verhältnisse* (1862, Former Conditions) and *Häuptling Abendwind* (1862, Chief Evening Breeze) reflect his personal concerns about the theater and his awareness of the social and political conditions of the time. In the 1840s and 1850s Nestroy as an actor and writer stood out as the unsurpassed favorite of the Viennese public.[5]

The Biedermeier period in Vienna granted relief from political repression in the theater, whether it was serious drama for the upper classes or farce and comedy for the lower classes. The absolutist regime in Austria after the Congress of Vienna (1815) wanted to preserve stability at all cost, and Franz I of Habsburg and his successor Ferdinand, through the agency of Chancellor Metternich, carried out the strictest censorship of letters, printed materials, and stage plays. Secret police and informants were everywhere; political dissent was severely punished, taxation was imposed without representation, and the popular assemblies could not participate in legislation. Although Nestroy did not attack the regime itself, his comic genius still found a fertile panorama for ridicule all around him. He made fun of outmoded traditions and stereotypes at every level of society, including the aristocracy, by often brutally and cynically exposing their weaknesses, skillfully adapting his language to the milieu he presented. Repression seemed to ignite his critical spirit even more. As early as 1826 he had his first encounter with the police in Brünn. Thereafter he would often substitute gestures and pantomime for his biting and more blatant verbal attacks. He turned to more social satire after 1836, expressing in his works a disappointment with the idealistic sense of bourgeois security. Without being a social reformer, Nestroy, whose sympathies lay with the common people, was keenly aware of the political shortcomings of the Metternich era. The majority of his characters come from the lower classes.[6]

As was the convention of the time, the material for his comedies was hardly ever original. He adapted existing plays, primarily comedies, from Germany, France, and England, and also borrowed plots from novels and stories as well. He relied on and adapted not only the Viennese folk play, but also the structure, plot, and stock figures of the European comic tradition. In his parodies he directed his criticism against the stilted and artificial language of many serious contemporary dramas and operas of his day.[7] While he usually did not change the original plot in his adaptations and was a rather superficial writer, he would often add unique figures. He was extraordinarily successful in transforming his sources into the local Viennese setting by utilizing a stylized Viennese language, not merely a dialect. In this respect he can certainly be considered a representative of Austrian literature as distinguished from German literature; his works would be impoverished by translations into High German and are most effective with actors and audiences of his own language community. His varied language styles and his gift for word play were among his lasting artistic achievements. He simplified existing plots, trivialized characters, and further developed ideas suitable for his verbal fireworks, while intrigue of every kind served as the propelling force of his comedies. Nestroy frequently added musical scenes or songs and in his early works transformed the traditional "Entree" song into his typical "Couplets," witty songs with a refrain presented in a parlando style, usually containing satirical comments about the play and its heroes. These songs allowed him to step out of his role in each act, turn to the public, and discuss strange cases of life and human nature from his own point of view. Such episodes were often followed by monologues which provided additional opportunities for criticism of political and social events of the day.

The lead roles of his plays were attuned to the specific talents of his outstanding co-performers, such as Wenzel Scholz and Karl Carl, with the best parts intended for himself (e.g. Knieriem, Schnoferl, Longinus, Weinberl, Titus, von Lips, Nebel, Kern, and Kampl, to name a few). By contrast the female roles are usually pale and depersonalized, often only caricatures with a penchant for money, love, and jewels with the exception of some simple peasant-like women characters, such as Salome (*Der Talisman*), Kathi (*Der Zerrissene*), or Pauline (*Kampl*) who display natural behavior and feelings. It often has been assumed that this treatment of women resulted from his companion Marie Weiler's jealousy over his many suspected and real affairs (the *Mädlerie*). Nestroy chose male characters to deliver his satire, and many of his leading roles utilized the traditional comical figures of the harlequin or *Hanswurst,* who become the central figures of his plays, and the satirical commentators (*Raisonneur*). Originally this latter character was a servant, but now he involved different trades and professions. It seems that the intrigues presented on stage continued into his private life, with secret letters, addresses, and appointments, rendezvous with his often casual women acquaintances, carefully prepared with the help of confidants. These activities soon became an open secret to all Vienna. Rumors and gossip only added to his attraction as a performer. No other actor was permitted to perform Nestroy's lead roles during his lifetime, and today his eccentricities and excesses on stage are viewed also as an outlet for his private shyness, repression, and secrecy.[8]

Nestroy's adaptations took the form of critical transformations, to which he would add his own comical effects accompanied by the music of the talented composer Adolf Müller.[9] Although Nestroy had started out in the tradition of the popular Viennese *Zauberstück* (magic play) he soon began to parody it. After a series of successful comedies he established himself firmly in the comic genre with *Der böse Geist Lumpazivagabundus oder das liederliche Kleeblatt* (1833, The Evil Spirit Lumpazivagabundus, or, The Three Scoundrels), based on the romantic story *Das große Los* (1827, The Winning Lottery Ticket) by Karl Weisflog. This comedy, which still remains one of his most popular works, represents a final parody of the magic genre which had reached its high point in Raimund's works. The simple plot, which does not yet display his later wit, and the play's dramatic form are considered still somewhat flawed. It is significant, however, that already at that early point in his career his pessimistic thoughts on human nature were in place. The keen observation of the everyday behavior of the people around him is already evident in the many realistic traits of his characters, in particular those of the three scoundrels. Even at this early stage of his career he was referred to as a folk dramatist. Critics of that day would judge his farces by their degree of realism.

Lumpazivagabundus, an evil spirit, destroys morals and order in the world, and seduces young people to a life of profligacy. Supernatural beings (Queen of Fairies, Amorosa, and Fortuna) provide plot motivation, yet prove to be essentially useless characters who have lost their power over men. A wager is made. Three carefree mortal workmen—the lovesick carpenter Leim, the dissolute tailor Zwirn, and the phlegmatic drinking shoemaker and would-be astronomer Knieriem—are put to the test by a big winning in a lottery. Material wealth was to transform these merrymaking fellows into solid citizens. Fortuna gives them two chances to change their ways. However, only Leim can successfully face the task, for he has always been a decent person. The unexpected happy ending lets Amorosa win her wager, but ultimately even love has lost its redeeming power. Indeed, in a brutally realistic and unsuccessful sequel to this play Nestroy shows the three men unhappy in marriage and life.

A measure of aggressive cynicism in Nestroy's acting became obvious at this point in his career, and from now on he would be censured again and again. The public, however, reacted enthusiastically, but more discerning observers mention a subtler, more differentiated manner of his acting style. Rather than concentrating on action, Nestroy had created three immortal comic archetypes of debauchery, written specifically to fit his own talents (he played Knieriem and sang his famous "Kometenlied" [Song of the Comet] 259 times, announcing the end of the world through a collision of planets), and those of his friends (Scholz as Zwirn and Carl as Leim). In this comedy Nestroy utilizes a variety of language styles, from dialect (lower class) to everyday parlance (Knieriem) and High German (supernatural beings). The comedy portrays a bourgeois class in decline; its representatives appear as mere caricatures. Nestroy also comments sarcastically on the economic instability of *Vormärz* Vienna, and depicts the deplorable condition of the unemployed artisans reduced to begging.[10]

After 1835 Nestroy turned away from the genre of the magic play. Many of his comedies in the 1830s contained details of his own personal life, among which the themes of marital infidelity and the conflict between family and artistic career recur. He himself was, it seems, forever undecided between his role as father and head of the family and that of a quite reckless adventurer for whom the bourgeois conventions have crumbled. The degree to which his personality appears in his lead roles, and the function of the theater in his life as an escape from his own reality, are matters of current scholarly discussion. His passion for gambling, however, has been accepted as a driving force of his work and life, and his weak personality stands in contrast to his powerful performances on stage. During this middle period his art evolved gradually towards its true form, falling between the satirical and the tragical farce with music, his lasting contribution to comedy.[11]

Nestroy's career as a playwright was not without complete failures, brought about by being under constant pressure, which sometimes caused him to work too hastily, as well as by the fickleness of the audiences who often wanted to be entertained, not criticized. During such times Nestroy was able to rely upon his comic genius as an actor and to turn quickly to another subject and mood for his next play. When his father died in poverty in 1834, he redoubled his efforts to promote his career. After success with a rather shallow adaptation of *Eulenspiegel* (1835), in which he and Scholz earned rave reviews for their acting, the press demanded more folk plays from him.

Nestroy earned the greatest critical acclaim in 1835 for the apparently moral qualities in *Zu ebener Erde und erster Stock* (1835, Life on the First and Second Floors), which was considered a new beginning for the popular theater. The plot traces the reversal of fortune for two families; the poor but honest Schluckers on the first floor, and the millionaire speculators, the Goldfuchses, on the second. Here for the first time Nestroy utilized a dual-level stage with parallel and contrapuntal actions performed simultaneously. Through the craft of the play he portrays both the upper and lower social classes as basically heartless, unscrupulous, and dishonest in their daily existence. In the same year, 1835, the actor/author was sentenced to a five-day prison term for indecent improvising on stage: Nestroy had verbally offended the inept critic Wiest.[12] He served his sentence in January 1836.

Subsequently, another of his musical farces, *Eine Wohnung ist zu vermieten* (1837, An Apartment for Rent), provoked a theater scandal by attacking the narrow-minded philistine Viennese petit bourgeois class in the person of Gundelhuber, in love with good food and drinking, but essentially heartless. The audience had expected a glorification of Vienna in a comedy in which the names of real streets and places were used, and reacted with outrage. In the same year he earned renewed enthusiastic approval with *Das Haus der Temperamente* (1837), a technical experiment. Here Nestroy used multiple staging to display representatives of the four humors and their children, treated as comic marionettes, succumbing to their moods and destinies. A sanguine, a choleric, a phlegmatic, and a melancholic father have each chosen a specific husband for their daughters who, however, follow their own hearts, thereby thwarting all plans, with Hutzibutz and Schlankl (played by Scholz and Nestroy) adding to the intrigue. Identical actions lead finally to a happy ending and four marriages. This time there was nothing but praise for Nestroy's ingenuity and his realism.[13] In 1839 Carl had left the Theater an der Wien for the Leopoldstädter Theater. From now on Nestroy would appear on two stages in Vienna. He successfully premiered in *Die verhängnisvolle Faschingsnacht* (1839, The Fateful Night at the Carnival), in which he parodied a boring contemporary tragedy by Holtei (*Tragödie in Berlin*), transforming it into a thrilling criminal comedy full of delightful confusion around the jealous woodcutter Franz with his exaggerated sense of honor. Henceforth Nestroy alternated his activity in Vienna with guest performances in various larger provincial towns.

By the beginning of the 1840s Nestroy had reached a high point in his dual career. He was very popular with his audiences and performed nearly every evening in a leading role. Every one of his plays during what is called "his classical period of the farce" was preceded by great audience anticipation, and his language, intonation, and jokes were widely imitated. His farces had become more humane and less grotesque, a new tone prevailed, and Nestroy's acting also took on a new and more humane quality. Nestroy's own roles, above all Schnoferl in *Das Mädl aus der Vorstadt* (1841, The Girl from the Suburbs), are endowed with heart and feeling. The year 1840 was a particularly happy one with the birth of his third child, his only daughter Maria Cäcilia (a second son, Karl, had been born in 1831), his triumphant guest appearances in Prague together with his friends Scholz and Carl, and the performance of two more of his comedies. One of these was *Der Färber und sein Zwillingsbruder* (1840, The Dyer and His Twin Brother), a parody of exaggerated values of courage and honor and in general of the ideas of Romanticism. A common, even timid and passive, Everyman, the dyer Kilian Blau, triumphs over all oppressive measures of the government system.

In December 1840 Nestroy marked a new milestone in his career with *Der Talisman oder die Schicksalsperücke* (The Talisman or the Fateful Wig), a farce that recreated a French vaudeville play about social hypocrisy, prejudice, snobbism, and greed in Viennese fashion. It is considered a classical example of a farce, in three acts, with the action taking place on one day, and Nestroy's wit and precision of language at its best. Nestroy uses discrimination against red-haired people to satirize prejudice, which he felt could be overcome only by love and understanding. He played the character Titus Feuerfuchs, one of his best roles, changing from aggression to fearful anxiety, in 112 performances and was celebrated by the public and critics.[14]

The play depicts the adventures of an unemployed barber's assistant Titus, and the goose-girl Salome Pockerl, both redheads and therefore ostracized by society. The fortune of Titus, the witty and resourceful outsider without scruples, turns around when he receives a black wig, the talisman; he immediately finds a job in the service of Lady Cypressenburg's houshold, becomes the target of all the ladies' affections, and climbs the social ladder. When he loses this wig, he continues his life succesfully with a blond wig, until he is found out and dismissed.

In a finale typical of Nestroy, Titus' long-lost millionaire uncle, the fat and slow-witted beer merchant Spund, turns up looking for an heir, on the condition that the candidate not be a redhead. Titus is hurriedly summoned back to the Cypressenburg villa, where three ladies are waiting to marry the rich heir. He reveals his true hair color, and, demonstrating his basically honest and decent nature, renounces the money in exchange for a barbershop. By this act he softens his uncle's heart. Titus is reunited with faithful Salome, one of the most touching female characters in Nestroy's plays, and they promise that many more future little redheads will help overcome society's prejudice.

In this farce a series of ladies are positioned as representative of the social prejudice against external features (red hair), and in four reflective "Couplets" Nestroy comments on such social discrimination. The critic Hans Weigel called this farce "a masterfully composed parable, the rare and happy example of a satirical comedy where the action is both the medium and object of the satire."[15] Today *Der Talisman* is Nestroy's most performed comedy. With it he had achieved a complex, yet homogeneous plot with the wittiest dialogue to this point in his career as a playwright, and he abandoned the prevailing tradition of the *Singspiel* with its arias and choruses.[16]

On a guest tour to Hamburg Nestroy had to confront initial hostile critical response prompted by his old enemy, the Viennese theater critic Moritz Gottlieb Saphir. Nestroy finally prevailed through the success of *Der Talisman*. Soon another success story would follow; he adapted the vaudeville play *La jolie fille du Faubourg* under the title *Das Mädl aus der Vorstadt* (1841), creating another starring role for himself as Schnoferl, the "honest" lawyer/detective who unmasks the dishonest speculator Kauz, played by Karl Carl. In Schnoferl Nestroy displayed his satirical genius and his talent for word play, aphorisms, and double entendre. Here three strands of action are interwoven organically as Nestroy illustrates again the sad state of the world, dominated by conventions, empty phrases, hypocrisy, deceit, and injustice.

Nestroy's next comedy, the four-act musical farce *Einen Jux will er sich machen* (1842, He Wants to Have a Good Time), was adapted from the English one-act farce *A Day Well Spent* by John Oxenford (1812-1877). It is considered Nestroy's most mature play and is praised for its masterful construction and characterization. The success of this play at its premiere on 10 March 1842 was overwhelming, and it was performed seventy times in the first year of its release in Vienna. It remains, next to *Der Talisman,* his most effective and popular work to this day. Nestroy played Weinberl, a character he had added to the original play. Weinberl continues the persona of Schnoferl but as a character who is more conciliatory and humorous than the early *Raisonneurs.*[17]

The entertaining action that abounds in comic situations deals with Weinberl, who works in a general store in a little town and aspires to an eventual partnership. While their employer, Herr Zangerl, is away arranging his marriage, the philosophical Weinberl wants to break out of his monotonous life for one rousing night of grand adventure in the big city. He sets out, accompanied by the witty and rash store apprentice Christopherl. Weinberl becomes involved in a series of mistaken identities, close calls with their employer, narrow escapes, and other comic twists. Finally, they arrive back home just in time to prevent a major robbery at the general store, enabling them to emerge as heroes.

Weinberl is juxtaposed with the phlegmatic Melchior, a foolish servant who follows orders strictly, a lead role designed for Nestroy's friend Scholz. Honest Melchior, with his standing comment, "That is classic" ("Das ist klassisch") is made light of by everyone else. Three marriages mark the happy end of this piece, whose structure is related to the tradition of the *Commedia dell'arte* (guardian-ward-lover scheme). Considered by critics as one of the best local farces ever written, the play abounds in dramatic tension, witty dialogue, and social commentary.

Einen Jux will er sich machen is the only one of Nestroy's plays that has been successfully recreated in a foreign language. Thus Nestroy remains one of the few Austrian writers known to the American public, albeit not under his own name: his farce served as Thornton Wilder's model for *The Merchant of Yonkers* which, first staged by the exiled Austrian director Max Reinhardt, did not meet with the taste of theater audiences in Boston and New York, where it was presented in 1938 and closed after only twenty-nine performances. It was felt by some critics that the comedy was too slow-moving and heavy; other critics point to the social context and the atmosphere of that special period of time shortly before the outbreak of World War II as reason for this lack of success. Wilder's second attempt in 1954 added a new and typically American character to the play, witty, charming, and realistic Dolly Levi who wants lots of money to improve her quality of life. With a new title, *The Matchmaker*, it resurfaced first in Great Britain in 1954, received a splendid reception in the United States in 1955, and became the progenitor of the musical *Hello, Dolly!* with Carol Channing and Barbra Streisand in the movie version from the early sixties. Another adaptation, Tom Stoppard's *On the Razzle* (1981), was an immediate popular success in England.[18]

In spite of a growing preference for French vaudeville plays in Carl's theaters, Nestroy enjoyed two more successful premieres: *Liebesgeschichten und Heiratssachen* (1843, *Love Affairs and Wedding Bells*), a comedy of errors satirizing both the newly rich and the traditional nobility, and *Eisenbahnheiraten oder Wien, Neustadt, Brünn* (1845, Weddings at Railroad Speed, or Vienna, Neustadt, Brünn). In the weaker comedies of this period some critics have noted that Nestroy's "wit was beginning to lose something of its freshness" and contained an "element of strain" as well as a certain "didactic tendency."[19] These qualities can also be evidenced to a certain degree in the changed atmosphere of such masterpieces as *Der Zerrissene* (1844) and *Der Unbedeutende* (1846), which were praised as true *Volksstücke* by the local theater critics, who envisaged a new popular theater espousing moral lessons for the lower classes.

Fashioned after the French vaudeville *L'homme blasé, Der Zerrissene* provided a splendid role for Nestroy as Herr von Lipp, a man who suffers from the fashionable romantic *Weltschmerz* and possesses so much money that he no longer knows what he wants. His counterpart is the revengeful and poor locksmith Gluthammer, played by Scholz. Poverty is considered by most characters in *Der Zerrissene* as the worst of fates, but wealth seems to destroy all sincere human relations. Von Lipp, who is surrounded by his three greedy and false friends, whom he, in his blind boredom, has also designated as his heirs, finally decides to marry.

First, however, he challenges his destiny in a most unusual way: in order to generate some excitement in his life, von Lipp decides to marry the first woman who crosses his path; she happens to be a somewhat destitute widow by the name of Madame Schleyer, in reality Gluthammer's former fiancée. It is also revealed that Madame Schleyer had inexplicably disappeared with all the couple's money the day before her marriage to Gluthammer. Likewise, the marriage between von Lipp and Schleyer does not take place. But her reappearance causes a physical struggle between von Lipp and Gluthammer, ending in apparent tragedy: both men fall into the river and von Lipp, who scrambles to safety, believes he has murdered his enemy, who, however, has also survived and thinks the same of his opponent. This first act has often been praised as a masterpiece of satirical comedy with respect to characterization and the "negative" love scene between von Lipp and Schleyer.

Afraid of the police, Gluthhammer and von Lipp hide in the same cellar, each believing to be haunted by the spirit of the other, until they realize no murder has occurred. After many confusions von Lipp has come to appreciate Kathi's care and honesty, and recognizes her love for him. Only the brutal shock he has experienced while thinking he was a murderer, has opened his eyes to true love and friendship and saves him from his total alienation and a deeply disturbed relation to his fellow men. He affirms that he suffered from being a person "torn in half," as the title of the play indicates, just because he had not yet met his better half. The comedy, with music from Nestroy's old friend Adolf Müller, became one of his greatest stage successes.[20] Although Kathi is an idealistic figure in her naive goodness, the underlying tone of the play is pessimistic, and von Lipp conveys Nestroy's own negative view of marriage early in the first act by saying it was invented exclusively for the purpose of being able to regret it when it is too late.[21]

The general economic climate was not conducive to the theater in the years 1845-1846. But despite the political and economic unrest everywhere, Nestroy still continued his celebrated guest performances during the summer months in a variety of European cities. However, times had changed, and events pointed to even greater changes and challenges to come. His adaptation of the French comedy *Le maitre d'école* could be performed for only eight weeks due to layoffs, riots, and serious labor problems in the Vienna suburbs—the consequences of a long smoldering dissatisfaction with repressive local conditions. In 1845 Karl Carl left the management of the Theater an der Wien, and in 1847 he had the Leopoldstädter Theater demolished and rebuilt under the name of Carl-Theater. It was inaugurated on December 10 with Nestroy's *Die schlimmen Buben in der Schule* (1847, The Naughty Schoolboys), a one-act farce with tall Nestroy in knee pants among real schoolboys, in the role of Willibald, an inferior student enrolled in a posh private school, where corruption and favoritism prevail, and teachers are totally dependent on the whims of the aristocracy. Real merit is overlooked here, and the seemingly harmless, hilarious, and sometimes even absurd events convey once more Nestroy's criticism, not only of the school system, but also of all authority. The various situations provide Nestroy with an excellent opportunity for word play and wit, juxtaposing the classroom with the real world. Life is presented as chaotic and unjust and ultimately threatened by disintegration.[22]

The year 1848 saw revolution in Vienna, and although Nestroy was not a spokesman for any political program or class, he introduced some democratic overtures into several of his plays. The massacre on 13 March 1848 in Vienna, and the resignation of Metternich, moved director Carl to arm and place his entire ensemble in uniform, though the gesture was made primarily for publicity. The Viennese witnessed their favorite actors marching for freedom from tyranny and censorship and for freedom of the press. Nestroy's creative spirit returned once again more powerful than ever. In quick order he produced five successful comedies in eighteen months. He also caused the greatest theater scandal of his career with a weak play, *Die Anverwandten* (1848, The Relatives), an adaptation of Dickens' *Martin Chuzzlewit*, in which he poked fun at the newly elected deputies to the *Deutsche Nationalversammlung* (German Parliament) in Frankfurt am Main.

Nestroy then regained favor with his audiences with *Die Freiheit in Krähwinkel* (1848, Liberty Comes to Krähwinkel), directing devastating criticism at the Metternich regime while also foreshadowing the specter of the returning reactionary times. His predictions proved correct, in fact, with the victory of the imperial troops on 1 November 1848 and the subsequent mass arrests and the reinstatement of censorship on 11 November. Nestroy presents a backward and isolated village totally dependent upon the local absolutist administration which successfully withholds information from all citizens. The revolutionary Eberhard Ultra, editor of the local newspaper, undermines and ultimately destroys the old regime through his intrigues. He plays a number of roles adopting different styles of language signifying different political groups. The town newspaper finally reveals the political situation instead of concealing it, and a constitutional regime can be established. While not regarded as one of his best plays artistically, recent criticism points out that Nestroy had realized here "the revolutionary and democratic potential of the *Volksstück*," a feature extremely important in bringing about the revitalization of this form by Ödön von Horváth in the 1930s.[23]

The vicissitudes of Nestroy's failures and successes as a comic theater author continued with a travesty of Friedrich Hebbel's now forgotten tragedy *Judith* under the title *Judith und Holofernes* (1849). Nestroy's version has survived as a parodic masterpiece attacking hero worship, megalomania, war, and dictatorship. The play was a huge success and today still dazzles with its witty remarks on every level. By ridiculing the insincere pathos of Holofernes' language, Nestroy anticipated the later negative judgment of Hebbel's early play, and also created one of the first portrayals of a vain and sadistic dictator.

In the same year, 1849, Nestroy produced two more comedies; neither met with success. Because of its critical political attitude Nestroy decided not even to submit his fine folk play, *Der alte Mann mit der jungen Frau* (1849, The Old Man with the Young Wife) to the state censoring office. Written during the worst period of the government repression during the October revolution in Vienna 1848, it was not performed until 1890 in a much altered version and then disappeared completely from the stage until 1948, when it was successfully revived in the Theater in der Josefstadt in Vienna. Only on the surface a political play, it is actually one of Nestroy's most mature works with a sensitive character study of the sixty-year-old protagonist, millionaire Kern. The play centers on his personality, his resigned wisdom, and his pessimistic insight into human nature which reveals Nestroy's own mature outook on life. Kern is deceived by his young wife, Regine, but he tactfully forgives her, recognizing that he has brought this dilemma on himself by unrealistically attempting to cross the generational lines. Jealousy never becomes the central issue here: Kern maintains the appearance of bourgeois propriety, although they decide to separate.

The second play, *Höllenangst* (1849, Hellish Fear), representing the post-revolutionary era, in which social criticism seemed more tolerated, resulted in a box-office flop. However, this comedy was revived successfully as a television play in Vienna in 1961 with the legendary comic actor Hans Moser as the cobbler Pfrim (a character related to Knieriem of *Lumpazivagabundus*). Since Nestroy had expressed some of his most personal views on the way of the world here, it is worthwhile examining the issues presented. Nestroy portrays the life story of Pfrim's son, young Wendelin, a born-again rebel against the wrong order of the world, against those responsible for it, and against an unjust destiny. Wendelin enters a pact with the devil, who in reality is a judge by the name Thurming, and from this confusion many comic and grotesque situations arise, providing Nestroy with opportunities to dispense his pessimistic social and political views. The action is set against a Kafkaesque background of mysterious secret crimes and political rivalries. This farce, one of the first plays to make use of black humor, deals in a grotesque, often even irreverent, anti-Catholic manner with transcendental issues. The anti-Catholic stance and the macabre humor must have baffled and offended deeply the Viennese theater audience and literary critics alike.

Nestroy wrote a dozen more plays in the period from 1850 to his death in 1862. Although a constitution had been granted in Austria, in reality the new emperor Franz Joseph continued an autocratic rule, and the conditions of life of the lower classes had not improved. Political censorship was still practiced. Since theater tickets had become progressively more expensive, excluding the lower ranks of the audience, Nestroy had to comply with the wishes of a more elegant and demanding theater public and responded with a more fashionable type of theatrical entertainment. Between 1853 and 1860 Nestroy resorted increasingly to one-act plays, which became the prevailing dramatic art form in Vienna. By that time a new comic actor, the elegant Carl Treumann, a specialist in one-act plays, had joined Carl's ensemble. After initial resistence Nestroy realized that Treumann proved an ideal addition to his comic team. Nestroy, Scholz, and Treumann now acted as a trio.

Nestroy's last full-length play was *Kampl* (1852), in which he repeats and further expands the basic pattern of *Zu ebener Erde und erster Stock*. Audiences recognized a mature self-portrait of Nestroy in well-meaning, witty, and wise Dr. Kampl, who abandons the city and his bourgeois and aristocratic patients in order to help those in the suburbs. Here a young aristocrat, Ludwig, defends simple working-class people against the idle and lazy members of his own rank. Nestroy places his hope for a future "rule of the heart" with representatives of the young generation, although these characters (e.g. Ludwig, Wilhelm, and Pauline) are pale compared with his "scoundrel" figures (Gabriel Brunner, a role for Scholz). Dr. Kampl's intrigues also help to bring the loving couples from opposite social camps together. Nestroy's satire is directed again against the widespread materialism, revealed in the dialogues of the upper classes. Although the action moves at a slower pace than usual, Nestroy paints convincingly realistic cultural portraits of the bourgeois and aristocratic milieu (especially in the two dancing parties), and his language displays his usual fireworks of paradoxes, aphorisms, antitheses, and parody.[24]

The taste of the theater-going public had turned to French vaudeville plays and farces, and later to operettas in the Offenbach style, a development furthered by the guest appearance of the successful Levassor-Teisseire company from Paris. Political resignation had, however, overtaken the bourgeois classes. A change in Nestroy's acting style was observed, it became more grotesque, spiritual, and objective-ironic.

After Karl Carl's death in 1852, Nestroy had accepted the directorship of the Carl Theater in 1854. He entrusted administrative matters mostly to the shrewd business acumen of his companion Marie Weiler and his friend Ernst Stainhauser, while he oversaw the artistic affairs. At that time he felt required to succumb to the public taste: a great number of inferior one-act plays were performed during his tenure at the Carl Theater.

The formerly so successful folk-comedy was soon in full decline, prompted by a significant change in the taste and the composition of the theater-going public. In addition, during the industrialization of the 1850s and 1860s, the heavy influx of a diverse range of people from the Austrian provinces into Vienna continued, doubling the city's population within the three decades between 1830 and 1860, brought about major social, financial, and political changes. Nestroy himself accepted the new operetta fashion of the day and appeared as Jupiter in Jacques Offenbach's *Orpheus*. He had suffered the loss of his good friend Wenzel Scholz in 1857 and encountered two serious private crises (1856 and 1858) in his relationship with Marie Weiler. She resented his many affairs, his passion for gambling, and his financial irresponsibility. In spite of his leading a double life he reproached her for spying on him (*Nachspioniererei*) and defended his actions, insisting that if she had not found out about them she would not have suffered and therefore had to blame herself for her unhappiness. He took great care to wipe out every possible trace of his affairs and destroyed his correspondence. Two paternity suits against him mar these late years. His relations with his companion and with women seem to have been overshadowed by ambivalence and reveal the double standard accepted in his time. However, he acknowledged the significant stabilizing element Marie Weiler had brought to his existence, his work, his household, and his fortune, and ultimately made her the sole heir of his considerable fortune. A difficult reconciliation with Marie was achieved only through his friend Stainhauser.

Nestroy now wrote and performed less. Although he remained interested in the theater, he devoted more time to private life. His letters often express melancholy thoughts and the desire for peace. Lengthy travels abroad followed, mostly to the North; he felt a particular attraction to the Baltic Sea. He resigned as theater director in 1860 and bought homes in

Graz and Bad Ischl. On 30 October 1858 Nestroy took leave from the stage at the Carl-Theater with a special performance and moved to Graz permanently. However, he continued writing and produced another farce, *Frühere Verhältnisse* (1862), on the theme of lies and deception, highly regarded by many as one of his masterpieces. The play unmasks the past lives of two couples, whose situations have changed into their opposite—the former servant has become the master, and vice-versa. The real opponents here seem to be reality and illusion.

Nestroy's retirement in Graz was interrupted by regular farewell and guest appearances each February and March at his friend Neumann's theater at the Franz Josef-Quai in Vienna. His last work shows his undiminished dramatic power: *Häuptling Abendwind oder Das greuliche Festmahl* (1862, Chief Evening Breeze, or The Horrible Banquet) was a political mardi gras burlesque aimed at the colonial imperialism and growing nationalism of the European powers of his time. Nestroy satirized the ongoing international political conferences that preceded the war by transposing them, in Swiftian manner, to an imaginary exotic South Sea island among cannibalistic tribal chieftains who meet for a diplomatic summit but end up in an eating orgy. The model for this farce, the French *Vent du soir ou l'horrible festin*, with music by Offenbach, had been a great success in Vienna, whereas Nestroy's play with the added political satire, was not understood by an indifferent audience. It was performed only a few times, in spite of the attendance of the emperor at the premiere.

The farce, which exposes and ridicules nationalistic tendencies and the Victorian pride in civilization, was successfully revived on the stage in this century, however, and the fierce satire of international conferences (originally directed at the meeting between Napoleon III and Wilhelm I of Prussia) at the highest level was finally recognized. The chieftains unknowingly devour each other's wives as dinner fare during their negotiations. The farce has been adapted by a number of modern dramatists who have seen its potential for satirizing contemporary politics, for example, Elfriede Jelinek's dramolet *Präsident Abendwind. Ein Dramolet. Sehr frei nach J. Nestroy* (1993, *President Evening Breeze*)[25] juxtaposes caricatures of the Bavarian politician Franz Josef Strauß and Austria's Kurt Waldheim as the discussing chieftains).

Nestroy last appeared on stage in Vienna in his favorite role as Knieriem in his *Lumpazivagabundus* on 4 March and again on 29 April 1862 in Graz. He died of a stroke on 25 May 1862, and was buried in Vienna's

Währinger cemetery accompanied by a procession of thousands of his loyal fans who mourned the great actor and private citizen they had come to know as one of them and who forgave him his weaknesses and his attacks on their own failings. He was moved to a grave of honor (*Ehrengrab*) in the Vienna Zentralfriedhof in 1881. Nestroy was considered the greatest of the true *Volksdramatiker* who had performed over 800 roles on stage during his forty-year theatrical career. His foremost aim had been to entertain his public with whom he identified, in contrast to his immediate followers who adopted a more didactic vein.[26] W.E. Yates best summarizes some of Nestroy's achievements by stating that he ". . . reshaped the nature of Viennese popular comedy; he burlesqued and abandoned the traditional 'Zauberstück' . . . ; in the fifties he introduced the operettas of Offenbach . . . and paved the way for the younger Strauss."[27]

In a final consideration of Nestroy's reputation in the twentieth century one might emphasize that his works and his tradition have become, in contrast to those of his predecessor Ferdinand Raimund, a point of reference and inspiration for a highly diverse group of modern Austrian, German, and Swiss writers, among them Ödön von Horváth, Marie Luise Fleisser, Jura Soyfer, Friedrich Dürrenmatt, Helmut Qualtinger, Peter Handke, Franz Xaver Kroetz, Werner Fassbinder, Wolfgang Bauer, Harald Sommer, Peter Henisch, Peter Turrini, Heinz R. Unger, Felix Mitterer, and Elfriede Jelinek.

Although there are also recent adaptations of Nestroy's plays such as Peter Henisch's *Lumpazimoribundus. Antiposse mit Gesang*,[28] his influence is perhaps a more general one, as a patron saint of the Austrian realistic-critical tradition in writing, in particular referring to the extraordinary production of socio-critical realistic farces as well as to his originality as a language creator. Nestroy's unique appeal lies in his fascination with mankind and its foibles, in the universality and timelessness of his concerns, in the satirical way in which he unmasked the incorrigible hypocrisy and greed of his fellow man, as well as the failures of the social system and government.[29]

While Kraus, Brukner, Rommel, and Mautner gave new initial impulses to Nestroy reception, a number of younger writers such as Horváth, Fleisser, Canetti, and Soyfer received inspiration from his social and political satirical qualities for their own socio-critical dramatic works in the first half of this century. The revival of their works on the German language stage during the sixties coincided with and at the same time reinforced the so-called Nestroy renaissance. His popularity remains undiminished at present. The authors of the new critical folk play of the recent decades refer constantly to Nestroy and attest to his modern appeal.

A second strand of influence stems from the more apolitical, aesthetic Nestroy concept, Nestroy as the creator of satirical language, of word play in different language styles, rediscovered by Karl Kraus and Franz Mautner, a Nestroy without whom writers such as Artmann, Qualtinger, Handke, and Jelinek could not be explained. Nestroy's achievement in exposing shallow, clichéd language was recognized at the same time that a trend of distrust of language and of unmasking its social, cultural, and political clichés emerged in Austria in the early twentieth century.

The theatrical, popular, and critical reception of this satirical writer has hardly ever been in agreement, and while the present scholarly efforts are getting closer to a more objective Nestroy image, he continues, as in his own time, to provoke, entertain, challenge, and inspire readers, scholars, writers, and audiences alike.

Notes

1. Karl Kraus, "Nestroy und die Nachwelt. Zum 50. Todestag," *Die Fackel*, XIV/349-350 (1912), 1-23. For the most comprehensive recent Nestroy biography and bibliography see Jürgen Hein, *Johann Nestroy* (Stuttgart: Metzler, 1990), to be henceforth abbreviated as Hein, *Johann Nestroy*.

2. See Franz H. Mautner, *Nestroy* (Heidelberg: Lothar Stiehm, 1974), pp. 61-91; abbreviated as Mautner, *Nestroy*.

3. See Hein, *Johann Nestroy*, pp. 2-7, 127ff; W.E. Yates, "Editing Nestroy," *German Life and Letters*, 36 (1983), 283-293.

4. See Hein, *Johann Nestroy*, pp. 22-43; Otto Basil, *Johann Nestroy in Selbstzeugnissen und Bilddokumenten* (Reinbek: Rowohlt, 1967), pp. 18-24, quoted as Basil, *Johann Nestroy*; Mautner, *Nestroy*, pp. 117-124. For further biographical information see Rio Preisner, *Johann Nepomuk Nestroy. Der Schöpfer der tragischen Posse* (Munich: Carl Hanser, 1968), abbreviated as Preisner,... *tragische Posse*, and Otto Rommel, *Johann Nestroy. Der Satiriker auf der Altwiener Komödienbühne* (Vienna: Anton Schroll, 1962).

5. For a discussion of Nestroy's early period see Siegfried Diehl, *Zauberei und Satire im Frühwerk Nestroys. Mit neuen Handschriften*

zum "Konfusen Zauberer" und zum "Zauberer Sulphur" (Bad Homburg: Gehlen, 1969), abbreviated as Diehl, *Zauberei*; see Hein, *Johann Nestroy*, pp. 68-69, and W.E. Yates, *Nestroy: Satire and Parody in Viennese Popular Comedy* (Cambridge: University Press, 1972), abbreviated Yates, *Satire*, pp. 25-28 about the relation to Raimund. For more information on Nestroy's artistic development see Hein, ibid, pp. 68-98; Mautner, *Nestroy*, pp. 117ff, 272ff, 306ff; Yates, ibid., pp. 55-77.

6. See Robert Harrison and Catherina Wilson, "Introduction" to *Three Viennese Comedies by Johann Nepomuk Nestroy. [The Talisman, Judith and Holofernes,* and *The House of Humors]*, transl. by R.H. and C.W. (Columbia, S.C.: Camden House, 1986), pp. 5-6. (Abbreviated as Harrison and Wilson, eds. *Three Comedies*); also see Mautner, *Nestroy*, chapter on "Die Revolution," pp. 281-305; Yates, *Satire*, chapter on "Radicalism," pp. 149-165.

7. See Yates, *Satire*, for a discussion of Nestroy's transposition of two plays, Holtei's *Ein Trauerspiel in Berlin* and Hebbel's *Judith und Holofernes*, pp. 99-119. See Reinhard Urbach, "Nestroy heute," *Suhrkamp Literaturzeitung*, 6/3 (1976), 3-4, about the adaptation of Nestroy into standard German by Rolf Schneider.

8. See Yates, *Satire*, pp. 75-77; also see Jürgen Hein, *Spiel und Satire in der Komödie Johann Nestroy* (Bad Homburg: Gehlen, 1970, abbreviated as Hein, *Spiel und Satire*), pp. 89-117, and pp. 38-41 for a discussion of the development of the "Couplet" and its function for Nestroy's leading roles as satirical commentator or *raisonneur* in his plays. Pp. 36-42 deal with characters in Nestroy's comedies.

9. See Basil, *Johann Nestroy*, p. 79. Also see Hein, *Johann Nestroy*, pp. 119-123, chapter about Nestroy's "Theaterlyrik und musikalische Einlagen" (Theater Lyrics and Musical Numbers).

10. See Basil, *Johann Nestroy*, pp. 79-82. Also see Mautner, *Nestroy*, pp. 170-181. Detailed discussion of Nestroy's use of language in Olga Stieglitz, *Syntaktische Untersuchung der Sprache Johann Nestroys am Beispiel seiner Zauberposse "Der böse Geist Lumpazivagabundus,"* vols. 1-2 (Vienna: Verband der wissenschaftlichen Gesellschaften Österreichs, 1974).

11. The exact designation of his plays has caused much debate. See in particular Hein, *Nestroy*, chapter 5, "Struktur- und Gattungsfragen," (questions about form and genre), pp. 101-113. Also see Mautner,

Nestroy, pp. 33-45; Preisner, . . . *tragische Posse*, for the concept of the "tragic farce"; Otto Rommel, *Johann Nestroy. Der Satiriker auf der Altwiener Komödienbühne* (Vienna: Schroll, 1948), pp. 81-132.

12. Basil, *Johann Nestroy*, pp. 91-92.
13. See Yates, *Satire*, p. 65; for a discussion of Nestroy's realism see Siegfried Brill, *Die Komödie der Sprache. Untersuchungen zum Werke Johann Nestroys* (Nuremberg: Carl, 1967), p. 108ff.
14. See Basil, *Johann Nestroy*, pp. 97-100. Helmut Herles' comparison between the French model "Bonaventure" and Nestroy's adaptation shows the creative process in *Nestroy's Komödie "Der Talisman."* (Munich: Wilhelm Fink, 1974). Also see Mautner, *Nestroy*, pp. 234-240.
15. Hans Weigel, *Johann Nestroy* (Hannover: Friedrich, 1972, abbreviated as Weigel, *Johann Nestroy*), pp. 35-36 (my translation). For a discussion of *Der Talisman* see Mautner, *Nestroy*, pp. 234-240.
16. Basil, *Johann Nestroy*, p. 102.
17. See Hein, *Spiel und Satire*, pp. 39-41.
18. Maria P. Alter, "The Reception of Nestroy in America as Exemplified in Thornton Wilder's Play 'The Matchmaker.'" In: *Modern Austrian Literature*, 20/3-4 (1987), 33-42. Also see Basil, *Johann Nestroy*, pp. 104-105; Hein, *Spiel und Satire*, pp. 148-158; Mautner, *Nestroy*, pp. 247-248. For a discussion of the English translations of Nestroy see Kari Grimstad, "Nestroy in English." In: *Momentum Dramaticum*. Eds. Linda Dietrick and David G. John (Waterloo, Ontario, University of Waterloo Press, 1990), pp. 439-449.
19. See Yates, *Satire*, pp. 65-66. Also see Mautner, *Nestroy*, pp. 252-271.
20. See Basil, *Johann Nestroy*, pp. 108-110. Also see Karl Kahl, *Johann Nestroy oder der Wienerische Shakespeare* (Vienna/Munich/Zurich: Molden, 1970), pp. 219-221.
21. See Introduction to Robert Harrison and Catharina Wilson, eds. *Three Comedies*, p. 24.
22. See Basil, *Johann Nestroy*, pp. 115-118. Also see Weigel, *Johann Nestroy*, pp. 48-52.
23. Craig Decker, "Toward a Critical *Volksstück*: Nestroy and the Politics of Language," *Monatshefte* 79 (1987), 45, 55-59.
24. Basil, *Johann Nestroy*, pp. 133-136. See also Mautner, *Nestroy*, pp. 317-321.

380 Maria Luise Caputo-Mayr

25. Elfriede Jelinek, "Präsident Abendwind. Ein Dramolet, sehr frei nach J. Nestroy. *TEXT + KRITIK,* 113 (1993), pp. 3-20. See also *President Evening Breeze,* translated by Helga Schreckenberger and Jacqueline Vansant, in: *New Anthology of Austrian Folk Plays,* ed. Richard H. Lawson (Riverside: Ariadne Press, 1995). Nestroy's *Häuptling Abendwind,* ed. Herbert Wiesner, inspired three more theatrical texts which, together with Jelinek's, appeared in Berlin in 1989.

26. Yates, *Satire,* p. 69.

27. Yates, "Editing Nestroy." *German Life and Letters,* 36 (1983), 283.

28. Peter Henisch, *Lumpazimoribundus. Eine Antiposse mit Gesang* (Eisenstadt: Edition Roetzer; Wien/München: Thomas Sessler Verlag /o.J./).

29. For a detailed discussion of Nestroy's influence on twentieth-century literature see Mautner, *Nestroy,* "Die Wirkung," pp. 349-373. See also Hein, *Johann Nestroy,* pp. 123-137.

Bibliography

I. Works by Johann N. Nestroy in German

Sämtliche Werke. Historisch-kritische Gesamtausgabe. Vols. 1-15. Ed. Fritz
Brukner and Otto Rommel. Vienna: Schroll, 1924-1930, 1974.

Johann Nestroys gesammelte Briefe und Revolutionsdokumente (1831-1862).
Nestroy und seine Bühne im Jahre 1848, ed. Fritz Brukner.
Vienna: Wallishausser, 1938.

Gesammelte Werke. Edited by Otto Rommel. 6 vols. Vienna: Schroll,
1948-1949, 1962.

Ausgewählte Werke. Introduced and edited by Hans Weigel. Gütersloh: S.
Mohn [1962].

Nestroy Gesamtausgabe. Historisch-kritische Ausgabe sämtlicher Werke in
14 volumes, eds. Jürgen Hein and Johann Hüttner. Vienna/Munich: Jugend und Volk, 1977. The edition is still in
progress and will comprise probably forty volumes. Presently
seventeen volumes have been published.

Briefe. Ed. Walter Obermaier. Vienna/Munich: Jugend und Volk, 1977.

Schwarz, Heinrich. *Johann Nestroy im Bild. Eine Ikonographie,* eds. Johann
Hüttner and Otto G. Schindler. Vienna/Munich: Jugend und
Volk, 1977.

Komödien. Ed. Franz H. Mautner. Vols. 1-6. Frankfurt am Main: Insel,
1979.

II. Selected Works in German

Der Zettelträger Papp. Komische Kleinigkeit. Vorspiel (prelude in one act).
Graz, 15 December 1827.

Der Tod am Hochzeitstage oder Mann, Frau, Kind. Zauberspiel (magic play
in two acts). Vienna, Josefstädter Theater
, 18 August 1829.

Der böse Geist Lumpazivagabundus oder Das liederliche Kleeblatt. Zauberspiel mit Gesang (magic play with songs in three acts). 11 April
1833.

Robert der Teufel. Parodierendes Zauberspiel (magic parody in three acts).
9 October 1833.

Zu ebener Erde und erster Stock oder Die Launen des Glückes. Lokalposse
mit Gesang (local farce with songs in three acts). 24 November
1835.

Das Haus der Temperamente. Posse (farce in three acts). 6 November 1837.

Die verhängnisvolle Faschingsnacht. Posse mit Gesang (farce with songs in three acts). 13 April 1839.

Der Färber und sein Zwillingsbruder. Posse mit Gesang (farce with songs in three acts). 15 January 1840.

Der Talisman. Posse mit Gesang (farce with songs in three acts). 16 December 1840.

Das Mädl aus der Vorstadt oder Ehrlich währt am längsten. Posse in three acts. 21 November 1841.

Einen Jux will er sich machen. Posse mit Gesang (farce with songs in three acts). 10 March 1842.

Eisenbahnheiraten oder Wien, Neustadt, Brünn. Posse mit Gesang (farce with songs in three acts). 3 January 1844.

Der Zerrissene. Posse mit Gesang (farce with songs in three acts). 9 April 1844.

Der Unbedeutende. Posse mit Gesang (farce with songs in three acts). 2 May 1846.

Freiheit in Krähwinkel. Posse mit Gesang (farce with songs in three acts). 1 July 1848.

Judith und Holofernes. Travesty mit Gesang (travesty with songs in one act). 13 March 1849.

Höllenangst. Posse mit Gesang (farce with songs in three acts). 17 November 1849.

Der alte Mann mit der jungen Frau. Volksstück mit Gesang (folk play with songs in four acts). No date.

Kampl oder Das Mädchen mit Millionen und die Nähterin. Posse mit Gesang (farce with songs in four acts). 29 March 1852.

Frühere Verhältnisse. Posse mit Gesang (farce with songs in one act). 7 January 1862.

Häuptling Abendwind oder Das greuliche Festmahl. Indianische Faschingsburleske (Indian Mardi Gras Burlesque in one act). 1 February 1862.

III. Works in English Translation and Adaptations

Thornton Wilder. *The Merchant of Yonkers. A Farce in Four Acts.* New York/London: Harper, 1939.

_____. *The Matchmaker. A Farce in Four Acts.* In: Wilder, *Three Plays.* New York: Bantam, 1958.

Liberty Comes to Krähwinkel. Farce in Three Acts with Songs, by Johann Nestroy. Adapted and translated by Sybil and Colin Welch. *The Tulane Drama Review,* 4/5 (June 1961).

Three Comedies. [*A Man Full of Nothing* = *Der Zerrissene; The Talisman; Love Affairs and Wedding Bells* = *Liebesgeschichten und Heiratssachen.*] Translated by Max Knight and Josef Fabry. Introduction by Thornton Wilder. New York: Frederick Ungar, 1967.

Tom Stoppard. *On the Razzle.* Adapted from *Einen Jux will er sich machen* by Johann Nestroy. London: Faber & Faber, 1981.

Three Viennese Comedies by Johann Nepomuk Nestroy. [*The Talisman, Judith and Holofernes,* and *The House of Humors.*] Translated by Robert Harrison and Katharina Wilson. Columbia, S.C.: Camden House, 1986.

IV. Secondary Literature in English

Alter, Maria P. "The Reception of Nestroy in America as Exemplified in Thorton Wilder's Play *The Matchmaker." Modern Austrian Literature,* 20/3-4 (1987), 32-42.

Barraclough, C.A. "Nestroy, the Political Satirist." *Monatshefte,* 52 (1960), 252-257.

Branscombe, P. "An Old Viennese Opera Parody and a New Nestroy Manuscript." *German Life and Letters,* 28 (1975), 210-217.

Bruckner, J.P. An Annotated Nestroy Bibliography. Dissertation, University of Virginia, 1973.

Decker, Craig. Challenging Social and Cultural Institutions: Nestroy, Horváth, Kroetz and the *Volksstück.* Dissertation, University of California, Irvine, 1986.

_____. "Toward a Critical 'Volksstück': Nestroy and the Politics of Language." *Monatshefte,* 79 (1987), 44-61.

_____. "The Hermeneutics of Democracy: Nestroy, Horváth, Turrini, and the Development of the 'Volksstück.'" *Seminar,* 27 (1991), 219-232.

Harding, Laurence V. *The Dramatic Art of Ferdinand Raimund and Johann Nestroy. A Critical Study.* The Hague/Paris: Mouton, 1974.

McKenzie, John R.P. "The Techniques of 'Verwienerung' in Nestroy's 'Judith and Holofernes.'" *New German Studies*, 1 (1973), 119-132.

_____. "Nestroy's Political Plays." In: W.E. Yates and J.R.P. McKenzie, eds. *Viennese Popular Theatre: A Symposium.* Exeter: University of Exeter, 1985.

Reese, Joe. "'Der Zerrissene' and 'L'Homme blasé': A Closer Look at Nestroy's Source." *Modern Austrian Literature*, 2/1 (1990), 55-67.

Reichert, Herbert W. "Some Causes of the Nestroy-Renaissance in Vienna." *Monatshefte*, 47 (1955), 221-230.

Seidmann, Gertrud. "Johann Nestroy." In: *German Men of Letters.* Vol. 5. Twelve Literary Essays Edited by Alex Natan. London: O. Wolff, 1969, pp. 275-299.

Stern, J.P. "German Literature in the Age of European Realism." In: *German Language and Literature: Seven Essays.* Edited by Karl S. Weimar. Englewood Cliffs, N.Y.: Prentice-Hall, 1974, pp. 223-306.

Straubinger, O.P. "The Reception of Raimund and Nestroy in England and America." In: *Österreich und die Angelsächsische Welt*, ed. Otto Hietsch. Vienna/Stuttgart: Braumüller, 1961, pp. 481-494.

Yates, W.E. "Convention and Antithesis in Nestroy's Possen." *Modern Language Review*, 61 (1966), 225-237.

_____. *Nestroy. Satire and Parody in Viennese Popular Comedy.* Cambridge: University Press, 1972.

_____. "Prospects of Progress: Nestroy Re-edited." *Journal of European Studies*, 9 (1979), 196-205.

_____. "Editing Nestroy." *German Life and Letters*, 36 (1983), 281-293.

_____ and John R.P. McKenzie, ed. *Viennese Popular Theater : A Symposium. Das Wiener Volkstheater. Ein Symposium.* Exeter: University of Exeter Press, 1985.

V. Selected Secondary Literature in German

Basil, Otto. *Johann Nestroy in Selbstzeugnissen und Bilddokumenten.* Reinbek: Rowohlt, 1967.

Brill, Siegfried. *Die Komödie der Sprache. Untersuchungen zum Werke Johann Nestroys.* Nuremberg: Carl, 1967.

Conrad, Günter. *Johann Nepomuk Nestroy: 1801-1862. Bibliographie zur Nestroyforschung und -rezeption.* Berlin: Erich Schmidt Verlag, 1980.

Diehl, Siegfried. *Zauberei und Satire im Frühwerk Nestroys. Mit neuen Handschriften zum "Konfusen Zauberer" und zum "Zauberer Sulphur."* Bad Homburg v.d.H.: Gehlen, 1969.

Grimstad, Kari. "Nestroy in English." In: *Momentum Dramaticum.* Festschrift for Eckehard Catholy, eds. Linda Dietrick and David G. John. Waterloo, Ontario: University of Waterloo Press, 1990, pp. 439-449.

Hein, Jürgen. "Nestroyforschung (1901-1966)." *Wirkendes Wort,* 18 (1968), 232-245.

_____. *Spiel und Satire in der Komödie Johann Nestroys.* Bad Homburg v.d.H./Berlin/Zurich: Gehlen, 1970.

_____. *Johann Nestroy. "Der Talisman." Erläuterungen und Dokumente.* Stuttgart: Reclam, 1975.

_____. *Johann Nestroy.* Stuttgart: Metzler, 1990. (Sammlung Metzler 258).

Herles, Helmut. *Nestroys Komödie: "Der Talisman." Von der ersten Notiz zum vollendeten Werk. Mit bisher unveröffentlichten Handschriften.* Munich: Fink, 1974.

Kahl, Kurt. *Johann Nestroy oder Der Wienerische Shakespeare.* Vienna/Munich/Zurich: Molden, 1970.

Kraus, Karl. "Nestroy und die Nachwelt. Zum 50. Todestag." *Die Fackel,* 14/349-350 (1912), 1-23.

Mautner, Franz H. *Nestroy.* Heidelberg: Lothar Stiehm, 1974.

Preisner, Rio. *Johann Nepomuk Nestroy. Der Schöpfer der tragischen Posse.* Munich: Hanser, 1968.

Rommel, Otto. *Johann Nestroy. Der Satiriker auf der Altwiener Komödienbühne. Gesammelte Werke,* ed. Otto Rommel. Vienna: Schroll, 1948, (vol. 1, 1962).

Stieglitz, Olga. *Syntaktische Untersuchung der Sprache Johann Nestroys am Beispiel seiner Zauberposse "Der böse Geist Lumpazivagabundus."* Vol. 1-2. Vienna: Verband der wissenschaftlichen Gesellschaften Österreichs, 1974.

Urbach, Reinhard. *Die Wiener Komödie und ihr Publikum. Stranitzky und die Folgen.* Munich/Vienna: Jugend und Volk, 1973.

_____. "Nestroy heute." *Suhrkamp Literaturzeitung,* 6/3 (1976), 3-4.

Weigel, Hans. *Johann Nestroy.* Hannover: Friedrich, 1972.

Betty Paoli

Ferrel Rose

Passing over the more obvious poets of Nikolaus Lenau and Anastasius Grün, Grillparzer once called Betty Paoli Austria's greatest lyricist.[1] By the twentieth century, however, her name had practically disappeared from record. To this day the published studies on Paoli tend to focus on her association with other key literary figures: Adalbert Stifter, Marie von Ebner-Eschenbach, and Conrad Ferdinand Meyer. Betty Paoli herself denied any pretense to lasting fame; nevertheless she became a model to the generation of women authors who immediately followed in her footsteps. An autodidact in art, languages, literature, and theater, she successfully negotiated the transition from home journal (*Taschenbuch*) poet to tone-setting literary critic. In the 1860s and 1870s she wielded considerable influence as essayist and reviewer for the *Neue Freie Presse,* the most widely read newspaper in educated liberal circles. Thus, at a time when the first stirrings of feminist agitation were often greeted with undisguised hostility, Paoli managed to become the first Austrian woman to gain recognition and to support herself as a feuilletonist. She also wrote social commentary, serving as an influential proponent of the women's movement in Austria.

Our knowledge of Paoli's youth is sketchy at best. Extremely guarded about her personal life, she refused to write her autobiography even when pressed to do so.[2] Since her papers appear to have been lost to the Nazis, we have little or no written record of her life other than the frequently quite subjective accounts of her friends. The surviving sources tend to contradict one another, no doubt reflecting the conflicting accounts that Paoli herself gave. While it is a common phenomenon for elderly people's memories to grow unreliable, it appears that Paoli may have relished the pose of a woman of mystery who had led several different lives. Many of her contemporaries colluded with the obfuscating by romanticizing her turbulent beginnings.[3] Also known under the epithet of "the battered traveler" ("die Vielumhergetriebene"), Betty Paoli provoked much speculation about her personal fortunes.

Barbara or Babette Elisabeth Glück (Paoli was a surname she adopted in the 1830s) was born in Vienna on 30 December 1814 to Theresia Glück, the wife of a high-ranking military doctor, who, as it was revealed only after the poet's death, was her father in name only.[4] Her real father appears to have been a prominent Hungarian aristocrat.[5] Since her mother was married only seven months before her daughter's birth, an accidental pregnancy may well have caused her real father to abandon an expectant mother whose lower social status formed an obstacle to marriage. Theresia may then have married Mr. Glück to avoid the disgrace of unwed motherhood. Mr. Glück died soon after their union, and Elisabeth had no recollection of him.

Mr. Glück's death did not immediately disrupt his family's comfortable lifestyle; his widow enjoyed a modest inheritance. Some posthumous accounts suggest that Theresia Glück's imprudence put her daughter's financial and psychological security at risk. Restless and neurotic, Theresia dissipated the family livelihood in risky speculations. Eager to learn, Betty could not look to her mother for guidance, and frequent changes of residence precluded any systematic rigor or continuity in her education. Paoli herself later spoke of maturing "à la diable," naming harsh experience as her first tutor. Only because she was an avid reader could she begin to compensate for her spotty education. For a time her mother left Betty in Hungary with the Schmidts, the family of a grammarian who tutored her in foreign languages.[6] By the time she was grown she had mastered English, French, and Italian; in the early 1850s she became proficient enough in Russian to produce beautiful translations of Turgenev and Pushkin. According to her early poem "Abschiedswort an Ungarn" (Farewell to Hungary), it was during this first stay away from home that she resolved to earn her own living.

As was the case with Marie von Ebner-Eschenbach, Schiller's idealistic vision of a better humanity was Paoli's earliest source of literary inspiration; it is said that by the age of ten Paoli know all of his poems by heart. She continued the practice of memorizing favorite poems into her old age, keeping her mind agile by reciting poetry to herself before she fell asleep at night and refreshing her memory the next morning if a line escaped her.

The mysticism of Angelus Silesius also appealed to her, making him the only writer of the distant past to influence her own writing.[7]

Paoli was in the midst of adolescence when financial catastrophe struck and mother and daughter were left penniless.[8] They scraped to make ends meet but with little success. Drawing on a remarkable self-sufficiency instilled by a lonely childhood, Paoli hoped that her work as a seamstress would enable her to provide for both herself and her mother. Compelled by increasingly dire finances, she accepted a position as governess in a Russian province close to the Polish border and departed from Vienna in 1830 or 1831, accompanied by her mother. While neither seemed particularly happy in their new surroundings, soon after their arrival Mrs. Glück was so overcome by homesickness and restlessness that she begged her daughter to quit her post. Betty was unable to obtain a release from her contract, so the Glücks fled on a cold winter night. Lacking passports, they resorted to traveling with a band of smugglers in order to cross the Polish border. The strenuous journey proved fatal to Theresia, who took ill and died shortly after they reached a Galician village.

Until she was twenty years old Paoli remained in Galicia, securing a position as governess in a family of Polish aristocrats. She seems to have felt demeaned by this position. However lonely her childhood had been, Betty had enjoyed a large degree of freedom. Her resulting strong-mindedness made her resent being at the beck and call of her employer. In defense she withdrew into herself.[9] The poet would later credit her precocious emotional development to the hardships of youth. The long months of isolated self-reflection instilled a seriousness of purpose that lasted throughout her life.[10] Her earliest poems date to this stay in Galicia. In them she described how poetry restored hope to her flagging spirits and gave her the courage to go on living. These verses were later lost by a careless friend who borrowed them.

The only extant works from the 1830s suggest that social concerns figured prominently in the young artist's imagination. In "An die Männer unserer Zeit" (To the Men of Our Time) the seventeen-year-old poet offers a rebuttal to critics of women's emancipation. "Die Dichterin" (The Female Poet) suggests how conscious the teenager was of the woman writer's predicament in being deprived of a literary ancestry: The "forest of German poets" nominally includes all of the muse's children, but in fact literary history considers only her sons eligible.

Indeed, Paoli's engagement for women's issues was a salient theme common to all phases and genres of her writing. In her essays Paoli would later apply her own experiences with misogyny to an analysis of broader social issues. An unpublished essay from the 1870s or 1880s surveys the "woman question" from Mary Wollstonecraft to the present.[11] In 1865 she published a report on the first women's congress in Leipzig.[12] And a year later in "Ein Wort Pombals" she offered a remedy for the economic plight of women, so many of whom had lost their male providers in the war with Prussia: put them to work in clerical jobs. Unmasking the absurdities of confining women to the home, she urged the Austrian state to follow the progressive examples of France and Switzerland in promoting employment for women.

During her two-year sojourn in Galicia Paoli worked hard to fill the gaps in her education. Acquiring a moderate proficiency in Polish, she must have studied English also, for it was here she first became acquainted with Lord Byron, who would have a lifelong impact on her. Perhaps this early awakening to Romantic poetry and pessimism conflated with her life experience. Scholars commonly assume Betty first fell in love in Galicia since in "Briefe an einen Verstorbenen" (Letters to a Deceased One) in *Nach dem Gewitter* (1843, After the Storm), the poet evokes a Byronesque Weltanschauung in her eulogy to her dead beloved. While the practice of teasing out the poet's biography from her poetry has its problems, numerous poems in Paoli's *oeuvre* refer to the discovery of a new love and its heartbreaking loss occurring soon after her mother's death.

Soon after returning to Vienna in the spring of 1835, she adopted the pen name Paoli with the publication of the short story "Clary" in Witthauer's *Wiener Zeitschrift* (Vienna Journal).[13] While the author attributed the initial adoption of a pseudonym to a mere whim, it was clearly a calculated move. She explained the assumed name as a conscious effort to blot out a "dark shadow" cast over her given name—perhaps an oblique reference to the question of her true father. Moreover, by selecting the name of Pasquale de Paoli, the Corsican freedom fighter, she embraced a foreign, male identity associated with revolutionary impulses. Until 1846 her poems appeared also in Saphir's *Humorist* and in Prague's leading journal, *Ost und West*. But initial forays into publishing did not provide Paoli with financial security. Like so many writers of the period, she had to rely primarily on tutoring and translating for her livelihood. Throughout her life she would look upon these labors as "hack" work, a chore necessary to provide the limited leisure time for the purpose of pursuing the "higher" calling of poet.

By 1841 she was able to put together a small volume entitled *Gedichte* (1841, Poems). Without support from patrons or other form of promotion Paoli's literary debut caused a sensation in Austria. *Gedichte* unveils with uncommon directness the inner life of a female poet. Here she unleashes all of the emotions—of burning passion, of existential melancholy, of recriminating anger toward the man who betrays her, of proud renunciation—that, as she claims in "Wahrheit in der Dichtung" (Truth in Poetry, 120-122) would be taboo admissions in her daily life. Although many of the poems address an unnamed beloved, this collection of verse is primarily the story of a woman whose painful past has led her to poetry as the one true source of consolation and redemption.

Given the restrictive mores of Biedermeier Austria, these poems raised a few eyebrows. Many a reader looked askance at a female poet's unrestrained display of emotion, considering such outbursts as selfishly unmindful of a woman's social duty. An even greater transgression against poetic tradition was Paoli's inversion of gender-specific metaphors. She clothes her poetic self in the medieval idiom of fortresses and chivalry, likening the poetic 'I' to warriors steeled in battle ("Verwahrung" [Protest, 113]) or to a victor showing off with pride the scars of honor inflicted by a life of pain ("Tagebuch" [Diary], #45, 232). Elsewhere the poet appears as a sheer cliff defying fierce elements ("Verschiedenes Leid," [Different Suffering], 204); by contrast the betraying lover is cast as the more flaccid, fearful nature, literally a flower snapped easily by ill fortune. She flaunts her proud self-reliance, urging others to come to the same realization: "Wherefore comes rescue [from troubles] than through myself?" ("Rettung" [Rescue], 92). And she proves herself the more valiant soul in refusing the advances of her lover whose affection is motivated only by a Pygmalion desire to be the sole spender of a lonely woman's happiness ("Liebesgroßmuth" [Magnanimity in Love], 82-89). The poet's appropriation of traits socially defined as masculine creates a tension for the female artist: "My misfortune can be summarized in two words: I was a woman and fought like a man!" ("Kein Gedicht" [No Poem], 72).[14]

However "manly" the poetic persona of some poems, others belie this stance and look back with longing at her foiled biological "destiny." "Kein Gedicht" shows the poet struggling to break free of conventional notions of a woman's calling. "Ins Album einer Braut" (Into the Album of a Bride,

98-99) greets a bride-to-be as being able to look forward to a fate that the poet would have wished for herself, had she been so blessed; in "Wo?" (Where? 119) she calls out to the life partner who has been created for her but whom a cruel fate has kept her from meeting or recognizing. An absolute contradiction of "Rettung," "Metamorphosen" (Transformations, 48) reasserts the redemptive value of a man's love in offering refuge to a woman who has been overexposed to life's harshness.

Notwithstanding her momentary lapses into more "natural" female longings, the assertiveness of the poet's male persona was enough to shock some critics, the harshest of whom labeled the collection "a profanation of the female soul."[15] In the second edition of *Gedichte* Paoli met the morally outraged with a sharp rebuttal: "Unwomanly idea: Oh how foolishly you speak! / For indeed, what does the mind have in common with gender?" ("Tagebuch," #65, 235). Paoli's insistence on a genderless aesthetic, paired with her commitment to improving women's lot in general, ought to have cautioned nineteenth-century critics against the common assumption that a woman's writings were by definition autobiographical. Werner, Beck, and Marchand among other scholars have searched futilely for the identity of the man or men who prompted the emotional outpourings of *Gedichte* and Paoli's later collections of verse. It is true that the poet does at times invite the reader to speculate on her biography: In referring to her mother's death in "Einem Jugendfreunde" (To a Friend of My Youth, 147f.) she suggests real-life models for the other two love relationships mentioned in the same lines: one of a platonic nature rendered eternal by the beloved's untimely death; the second an erotic love cut short by the death of passion and the man's betrayal. This second relationship was considered more significant because it enhanced the poet's link to the divine source of poetry by introducing her to a deeper agony, which was to become her muse. As the motto she borrowed from Byron suggests ("Tagebuch," 208), these poems are to be read as the tomb of her heart. And for every poem hinting at biography there is at least one poem that presents the conflict between man and woman in universal terms. A parallel poem to "Einem Jugendfreunde" can be found, for example, in "Entgegnung" (Reply, 150-159), which restates the tension between eros and philos as a part of the human condition. The pain of the poet is a result less of being forsaken by a specific individual than of her despair over the impossibility of having a strong physical and spiritual bond of love reciprocated fully by both partners.

Thus Paoli was striving to convey paradigmatic experiences to a broad audience. Surely "Einem Weltling" (To a Man of the World) was addressed not only to the faithless lover but to other betrayed women who had had to swallow their helpless rage:

> Before you I have cried in vain
> And raved in throes of agony;
> But you the world will not disdain,
> Because you have abandoned me.
>
> A clever man, no doubt, will find
> Such victims to abuse,
> Whom no one out of all mankind
> Would defend, avenge, excuse!
>
> A clever man, no doubt, disdains
> Old ties when love abates!
> Tell me, don't you feel the blame
> That such praise articulates?[16]

But while women constituted the majority of her admirers, Paoli's poetry did elicit glowing praise from men. Among her enthusiastic readers were the politically engaged writers Moritz Hartmann and Alfred Meißner. In his letters to Meißner in 1841 and 1842 Hartmann describes Paoli as "brilliant" and "the only woman with whom I have ever been able to enjoy uninhibited conversation."[17]

Her first book gained Paoli admittance to the salon of Henriette Wertheimer, the wife of a prominent Viennese philanthropist. As Wertheimer's companion Betty Paoli soon found herself in frequent contact with the writers Hieronymus Lorm, Grillparzer, Leopold Kompert (novelistic chronicler of Jewish life), Ernst von Feuchtersleben, Ottilie von Goethe, and Hammer-Purgstall (the founder of Oriental studies in Austria). For a time at least Paoli was relieved of financial worry and benefited from the exchange of ideas with colleagues.

During a vacation with the Wertheimers in the resort town of Baden Paoli met the Austrian poet who had most inspired her: Nikolaus Lenau happened to visit the home of a mutual acquaintance, where Paoli was staying for a few days. She gave him a copy of her *Gedichte,* which includes two poems dedicated to Lenau. While attributing to Paoli an agreeable and level-headed personality, Lenau was unable to return her admiration: "I could not force from my usual reserve that measure of friendliness that the good worthy soul had deserved. O you kind-hearted women, read my songs, but leave me myself to growl in my corner."[18] Flattered by Paoli's intelligent praise, Lenau qualifies his favorable impression with a patronizing gloss. This response also anticipates the unfortunate assessment of so many later critics, namely, that Paoli's literary output deserved less attention than did her person (biography).

In 1843 Paoli published her second collection of poems entitled *Nach dem Gewitter* (After the Storm). In the spring or summer of the same year she became reader and companion to Princess Marie Anna Schwarzenberg, the widow of the victor at Leipzig (1814). Princess Schwarzenberg had lived with her husband in several European capitals and accompanied him on his military campaigns. As an old woman she still conducted an extensive correspondence and subscribed to numerous journals, eager to keep informed about world events such as had dominated her young married life. In the beginning at least Paoli's new position afforded her considerable leisure time. She had the mornings to herself; the afternoons and evenings were spent reading aloud to the Princess and assisting her with correspondence.

Paoli had met Anna Schwarzenberg through her son Friedrich, who had become a literary personality after the publication of his memoirs under the pseudonym of the "Lanzknecht." As a distraction from an unrequited love, he had traveled the globe in pursuit of noble causes to defend in battle.[19] According to Metternich, the hot-headed adventurer was "to be found wherever there was shooting."[20] Balzac, Hebbel, and Eichendorff were among those writers inspired by Schwarzenberg's poetic accounts of his wanderings.[21] Initially attracted to each other by a common peripatetic existence, Paoli's and Schwarzenberg's devotion to his mother produced an almost forty-year correspondence between them. Paoli's admiration for Schwarzenberg also left its imprint on at least two works of fiction: In "Merced" the narrator's presentation of her friend Leo M. parallels the characterization of Schwarzenberg by his contemporaries as an eccentric but misunderstood "anachronism . . . a truly chivalrous, powerful, and nonetheless sensitive nature."[22] Just as Friedrich Brüder had done, Zdenko Lozensky (1847, "Die Brüder" [The Brothers]) cedes his rights of inheritance to his younger brother and seeks the uncertainty of adventure abroad so that he might extinguish his longing for an unattainable woman.

In her letters to Friedrich, Paoli underscored her gratitude for her new position as companion; during one period of depression she even claimed the Princess was her only reason to go on living.[23] Under her influence Paoli developed an "inner balance and an intellectually broad view and understanding of people and things."[24] Most importantly, Anna Schwarzenberg compensated Paoli for the inadequate mothering she had experienced in childhood. Her response to the Princess's death in 1848 reveals the poet's deprivation of motherly affection: "Having been thrust out into the world at a tender age, and being accustomed to struggles of all kinds, I feel so helpless now that I have lost her—like an orphaned child."[25]

Anna Schwarzenberg also became the catalyst for an important friendship in Betty Paoli's life: Adalbert Stifter's tenure in 1842 and 1843 as reader to the Princess overlapped with Paoli's. Their daily contact formed a close friendship that would dissolve only after 1848, when Stifter's artistic development led him in a direction different from Paoli's. The portrait of the Princess and Paoli in *Nachsommer* is a monument to this period in Stifter's life; according to one interpretation of this episode of the novel, the figure of the female reader (modeled after Paoli) foreshadows the narrator's muse, which makes its appearance a few scenes later in the form of a marble statue.[26]

When they were not in Worlik, the Schwarzenberg estate in Bohemia, or in Jakoberhof, their winter residence in Vienna, the Schwarzenberg household traveled. During an 1844 trip to Berlin Paoli was received enthusiastically among the writers surrounding Rahel von Varnhagen. In Ludmilla Assing's words: "She [Paoli] entered our midst as a muse."[27] Bettina von Arnim had just completed her *Buch an den König,* an appeal for social justice, and Paoli was attracted by the vital liberal ideas of the Berlin salon.[28] Brief as Paoli's stay in Berlin was, it left its mark on her next book, *Romancero* (1845); dedicated to Bettina in memory of the happy time they spent together, this volume contains Paoli's most remarkable epic poems, two of which evoke the yearnings of freedom fighters in Italy.

Most of Paoli's novellas date to the early part of her stay with Princess Schwarzenberg. All but a handful of her extant prose narratives were completed by 1844, enough to constitute a three-volume collection, *Die Welt und mein Auge* (The World and My Eye). Often approaching the length of a novel, these narratives inspired confidence in some colleagues such as Stifter, who encouraged her to try writing a full-length novel. Probably because of unfavorable reviews Paoli disparaged her narrative writings later in a letter to Moritz Hartmann: "It would behoove everyone to spare my novellas their criticism, they do not bore anyone so much as me. Just let me win the big lottery and you will see whether I ever write a single one again, but until then I will continue [with novellas], since I, cursed as I am, do not know how to make hats and bonnets."[29] Paoli implied that only financial necessity forced her into the "unwomanly" profession of authorship. This prickly denial of literary ambition echoes many similar statements by women embittered by a critical establishment that tended to reward female creativity only when it was practiced at home (as in millinery).

Publication of Paoli's novellas ceased in 1857. Having experienced immediate success with her first published volume of poetry, she probably saw no reason to persist in a genre that met with disheartening reviews. Yet with a little more encouragement from admirers like Adalbert Stifter, Paoli may well have continued in this direction, for in the spring of 1845 she had begun work on a novel.[30] Recent critics have suggested Paoli's prose writings merit reevaluation.[31] Some of the novellas are very well crafted and call for fresh interpretation.

The spring of 1846 found Paoli pleading with Friedrich to arrange a vacation for her. Fond as she was of the Princess, the moving about from inn to inn in the summers and the steady stream of visitors in the winters were too disruptive. Aristocratic pastimes such as the hunt were consuming time she would have liked to devote to her own work. A year earlier she had even considered resigning from her post; she feared her artistic growth was stagnating amid such frivolity.[32] Yet Paoli could not bring herself to abandon the Princess, and she persevered until 1846, when she suffered acute depression and illness. Having obtained her leave, Paoli went to Florence in late June to be treated for a nervous disorder, and by late summer she was residing in Venice.[33]

Here Paoli associated with a German colony of artists and writers, including the painter Rottmann and the eccentric writer Heinrich Stieglitz, who had been living in self-imposed exile from Germany since his wife's suicide in 1834. Despite his essentially kind and affectionate nature Paoli found his company insufferable. As Heinrich's newest friend she was obliged to read all his manuscripts, with notes crowded in the margins for the second edition that would never appear. According to Paoli, Stieglitz had been a victim of his own premature literary success, which had stunted his artistic potential and caused the writer to delude himself about his own lack of talent. As his fame waned with each successive publication, his defiance toward his unappreciative public grew, much to the detriment of his character and the people who had to live with him.[34] Despite her reservations about Stieglitz, Paoli's occupation with another's troubles distracted her from her own misery and contributed to her recovery.

When Paoli returned to Vienna in January 1847, her health and spirits had improved. By this time her reputation as poet was attracting fan mail. She was in Worlik that summer when she received a writing sample from an ambitious seventeen-year-old, Marie Dubsky, who requested the older woman's estimation of her literary prospects. Paoli was encouraging in her response but cautioned the younger poet against some of the same pitfalls she herself had experienced: in Ebner-Eschenbach's (née Dubsky) earliest literary attempts Paoli spotted a tendency to overlook the rules of versification. Some thirty years later Paoli would reciprocate Marie Dubsky's reverence by publishing glowing reviews of Ebner-Eschenbach's early narratives. In her 1894 eulogy to her deceased friend, Ebner-Eschenbach sealed this mutual admiration by recalling an acquaintance who read Paoli's poetry "only on her knees."[35]

Despite the salutary interlude in Venice Paoli still found her surroundings in Vienna less than stimulating. Other than Anna Schwarzenberg she lacked any friends in whom she could confide. While she was saddened by the Princess's death the following April 1848, it relieved her of the burdens that accompanied that relationship. For Paoli the disruptions of the March uprisings overshadowed the Princess's death. For the next four years her finances were again precarious. Until 1848 her publications had appeared primarily in *Taschenbücher* (pocket books), a genre targeting women and families and steering clear of political controversy—the quintesssential expression of Biedermeier culture. The 1848 revolt threatened the *Taschenbuch* industry, and Paoli lost her primary source of publishing revenue at the same time her aristocratic patron died.

As for the political implications of the revolution, Paoli was initially enthusiastic, even overjoyed by the promise of change.[36] Along with her more radical colleagues she had engaged in criticism and even mockery of a repressive regime that had only itself to blame for the mounting crisis. As she advised Hartmann in February 1847: "You wouldn't tolerate it here anymore. All they need to do now is forbid the sale of scissors and knives so that by all means the dear little children don't prick or cut them-selves."[37] As a writer she was most affected by the censorship laws, and she used one of her next publishing opportunities to air her exasperation on this subject.[28] But as words turned into actions, she lost faith in liberal politics. The rioting students and proletariat soon struck her as a frenzied mob that had taken leave of its senses. Revolutionary leaders and political poets became suspect as sheer opportunists who glossed over the struggle and pain that would be exacted in creating a new political order.[39] Paoli increasingly believed true democracy was a very gradual process that had to be prepared over generations. Above all it required the intellectual and moral education of the lower classes. She feared democracy as a political realization of a crude materialism, which she correctly predicted would bring an end to the aesthetic ideals she cherished: "A society that considers the solution of the most profound problem to consist of uniformly feeding all of its members must, insofar as it can, seek to root out those ideal impulses that would attack its principle at the roots."[40]

Shortly after the Emperor's flight from Vienna to Innsbruck in May, Paoli retreated to the estate of Schwarzenberg's niece, Countess Palffy, in Malaczka. Partly because of her connections with the Schwarzenberg clan she was biased toward the army, believing only its intervention could restore order. By August poems such as "An Radetzky" (*Nach dem Gewit-ter*, 235) displayed an Austrian patriotism new to Paoli, reversing attitudes that had enabled her to embrace her fellow Germans in Berlin just a few years earlier. A later poem, "23. Februar 1853" expresses her utter devotion to Franz Joseph.

As long as violent rhetoric and acrimonious debate raged in Vienna, Paoli kept her distance from the capital, delaying her return until the fall when the Imperial flag was hoisted over St. Stephan's. Politics caused her to become estranged from several colleagues in opposing ideological camps who had been dear to her, most notably Jakob Kaufmann. To avoid fur-ther conflict she secluded herself and became known to her detractors as the "schwarzgelbe Hyäne" (black and yellow hyena), a reference to a club that attracted loyalists to the throne. In 1849 Paoli was relieved to find an escape from this controversial setting by accepting a temporary post as companion to Countess Bünau in Dahlen near Dresden. Dresden proved to be one of Paoli's favorite homes, a city she would describe with great affection in Vienna's leading newspaper, the *Neue Freie Presse,* in 1870.

Her new post also allowed Paoli a bit more independence than she had experienced in the Schwarzenberg household. Paoli was relieved of her duties whenever relatives came to visit or to escort the Countess on her travels, which was often. There was little to draw Paoli back to Vienna, however, since she felt publishing conditions there offered her little prospect for financial survival.[41] When she revisited Berlin in the fall of 1849, the shift in her political mood dampened her enthusiasm for her former literary friends. What she perceived as incessant gossip in the Savigny household jarred her nerves, and she was all too glad to look for intellectual sustenance elsewhere. In taking up with the painter Peter Cornelius, she continued the education in art history she had begun under Rottmann's tutelage in Italy.[42]

Financial difficulties bound her to Dessau for the winter, but by the spring of 1849 she had arranged to transfer to Paris: she would cover her expenses by offering the *Neue Freie Presse* her skills as a freelance correspondent to the French capital. Lasting only three months, her Paris sojourn left an indelible impression. According to a French scholar, Paoli considered it a great misfortune that she had not been born in France.[43] Letters of introduction enabled her to meet Heinrich Heine and George Sand. The Dutch painter Ary Scheffer, whose royalist sympathies also appealed to Paoli, became her guide to Paris's art treasures. She was a frequent guest in the home of the critic Jules Janin, and became enamored of the stage talent of Rachel, probably the most famous French actress of the day. It was possibly Janin who along with Paoli's first successes as a correspondent convinced the poet of her critical aptitude.

Bünau's marriage in late 1854 to a Count Sahr brought Paoli's position in Dahlen to a definite end, although her friendship with Countess Sahr continued for many years afterward. When Paoli returned to Vienna in 1852, the times were ripe for a journalistic career. A rapidly expanding population and the political excitement of 1848 had stimulated the demand for daily newspapers, which now numbered fourteen in Vienna alone. But it took Paoli a few years to gain a foothold in her new line of work. Beginning in January 1852, her first articles were printed in Warrens' *Wiener Lloyd* as a stop-gap in place of reviews that the regular critic had failed to supply. She could not have enjoyed writing on predetermined topics, but her employment with a journal with an international profile positioned her well for later assignments.

Warrens refused Paoli a regular contract, however, thus clouding her financial outlook. She worked at a frenzied pace during 1852 but was still unable to make ends meet. After only seven months in Vienna she was a physical wreck and took the cure in Doblbad. Determined as she was to remain independent—she had already refused Stifter's offer to take up residence in an apartment he purchased for her near his home in Linz—her plight was desperate enough that she reluctantly accepted Fritz Schwarzenberg's assistance. Just at this time a Russian expatriate, Madame Bagréef-Speranski, asked her to be her companion, thus sparing the proud writer the embarrassment of accepting "charity" from her friends. Bagréef-Speranski was herself a writer and endeavored to reproduce in her Vienna home the salon culture that had waned with the end of the Biedermeier era. Paoli was one of several personalities to grace Bagréef's smoking hour after Sunday dinner, a salon that also welcomed Bauernfeld, Grillparzer, and Heinrich Laube.

From 1853 to 1855 Paoli took on the role of theater critic for the Hofburg and reviewed the monthly art exhibitions. Though she was not a painter, she had a first-hand knowledge of art treasures in Italy, France, and Germany, having also benefited from the expert guidance of painters such as Cornelius, Scheffer, and Rottmann. In 1855 Paoli mended the rift that had developed with her publisher in the previous year in order to continue as theater and art critic for the *Österreichische Zeitung,* a journal Warrens had founded to replace the now defunct *Lloyd.* Until 1860 Paoli reviewed as many as six to eight premieres a month.[44]

Paoli's entry into theater criticism coincided with the heyday of the Burgtheater under the reforms of Heinrich Laube. It is curious that in this most public of literary domains, the theater, Paoli resorted to yet another pseudonym. Under the stage name Branitz she translated a number of plays from the French. Laube preferred her to any other translator because she captured the humor of these society plays without deviating too much from the original; among her greatest successes were Dumas' *Biedermänner* and Beauville's *Gringoire.*[45] Paoli became a regular at luncheons in the Laube home, conversing with the most renowned performing artists of her time including LaRoche, Anschütz, and Fanny Elßler. True to the ideals of the moderate women's movement, Paoli stopped short of suggesting a radical revision of gender roles. Her eulogy to Julie Rettich celebrated the female actress as an embodiment of her emancipatory ideal. An enlightened upbringing coupled with an innately sweet disposition and acting talent had created the most extraordinary feat of all: a female artist who did not sacrifice her "femininity" to professional ambition. In embracing a more "conservative" feminism, Paoli astutely recognized the limits of her culture's tolerance for change.

She also boosted the careers of actors just starting out, introducing Josef Lewinsky to the prominent dramatist Otto Ludwig. She helped Zerline and Ludwig Gabillon through some difficult times at the beginning of their Vienna engagement.[46] Her bond to the Gabillons was strengthened by the birth of their children; Paoli associated with them as an aunt and indeed was godmother to one daughter; another daughter, Helene, went on to write the studies that have become crucial sources for all later scholarship on Paoli.

A hazard of her new role as critic was that it exposed her to the wrath of more powerful male colleagues. Paoli did not mince words when reviewing works that fell short of her aesthetic standards. Perhaps the most notable example occurred with her review of Hebbel's *Magellone* (since renamed *Genoveva*), a production she felt had debased a tender folk legend into a contrived melodrama of insanity.[47] Despite her general acknowledgement of the playwright's talent and a more flattering review published later, Hebbel bore a long-standing grudge, referring to her as a female "Puss in Boots." Years later Emil Kuh did not dignify Paoli by naming her in his Hebbel biography but embedded his critique of Paoli in a diatribe against Laube, whose whimsical handling of *Agnes Bernauer* had embittered Hebbel a few years earlier. To Kuh, Paoli is an "unwomanly" critic and jealous poet "masquerading as the dramaturge Lessing."[48] This misogynistic response to Paoli's blunt criticism suggests a key reason for the negative view of her essays. By contrast, her poems, veiling as they did her critique of patriarchal norms, were more palatable, and consequently they found a broader, more enduring, reception.

While pursuing her new career as a critic, Paoli wearied of life in the Bagréef household. This jadedness set in despite or rather because of her host's literary pretensions. She wrote voluminously in French and German, and her descriptions of Russia were especially valued as a source on conditions in a country that was little known in Western Europe. Although Bagréef's ambitions were futile, she persisted stubbornly, blind to the flaws in her writing. She sought honest opinions of her work but ignored any criticism, which Betty Paoli did not shrink from meting out. The growing awkwardness of her position in Bagréef's household increased Paoli's relief at finding a better offer. In the late spring of 1855 she moved in with Ida von Fleischl-Marxow and her family, where she remained for nine or ten months of every year until her death in 1894. Paoli later reflected on this change as a complete caesura in her life; after years of restlessness and dependence on the whim of various employers she had found a safe haven with Ida Fleischl, who required no services from the poet.[49] To the somewhat envious Ebner-Eschenbach this new position afforded Paoli all of the comforts of family life without any of its obligations.[50] Although Fleischl never published a line herself, her literary judgment was valued as if she had been the publishing artist. Fleischl was Ebner-Eschenbach's closest literary adviser, reviewing all of her final manuscripts before they went to press. In the last two decades of Paoli's life Fleischl was the critical link in this triad of women. Ebner would visit the two housemates for weekly and later triweekly tarok games, during which they would take frequent time-outs for literary and political discussion.[51]

Fleischl was one of the few people Paoli addressed with the familiar "du." The poet's deep gratitude to her friend is attested in a number of poems, most notably in her last volume, in which the opening dedication calls her younger friend "the greatest blessing of her life" ("Widmung" [Dedication], *Neueste Gedichte*). "Am 5. September" (Fleischl's birthday) is an apotheosis of her generous friend as her savior, a soul doctor for her disillusioned spirit (*Neueste Gedichte*, 83). Paoli became an adopted member of the Fleischl household, corresponding regularly with Fleischl's grown children and offering her advice on how to handle family affairs. Paoli chastized her friend for dissipating too much of her valuable energies on demanding family members, suggesting she was too selfless for her own good in fulfilling the roles of wife, mother, and daughter. Her revealing commentary on Ida von Fleischl's familial hardships is probably our best source of information on this woman.[52]

Ebner-Eschenbach and others may have exaggerated the life of ease Paoli led in her old age. It is true that she had hardly a financial care in the winters, but she was on her own in the summers.[53] While Ebner and Fleischl were able to vacation at their Swiss summer retreat, Paoli had to improvise her plans from year to year, rotating her stays with friends at their country estates. Her pride seemed to prevent her from accepting this hospitality for long, and as her friends of old passed on and doctors increasingly prescribed spa treatments, she would seek out the cheapest apartments available at various European retreats. Her nervous disorders took her to the baths in Blankenberghe (Belgium), Franzensbad, Vöslau, Pystian, and Bad Kreuzen, among others. Her letters speak of suffering excruciating pain every other day and feeling just well enough on the alternate good days to handle her voluminous correspondence. In the 1880s she underwent treatment for an addiction to chloral, a sleeping medication.

Her low literary output in the last two decades was no doubt due to her deteriorating health and spirits. Her last important literary essay continued in the tradition of previous studies that sought to bring an undeservedly neglected writer into the limelight. Her review of Ferdinand von Saar's *Die Steinklopfer* (*The Stonebreakers*) includes a survey of the novelist's work to date. Her focus on Saar's compassionate portrayal of the suffering working class reflects the aging Paoli's growing philanthropic impulse, which is also apparent in her last volumes of poetry. In "Der Minotaurus," for example, she pleads for social welfare programs to stave off the impending struggle between rich and poor (*Neueste Gedichte*, 8).[54]

Yet the strongest bond between Paoli and Saar was their belief that the ideal aesthetic of poetic realism was only temporarily threatened and would enjoy a resurgence after the current Naturalist "fad."[55] Because Paoli was so firmly convinced that Saar's production anticipated the best literature the future would offer, she entrusted her papers to his care, leaving the selection of her planned *Letzte Gedichte* (Last Poems) to his judgment.[56] Feeling that Ebner-Eschenbach and Fleischl had greater claims on their deceased friend, Saar declined this honor, but he did contribute a "Requiem für Betty Paoli" as the lead poem for the posthumous *Ausgewählte Gedichte* (Selected Poems).[57]

During the last few years of her life ailing joints practically immobilized the elderly poet, but she remained an avid reader. She was immersed in a biography of George Eliot shortly before she died of heart failure in Baden on 5 July 1894. Paoli is buried in a corner of Vienna's main cemetery among the so-called "Halbberühmtheiten" (the half-famous).[58]

Paoli's language is simple and direct. It is the very antithesis of Droste's obtuse style that insists readers bring their own associations to a poem. Paoli favors rhetorical structures such as anaphora, extended conditional clauses, and analogies of her inner state to natural phenomena. Because of her tendency to build on a series of premises to a surprising pointed climax, the sonnet is the most common form in all her volumes of poetry. The reader is spared unrelenting melancholy in that the increasingly ponderous and despairing tone of several poems is broken up by two or three optimistic poems, usually accompanied by the adjustment of the meter to a shorter, bouncy line reminiscent of Heine. *Gedichte* contains most of the primary themes to be found in her later works.

One of her favorite paradoxes is the representation of *Weltschmerz* as a living death worse than death itself. The poet repeatedly implies that the ability to feel pain deeply has lifted her above the ordinary female dependence on men. The retreating lover proves unworthy, deserving not her tears of regret but her pity, for he has lost sight of the essential human values of compassion and inner balance ("Ein Menschenende. An ***" [The End of a Human. To ***], 160-162). Her "proud, noble blood" ("Zu spät" [Too Late], 50) prevents her from playing the role of tearful entreating woman ("Nachruf" [Obituary], 27). The poet's defiant notes are juxtaposed with effusive avowals of an idolatrous love expressed in poems such as "Antwort" (Answer, 69). The seesawing of the emotions between an unsustainable romantic joy and moments of contemptuous indifference reflects a pattern found throughout Paoli's poetry. One moment will yield rapture such as a love so sacred it precludes the possibility of ever hating ("Bewältigung" [Coping], 76; and "Tagebuch," [Diary], #9); the next moment the poet finds herself flirting with vengefulness ("Beruhigung" [Calming], 138; and "Tagebuch" #79).

Heterosexual love is but one of several recurring motifs in *Gedichte*. Still in her twenties, the author of *Gedichte* presents herself as a world-weary woman prematurely attuned to the transience of human happiness. This unfortunate precociousness is traced back to the seminal experience of losing her mother, the one person on earth who assured her of unconditional love ("An die Heimgegangene" [To the Deceased], 42). In "Dunkle Einsamkeit" (Dark Loneliness) this death takes on a double meaning, connoting also the deprivation of typically domestic or "female" sources of comfort:

> When my mother lay ill after the last journey,
> Thereupon much was changed in manifold ways.
>
> First the doctor carried away the flowers
> That she had so liked to tend in earlier, better days.
>
> Then the daylight was barred all entry

So that, it was said, the patient's rest be undisturbed.

And when the priest came to give her the last rites,
Even her child had to withdraw from her room.

Long since broken off and already wafting away
She breathed only a semblance of life in the end.—

From me too they gradually removed fragrance, light, and love,
I lie in silent night—will death perhaps come soon?

Representing intellectual and spiritual authorities, the doctor and priest
heartlessly intervene in the most painful moment of the daughter's life; the
rational forces of the patriarchy intercept the bonding between mother and
daughter. With its obvious association with death, night is also linked to
the curse of being an artist. Her body is but a daytime prison, from which
she is liberated only during nocturnal wanderings with deceased loved ones
in an otherwordly paradise. The reunions with the dead are what steel her
heart to persevere and inspire her to creativity ("Psyche," 47).

Paoli longs in vain for the joys of youth, but the colors of winter and
fall suit her melancholy best ("Herbstgefühl" [Feeling of Autumn], 8;
"Versprechen" [Promise], 116). In juxtaposition to her internal state
springtime scenes are also employed to depict her particular torture, all the
more tantalizing when the external beauty of nature is only seemingly
within reach ("Frühlingsgaben" [Gifts of Spring], 7). Prone to suicidal
longings, the poet envies Ophelia for her relatively smooth and unconscious slip into death:

O happy is he, who achieves the grave,
Without having to court it wildly,
And he, who sweetly caressed by hope
Dies in searching for flowers! ("Ophelia," 20)

In *Nach dem Gewitter* the poet validates suicide as a metaphor for idealistic
striving—where, for example, she romanticizes the divided self of the
English poet Landon (208-213), who poisoned herself in Senegal in 1841.
The theme of suicide functions as part of a matrix of devices, all serving
to remind the reader of the poet's link to the divine through her frequent

encounters with death. Paoli even takes on the pose of speaking to the living as a voice from the beyond, referring to her autograph as the "dark, rigid letters of a tombstone inscription" ("In ein Album," 123). Repeated images of the self suspended precariously over a threatening abyss reinforce a sense of longing that verges on destruction.

In her eulogy to Droste-Hülshoff she reminds us of that poet's proverbial gift of second sight, drawing out elsewhere the association of poetic powers with the prophetic eye. "Das zweite Gesicht" (Second Sight, 156-161) poses as an Irish ballad but is also an artist poem: the innkeeper who is cursed/blessed with prophetic power is shunned (and eventually murdered) by the society who fears the truth. It is on this second or inner sight, the fearless standing up for the truth, that Paoli bases her claim to a literary calling, as she pointedly states in "Mein Ruhm" (My Fame, 122). Thus it is not surprising Paoli soon had the reputation of a modern-day Cassandra, a persona the poet embraced not only in her poetry but in her personal interactions as well; in her correspondence she often referred to her death as imminent—only to live well into her eighties.

Paoli's second collection of verse marks a transitional phase between the fervent longings expressed most forcefully in *Gedichte* and her later mellower poems (*Neue Gedichte* and *Neueste Gedichte*), which take a more philosophical view of her sufferings. As the title *Nach dem Gewitter* suggests, the emotional upheavals of *Gedichte* have subsided. The twenty-eighth poem in the opening cycle of her second volume, "Astern" (Asters, 30) obscures the causes of the parting of the ways between the lovers, thus suppressing the feelings of bitter recrimination so she might on occasion vicariously relive the moments of their joyous union through her verse. The opening dedication "An ***" suggests the extension of their relationship through the rose-colored glass of verse is to haunt her betrayer.

Two of the five narrative poems in Paoli's third volume of poetry evoke scenes from recent Italian history, glorifying the martyrdom of those who died for freedom from foreign oppression. At first glance the political engagement of *Romancero* (1844) seems an anomaly within Paoli's corpus, but the poet employs political themes to other ends. In consequence of his political agitation Silvo Pellico was still incarcerated in 1844, and so Paoli's version of his story in "Maria Pellico" was immediately relevant to the current Austrian situation. Around the empire ethnic minorities were mobilizing to free themselves from the Habsburg yoke. But Paoli is less interested in Pellico himself than in his sister, so closely bonded to Silvo from earliest childhood their identities appear to merge. Recalling the history of martyrs from ancient times (e.g., Tasso's Leonore), Maria is haunted by memories of a happy childhood with her brother. Aching to shoulder some of his pain, her role as passive observer is more unbearable than her brother's punishment. In renouncing all earthly pleasure Maria's decision to enter a convent is paradoxically an emancipatory act; she is no longer captive to her family's insensitivity. As she has already witnessed her family's relative indifference to their son's departure, so too will she in her cloister be as dead to them.

Evoking paradoxical associations with freedom in death, the cloister is a leitmotif linking "Maria Pellico" with "Die Beichte des Mönchs" (The Monk's Confession) in the same collection, but the monk is able to undergo self-abnegation only after having been tormented by and succumbing to temptation. Although this poem is a reworking of an Italian legend, its similarity to a more autobiographical poem in her previous collection suggests a reason for its appeal to the poet at this stage of her life. She has clung to earth's pleasures only to realize the somber truth of a prophetic voice that once informed her "You will find your end among the silent walls of a cloister" ("Plan," *Nach dem Gewitter,* 140). Now all the wiser from her internal strife, she directs her longing gaze to a secluded garden among cypress trees enveloped in calm, stillness, and oblivion.

Her longing to forget presents itself also in a more menacing fashion through the recurring image of the abyss, evidencing Paoli's attraction to the forces of the unconscious in her mid-years. Freely improvising on the sketchy details of Pergolesi's biography, "Stabat Mater (*Romancero*) psychologizes the genesis of Pergolesi's musical masterpiece. Having repressed an early childhood trauma, the witnessing of his father's execution, the early modern composer's greatest artistic achievement ensues from the resurfacing of this very trauma: as he himself is near death, a vision of his mother, dying from the shock of seeing her husband murdered, comes to him in a dream, and her voice supplies the melodic thread of his last and finest composition.

A few poems in Paoli's early poetry anticipate the tone that will predominate in the collections published after 1848. "Probatum est" (Tested, *Gedichte* 29-30) proposes a cure for sufferers from melancholy: patience and adaptability. Particularly in the "Tagebuch," a later addition to *Gedichte,* an aphoristic impulse supplants the subjective preoccupations so pronounced in the 1840s. Here she offers her readers wisdom to live by, the fruits of her long years of suffering.

Aside from being meticulously crafted, Paoli's late poetry contains little that is completely new in content. Here and there the superb style of a poem merits republication in a new edition. But after 1848 her lyrics offer fewer fresh insights than her critical essays. And for all her avowals of poetry as the highest art form Paoli probably ranked her prose higher at the end of her life. When her late discovery of Conrad Ferdinand Meyer's poetry filled her with awe, she expressed shame over the lyrics of her youth, detecting in them only affectation and self-absorption. Without quite condemning her former self Paoli attributed her poorly realized talent to the unfavorable conditions of her upbringing.[59]

While the older Paoli may have judged her lyrical outpourings too harshly, it has nonetheless been to the detriment of her twentieth-century reputation that this genre was the basis of her fame—this at a time when lyric poetry was rapidly becoming obsolete with the social transformations wrought by industrialization. Paoli astutely recognized the signs of a rapidly evolving literary marketplace and quickly acted to transfer her skills to the more promising field of journalism; thus she salvaged her career if not for posterity, at least for her personal livelihood. Nevertheless, Paoli's distinction as a poet has continued to eclipse her other contributions of potential interest to contemporary readers.

Like her poetry, Paoli's novellas were concerned firstly with the interior world of personal tragedy with its attendant inner conflicts, which constitute the focal point of her plots. It is true, as many critics have been quick to point out, she is prone to casting the protagonist as an all too transparent version of herself, and she relies heavily on stock characterizations for the depiction of the secondary figures. But her narrative plots are often more complex than meets the eye, and Paoli's ability to delineate with sensitive insight the social and psychological hardship of talented indigent women offers unexplored terrain for social historians.

The heroines of her novellas frequently bear a strong physical likeness to the author and echo her biography in that they are orphans or suffer from neglect by a mother figure. One of her orphans, Leonore in the narrative bearing the same name, reacts with angry defiance when the honor of her deceased mother is called into question; she is very uncomfortable about accepting the charity of her haughty aristocratic benefactors, who make her feel her subordinate position all too keenly. The mother-daughter bond takes on particular significance in light of the lack of mention of her father; even in the novellas father figures rarely appear and then recede far into the background of the plot. The plot line of "Auf- und Untergang" bears the strongest biographical parallels, which lead some readers to see Paoli's account of her own childhood superimposed on her retelling of Elise Mercoeur's life. Like Mercoeur, a well-known French writer, the young Betty may have embarked on an early struggle to explain to her mother that her penchant for writing stemmed from a deep inner need and was not intended to break social taboos against female authorship.[60]

One of Paoli's novellas, "Ein einsamer Abend" (A Lonely Evening), blurs the genre distinction between story and essay. To convey the illusion of a novella a fictive setting frames reflections on the status of literature in the industrialized world. The suicide of a writer prompts the narrator's probing of the social causes leading to so desperate a step; she views this case as symptomatic of a secular industrial society's contempt for poesy. Yet her prosaic times are merely a passing phase, the "awkward adolescence" ("Flegeljahre") of human history; it is quite natural that practical concerns will dominate in this period of flux, and that the weaker among poetic souls will be traumatized by society's turn from transcendental sources of knowledge. Nevertheless the narrator holds out hope that humankind will ultimately mature to a recognition of the indispensability of art to the wellbeing of the soul. Revealing an uncommonly open mind. "Ein einsamer Abend" does not condemn technical progress, for positive contributions are also noted; in the more advanced countries of France and England, for example, industrialization has helped create conditions in which women writers enjoy a higher status than ever before.

This last point typifies a number of Paoli's articles, which commonly adopted a cosmopolitan tone. Austria was fortunate to have so broadminded an essayist at a time when the country was increasingly looking inward. Straddling the Romantic and Realist eras—in her literary production as in her lifespan—Betty Paoli was also a pivotal figure among nineteenth-century German women writers. Certainly not all of her works warrant renewed analysis; indeed both her lyrics and critical writings become monotonous when read back to back. But in all of the genres in which she published, occasional literary gems await rediscovery. It would be a great disservice to Betty Paoli's unrecognized accomplishment if another seventy years were to pass again before the next English publication on this "veritable bard of the female soul."[61]

Notes

1. Helene Bettelheim-Gabillon, "Zur Charakteristik Betty Paolis," *Jahrbuch der Grillparzer-Gesellschaft*, 10 (1900), p. 198. Henceforth cited as "Charakteristik."

2. Paoli to Kompert, 31 July 1856, quoted in Stefan Hock, "Briefe Betty Paolis an Leopold Kompert," *Jahrbuch der Grillparzer Gesellschaft*, 18 (1908), p. 201.

3. To the artist Friedrich Pecht, for example, she seemed "more fit to live romances than to write them." *Aus meiner Zeit. Lebenserinnerungen*, vol. 2 (Munich: Verlagsanstalt für Kunst und Wissenschaft, 1894), p. 3.

4. Theresia Glück, née Grünnagel, was probably not Belgian, as most sources state. Rather her name suggests she was born to Austrians residing in the Netherlands; the cession of this former Habsburg territory to France in 1797 would have occurred during Theresia's childhood. Jolan Gluck, "Betty Paoli: Die Dichterin im Spiegel ihres Jahrhunderts," dissertation, City University of New York, 1989, p. 17.

5. Helene Bettelheim-Gabillon, "Betty Paoli. Ein Gedenkblatt zu ihrem hundertsten Geburtstag," *Westermanns Monatshefte*, 177 (1915), p. 666. Henceforth cited as "Gedenkblatt."

6. "Charakteristik," p. 197.

7. Annie Alice Scott, *Betty Paoli: An Austrian Poetess of the Nineteenth Century* (London: Routledge and Sons, 1926), pp. 21, 204.

8. The sources conflict on whether the inheritance was lost primarily through Theresia's foolhardy speculations or through the bankruptcy of a businessman who was charged with managing the Glück's finances.

9. Friedrich Beck, "Betty Paoli," *Österreichische Rundschau*, 9 (1 November 1906), p. 261.

10. "Gedenkblatt," p. 666.

11. "Die Wandlungen der Frauenfrage," inventory number 106.380. Wiener Stadt- und Landesbibliothek.

12. "Eine Zeitfrage," *Neue Freie Presse*, 4 November 1865.

13. Scott, p. 33.

14. Here there are clear parallels with the poetry of Droste-Hülshoff, to whom Paoli paid homage in several essays. See *Betty Paolis Gesam-*

melte *Aufsätze,* ed. Helene Bettelheim-Gabillon (Vienna: Verlag des Literarischen Vereins in Wien, 1908), pp. 1-45.

15. Bettelheim, "Gedenkblatt," p. 668.
16. *The Defiant Muse: German Feminist Poems from the Middle Ages to the Present.* Translated by S.L. Cocalis and G.M. Geiger (New York: The Feminist Press, 1986), p. 51.
17. Hartmann to Meißner, quoted in Otto Wittner, *Briefe aus dem Vormärz* (Prague: J.G. Calve, 1911), pp. 121, 166.
18. *Lenaus Briefe an Emilie von Reinbeck,* ed. Anton Schlossar (Stuttgart, 1896), p. 167, quoted in Richard Maria Werner, *Betty Paoli* (Pressburg/Leipzig: Heckenast Nachf., 1898), p. 24.
19. Among the battles Friedrich took part in were the French expedition to Algiers (1830), the Carlist war in Spain (1838), the unsuccessful Catholic movement in Switzerland (1846), and the conflicts waged to put down the uprisings in Galicia (1846) and Hungary (1849).
20. Helene Bettelheim-Gabillon, "Betty Paoli und die Familie Schwarzenberg," *Österreichische Rundschau,* 15, p. 195. Henceforth cited as "Schwarzenberg."
21. Quoted in "Gedenkblatt," p. 670.
22. "Merced," *Iris,* 6 (Pesth, 1845), p. 149.
23. Paoli-Schwarzenberg, 26 September 1846, quoted in Bettelheim, "Schwarzenberg," p. 200.
24. Hock, p. 203.
25. *Gesammelte Aufsätze,* pp. VI–VII.
26. Karl Hugo Zinck, "Betty Paoli und Adalbert Stifter," *Vierteljahresschrift des Adalbert-Stifter-Instituts des Landes Oberösterreich,* 22 (1973), pp. 123, 127f.
27. Marie von Ebner-Eschenbach, "Einleitung," *Ausgewählte Gedichte von Betty Paoli* (Stuttgart/Berlin: Cotta, 1894), p. 9.
28. Gluck, p. 30.
29. Paoli-Hartmann, 18 February 1847, quoted in Wittner, p. 425.
30. Ibid., 27 May 1845, quoted in Wittner, p. 355.
31. Aurelia Rabitsch, "Betty Paoli als Epikerin," dissertation, Graz, 1972.
32. Paoli-Hartmann, 27 May 1845, quoted in Wittner, p. 354.
33. Gluck, p. 31.
34. *Gesammelte Aufsätze,* pp. 161-175.
35. Ebner-Eschenbach, p. 6.
36. See for example "In denselben Tagen" (*Neue Gedichte*).

37. Quoted in Wittner, p. 426.
38. "Censor und Setzer," *Nach dem Gewitter*, 2nd edition (1850), p. 264.
39. "Einigung. Frühling 1848," *Neue Gedichte*, p. 42.
40. Quoted in "Charakteristik," p. 207.
41. 18 August 1849, quoted in Gluck, p. 87.
42. *Gesammelte Aufsätze*, p. 68.
43. Alfred Marchand, "Betty Paoli," *Les Poètes Lyriques de L'Autriche* (Paris: Fischbacher, 1886), p. 208.
44. Her experience with theater led her to write a drama, which was apparently never performed. *Eine Herzenswahl. Drama in 5 Aufzügen* (Vienna: Keck, 1857).
45. Ebner-Eschenbach, p. 12.
46. *Ludwig Gabillon. Tagebuchblätter. Briefe. Erinnerungen*, ed. Helene Bettelheim-Gabillon (Vienna/Pest/Leipzig: Hartleben, 1900), p. 76.
47. *Wiener Lloyd*, 22 January 1854, quoted in Gluck, p. 124.
48. Emil Kuh, *Biographie Friedrich Hebbels*, vol. 2 (Vienna/Leipzig: Braumüller, 1907), p. 371.
49. Marchand, p. 209.
50. Ebner-Eschenbach, p. 10.
51. Ibid., p. 14.
52. Paoli's letters to the Fleischls are fairly complete for the period from 1871 to 1891. Wiener Stadt- und Landesbibliothek.
53. Unpublished correspondence reveals that Paoli received a state pension, but it is unclear when and how it was initiated. See, for example, letter dated 27 July 1884, Wiener Stadt- und Landesbibliothek, inventory number 48452.
54. See also in the same collection "'Ich dien'!'" (45-47) and the final lines of "Unsere Zeit" (110).
55. Friedrich Adamec, "Betty Paoli und ihr Freundeskreis," dissertation, Vienna, 1951, p. 55f.
56. Ibid., p. 56.
57. *Gedichte, Auswahl und Nachlaß*, ed. Anton Bettelheim (Stuttgart: Union Deutsche Verlagsgesellschaft, 1895), pp. 22-24.
58. Scott, p. 211.
59. See especially Paoli-Meyer, 9 May 1883, quoted in A. Schaer, "Betty Paoli und Conrad Ferdinand Meyer," *Euphorion. Zeitschrift für Literaturgeschichte*, ed. August Sauer, 16 (1909), p. 507.
60. Werner, p. 21ff.

61. Leopold Kompert, "Betty Paoli," *Gedenke Mein! Taschenbuch für 1857,* 26 (Vienna: Pfautsch & Voß), p. xviii.

Bibliography

I. Works by Betty Paoli in German

Books

Gedichte. Pesth: G. Heckenast, 1841. Second expanded edition, 1845.

Nach dem Gewitter. Pesth: G. Hecknast, 1843. Second expanded edition, 1850.

Die Welt und mein Auge. Novellen. Pesth: G. Heckenast, 1844.

Romancero. Leipzig: Wigand, 1845.

Neue Gedichte. Pesth: Heckenast, 1850. Second expanded edition, 1856.

Lyrisches und Episches. Pesth: Heckenast, 1855.

Julie Rettich. Ein Lebens- und Charakterbild. Vienna: Leopold Sommer, 1866.

Wiens Gemäldegalerien in ihrer kunsthistorischen Bedeutung. Vienna: Gerold, 1865.

Neueste Gedichte. Vienna: Gerold, 1869.

Grillparzer und seine Werke. Stuttgart: J.G. Cotta, 1875.

Ausgewählte Gedichte, ed. Marie von Ebner-Eschenbach. Stuttgart: Cotta, 1894. Expanded edition, Anton Bettelheim, 1895.

Die Brüder. Anna. Zwei Erzählungen. Vienna: Daberkow [no date].

Gesammelte Aufsätze, ed. Helene Bettelheim-Gabillon. Vienna: Verlag des Literarischen Vereins, 1908.

Die schwarzgelbe Hyäne, ed. Josef Halper. Graz/Vienna: Stiasny, 1957. Selected poems, letters, and essays.

Early Poems

Betty Glück. "Abschiedswort an Ungarn." *Der Spiegel für Kunst, Eleganz und Mode.* Pesth: Tonala, 1832, vol. 48 (16 June 1832), pp. 383-384.

————. "An die Männer unserer Zeit. Halb Ernst, halb Scherz." *Wiener Zeitschrift für Kunst, Literatur, Theater und Mode,* 102 (25 August 1832), pp. 821-822.

————. "Die Dichterin." *Der Humorist.* Vienna (20 August 1837), p. 494.

Novellas

Betty Glück. "Alfred." *Der Spiegel für Kunst, Eleganz und Mode*. Pesth: Tonala, 18/137-139, 145-149; 19/154-157; 20/162-164.

Betty Paoli. "Merced." *Iris. Zeitschrift für Wissenschaft, Kunst, und Literatur,* 1845.

_____. "Das Mädchen von San Giorgio." *Iris,* 1846.

_____. "Die Brüder." Rheinisches Taschenbuch für 1847. Frankfurt am Main: J.D. Sauerländer, 1847.

_____. "Anna." *Österreichische Zeitung*. Vienna: April-May, 1857.

Selected Articles and Reviews

"Deutsche Briefe." *Presse*. Vienna, 25 and 29 August, 27 September, 4 October 1848.

"Bücherecke." *Wiener Lloyd:*
    On Julie Burov. 5 January 1852
    On Birch-Pfeiffer. 11 January 1852
    On Bagréef-Speranski. 23 March 1852
    On Hebbel's *Genoveva*. 22 January 1854

"Die Kunstausstellung im Juni." *Österreichische Zeitung,* 23 June 1861.

"Eine Zeitfrage." *Neue Freie Presse,* 4 November 1865.

"Ein Wort Pombals." *Neue Freie Presse,* 12 August 1866.

"Ein Ausflug nach Dresden." *Neue Freie Presse,* 13 July 1870.

"Reisestationen." *Neue Freie Presse,* December 1870-March 1871 (Report on her Italian journey).

"Franz Grillparzer." *Neue Freie Presse,* 7 April 1872.

"In Sachen der Literatur." *Neue Freie Presse,* 21 April 1879.

Correspondence

Bettelheim-Gabillon, Helene. "Betty Paoli und die Familie Schwarzenberg." *Österreichische Rundschau,* 15 (1908), 194-220.

_____, ed. "Einführung." *Gesammelte Aufsätze*. Vienna: Verlag des Literarischen Vereins (1908), pp. 5-111.

_____, ed. *Ludwig Gabillon. Tagebuchblätter Briefe. Erinnerungen.* Vienna/Pesth/Leipzig: A. Hartleben, 1900.

Hock, Stefan, ed. "Briefe Betty Paolis an Leopold Kompert." *Jahrbuch der Grillparzer Gesellschaft,* 18 (1908), pp. 177-209.

Ilwof, Franz. "Betty Paoli und Ernst Freiherr von Feuchtersleben." *Jahrbuch der Grillparzer Gesellschaft,* 12 (1902), pp. 199-211.

Schaer, A., ed. "Betty Paoli und Conrad Ferdinand Meyer. Zeugnisse einer Dichterfreundschaft in elf Briefen (1877-1886)." *Euphorion. Zeitschrift für Literaturgeschichte,* 16. Leipzig/Vienna: Carl Fromme, 1909.

Wittner, Otto, ed. *Briefe aus dem Vormärz. Eine Sammlung aus dem Nachlaß Moritz Hartmanns.* Prague: J.G. Calve, 1911.

II. Works by Betty Paoli in English Translation

"To a Man of the World." Translated by Susan L. Cocalis and O.M. Geiger. *The Defiant Muse: German Feminist Poems from the Middle Ages to the Present,* ed. Susan L. Cocalis. New York: The Feminist Press, 1986, p. 51.

III. Secondary Works in English and French

Marchand, Alfred. "Betty Paoli." *Les Poètes Lyriques de L'Autriche.* Paris: Fischbacher, 1886.

Scott, Annie A. *Betty Paoli. An Austrian Poetess of the Nineteenth Century.* London: Routledge, 1926.

Major Studies in German

Adamec, Friedrich. "Betty Paoli und ihr Freundeskreis." Dissertation, Vienna, 1951.

Beck, Friedrich. "Betty Paoli." *Österreichische Rundschau,* 9 (1 November 1906), 260-272.

Bettelheim-Gabillon, Helene. "Zur Charakteristik Betty Paolis." *Jahrbuch der Grillparzer Gesellschaft,* 10 (1900), pp. 191-250.

_____. "Betty Paoli. Ein Gedenkblatt zu ihrem hundertsten Geburtstag." *Westermanns Monatshefte,* 17 (1915), pp. 666-674.

_____. "Betty Paoli und die Familie Schwarzenberg." *Österreichische Rundschau,* 15, 194-220.

_____. "Betty Paoli." *Neue Österreichische Biographie,* 5. Vienna: Amalthea, 1928, pp. 48-65.

Ebner-Eschenbach, Marie von. "Einleitung." *Ausgewählte Gedichte.* Stuttgart: Cotta, 1894.

Gluck, Jolan. "Betty Paoli: Die Dichterin im Spiegel ihres Jahrhunderts." Dissertation, City University of New York, 1989.

Hacker, Hanna. "Betty Paoli." In *Die Frauen Wiens: Ein Stadtbuch für Fanny, Frances und Francesca*. Vienna: AUF-Ed, Verlag der Apfel, 1992, pp. 184-203.

Kompert, Leopold. "Betty Paoli." *Gedenke Mein! Taschenbuch für das Jahr 1857*. Vienna: Pfautsch & Voß, 1857.

Lewinsky, Josef. "Gedenkrede auf Betty Paoli." Vienna: Verlag des Vereins der Schriftstellerinnen und Künstlerinnen in Wien, 1895.

Rabitsch, Aurelia. "Betty Paoli als Epikerin." Dissertation, Graz, 1972.

Wallner, Victor. "Betty Paoli." In his *Zwischen Fächer und Bubikopf: Die "vergessene" Emanzipation in Baden*. Baden: Gesellschaft der Freunde Badens und städtischer Sammlungen, 1993, pp. 28-33.

Werner, Richard Maria. *Betty Paoli*. Pressburg/Leipzig: G. Heckenast Nachf., 1898.

Wozonig, Karin. "Die Literatin Betty Paoli: Eine Studie zur weiblichen Nobilität im 19. Jahrhundert." Vienna Diplomarbeit, 1995.

Zinck, Karl Hugo. "Betty Paoli und Adalbert Stifter." *Vierteljahresschrift des Adalbert Stifter Instituts des Landes Oberösterreich*, 22, 3/4 (1973), 121-132.

_____. "Betty Paoli (1814-1894) und Dr. Josef Breuer (1872-1975) in ihrer Zeit." *Vierteljahresschrift des Adalbert Stifter Instituts des Landes Oberösterreich*, 25 (1976), 143-159.

Caroline Pichler

Barbara Becker-Cantarino
assisted by Gregory Wolf

"Madame Pichler is neither beautiful nor ugly, quite tolerable, and either childless or blessed with just one boy and one girl. She is a woman present when the children are bathed; only in *pressing* cases, and only when the printer presses on (two sturdy volumes must be written and published!), does she let the soup and pap burn."[1] This condescending picture of Caroline Pichler (1769-1843) as a little housewife dabbling in writing during her spare time was composed by the anonymous critic "Gk" (Göckingk) in a review of her first novel *Leonore. Ein Gemählde aus der großen Welt* (1804, Leonore, a Picture from the Great World). In spite of Gk's unflattering portrayal, Pichler became a much admired, widely read, productive, and prolific writer: *Die sämmtlichen Werke der Frau Caroline Pichler, gebornen von Greiner. Octavformat* (The Collected Works of Mrs. Caroline Pichler, neé von Greiner, in Octavo) published from 1824 to 1844, consists of fifty-three volumes of "novels, dramas, essays, lyrical works, and short stories"[2] and is only one of three "complete editions" published during her lifetime." Her most famous work, the detailed autobiography *Denkwürdigkeiten aus meinem Leben* (1844, Memorable Events from My Life),[3] provides a firsthand account of the cultural and literary life in Old Vienna during the Wars of Independence and the Vienna Congress. In those decades Pichler became known for her role in the salon of her mother Charlotte von Greiner and later in her own, and as an author whose popularity far exceeded the borders of Austria.

In her life and works Caroline Pichler represented the views of the educated "middle class," that is to say, of those who, unlike the aristocrats of the upper social strata, gain social status because of personal accomplishments and not through birth and heredity. Men of the educated middle class served as civil servants and officials in Vienna; although not members of the aristocracy and court circles, they were important in Austria's literary and cultural life during the late eighteenth and early nineteenth centuries. Caroline's father, Franz Sales von Greiner, was knighted by Maria Theresa in 1771, and was later named court adviser and privy counselor to the court chancellery in 1773. Sales displayed his gratitude by marrying the Empress's favorite attendant, Charlotte Hieronymus, in 1776. Maria Theresa had taken Charlotte in as a five-year-old orphan and had had her trained to become her favorite reader (not of literature but of letters and documents in German, Italian, French, and Latin), thus providing the young and highly intelligent Charlotte with an unusual education. After her marriage Charlotte was received privately by the Empress on several occasions during the 1770s, and her young daughter Caroline, who accompanied her, fondly remembered these visits in her memoirs.

One may assume the Empress, as a living model of important women, had a considerable effect on Caroline. Many years later in her last novel *Elisabeth von Guttenstein. Eine Familiengeschichte aus der Zeit des Österreichischen Erbfolgekrieges* (Elisabeth von Guttenstein. A Family History from the Time of the Austrian War of Succession), written in 1833/1834, she portrayed the Empress in a very affectionate way: "Everything that could make a woman attractive, beauty, charm, intellect, modesty, compassion, loyalty to the spouse, tender love for the children, respect for what is right and virtuous, unite in a wonderful union with the sagacity and intellectual strength of a man and all other characteristics which dignify a Monarch of the Crown."[4] Idealized womanhood as described by the Romantics, especially Schleiermacher,[5] is an important aspect of Pichler's depiction of the Empress, yet even more important is the explicit reference to her "male intellectual strength." In this novel, Pichler intended to glorify Maria Theresa by comparing her to Frederick the Great and presenting her as his equal, a thought that angered the German critic Laube: "The days and wars of Frederick the Great are no topic for a woman" (*Denkwürdigkeiten,* II, 288). The novel's Austrian patriotism troubled Laube somewhat, but he found even more disturbing the idea of a woman writing about such "male" topics as the glorious wars of Frederick the Great. Another male critic who lamented that Pichler's male characters were nothing more than costumed women hoped that another such work would "dislodge these (bad novels) from the hands of young women and from the shelves of libraries" (Ibid., 289). The fact that an author was a woman was a major factor in contemporary critical reception. One expected "womanly" topics; the old days and wars of Frederick the Great were not suitable for a woman. One presumed to find a female flaw in the mode of representation, such as the men being only costumed women, and one recommended literature written by women only to a female audience.[6] This narrow focus for "women's literature," as literature written by women, from a woman's perspective, and read almost exclusively by women, served to constrain Pichler's concept of herself as an author, just as it did for almost all women writers of her time.[7]

Eighteenth-century discussion about the worth of women and the necessity of educating them, propagated by Joseph von Sonnenfels in his moral weekly and especially in *Theresie und Eleonore* (1767)[8] following Fenelon's example, undoubtedly left its mark on Caroline's upbringing. The family's social position was also crucial for her education, as well as were her parents' many intellectual and artistic interests, which made the Greiner household a center for artists and intellectuals. According to Caroline Pichler, among the most prominent visitors were:

> Sonnenfels, to whom his fatherland is more indebted than it realizes. Denis, Abbot Metastasio, Mastalier, Haschka, Alxinger . . . Professors Well, Wollstein, Ekhel, Dr. Stoll, Ratschky, Leon, Blumauer, Hofstätter, Barons von Sperges and von Swieten were some of the many guests during evening discussions at my parents' house. Spirited, sophisticated conversation, literary and political news, everything in the field of art, especially music . . . everything new and exciting would be discussed. And although as children and young adults educated to proper behavior it would not have occurred to us to join in the conversation, we did listen to it, and many a seed was cast in our young minds. (*Denkwürdigkeiten*, II, 398)

Such was Caroline Pichler's description of the salon and characterization of her acquired role of "modesty"; the passage was already contained in *Überblick meines Lebens* (1819, Reflections on my Life).

Pichler's literary activity began early. She was tutored privately by the writers von Haschka and Gottlieb Leon, among others, and her first poem appeared as early as 1782 in the prestigious *Wiener Musenalmanach* (Vienna Almanac of the Muses). She subsequently wrote idylls in the then popular hexameter style of Geßner and J. H. Voß. The dedication of her volume "An meine Mutter" (1803, To My Mother) is revealing:

> Take the most innocent thanks for all grief,
>> all love, which a child does not appreciate,
>> which only the mother understands!
> Take, as a gift from me, the pictures of rural simplicity,
>> of domestic peace and happiness, and deep satisfying
>> stillness.
> If I, in the noise of this world, harbor a sensitivity for
>> the purer joys, for nature,
> it is, o Mother, your work.
> It is likewise your work
> when I attempt to write about the flowers blooming in
>> a happy domestic garden,
> When the beautiful reality bears likeness to poetic
>> happiness,
> And my satisfied heart manifests itself in the songs.[9]

The poem provides an early example of the "Mutterkult" (cult of motherhood) and "Lob des Hauses" (praise of the home), themes which were to become prominent during the Biedermeier period.[10] Such feelings of security and contentment are characteristic of Pichler's verses, which are quite similar to and compare favorably with those by Voß or Geßner; these particular lines embody Caroline Pichler's striving for domestic happiness, a central theme of her later and more important prose.

Pichler's extensive private tutoring was not intended to prepare her for a professional career; such an education was merely typical for a woman of her class as preparation for her role as educated wife and good mother. Reading, writing, and playing music—when domestic and familial chores were finished—were quite fashionable and accepted pursuits for women, but not so was publishing or a writing career. Caroline Pichler began her successful career as an author, therefore, only after several tumultuous events. Following a dissolved engagement and an unhappy love, she married Andreas Pichler in 1796, an official in the court chancellery. She bore a child in 1797, a daughter named Elisabeth, who was to remain her only child. Most important perhaps was her father's sudden death in 1798, whereupon the family was forced to move from their stately city home into a modest suburban dwelling in the Alservorstadt. Caroline Pichler then turned to serious publishing, no doubt in order to improve the family's finances.[11] As she so often pointed out, her husband was the person who persuaded her to revise her *Gleichnisse* (Parables), short prose pieces in which she compares natural phenomena with human experiences and thus attempts to interpret and understand them. Published in 1800, they won acclaim.

Novels and stories followed, among which *Leonore* (1804), *Agathokles* (1808), and the novella "Stille Liebe" (1808, Quiet Love) earned her popularity. She also wrote ballads, poems, historical-patriotic dramas, two Catholic devotional books based on Fénelon's model, many journalistic essays, such as commemorative pieces on famous persons, and essays on contemporary cultural (not political) topics. Her *Zeitbilder* (1839, Pictures of the Times), "Wien in der zweiten Hälfte des 18. Jahrhunderts" (Vienna in the Second Half of the 18th Century), and "Wien im Anfange des 19. Jahrhunderts" (Vienna at the Beginning of the 19th Century) depicted history in fictional form, thereby circumventing strict censorship. In 1844, one year after her death, her memoirs, the *Denkwürdigkeiten aus meinem Leben,* were published.

As knowledge of her literary prowess grew, Caroline Pichler's house became a salon for Austria's cultural and literary élite. Although her mother presided at the gatherings until her death in 1815, Caroline was the major attraction. Many important champions of the patriotic-dynastic movement in Austria visited: among them Hormayr, Haschka, Karl Streck-fuß, Hammer-Purgstall, the Collin brothers, Privy Counselor von Ridler, and later Grillparzer and Lenau. Visitors to Vienna, such as Tieck, Brentano, Theodor Körner, Madame de Staël, Friedrich, Dorothea, and A. W. Schlegel, also came to the Pichler house. Just as Vienna during the first two decades of the nineteenth century was the political center for the anti-Napoleonic resistance and national movements, the Pichler salon, as well as the more elegant houses of Fanny Arnstein,[12] Henriette Pereira and Eleonore Fliess, offered a meeting place for the literati and the intellectuals. Caroline Pichler not only provided for sophisticated conversation, she also served as mediator between factions. As hostess she played an active role in these gatherings; she controlled the discussions and arranged and took an active part in the literary, musical, and theatrical presentations. This form of social life was quite important, as it facilitated communication among like-minded and dissenting individuals of the educated middle class; almost all other forms of social intercourse outside of the domestic sphere were quite restricted, if not prohibited, for men and women who were not members of the aristocracy.

Caroline Pichler lived by the notion that "intellectual development" and the "job of the woman as housewife and mother" belong together and that these could and should be pursued simultaneously. She wrote:

> As soon as everything that we learn, practice, and think is subordinated to the highest purpose—not only that of the woman, but that of mankind—to the purpose of moral ennobling, and as soon as the educated and therefore the better woman becomes the competent housewife, the experienced educator, and her husband's faithful, reliable friend, then all of the complaints about the wrong direction and damaging consequences of the higher education of the female sex will disappear."[13]

Pichler propagated education for women as a necessary "moral ennobling," a position which in 1807 was not universally accepted. It should also not be forgotten that such a goal was by no means realized. Education as a road to moral ennobling, while neither new nor emancipatory in the modern sense, was nevertheless pragmatic for her time and suitable for her social class; with it Pichler attempted to reconcile and combine the Christian image of woman with the Enlightened desire for intellectual development.

Only under the impact of the War of Independence did Caroline Pichler voice her concerns in the essay "Über die Bildung des weiblichen Geschlechts" (1810, On the Education of the Female Sex).[14] This work propagated a more dignified and more secure existence for women at a time when their traditional life-style, support through marriage, threatened to disintegrate. She pointed to women's "educational ability and capacity for perfection in many areas," which should be developed in order to "make woman a more self-supporting and more useful being to the state than had been the case until now" (295). For "women from the lower classes" she suggested jobs in millinery or sales-clerking, for the "educated classes" she pointed to office work and educational employment, domains in which the majority of women are employed even today. In 1807, however, such a call for employment and professional activities for middle-class women was new and socially revolutionary. Pichler ended her essay with a statement that even today is not entirely accepted in all quarters of Austria: "The well-educated woman will be—whether she marries or not—a highly valued human being—a complete person" (301). These are cautious assertions suggestive of an awakening self-confidence and a striving toward independence, cautious when compared to the emancipatory demands of a Mary Wollstonecraft or Olympe de Gouge.[15] Caroline Pichler, however, was not forced to test her emancipatory stance in a real life situation. Her relatively good fortune during the years of the Restoration allowed her to overlook other women's different circumstances, especially those of the less-privileged lower classes, while she herself was able to realize the cult of the family and the home. She had accepted for herself the view of her contemporaries that a natural difference between man and woman was predetermined, and that each sex had been destined for a different role in society. It must be stressed, however, that she came to embody the companionate and educated spouse who rejected the role of the subordinate housewife. She dismissed the notion there was any intellectual difference between men and women.

In her narrative and dramatic works Caroline Pichler depicted the world from the perspective of her own personal experiences and her social milieu. She is the most important representative from the *first* generation of literary women active in Austria. (Before her there are only a few outstanding women writers such as Katharina Regina von Greiffenberg in the seventeenth century.) Thus her voluminous production has a special meaning, not to be judged by the standards and aspirations of (contemporary) German Classicism.[16] Her first major family novel *Leonore* (1803) originated "from a greater plan, from cheerful and sad memories of my childhood, from many incidents and persons I had encountered in my life, which I modified in a way required by poeticizing and idealizing" (*Denkwürdigkeiten*, vol. 2, 405). Her fictional protagonists, however, are not quite as idealized in her memoirs as she claimed retrospectively. The novel *Leonore,* for example, concerns a rich orphan who is placed by her calculating guardian, Mr. von Wichman, with his sister, Frau von Schöndorf, in order to "marry her off" to her nephew and thereby inherit her wealth. The luxury and the mindless entertainments and preoccupations in the Schöndorf household finally lead Leonore to a clash with her childhood friend and fiancé Blum. Their conflict culminates in estrangement after an elderly gentleman, Herr von Wallner, who covets Leonore's money, wins Leonore's attention and confuses her real feelings. In his disappointment Blum, who because of financial reasons and familial considerations has been forced to postpone the marriage, departs for England. In the end, Leonore sees through Wallner's plans, ultimately refuses him, leaves the Schöndorf house, and moves to the country to live with her friend Theresa. A secondary plot involves Juliane von Schöndorf's failed attempt to supplant Leonore with scheming and flirtation; she settles for a marriage of convenience in order to obtain a title and wealth but is bitterly disappointed. Meanwhile, with the help of a friend, Leonore finds her way back to Blum and to happiness.

Leonore contains obvious parallels to *Clarissa Harlowe* (1749), the English family novel by Richardson, especially when, for example, Leonore's suitor Baron von Wallner is called "this second Lovelace,"[17] and is depicted as a sophisticated but unscrupulous calculating dandy. There is, however, a significant difference in that Leonore is not ruined like Clarissa. Rather Leonore is capable of rethinking her situation when she sees through Wallner's scheme and moves to the country; she undergoes a certain character development. Caroline Pichler was also certainly familiar with Sophie La Roche's *Geschichte des Fräulein von Sternheim* (1771, The Story of Lady Sophia von Sternheim). The ballroom scene, for example, where Leonore's lover disapproves of her fashionable clothes and thus drives her into the arms of a scheming courtier, is similar to a scene from La Roche's work; both heroines ultimately achieve rural bliss and solitude with loving husbands. Such intentional parallels and unintentional similarities[18] reveal Pichler to be well-read and attest to her familiarity with contemporary literature.

Pichler's fictional characters and the events in *Leonore* mirror her own social circle and contemporary events. The atmosphere of her parents' salon is reproduced in the fashionable gatherings in the home of the educated Frau von Valsin, and Pichler's uneasy fascination with revolutionary France is expressed through her fictional character Juliane von Schöndorf as she writes in a letter to her French confidante:

> Why could I not see the light in your fatherland? Then if I could have witnessed the great battle of fighting forces, which would decide the welfare of humanity for the next centuries, then I might have, would have taken part and

> would have played a role in it like the exalted goddesses of
> the Seine, like Tallien, Louvet, and Staël, or else I would
> have perished in the storm. (I, 38)

We are not dealing with an autobiographical account of particular events in Caroline Pichler's life, but rather with typical situations, problems, and behaviors that were characteristic of the educated middle class. For this reason her novels as well as her memoirs of the cultural life in "Old Vienna" exhibit a certain documentary character in fictional form: they reflect feelings, memories, opinions, and aspirations of Pichler's contemporaries, and for the first time in Austrian literature also of women. Central problems involve the emotional and social relationships of man and woman, played out in many variations from the romantic love of Blum and Leonore, to the marriage of convenience of Juliane and the count and the affair of Mrs. von Valsin and Wallner. Pichler's social novels portray the real difficulties that developed in the transition from a system of marriage of convenience to one of bourgeois partnerships grounded in romantic love as well as the difficulty which in turn evolved from this new concept of marriage and relationships between the sexes. In these novels misunderstandings, fears, or harmonic gratifications in the relationships between men and women are closely linked to social realities (poverty, need, wealth, ties to parents, consideration for relatives) and to the character traits of individual human beings (envy, jealousy, hate, good nature, good faith, etc.). In Pichler's fictional world, conflicts between men, or likewise between women, are rarely portrayed, except where such conflicts arise from rivalries or jealousies stemming from male-female relationships. In contrast to these conflicting opposite-sex relationships Pichler depicted true and lasting same-sex friendships (Blum and Seltig, Wallner and Count Feldern, Leonore and Therese), which seem to provide a strong framework for this society. In addition, Pichler's depiction of women's friendships, a late and little observed phenomenon during Germany's great "friendship period" (ca. 1750-1850), is noteworthy.[19] As was the case in Caroline Pichler's own correspondence with Therese Huber,[20] with Caroline von Wolzogen,[21] and with Dorothea Schlegel,[22] like-minded human and literary interests lay at the heart of these relationships.

Most of Pichler's novels are narrated through the correspondence of friends. The letter, popular and effective as a narrative form in German literature since La Roche's *Geschichte des Fräuleins von Sternheim* (1771,

The Story of Lady Sophia von Sternheim) and Goethe's *Werther* (1774, *The Sorrows of Young Werther*), allows the individual to discuss affectionately and subjectively complex feelings, relationships with others, and personal experiences. Such a form also allows for the representation of experiences from different points of view. On the one hand, this explains the lack of a definable plot in Pichler's novels (a feature often pointed out by contemporary critics), and, on the other hand, the repetition of an event from several subjective perspectives creates a detailed, psychologically empathetic picture that underscores the importance of the individual emotional world and should not be dismissed lightly as outmoded sentimentality of the eighteenth century. This emotional world, with its complications and entanglements of human bonds and relationships with the opposite sex, was an important area of everyday life for the middle class, a politically weak, yet economically and socially increasingly important class, and its emancipation. The individual's conscious experience of his or her emotional world was not a flight from reality, but rather the actual everyday experience of this class, and especially of its women.

This is not to say, however, that *Leonore* is merely a "women's novel" in which a woman exclusively addresses female concerns for a female audience. In this family novel of the middle class Pichler describes all characters, male and female, with equal care and psychological attention to detail. Leonore is a heroine, and, as in other novels since Gellert's *Die Schwedische Gräfin* (The Swedish Countess), female protagonists assume a central role. The letters written by Pichler's male characters such as Blum or Wallner illustrate that the author is capable of moving beyond a female perspective and point of view; she is able to depict her characters and their world not in strictly female terms, but in general human ones with attention to morality—Pichler was a devout Catholic. Her male figures, such as Blum, Wallner, and Count von der Wahl are articulate and independent men. Her female figures are likewise individuals in traditional female roles, while the roughly contemporary heroines like Schlegel's Lucinde or Goethe's Ottilie are still largely conceived from male perspectives and for the needs of the male protagonist.[23]

Pichler's later novels and historical dramas, which have been interpreted too narrowly as an expression of her Austrian patriotism,[24] contain many fine examples of successful psychological depictions of typical sentimental and emotional individuals from the middle class. Stimulated by Friedrich Schlegel's lectures in 1812 during the War for Austrian Independence, Pichler quite naturally turned to historical subjects. Her drama, *Ferdinand der Zweyte König von Ungarn und Böhmen* (Ferdinand the Second King of Hungary and Bohemia) was initially censored, and the Burgtheater's production was canceled although Pichler had an audience with Metternich. Not until 1816 was the drama finally performed by a lay theater group in Graz after Hormayr persuaded Pichler to change the title to the very unpolitical "Wankelmuth und Vertraun" (Wavering and Trust); it was also read in Pichler's salon with audience participation. In this drama Caroline Pichler sought to portray "inner action, what happens in the minds of people" and thereby hoped to "replace the lack of external action, events, and spectacles."[25] Her concept of history was a non-tragical, sentimental one; she understood history as a shift between human relationships and conflicts. These conflicts became the center of her dramas, rather than actual political or historical events; in any case, after 1815 censorship would not have allowed plays with political implications to be performed. But she did achieve success with several of her plays; for example, her benefit performance of *Heinrich von Hohenstauffen, König der Deutschen* (Heinrich von Hohenstauffen, King of the Germans) was performed twenty-seven times at the Hofburgtheater in 1813.

These accomplishments, along with a generally positive critical reception, allowed Caroline to step into the background in her memoirs when she almost apologized for her dramatic works, saying: "I have now been convinced by the often quoted saying that women should not venture out onto the stage" (*Denkwürdigkeiten,* I, 428). It appears that during the eventful period from 1812 to 1815, Caroline Pichler could be creative in dramatic works when her dramas were no longer performed and when, during the restrictive Restoration period, her interest in writing drama waned. In spite of her earlier dramatic successes she succumbed to the contemporary opinion that women are not suited for this "male" genre.[26] She wrote in her memoirs that "the heroic Tragedy is something whose adaptation goes beyond the horizon of womanly powers" (*Denkwürdigkeiten,* I, 400). Caroline Pichler's later comment is, however, much more to the point and relatively free from contemporary prejudice:

> My entire philosophy of life was not suited for the dramatic and visual, which presents an important event with all its motives and consequences in quick succession. I much preferred to follow, with observant eyes and good

> measure, the course of feelings and the minute per-
> mutations in the human mind. For this the novel is the
> most suitable form, especially the epistolary novel. (*Denk-*
> *würdigkeiten,* I, 398)

Not surprisingly, Pichler's greater accomplishments and more enduring
works lie in the area of narrative prose. Another famous novel is the
historical work *Agathokles* (1808), which was written under the influence
of Wieland's style and takes place in the last year of Diocletian's rule. It
pleased even Goethe, but he never got around "to saying a kind word
about Caroline Pichler and her sisters in Apollo."[27] L. L. Haschka's comment in a letter to his friend Reinhold in Jena appropriately characterizes
the importance of this novel: "Now I must tell you about a book; it's only
a novel and was written only by a woman, but a man of my age and a
philosopher of your stature will not be ashamed to have read it and would
even boast about it. It is *Agathokles.*"[28] Although *Agathokles* was "only" a
novel written by a woman, the in-depth psychological portrayal of the
characters and the didactic-philosophic discussions in the novel earned
praise.

Even more important and more original is Pichler's novel *Frauenwürde*
(1818, The Dignity of Woman), in which she deals with different female—as well as male—characters set against the background of the Austrian War for Independence. Here she portrays contemporary society in
the same manner as in her last non-historical novel, *Die Nebenbuhler*
(1821, The Rivals). The plot of *Frauenwürde* revolves around a couple and
their friends: Rosalie von Sarewski, a famous author and talented painter,
begins a relationship with Baron von Fahrnau, from which she cannot
escape. When Fahrnau believes his wife Leonore loves her childhood
friend, Julius von Tegenbach, he joins the war in hopes of being killed;
Julius, however, is the one to be killed. Fahrnau and Leonore resolve their
differences, and Rosalie commits suicide. *Frauenwürde*'s plot is reminiscent
of Goethe's *Wahlverwandtschaften* (*Elective Affinities*), but Pichler consciously pursues different solutions to the entanglement.

The four main characters are especially of interest. Baron von Fahrnau
and Julius von Tegenbach represent two major political views of the
period, royalism and liberalism, which were much discussed during the
time the novel takes place (1810-1814) (*Denkwürdigkeiten,* II, 109). These
socio-political problems remain in the background, however; more impor-

tant are the human and familial concerns. Rosalie, who is portrayed as an elegant, educated, and sophisticated woman, triggers the emotional and human confusion and aberrations. She is conscious of being different in her feelings and actions when she calls herself "an eternally shunned foreigner because of her feelings and desires,"[29] and observes "the eternally growing germ of dissatisfaction resides in a divided heart" (Ibid., 21). On the other hand, Leonore von Fahrnau is the educated wife neglected by her husband; only after many bitter turns does a reconciliation occur.

As a caption for this novel Caroline Pichler chose the second verse from Schiller's *Braut von Messina* (*The Bride of Messina*): "Life is not the greatest good, but guilt is the greatest of evils." The title of the novel can be traced also to Schiller and his poem identically titled "Frauenwürde" (1796), whose view of woman amused the Schlegel circle in Jena and was ridiculed in A. W. Schlegel's (then still unpublished) parody.[30] Caroline Pichler consciously connects with Schiller's concept of dignity; according to Schiller, woman finds her dignity only in the spiritual-intellectual fulfillment through the roles of wife and mother. This is the moral-didactic message in her novel *Frauenwürde,* a conservative message even in her day. Since the difficulties and problems in the attainment of this goal are thematized in a subjective epistolary form, the importance of this novel lies in its psychological, empathetic portrayal and problematizing of the characters. The (Austrian) Restoration is evident in this message; Austrian Biedermeier speaks through the personal-familial problematic of the characters.

Caroline Pichler was the most famous and successful representative of the first generation of female authors in Austria. Her world and the way she perceived it manifested themselves in her works while she remained conscious of the restrictions placed upon her by society. With her the realm of women entered literature, albeit as *Frauendichtung,* women's literature, and was only gradually accepted, not as high art, but as (trivial) entertainment and (useful) teaching for female readers. Nevertheless, even a passing glance at her numerous works shows she did not merely produce a gender-specific genre of literature, but recreated the mood, feelings, and emotions of her epoch. Caroline Pichler was a major representative of the early Biedermeier, of a sociable literary culture much influenced by this sophisticated woman and emotionally sensitive author.

Notes

1. *Neue allgemeine deutsche Bibliothek* 41 (Berlin, 1804), p. 96.
2. The edition was published "Im Verlage von A. Pichlers sel. Witwe in Wien." Caroline Pichler's brother-in-law, Anton Andreas Pichler, was the owner of the publishing house managed by the widow Elisabeth Pichler after his death in 1825. Her first set of "complete works" was published by Anton Strauß in Vienna in 1813-1817 and consisted of twenty volumes. A third complete set of her works, consisting of sixty volumes in the miniature 16* format, also was published by Pichler in Vienna between 1828 and 1845.
3. I am quoting from the edition by Emil Karl Blümml in *Denkwürdigkeiten aus Alt-Österreich,* vols. 5 and 6 (Munich, 1914). Blümml included almost all of the edited passages from the first edition in 1844 and a detailed biographical commentary.
4. *Gesamtausgabe 1828-1845,* vol. 49, p. 48.
5. See Barbara Becker-Cantarino, "Priesterin und Lichtbringerin. Zum Frauenbild der Frühromantik," *Die Frau als Heldin und Autorin. Neue kritische Ansätze zur deutschen Literatur,* ed. Wolfgang Paulsen (Bern: Francke, 1979), pp. 111-124.
6. See Barbara Becker-Cantarino, "Joseph von Sonnenfels and the Development of Secular Education in Eighteenth-Century Austria," *Studies on Voltaire and the Eighteenth Century,* 163 (1977), pp. 29-47.
7. German women writers of her generation (e.g., Therese Huber) emphasized their roles as mothers and housewives with, which their writing would not interfere, or they gave up writing and publishing altogether, as did most women aligned with German Romanticists (e.g., Dorothea Schlegel or Sophie Mereau).
8. About the Greiner salon: Roswitha Strommer, "Wiener literarische Salons zur Zeit Joseph Haydns," *Joseph Haydn und die Literatur seiner Zeit,* ed. Herbert Zeman (Eisenstadt, 1976), pp. 97-122.
9. *Gesamtausgabe (1820-1844),* vol. 15, p. 5.
10. For "Mutterkult" and "Lob des Hauses" see Friedrich Sengle, *Biedermeierzeit* (Stuttgart: Metzler, 1971), vol. 1, pp. 59-63.
11. No Pichler biography exists; Goedeke and Wurzbach are incomplete. For an alphabetical list of works see Blümml, *Denkwürdigkeiten aus Alt-Österreich,* vol. 2, pp. 720-730.

12. See the excellent historical biography by Hilde Spiel, *Fanny Arnstein oder die Emanzipation 1758-1818* (Vienna, 1962).

13. "Über die Corinne der Frau von Staël" (1807), *Gesamtausgabe* (1813-1817), vol. 13, pp. 172-173.

14. *Gesamtausgabe* (1813-1817), vol. 1, pp. 292-302.

15. Regarding the increased scholarship about emancipation in the late eighteenth century, refer to the historically based essay by Jane Abray, "Feminism in the French Revolution," *American Historical Review* 80 (1975), 43-62.

16. Lesli Bodi comments about such criteria for Austrian literature during the Enlightenment, *Tauwetter in Wien. Zur Prosa der österreichischen Aufklärung 1781-1795* (Frankfurt: S. Fischer, 1977).

17. *Gesamtausgabe,* 1820-1844, vol. 11, p. 42.

18. Concerning parallels with Rousseau, Goethe, Schiller, and others: Lena Jansen, *Karoline Pichlers Schaffen und Weltanschauung im Rahmen ihrer Zeit* (Graz, 1936). Deutsche Quellen und Studien 13, pp. 101-107.

19. See *Frauenfreundschaft—Männerfreundschaft.Literarische Diskurse im 18. Jahrhundert,* Wolfram Mauser and Barbara Becker-Cantarino, eds. (Tübingen: Niemeyer, 1991).

20. Carl Glossy, "Briefe von Caroline Pichler an Therese Huber," *Jahrbuch der Grillparzer Gesellschaft* 3 (1893), 269-365, contains eighteen letters from 1818 to 1828; Ludwig Geiger, "Briefe von Therese Huber an Caroline Pichler," *Jahrbuch der Grillparzer Gesellschaft* 17 (1907), pp. 190-201, contains the reciprocal nineteen letters. Therese Huber, who lived in Stuttgart and who edited the respected journal *Morgenblatt für gebildete Stände* until 1823, did not personally know Caroline Pichler.

21. Caroline von Wolzogen visited Vienna in 1813 and a correspondence ensued from her relationship with Caroline Pichler; only two letters from 1834 and 1840 can be found in *Literarischer Nachlaß der Frau Caroline von Wolzogen* (Leipzig, 1867), vol. 2, pp. 396-399.

22. After a long friendship in Vienna (1808-1829) a correspondence arose between Dorothea Schlegel and Pichler when Dorothea left Vienna after Friedrich Schlegel's death in January 1829.

23. Regarding *Lucinde,* see Barbara Becker-Cantarino, "Schlegel's *Lucinde,*" *Colloquia Germanica* (1976-1977), 128-129. About the

male perspective, see Hannelore Schlaffer, "Frauen als Einlösung der romantischen Kunsttheorie," *Jahrbuch der deutschen Schiller Gesellschaft* 21 (1977), pp. 276-296.

24. André Robert characterized Pichler's ballads and dramas in this manner: *L'idée nationale autrichienne et les guerres de Napoléon. L'apostolat du Baron de Hormayr et le salon de Caroline Pichler* (Paris, 1933).

25. "Vorrede," *Neue dramatische Dichtungen* (Leipzig: Aug. Liebeskind, 1818), p. 22.

26. See "Über die Diotima," *Friedrich Schlegels sämtliche Werke* (Vienna, 1822), vol. 1, pp. 126-127.

27. August Sauer, *Goethe und Österreich* (Vienna, 1902-1904), vol. 2, pp. 272, 389-395.

28. Robert Keil, *Wiener Freunde 1784-1808* (Vienna: Kurzböck, 1883), p. 98, letter of 12 November 1808.

29. *Gesamtausgabe 1820-1844,* vol. 11, p. 22.

30. See Friedrich Schlegel, *Dichtungen,* ed. Hans Eichner. Kritische Friedrich Schlegel-Ausgabe, vol. 5 (Paderborn: Schöningh, 1962), p. xxviii.

Bibliography

I. Works by Caroline Pichler in German

Gleichnisse. Vienna: A. Pichler, 1800.

Idyllen. Vienna: A. Pichler, 1803.

Leonore. Gemählde aus der großen Welt. Vienna: A. Pichler, 1804.

Agathokles. Briefroman aus der Antike. Vienna: A. Pichler, 1808.

Die Grafen von Hohenberg. Vienna: A. Pichler, 1811.

Biblische Idyllen. Vienna: A. Pichler, 1812.

Olivier. Vienna: A. Pichler, 1812.

Dramatische Dichtungen. Vienna: A. Strauss, 1815: *Heinrich von Hohen-stauffen; König der Deutschen,* Trauerspiel in fünf Aufzügen; *Wiedersehen,* Schauspiel in zwey Aufzügen; *Mathilde,* Tragische Oper in drey Aufzügen.

Ferdinand der Zweyte König von Ungarn und Böhmen. Historisches Schauspiel in fünf Aufzügen. Leipzig: G. Fleischer, 1816.

Frauenwürde. Leipzig: A. Liebeskind, 1818.

Die Nebenbuhler. Vienna: A. Pichler, 1821.

Kleine Erzählungen. Vienna: A. Pichler, 1822-1828. 10 vols.

Gedichte. Vienna: A. Pichler, 1822.

Die Belagerung Wiens. Vienna: A. Pichler, 1824.

Die Schweden in Prag. Vienna: A. Pichler, 1827.

Die Wiedereroberung von Ofen. Vienna: A. Pichler, 1829.

Friedrich der Streitbare. Vienna: A. Pichler, 1831.

Henriette von England. Gemahlin des Herzogs von Orleans. Vienna: A. Pichler, 1832.

Elisabeth von Guttenstein; eine Familiengeschichte aus der Zeit des österreichischen Erbfolgekrieges. Vienna: A. Pichler, 1835.

Zerstreute Blätter aus meinem Schreibtische. Vienna: A. Pichler, 1836.

Zeitbilder. Vienna: A. Pichler, 1839-1841.

Denkwürdigkeiten aus meinem Leben 1769-1843. Vienna: A. Pichler, 1844.

II. Works in English Translation

The Artist Lovers; Quentin Matsys and Johannes Schoreel. Two Romances. London: E. Lumley, 1845.

"The Swedes in Prague, or the Signal Rocket. A Historical Romance." In: J.D. Haas, *Gleanings from Germany,* 1839.

Waldstein; or, the Swedes in Prague. Translated from the German by J.D. Rosenthal. London, 1828.

"The Wife Hunter." Translated from the German. In: *Omnibus of Modern Romance,* 1844.

III. Major Studies in German

Becker-Cantarino, Barbara. "Caroline Pichler und die 'Frauendichtung,'" *Modern Austrian Literature,* 12 (1979), 1-23.

Bittrich, B. "Österreichische Züge am Beispiel der Caroline Pichler," *Literatur aus Österreich—Österreichische Literatur* (1981), 167-89.

Glossy, Carl. "Briefe von Caroline Pichler an Therese Huber," *Jahrbuch der Grillparzer-Gesellschaft,* 3 (1893), pp. 269-365.

Jansen, Lena. *Karoline Pichlers Schaffen und Weltanschauung im Rahmen ihrer Zeit.* Deutsche Quellen und Studien 13. Graz 1936.

Neunteufel-Metzler, A. *Karoline Pichler und die Geschichte ihrer Zeit* Dissertation, Vienna, 1949.

Prohaska, Gertrud. *Der literarische Salon der Caroline Pichler.* Dissertation, Vienna, 1946.

Strommer, Roswitha. "Wiener literarische Salons zur Zeit Joseph Haydns." *Joseph Haydn und die Literatur seiner Zeit.* Ed. Herbert Zeman. Eisenstadt, 1976.

Ferdinand Raimund

Dorothy James

The Carpenter's Song

Some say that and some say this,
They argue high and low,
What happiness and fortune is
They simply do not know.
The very poorest man to me
May be too rich for you
But Fate's the carpenter, you see,
Who planes and smooths the two.

With might and main young people try
To find true happiness,
But as the years go flying by,
They settle for much less.
My wife gets mad, it's such a pain,
But I won't pick a fight,
I knock the shavings from my plane
And think, it serves me right.

When Death politely pays his call,
"Come, little brother, come,"
I simply won't turn round at all,
Pretend I'm deaf and dumb.
"Come on, dear Valentin," he'll say,
"Don't make a fuss! Oh my!"
And I'll just put my plane away
And tell the world Good bye.[1]

Ferdinand Raimund sang the song of Valentin the carpenter at the première of his last play, *Der Verschwender* (The Spendthrift) at the Josefstadt Theater in Vienna on 20 February 1834. The play was an immediate and enormous success. The performance lasted for four hours before a house filled to overflowing. Thunderous applause and eight curtain calls at the end of the play testified to the warmth of feeling flowing from the audience to Raimund/Valentin, the heart and soul of the play. The carpenter's song came into being that night as a true folk song, from the pen of the dramatist-poet Raimund, through the voice of the actor-dramatist Raimund, and through the instant acceptance by the audience as a song of its own.

Raimund's Viennese contemporary, Franz Grillparzer, trying to capture the essence of Raimund's particular genius as a dramatist, wrote in 1837 the often quoted words: "It does not detract from Raimund's great talent to say that the public contributed as much to his writing as he did himself. His half unconscious gift was rooted in the spirit of the masses."[2] This is an insider's comment, and it has been echoed in various ways by many writers since then. The present-day outsider to Vienna may be skeptical about what sounds like a mystical explanation of eight plays, popular in their day, still funny and moving in parts, belonging to that singular genre, the Viennese musical-magical play. It is for this outsider that I have begun my discussion of Raimund with the tangible birth of the folk song, the carpenter's song, on 20 February 1834, real yet hardly explicable outside the magic of the folk theater. In Raimund's own language, the song is unabashedly sentimental, the words simple, the thought hardly original, even banal. Yet it has survived the century and a half since Raimund first sang it himself, and it has great dramatic and lyrical force in the Viennese theater where it can still stop the show. It is hard to translate the dialect verse into English and even harder to translate the atmosphere in which Ferdinand Raimund reached the heart of his audience when he stood on the stage of the local theater in the role of the loyal and good-natured carpenter Valentin and sang of the fate of the carpenter who smooths and planes away the inequities of life.

Close to a century later another Viennese poet tried to describe Raimund and took his description to a higher degree of abstraction than Grillparzer had done: Hugo von Hofmannsthal saw in Raimund a perfect unity of life and work, work and environment, a kind of vegetative growth. "From time to time," he wrote in 1920, "individuals emerge in whom a social whole blossoms forth, fatefully and, one might say, effortlessly" (473). This attractive but imprecise notion has colored some of the important criticism of Raimund in our century. Otto Rommel, the greatest historian and critic of the Viennese Popular Theater, argues in 1952 that one cannot be just to Raimund's work unless one seeks to grasp it as a unified whole, appreciating the attempts at serious drama along with the comedy (911f). By contrast, the German critic, Friedrich Sengle, writing in 1981 in his monumental work on the Biedermeier period, sees quite clearly that the concept of Raimund's work as springing full-blown from a naive folk-genius, actually stands in the way of a fair judgment of the individual plays, some of which are simply better than others. Sengle suggests that Grillparzer, when he wrote in Raimund's own time about the "mass-spirit," was more probably thinking in a quite concrete way of the audience of the popular theater than of the legendary Austrian folk-spirit invoked by twentieth century neo-romanticists (1-2).

Critics of recent decades have tended to divide those seeking explanations for Raimund's work in his psyche from those, more numerous, seeking connections with his own and his contemporaries' social and political attitudes. It does not seem to me that concentrating attention upon any one of the formative forces at work in his drama can really do justice to Ferdinand Raimund. He was a theatrical phenomenon in a *popular* theater as well as a talented and temperamental man of artistic, personal, and social ambition. I would not, however, by any means argue for one all-inclusive judgment of his total life's work. In the short span of this essay I shall look at the life, works, and environment of Raimund in complicated conjunction, but not as a mystical or "vegetative" whole.[3] We shall follow the progression of Raimund's life in Vienna, commenting on the genesis and development of individual works, and making some judgments of them, until we come back in the end full circle to the carpenter's song where we began.

On that triumphant first night of *Der Verschwender*, standing on the Josefstadt stage in the cheerful guise of Valentin, receiving the adulation of his audience, of his own people, was the man, Ferdinand Raimund, forty-three years old, caught in a mesh of inner paradoxes and ambiguities, two and a half years away from his own unkind death in a botched and painful suicide. How are we to understand the unique, idiosyncratic yet enormously popular work of this melancholy and complicated man, playing out his life's drama in a theater of comedy for "simple folk"?

438   Dorothy James

Setting the Scene (1790-1823)

Herr Raimund plays everything.

Ferdinand Raimund, born in 1790, grew up in the early years of the reign of Emperor Franz. These were years of privation for the Viennese people, years when Franz was forced to relinquish the title of Holy Roman Emperor and the capital of his shrinking empire was twice invaded and occupied by Napoleon and the French army. They were years of rising prices and falling money values, culminating in the state bankruptcy of 1811—hard times for many citizens, not least small tradesmen.

Jakob Raimann, father of Ferdinand, was a master turner whose workshop was in the main street of Mariahilf, one of the urban districts surrounding the inner city outside the city walls. He lived and died in the outer city. His son, orphaned in 1804, worked his way up from poverty to die a much richer and more successful man than his father, but he too made his career in the outer, not the inner, city. Heinrich Anschütz, an actor of the Burgtheater inside the city walls, wrote of Raimund after his death: "And this great spirit had the small weakness to complain that he could not be a court actor, and that his dramas were excluded from the Burgtheater. Yet how great was his stature and how much more effective he was as Raimund."[4] As Raimund, he was completely identified with the "Vorstadttheater," the outer city theaters where popular comedy, banished from the court theater and the city center, had found its new home and new life. In the last decades of the eighteenth century small theaters had begun to appear in every district outside the walls; little groups of actors playing on makeshift stages with inadequate properties and costumes performed all the plays in the repertoire of the Burgtheater as well as their own popular comedies. By the turn of the century the Leopoldstadt, Josefstadt, and Wieden theaters had established their superiority, and the smaller companies gradually died out; but by that time the habit of theater going was firmly entrenched in all classes of the population. It is often said that Raimund's dream of a theatrical career began in the Burgtheater, where as a boy he worked as a confectioner's apprentice selling refreshments, and this may be so. But it was surely among the apprentices and shopkeepers, the serving maids, and street vendors who constituted the regular audience of the outer city theaters that he must first have seen the practical possibilities of entering the acting profession.

He spent the years 1808 to 1814 touring with companies in the provinces. His contribution to the Kunz company with whom he toured the region of Raab and Odenburg is summed up in one of the few extant reviews of that period: "Herr Raimund plays everything."[5] These undoubtedly grueling years earned him his first important contract. He was engaged to play villains and secondary comic roles at the flourishing Josefstadt theater. In 1815 Josef Alois Gleich created a leading comic role, the fiddler Adam Kratzerl, for Raimund himself. Two more plays starring Raimund/Kratzerl followed in quick succession, and Raimund's name as a local Viennese comedian was made.

In 1817, at the age of twenty-seven, Raimund was engaged by the Leopoldstadt theater to play major comic roles. He went to live near the theater and was then to spend most of his life in the district of Leopoldstadt. The theater stood on the Jägerzeile, the main street out of the city over the Ferdinandsbrücke to the Prater, the large amusement park opened to the public by Joseph II in 1766 and still drawing all sections of the Viennese population, from the Emperor and his court driving in their carriages along the main promenade to the masses of people jostling their way through the stalls and games booths, the puppet theaters and beer houses.

The Leopoldstadt theater was smaller than its two main rivals in the outer city, but it was very popular, not least as the home stage of the famous character Kasperl, created by Johann Laroche (1745-1806). The building had changed very little since its opening in 1781, and even then it had not been noted for its comfort. It remained poorly lit, and it must still have smelled strongly of beer and sausages sold throughout the performances. Thus as late as the 1820s the theater retained much of the atmosphere of the local stages of the previous century. This endeared it to its audiences who still went to Kasperl's theater for an evening of uproarious entertainment. In Raimund's early years with the company there were three resident playwrights, Adolf Bäuerle (1786-1859), Karl Meisl (1775-1853), and Josef Alois Gleich (1772-1841). Successful writers for the popular stage since the turn of the century, they understood and worked with the potentialities and limitations of their actors, of their stage and its machinery, and above all of their audience.

At the height of popularity at this time were the musical-magical burlesques or parodies, shifting in scene between Vienna and fairyland. Such plays were exhibition pieces for leading actors who excelled in quick-change roles, sometimes four or five in one play. Raimund's hard-earned versatility as an actor stood him in good stead. The playwrights for the theater produced large numbers of plays of a similar type,[6] and Raimund had become well accustomed to eking out the inspiration of his script writers with his own interpolations. Urged by friends and admirers to write his own plays, he hesitated for some time to do so. He was very sensitive to criticism, and always inclined to attribute adverse comments on his acting to the machinations of jealous rivals. Costenoble, an actor in the Burgtheater, a life-long admirer of Raimund's art, tells of his reaction to the idea of writing his own plays: "'My God,' was Raimund's melancholy cry, 'Haven't I got enough enemies and hissers in the parterre? Do you want me to write away the few friends that I still have?'"[7] In the small theater world of Vienna there were undoubtedly rivalries and intrigues, but Raimund, always suspicious of his fellow men, often saw insults where none were intended.

Before he wrote his first play in 1823, he had already set his foot on a road that was to lead him away from the comfortable bourgeois family existence to which he aspired. In 1819 he fell in love with Antonie Wagner, second eldest daughter in the very well-placed family of Ignaz and Therese Wagner. Ignaz Wagner had renovated and rebuilt two floors of his large house on the Taborstraße as one of the most popular coffeehouses in Leopoldstadt. His wife was the daughter of a well-to-do wine merchant, and she would not accept the young actor as a desirable suitor for her daughter. Not only was he poor, but he had already made a name for himself in Vienna by landing in jail for three days after physically abusing a young actress whom he regarded as unfaithful to him. Such behavior matched the shiftless reputation that solid citizens associated with actors, and the Wagners refused the couple permission to marry. Raimund consoled himself with the actress daughter of his fellow playwright, Alois Gleich. Luise Gleich was young and beautiful but had already a somewhat shady reputation. When she told Raimund he was the father of the child she was expecting, he was in no position to deny it, and he agreed to marry her. The episode turned into a public scandal when he failed to turn up at the church for the wedding. At his next appearance in the theater he was booed and hissed by the audience. Thus coerced in public as well as in private, he married Luise some days later on 8 April 1820. The daughter, born in October, died within weeks, and the marriage did not last much more than a year. In January 1822 the couple divorced, but under the law of Roman Catholic Austria, Raimund could not marry again.

This youthful melodrama prevented Raimund from marrying Antonie

Wagner but proved to be not much more than an interlude in their relationship. On 10 April 1821 the couple solemnly vowed faithfulness to
each other before the statue of the Virgin Mary in Neustift and informed
Antonie's parents of their decision. It was not until 1827, however, that
the Wagners recognized their union. The jealousies and mutual suspicions,
the constant quarrels and ecstatic reconciliations that marked their relationship are revealed in the letters of Raimund to Antonie (1819-1830).
The sad drama of his life was already unfolding when his first comedy was
an instant success in 1823.

Quecksilber and Florian: Local Clowns (1823-1824)
Raimund has won his laurels . . . as a local poet.

In 1823 Meisl was writing a play based on a fairy tale from Wieland's
Dschinnistan, and Raimund became so impatient with his repeated delays
that he wrote the play himself. Audience and critics welcomed his first
play, *Der Barometermacher auf der Zauberinsel* (The Barometer Maker on
the Enchanted Island) and greeted his "debut as a local poet"[8] with enthusiasm and good will. When his second play *Der Diamant des Geisterkönigs* (The Diamond of the Spirit King) was performed a year later in
1824, a critic wrote: "For the second time Raimund has won his laurels
as a local poet. He knew how to present a picture so that from beginning
to end the audience was completely breathless with laughter."[9] Raimund
knew well how to write a play with all the elements of a box-office success in the Leopoldstadt theater—cheerful songs and dances, spectacular
use of stage machinery, comic characters speaking in local dialect and
alluding constantly to Vienna and its environs in a dialogue of puns, jokes
and all manner of witticism.

The decade following the Congress of Vienna in 1815 was one in which
the Viennese people were glad to see their city rise again from the ig-
nominy of defeat. They had seen the most powerful men in Europe assemble within their walls and for months had been witness to the lavish
social life of the Congress. Vienna seemed to them to be the capital of
Europe, and while popular dramatists can certainly be said to have performed useful propaganda for the ruling class when they introduced songs
in praise of Vienna and Austria into their plays, they can equally well be
said to have reflected the mood of the theater-going populace. The characters of the magical-musicals, often transplanted or exiled to various kinds

of fairyland, sang to great applause their songs of homesickness for the best country in the world: "You're safest of all on Austrian land," "In Austria your good luck will never run out," or "Everyone knows Vienna's the best!"—these are all fragments of Raimund's early songs. He played very successfully to the prevailing mood of self-congratulation, filling his dialogue and his stage sets with local color.

Popular dramatists did not use local color in their plays in order to present a realistic picture of their society. Rather it was their best source of comic effect. They parodied high drama or myth or fairy tale by bringing it down to the local level. Fairy-tale action was given a Viennese setting, supernatural beings were endowed with human characteristics, and royalty and the nobility with middle-class habits. Stage scenery was often used to strengthen the local impression; familiar pieces of the Viennese scene were set up on stage, such as the Chinese summer house in *Der Barometermacher auf der Zauberinsel.* Various forms of transportation familiar to the Viennese, from post-coaches to balloons, appeared on the scene complete with wings and fairy coachmen speaking Viennese who whisked characters through the air from one magical set to another. Raimund called his first play "a parody of the fairy tale, Tutu." He applied to the fairy tale the stock process of "Verwienerung"—translated literally, "Viennafication." The inhabitants of the Magic Island as well as the strangers from Vienna speak dialect throughout and allude frequently to Viennese life and customs.

In Raimund's time the stock comic character of the popular theater was essentially still a joker, something of a wag and something of a buffoon. He had replaced the stock clown, who had always appeared in his own costume—Hanswurst/Stranitzky (1676-1726) in the Salzburg peasant's costume with a heart on his jerkin, or later Kasperl/Laroche in his baggy trousers, floppy hat, and false pointed beard. Now favorite leading actors appeared in a variety of roles often with comic sounding names which signified their trade and sometimes their temperament, thus Quecksilber (Mercury), the Barometer Maker. They retained for comic effect many of the characteristics handed down by their predecessors as far back as Hanswurst—preoccupation with food, for example, shows of bravado, exhibitions of cowardice, outbursts of weeping, and childish behavior of all kinds. Many stock verbal witticisms were also retained: the nonsense speech, the catch phrase, repetition of single words, and deliberate misunderstanding. One basic rule of characterization remained unchanged from Hanswurst to the local parodies and magical extravaganzas of the post-Congress period: comic characters spoke in Viennese dialect prose and were drawn from the lower orders of society while serious characters used a more elevated High German and often poetic language. Local parody in Raimund's day did not violate this rule. It had changed the balance of the traditional pattern in that most of its characters were local and comic, but in endowing noble or allegorical characters with lower-class characteristics, it simply transferred them to the sphere of the local comic characters. Any noble characters who were *not* localized were also not funny, nor were local characters serious.

Raimund's first two plays do not transgress these traditional boundaries. In his second play, *Der Diamant des Geisterkönigs*, he returns indeed to the traditional pattern as old as Hanswurst himself, whereby the actions of the serious characters are paralleled and parodied by those of the comic ones. Florian Waschblau, the servant, is the traditional comic counterpart to his serious young master Eduard. They engage in a series of unlikely adventures; transported by balloon to the Land of Truth, they succeed in their search for a girl who has never told a lie and fly back with her to the cloud palace of Longimanus. All ends well, and audience and critics are delighted with their new "local poet," convinced he understands them well and knows how to please them.

Before he wrote his first two successful plays and for many years afterwards, Raimund was considerably less than convinced that his audience understood him. In October 1822, the year after his unfortunate marriage and divorce and his renewed plighting of his troth to Antonie, he pleaded with her in one of his many letters to trust him and abandon her jealous suspicions:

> A small part of the public hates me because the other part loves me. This public only ever wants me to be unhappy in my life as a private citizen because it has no understanding of my way of thinking, of my heart, and considers me to be a quite ordinary actor from the moral point of view. This has already caused me many miserable hours, yet it doesn't surprise me, it has already once robbed me of the happiness of my life. This public might once again look on with pleasure as a man who sacrifices himself completely to its pleasure is morally destroyed. (W, 385)

He longed for Antonie to believe him, to take him seriously, to see him, as he constantly repeats in his letters, as a respectable, honest, and morally upright man. In a similar way he longed for his audience not to regard him as an ordinary actor from the moral point of view. Their favorite and beloved comedian, he desperately wanted them to take him seriously. In the July before he began writing his own dramas, he played in the summer theater of Baden, outside Vienna, to no less an audience than the Emperor and Empress themselves; he describes with tongue in cheek his success in his comic role in a play by Karl Meisl, writing in a letter to Toni:

> I cannot produce a better mood from Baden than the one I arrived in. I came here thinking sad thoughts about our fate, and I shall return in the same state, despite the fact that I was greatly applauded in the *Ghost*, and the Emperor and Empress were extraordinarily delighted. You know that I am not so simple as to be vain about such things, but the very biased, prejudiced public rates this sort of thing highly, and there were many people in the theater who were looking at the face and reactions of the Emperor all the time and not at the play. I may therefore strew flowers of thanks before the Good Fortune who perhaps made my victory over the serious countenance of His Majesty easier by sending him a good digestion. On such things hang the fortunes of an artist.

And he goes on to describe "the ineffable sadness of his soul" (W, 393).

In the following months this ineffably sad man wrote and played himself into high favor with his own audience in the Leopoldstadt theater as the local clown figure, Quecksilber, a year later with the even more popular Florian. His financial situation improved. He was able to buy a horse and carriage, and later to take a manservant. He could make those excursions into the countryside around Vienna which throughout his life brought him some measure of peace. Even so, illness, diagnosed by his doctor as "sickness of the emotions" (W, 439), kept him away from the stage for several months in 1825. In this same year he began to write a new play in which he struck a chord not heard before on the popular stage. Comments on his off-stage personality by his contemporaries often refer to his "serious-comic" temperament, which in a circle of friends could produce much hilarity.[10] Early in his acting career, critics had observed his ability to impart an air of "comic melancholy" to a stereo-typed comic role.[11] In the play he completed in 1826 he explicitly created dramatic opportunity for this aspect of his private and his stage person-ality. It was *Das Mädchen aus der Feenwelt* or *Der Bauer als Millionär* (*The Girl from the Fairy World* or *The Peasant as Millionaire.*)

Peasant Wurzel: Clown as Time's Fool (1826)
. . . this piquant mixture of the touching and the comic . . .

The title of Raimund's third play is *Das Mädchen aus der Feenwelt,* but it is the peasant of the subtitle, Fortunatus Wurzel, peasant turned million-aire, who remains in the mind long after one has forgotten the girl Lott-chen, his foster-daughter, sent to him by the fairy Lacrimosa. The play is another local extravaganza: fairy-tale elements go hand in hand with local ones in a complicated story plot where magical and allegorical figures play havoc with the lives of human (Viennese) beings. It has also, however, a unifying theme—the simple proverbial truth that pride goes before a fall—and this theme, played out as it is by the powerful comic character, Peas-ant Wurzel, stays in strong pictorial images in the mind of anyone who has seen the play.

Wurzel first appears as a gauche but jovial newly rich millionaire living a life of brash luxury and rowdy dissipation in the city. Having failed to fulfill the obligations under which his wealth was magically bestowed on him, he is first visited by Youth, who has come to take leave of him and then by Old Age, who swears him eternal friendship. The simple poetry of Youth's song of farewell to Wurzel has haunted many people as it haunted Heinrich Heine in Paris in 1837. Pondering the passing of time in his preface to the second edition of his *Buch der Lieder,* he recalled this scene and quoted the song from memory, years after seeing the play per-formed in Munich: "The sun is shining bright and yet / One fine day the sun must set." Haunting too is the transformation of the peasant himself. Wurzel changes before the eyes of the audience from a blustering robust man into a tottering invalid.

When he next appears it is in a costume modeled exactly on that of a figure of the Viennese street scene, the ash man. An old or destitute man, he would beg or buy ash for a paltry sum and make a meager living from selling it to soap manufacturers. The authentic dialect cry, "An Oschen!" (Ashes!), an echo of the streets and courtyards of the real city, now sounds

in the wings, and Wurzel the peasant, recently a millionaire, appears leaning on his stick, bowed beneath the weight of his ash can, immediately
recognizable to the audience, a graphic local personification of the transience of fortune and the folly of pride. He sings the simple song that
points the moral of the play:

> He struts around the town,
> Pride will bring him down,
> He wears a fancy suit,
> Is stupid as a coot,
> He's all puffed up and vain,
> My friend, it's quite insane!
> Soon time will take its toll,
> You'll play the ash man's role!
> Ashes! Ashes! (I, 4, 217-218)

The ash man goes beyond the stock caricatures of street figures so common in magical parodies and is more powerful than most caricatures of
allegorical figures. The local character itself has allegorical force. It has
escaped from the stereotyped categories of comic and serious characters
that shackle many of the stage personalities of the popular theater. Wurzel,
the clown figure, has grown into a melancholy image of man as time's
fool.

Considerably less universal in appeal is another aspect of the play's
serious vein—its periodic straight moralizing. The whole play is pervaded
by the conventional attitude that everyone has a place in society and that
contentment and self-respect are best found in that place. The allegorical
character, Contentment, pointedly conveys this lesson to Lottchen. Looking out from her thatched cottage in a pretty little garden to the high
mountains in the distance, she says: "You belong in the valley. Do you see
that high, shimmering mountain? That is the Alp of Riches, and opposite
him is that even more gleaming suitor, the Großglockner of Fame. They
are beautiful mountains, but never send your wishes up to them! The air
is strong and uplifting on their heights, but the storm-wind of envy blows
around their peaks, and even if he cannot extinguish the flame of your
happiness, yet he will certainly put out forever the lovely spark of trust in
your breast" (II, 3, 189-190). A critic of the première who calls the scene
meaningful and beautiful also writes approvingly: "Wise restriction of life's
needs is the basis of contentment. The opposite throws the passions into

turmoil."[12] The out and out moralizing of such a scene could only be cheerfully accepted by critics and by audiences who approved of the sentiment expressed, and moreover did not resent a little direct preaching from the stage. Such an audience clearly existed in the Leopoldstadt theater.

Modern critics have seen other reasons for the popularity of this play in the Vienna of 1825. Volker Klotz has argued convincingly that the spectators in this age of beginning industrialization and encroaching faceless capitalism found themselves caught in forces they could not control, tempted as well as frightened by new possibilities for speculation and by plentiful examples of rapid financial rises and falls among fellow citizens. In *Das Mädchen aus der Feenwelt*, contests between supernatural forces control the fortunes of human characters, pawns in a game they do not understand, and for the Viennese audience, Klotz suggests, the play is a grand metaphor for contemporary experience to which it responds at a semiconscious level (79). This is, of course, entirely possible. One tends to doubt, however, that among the people of the Austro-Hungarian Empire a deep sense of being at the mercy of uncontrollable forces is especially unique to the early industrial period. In the personal world of Raimund, most clearly revealed in his letters to Antonie, the sense of being at the mercy of higher powers is very strong. The natural language on which he draws to express this sense is quite conventional with a strong religious or metaphysical flavor. Depending on whether he is in an optimistic or pessimistic mood, he sees the fateful powers in his life as benign or malignant. Trying to bolster the spirits of Antonie, he assures her simply and hopefully, "A God lives up there in the clouds" (W. 442), and he frequently invokes the power of the angels or of the Holy Mother to protect her. The single word he uses most often to describe a higher power is Fate. Fate will tear Antonie away from him, but at the same time Fate has given Antonie to him. Fate which gives him Antonie's love also breaks up mountains to rob him of the innocent joy of an alpine excursion. No doubt Raimund, Antonie, and their fellow citizens were at the mercy of arbitrary economic forces, but it seems likely that deep in their psyches as well as in their everyday language, they *felt* themselves at the mercy of what were to them higher powers still.

A very unsettling sense of economic unpredictability must certainly have been in the air. It seems to me, however, that precisely in such unstable times so-called ordinary people cling ever more outspokenly to standards they see as fixed and solid and their own. One can object from our vantage point that this did not help to make Raimund's contemporaries into politically active citizens. One can suggest disapprovingly, as Klotz does of Wurzel, Lottchen, and Karl, that they sought private solutions to their problems rather than public improvement. However, it does not seem to me to capture the essence of the play or of the times if one deduces then, as Klotz does, that Raimund sends the audience home at the end of the play with only "a threadbare suggestion of happiness" (86); nothing has really changed; the good powers have defeated the bad powers, but the powers are still powers, and the peasant only returns to the plough, and Lottchen to the poor fisher boy whom she loves. Only a private solution? Yes, but the fact that the good powers defeat the bad powers is a cause for genuine rejoicing among the powerless, and the happy end of *Das Mädchen aus der Feenwelt* is, I believe, a devoutly wished happy end on Raimund's part, and a real one on the play's own terms and on those of its audience.

The play was enthusiastically received by audiences and critics in its day, and it was precisely the mixture of amusement and morality that led contemporary critics to regard it as reaching new heights in the popular theater. A first-night critic of the *Theaterzeitung* welcomed what he called the serious aspects of the play but expressed relief that Raimund had nonetheless kept the requirements of the popular stage in mind. It would be difficult, he said, for anything which addressed itself exclusively to reason and to the mind to take root in this theater. There was, however, enough to laugh at: "This alternation of merry jest and instructive seriousness, this stimulation of imagination and of the heart, in short this piquant mixture of the touching with the comic will long ensure that this play will have precedence over many others on the Leopoldstadt stage."[13] The critics were well satisfied, but Raimund was not. He had found a winning combination of ingredients for the popular theater of the 1820s, but he never again wrote a play quite like *Das Mädchen aus der Feenwelt*.

Peasant Gluthahn: Anti-Clown (1827)
I don't want to write local plays at all.

After Raimund's death his friend Costenoble told the story of a lady who wanted to say something nice to Raimund on a social occasion and so said how salutary it had been for art that with his plays he had given a higher and nobler direction to the popular theater and to local comedy. "Raimund started up as if pinched by tongs and shouted, 'Local comedy? Popular theater? I don't want to write local plays at all and I don't want to know about the popular theater.'" And that, commented Costenoble, was Raimund's sickness.[14]

Sickness or not, Raimund's ambition to write something other than local plays probably did prevent him from developing his natural talents in a linear fashion and writing better and better local comedies. Obviously he would have been well equipped to do this. The fact he did not *want* to move steadily along the valley path of gently moralizing humor led him into some dangerous mountains. It resulted in his least successful dramatic experiments, but through experimentation, I would submit, he also arrives at his greatest dramatic achievement. It is fairly standard to consider three of Raimund's plays his best, namely, *Das Mädchen aus der Feenwelt* (1825), *Der Alpenkönig und der Menschenfeind* (1828, The King of the Alps and the Misanthrope), and *Der Verschwender* (1834, The Spendthrift), and to see these as stemming directly from the popular tradition, thus most in touch with the "folk spirit." His other plays, *Die gefesselte Phantasie* (1826, Fettered Fantasy), *Moisasurs Zauberfluch* (1827, Moisasur's Magic Curse), and *Die unheilbringende Krone* (1829, The Fateful Crown), are seen rather as products of his own particular and personal ambition. They are then judged successful or unsuccessful, depending on whether the critic considers that Raimund's forays into serious drama are a heightening of the popular theater tradition or an unfortunate deviation from it. It seems to me, however, that while Raimund's development as a dramatist is not linear in any simplistic sense, it does not quite proceed along these two parallel lines either. Every one of his plays from *Das Mädchen aus der Feenwelt* on is an experiment, and I would suggest that in one of his most ambitious and ultimately unsuccessful attempts at serious drama, *Moisasurs Zauberfluch*, are the seeds of his most ambitious and highly successful comedy, *Der Alpenkönig und der Menschenfeind*.

Raimund set out deliberately in *Moisasurs Zauberfluch* to escape the time-honored form of local and popular comedy. He called it an "Original Magical Play." Knowing that it would not go down well in the Leopoldstadt Theater, he had it produced in the Theater an der Wien in 1827, with Karl Carl in the role of Gluthahn, the comic lead. It was an altogether darker play than anything Raimund had written before. Not only was the main plot intended to be deeply serious, but audience and critics found themselves asking whether or not the central comic character was really comic at all. Certainly by popular theater standards he was not. The well-to-do peasant Gluthahn is in fact the villain of the piece and—a switch on the normal character parallelisms of popular comedy—a *nasty* comic and local counterpart to the serious and High-German-speaking Moisasur, a monstrous Demon of Evil with a scaly body, dragon's wings, and snakes writhing about his head. Gluthahn is cruel, avaricious, and completely self-centered. He mistreats his wife, torments his neighbors, and grinds the last penny out of his debtors. His antics do make the audience laugh, but the laughter sends a shiver down the spine which was unusual in the cheerful atmosphere of the popular theater. The heroine of the play, Alzinde, the virtuous Queen of the Diamond Kingdom, is turned into an old woman by Moisasur and banished to the Austrian mountains. She lands on Gluthahn's doorstep, and when he discovers that she weeps diamonds, he drags her off and tries to sell her to a jewel merchant. The local magistrate then sends both Gluthahn and Alzinde to prison.

The primary source of humor in Gluthahn's character lies in the fact that his blatant cruelties and misdeeds are accompanied by constant re-iteration of his own good intentions and soft-heartedness. At first the impression made on the audience is that his words, so much at variance with his actions, must be deliberate irony on his part: in his first scene, after abusing his exhausted and ill wife, he eventually gives in to her pleading and graciously allows her to take the extravagant step of sending for a doctor, saying confidentially to the audience: "I shouldn't have given in, but my word, I'm simply too good." This "I'm too good" develops into a catch-phrase but one that is not primitively funny by virtue of mere repetition. It pinpoints the basic feature of Gluthahn's character, namely, that in all his meanness and cruelty he really believes he is good-hearted. The audience becomes gradually aware that they are laughing at a character in the grip of chronic self-deception. There is a shift in what initially seemed to be Gluthahn's own irony: the real irony of the situation lies in the fact he cannot see his own misdeeds or believe in his own downfall.

Gluthahn disturbed the comfortable audiences of Vienna, and as a single character he represents a new strength of character-drawing for the popular stage, away from the cheerfully implausible clown figure in the direction of the grotesquely plausible comic character. Unfortunately, his dramatic impact is diminished by the paraphernalia of the "serious" plot of the play, the tussle between the good Queen Alzinde, supported by the Spirit of

Virtue, and Moisasur, the Demon of Evil. The play is an attempt at a philosophical allegory, dramatizing the warring forces of good and evil in the world. The moral that virtue must fight and must prevail is solemnly intoned by the Genius of Virtue. The world is a battlefield and evil has been put there especially to fight with good:

> Virtue is allowed to falter,
> But it's your fault if she falls.
> All on earth received the power
> To resist temptation's hour
> But the weak will lose the fight.
> Victorious is the man of might.
> So on earth the great behest,
> Put all Virtue to the test. (I, 10, 313)

Though phrased more grandly and in verse, such thought is as conventional as anything Contentment might have said in *Das Mädchen aus der Feenwelt*. This particular passage shows the other side of the coin in a world governed by morals as well as by almighty and arbitrary forces: The human being has very little actual power but a great deal of personal responsibility! In Raimund's magical-allegorical world, however, Alzinde is not left to battle on with only her personal virtue to sustain her. She can escape from the evil curse by weeping tears of joy in the arms of death, and the Spirit of Virtue in person enables her to fulfil this impossible condition by descending into the Underworld and commanding its ruler, Mutability, to assist in her rejuvenation. When her earthly adventures end in prison, Mutability appears and offers death as a solace from the world's woes. On the point of succumbing she falls into his arms and immediately Hoanghu appears with Virtue. In tears her husband offers his youth and strength for her life, and Alzinde is so moved that in the arms of death itself she weeps tears of joy and so gains her lost youth. This scene holds the potential for great visual-allegorical effect—the potential Raimund realized so hauntingly in *Das Mädchen aus der Feenwelt*—and it is one of the scenes in the play which academic critics of our own times have commended.[15] Critics of the première applauded it for its beauty, and it assuredly moved contemporary audiences. In the Theater an der Wien, where serious as well as comic plays were often performed, the audience responded with great enthusiasm to the play as a whole. Raimund, who was not performing, was called to the stage six times and could scarcely give his prepared speech for tears of emotion. Critics did not take issue with the hollowness of the serious characters or of the language, indeed, they remarked that Raimund had made great strides in this respect. "The language, where the plot requires it, is powerful, rich in images, often elevated and zestful," wrote the critic of the *Sammler* after the opening night.[16] The modern ear, however, can scarcely but hear doggerel in such passages as Alzinde's and Hoanghu's ecstatic and exclamatory reunion:

> Hoanghu: O Alzinde!
> Alzinde: My Hoanghu!
>   You are mine eternally!
> Hoanghu: Death shall never part us two!
> Alzinde: For we die communally! (II, 10, 345)

The play's capacity to move audiences today is limited because it is so hard to take these serious characters seriously. They are not flesh-and-blood creatures but figures in outline who talk in abstractions; they posture, exclaim, and protest, but we do not believe in their sufferings.

It was certainly not to the serious characters or to the sentiments expressed in the serious parts of the play that contemporary critics objected, but rather to the kind of comedy presented by the leading comic character. "This character hurts more that he delights," was their disapproving response.[17] The next time Raimund tried his hand at tragi-comedy, in *Die unheilbringende Krone*, he had no reason to fear the audience would not accept the comic lead, because he returned to the old familiar devices of the popular theater to put this character together. This time, however, the audience had a different problem.

The Harpist and the Tailor: Pure Clowns (1826/1829)
"Are we supposed to laugh or cry?"

Earlier, in 1826, Raimund had written *Die gefesselte Fantasie* which he also called an "Original Magical Play." He called *Die unheilbringende Krone* of 1829 a "Tragic-Comic Original Magical Play," and this is held to be Raimund's most ambitious attempt at tragic drama. In both of these plays Raimund poured all his dramatic ambition into the serious parts. The comic leads are both characters whom Raimund, the local actor-playwright, could create out of his back pocket. Nachtigall (Nightingale), who is named in time-honored fashion to reflect character and profession, is a singer, harpist, and beer-house entertainer, and Simplizius Zitternadel (Trembleneedle) is a foolish and cowardly tailor.

Nachtigall first appears on stage in the setting of a Viennese beer-house, performing the realistic task of singing and insulting the customers. This is one of the few scenes in Raimund's works which straightforwardly reflects a slice of Viennese life in an authentic setting. Lightning soon splits the back wall, however, and the two wicked fairies in their cloud-carriage spirit the harpist away to the land of Flora, there to play a part in the serious plot of the play. With the change of scene he becomes very much a *caricatured* Viennese harpist, a figure of fun, comically local in a fantastic setting. Not far removed from Hanswurst, he parades his bravery, then catching sight of lions, he falls to his knees groveling in ludicrous terror. He weeps as easily as Kasperl when denied help by Fantasy in writing a prize poem, and then hops about in childish glee when he thinks he has after all won the prize, crying "I'm going to be king!" And all these antics ostensibly serve the ends of a serious allegory of poetic imagination which cannot be forced into the service of a coarse rhymester, nor persuaded to answer the call of the professional writer; it comes freely only to the man whose poetry springs from the love in his heart. This romantic notion is portrayed by Raimund in picturesque terms. Fantasy is captured by the wicked fairies and appears in chains, her wings clipped. She refuses to help Nachtigall write the prize poem, and she does not assist the pedant Distichon either. It is the young shepherd-prince, Amphio, to whom she whispers her inspiration and it is he who wins the hand of the Queen.

The hero and heroine of the play are Amphio and Hermione the Queen of Flora. Their scenes in romantic valleys where sheep graze on the hillside are idyllic and without a trace of humor. Fantasy herself aspires to seriousness of character and loftiness of language but lapses at times into jollity and hops about the stage like any cheery chambermaid of popular comedy. Raimund's own role, Nachtigall, is by far the most powerful theatrically, and while Amphio, with the aid of Fantasy, wins the contest and the Queen, it is indubitably Nachtigall who wins the audience.

We know from Raimund's own testimony that not only did he quite explicitly set out to make a serious point in this play, but also that he failed to grasp why his audience balked at it. In his fragment of an autobiography he explains he wrote the play as a response to those envious persons who doubted he could really have written *Das Mädchen aus der Feenwelt*. He wanted to demonstrate in his new play that, without being a scholar, one could create "an innocent poem." He explained the cool reception awarded the play: "It wasn't funny enough for the public, and the idea was not popular."[18] His own heart was certainly with the innocent poet Amphio, writing out of love. That his talent was rather with the comic singer Nachtigall he did not see. To the detriment of his own development as a dramatist, he allowed his characteristic scorn for the public taste to blind him to his own strengths and weaknesses as a writer and as a dramatist. The reactions of the first-night audience were predictably mixed. The critic of the *Sammler* wrote: "Some people objected to the overly serious tendency of the whole thing. Others thought the comic lead was too little in evidence. Some did not think the play was well cast, and others held that the play just did not belong in this theater."[19] This kind of criticism no doubt confirmed Raimund's own belief that the fault was not with the play but with the inability of the audience in the Leopold-stadt to respond to it.

He repeated the mistakes of *Die gefesselte Fantasie* on a grander scale in his next and last attempt at high drama, *Die unheilbringende Zauberkrone* of 1829, where he again relied in the comic scenes on stock theatrical devices. The poor village tailor, Zitternadel, is a wisecracking debtor, who awaits arrest at the hands of his creditors and escapes in the company of Ewald, a serious young poet. His ludicrous terror in the land of Massana provides a comic contrast to Ewald's noble bearing and dignified courage. Viennese jokes abound, and in the best traditions of magical burlesque Zitternadel performs ludicrous antics on the back of a winged bison. These do not differ essentially from the antics of Quecksilber in Raimund's very first play when he flies through the palace window on the back of a crowing cock. In writing Zitternadel's lines Raimund resorts more frequently than in any of his other plays to mime and to such stock devices as the nonsense speech and the comic repetition of a single word. He has obviously devoted most of his attention to the serious plot of the play involving an imaginary kingdom of Agrigent in which Phalarius, a general, tries to overthrow the king, Creon, with the help of a crown given to him by the Prince of the Underworld. The Goddess Lucina saves Creon by fulfilling the three impossible conditions Phalarius lays down: she produces the required "king without a kingdom, hero without courage, beauty without youth." She does this with the help of Ewald and Zitternadel, who fly away on a cloud and together encounter a series of adventures in much the same way as Eduard and Florian or any other master and servant of popular comedy, except their absurd adventures are serving the ends of a plot enacted in an atmosphere of high tragedy. Raimund had played this kind of role to great comic effect many times. He uses it here to provide easy comic relief for people whose taste in drama he does not really respect and who, he always fears, do not really respect his true talent.

He underestimated the good sense of his audience. They were not at all pleased with the tragic plot of this play, and the comic scenes did not appease them. The critic of the *Sammler* voiced general dissatisfaction when he wrote: "When dead victims of plague . . . are carried across the stage, when we experience the horrible end of a whole city and its inhabitants in an earthquake . . . are we then supposed to laugh at the jokes of a tailor? Are we supposed to laugh or cry? The demand is against all psychology."[20] Used as they were to the traditional interweaving of comic and serious strands of plot, the public and the critics found the contrast here glaring and unacceptable and were bewildered by the ambiguity of the playwright's intention.

The traditional divisions of "comic" and "serious" must have seemed to Raimund to hold a simple solution for his particular problems as a comic actor with ambitions in serious drama, but resorting to them in too simplistic a way was a retardation in his development towards well-constructed "serious" local comedy of character. It is doubtful whether Raimund himself realized this. The critic Hans Weigel has suggested that Raimund so much wanted to be Schiller and Shakespeare he could never completely be Raimund (45). It is surely true that the one play in which he came nearest to being completely Raimund was also his best play, and that was *Der Alpenkönig und der Menschenfeind*.

Herr von Rappelkopf: Anti-Clown as Hero (1828)

> *The task of art does not lie in the idea,*
> *but in giving life to the idea.*

A year after he wrote *Moisasurs Zauberfluch*, Raimund wrote *Der Alpenkönig und der Menschenfeind* in which he turned the failed Gluthahn experiment into a major success. The leading comic character, Rappelkopf, is as far from being a stock funny man as Gluthahn is. He is a misanthrope who maltreats his family and servants yet persists in believing himself to be a victim of the cruelty and misdeeds of others. Rappelkopf, however, unlike Gluthahn, is not shunted to the side of a serious play that is supposed to be about someone and something else. This play is straight-forwardly about Rappelkopf and about misanthropy. There is a super-natural element in the play, but it enters the play strictly in relation to Rappelkopf himself: the King of the Alps decides to show Rappelkopf the error of his ways by assuming the misanthrope's unlovely personality and parading it in front of him. Rappelkopf is transformed for this purpose into his own brother-in-law, and in a series of hilarious scenes, he watches himself in all his paranoid splendor. More and more convinced he has been behaving like a madman, he is driven to a dramatic conversion by the threat of the King of the Alps to kill himself. Since they have at this point only one life between them, Rappelkopf sees his own death ap-proaching and swears he is cured of misanthropy. This change of heart saves his life, cures him of his persecution mania, and brings happiness to his long-suffering family.

The play is a far cry from the local parody. The audience certainly laughs at Rappelkopf, but he never gives the impression of playing the fool to amuse the audience. On the contrary, he takes himself very seriously. His exaggerated fears of his loving family and his harmless servants are themselves farcical, and ridiculous situations arise out of this fear, such as when he intercepts the foolish servant Habakuk on his way to the kitchen garden to cut chicory and flies into a paroxysm of rage at the sight of the knife, accusing the bewildered servant of attempted murder. Absurd as his exhibitions of paranoia are, such is the pace of the action in the scenes of his anger, such is his total domination of his environment, the audience is swept, protesting with laughter, into *his* world, and, reeling, sees the outside world with his fevered imagination. Occasional rational thoughts are swallowed up rapidly and comically in his self-sustaining hatred. "She might not be so bad," he says, half-relenting at the sight of the pretty chambermaid, but, hastening at once to fan the flames of his own ani-mosity, he shouts, "But I have such a hatred for her, a hatred without end." His inability to admit his own unreasonableness is complete in his monologues and asides to himself. Thus gross insults to the chambermaid are accompanied by such straightfaced assertions as "I must restrain myself so that I am not impolite to her." This, the personal duplicity of a self-deceiver, is brilliantly matched in the heat and anger of conversation by blatant but equally unaware admissions of his irrational attitudes: asked what he has against Augustus, his daughter's suitor, "as a human being," he blurts out the answer, "Nothing, except that he is one," only to revert as soon as he is alone to his stance of injured virtue with the whining cry of self-pity, "Everything is against me, and I never hurt anyone." Thus the audience is carried up and down on the tide of his passion, and his most ludicrous excesses are comprehended on his own illogical terms. Just as Gluthahn's own reality was conveyed to the audience and shown to be a delusion, so again the audience glimpses a personal reality at variance with the world's facts. But in this play Raimund goes a stage further: the process is reversed in the second part of the play as Rappelkopf incredulously and at all times comically comes face to face with the other reality, that of the people around him.

The two-act play is tightly constructed: the plot hinges entirely on the character of Rappelkopf himself. The dialogue is not in the least dependent on local jokes for its effect, and Raimund himself insisted that he did not play Rappelkopf in the local dialect. The play is anything but typical of comedy as it was performed night after night on the Leopoldstadt stage, yet it was an enormous success when it was first performed there in 1828. After the thirtieth performance the *Theaterzeitung* reported: "The house is still stiflingly full; one has to book weeks in advance for boxes and stalls, and so far on no single day have they taken less that 1000 florins at this *King of the Alps.*"[21] No one suggested, as they did a year later of *Die unheilbringende Krone,* that this play did not belong on the stage of the Leopoldstadt. Rappelkopf's emergence from his psychically disturbed state into an understanding of himself is presented in the simple but striking terms of the popular theater at its best.

Leigh Hunt, reviewing an English adaptation at the Adelphi Theater in London in 1831 wrote in *The Tatler:* "Though in general we do not like to have a moral thrust in our faces, especially if there be vice in it (which is not seldom the case) yet the one inculcated by this new piece is so truly deserving of the name, so undogmatical, so good-natured, as well as enforced in so very new and surprising a manner that everybody is interested in giving it precedence. It is a comment but a very general one, upon the wish expressed by the poet that heaven would give us the power 'to see ourselves as others see us.'"[22] While stage symbolism of this kind was hardly "new and surprising" on the Viennese stage, the central function of this particular dramatic image was no commonplace there either. Largely because of it the play stands out as a high point in the development of popular comedy and as the most perfectly realized of Raimund's dramatic concepts. The figurative presentation of an obvious moral, however, would have had a very different effect if it had been solemn and pompous in tone. It is doubtful whether Leigh Hunt would have wanted a moral thrust in his face by the dogmatic Genius of Virtue, or even by the pious and pretty Contentment, and certainly the average modern audience would not appreciate it. At the same time, we have to see the contemporary Viennese enthusiasm for the play would have been limited if the characterization of Rappelkopf, like that of Gluthahn, had involved *no* moralizing overtones and *no* optimistic outcome. While a plain moral, if it is to be generally acceptable in the theater has to be "undogmatical," a comedy, in order to meet with the complete approval of Raimund's own local audiences and critics in the 1820s, needed to be "good-natured." By satisfying all these requirements at once Raimund created one whole and unified moralizing comedy which not only appealed to his own local audience, but also held general and (so far) lasting appeal. It is not surprising this was the one of his plays which Grillparzer esteemed most highly. He expressed the wish that all German poets, far better educated than Raimund as they were, would study this play to grasp that "the task of art does not lie in the idea but in giving life to the idea." If Raimund had written three works of this quality, wrote Grillparzer, his name would have been assured a place in the annals of German poetry.

But Raimund did not. Juggling as he was the demands of his audiences, the demands of his own ambitions, and never consciously grasping where his own strength lay, it is perhaps surprising not that he wrote only one *Alpenkönig* but that he wrote one at all. In the face of the enormous struggle he had in combining what he was good at with what he wanted to do and what his audience wanted him to do, Hofmannsthal's sense of his life's work as a vegetative growth, a fateful and effortless whole, seems to be something of a fantasy. Yet many people have been tempted to take Hofmannsthal's judgment at face value because Raimund has come to represent for subsequent generations the spirit of his era. This is not all fantasy and it is time we came full circle to Raimund's last years and to Valentin the carpenter.

Valentin, Loyal and True (1834)

Valentin's loyalty is a rare find
for an arrogant man down on his luck.

By the end of the 1820s, the Leopoldstadt theater was in financial difficulty. It was sold in 1828 to Rudolf Steinkeller who knew very little about Vienna and still less about the theater and who brought about the disintegration of the company by dismissing many of the older actors and engaging only mediocre actors to take their place. Raimund, then director of the theater, became more and more angry about these changes and resigned from the company in August 1830.

During the last years of his life he gave guest performances, mainly in his own plays, in Prague, Munich, Hamburg, and Berlin, where he was acclaimed with enthusiasm by audiences and critics. His appearances in Vienna also met with great success, particularly the series at the Josefstadt theater in 1834 where his last play was performed. He had taken up a more stable domestic life in the Wagner household in 1829 and he was by now in a strong financial position. In 1835 he bought a country house for himself and Antonie in Gutenstein in the pleasant valley of Piesting just outside Vienna. The outward circumstances of his life spelled success, and his last great comic character, Valentin, was a happy man.

Five years had passed since *Die unheilbringende Krone*, and Raimund did not repeat the disastrous combination of high tragedy and low comedy that marked the play. However, in *Der Verschwender* he did divide his attention and the attention of the audience between two sets of characters—the comic/local ones and the serious/"high-born" ones. *Der Verschwender* does not therefore achieve the coordination of plot, character, and theme that made the *Alpenkönig* a great play. Flottwell, a rich and extravagant nobleman, is pestered for a year of his life by a beggar to whom he carelessly throws quite substantial sums of money. His lifelong extravagance leads to his downfall, and on his fiftieth birthday, alone and penniless, he meets the beggar and recognizes him as himself at the age of fifty. The fairy Cheristane who loved him had taken a year of his life and used it to collect from his youthful self the small fortune that now saves him from penury.

This picturesque idea does not make as great an impact as the confrontation of Rappelkopf with himself because Flottwell is a wholly serious and comparatively uninteresting character. He is overshadowed in the play by

Valentin, his servant. Valentin turns out to be more than a traditional comic-servant counterpart. He first hops onto the stage like any other stock local character singing a comic song. His antics amuse Flottwell, his guests, and the audience through two acts of the play, but when he next appears, he is twenty years older and no longer in servant's livery but wearing carpenter's clothes. He meets Flottwell who is now tattered and unkempt, scarcely recognizable. Valentin is about to throw him a small coin, but then he stops and after a moment of hesitation, so the stage directions tell us, "he cries out quickly, 'My noble Lord!' (a mixture of joy, sadness, and astonishment makes him tremble, he does not know how to control himself. Calls out again) 'My noble lord!' (Tears appear in his eyes, wordlessly he kisses his hand)" (III, 4, 585).

When Raimund played this scene, he never failed to bring tears to the eyes of his audience, and it is still one of the great moments of the play. Comic, yet touching, the scene draws on Raimund's particular well of laughter and tears. Valentin takes Flottwell home with him and is over-joyed at being able to help him. Before his naive delight is shattered by the cold reactions of his sharp-tongued wife Rosel, the former pert and pretty chambermaid of Act I, he stands alone on the stage pondering the downfall of Flottwell and the inability of man to control his fate. The trite saying: "Man proposes, God disposes," leads into Raimund's best-loved song. Valentin, the carpenter, sees the inequalities of man smoothed and planed by a carpentering fate, and as he stands there, a struggling artisan with a family to support yet so fortunate and well-loved in comparison with the beggared and lonely Flottwell, he embodies his own words.

A critic wrote in 1834: "People who have stayed away from the local plays for years come back time and again to the performance of this moral and entertaining local play."[23] Who were these people who were attracted into the theater by Raimund's particular gift of combining entertainment with a high moral tone?

The public face of wellbeing and complacency shown by the broad cen-ter group of the Viennese who were neither assailed by the extreme doubts and frustrations of the intellectuals nor troubled by the extreme cares of the poor and destitute did not remain unclouded in Raimund's lifetime. By the 1830s, growing numbers of the proletariat were beginning to make their presence felt in the city. In 1789, describing the leisure activities of the "common man," Johann Pezzl defined the term thus: "That is what I call, not the lowest rabble, but the citizens, or, to put it more precisely, the tradesmen and artisans, the servants of the court and the nobility, the small merchants, in short, the usual class of people between the nobles and menial servants."[24] By the time that model serving man and artisan, Valentin, appeared on stage in the 1830s, it may not have been possible to discount the "lowest rabble" as blithely as Pezzl does, but the audience of the Leopoldstadt theater was still primarily drawn from the broad center group he describes. This "usual class of people" essentially set the tone, though the aristocrats continued to drive out to take their places in the higher priced boxes and there were cheap seats for the poorer fringes in the gallery. At the upper end of the social scale, intellectuals, long restive, had after the July revolution of 1830 in Paris begun to hope the stranglehold of the Imperial Government might begin to loosen, but undercurrents of discontent had not yet noticeably disturbed the tranquil surface of the city's "usual class of people." In 1831 Emperor Franz was assured by his advisers that there was no sign of the Paris disorders spreading to his own capital city. Nevertheless precautions were increased and strict measures were taken against strangers in the city to prevent the unwelcome infiltration of liberal ideas. The Emperor himself while supporting these measures wrote: "I am not worried about the true Viennese citizens. I can count on them in all circumstances."[25] Although some thirteen years later many of these citizens took to the barricades, the kind of confidence placed by the Emperor in his loyal subjects would not have been misplaced in Raimund's Valentin, nor probably in the people to whom he most appealed.

The lack of outright political commentary, positive or negative, in Raimund's plays is unremarkable, given the censor's close surveillance. The complete absence of satirical tone is however significant. There is a world of difference in tone between Nestroy's *Lumpazivagabundus*, first performed in 1833 and Raimund's only play of the thirties. The artificially contrived closing scene of *Lumpazivagabundus* in which Nestroy's entertaining ne'er-do-wells are shown converted to a most unlikely state of domestic bliss leaves the indelible impression of a tongue-in-cheek concession to a fading public taste. Raimund's *Verschwender*, on the other hand, performed a year later, is still pervaded by the standards set in the heyday of this taste, and it still appealed without irony to the worthy citizen whose life was based on these standards. There is an attempt at domestic revolution in the last act when Valentin's wife Rosa, quite lacking in the respectful attitude of Valentin, refuses to take Flottwell into her home. In her barely veiled insolence there is an attitude that had no official place in the old social order and certainly not in the stage version of that order. But Raimund clearly intends her behavior to seem outrageous. The dominant note of the play is struck by Valentin, and it is one of wry good humor.

There is no reason to assume Raimund intended to bolster the state when he created in Valentin a character close in spirit to a "true Viennese" on whose loyalty Emperor and State could rely. Equally there is no reason to assume from this or any other of his plays that he consciously or subconsciously opposed the political status quo. There seems to be a concern among critics of both such persuasions to rescue him from a reputation of political passivity and to protect him from the charge of being "harmless."[26] The only surviving personal comment of Raimund himself on politics is in a letter of his later years: "As far as the world in general is concerned, the rage for talking politics and despising all morality while you're at it, is becoming more and more disgusting. I long for a small circle in which I might still find feeling and loyalty."[27]

Raimund's concern for morality was itself a quite aggressive one, and not the passive and "harmless" stance it may appear to be in the eye of the modern beholder. Moral indignation is frequent in his letters and is expressed clearly, for example, to a friend who suggested that he ought to have reunited Flottwell with his long-lost daughter at the end of *Der Verschwender*: "It is not my intention to reward Flottwell . . . at the end of his botched career. Really he ought to come to a bad end. I only want to save him from undeserved shame and from the terrible ingratitude of people. His own generosity did not always occur out of true virtue, and his reward for it, he owes to heaven. The children are nice to him, and Valentin's loyalty is a rare find for an arrogant man down on his luck."[28] Raimund himself, it seems to me, did not particularly regard Valentin as typical of a class or of a countryman. He regarded him as "a rare find" and an ideal. And so, quite probably, did those solid citizens who flocked to see the play and wiped tears from their eyes when he sang his carpenter's song.

Fate is the Carpenter
His half unconscious gift was rooted in the spirit of the masses.

Valentin's cheerful temperament seems far removed from Raimund's own. The quiet and cheerful resignation to the prospect of death sung in wryly comic tones in the last verse of Valentin's famous song is a far cry from the agonizing death of Raimund himself. His attacks of "melancholy" or extreme depression, did not go away when at last he was able to live with Antonie in their own house in the countryside he loved so much. It was in this house he was bitten by a dog and stricken with fear the dog was rabid. For years he had been pathologically afraid of illness. He became obsessed with the idea the dog had infected him. On his way to Vienna to seek medical help, he and Antonie were forced by bad weather to stay overnight in an inn in Pottenstein. Antonie went to fetch him some water, and in her absence he shot himself in the mouth. He lived in agony for five days. He was transported to Vienna but the doctors who operated on him were unable to save his life.

His suicide is sometimes associated with his sense of failure, a sense that his day as the darling of the Viennese audiences was over because a new idol was winning their affection. Yet he had always lived with a fear of rivals and foes, even when there were none of any consequence. He killed himself in the grip of pathological fear, trying unsuccessfully to escape a horrible death. Perhaps his career was at a turning point. Certainly a potential rival had appeared on the Viennese stage in the shape of Nestroy. There is no way of determining whether Raimund would have been capable of meeting the challenges of a changing situation in society and in the theater. In taking his life when he did, he escaped them. All Raimund's plays were written in the latter part of the reign of Emperor Franz, a time when the broad mass of the people appeared more interested in achieving a comfortable life than in battling social and political issues. The Emperor died in 1835, and a year later Raimund committed suicide.

Raimund was a common man of the Vienna of Emperor Franz. He was born into the broad center group of the city's population, the class among whom he lived and whose standards he accepted. As an actor and producer he was hardworking and painstaking. He was thrifty, and, in accumulating his own small fortune, he prided himself on being a man "who had *earned* his own living from the beginning" (W 397). His attitude toward the bourgeois standards of his day cannot be fairly assessed without regard for the crucial fact of his having emerged from poverty. Unlike latter-day academic critics who belong to the modern "middle class" themselves, and are in a comfortable enough position to hold the less enlightened bourgeoisie of Raimund's day in some contempt, Raimund *aspired* all his life to middle-class status. His youthful folly had robbed him of conventional domestic happiness, and he bitterly regretted this to the end. He endeavored to live the life of a worthy member of society and is constantly at pains in his letters to Antonie to assure her of his uprightness. The word *rechtschaffen* (upright or respectable) occurs again and again in his avowals of good faith. He knew his own temperament flew in the face of convention, and this disturbed and upset him. In 1823 he wrote to Antonie: "I behave as an upright man, to you and to all people . . . If I have a great weakness, it is my violent temperament, to which, on the other hand, I owe the birth of my art. I strive constantly to put aside this failing" (W 399).

He could not personally resolve the paradox in this assertion, but an artistic resolution did emerge in his greatest play in which he played the misanthrope and cured himself. That there was a suspicious misanthropic streak in Raimund is clear from the testimony of his contemporaries and from his own statements and letters. One hears in his letters the voices of his stage misanthropes: he protests to Antonie, "I am much too good to false, ungrateful people. If only I could live contentedly with you in isolation" (W 419). He allowed the darker side of his temperament an outlet in the peasant Gluthahn and, then again, in flamboyant and triumphant form in Rappelkopf, of whom Grillparzer wrote with polite restraint: "Raimund had the advantage in this eccentric central character of being able to copy himself a little." A critic of our times, Heinz Politzer, has viewed the split personality of Rappelkopf without reserve as the "personal fear-vision" of Raimund himself. He disputes the traditional view of Rappelkopf's "conversion," claiming the self-knowledge professed by Rappelkopf at the end of the play is itself ambiguous, not to be taken at face value, but to imply he knows he is incurable.[29] Yet the sting is gradually and deliberately taken out of Rappelkopf's bitterness by the hilarious pantomime that ends in the triumph of his "better nature." The conversion of Rappelkopf is integral to the theme and construction of the play and not insignificant as an expression of Raimund's personal feeling. The dramatist himself lived perpetually torn between his own two realities. As "an upright man," he strove all his life to overcome his own misanthropic, violent, and melancholy tendencies. We know he did not succeed. He sank ever deeper into the fears of life and death that ended in his grotesque suicide. A cure for his own paranoia and misanthropy was certainly beyond his reach in life; for the dramatist it was surely a wishful dream converted into unambiguous reality for his stage misanthrope, Rappelkopf.

To use present-day psychological hindsight to suggest Rappelkopf is not really cured seems to me to fall into the same category of critical error as to use present-day political and sociological hindsight to suggest Lottchen finds only a threadbare happiness with her fisherman Karl. Raimund himself did not seek social revolution any more than he wanted to be a melancholic. He longed to be a part of established middle-class society, just as he longed to be contented and at peace with himself and other people. His greatest personal desire was to be loved and trusted by the daughter of a wealthy coffeehouse owner and to be accepted by her family as a respectable and upstanding man worthy of her. His greatest professional desire was to be loved and respected by bourgeois Viennese audiences and to be accepted by them as a serious, thinking poet. The fact that both these desires were partially met but never in a way that completely satisfied him drove him farther and farther into melancholy. But is there not in the end some poetic justice for Raimund? The plays that appealed most deeply to the respectable Viennese audiences of his day have turned out to be his greatest and most lasting plays—*Das Mädchen aus der Feenwelt, Der Alpenkönig und der Menschenfeind*, and *Der Verschwender*. He, the struggling outsider, gave lasting shape to the dreams and ideals of the comfortable insider and went down in history as the voice of the folk-spirit. "Fate is the carpenter, you see, who planes and smooths the two."

Notes

1. III, 6, 591-592. The translations of Raimund's texts (and of all other texts) in this essay are my own. References are to the original German texts. The few existing translations of Raimund's plays are listed in the Bibliography but I do not refer to them as such in my essay. The translated titles of the plays are my own. References to the plays are to one of the reasonably accessible German editions of the plays, Otto Rommel's edition of 1961 (see Bibliography). To facilitate the use of other editions, act and scene references are given as well as page numbers. References to the reviews of the plays, contained in Volume V of the *Historisch-kritische Säkularausgabe* (see Bibliography), are given as HKA, V, with the page number. References to Raimund's letters are to the second volume of the reasonably accessible edition by Franz Hadamowsky (*Werke*, 1971, see Bibliography) and are given in the text as W with the page number.

2. Written by Grillparzer on the occasion of the appearance of the first volume of Raimund's works in 1837. For this and other references cited in the text only by page number the works are given in the bibliography.
3. I am drawing to some extent on my own earlier work on Raimund published in 1970 under the name of Prohaska (see Bibliography). Further discussion, particularly of the connections between the plays and the city of Vienna, may be found in that book.
4. See Heinrich Anschütz, *Erinnerungen aus dessen Leben und Wirken*. Vienna, 1866, p. 411.
5. *Theaterzeitung*, 343, 1813; HKA, V, p. 9.
6. According to Otto Rommel's index of the plays of these three dramatists (Rommel, 1952, pp. 1028ff), Bäuerle wrote at least 70 plays, Meisl 184, and Gleich 224; by 1823, Bäuerle had already written 55, Meisl 94, and Gleich 151.
7. HKA, V, p. 227.
8. *Abendzeitung*, 340, 1823; see HKA, V, p. 226.
9. Ibid., p. 169, 1825; HKA, V, p. 250.
10. See e.g. the comments of the actor Costenoble, 15 April 1822; HKA, V, p. 180.
11. See e.g. *Theaterzeitung*, 428, 1819; HKA, V, p. 93.
12. *Theaterzeitung*, 571, 1826; HKA, V, p. 306.
13. *Theaterzeitung*, 571, 599, 603, 1926; HKA, V, p. 309.
14. HKA, V, p. 761-762.
15. Otto Rommel, for example, and Claude David.
16. *Sammler*, 476, 1827; HKA, V, p. 375.
17. *Theaterzeitung*, 503, 1827: HKA, V, p. 371.
18. HKA, V, p. 836.
19. *Sammler*, 35, 1828; HKA, V, p. 398.
20. *Sammler*, 474, 1830; ibid., p. 257.
21. *Theaterzeitung*, 607, 1828: HKA, V, p. 463.
22. See Introduction to *The King of the Alps*, pp. 2-3. This is an adaptation rather than a translation of Raimund's play. Substantial alterations were made to suit the English ensemble at the Adelphi.
23. *Federstunden*, 647, 1834; HKA, V, p. 621.
24. Johann Pezzl. *Skizze von Wien*. Vienna, 1789, p. 90f.
25. See Carl Glossy. *Literarische Geheimberichte aus dem Vormärz, Jahrbuch der Grillparzer-Gesellschaft*, 21, 1912, p.v.

26. See e.g. Gerd Müller, "Certainly he is not 'harmless.' Rather he shows himself in content and thematic value system to be an altogether political author" (24).
27. Letter to Therese von Isenflamm, Munich, 20 November 1831. W, 509.
28. Letter to Friedrich Ludwig Schmitt, 20 December 1835 (W, 2, 518).
29. Heinz Politzer, "Ferdinand Raimunds 'Der Alpenkönig und der Menschenfeind,'" in: H.P., *Das Schweigen der Sirenen* (Stuttgart: Metzler, 1968), p. 188.

Bibliography

I. Works

a) Individual Plays

The nature of the popular theater was such that the scripts of plays were adapted for different performances often by the authors themselves. Thus texts submitted to the censors, scripts for the actors, and original manuscripts by the playwright often contained variant passages. Raimund's plays were not published until after his death and he had not himself revised them for publication. They were first published in Vogl's edition of 1837 (see below) and this version was based on manuscripts prepared by Raimund for his last performances and sold by Antonie Wagner to the book dealers Rohrmann and Schweigerd. The simplest way to date the individual plays themselves is by first performance, as follows:

Der Barometermacher auf der Zauberinsel. 18 December 1823.
Der Diamant des Geisterkönigs. 17 December 1824.
Das Mädchen aus der Feenwelt or *Der Bauer als Millionär.* 10 November 1826.
Moisasurs Zauberfluch. 25 September 1827.
Die gefesselte Phantasie. 8 January 1828.
Der Alpenkönig und der Menschenfeind. 17 October 1828.
Die unheilbringende Krone or *König ohne Reich, Held ohne Mut, Schönheit ohne Tugend.* 4 December 1829.
Der Verschwender. 20 February 1834.

The only play written outside the chronological order of performance presented here is *Die gefesselte Phantasie,* written in 1826, completed 24 September 1826.

b) Collected Works

Sämtliche Werke, ed. Johann Nepomuk Vogel. 4 vols. 1st edition. Vienna: Rohrmann and Schweigerd, 1837. 2nd edition. Vienna: Karl Hölzl, 1855.
Sämmtliche Werke. Nach den Original- und Theatermanuscripten nebst Nachlaß und Biographie, eds. Karl Glossy and August Sauer. 3 vols. Vienna: C. Konegen, 1881.

Sämtliche Werke, ed. Eduard Castle. Vienna: Hesses Klassikerausgabe, 1903.

Liebesbriefe, ed. Fritz Brukner. Vienna: Moritz Perles, 1914.

Sämtliche Werke, Historisch-kritische Säkularausgabe, eds. Fritz Brukner and Eduard Castle. 6 vols. (Vols. 1 and 2, *Dramen;* vol. 3, *Nachlaß;* vol. 4, *Briefe;* vol. 5, parts 1 and 2, ed. Franz Hadamowsky, *Ferdinand Raimund als Schauspieler: Chronologie seiner Rollen nebst Theaterreden und lebensgeschichtlichen Nachrichten;* vol. 6, ed. A. Orel, *Die Gesänge der Märchendramen in den ursprünglichen Vertonungen.* Vienna: Anton Schroll, 1924-1934.) (Nachdruck. Nendeln/ Liechtenstein: Kraus Reprint, 1974).

Sämtliche Werke. Nach dem Text der von Fritz Brukner und Eduard Castle besorgten Gesamtausgabe, ed. Friedrich Schreyvogel. Munich: Winkler, 1960.

Gesammelte Werke, ed. Otto Rommel. Gütersloh: Sigbert Mohn, 1961.

Werke, ed. Franz Hadamowsky. 2 vols. Salzburg/Stuttgart/Zürich: Bergland Buch, 1971.

II. English Translations

The King of the Alps. Adapted by J.B. Buckstone. London: Lacy's Acting Edition of Plays, vol. 6, 1852.

The Spendthrift. Translated by Erwin Tramer. New York: Frederick Ungar, 1949.

The Theater of Ferdinand Raimund: The Maid from Fairyland or The Peasant as Millionaire, Mountain King and Misanthrope. Translated by Corliss Edwin Phillabaum. Unpublished dissertation, Ohio State University, 1962.

III. Secondary Works In English

Branscombe, Peter. "Reflections on Raimund's Artistic Relationships with his Contemporaries." *Viennese Popular Theatre: A Symposium,* eds. W.E. Yates, John R.P. McKenzie. Exeter: University of Exeter Press (1985), pp. 25-40.

Crockett, Roger. "Raimund's 'Der Verschwender.' The Illusion of Freedom." *German Quarterly,* 58 (1985), 184-193.

Harding, Laurence Victor. *The Dramatic Art of Ferdinand Raimund and Johann Nestroy. A Critical Study.* The Hague: Mouton, 1974.

Jacobs, Margaret. "Legitimate and Illegitimate Drama: Ferdinand Raimund's 'Der Alpenkönig und der Menschenfeind' and John Baldwin Buckstone's 'The King of the Alps.'" *German Life and Letters,* 31 (1977), 41-52.

Jones, Calvin N. *Negation and Utopia: the German Volkstück from Raimund to Kroetz.* New York/Frankfurt am Main/etc.: Peter Lang, 1993.

Michalski, John. *Ferdinand Raimund.* New York: Twayne, 1968.

Nash, Martin A. "'Die gefesselte Phantasie' and Ferdinand Raimund." *The German Quarterly,* 36 (1963), 14-23.

Prohaska, Dorothy. *Raimund and Vienna. A Critical Study of Raimund's Plays in their Viennese Settting.* Cambridge: University Press, 1970.

Roe, Ian F. "Raimund's 'viele schöne Worte.'" *Viennese Popular Theatre: A Symposium,* eds. W.E. Yates, John R.P. McKenzie. Exeter: University of Exeter Press, 1985, pp. 13-24.

Straubinger, O. Paul. "The Reception of Raimund and Nestroy in England and America." *Österreich und die angelsächsische Welt,* ed. Otto Hietsch. Vienna/Stuttgart: Wilhelm Braumüller, 1961, pp. 481-494.

IV. Major Works In German

David, Claude. "Ferdinand Raimund: 'Moisasurs Zauberfluch,'" *Das deutsche Lustspiel* I, ed. Hans Steffen. Göttingen: Vandenhoeck & Ruprecht, 1968. pp. 120-143.

Hein, Jürgen. *Ferdinand Raimund.* Stuttgart: Metzler, 1970.

_____. "Ferdinand Raimund (1790-1836)." *Das Wiener Volkstheater.* Darmstadt: Wissenschaftliche Buchgesellschaft, 1978.

_____, ed. *Theater und Gesellschaft. Das Volksstück im 19. und 20. Jahrhundert.* Düsseldorf, 1973.

Helmensdorfer, Urs, ed. *Ferdinand Raimund. Das Mädchen aus der Feenwelt oder Der Bauer als Millionär. Text und Materialien zur Interpretation.* Berlin: Walter de Gruyter, 1966.

Hofmannsthal, Hugo von. "Ferdinand Raimund." *Gesammelte Werke in Einzelausgaben, Prosa III.* Frankfurt am Main: Fischer, 1964, pp. 471-478.

Kahl, Kurt. *Raimund.* Velber: Friedrich, 1967.

Kim, Yong-Ho. *Der Ernst von Ferdinand Raimunds Spielen—unter besonderer Berücksichtigung der Traditionsbezüge und der gesellschaftlichen Funktion seines Theaters.* New York/Frankfurt am Main/etc.: Peter

Lang, 1991.

Kindermann, Heinz. *Ferdinand Raimund: Lebenswerk und Wirkungsraum eines deutschen Volksdramatikers.* Vienna/Leipzig: Adolf Luser, 1940.

Klotz, Volker. "Raimunds Zaubertheater und seine Bedingungen." *Dramaturgie des Publikums.* Munich: Carl Hanser Verlag, 1976. pp. 50-88.

Kreissler, Felix. *Das Französische bei Raimund und Nestroy.* Vienna: Notring der wissenschaftlichen Verbände Osterreichs, 1967.

Müller, Gerd. "Die klassischen Vertreter des Alt-Wiener Volksstücks: Raimund, Nestroy." *Das Volksstück von Raimund bis Kroetz. Die Gattung in Einzelanalysen.* Munich: Oldenbourg, 1979.

Politzer, Heinz. "Raimund. 'Der Alpenkönig und der Menschenfeind.'" *Das deutsche Drama,* ed. Benno von Wiese. Vol. 2. Düsseldorf: Bagel, 1958, pp. 9-22.

_____. "Zauberspiegel und Seelenkranker. Ferdinand Raimunds 'Der Alpenkönig und der Menschenfeind.'" *Das Schweigen der Sirenen.* Stuttgart: Metzler, 1968, pp. 185-205.

Pongs, Hermann. "Ferdinand Raimund. 'Der Alpenkönig und der Menschenfeind.'" *Das Bild in der Dichtung.* Vol. 4. Marburg: Elwert, 1973.

Rommel, Otto. *Die Alt-Wiener Volkskomödie: Ihre Geschichte vom barocken Welttheater bis zum Tod Nestroys.* Vienna: Anton Schroll, 1952.

Sauer, August. "Ferdinand Raimund. Eine Charakteristik." *Gesammelte Reden und Aufsätze zur Geschichte der Literatur in Österreich und Deutschland.* Vienna: Carl Fromme, 1903, pp. 240-274.

Schaumann, Frank. *Gestalt und Funktion des Mythos in Ferdinand Raimunds Bühnenwerken.* Vienna: Bergland Verlag, 1970.

Sengle, Friedrich. "Ferdinand Raimund." *Biedermeierzeit. Deutsche Literatur im Spannungsfeld zwischen Restauration und Revolution 1815-1848.* 3 vols. Stuttgart: Metzler, vol. 3, 1980, pp. 1-56.

Urbach, Reinhard. *Die Wiener Komödie und ihr Publikum.* Vienna/Munich: Jugend und Volk Verlagsgesellschaft, 1973.

Wagner, Renate. *Ferdinand Raimund. Eine Biographie.* Vienna: Kremayr and Scheriau, 1985.

Weigel, Hans. *Flucht vor der Größe. Beiträge zur Erkenntnis und Selbsterkenntnis Österreichs.* Vienna: Wollzeilen-Verlag, 1960.

Wiltschko, Gunther. *Raimunds Dramaturgie.* Munich: Wilhelm Fink, 1973.

Leopold von Sacher-Masoch

Michael T. O'Pecko

The appearance of Leopold von Sacher-Masoch's first obituaries in Berlin, Cologne, and Frankfurt almost a year before his death signaled both the celebrity he had achieved as a young writer and the obscurity into which he had fallen in his later years. While he was justly, if sometimes excessively, celebrated as a major new talent in Austrian literature after the publication of his earlier works, this initial admiration was eventually eclipsed by an unhealthy curiosity about his personal life. Many critics and readers speculated about the relationship between autobiography and fiction in Sacher-Masoch's work, encouraged by his preoccupation with unconventional sexual behavior (which eventually led Richard von Kraft-Ebbing to coin the term "masochism" in his *Psychopathia sexualis*) and by the bitter and self-serving memoirs of his estranged wife, Aurora von Rümelin, better known as Wanda von Sacher-Masoch. Finally, his distaste for the rising tide of materialism, militarism, and nationalism in the newly united German Reich, which he first voiced in his novel *Die Ideale der Zeit* (1873, The Ideals of the Time), and his sympathetic and knowledgable portrayals of Eastern European Jews in his works encouraged many of his critics to forego literary analysis in favor of anti-Semitic or anti-Slavic attacks.

The author's father, Leopold von Sacher, a member of the Austrian hereditary nobility with the title "Ritter von Kronenthal" (Knight of Kronenthal) was a highly placed official in the Austrian civil service, serving first in Lemberg (now the Ukrainian city of Lvov), then in Prague, and finally in Graz. His mother was the daughter and only surviving child of a prominent Ruthenian[1] physician, Dr. Franz Masoch. Since Dr. Masoch had no male children to carry on the line, he requested that his son-in-law seek permission from the Austrian Emperor to add his father-in-law's name to his own, thus becoming the first of the Sacher-Masochs.

The writer, his son and namesake, was born on 27 January 1835, in Lemberg, then the capital of Austrian Galicia. According to an autobiographical sketch,[2] it was a Ruthenian peasant woman serving as his nanny who first stimulated his imagination by singing him folk songs and telling him stories and fairy tales. According to another source,[3] the boy spoke only Polish and Ruthenian until he was thirteen years old, when he learned German for the first time. Moving with his family to Prague, he began his university studies there, earning a doctorate in history when he was only twenty-one years old at the University of Graz, where he lectured for the following ten years.[4]

Sacher-Masoch's first major work of fiction, a novel entitled *Eine galizische Geschichte: 1846* (1858, A Galician Story), took as its theme the Polish insurrection of 1846, which had impressed itself on his memory during his childhood in Lemberg. In this novel, Sacher-Masoch painted a picture of the larger social order in Austrian Galicia, including portraits of the Austrian bureaucracy and military, the German settlers, the Ruthenian peasantry, and Jews, while focusing on a group of aristocratic Polish conspirators whom he depicted as elegant, dashing, courteous, and chivalric among themselves, but as romantic and unrealistic in their political scheming, and often cruel and inhumane in their treatment of their peasants. The novel implies that the insurrection failed because of the peasants' unwillingness to follow their Polish overlords in a campaign against the Austrian Emperor, whom the peasants considered a "good master."

In this novel Sacher-Masoch introduced several themes which would characterize much of his later work, including sexual domination of men by women. In Sacher-Masoch's works, such women, while clearly intriguing to the author, exercise despotic power in social or political realms (which Sacher-Masoch's works consistently condemn), reflect their male partner's immaturity, or use their cruelty to attain social and economic ends otherwise beyond their reach. In *Eine galizische Geschichte,* for example, the Princess Wanda Solnikoff, like most of Sacher-Masoch's heroines, who are separated, divorced, or widowed, has left her husband and returned to her family's estate in Galicia. Her beauty and charm are matched only by her arrogance and her cruelty, as she demonstrates when she explains with a smile that her exquisite fur was taken from an animal caught by a Siberian exile who would rather have wrapped it around his frozen feet than have relinquished it so it could be made into a lining for the jacket of a woman leading a luxurious life.[5] Thus, in one of his first uses of this motif Sacher-Masoch employs the fur, which plays such a large role in the erotic obsessions of many of his male characters, as a symbol of oppression and inequality.

Her admirer, Count Stanislaus Donski, the novel's most aggressively, even stereotypically, masculine character and a leader of the revolt, acknowledges Wanda's nature when he toasts her as "our Amazon," drinks champagne out of her slipper, and then places it back on her foot as "humbly as a slave" (94). In fact, Donski displays a disconcerting preoccupation with Wanda's feet and is repeatedly inclined to describe himself as her slave. Donski's attitude toward the peasants is as cruel and inhumane as Wanda's is toward the unknown Siberian exile; he contemptuously denies, for example, that "the peasant, this animal, this beast, [could have] the same rights as I" (44).

The novel's most brutally described deaths are reserved for Wanda and Donski, who are, fittingly, clubbed to death by enraged, rebellious peasants. That these deaths are meant to be understood as punishment for Wanda's and Donski's thoughts and deeds is underlined by the fate of a second pair of lovers, Julian Mislecki and Minia Rozminski (Wanda's younger sister), whose love is not distorted by the mistress-slave relationship that characterizes the former couple, and who are recognized by their peasants as good, kind human beings; they are virtually the only conspirators who survive the revolt and come to a happy ending.

Except for *Der Emissär: Eine galizische Geschichte* (1863, The Emissary: A Galician Story), which built upon the success of *Eine galizische Geschichte: 1846,* the next phase in Sacher-Masoch's career consisted of a more rigorous attempt to marry his historical training to his literary ambitions. However the historical novels *Kaunitz* (1865), *Der letzte König der Magyaren* (1867, The Last King of the Magyars), and the historical drama *Der Mann ohne Vorurtheil* (1866, The Man without Prejudice) did little to further his reputation as a writer.

According to yet another autobiographical sketch,[6] Sacher-Masoch found his own authorial voice with the aid and encouragement of the eminent writer and critic Ferdinand Kürnberger. Kürnberger had rejected Sacher-Masoch's earlier work as worthless because, he claimed, it was "manufactured," like all German literature since Goethe. When Sacher-Masoch told him tales of his "Little Russian" homeland, however, Kürnberger listened "with rapture" and finally declared that if Sacher-Masoch could only write what he narrated so cleverly, he would be a true poet. Sacher-Masoch claims he set to work that very evening and two weeks later was able to read the completed manuscript of the *Novelle* "Don Juan von Kolomea" (Don Juan of Kolomea) to Kürnberger, who was so impressed with this work he volunteered a foreword in which he compared his young friend to Goethe and Turgenev.

"Don Juan von Kolomea" was the first completed work to be included in the ambitious, uncompleted cycle of *Novellen* that Sacher-Masoch conceived under the title *Das Vermächtnis Kains* (The Legacy of Cain). Sacher-Masoch intended to portray "all of mankind's great problems, all the dangers of existence, all of humanity's ills."[8] Six groups of *Novellen,* each consisting of six *Novellen,* were to be composed on the themes of love, property, the state, war, work, and death. Of the six novellas Sacher-Masoch planned for each of the six themes, five would explore the questions raised by the theme, and the sixth would propose an answer to those questions.

The first cycle, *Die Liebe* (Love), appeared in 1870 and consisted of a prologue entitled "Der Wanderer" (The Wanderer), reprints of three previously published works, "Don Juan von Kolomea," "Der Capitulant" (The Man Who Re-enlisted), and "Mondnacht" (Night of the Moon), and three new works entitled "Venus im Pelz" (Venus in Furs), "Die Liebe des Plato" (Plato's Love), and "Marzella" (Marcella).

"Der Wanderer" articulates the philosophical framework for the entire series of six cycles in the form of a conversation between two characters: the narrator, presumably the same person in all six *Novellen* of *Die Liebe,* a young man of means out hunting (apparently modeled on the narrator in Turgenev's *A Huntsman's Sketches*), and the Wanderer, a member of a Russian religious sect that believes the world is ruled by Satan and therefore considers it sinful to marry, own property, or acquiesce in the laws of the state, since such actions would be tantamount to accepting the authority of a corrupt world; thus, the Wanderer roams ceaselessly throughout the world, always "fleeing from life."

The Wanderer's philosophy reveals the author's apparent familiarity with the Ruthenian peasant's outlook as well as the influence of Schopenhauer and, probably, Darwin. The Wanderer rejects the concept of love, stating that men and women are, like all creatures, enemies by nature, united for only a short time by lust and nature's blind drive to reproduce the species. Property, the state, and war arise only through the human propensity to exploit the work of others. The great secret of existence, according to the Wanderer, is that work is the only activity that can free man from his misery. Inescapable death, the only source of complete release, peace, and freedom, should be welcomed rather than feared. The narrator's reception of the Wanderer's precepts seems uncritical, but its effect upon him is more positive, leaving in him a "holy yearning for knowledge and truth."[9] These principles articulated by the Wanderer underlie virtually all of Sacher-Masoch's work throughout his long career.

Only two of the projected six cycles, *Die Liebe* and *Das Eigenthum* (Property), were completed,[10] but *Die Liebe* contains what is arguably Sacher-Masoch's best work, provocative in its ideas and startling in its succinctly powerful descriptions. Since the reception of "Venus im Pelz" has played such an important role in determining Sacher-Masoch's reputation, and since "Venus im Pelz" can be properly understood only in the context of *Die Liebe,* it will be necessary to devote attention to each of the *Novellen* in the cycle.

"Don Juan von Kolomea," like the other *Novellen* of *Die Liebe,* is a *Rahmennovelle,* in which the narrator of of the cycle encounters the central figure of the tale, who then tells his or her own story. Demetrius, a "Russian" (i.e., Ruthenian) estate owner, relates his marriage was originally a happy one that provided deep satisfaction to himself and his wife, Nikolaja, until the birth of their children, when her excessive devotion to her children led her to neglect him, thus provoking the distortions in his personality that led to repeated and obsessive adultery.

The text indicates a successful relationship between a man and a woman must necessarily be based on equality between the sexes; such a relationship was enjoyed by Demetrius and Nikolaja in the earlier, happy stage of their marriage: "Among our people, the husband has no special privileges; we have one law for man and wife" (55). That equality, which Demetrius describes as "two monarchs negotiating with one another," is destroyed by Nikolaja's withdrawal of her affections from him in favor of her children. The inability to achieve or maintain equality between the sexes motivates many of the conflicts in Sacher-Masoch's fiction and is the basis for the repeated depiction of the mistress-slave relationship in much of his work.

The quality of the love in Demetrius' adulterous relationships is very different than the love he experienced within the marriage, as becomes apparent in his description of the peasant girl with whom he first went astray. When he first describes her dirty, unkempt appearance, her red scarf and the red sky behind her, her dark complexion, her hawk-like nose, and the snake-like hissing of her eyes ("ihre Augen zischen gegen mich auf") all indicate a natural, passionate sensuality, but one that is dangerous and threatens to destroy its object (53).

Thus, while Sacher-Masoch explored uncommon forms of love with sympathy and tolerance throughout his career, his texts are often structured around nineteenth-century bourgeois values, as in "Don Juan von Kolomea," where the extramarital experience is presented so vividly and so negatively in contrast to an idealized partnership of equals within the conjugal state.

At first glance, "Der Capitulant" is a more conventional tale of unhappy love: two young Ruthenian peasants, Katharina and Frinko, fall in love, but she attracts the eye of the local nobleman and eventually becomes mistress of his great estate, causing Frinko to join the army. The unusual aspect of the tale is the attempt on the part of Frinko and the other peasants in the tale to understand the economic necessity that underlies Katharina's decision. Kolanko, who is said to be over a hundred years old, articulates the story's point most clearly: "[A woman] can't work like a man . . . By nature she has no stamina, that is sure, and besides, she doesn't learn anything worthwhile, no craft; so naturally she tries to live off a man. . . . Just think of what a man has to do to get ahead—while some pretty thing just has to show her face or, at most, something else as well, and the girl who tended the cows turns into a lady" (98). While such insight suffices to allow Frinko to maintain a pure-hearted love for Katharina, it leads him to the startling conclusion that, while a man can love romantically with his whole heart, a woman's position precludes her from doing so.

Katharina is in some ways typical of Sacher-Masoch's female characters: her predatory eroticism does not result from distorted biological theories or philosophical mysogynism, but from the author's belief that women, a disadvantaged, even oppressed, sex, have only their erotic domination over men to achieve the advantages men realize by other means, such as birth, education, or economic independence.

"Mondnacht," the third *Novelle,* is the story of Olga, the wife of a Ruthenian estate owner, Mihail, who forces her to live in isolation from the larger world of the district capital and who loses interest in her as he becomes involved in the district's political life. Olga resolves to take a lover, Wladimir, to make her husband jealous. Wladimir, a gifted, hard-working man, is originally contemptuous of this frivolous and spoiled crea-ture, but they eventually fall passionately in love with each other. After a year in which Olga shares Wladimir's life and assimilates his view, their affair is discovered, and her husband kills Wladimir in a duel. Olga, who remains with Mihail for the sake of their children and because of her need to be loved, becomes a somnambulist driven to tell her story to the nar-rator (identified as "Leopold"). She says her only sin is "that she is a woman and that she was raised like a woman, for *pleasure* and not for *work*" (115, emphasis original).

A common theme links "Die Liebe des Plato" and "Venus im Pelz," the first two *Novellen* of the second volume of *Die Liebe:* Their central characters are conceived in the tradition of Don Quixote or, more pre-cisely, Wieland's Don Sylvio. They are "Schwärmer," unrealistic dreamers, whose imaginations have been overly stimulated by literature, philosophy, and art. While each of them "learns his lesson" in the end, neither is suffi-ciently cured to construct a way of life in which sexuality plays a healthy role.

"Die Liebe des Plato," while professing to explore "platonic" love, i.e., spiritual love free of sensuality, is in fact a remarkably candid and sympa-thetic portrayal of a young man with a clearly homoerotic orientation.[11] Count Henryk Tarnow, described as looking like "a girl in disguise," is a philosopher and idealist who avoided women but who "treated men with a delicacy and a charm similar to that with which others treat our women."[12]

Predisposed to avoid romantic involvement because of the example of his parents' unhappy marriage, Henryk falls under the spell of Plato's "Symposium," reading it so frequently he can almost recite it by heart. Convinced by his reading that spiritual love must be valued more highly than physical love, he rejects all involvements with women, arguing that women, who are of a purely sensual nature, are incapable of spiritual love. He concludes "the most noble, the best feeling, the one that gives us the greatest satisfaction seems to me to be the friendship of one man to another, because such friendship alone is based on equality and is com-pletely spiritual" (38).

His theories are tested by Countess Nadeschda Baragreff, a rich, di-vorced Muscovite, who possesses a slender and fine build as well as a spiritual quality "expressed not so much in the shape of her body as in her stance and in her movements, not in the features of her face, but rather in its expression" (49-50).[13] Henryk, whose behavior and convictions are now so well known as to have earned him the nickname "Plato," tells Nadeschda openly, "I could love you if you weren't a woman" (57). She replies she is sure he will enjoy the company of her brother, Anatol, whose physical appearance is strikingly similar to her own, but whose philosphy of love is virtually identical to Henryk's.

Nadeschda disguises herself as a man, takes the name Anatol, and begins a series of midnight assignations with Henryk. At their first meeting Anatol remains behind a curtain, but he and Henryk grow ever more intimate until, upon seeing Anatol in form-fitting clothing for the first time, he felt "that force of nature that no living creature can completely oppose and avoid. I felt the mysterious working of sensual beauty" (108). But when Anatol reveals himself to be Nadeschda, Henryk is shattered and ends the relationship.

Six years later, Henryk again encounters Nadeschda, yields to her in her boudoir within the hour, and marries her, but they are divorced within the year. At the time of the narration he leads an apparently celibate life in his own dwelling on the Hungarian estate of a friend who holds similar views.

Henryk fears women because he considers their pure sensuality to be inimical to his own more spiritual nature (25), thus subscribing to the image of the demonic woman that would become fashionable at the turn of the century. He never seizes the repeated opportunities to correct his view, such as when he acknowledges his mother's spiritual superiority as an exception to his thesis and her example as the major influence on the development of his own personality. In addition, the narrator, whose function in the collection is often to correct the mistaken perceptions of the central character who has narrated his or her own story, calls him "quite exaggerated" in the final scene of the *Novelle* (118). The most potent argument against Henryk's position and the *Novelle*'s most eloquent defense of a woman's ability to be a man's equal in spirituality, however, comes from Anatol, who states men would have to be patient with women, who, having previously been accustomed to being treated and indulged like children, were now being asked, as equals, to give up all their sweet bonbons (79).

Thus, although "Die Liebe des Plato" illustrates the Wanderer's belief that men and women are enemies by nature, it also quietly articulates Sacher-Masoch's belief in the possibility of transforming male-female enmity into harmonious relationships based on equality.

Severin Kusiemski, the young, central character of "Venus im Pelz," has also derived his ideas about love from literature and art. Severin's eccentricity, not dissimilar to Henryk's ideal Platonic love, is "Übersinnlichkeit," or pretersensuality, by which he means the state of being beyond the grasp of the merely sensual. But whereas a platonic relationship finally seems to have provided Henryk with some modicum of satisfaction, Severin has deluded himself about his pretersensual character; he has zealously sought out examples of women's erotic domination of men from sources ranging from the Bible to Goethe and has become obsessed with them. Thus, while Henryk fears becoming enslaved to a woman, Severin works actively to place himself in that same position.

While vacationing at a Carpathian resort, where he spends his time reading and dreaming in self-imposed isolation, Severin meets Wanda von Dunajew, a beautiful, young widow from Lemberg. He falls in love with her, but they hold contradictory views on love: she considers "pleasure without pain" and "the serene sensuality of the Hellenes" the ideals she wishes to realize in her life, whereas he believes love to be a "sweet torture."[14] Their relationship becomes ever more unequal, with the juvenile and inexperienced Severin becoming ever more attracted to and dependent upon Wanda's mature and autonomous personality. He finally declares that, since he cannot fully enjoy the happiness of love, he would drink its pain and torture to the last drop; that, he proclaims, is also a kind of pleasure (55).

Eventually, after much persuasion, Wanda agrees to make him her slave, and they enter into a contract binding Severin to her for six months. They travel together to Florence, where Wanda banishes him from her presence and orders him to work in the gardens for long periods at a time; she is annoyed by his ceaseless desire to be punished and beaten. This unnatural situation comes to a close when Wanda meets a handsome Greek, who at Wanda's instigation gives Severin the beating of his life before they leave Florence (and Severin) to begin their life together.

Severin then returns to Galicia, where he takes over the management of his father's estate and settles into a more productive, satisfying existence, learning ". . . what I didn't know before, something that restored me like a drink of fresh water; [I learned] *to work* and *to fulfill my obligations*" (139). As the Wanderer had predicted in the prologue, work was the only thing that could free him from his misery.[15]

The final *Novelle* of *Die Liebe* is "Marzella, oder das Märchen vom Glück," in which the "solution" to the problems occasioned by love is proposed. Marzella, a peasant girl, rejects the advances of Count Alexander Komarow, until, when asked what she wants from him she demands to be educated. She quickly proves her superior ability, and in the course of time they are married. In this ideal household, Marzella shares the tasks and interests of her husband as an equal, and even states that only when women have the appropriate intellectual ("geistig") work can women's "emancipation" (her word) be achieved.[16]

Sacher-Masoch has been forgotten as a champion of women and their rights. As the most frequently published and widely translated of his works, "Venus im Pelz" is virtually the only work for which he is known today, and its reception has been exceptionally narrow, focusing almost exclusively on the the plot's more scandalous aspects as can be seen even in various editions and translations of the work[17] as well as in the secondary literature.[18]

The unconventionality of the plot of "Venus im Pelz" and the situations in which Henryk and Severin find themselves can be disconcerting even today. It is probable Sacher-Masoch was what is today called a masochist, and it is likely his portrayal of the physical pain and humiliation, sometimes possible in love, was born of his own obsessions. But his extremely chaste portrayal of potentially erotic scenes and his attempt to address major social and aesthetic issues, such as the role of women in society or the influence of art and literature on their admirers, elevate "Die Liebe des Plato" and "Venus im Pelz" above their unfortunate, narrow reputations.

Sacher-Masoch's life and his fiction are confusingly intertwined. In December 1869, for example, he is supposed to have signed a "contract" that obligated him to be the "slave" of Fanny Pistor Bogdanow for a period of six months. Assuming the contract itself was not fiction, as was suggested by Karl Demandt,[19] it seems impossible to say with certainty whether "Venus im Pelz" imitates an episode in his life or whether, inspired by his fiction, he determined to live out his fantasy.[20]

Another, earlier liaison with a married woman, Anna von Kottowitz, supplied him with the background for *Eine geschiedene Frau* (1870, A

Divorced Woman), which, despite its title, revolves around a young man whose idealism prevents him from forming a realistic assessment of a woman with whom he has a passionate affair. Like Severin in "Venus im Pelz," Julian von Romaschkan must undergo mistreatment, psychological and physical, before he learns his lesson, as the novel's subtitle "Passions-geschichte eines Idealisten" (The Passion Story of an Idealist) indicates.

Next Sacher-Masoch began receiving pseudonymous letters from a young woman in Graz named Aurora von Rümelin, who styled herself "Wanda" in imitation of the heroine of "Venus im Pelz." Whatever the truth of their ill-starred courtship and marriage may be,[21] there can be no question that the financial obligations brought on by his growing family's needs exercised a negative influence on his art. Often writing hurriedly to survive, he found little time to polish and revise his work, which remains interesting primarily because of his talent as a born raconteur and his sometimes startling insights into social and aesthetic trends.[22] He divorced "Wanda" in 1886 and subsequently married Hulda Meister, who had worked as a translator for the journal *Auf der Höhe* (On the Heights), where Sacher-Masoch served as editor from its inception in 1881 until its demise in 1885.[23]

A great deal of Sacher-Masoch's later work can be characterized as "pi-quant tales," as they were known during his lifetime, since his straitened circumstances made it necessary for him to concentrate on work that sold well.[24] But even these works, whose plots most frequently take place in the theater, the Russian court, or Viennese society, do not abandon his views on women as articulated in *Die Liebe*. In "Eine grausame Reclame" (1873, A Cruel Advertisement), for example, an aging actress encourages a young officer's attention only to scream for help at the compromising moment. After she complains to his commanding officer and the local newspapers that he forced himself upon her, he commits suicide; she is using her only assets to assure her economic survival. In his posthumously published "Die Daumschrauben" (1907, The Thumbscrews), the friendship of Justus Mö-ser with a beautiful duchess moves her to abolish torture as a means of obtaining confessions, but she must first convince their prime minister and her husband. When the prime minister denies torture could force anyone to confess to anything falsely, she uses thumbscrews on him to force him to confess his passion for her and his hatred of the duke (both lies), there-by winning his support for her campaign; her cruelty was her only means to exercise political power.

The principles articulated by the Wanderer in *Die Liebe* also underlie his Jewish and Ruthenian tales, the two most important subsets of Galician tales that constitute the greater part of his remaining work.

Having observed Jewish life in the Galician ghetto as a child when he accompanied his uncle, a doctor, to Jewish homes, Sacher-Masoch portrayed the Jews frequently and sympathetically in his work, leading anti-Semitic, German nationalist critics to dismiss his work because of his alleged ethnic heritage.[25] These works on Jewish themes, including the collections *Judengeschichten* (1878), *Neue Judengeschichten* (1881), *Polnische Ghetto-Geschichten* (1886), and *Jüdisches Leben in Wort und Bild* (1891; originally published in France as *Conte Juifs,* 1888), the *Novellen* "Hasara Raba" (1874), "Der Judenraphael" (1882) and "Der Iluj" (1882), consciously attempted to battle the rising tide of anti-Semitism that arose throughout German-speaking Europe after the founding of the German empire in 1871. Adolf Opel praised the literary quality of the Jewish tales for their realistic characterizations and the unrelenting psychological illumination of the protagonists; with the publication of *Jüdisches Leben in Wort und Bild,* however, he asserts that Sacher-Masoch's literary ambitions yielded to didactic ones, resulting in an idealization and an apotheosis of the Jewish character set in a landscape of comforting idylls.[26] Despite the philo-Semitism of these works, it must be pointed out that Sacher-Masoch's characterizations, like those of other authors sympathetic to Jewish aspirations in late nineteenth-century Austria, were not infrequently crude and stereotyped.[27]

Like Karl Emil Franzos, who also frequently set his work in the Galician ghetto, Sacher-Masoch seems to advocate Jewish secularization and assimilation. Not surprisingly, he expected education and work to transform the Jews' position in society as throroughly as he expected them to alter women's status. Unlike Franzos, however, he could be sympathetic to the Chassidim,[28] whose exotic Eastern ways embarrassed Franzos, an assimilated Jew. Because of this sympathy for the full spectrum of Jewish society in Galicia and his seemingly encyclopedic knowledge of the religious practices and social mores of the Galician Jews, Sacher-Masoch's Jewish tales are of ethnographic as well as literary interest.

Sacher-Masoch's tendency in the Ruthenian tales is the same as in *Eine galizische Geschichte: 1846:* to demonstrate the injustices the peasantry[29] suffered at the hands of the Polish aristocracy. A major weakness in these works, which include the collections *Galizische Geschichten* and *Basyl der*

Schatzgräber, as well as individual *Novellen* such as *Das Volksgericht* or *Der Hajdamak,* is his inability to portray the peasants as three-dimensional characters; he is generally far less successful in this respect than Berthold Auerbach or Jeremias Gotthelf; in these works it is usually the Austrian officials, the clergy, or the local aristocracy whose characterizations dominate the narrative. The suspicion that many of these tales were written as an Austrian counterpart to tales of the American "wild west" is borne out when one of them characterizes the Ruthenians as "primitive people, like in the American prairies" and then explicitly compares them to the American Indians.[30]

In 1893, two years before his death, Sacher-Masoch, then living in the German town of Lindheim, founded the Upper-Hessian Association for Public Education (Oberhessischer Volksbildungsverein), whose stated aims were to further the practical and intellectual interests of the Upper Hessian peasants by founding public libraries, organizing concerts, plays, and lectures, and providing financial support for young men and women to attend agricultural and trade schools.[31] Despite impressive accomplishments in the two years of its existence, the Association did not survive its founder's death.

Subsequent reissues of Sacher-Masoch's work were largely limited to the "piquant" literature and the Jewish tales. With a few exceptions, notably the works of Eberhard Hasper, Rudolf Latzke, and Hartmut Steinecke cited in the bibliographic section of this article, serious literary scholarship largely ignored Sacher-Masoch after his death. Beginning in the 1960s, several scholars attempted to use his works as a basis for the articulation of a psychological theory of masochism.[32] More recently, Michael Farin has provided the foundation for a fresh appraisal of Sacher-Masoch's work by gathering together widely scattered biographical and critical materials in one major volume and by reissuing several of the more important out-of-print works. In addition, with the growth of interest in village and ghetto literature, there has been a renewed interest in the Jewish tales.[33]

Sacher-Masoch's work cannot easily be assigned to any single style or period. An heir to the humane beliefs of German classicism and the progressive social ideas of Young Germany, and a forefather of some of the stylistic and thematic experiments of Naturalism, Impressionism, and Jugendstil, his works must be considered one of the finest products of Realism in the German language, portraying as they do his characters and their stories within their social and economic context in the most distant corners of the Austro-Hungarian empire; in addition, the best of his prose style, distinguished by its musicality and richness of detail, has been favorably compared to Stifter and Turgenev.[34] While he has been granted some recognition for his achievements in a period when "gender norms were being protested and redefined from a variety of standpoints," his work in this area still requires an objective evaluation free of the taunt of pornography. Finally, because of his unending attempt to discover and portray the humanity of scorned and neglected ethnic groups and social classes, he deserves the respect of our more tolerant century.

Notes

1. Ruthenian was the term used in Austria-Hungary to denote the Ukrainian or Rusyn population of Galicia. Sacher Masoch also used the term "Little Russian."

2. Originally sent to Paul Heyse, and published in Leopold von Sacher-Masoch, *Don Juan von Kolomea: Galizische Geschichten,* ed. Michael Farin (Bonn: Bouvier, 1985), pp. 198-199.

3. Franz Brümmer, *Deutsches Dichter-Lexikon* (Eichstatt/Stuttgart), 1877, reprinted in Michael Farin, *Leopold von Sacher-Masoch: Materialien zu Leben und Werk* (Bonn: Bouvier, 1987), pp. 28-30.

4. A detailed account of Sacher-Masoch's years at the University of Graz can be found in Walter Höflechner, "Leopold von Sacher-Masoch Ritter von Kronenthal und die Universität Graz," *Publikationen aus dem Archiv der Universität Graz,* ed. Hermann Wiesflecker (Graz: Akademische Druck- und Verlagsanstalt, 1975), vol. 4, pp. 125-138, reprinted in Farin, *Materialien,* pp. 252-272.

5. (Schaffhausen: Hurter, 1858), p. 323.

6. *Deutsche Monatsblätter* (Bremen) II, 3 (June 1879), 263-264. Reprinted in Sacher-Masoch, *Souvenirs,* ed. Susanne Farin (Munich: edition belleville, 1985), pp. 66-67.

7. Reprinted in Sacher-Masoch, *Don Juan von Kolomea: Galizische Geschichten,* ed. Michael Farin (Bonn: Bouvier, 1985), pp. 188-194.

8. "Prospekt des Werkes *Das Vermächtnis Kains,*" sent by Sacher-Masoch to J.G. Cotta and reprinted in ibid., pp. 179-180. All translations are mine.

9.   Ibid., p. 18. All page numbers referring to "Don Juan von Kolomea," "Der Capitulant," and "Mondnacht" also refer to this edition.

10. In addition, Michael Farin believes a number of the later *Novellen* can be ascribed to the uncompleted cycles (Sacher-Masoch, *Don Juan von Kolomea,* ed. Michael Farin, p. 184).

11. Paul Derks, in his *Die Schande der heiligen Päderastie: Homosexualität und Öffentlichkeit in der deutschen Literatur 1750-1850* (Berlin: Verlag Rosa Winkel, 1990), maintains that "Platonic" was occasionally used as a code word for "homosexual."

12. Sacher-Masoch, *Die Liebe* (Stuttgart: J.G. Cotta, 1878 [third edition]), vol. 2, pp. 6-7.

13. Sacher-Masoch here touches on another of Wieland's themes, the difference between "Anmut" (grace), which is the expression of the soul as revealed in movement or expression, and "Reiz" (physical charm), which was the emanation of the mind as revealed in the beautiful form of the charming object.

14. Leopold von Sacher-Masoch, *Venus im Pelz* (Frankfurt: Insel, 1968), p. 22. All translations are mine.

15. For a more detailed analysis of "Venus im Pelz," see Michael O'Pecko, "Comedy and Didacticity in Leopold von Sacher-Masoch's *Venus im Pelz,* in: *Modern Austrian Literature,* vol. 25, no. 2 (June 1992), pp. 1-13. Rita Felski's "The Counterdiscourse of the Feminine in Three Texts by Wilde, Huysmans, and Sacher-Masoch" (*Publications of the Modern Language Association,* 106 (1991), pp. 1094-1105 reaches a different conclusion, contending that "the parodic subversion of gender norms reinscribes more insistently the divisions that the text ostensibly calls into question" (1094).

16. Sacher-Masoch, *Die Liebe,* vol. 2, p. 463.

17. Ledos de Beaufort's 1902 translation published in Paris by Charles Carrington, for instance, carries the glaring subtitle "roman sur la flagellation," and the 1968 edition published by the prestigious Insel Verlag was bound in purple velvet.

18. Titles such as Leopold Stern's *Sacher-Masoch ou l'amour de la souffrance* (Paris: Bernard Grasset, 1933; Mark Amiaux' *Un grand anormal: Le Chevalier de Sacher-Masoch* (Paris: Les éditions de France, 1938); Reinhard Federmann's *Sacher-Masoch oder die Selbstvernichtung* (Graz: Stiasny, 1963); Gilles Deleuze's *Présentation de Sacher-Masoch: Le froid et le cruel* (Paris: Editions de Minuit, 1967);

and James Cleugh's *The First Masochist* (New York: Stein & Day, 1967) make the direction of this work's reception clear.

19. "Leopold von Sacher-Masoch und sein Oberhessischer Volksbil-dungsverein zwischen Schwarzen, Roten und Antisemiten," *Hessiches Jahrbuch für Landesgeschichte,* 18 (1968), pp. 160-208. Reprinted in Farin, *Materialien,* pp. 272-331.

20. The text of the contract is contained in Carl Felix Schlichtegroll, *Wanda ohne Maske und Pelz* (Leipzig: Leipziger Verlag, 1906), pp. 24-25, and reprinted in Sacher-Masoch, *Don Juan von Kolomea,* p. 181. Michael Farin states that Sacher-Masoch was writing "Venus im Pelz" at the time of the contract (*Don Juan Kolomea,* p. 181), but C.F. Schlichtegroll indicates that a substantially completed version of "Venus im Pelz" existed at the time of Sacher-Masoch's relationship with Anna von Kottowitz, before the alleged signing of his contract with Fanny Pistor (quoted in Sacher-Masoch, *Die geschiedene Frau* [Nördlingen: Greno, 1989], p. 198).

21. Neither Wanda's self-serving autobiography, *Meine Lebensbeichte* (1906, Confession of My Life) nor Carl Felix von Schlichtegroll's tendentious rejoinder, *"Wanda" ohne Maske und Pelz* (1906, "Wanda" *sans* Mask and Fur) can be considered completely reliable, and they disagree on most major points. Schlichtegroll's work, none-theless, more often has the ring of truth than *Meine Lebensbeichte.*

22. As early as the 1870s Sacher-Masoch was describing the effects of technology in terms that are identical to those used by German and American Impressionists at the turn of the century. In *Die Ideale unserer Zeit* (1875, The Ideals of Our Time), for example, he wrote, "In our day life rushes ahead as if it were driven by steam. Just as the smoking-snorting monster with the glowing, red eyes carries us off so that forest and field, river and mountains fly past, so we, too, change the human images around us. We demand rapid change in everything . . ." (Bern: B.F. Haller, 1876 [third edition], vol. 3, p. 2). In the same novel the narrator states that "our material, nervous age knows no higher purpose in art than its effect on the nerves" I, 32).

23. He was also connected with the *Gartenlaube für Österreich* from 1866 to 1867 and a short-lived effort called *Belletristische Blätter* in 1880.

24. Hulda Meister complained that although no one wanted to reissue his serious works, the *Novellen* of *Das Vermächtnis Kains,* for example, his piquant works were best-sellers and continually reissued although the family did not profit from their sales ("Erinnerungen an Sacher-Masoch," *Wiener Leben,* 17 April 1910, pp. 1-3. Reprinted Farin, *Materialien,* pp. 9-16).

25. See Farin, *Materialien,* for example.

26. Adolf Opel, "Nachwort," *Der Judenraphael,* by Leopold von Sacher-Masoch, ed. by Adolf Opel (Vienna: Böhlau, 1989), p. 457.

27. Egon Schwarz, "Judische Gestalten bei Marie von Ebner-Eschanbach und Ferdinand von Saar," *German Quarterly* 63.2 (1990), 173-186.

28. See especially Sacher-Masoch's portrayal of the miraculous rabbi of Sadagora in "Hasara Raba."

29. Wilhalm Goldmann's comment in his *Literarischen Physiognomien* (Vienna, 1884; quoted by Adolf Opel in his edition of *Der Judenraphael,* p. 452) that Sacher-Masoch hated the Poles, pitied the Ruthenians, and loved the Jews is only correct insofar as the Poles in question were aristocrats. The Polish peasant received the same sympathy as the Ruthenians, but since Sacher-Masoch's work was set primarily in Eastern Galicia, where the Ruthenians predominated, the portrayal of Polish peasants is infrequent.

30. Sacher-Masoch, "Magaß der Räuber," *Galizische Geschichten* (Leipzig: Ernst Julius Günther, 1875), p. 16.

31. Kaarl E. Demandt's admirable essay, "Leopold von Sacher-Masoch und sein Oberhessischer Folksbildungsverein zwischen Schwarzen, Roten, und Antisemiten" (Farin, *Materialien,* pp. 272-331 demonstrates that another important, if unstated aim was to struggle against the rising tide of anti-Semitism in the Hessian lower classes.

32. See especially Gilles Deleuze, *Présentation de Sacher-Masoch: Le froid et le cruel* (Paris: Éditions de Minuit, 1967) and Zbigniew Swiatlowski, Sacher-Masoch oder die bedrohte Normalitat," *Germanica Wratislaviensia* 27 (1976), 149-171.

33. See especially Hans Otto Horch, "Der Außenseiter als 'Judenraphael': Zu den Judengeschichten Leopolds von Sacher-Masoch," *Conditio Judaica: Judentum, Antisemitismus und deutschsprachige Literatur vom 18. Jahrhundert bis zum Ersten Weltkrieg* (Tübingen: Niemeyer, 1989), pp. 258-286; Andrea Wodenegg, *Das Bild der Juden Osteuropas: Ein Beitrag zur komparatistischen Imagologie an*

Textbeispielen von Karl Emil Franzos und Leopold von Sacher-Masoch (Frankfurt am Main/Bern/New York: Peter Lang, 1987), and David Biale, "Masochism and Philo-Semitism: The Strange Case of Leopold von Sacher-Masoch," *Journal of Contemporary History,* vol. 17, no. 2 (April 1982), 305-323.

34.   Opel, p. 437.
35.   Felski, p. 1094.

Bibliography

1. Works by Leopold von Sacher-Masoch in German

Eine galizische Geschichte: 1846. Schaffhausen: Friedrich Hurter, 1858.
Later printed in abridged form under the title *Graf Donski.*

Der Emissär: Eine galizische Geschichte. Prague: F.A. Credner, 1863.

Die Verse Friedrich des Großen: Historisches Lustspiel Schaffhausen: Friedrich Hurter, 1864.

Kaunitz: Culturhistorischer Roman, 2 vols. Prague: F.A. Credner, 1865.

Der Mann ohne Vorurtheil: Historisches Lustspiel. Leipzig. 1866.

Der letzte König der Magyaren: Historische Roman. Jena: Hermann Costenoble, 1867.

Unsere Sclaven: Eine sociale Komödie in 5 Acten. Vienna: L.W.Seidel, 1869.

Die geschiedene Frau: Passionsgeschichte eines Idealisten, 2 vols. Leipzig: Paul Kormann, 1870.

Aus dem Tagebuche eines Weltmannes. Leipzig: Paul Kormann, 1870.

Das Vermächtniß Kains: Novellen: I. Theil: Die Liebe, 3 vols. Stuttgart: J.G. Cotta, 1870.

Zur Ehre Gottes! Ein Zeitgemälde. Leipzig: Ernst Julius Günther, 1872.

Die Keuschheitskommission in Wien 1758. Lustspiel. Goslar, 1872.

Falscher Hermelin: Kleine Geschichten aus der Bühnenwelt. Leipzig: Ernst Julius Günther, 1873. A second volume, containing additional works, was published in Bern: Georg Frobeen, 1870.

Soziale Schattenbilder: Aus den Memoireneines österreichischen Polizeibeamten: Ein Seitenstück zu 'Falscher Hermelin.' Halle: Hermann Gesenius, 1873.

Ein weiblicher Sultan: Historischer Roman, 3 vols. Leipzig: Ernst Julius Günther, 1873. Later published as *Sklave und Gemahl.*

Die Messalinen Wiens: Geschichten aus der guten Gesellschaft. Leipzig: Ernst Julius Günther, 1873.

Wiener Hofgeschichten: Historische Novellen, 2 vols. Leipzig: Ernst Julius Günther, 1873.

Über den Werth der Kritik: Erfahrungen und Bemerkungen. Leipzig: Ernst Julius Günther, 1873.

Russische Hofgeschichten: Historische Novellen, 4 vols. Leipzig: Ernst Julius Günther, 1873-1874.

Gute Menschen und ihre Geschichten: Novellen. Leipzizg: Ernst Julius Günther, 1877.

Liebesgeschichten aus verschiedenen Joharhunderten: Novellen, 3 vols. Leipzig: Ernst Julius Günther, 1874-1877.

Galizische Geschichten: Novellen. Leipzig: Ernst Julius Günther, 1875. A second volume, containing new works, was published in Bern/-Leipzig: Georg Frobeen, 1881.

Die Ideale unserer Zeit: Roman, 4 vols. Bern: B.F. Haller, 1875.

Das Vermächtniß Kains: Roman, 4 vols. Bern: B.F. Haller, 1875.

Der neue Hiob: Roman. Stuttgart: J.G. Cotta, 1878.

Die Republik der Weiberfeinde: Roman, 2 vols. Leipzig: Johann Friedrich Hartknoch, 1878.

Harmlose Geschichten aus der Bühnenwelt. Leipzig: Johann Friedrich Hartknoch, 1878.

Judengeschichten. Leipzig: Johann Friedrich Hartknoch, 1878.

Ein Mann wird gesucht: Roman. Berlin: Teschner und Rosenhauer, 1879.

Silhouetten: Novellen und Skizzen, 2 vols. Leipzig: Schulze & Co., 1879.

Die Aesthetik des Häßlichen: Erzählung. Leipzig: Richard Eckstein, 1880.

Basyl der Schatzgräber und andere seltsame Geschichten. Leipzig: Wartig, 1880.

Neue Judengeschichten. Leipzig: E.L. Morgenstern, 1881.

Der Ilau. Leipzig: E.L. Morgenstern, 1882.

Das schwarze Kabinett: Novelle. E.L. Morgenstern, 1882.

Der alte Castellan: Novelle. E.L. Morgenstern, 1882.

Der Judenraphael: Novelle. E.L. Morgenstern, 1882.

Die Gottesmutter. E.L. Morgenstern, 1883.

Frau von Soldan: Roman. E.L. Morgenstern, 1884.

Der kleine Adam. Sascha und Saschka. Berlin/Stuttgart: W. Spemann, 1885.

Polnische Ghetto-Geschichten. Munich/Leipzig: G. Franz, 1886.

Kleine Mysterien der Weltgeschichte. Leipzig: Oswald Schmidt, 1886.

Die Seelenfängerin: Roman. Jena: Hermann Costenoble, 1886.

Deutsche Hofgeschichten: Geschichten aus der Zopfzeit. Leipzig: Oswald Schmidt, 1888.

Polnische Geschichten: Novellen. Breslau: S. Schottländer, 1887.

Seraph. Zwei Königinnen. Die vier Temperamente. Breslau: S. Schottlander, 1888.

Rococo: Bilder aus der Zopfzeit. Leipzig: G. Laudien, 1888.

Der Flötenspieler von Bornim. Weimar: Weißbach, 1889.

Die Schlange im Paradies: Russischer Sittenroman, 3 vols. Mannheim: J.
  Bensheimer, 1890.
Die Einsamen. Mannheim: J. Bensheimer, 1891.
Im Reich der Töne: Musikalische Novellen. Mannheim. J. Bensheimer,
  1891.
Zu spät. Die Kartenschlägerin. Breslau: Schlesische Verlagsanstalt, 1891.
Jüdisches Leben in Wort und Bild. Mannheim: J. Bensheimer, 1891.
Die Abenteuer des Franz von Mieris und andere Malergeschichten. Mann-
  heim: J. Bensheimer, 1891.
Zoë von Rodenbach: Märtyrer der Liebe: Roman. Mannheim: J. Bensheimer.
  1892.
Bühnenzauber: Theater-Roman, 2 vols. Mannheim: J. Bensheimer, 1893.
Neue Erzählungen. Mannheim: J. Bensheimer, 1893.
Lustsige Geschichten aus dem Osten. Breslau: Schlesische Verlagsanstalt,
  1893.
Terka. Die Maus. Maria im Schnee: Novellen. Breslau: Schlesische Verlag-
  sanstalt, 1894.
Die Satten und die Hungrigen: Roman, 2 vols. Jena: Hermann Costenoble,
  1894.
Im Böhmerwald. Mein Freund Wodakoski. Prague: Jakob B. Brandeis,
  1895.
Die Schlange im Paradies: Lustspiel. Hannover, 1895.
Die Stumme. Turandot: Roman. Berlin: Hermann Hillger, 1897.
Entre Nous, Roman. Berlin: Hermann Hillger, 1898.
Afrikas Semiramis, Roman, ed. C.F. von Schlichtegroll. Dresden: H.R.
  Dohrn, 1901.
Hinterlassene Novellen: Grausame Frauen, 3 vols. Dresden: H.R. Dohrn,
  1901.
Grausame Frauen, 6 vols. Leipzig: Leipziger Verlag, 1907. Significant
  overlap with *Hinterlassene Novellen.*
Ausgewählte Ghetto-Geschichten. Leipzig: Sally Rabinowitz, 1918.

A more extensive biography, including the titles of individual *Novellen,*
works published only in journals, and new collections of previously issued
Novellen is contained in Michael Farin, ed. *Leopold von Sacher-Masoch:
Materialien zu Leben und Werk.* Bonn: Bouvier, 1987.

II. Works in English Translation

Jewish Tales. Translated by Harriet Lieber Cohen. Chicago: A.C. McClurg & Co., 1894.

The New Job. Translated by Harriet Lieber Cohen. New York: Cassell, 1891.

Seraph: A Tale of Hungary. Translated by Emma M. Phelps. New York: Allen, 1893.

Venus and Adonis, and Other Tales of the Court of Catherine II. London: Mathieson, 19??

Venus in Furs. Five editions since 1921. Translated by Uwe Moeller and Laura Lindgren. New York: Blast Books, 1989. Includes letters of Sacher-Masoch to Emilie Mataja.

A Light for Others and Other Jewish Tales from Galicia. Translated by Michael T. O'Pecko, Riverside: Ariadne Press, 1995.

III. Secondary Works in English

Biale, David. "Masochism and Philo-Semitism: The Strange Case of Leopold von Sacher-Masoch," in: *Journal of Contemporary History,* vol. 17, no. 2 (April 1992), 305-323.

Felski, Rita. "The Counterdiscourse of the Feminine in Three Texts by Wilde, Huysmans, and Sacher-Masoch." *Publications of the Modern Language Association,* vol. 106, no. 5 (October 1991), 1094-1105.

Hart, Gail K. "Das Ewig-Weibliche nasführet dich: Feminine Leadership in Goethe's *Faust* and Sacher-Masoch's *Venus,*" in: Jane K. Brown, ed. *Interpreting Goethe's Faust Today.* Columbia, SC: Camden House, 1994, pp. 112-122.

Kore, Clea Elfi. *Decadence and the Feminine: The Case of Leopold von Sacher-Masoch.* Dissertation, Stanford University, 1983.

Noyes, John K. "The Importance of the Historical Perspective in the Works of Leopold von Sacher-Masoch," in: *Modern Austrian Literature,* vol. 27, no. 2 (1994), 1-20.

O'Pecko, Michael T. "Comedy and Didacticism in Leopold von Sacher-Masoch's *Venus im Pelz,*" in: *Modern Austrian Literature,* vol. 25, no. 2 (1992), 1-13.

IV. Secondary Works in German

Farin, Michael, ed. *Leopold von Sacher-Masoch: Materialien zu Leben und Werk.* Bonn: Bouvier, 1987. Invaluable collection of previously published material.

Hasper, Eberhand. *Leopold von Sacher-Masoch.* Dissertation, University of Freiburg, 1931.

Horch, Hans Otto. "Der Außenseiter als 'Judenraphael': Zu den Judengeschichten Leopold von Sacher-Masochs, vol. 2, in: Hans Otto Horch, ed. *Conditio Judaica: Judentum. Antisemitismus und deutschsprachige Literatur vom 18. Jahrhundert bis zum Ersten Weltkrieg.* Tübingen: Niemeyer, 1989.

Latzke, Rudolf. "Die Realisten," in: Johann W. Nagl and Eduard Castle, eds. *Deutsch-Österreichische Literaturgeschichte.* Vienna: Carl Fromme, 1930. Vol. 3, pp. 954-973; reprinted in Farin, Sacher-Masoch, *Materialien.*

Noyes, John. "Deleuze liest Sacher-Masoch: Zur Ambivalenz des literarischen Kanons," in: *Acta Germanica,* Supplement 1 (1990), 69-80.

————. "Der Blick des Begehrens: Sacher-Masochs 'Venus im Pelz,'" in: *Acta Germanica,* 19 (1988), 9-27.

Sacher-Masoch, Wanda von. *Meine Lebensbeichte: Memoiren.* Berlin/Leipzig: Schuster & Loeffler, 1906.

Sauter, Michiel. "Marmorbilder und Masochismus. Die Venus Figuren in Eichendorffs *Das Marmorbild* and in Sacher-Masoch's *Venus im Pelz,* in: *Neophilologus,* vol. 75, no. 2 (January 1991), 119-127.

Schlichtegroll, Carl Felix von. *'Wanda' ohne Maske und Pelz: Eine Antwort auf 'Wanda' von Sacher-Masochs "Meine Lebensbeichte" nebst Veroffentlichungen aus Sacher-Masochs Tagebuch.* Leipzig: Leipziger Verlag, 1906.

Sebald, W.G. "Aporien deutschsprachiger Ghettogeschichten," in: *Literatur und Kritik* no. 233/234 (April-May 1989), 161-177.

Swiatlowski, Zbigniew. "Sacher-Masoch oder die bedrohte Normalität," in: *Germanica Wratislaviensia,* 27 (1976), 149-171.

Wodenegg, Andrew. *Das Bild der Juden Osteuropas: Ein Beitrag zur komparatistischen Imagologie an Textbeispielen von Karl Emil Franzos und Leopold von Sacher-Masoch.* Frankfurt am Main/Bern/New York: Peter Lang, 1987.

Charles Sealsfield

Karl J. R. Arndt

When in May 1823 Karl Postl, Secretary of the Kreuzherren Orden mit dem Rothen Stern in Prague, vanished into the underground, he managed to elude the careful search for him by the Austrian Police and did not surface again until he reached the safety of Pittsburgh, Pennsylvania. From there, on 20 September 1824, he wrote to Goethe's publisher Cotta in Stuttgart offering to send him monthly reports for his journals and publications, if the conditions suggested to him through Hofrath André still existed. He signed this letter as Sidons and stated this was not his real name but that Cotta would readily recall his correct name when he thought of the young man who visited him and to whom he showed such kindness.[1] In a postscript he then added that he could be reached under the name Sidons in care of von Bonnhorst Esq. in Pittsburgh or Dr. Eberle in Philadelphia, because both were his friends. The letter was marked as received on December 20 and answered on 10 March 1825. Both von Bonnhorst and Eberle were prominent German-Americans who acted as city greeters to German immigrants. Cotta's reply to this letter has not been found, but judging by what followed, it probably was not encouraging.

When two years later Sidons (Postl) returned to Germany, he waited six weeks before he informed Cotta on 16 September 1826 that he had arrived in Germany and was interested in publishing a book on the United States. Before writing that letter he had tended to concerns which were closer to his heart and continued to remain so as long as he lived: espionage and politics. On 18 August 1826 from Wiesbaden he wrote the following letter in English to Prince Metternich:

[18. August 1826]

Serene Highness!

The Undersigned begs leave to lay before You the following:

He is informed from very good sources that the revolutionizing policy of Great Britain or rather of a powerful party with a popular minister at their head is even now principally directed against Austria whose growing influence seems to become obnoxious especially to the said party.

Among other measures which have been adopted, Englishmen as well as Germans, the latter from different countrys, mostly however Hanoverans, are employed in Hungary, & several other provinces.

One of the emissaries the undersigned met with. The conversation of this gentleman, of course less restrained towards an American, showed plainly the purport of his mission. A variety of other plots have the same tendency.

Though not a European, the standing of the undersigned in society, his being conversant:/ besides his own:/ with two other languages, & a thorough knowledge of America and England induce him to believe his services in this respect could be highly useful to the interest of His Austrian Majesty & Your Serene Higness [!].

Should they be desired a few lines addressed to Mr. Sidons & directed to the post office at Frankfurt "Poste restante" would inform him of the further pleasure.

As the particular character of his native country as well as the business in question preclude every publicity, He will not decline an interview with intermediate persons, though an audience with Your Higness[!] may be, He presumes to say, the best & only means of giving satisfaction for the present, & granting important services for the future.

Will Your Higness [!] condescend as far the undersigned is willing to hasten to any place & at any time, & to give most satisfactory proofs of his willingness to promote the interests above named.

He intends to leave Germany, as soon as he has recovered his health for England, where private affairs are most likely to keep him for some years from home.

Your Serene Highness [!]

Wiesbaden, the 18 August 1826   most humble & most
obedient servant
H. Sidons.[2]

This letter was sent to Metternich's representative von Neumann who was instructed to interview Sidons. On the verso of this letter the following was noted in ink by von Neumann: "Charles Sealsfield, Clergyman domicilié en Pennsylvania, passeport de la Louisiane Mr. Bunsen Pfingstweide." The Bunsen reference was the address where Sealsfield could be reached.

On 28 August 1826 Sidons, again in English, replied to a letter arranging an appointment with Metternich's representative Philipp von Neumann, that late receipt of the letter prevented keeping the suggested appointment but that he would meet von Neumann in Wiesbaden at the named hotel as soon as possible.[3] On 31 August 1826, then, Philipp von Neumann sent Prince Metternich a full report (in French) of his meeting with Mr. Sidons. Von Neumann had addressed Sidons in English but at once noticed that he did not have a good command of this language and spoke with a heavy German accent. At first von Neumann carried on the interview as though he did not notice this, and questioned Sidons about the information that he wanted conveyed to Metternich. Sidons indicated he had information about English plans for starting a revolution in Hungary, but further questioning convinced von Neumann that he was dealing with an adventurer who was trying to make himself important in order to get money out of them. Because the information was so vague, von Neumann told Sidons he would be reimbursed generously if he could produce some positive evidence for his claims; evidence which would make it possible for them to take preventive measures. To this Sidons replied that as an American, he was in a position to get much information because people did not mistrust him. He added that he knew General Lafayette in America and had seen him again in Paris, where in his house he had heard things which would leave no doubt about the plans against Metternich's lands.

Sidons then produced a passport issued to Charles Sealsfield by the Province of Louisiana; he said this was his real name. Von Neumann reported: "He is entered under this name as a Protestant Minister born in Pennsylvania. I therefore remarked that by his accent he could be taken to be a German. He told me that his father was of German descent, that he was at the head of a German colony in Pennsylvania, and that that explained his German accent." Sidons/Sealsfield went on to say that he would be returning to Paris in four or five weeks and would later go to England where he would look up the persons who could give him important information. He offered to put himself fully at their service if they would assure him of a sum per month or per year, but von Neumann refused to enter into such an agreement without more convincing evidence of its value. He suggested instead that since Sidons/Sealsfield would be going to Paris anyway, he could convey any important information to Baron von Binder there, or to the Austrian Embassy in London; both would be informed of his identity. When von Neumann asked where he could be reached in Paris, Sidons/Sealsfield gave the name of Mr. Brown, the American minister there (Brown, he claimed, knew him): he gave Mr. Bunsen in Pfingstweide as his Frankfurt address. In a postscript von Neumann explained that he introduced himself to Sidons/Sealsfield as Mr. Weber and hoped that this would not be changed.[4]

On 7 September 1826 Metternich sent a copy of von Neumann's Sidons/Sealsfield interview to Baron Binder in Paris for his information, asking him to be cautious about this man who claimed to be an American and to discover what he could about his past, his principles, etc. The letter was written in French, and Baron Binder's reply on 24 September 1826 was also in French; it said that he would act according to instructions should Sidons or Sealsfield present himself. In preparation for his arrival Baron Binder tried to gather what information he could. He had asked the American minister Mr. Brown about Sidons/Sealsfield and was informed that Brown did not know him. "This circumstance alone, which destroys one of Sealsfield's assertions, would strengthen the opinion of Mr. von Neumann that this is an adventurer who is reporting either false or unimportant information to get some money."[5] For that reason Baron Binder believed he need not further assure Prince Metternich that he would use the greatest caution in dealing with Sealsfield. That ends the known information about Sealsfield's passport and his willingness to serve Metternich as a spy against England, although as a Roman Catholic priest supposedly, according to scholars, he had fled Metternich's Austria for liberty.

Because it is so unusual that Louisiana would issue a passport for a Protestant Minister with an Anglo-American name such as Charles Sealsfield who claimed that he was a citizen of the state of Pennsylvania, the author of this essay looked into this matter and even obtained the friendly and interested cooperation of the State of Louisiana and its Department of State in his search. On 9 October 1982 the author was informed by the Archives and Records service of the State of Louisiana: "We have pursued all of our available avenues of research, but could find no information which would lead us to believe that the State of Louisiana has ever issued passports; the Secretary of State's legal department has confirmed for us that only the federal government has the authority to do so." Further search with the State Department of the United States on 22 December 1982 brought this enlightening reply from the Legislative and Diplomatic Branch of the Civil Archives Division of the U.S. National Archives: "The Department of State was not given sole authority to issue passports until 1856 and up until that time States and judicial authorities issued them as well."

Investigation in the U.S. Archives, which contain U.S. Consular records as well, revealed no record of a passport being issued to Charles Sealsfield, but an examination of the excellent research study *THE UNITED STATES PASSPORT PAST, PRESENT, FUTURE*[6] revealed how irregularly passports were issued in the time of Charles Sealsfield. This irregularity is confirmed by research in the records of Rapp's Harmony Society, one of America's and particularly Pennsylvania's richest but comparatively unknown sources of original information about immigrants to America and their needs for identification.

While Sealsfield's letter to Metternich showed that his first interest was in establishing a political connection which he could serve, he was not forgetful of his literary ambitions and the fact that an American literary career began in Europe. He wrote to Goethe's publisher Cotta from Frankfurt on 16 September 1826, noting that he had arrived from the United States about six weeks ago, was interested in publishing a book about the United States, and was enclosing an example of his style of writing. The book was in two parts. The first part described the political and social conditions of the United States and the second a journey to the Western States and to New Orleans. He was making no conditions, but if Cotta accepted his offer he would not look for another publisher. On 27 October 1826 he again wrote to Cotta from Stuttgart, stating that he had just arrived from Frankfurt and asking him to determine a time when he could have the honor of delivering his book about America. The first part was ready and the second part was in the process of completion. Because his German style was inclined to be influenced by English, some important men in

Frankfurt had undertaken to polish it. He was in a hurry to get back to America and wanted to be paid either in cash or partly in books. Although it was his first book, he had had great expenses with it, especially the second part covering the West to New Orleans. He wrote with great confidence but in a hurry about a book not yet finished.

On 31 October 1826 a contract for his book was signed with Cotta, and he acknowledged receipt of the advance payment. He was off to England and did not wait to see his first book through the press. He was confident of a quick sale, which proved to be wrong, although Cotta gave the book a good sendoff with an advertisement placed side by side with Goethe's large edition of his writings, known as the "Ausgabe letzter Hand" (final, definitive edition).

Soon complications developed, because Sealsfield's Anglo-American ambition took him to England and delayed him there so that he could have an adapted English version of his *Vereinigten Staaten* (1827, United States) and his *Austria As It Is* (1828) printed. This was the start of his difficulties with Cotta, who complained of the form in which Sealsfield submitted his reports. Anyone who has struggled with Sealsfield's bad handwriting wonders how his manuscripts ever got into print.

After this noteworthy introduction to the international world of letters, Cotta let Sidons (Sealsfield) speak for himself in Cotta's *Neue allgemeine politische Annalen* (New General Political Annals) in the first issue of volume 23, in 1827. The contribution was entitled: "Über Administration and Politik der gegenwärtigen Regierung der Vereinigten Staaten von Nord-Amerika" (About the Administration and Politics of the Present Government of the United States of North America).

Sealsfield's proposal to Cotta for a contract covering his contributions to Cotta's journalistic empire has been printed under the date of 31 October 1826 in the second volume of Castle's Sealsfield biography. We refer to this contract and to the documents following it for documentation of Sealsfield's further dealings with Cotta. His additional publications in the Cotta journals have been identified in the Heller and Leon bibliography of the writings of Charles Sealsfield published by Washington University in September 1939. They are mostly advance extracts from his book *Die Vereinigten Staaten* to promote the sale of that volume, but Cotta's help in launching the literary career of an Austro-American prepared the way for the second stage in London, without which no American could hope for literary success in the United States.

On 7 November 1826 Sealsfield wrote Cotta from Frankfurt that he was leaving for London, and on 29 January 1827 he informed Cotta that he had signed a contract with John Murray for *The United States of North America As They Are* (1828). He made frequent references to Mr. Akermann, an important German publishing contact man in London, who also had direct contacts with the most prominent Philadelphia publisher, Carey, Lea and Carey. It became clear that Sealsfield was very busy attending to the building of his literary base in London through which, as was the case for all American writers at that time, a literary career in America could be launched. Obsessed by this consideration of the future and dominated by his political interests and spying activity which took him to Paris for several interviews with Prince Esterhazy, he came into financial difficulties as he prepared his "spy who came in out of the cold" book *Austria As It Is*. In his distress and his struggle to establish his future he made serious mistakes, imposing on friends in order to raise money for his continued stay in London. But he did make contacts with literary men and with Akermann, through whom he had direct contact with the important American publisher Carey, Lea and Carey. He contributed articles to Cotta from London but realized that he could not be of real help to Cotta until he had been there much longer.

Sealsfield's letters to Cotta were nervous, distraught, unreasonable, frantic, and not such as to inspire confidence in a man who was to act as Cotta's American correspondent. Sealsfield, the fugitive but fascinated political spy, was in a struggle with Sealsfield, the fugitive man of letters. Duty as a reporter for Cotta in America was calling, but love of Europe and the political scenes of activity in Paris and London were holding him back. Even after his return to Kittaning near the gateway to the west, the lively scene of future activity described in his works, he wrote to Cotta on 3 January 1828, "My work, my hopes are in England, where you will always find me or my capital."[7] It was with obvious reluctance that Sealsfield left via Le Havre on 15 June 1827, after having had the satisfaction of mailing Cotta a copy of Murray's publication of *The United States of North America*. Sealsfield had achieved his purpose: his career as an Austro-American writer had been launched in Germany and England with the foremost publishers of these nations, and he could now face America as the author of one German and three English works.

While seeing his three English books through the press, Sealsfield always remained in close touch with Goethe's publisher Cotta, not forgetting to urge Cotta to write to the publisher Murray in London to boost publication of the English translation of his first German book *Die Vereinigten Staaten von Nordamerika* by C. Sidons.[8]

While this international literary business was going on between London and Stuttgart, Goethe in May of 1827 published an article recommending to young German poets some publications that would inspire them in their work: "Stoff and Gehalt. Zur Bearbeitung vorgeschlagen (Subjects Proposed for Adaptation)."[9] He showed particular interest in Ludwig Gall's *Meine Auswanderung nach den Vereinigten Staaten von Nord Amerika*[10] (My Emigration to the United States of North America) noting especially, however, that any writer choosing this field would have to have the pride "to compete with Cooper." That Sealsfield was in agreement with Goethe's statement is shown by the fact that after his return to America he retired to Kittaning and began working on his first English novel *Tokeah*, a work which was a direct challenge to Cooper's popularity.

Sealsfield left for the United States on 15 June 1827, but his correspondence in this period shows a worsening relationship with Cotta because of his constant pressure for the advancement of money and his imposition on Cotta and others to help him in his embarrassed financial situation. On 3 January 1828 he wrote from Kittaning that he had almost completed a work named *Canond ah* and would be ready to send this to Cotta by 15 May from Philadelphia. He would direct Carey, Lea and Carey to hold back funds sent to him by Cotta until he had delivered the manuscript to them for shipment. He already had inquiries for this book from two leading publishers in Germany but preferred to deal with Cotta.[11]

His "Canond ah," as described at this time, is the earlier title for his *Tokeah*, and the claim that two publishers in Germany were interested is an obvious overstatement to impress Cotta and to get some advancement of funds, because when he later approached Brockhaus for publication his offer was rejected. Sealsfield was in great financial distress, and Cotta not only resented his requests for money, but also the careless form in which he submitted his manuscripts. On 18 September 1828 Cotta received a letter from Sealsfield stating that he could no longer be at his service.[12] After his letter there is a break in the correspondence as published by Castle, and the next letter published is in English to Brockhaus dated 28 March 1829 from Francisville, Louisiana, offering him a book for publication.[13] Brockhaus declined in a letter dated 10 June 1829 and addressed to Sealsfield care of Messrs. Carey, Lea & Carey. The publication of Seals-field's *Tokeah* took place in this chronological gap in Castle's *Der große Unbekannte. Das Leben von Charles Sealsfield, Briefe und Aktenstücke* (The Great Unknown. The Life of Charles Sealsfield, Letters and Documents).

On 14 January 1829 Carey, Lea & Carey registered in the office of the Clerk of the Eastern District of Pennsylvania "the Title of a Book, the right whereof they claim as proprietors, in the words following, to wit":

Tokeah: or The White Rose

Knowest thou the land where the lemon trees bloom?
Where the gold orange glows deep thicket's gloom
Where a wind ever soft, from the blue heaven blows,
And the groves are of laurel and myrtle and rose?
Knowest thou it?
         Thither! O, thither!
My dearest and kindest with thee would I go.

Tokeah was widely advertised in the newspapers of the country and immediately put on sale in Philadelphia, New York, and Boston, and the reviews published in these main American cities of the time now follow in chronological order. On 12 and 13 February 1829 *The New York Evening Post* announced: NEW NOVEL—*Tokeah*, or *The White Rose* in 2 vols. 12 mo. Just rec'd for sale for G. & C. Carvill, 108 Broadway." On 21 February 1829 *The Philadelphia National Gazette and Literary Register* published a review of *Tokeah* praising it as an American work:

> We have been induced to read and notice this book, chiefly because it is an American novel—written in this country and descriptive of its scenes, people, habits, and manners. We are not indeed of that excessive literary patriotism which leads to the indiscriminate praise of every native author; nor do we consider it absolutely necessary for all our countrymen who write, to drag before us Indians and republicans. We do not think that Washington Irving is rendered less American by describing the humors of Brace-bridge Hall, any more than Milton is changed into an Antediluvian because he selected the garden of Eden for his

scene, or Corneille into a Spanish knight-errant from depicting the heroism of the Cid. We are willing to give to American authors the privilege which those of all other nations have had, to write about whatever times, manners and regions they may choose, being fully satisfied if their country is honored by the exercise of such genius as may place her sons in fair rivalry with those of any other nation.

Still we are ready to confess that we feel great pleasure in the delineation of incidents which are peculiar to America. We are glad when talent is exercised on so broad and untried a field and we believe that an originality and novelty may be imparted, which the more frequently described scenes of civilized and fashionable life do not afford.

The novel we have named is purely American; and we venture to say that in the delineation of Indian character, habits, ceremonies, etc. it has rarely been surpassed and seldom equalled. The same skill is exhibited in depicting the singularly original manner and pursuits of the early settlers on the frontier—a race of men who are not less remarkable than the Aborigines for bodily strength, patience, and courage, far superior to them in shrewdness, and who mix in a strange manner many of the pursuits of social life with those of their wilder neighbors.

The work opens with a description of one of these settlements on the frontier of Georgia, depicting, with great truth, the manners and character of Captain Copeland and his family, and a visit they received from a chief of the tribe of Oconee Indians, who confides to the care of the backwoodsman's wife, a beautiful child whom he had carried off in a skirmish with the whites. This child, "The White Rose," is educated by the clergyman of a neighboring missionary station, but after ten or twelve years is again claimed by the chief Tokeah, who is about to retire with his tribe beyond the Mississippi. The new settlement of the tribe becomes the scene of the principal adventures. Lafitte, pirate of Barataria, intrigues with the Indians, endeavors to excite them to take part against the Americans in the war with England, which had lately broken out, and succeeds in persuading the old chief to betroth him to Rosa. His schemes, however, are defeated by the wisdom and bravery of a young Pawnee chief, who is married to Canond ah, the daughter of Tokeah. The pirate is taken prisoner and carried to New Orleans, where General Jackson is at that time encamped. Rosa is married to an officer who had previously sought refuge with the Oconees; and the old chief, after paying a visit to the graves of his fathers on the frontiers of Georgia, returns home and dies in the midst of his tribe.

This is a meager sketch of a plot filled up with some extremely interesting episodes and details. The character of Canond ah, the Indian girl, and her Pawnee lover, are described with great truth and luxury. There is a night scene, when the pirate attacks and sets fire to the village, which is depicted with no common talent; and we could dwell with pleasure on more than one description, and on many striking incidents and dialogues, did our limits admit of it.

On 10 March 1829 the *New York Commercial Advertiser* printed the following review of *Tokeah*, which the *New York Spectator* reprinted on 13 March 1829:

Tokeah or the White Rose. Is Mr. Cooper to have a Rival, or has a greater than Cooper arisen? is a question which will naturally occur to the admirers of the Prairie and the Last of the Mohegans, on reading the two volumes published by Carey, Lea & Carey, under the above title. Having read the first volume, we feel that we are doing no injustice to the distinguished author of the works above mentioned in comparing *Tokeah* with them. The scene is laid in the province of Texas and the surrounding country. The historical characters introduced are calculated to give deep interest to the story; and the fiction is exceedingly well managed.

The April 1829 issue of the *American Monthly Magazine*, Boston, edited by N.P. Willis, commented:

This book deserves more than the cursory notice to which
we are at present limited. It is in the same walk with Mr.
Cooper's novels, and will bear a very fair comparison with
them. With less originality and power in single characters
and scenes, there is a more sustained and uniform beauty
throughout, and, in the delineation of female characters, a
skill to which Mr. Cooper has not approached. We do not
know of two more beautiful creations than Canond ah and
Rosa. The latter, especially, a Spanish captive reared in the
hut of the chief Miko of the Oconees, is drawn with exquisite tenderness. The descriptions are evidently the work
of a man who has been accustomed to observe, and who
has looked at nature with the eye of a poet. It is altogether
a most delightful book, and a credit to our literature.

On 2 May 1829 *The Ariel; a Semimonthly Literary and Miscellaneous
Gazette* of Philadelphia published a lengthy review, examining *Tokeah* as
a serious challenge to Cooper but concluding that the latter's preeminent
position was safe:

The author of this novel is not known. It is one of those
works, which fall dead-born from the press, serving, however, for a few weeks, the temporary purposes of a circu-
lating library, ever afterwards to lie like useless lumber, on
the dusty shelves of the booksellers. The story is too tame
to be made endurable in the hands even of the most accomplished writer; but when told in language so commonplace and rude, copiously interspersed with oaths, and
other positive vulgarisms equally offensive, its author must
expect no better fate for it. The American public have been
too much used to language free from all contamination of
this kind, to brook the absolute indignity of seeing such
profanity put forth for their perusal and encouragement.

This review so completely demolished Sealsfield's proud Anglo-American
challenge to Cooper in his own language and on his home ground that it
changed the course of Sealsfield's life. He published his novel in London
under the changed title *The Indian Chief* in the same year, and Carey, Lea

& Carey did publish his "Early Impressions" in the *Atlantic Souvenir* for 1831 as "By the author of *Tokeah*," but that was the end.[14] His pride had caused him to break off with Goethe's publisher Cotta, and now the German publisher Brockhaus rejected a book on the United States which Sealsfield offered him. He found anonymous employment in the Franco-American journal *Courrier des Etats-Unis* but not for long.[15] As an Austrian Roman Catholic priest who had fled from Prague and changed his name from Postl to Sealsfield, he did not have the courage to seek employment with one of the many German-American journals or newspapers,[16] although his Louisiana-issued passport had identified him as a Protestant clergyman from Pennsylvania.

Sealsfield wanted to get back to the sources of world political power, so sometime in December 1830, when he was interviewed for employment by the then editor of the *New York Morning Courier and Enquirer*, he presented himself as a "learned foreigner, then on a visit to this country"[17] as evidenced by the following letter written to the American consul, David Warden:

Paris the 23 Decr 1830

D Sir!

I thank you sincerely for your kindness and shall previously to my seeing Bishop Gregori,[18] take the liberty of paying you my compliments. As Mr. Stewarts visit gives me an opportunity of writing I beg you not to forget Mr. O Reilly—He has not yet sent the letters—If you can dear Sir effect anything with respect to my having access to public papers & connection with the press I shall feel very gratified—the more so as this business having been engaged for a couple of years in it would impede but little the progress of the rest of my studies—[19]

I am just now writing to Washington for the T—& V.B.[20] the Courier or the public voiture starting tonight— If you are willing to write to New York please to have your letters ready I shall at any rate call at your house—where I beg you in case you should not be at home, to leave those letters—

With the highest regard

Your obedient humble servant
Ch. Sealsfield

Warden Esqr.
Addressed: D.B. Warden Esqr. forwarded by Mr. Steward
Present

In an undated letter, marked as received by Cotta on 11 January 1831 in Stuttgart, probably written from London after the above letter to Consul Warden in Paris, Sealsfield stated that he had just arrived from the United States, had given up his connection with the *Courrier des Etats Unis* and was serving as correspondent for the New York *Morning Courier and Enquirer*, "der Hauptadministration Zeitung von Newyork," (the official organ of the administration). He again offered his services to Cotta, stating that Cotta could probably nowhere find a person having a more exact and complete knowledge of the United States and England.[21] Although Cotta noted that he had answered this letter on the 28th, his reply has not been found. On 10 February 1831 Sealsfield was introduced as London and Paris Correspondent of the New York *Morning Courier and Enquirer* and continued on and served loyally until he retired to Switzerland in 1832 to publish his American experiences in his mother tongue. His last communication, dated 24 February 1832, praised Andrew Jackson for president. Sealsfield withdrew as London and Paris Correspondent for the New York *Morning Courier and Enquirer* probably because of Andrew Jackson's serious political troubles at home, which Sealsfield described frankly in a letter of 29 May 1831 to David Warden. These troubles reached a climax on 23 August 1832, when the New York *Morning Courier and Enquirer* removed the names of Andrew Jackson and Van Buren from the top of its editorial column and replaced them with the motto "Principles, not men." Notice was served that the partnership of Mordecai Noah and James Watson Webb had been dissolved. Thus Sealsfield and Jackson had lost their most influential friend and supporter.[22]

Sealsfield's first publication after retirement to Switzerland was *Der Legitime und die Republikaner: Eine Geschichte aus dem letzten amerikanisch-englischen Kriege* (1833, The Legitimist and the Republicans: A Story From the Last American-English War), the German revision of *Tokeah*. The first volume was translated into German while the second was made over into a glorification of Andrew Jackson's part in the late American war with England. The work was so well received that Sealsfield's next publication, *Transatlantische Reiseskizzen und Christophorus Bärenhäuter im Amerikanerland* (1834, Transatlantic Travel Sketches and Christophorus the Loafer in America) was identified as "by the Author of *Der Legitime und die Republikaner.*" As a supplement to this work, dated May 1832, the publishers included a review of *Der Legitime* which had appeared in the Leipzig *Blätter für literarische Unterhaltung:*

> If Cooper's more experienced pen had carried out this plan, the execution might have gained some. On the whole however we, due honor to Cooper's talent, give this conception the preference to one by Cooper, because it is more intellectual and greater. The author is probably a man who as a statesman already holds an important place in the republic, or surely will still do so. Whoever has studied the interests of his nation so exactly as he, is called to take a part in its leadership. In any case this novel is by far more instructive than any one by Scott or Cooper and deserves to be observed especially by those Germans, who with one foot have already left their native hut in order to begin the great emigration.

The very favorable review of *Der Legitime* belongs to the history of *Tokeah* because it anticipates Professor Mundt's critical comparison of Cooper and Sealsfield in which he gave Sealsfield the preference. *Der Legitime und die Republikaner* was a strong factor in winning for Sealsfield the cherished title of "Greatest American Author,"[23] which resulted from the national and international inquiry into the validity of Professor Theodor Mundt's judgment as quoted by the editor of the *Boston Daily Advertiser* on 29 March 1844. The excitement caused by this extensive controversy moved the successors of the original publishers of *Tokeah*, Lea and Blanchard, in 1845 to publish a second edition of *Tokeah* in a condensed pamphlet form containing a statement of Sealsfield's identity:

> The question has very often been asked "Who is Sealsfield? Could any but an American have acquired a knowledge of the manners and peculiarities of all classes in this country, as minute and perfect as that displayed in his works?" The publishers take pleasure in stating that, notwithstanding the apparent evidence to the contrary, C. Sealsfield (as his name is correctly written) was a German of singular erudi-

tion, obliged to exile himself on account of political difficulties in which he became involved. He came to this
country, where he remained for several years, traveling
extensively, especially through the South and West, during
which time he obtained that thorough and accurate knowledge of the inhabitants of those regions which imparts such
a vivid and life-like appearance to his portraiture of their
characters and adventures. It was at this period that he
wrote the following tale, in English—presenting the remarkable instance of a novel, American in character and
language, produced by one who had been but a year or two
in the country. The striking and truthful sketches of Indian
life and character impart much interest to the story. It was
published in 1829, during the Author's residence in this
country, by the predecessors of the present firm.

Philadelphia, June, 1845.

After this digression from the chronological sequence of this essay, which
is justified by the importance of Sealsfield's first novel and the impact
which *Der Legitime und die Republikaner* had on his reputation internationally, we return to our point of departure. In the year 1834 *Transatlantische Reiseskizzen und Christophorus Bärenhäuter* (Transatlantic Travel Sketches and Christophorus the Loafer) was published in Zurich by
Orell, Füssli and Company. *Christophorus Bärenhäuter* is a charming,
humorous short story inspired by "Jemima O'Keefy," published in Flint's
Western Magazine and Review. It is the first time in Sealsfield's works that
he managed to portray a hardworking and honest German-American with
kindness and humor. Unfortunately, it was never republished. In 1835 this
volume was followed by *Der Virey und die Aristokraten oder Mexico im
Jahre 1812* (The Virey and the Aristocrats or Mexico in the Year 1812),
which in a vein similar to *Der Legitime und die Republikaner* deals with the
social and ethnic problems of Mexico. It is significant that in publishing
Die Große Tour (The Great Journey) anonymously, he identified this as
by the author of *Legitime, Transatlantische Reiseskizzen* and *Virey*. At this
point Sealsfield started to run into difficulties with his publishers, and
titles and locations of publication present problems going beyond the
scope of this essay. For clarification, Dean Heller's *Charles Sealsfield:
Bibliography of his Writings* goes to great length to explain these compli-

cations. We have Dean Heller's holograph notes for this complicated period from which we cite this unpublished comment: "Some experience with Sealsfield's own dates makes one inclined to withdraw from him even the benefit of the doubt." To keep within the scope of this essay, we therefore consider it proper at this point to use the assistance of recognized specialists such as Henry T. Tuckerman.[24] He compressed the complexities of Sealsfield's life and works in the following laudable lines:

> In 1832, he [Sealsfield] visited Switzerland, and there published a translation of *Tokeah.* So popular was the work abroad, that he resolved to compose a series of romances illustrative to American Life. His keen observation, strong sympathies, and imaginative zest enabled him to mould into vivid pictures the scenes and characters with which he had become familiar in America, where the six novels devoted to that subject soon became known through partial translations which appeared in *Blackwood's Magazine.* The intensity and freshness of these delineations excited much interest. They seemed to open a new and genuine vein of romance in American life, or, rather, to make the infinite possibilities thereof charmingly apparent. This was an experiment singularly adapted to a German, who, with every advantage of European education, in the freshness of life had emigrated to this country, and there worked and travelled, observed and reflected, and then, looking back from the ancient quietude of his ancestral land, could delineate, under the inspiration of contrast, all the wild and wonderful, the characteristic and original phases and facts of his existence in Texas, Pennsylvania, or New York. "Life in the New World" was soon translated and published in the latter city. It was followed by "The Cabin Book; or, Sketches of Life in Texas," and others of the series which abroad have given to thousands the most vivid impressions of the adventures, the scenery, and the characters of our frontier, and of many of the peculiar traits of our more confirmed civilization.

Tuckerman's view is substantiated by the following lines from *The Cambridge History of American Literature*,[25] evaluating Sealsfield:

> Foremost among them [German travelers in the United States] was the Austrian Charles Sealsfield (Karl Postl) proud to call himself "Bürger von Nordamerika" [citizen of North America] who held up to view virile, reckless, self-reliant types of American manhood as objects for emulation, to enthralled Europeans. Longfellow was especially fond of Sealsfield's depictions of the Red River country and its Creole inhabitants. *The Cabin Book* (*Das Cajütenbuch*) has for its historical setting the Texan war of independence against Mexican misrule. *Morton oder die große Tour* presents a view of Stephen Girard's money-power and personal eccentricities. *Lebensbilder aus der westlichen Hemisphäre* introduces the lure of pioneer life, with its gallery of southern planters, hot-tempered Kentuckians, Eastern belles and dandies, alcaldes, squatters and desperadoes, American types as they appeared between 1820-1840. Sealsfield's Mexican stories (*Virey, Nord und Süd*) contain nature pictures in wonderful colours, a striking instance of which is found also in the *Cabin Book*, in the chapter called "The Prairie of St. Jacinto."

In spite of such glorification of the United States, Sealsfield remained an Austrian and American expatriate and settled in Switzerland. He did return to the United States in 1837 and addressed an English letter to Joel Poinsett, reprinted in Castle's edition of his letters[26] (*Briefe*, 161). In this letter he returns to his favorite subject, politics, and makes the following offer to Poinsett:

> I have access to coteries, which would enable me to give You & our worthy Chief magistrate more accurate hints as to the secret springs & the political movements, than perhaps even some well paid Ministers ever could do. I do therefore think it not amiss to lay this before You, leaving it to You, whether You will make any use of my confidential proposal—(which I beg You of course to consider con-

fidential) or not. Having been, many years ago Editor of the Courier des Etats Unis & Correspondent both of the Times, the Morning Courier & Enquirer & of the leading Paris Journal now—I am led to the belief that my letters might perhaps be *desirable to an elevated friend of Yours.*—If they should be, a letter informing me of Your wishes and directed under my address to Zürich (en suisse) will always find me ready to comply with them.

In 1857 he again returned to the United States but expressed his displeasure in the following words taken from a letter written in Richmond, Virginia, on 4 November 1857 to Brantz Mayer in Baltimore:

There is no doubt that the enormous immigration which overflows New York City as well as the State begins to create a serious inconvenience affecting the sound & healthy part of the native population. A healthy immigration is certainly a blessing to any country. It produces exactly what the circulation of blood produces in the human frame. As in countries, when there is no foreign immigration the inhabitants will retrograde, so in those countries when the influence is too strong the immigration will not only vitiate & corrupt but give the tone to the whole country. It is to be feared that this will be the case with some of your northern & northwestern states. You have a bulwark in your slave population against this very inundation—these groveling sensual low born & bred sensual agronous & mechanical tools, who come over merely because they can fill—(sit venia verbo) their bellies better & ride here & spurn those very people before whom they were creeping & cringing in Europe.[26]

Many biographical relationships remain unclear about the dark and devious peregrinations of this self-tormented wanderer between two worlds who spent so much time and energy of his second life trying to cover all traces that might lead to the discovery of his previous existence as a Roman Catholic priest. Anyone who doubts that he was ever able to erase the character *indelebilis* conferred upon him with his priestly vows should make very careful study of his tombstone inscription at Solothurn, Switzerland, placed there by his instructions and finally putting Sealsfield's divided self together again in a remarkably concentrated form in a final confession before he faced his Supreme Judge.

Sealsfield's grave beside St. Niklaus Church is suitably marked by two large stone slabs, one bilingual and religiously autobiographical, the other in German and politically of autobiographical significance. The first is the headstone leaning against the north wall of the church and is inscribed:

CP

CHARLES SEALSFIELD
geboren den 5. März 1795
gestorben den 26. Mai 1864
Psalm 145. And enter not into judgment with thy servant,
for in thy sight shall no man living be justified.
Psalm 51. Have mercy upon me my God,
according to thy loving kindness,
according to the multitude of thy tender mercies
blot out my transgressions.

The second large stone slab covers the remains of the body and is inscribed in German:

Charles Sealsfield Bürger von Nord Amerika.

The "CP" at the top of the headstone is the anglicized form of his original name Karl Postl, and the first date given under the name of "Charles Sealsfield" is the birth date of Karl Postl, while the second date is the date of death of Charles Sealsfield (the haunted Karl Postl). It is very significant that the two scripture passages, so profound and concentrated in this fugitive priest's final confession to Him whom he had sworn to serve, are in English—open, yet concealed to the public. They should properly have been rendered in Latin or in Luther's German, for they are taken from the Catholic prayer books chosen for persons facing the last agony of death, as Postl/Sealsfield faced it in his last hours of solitude before the dissolution of his physical existence.

The stone slab covering his earthly remains, as it were, speaks with the defiance of a free American citizen: "Charles Sealsfield, Citizen of North America," in other words, a notice to the Austrian police: "You cannot touch my body or property, I am a citizen of North America." This was important because it protected his testament from possible confiscation by the Austrian government as a fugitive from its justice.

Notes

1. Edward Castle. *Der große Unbekannte, das Leben von Charles Sealsfield: Briefe und Aktenstücke* (Vienna: Karl Werner, 1955), p. 107. Henceforth cited as Castle, *Briefe.*
2. Ibid., p. 108.
3. Ibid., p. 109.
4. Ibid., p. 111.
5. Ibid., p. 113.
6. *The United States Passport: Past, Present, Future* (Washington, DC: Government Printing Office, 1974.
7. Castle, *Briefe,* p. 144.
8. Ibid., p. 139.
9. *Goethe's Werke, Vollständige Ausgabe letzter Hand* (Stuttgart, 1837, LV, 420-424, reprint of 1827 edition.
10. Ludwig Gall, *Meine Auswanderung nach den Vereinigten Staaten von Nord Amerika, Frühjahr 1819 und Rückkehr nach der Heimath im Winter 1820* (Trier, 1822).
11. Castle, *Briefe,* p. 144.
12. Ibid., p. 149.
13. Ibid., p. 150.
14. Karl J.R. Arndt, "Early Impressions: An Unknown Work by Seals-field," in *The Journal of English and Germanic Philology* 55 (January 1956), 100-116.
15. Karl J.R. Arndt, "Charles Sealsfield and the Courier des Etats Unis," *Publications of the Modern Language Association,* pp. 67, 170-188.
16. Karl J.R. Arndt and May Olson, *The German Language Press of the Americas* (Munich: Verlag Dokumentation, 1965-1980), 3 volumes.
17. *Morning Courier and Enquirer* (New York, 10 February 1831), page 2, column 1.
18. Warden in 1810 had published *An Enquiry Cncerning the Intellectual and Moral Faculties and Literature of Negroes,* translated from the French of B. H. Gregoire.

19. Sealsfield always worked behind the scenes on friends, pressing for favors of this kind or for favorable reviews of his works. He was quite brazen about it, so that some American critics remarked, without revealing too much, that the author might readily be found close to the reviewer.

20. This is a cryptic remark. He was writing for the Jackson and Van Buren *Morning Courier and Enquirer* of New York (T&VB stands for Tammany and Van Buren). Since he was writing in great haste and wanted to impress Warden, he probably wanted to say: I am just now writing to Washington and for the Jackson *and* Van Buren *Courier* in New York. He liked to pose as a man having the confidence of powerful political individuals like Jackson and Van Buren, but so far nothing has surfaced in the political papers to identify him in that way.

21. Castle, *Briefe,* p. 154.

22. James L. Crouthammel, *James Watson Webb: A Biography* (Middletown: Weslyan University Press, 1969).

23. Karl J.R. Arndt, "Charles Sealsfield, 'The Greatest American Author,'" in *Proceedings of the American Antiquarian Society* (October 1964), 249-259.

24. Henry T. Tuckermann, *America and Her Commentators* (New York: Kelley, 1970), p. 311.

25. William B. Trent, John Erskine, Stuart P. Sherman, and Carl Van Doren, eds. *The Cambridge History of American Literature* (New York: Macmillan, 1945), p. 579.

26. Castle, *Briefe*, p. 161.

Preface to the Bibliography

The reconstruction of the mosaic which pictures the various lives of Postl/ Sidons/Sealsfield is a work to which generations of scholars, priests, musicians, and laymen have contributed through painstaking research. For America it was Professor Albert Faust who discovered Sealsfield and who gave him his first biography; Albert B. Faust, *Charles Sealsfield (Carl Postl) Der Dichter beider Hemisphären. Sein Leben und seine Werke* (Weimar, 1897). It is characteristic of the pusillanimity of American publishers that Faust had to go to Germany to publish his work and that he published it in German.

The next great step forward in Sealsfield research was made by Dean Otto Heller with the important publication: Otto Heller and Theodore Leon, *Charles Sealsfield. Bibliography of his writings together with a classified and annotated Catalogue of Literature relating to his works and his life.* Washington University Studies New Series, Language and Literature, No. 8, September 1939.

Heller and others prior to World War I had planned to publish a definitive edition of Sealsfield's works and had already issued an invitation to subscribe to the works, indeed had started preparations of the texts for publication, when the war destroyed the Society for the Advancement of German Science, Art, and Literature in Bohemia, which had supported the project, and thus put an end to the project.

The German and English announcements of the complete, critical edition of the works of Charles Sealsfield listed Otto Heller as general editor cooperating with A.B. Faust of Cornell University, H.S. Goodnight of the University of Wisconsin, James Taft Hatfield of Northwestern University, K.D. Jessen of Bryn Mawr College, M.D. Learned of the University of Pennsylvania, and A. Ravize, then at Bordeaux. Sealsfield's works were to run to seventeen volumes uniform in size and make-up with the edition of *Adalbert Stifter* by A. Sauer. The entire edition had been very carefully prepared, and it is a great pity that it was never published.

In France during these years it was Professor A. Ravize who had laboriously collected a great number of Sealsfield letters which were to go into the volume of letters that was planned for the definitive edition. These fortunately came into the hands of Professor Eduard Castle who included them in his later Sealsfield biography.

After World War I the author of this essay and Albert Kresse, a musician in Stuttgart, started collecting Sealsfieldiana and by great labor and sacrifice assembled the greatest collection of Sealsfieldiana in existence today. It has been my privilege to work with this collection and to complete my own by exchange with it. My own collection started with my purchase of the Heller collection, to which I have added constantly.

From Faust, Heller, and Kresse we come to the greatest publication efforts made on the life and work of Sealsfield to date, that of Eduard Castle. He was greatly favored in his research by a revival of the Sealsfield interest once propagated by the former Society for the Advancement of German Science, Art, and Literature in Bohemia. German research interest in Sealsfield was running high in the days of Nazi ascendancy, but the same nazistic zeal which helped Castle assemble his first attempt at a biography, also again brought its destruction because World War I, due to the Versailles Treaty, proved to be nothing but an Armistice. Before the full fury of the bombing attacks was unleashed over Hitler's empire, Castle managed to publish much of the material assembled in the Heller-Leon bibliography. In this he was greatly aided by the Kresse collection. The volume referred to is now a basic work for Sealsfield study, although published in 1941 in an edition limited to one hundred and eighty copies: Eduard Castle, *Das Geheimnis des Grossen Unbekannten, Charles Sealsfield-Carl Postl. Die Quellenschriften mit Einleitung, Bildnis, Handschriftenproben und ausführlichem Register* (The Secret of the Great Unknown, Charles Sealsfield–Carl Postl. The Sources with Introduction, Illustrations, Samples of Writing and Detailed Index).

Having assembled and published these sources, Castle wrote his definitive biography of Charles Sealsfield and had already seen it into proof when the entire press, including the plates to the Sealsfield work, were destroyed by American bombs in an attack on Berlin.

When the writer of this essay came to Berlin with U.S. Military Government in 1945, he took a jeep and went searching for the manuscript. At that time all communications had broken down, except those in the hands of the victorious Allies. Before the war he had been in contact with both Kresse in Stuttgart and Castle in Vienna, hence his first act as soon as possible after the war was to reestablish relations with both Kresse and Castle.

He finally managed to get Castle's Sealsfield biography accepted and cleared for publication in Baden-Württemberg, but the project failed to get approval of the Control Council in Berlin. When he returned to civilian life he approached the U.S. Ambassador to Austria in Vienna, the Hon. Walter J. Connelly, and obtained through the Cultural Affairs Branch in Vienna the financial support which finally resulted in the publication of Castle's great two-volume definitive biography, an assistance which Castle gratefully acknowledged on pages 660 and 661 of his work.

This life and work essay overview of the Austro-American Postl/Sealsfield was prepared especially for the volume edited by Professor Donald G. Daviau of the University of California at Riverside. It is based on the Arndt collection of Sealsfieldiana beginning with the start of Postl's internationally diversified and multilingual life. Because this volume is designed especially for the information of English readers, Sealsfield's Anglophilism which caused him to write to his first publisher Cotta that he would always be able to find his resources and capital in England is well documented in this essay. It is also documented in the publication of the American Antiquarian Society's "Charles Sealsfield, 'The Greatest American Author'" in volume 74 of its *Proceedings.* This was the conclusion reached by the inquiry and search launched by the *Boston Advertiser* for the greatest American writer in 1844.

It was only the limitation of time and space that kept the author from including in this volume more fully the contributions of Sealsfield to the New York *Morning Courier and Enquirer* which show how much joy Sealsfield took in politics and in reporting to readers what he managed to obtain from "sources to which no other person has access."

Bibliography

Because a complete bibliography of Sealsfield's books transcends the reasonable scope of this essay, we refer to Dean Heller's excellent standard bibliography as listed under secondary sources. Dean Heller's bibliography is a striking example of the difficulties encountered in an accurate listing of Sealsfield's works. Sealsfield was a very suspicious fugitive author publishing anonymously and consequently suffering from pirates in France, Germany, and Scotland, for which reason he constantly varied the published forms of his works. In this situation the author entrusted with the preparation of this essay has, as editor-in-chief for Olms Verlag, prepared the following final facsimile reprints of Sealsfield's writings:

Volume 1: *Die Vereinigten Staaten von Nordamerika*, nach ihrem politischen, religiösen and gesellschaftlichen Verhältnisse betrachtet.
Stuttgart/Tübingen: Cotta, 1827.

Volume 2: *The United States of North America As They Are*. London: Murray, 1828. *The Americans As They Are* described in a tour
through the valley of the Mississippi. London: Simkin and
Marshall, 1828.

Volume 3: *Austria As It Is* or, *Sketches of Continental Courts*. London:
Hurst, Chance, and Co., 1828.

Volumes 4-5: *The Indian Chief* or *Tokeah and the White Rose*. London:
Newman, 1829.

Volumes 6-7: *Der Legitime und Die Republikaner*. Stuttgart, 1845.

Volumes 8-9: *Der Virey und Die Aristokraten*, or *Mexiko im Jahre 1812*.
Stuttgart, 1845.

Volume 10: *Morton oder Die große Tour*. Stuttgart, 1846.

Volumes 11-12: *Lebensbilder aus der Westlichen Hemisphäre*. George Howard's Esq. Brautfahrt.—Ralph Doughby's Esq. Brautfahrt.
Stuttgart, 1846.

Volumes 13-14: *Lebensbilder aus der Westlichen Hemisphäre*. Pflanzer-
leben.—Die Farbigen. Stuttgart, 1846.

Volume 15: *Lebensbilder aus der Westlichen Hemisphäre*: Nathan, der
Squatter-Regulator. Stuttgart, 1846.

Volumes 16-17: *Das Cajütenbuch oder Nationale Charakteristiken*. Stuttgart, 1847.

Volumes 18-20: *Süden und Norden*. Stuttgart, 1842.

Volumes 21-23: *Die Deutsch-Amerikanischen Wahlverwandtschaften*. Zurich, 1839.

II. Works In English
See Volumes 2-5 above.

III. Secondary Works in English
Arndt, Karl J.R. "Charles Sealsfield and the *Courrier des Etats-Unis*." In
Publications of the Modern Language Association 68 (1953), 170-
188.

_____. "Charles Sealsfield, 'The Greatest American Author.'" In *Pro-
ceedings of the American Antiquarian Society* 74 (1964), 249-
259.

_____. "'Early Impressions:' an Unknown Work by Sealsfield." In *Journal of English and Germanic Philology* 55 (1956), 100-116.

_____. "The Litigious Mr. Sealsfield." In *Modern Language Notes* 78 (1063), 527-532.

_____. "New Light on Sealsfield's *Cajütenbuch* and *Gesammelte Werke*." In *Journal of English and Germanic Philology* 41 (1942), 210-222.

_____. "Newly Discovered Sealsfield Relationships Documented." In *Modern Language Notes* 81 (1972), 450-464.

_____. "Plagiarism: Sealsfield or Simms." In *Modern Language Notes* 69 (1954), 577-581.

_____. "Recent Sealsfield Discoveries." In *Journal of English and Germanic Philology* 53 (1954), 160-171.

_____. "Sealsfield's Claim to Realism." In *Monatshefte für Deutschen Unterricht* 35 (1943), 271-285.

_____. "Sealsfield's Command of the English Language." In *Modern Language Notes* 67 (1952), 310-313.

_____. "Sealsfield's Early Reception in England and America." In *Germanic Review* 18 (1943), 176-195.

_____. "The Cooper-Sealsfield Exchange of Criticism." In *American Literature* 15 (1943), 16-24.

Barba, Preston A. "Sealsfield Sources." In *German-American Annals* 9 (1911), 31-39.

Carrington, Ulrich S. *The Making of an American: An Adaptation of Memorable Tales by Charles Sealsfield*. Dallas: Southern Methodist University Press, 1974.

Friesen, Gerhard. "Charles Sealsfield and the German Panoramic Novel of the 19th Century." In *Modern Language Notes* 84 (1969), 734-775.

Heller, Otto and Theodore H. Leon, compilers. *Charles Sealsfield: Bibliography of his Writing together with a Classified and Annotated Catalogue of Literature Relating to his Works and his Life*. St. Louis: Washington University Press, 1939.

Jordan, E.L. *America—Glorious and Chaotic Land: Charles Sealsfield Discovers the Young United States: An Account of Our Post-Revolutionary Ancestors by a Contemporary*. Englewood Cliffs: Prentice-Hall, 1969.

Schuchalter, Jerry. *Frontier and Utopia in the Fiction of Charles Sealsfield.* New York: Peter Lang, 1986.

Trent, William Peterfield, et al., eds. *The Cambridge History of American Literature,* 3 volumes. New York: Macmillan, 1945.

Tuckermann, Henry T. *America and Her Commentators: With a Critical Sketch of Travel in the United States.* New York: Kelley, 1970.

IV. Major Studies in German

Castle, Eduard. *Das Geheimnis des Großen Unbekannten Charles Sealsfield–Karl Postl: Die Quellenschriften mit Einleitung, Bildnis, Handschriftproben und ausführlichem Register.* Vienna: Wiener Bibliophilen Gesellschaft, 1943.

————. *Der große Unbekannte: Das Leben von Charles Sealsfield (Karl Postl).* Vienna: Karl Werner, 1955.

Djordjewich, Milosch. *Charles Sealsfields Auffassung des Amerikanertums und seine literarhistorische Stellung.* Dissertation, Munich, 1926. Hildesheim: Gerstenberg Verlag, 1978.

Faust, Albert B. *Charles Sealsfield, der Dichter beider Heimsphären.* Weimar: E. Felber, 1897.

Kresse, Albert. *Erläuternder Katalog meiner Sealsfield-Sammlung.* Stuttgart: Charles Sealsfield Gesellschaft, 1974.

List, Rudolf. *Karl Postl–Sealsfield: Leben and Werk.* Niederdonau: Gaupresseamt, 1943.

Schüppen, Franz. *Charles Sealsfield/Karl Postl: Ein österreichischer Erzähler der Biedermeierzeit im Spannungsfeld von Alter und Neuer Welt.* Frankfurt am Main: Peter Lang, 1981.

————. "Charles Sealsfield (Forschungsreferat)." In *Zur Literatur der Restaurations-Epoche 1815-1848.* Eds. Jost Hermand and Manfred Windfuhr. Stuttgart: Metzler, 1970.

Sengle, Friedrich. "Die Dichter." In *Biedermeierzeit: Deutsche Literatur im Spannungsfeld zwischen Restauration und Revolution, 1815-1848.* Stuttgart: Metzler, 1980.

Spiess, Reinhard F. *Charles Sealsfields Werke im Spiegel der literarischen Kritik: Eine Sammlung zeitgenössischer Rezensionen mit einer Einleitung herausgegeben.* Stuttgart: Charles Sealsfield Gesellschaft, 1977.

Adalbert Stifter

G. H. Hertling

Stifter was born in 1805 in the formerly Upper Austrian, later Czecho-slovakian town of Oberplan in Southern Bohemia of lower middle-class parents; he died of suicide in 1868 in Linz, Upper Austria, after having spent the greatest part of his life within the boundaries of the Austro-Hungarian Empire. From 1818 to 1826 we find him from age twelve to twenty-one as a student at the (still) renowned Benedictine Abbey School of Kremsmünster (Upper Austria). Kremsmünster's educational philosophy was based upon an enlightened Catholicism under Austria's Emperor Joseph II, thus giving Stifter the foundation of his life-long rational-humanistic philosophy—a precious gift indeed for anyone struggling to preserve the moral and ethical values once espoused by Germany's classical humanists of the eighteenth century. The eight years at the Abbey were spent studying the natural sciences, classical languages and literatures, especially the eighteenth-century German classics. Drawing and painting were not neglected educational activities. These years Stifter later called the happiest years of his life.[1] These were indeed the most important years for shaping his philosophy of life, especially through the works of Leibniz, W. v. Humboldt, Herder, Winckelmann, Goethe, Schiller, and many other eighteenth-century German idealists.

After concluding his classical studies at Kremsmünster, Stifter remained in Vienna for twenty-two years, from 1826 to 1848, initially with the intention to study Law and to pursue his interest in the natural sciences at the University of Vienna. There he attended lectures on Law, Mathematics, Physics, and Astronomy, however without completing his studies. Although Vienna's programs at that time could not be compared with the curricula offered by German universities, it was Vienna's cultural life that blossomed, particularly music and the theater. Completely self-supporting, Stifter took on various tutorial positions, at first with the family of the extremely cultured Baroness von Mink in whose home he could also pursue his love for painting, and later, still as a student at the University, as a tutor of the young Richard Metternich, the son of Austria's Chancellor Klemens Metternich. It was in the house of the Baroness that Stifter wrote the first three of his early novellas (or stories),[2] *Der Condor* (The Condor) which first appeared in 1840, later to be revised and to be published with twelve additional stories under the collective title *Studien* (Studies), thirteen stories in all that appeared in six volumes between 1844 and 1850 (1844, volumes I and II; 1847, III and IV; 1850, V and VI): *Der Condor, Feldblumen* (Wildflowers), *Das Heidedorf* (Heath Village), *Der Hochwald* (High Forest), *Die Narrenburg* (Fools' Castle), *Die Mappe meines Urgroßvaters* (My Greatgrandfather's Portfolio), *Abdias, Das alte Siegel* (The Old Seal), *Brigitta, Der Hagestolz* (The Recluse), *Der Waldsteig* (Forest Trail), *Zwei Schwestern* (Two Sisters), and *Der beschriebene Tännling* (The Designated Young Fir). Of these, *Der Condor, Der Hochwald, Brigitta, Der beschriebene Tännling,* and especially *Abdias* have become the best-known novellas with the most favorable of critical acclaims.

The collective title *Studien* clearly links the author to his sketches and paintings, the first three of which he finished in 1839, entitled "Blick in die Beatrixgasse" (View into Beatrix Street), "Blick auf die Vorstadthäuser" (View of Suburban Houses), and "Ruine Wittinghausen" (The Ruin of Wittinghausen).[3] Before characterizing the *Studien* briefly, it is necessary to address a sequence of events which led to Stifter's "escape into imaginative prose."[4] To begin with, he felt ever more disillusioned with his university studies, then suffered the shock of unrequited love—his love for a wealthy merchant's daughter, Franziska ("Fanny") Greipl whom he had met during a summer vacation after his first year at the University of Vienna in the town of Friedberg, near his native Oberplan. His pleading letters and his lyrics to Fanny were to no avail: Fanny yielded to her parents' request to terminate her relations with Stifter once and for all. Stifter then became increasingly disgruntled by the repressive political developments during the late thirties and early forties—by the censorship and police restriction of political, economic, and intellectual freedoms under the rule of Metternich (1815-1845). Initially sympathetic with Austria's middle-class liberalism, he soon became utterly disheartened by Metternich's oppressive measures which attempted to thwart any liberal, i.e., "revolutionary" development, whereupon he became equally disgusted with the 1848 Revolution itself. Fully identifying with an evolutionary, i.e., organistic philosophy of history as promulgated by German classical idealists of the previous century, it is no surprise that Stifter became ever more disheartened with the revolutionary materialism of nineteenth-century Vienna and of Austria in general. Small wonder that he rejected the politically tainted *littérature engagée* of the Young Germans (*Junges Deutschland*) whose exponents had "dared" to meddle with imaginative literature intended to disseminate morality, humaneness, and beauty.[5]

The *Studien* novellas, all of which initially appeared between 1840 and 1845 before their revisions for the six-volume *Studien* collection (1844-1850), present Stifter as an increasingly meticulous and detailed painter of landscapes. Their locations encompass the mountainous areas of the Bohemian Forest some distance north of the Danube, approximately north of Passau (Upper Bavaria) and north of Linz (Upper Austria), that is to say, in the native settings of Stifter's homeland. Forests, often impenetrably dense, hillsides, and mountain ridges, often with a view of a river valley (usually the Moldau), bathed in early or late sunlight, sometimes punished by drought, by fire, rain, or hail storms, provide for magnificent settings. Stifter's landscapes are either carefully cultivated or else ominous, the houses meticulously kept and carefully furnished, yet an ill-boding air of some sort of impending intervention from the outside looms over these idyllic settings.

In Stifter's early novellas, particularly in the revised *Studien,* an increasing reduction in dialogue becomes evident. This gradual decline expresses a profound understanding of people living and working together so harmoniously that linguistic communication is no longer necessary. Descriptive depictions increase with Stifter's development as a writer. Only two of the thirteen novellas have their settings far away from Stifter's homeland: *Abdias* with its exotic *mise en scène* in the Atlas mountain range of northern Africa, and *Brigitta* in the Hungarian puszta. All in all, with his early narratives Stifter escapes the city, which he uses only in a series of narrative sketches (meant to introduce Vienna to the visitor), entitled *Wien und die Wiener* (Vienna and the Viennese), two of which bring the most ominous accounts of frightening experiences: the autobiographical *Die Sonnenfinsterniß* [sic] *am 8. July 1842* (The Solar Eclipse of 8 July 1842) and the other autobiographical account, *Ein Gang durch die Kata-komben* (A Stroll through the Catacombs) beneath Vienna's St. Stephen's

Cathedral (1844).

Whereas the first versions of the later *Studien*-novellas reveal Stifter's close reading of Jean Paul, the early novellas in general often convey a fatalistic world view, the loss of identity or an awareness of existential isolation. In his revisions for the *Studien* collection Stifter clearly attempts to reduce these fatalistic-deterministic elements: resignation, moderation, self-control, and a love symbiosis with nature, with the family, and with people within the social environment, become dominant features. Thus, the dramatic elements wane as the story lines become lengthier. In this tendency the *Studien* novellas foreshadow the stories—or better: the small novels[6]—of the subsequent collection of six narratives, collectively entitled *Bunte Steine* (Many-Colored Stones) of the year 1853. When looking once more at the thirteen early novellas before turning to *Bunte Steine*, a number of paradoxical features both as to form and content become evident: certain classic-romantic characteristics stand in opposition to anti-romantic, drastically realistic, and existential features. Many of the protagonists' conciliatory, harmonious lifestyles are the result of conformist and resigned attitudes. The *Studien* novellas in their chronological sequence become more and more descriptive, their themes are frequently quite similar and vary only slightly. The paradoxical nature of their author becomes increasingly discernible, especially when comparing the original versions with the *Studien* revisions.

The period from 1838 to 1848 represented ten very productive years for Stifter both in writing and in painting. Because of this early success, creative writing was not so much a refuge any longer but became a mission to him. As of about 1848 his imaginative prose was to become the "highest earthly possession" to him; the stories themselves he conceived ever more as "ethic revelations,"[7] his language becoming increasingly perpetual, graphic, and highly metaphoric, oftentimes strikingly biblical and Goethean. The favorable reception of the *Studien* by most critics of Stifter's time was echoed by the late Romantic Joseph von Eichendorff (1788-1857), who claimed in 1846 there was "not a trace of modern frag-mentation, of conceited frivolity, or of morally experimental self-torture."[8] Such claims stand in direct contradiction to Thomas Mann's assessment that "an efficacious propensity for the Excessive, for the Elemental-Catastrophic, for the Pathological" finds its "frightful expression" in the early novellas, in spite of Stifter's efforts to set his course in search of the "Gentle Law"—traces of which are already visible in the revised versions of his early *Studien*. Stifter's early literary success even reached England where a reviewer in 1848 introduces Stifter as "a young [Viennese] writer . . . of more than ordinary promise," although aspects of his uniquely "true descriptive poetry" are reprimanded for their narrative detail.[9]

When comparing tone and content of Stifter's thirteen early stories with his profuse correspondence from the thirties to the late forties and beyond, especially the letters to his publisher and friend Gustav Heckenast in Budapest, then another striking paradox becomes noticeable: whereas the *Studien* revisions reveal a quest for moral and social stability and, for the most part, resolve all conflicts within the realms of artful and artistic spirituality, Stifter's letters convey a moody and brooding skepticism, reveal fears and depressive flights into pessimism, psychological experiences which stand in striking opposition to his poetological and narrative theme on order, harmony, and the "Gentle Law." Thus, Stifter's early stories, then his *Studien* revisions, followed by his *Bunte Steine* collection and his smaller narratives published between 1843 and 1862: *Der späte Pfennig* (1843, The Late Penny); *Die Barmherzigkeit* (1843, Compassion); *Die drei Schmiede ihres Schicksals* (1844, The Three Smiths of Their Fate); *Zuversicht* (1846, Trust); *Der Tod einer Jungfrau* (1847, Death of a Maiden); *Menschliches Gut* (1854, Human Possessions); and *Zwei Witwen* (1862, Two Widows), as well as his collection of five impressionistic essays of high psychological fervor in *Wien und die Wiener* (1844, Vienna and the Viennese), all these works with few exceptions register Stifter's increasing fears of chaos—of darkness and of death—as if his many Happy-End stories and novellas express his longing for happiness and harmony. But unforeseen natural catastrophes loom: conflagrations (*Katzensilber* [Mica]), an attack by wolves (*Brigitta*), hail (*Katzensilber*), and lightning storms (*Abdias*), or ominous snow storms (*Bergkristall [Rock Crystal]*) threaten to destroy order and harmony—frightful experiences that culminate in Stifter's horrifying description of a blizzard in his work written two years before his death: *Aus dem Bayrischen Walde* (1867, From the Bavarian Forest).[10] These and other (potentially) catastrophic disturbances seem to be divine interventions and occur either completely unforeseen or else at times when protagonists and others are unmindful, that is to say, "blind" and neglectful of working toward the good and the harmony of all. Manifestations of chaos appear, quite in the spirit of the "Foreword" to *Bunte Steine*, when mankind loses sight of the totality of life, when it becomes selfish and disrespectful of others.

Stifter's life in Vienna from 1826 to 1848 was restless and uneven: the terminated relationship with Fanny Greipl was crushing, yet his early literary activities, especially between 1840 and 1848, were intensive and successful. At first fully sympathetic with middle-class liberalism, the revolution became offensively "bestial" to him.[11] This monstrous antagonist stood against all principles of benevolent humanitarianism. As his despair of unrequited love grew, he began his relationship with Amalia Mohaupt around 1832, a completely uneducated woman of peasant stock who shared no literary (let alone other intellectual) interests with him, but whom he married in 1837.

Soon after the political upheavals of 1848 in Vienna and the publication of some small narratives (see above), along with a series of educational and political anti-revolutionary essays in the *Wiener Bote* (Viennese Messenger), published with Gustav Heckenast between 1848 and 1850, the most noteworthy being "Der Staat" (The State), "Rückkehr nach der Revolution" (Return after the Revolution), "Die oktroyierte Verfassung" (The Imposed Constitution), "Was ist Freiheit?" (What is Freedom?), and "Was ist Recht?" (What is Justice?), all of which express Stifter's profound disgust for non-evolutionary modes of history, he and Amalia moved to Linz. His ardent anti-revolutionary philosophy is echoed with equal vigor in his correspondence between 1848 and 1850.[12] Two years after his arrival in Linz, Stifter was appointed Adviser and Inspector (*Schulrat*) to Upper Austria's State Commission on Secondary Education under the general direction of Count Felix Ludwig Johann von Schwarzenberg, a government position he held from 1850 to his early retirement in 1865 (three years before his death).

When reading his "philosophical-political" essays from the late forties and early fifties with his stories and novellas of that time, especially the six entitled collectively *Bunte Steine* that appeared in 1853 in two volumes, Stifter's "mission" becomes self-evident: it is his calling to educate the "young at heart" through imaginative prose, through his work as School Inspector and, he so much hoped, through his (and his friend Johann Aprent's) literary anthology of 1854, the *Lesebuch zur Förderung humaner Bildung* (Primer for the Educational Advancement of Humankind). Thus, from the late forties to his death in 1868, Stifter devoted all of his time and energy to transmitting the educational ideals advanced by Germany's eighteenth-century Classicists, particularly Herder and W. v. Humboldt.[13] In conceiving and creating their primer, as Stifter and Aprent state in the

"Foreword," they "adhered to one particular idea and have compiled the materials in accordance to the idea of a *general education of mankind* [their italics] (Humanism), the cultivation of which modern times have rightfully added to the sciences so that the young, striving for factual knowledge, i.e., the pupils of secondary schools, of technical schools, etc., also be introduced to the worlds of higher, altogether human thinking and feeling, so that they may continue to progress on this now familiar path. . . ."[14] To understand and appreciate Stifter's restorative educational philosophy and his evolutionary views concerning history, it is necessary to study his polemical and programmatic "Foreword" to his *Bunte Steine* as well, since it contains the key to his aesthetic, educational, and philosophical concerns.[15] By the early fifties Stifter was convinced that only through educational reforms and through his own artistic and now also administrative engagements relative to humanistic-idealistic principles, could the deterioration of such values be held in check.

To Stifter's and Aprent's profound disillusionment their *Lesebuch* of 1854 was rejected for adoption in secondary schools (Upper Austria) by the Austrian Ministry of Education on the grounds that Stifter's and Aprent's selection of literary texts in two parts did not meet Austria's educational goals. In reality, the referee, himself a publisher of school primers, had feared competition. The text selections, comprised of eighteenth- and some nineteenth-century German prose and lyric poetry, clearly reflect Stifter's and Aprent's concept of intellectual and spiritual development in the young, i.e., the teachers' (and, with that, the parental) obligation toward one's psychological, spiritual, and aesthetic development, in place of educating the young toward physical and materialistic satisfactions. The text selections and, indeed, the title of the two-part anthology evidences Stifter's deep-rooted identification with the educational philosophies of eighteenth-century German thinkers.[16]

Stifter held office as Inspector of Public Schools (*Schulrat*) for some fifteen years (from 1850 to his "forced" retirement in 1865), although with diminishing involvement. His activities as *Schulrat* became more and more restricted as time went on, since Austria's public instruction returned to the jurisdiction of the Church soon after the failed Revolution of 1848. In the fifties the State no longer controlled educational matters, and the influential position of the *Schulrat* waned. Stifter's deep-felt disillusionment and bitterness grew as of 1856, the year in which his position as Inspector of the *Schulrat* in Linz, which he helped found in 1850, was eliminated.

It seemed as though imaginative literature was to become the sole vehicle left to him to educate his "young hearts"[17] toward a discovery of the "Gentle Law" which Stifter had set out to establish for himself and for his contemporaries with ever greater anguish: a law of nature that stands in opposition to manifestations of vehemence and violence, of selfishness and materialistic complacency.[18] Ever since the successful *Studien* novellas of the early and late forties, his correspondence with his friend in Budapest, Gustav Heckenast, intensified. Heckenast continued to encourage and urge Stifter to literary productivity. Once settled In Linz with Amalia, royalties were quickly spent, making Stifter ever more dependent upon Heckenast's prepayments, finally obliging Stifter to relinquish all his publishing rights to Heckenast exclusively. From the fifties onward Stifter grew ever more weary of this and ever more disheartened for other reasons as well: the rejection of his *Lesebuch zur Förderung humaner Bildung*, the suspension of his administrative and pedagogic efforts as *Schulrat*, his "forced" retirement from that office in 1865, the amplification of many negative voices now even concerning his *Studien* and the *Bunte Steine* novellas as well, then the so horribly tragic suicide of his adopted eighteen-year-old daughter Juliane Mohaupt (a niece of his wife Amalia) by drowning in the Danube at Linz in the year 1859, the increasing concern of Amalia's and his own health—all of these events became unbearable experiences. It is a wonder he was yet to write his only two novels: *Der Nachsommer* (*Indian Summer*) and *Witiko*, the former appearing in 1857, the latter from 1865 to 1867, both in three volumes. Horrifying was the death of his adopted daughter and shattering were the critical reviews of his works and of his lifestyle: that his novellas, stories, and then his novels were largely "undramatic," "far too detailed" and "cumbersome" in their "endless descriptions"—a "reflection," it was said, "of his apolitical lifestyle."[19]

Stifter's *Bunte Steine* of 1853 are a collection of six stories (or novellas or, as can be argued, of six "small novels"),[20] with the following titles: *Bergmilch* (Lublinite), which had appeared in 1843 as *Die Wirkungen eines weißen Mantels* (The Effects of a White Coat); *Bergkristall* (*Rock Crystal*), originally published as *Der Heilige Abend* (Christmas Eve) in 1845; *Kalkstein* (*Limestone*), originally published as *Der arme Wohltäter* (The Poor Benefactor) in 1848; *Granit*, first as *Die Pechbrenner* (The Charcoal Makers) in 1849; *Turmalin* (*Tourmaline*), originally entitled *Der Pförtner im Herrenhaus* (The Estate's Caretaker) in 1852; and lastly *Katzensilber* (Mica) of 1853. Of these, *Bergkristall*, *Kalkstein*, and *Granit* are perhaps the most widely known, with *Turmalin* being exceptionally stirring. Only *Kalkstein* was written for the collection itself; the others were revisions of stories from the forties, altered to correspond more precisely to Stifter's educational pronouncements than they had before. Although originally thought of as stories *for* children, most became stories *about* children, particularly *Bergkristall* and *Kalkstein*, the collection having been dedicated to Juliane.[21]

Similar to the collective title *Studien* with its metaphoric association to "sketches," "drafts," i.e., to preliminary, unfinished works of art, so too the *Bunte Steine* impart the notion of a colorful array of semi-precious stones found and "gathered" in nature. The title conveys a kind of unintentional collection of natural objects, suggesting the simplicity, purity, and therefore the beauty, of "things" natural. Every story clearly carries Stifter's ethical and moral concerns relative to the humanization of mankind, now endangered by "modernism." The central themes and motifs unifying the six stories lie in the endangerment, the rescuing and the sheltering of young individuals in the attempt to establish, to preserve and to protect harmonious families within the symmetry and oneness of nature. Time and again this "oneness" is challenged and endangered by elemental forces of unforeseen magnitude and violence, yet ethnologic, ecologic, and anthropologic concerns and actions generally lead to a fairy-tale-like triumph of symbiotic harmony. As with the *Studien* of 1844 to 1850, so too *Bunte Steine* of 1853 are set in the landscapes of Upper Austria; only *Turmalin* is mirrored against the backdrop of a city (Vienna)—with pitiful consequences.

For the sake of completing the references to Stifter's imaginative prose, an array of six smaller narratives—for the most part moralizing parables—should be mentioned here, all of which are rather sentimental stories, placing mankind's inner values above all else. They appeared between 1843 and 1862: *Der späte Pfennig* (1843, The Late Penny); *Die Barmherzigkeit* (1843, Mercy); *Zuversicht* (1846, Trust); *Der Tod einer Jungfrau* (1847, Death of a Maiden); *Menschliches Gut* (1854, Human Possessions), and *Zwei Witwen* (1862, Two Widows).

When *Bunte Steine* appeared in 1853, Stifter had already served for three years as *Schulrat* and was now appointed Curator of Upper Austria's Architectural Monuments. It was the year in which he began work on his utopian family- and educational-novel *Der Nachsommer*.[22] Stifter had already conceived it in the late forties and early fifties, that is, quite soon after his move to Linz. He was to spend four years writing it (in part, simultaneously with his following novel, *Witiko*), before it appeared in 1856 in three volumes. Although Stifter initially prioritized *Der Nachsommer*, which concerns itself with the aesthetic and moral education of a young man developing toward a world citizenry, he continued to work on the historical and political novel *Witiko* (1865-1867). The totally undramatic and therefore negatively received "narration"[23] concerns itself with the harmonious coexistence of two families, representing the bourgeoisie (Heinrich Drendorf) and the aristocracy (the Baron von Risach, Natalie, and her mother Mathilde, the Countess of Tarona), living in aesthetic harmony.

Stifter's didactic and philosophical intentions are clear: to show that scientific and artistic endeavors are complementary, not mutually exclusive. Briefly outlined, the protagonist's (Heinrich Drendorf's) "narration" about his educational upbringing some thirty years ago, is the story of this middle-class son of a Viennese merchant who is educated and matures ever so gradually within the ideal environment of the Asperhof (the Asper Estate) under the sensitive tutelage of an aging "noble" man, the *Freiherr* (Baron) von Risach. After years of carefully structuring Heinrich's educational experiences, the young man of "ethical nobility" finally becomes worthy of marrying his beloved Natalie, the daughter of the Countess of Tarona Mathilde, Risach's platonic love of many years. To interpret Heinrich's and Natalie's marriage as an expression of conciliation between the bourgeoisie and the nobility would be erroneous,[24] since Heinrich may identify with the world of the "noble" only through the presence of his mentor and benefactor, the Freiherr von Risach, who has taken it upon himself to "raise" Heinrich into becoming an individual of *inner* nobility.

Heinrich Drendorf here narrates in meticulous (and, to many a critic, tiresome) detail his educational experiences in von Risach's idyllic, ideal, and utopian environment, in and about his Rosenhaus (House of Roses), in a harmonious humanistic setting of practicality *and* beauty, tolerant of studies in the natural sciences, which are then followed by studies in the arts, aesthetics, ethics, psychology, and, ultimately, in humanistic philosophy. Heinrich's education is neither socially nor professionally oriented but is an end in itself, in sharp contrast to an education geared toward specialization. Thus, *Der Nachsommer* is the *summum bonum* of Stifter's philosophy of education, a utopian novel containing and advocating restorative ideals, presenting a "family" world devoid of tensions or dialectical strife between the objective and the subjective, a world of total harmony, a world without resistive elements which might hinder spiritual and intellectual development. Here Stifter succeeded in presenting "a prevailing grand and ethical force in contrast to the miserable degeneracy . . ." of the contemporary world perverted by materialistic values.[25]

It is no surprise that this Stifterian world of humanistic harmony in which utilitarian objects or "things" have become aestheticized, a world in which the "restoration of beauty" becomes the principal mode of action, a realm in which beauty, utilitarianism, ethics, and aesthetics are one, that this "pedagogical province" provoked then—and still today—considerable negative reception. Small wonder that Hebbel, in an ironic review of *Der Nachsommer* in 1858 entitled "Das Komma im Frack" (The Comma in Tail-Coat), criticized the undramatic narrative as one of excessively "painted" detail, a narrative technique, according to Hebbel, totally un suitable even for the novel as genre.[26] In Hebbel's view, Stifter again "for got" the "oak tree" for the sake of discerning the "moss," disregarding the "dance of planets" in favor of observing the "dance of gnats," in short, the comma puts on the tail-coat and looks down disdainfully at the sentence to which it is, after all, indebted for its existence."[27] For Hebbel, Stifter continues to be the "sedate man of eternal studies"[!], completely "losing sight of things human."[28] Little did Hebbel understand Stifter's pedagogical intentions, little could he grasp the novel's philosophical content, which, by its very nature, would not submit to "acrobatic theatrics." The most caustic critic of German literature and culture, Friedrich Nietzsche, spoke altogether differently of *Der Nachsommer* in 1880, when he added this particular work to the otherwise limited "Treasury of German Prose":

> Aside from Goethe's writings and especially aside from Goethe's *Conversations with Eckermann,* the best German book available, what is left of German prose literature that would deserve to be read again and again? Georg Christoph Lichtenberg's *Aphorisms,* the first book of Johann Heinrich Jung-Stilling's biography, Adalbert Stifter's *Nachsommer,* and Gottfried Keller's *Die Leute von Seldwyla* (The People of Seldwyla)—and that will be all for awhile.[29]

Whereas *Der Nachsommer* idealizes family, beauty, and ethical behavior,

Stifter's other novel, the historical, political, and sociological *Witiko* presents the ideal state in socio-political terms, a state restoratively and thus artistically reconstructed in a twelfth-century setting. Although Stifter first mentioned a plan for this novel in 1850, considering the romantic title "Der schwarze Ritter" (The Black Knight) for volume one of a historical trilogy about the Bohemian family of the Rosenberger, much of the work was not written until the late fifties, concurrently with *Der Nachsommer*. The first symptoms of Stifter's mortal illness[30] brought about more and more interruptions, but with the constant encouragement of his publisher Heckenast, Stifter managed to complete the three volumes in 1867, one year before his death.

Witiko relates the "fictitious history" of the medieval fortress of Wittinghausen,[31] the ruins of which are located in the vicinity of Ober-plan, Stifter's place of birth. Stifter's research concerning the ruins revealed only that the fortress had belonged to the powerful Bohemian House of Rosenberger in the twelfth century.[32] Stifter had used this castle fortress and its surroundings earlier in his masterful *Studien* novella *Der Hochwald* (1842), a highly dramatic tragedy in which the fortress is ultimately destroyed during the Thirty Years' War by the intrusion of chaos into the paradisiacal idyll. Whereas the *Hochwald* novella is a tragedy of intrusion and destruction, the novel *Witiko* tells of the castle's construction at the time of the Bohemian civil war of succession: Witiko serves and fights in support of the elected Duke, who victoriously perseveres in his struggle against the revolutionaries. When peace is restored, Witiko is rewarded with territory and feudal tenure. Finally, he can marry Berta, who had waited patiently for his rise to fame and glory. Bohemia, now part of the Holy Roman Empire, prides itself on the structuring of the Wittinghausen fortress. Here Stifter contrasts the harmonious historical, political, and social situation at the time of a united Habsburg Empire within the constellation of the Holy Roman Empire, a grandiose Empire, obviously mirrored against the disintegration and destruction of Habsburg-Austria at the time of the Revolution of 1848. In describing in great detail the construction of a medieval feudal state which culminates in the building of the fortress, Stifter clearly voices his grief concerning the fall of the Habsburg Empire and the dissolution of a dis-harmonious state.[33] The novel clearly evinces Stifter's utopian conception of a supranational "United Nations" founded on Christian values, a *Völkergemeinschaft* (community of nations) at the time the Habsburg Empire had dissolved, splintering into separate nationalistic states. Stifter's identification with the philosophy of history espoused by Herder, W. v. Humboldt, and now by the Romantic political and sociological theorist Adam Müller (1779-1829), i.e., with the conception of an organic, progressive, and cyclical development of history, is amply demonstrated in *Witiko*. This correspondence is perhaps best expressed in his own words: "A grand law manifests itself in national destinies—a law which, related to our own destiny, we call the law of ethics; the changes in the lives of people are but transfigurations of this law."[34] Stifter's idealization of the state in the general context of a humanitarian individualism tolerant of other states and nations is indeed restorative in spirit; but is it utopian? It is therefore not surprising that Witiko, as the archetypal protagonist of the ideal statesman, always acts correctly because he follows the natural "law," the "Law of Ethics."[35] He acts in accordance with natural occurrences which, according to Stifter, are based upon the "Grand Law of Ethics."[36]

Like *Der Nachsommer*, *Witiko* too was received rather unfavorably: like the first novel it stood counter to everything revolutionary. For this reason both novels, together with Stifter's *oeuvre* as a whole, were actually "discovered" and favorably received, along with similar literature and art forms rooted in eighteenth-century Idealism, only after the two World Wars. Just as the *Lesebuch zur Förderung humaner Bildung* of 1854 is a reflection of Stifter's literary tastes, just as this anthology was meant to be an educational primer,[37] so are the educational novel of aesthetization, *Der Nachsommer,* and the historical novel of political idealization, *Witiko,* "Pedagogical Provinces" which evince Stifter's philosophical ideals at their best—the Brotherhood of Man based upon moderation, faith, humility, love, family, tolerance, and gentleness.

The ten years between the publication of *Der Nachsommer* (1857) and the appearance of the third volume of *Witiko* (1867) became increasingly burdensome for Stifter. His failing health, the fear of a cholera epidemic in the area around Linz, the increasing dread of isolation and loneliness led him to numerous vacation "escapes," one of which was to Lackenhäuser in the Bavarian Forest in late autumn 1866. Here he became panic-stricken by the ominous claustrophobic experience of that fateful November blizzard, chronicled in 1866 under the title *Aus dem Bayrischen Walde* (From the Bavarian Forest). This poetic essay appeared the year before Stifter's death and, as said earlier, belongs to the most dramatic, intense, and existential experiences of his autobiographical narratives, i.e., to *Die Sonnenfinsterniß am 8. July 1842* and to *Ein Gang durch die Kata-komben* of 1842 (the latter published again in 1844 in Stifter's collection of five autobiographical observations, *Wien und die Wiener*).[38] When one reads these three anguishing, yet very poetic accounts of 1842, 1844, and of 1866/1867 collectively and compares them with his four in part frag-mentary novel-like versions of *Die Mappe meines Urgroßvaters* (My Great-grandfather's Portfolio), the last version having been halted by Stifter's death, then Stifter's Kafkaesque and highly paradoxical nature becomes evident: The "Gentle Law" of the "Foreword" to *Bunte Steine* of 1852, followed and magnified by his conception of the "Grand Law of Ethics" in the 1860s, is eminently vulnerable to and endangered by unforeseen and uncontrollable catastrophic events—by sudden and unexpected interventions which induce fear, horror, and in the case of the blizzard, panic.[39]

At the time of his final effort to return to his life-long preoccupation with his "novella-novel," *Die Mappe meines Urgroßvaters*, Stifter wrote four more short stories, all on the common theme and problem of "marriage" and "family," all written between 1864 and 1866: *Die Nachkommenschaften* (1865, Descendants), *Der Waldbrunnen* (1866, Forest Well); *Der Kuß von Sentze* (1866, Kiss of Sentze); and *Der fromme Spruch* which appeared posthumously in 1868 (The Pious Dictum). In considering *Die Mappe,* critics have correctly maintained that comparative analyses of the four versions that appeared between 1841 and 1938 (!), the so-called "Ur-mappe" (Original Portfolio) of 1841/1842, then the "Studienmappe" (The Studies Portfolio) of 1847, the "Letzte Mappe" (The Last Portfolio), a fragment written in 1864 and first printed in 1870, and lastly the "Vierte Fassung" (The Fourth Portfolio Version), not printed until 1938,[40] most succinctly illustrate Stifter's development as a poetic writer, particularly the changes that occurred in his concept of Realism. Before highlighting these developments and philosophical changes, a glance at the story lines becomes necessary, also because they remain basically the same with little variations: all four versions are "two" stories "within a story," carry a central story framed by two secondary ones. The narrator, using the first person, tells about his grandfather's autobiographical portfolio, that is, of the materials recorded by Augustinus, the physician. Thus, the narrator retells Augustinus' life—how he had settled down in (Stifter's beloved) Bohemian Forest, had fallen in love with Margarita and had lost her because of her possessive father and his own subjective and youthful manner.[41] Beside himself with grief, he had contemplated suicide but was saved by Margarita's father, the "sanftmütige Obrist" (the gentle Colonel) who, for didactic reasons, then told Augustinus about his own life: he too, as a young man, had been brash but had learned to compose himself by keeping a diary. Augustinus thus learned from Margarita's father, the "Obrist," that we mature through painful experiences.

Following the "Obrist's" model, Augustinus begins to keep a portfolio in order to search for and find his own identity. Augustinus now submits himself completely and unselfishly to the service of the common good. During his years of service as a physician, Augustinus learns that when his past and present experiences become synthesized, it will no longer be necessary to keep a portfolio.[42] After years of dedicated work, he encounters Margarita again at a folk festival and, like Stefan Murai's ever so late "discovery" of *Brigitta,* he too has become worthy of her in marriage. In spite of some minor variations in this story line, the "Letzte Mappe" of 1864 (published posthumously in 1870) and the last, the "Fourth Portfolio," are quite similar to each other in content, also in that both show Augustinus' life-long yearning to find his vanished friend the poet Eustach again. When in 1864 Stifter returned to revising the "Second" *Mappe*, the "Studienmappe" of 1847, he admitted the healing effect it had on him:[43] Just as Augustinus found solace in composing *his* portfolio, so does imaginative prose become a refuge for the ailing and failing poet Stifter.

In assessing Stifter's development as a poetic writer and thinker when overviewing the chronology of the four "Portfolios," one notices the following: The "Urmappe" of 1841/1842 is subjective, expressive, full of imagery and exact descriptions of nature. Loss of identity, physical and psychological isolation, feelings of determinism through hereditary and historical factors, and occasional pessimistic-fatalistic experiences make this "Urmappe" seem quite modern. Stifter then attempted to "delete" such "disturbing" experiences and behavior patterns by emphasizing Augustinus' ethical behavior in social terms. Dramatic and turbulent passages concerned with strife and conflict are avoided altogether in the "Studienmappe" of 1847. No longer is the reader "surprised" by the interventions of unforeseen occurrences. These have given way to ordinary actions such as taking walks, domestic care of house and garden, to the preoccupation of collecting "things" natural. As is seen already in such early novellas as *Brigitta* (1843) and in *Bergkristall* (1845/1843), for example, the use of dialogue diminishes sharply so as to express a profound spiritual and psychological "understanding" of the "other," a deep relationship which makes oral communication obsolete. All potentially selfish actions are surrendered and give way to actions based upon that "Grand Law of Ethics": resignation, self-restraint, and composure to the extent of self-sacrifice become Augustinus' dominant characteristics. The ever so undramatic and gentle flow of two new chapters, "Margarita" and the "Thal ob Pirling" (Valley near Pirling), move this formerly dramatic novella closer to the undramatic and restorative novel in the tradition of *Der Nachsommer* and *Witiko*. The profoundly ethical and therefore undramatic qualities of Stifter's late works have led many critics, particularly Friedrich Sengle in recent years, to characterize Stifter as a major exponent of Biedermeier in the literature and *Weltanschauung* of nineteenth-century German Realism.[44]

In comparing the "Studienmappe" of 1847 with the fragmentary "Letzte Mappe" of 1864, it becomes evident that language and syntax have become almost frigid, have been "objectified" as though the late Stifter began to "construct" his thoughts too rigidly and consciously. The "Letzte Mappe" of 1864, when mirrored against his correspondence from the sixties to his death in 1868, shows a Stifter becoming frightened and hardened; his late correspondence often shows him panic-stricken by the events of the times—so much so that only his literary activities offered him escape and asylum. Overviewing the *Mappe* summarily, the physician Augustinus becomes increasingly a symbolic figure of healing. More so than the "sanftmütige Obrist," he heals for the good of all, thus assuming the position as a progenitor of humanism, of culture.

From the autumn of 1863 to the year of his death by suicide on 26 January 1868, Stifter's illness—it is assumed he suffered from cirrhosis of the liver—became progressively unbearable, finally reaching levels of intolerable anguish and pain. Frequent "escapes" to spas such as Karlsbad and Marienbad, to Lackenhäuser, or visits to his beloved village of Kirchschlag near Linz brought no sustained relief, but instead increased anguish, fears, and depressions. In his letters to Heckenast during his last years, he blamed the worsening of his condition on the "disappointments" suffered while serving as Inspector of Public Schools, but particularly on the dehumanization of late nineteenth-century Austrian values, manifest, for example, in the Prusso-Austrian War of 1866, another manifestation of "bestiality" that horrified him. For a short time "happy" at having been retired and pensioned by the State in 1865, he sought escape, solace, and moments of recuperation elsewhere, especially in his imaginative prose which, to him, was to serve the advancement of humanity.

Of the four late novellas, *Nachkommenschaften* (1865, Descendants), *Der Waldbrunnen* (1866, The Forest Spring), *Der Kuß von Sentze* (1866, Sentze's Kiss), and *Der fromme Spruch* (The Pious Saying) of the same year, the first bears considerable significance with reference to Stifter's lifelong preoccupation with painting. *Nachkommenschaften* is, to a large extent, an autobiographical confession concerning his concept of art and aesthetics in general which is astonishingly Schillerian.[45] *Nachkommenschaften* is the first-person narrative of an eccentric twenty-six-year-old landscape painter, Friedrich Roderer, who after some time begins to doubt the value of his work and is ultimately forced to relinquish his profession as an over-eager painter, whereupon he leads a happy bourgeois life: love and family are ultimately triumphant. In near-comedy form, Stifter, with a strong dose of self-irony and self-parody, depicts Friedrich as a "Kauz," a "Narr" (a fool) in the long line of persistent but odd "descendants," who is finally cured of his artistic "aspirations" and endeavors. As a young artist he had yearned to portray an "absolute" reality ("die wirkliche Wirklichkeit"), as well as the "idea" of it simultaneously. To accomplish this he continues to paint a marshscape for months on end, living in a hut next to his marshlands in order to always remain in contact with this reality. He creates numerous sketches and paintings, burning just as many as he produces. Soon he realizes the futility of his actions: he burns his huge canvas, gives up painting, and marries a distant relative, Susanna Roderer. Meanwhile Susanna's father, Peter Roderer, drains the marsh to destroy it as an unhealthy, romantic attraction for Friedrich and for the purpose of cultivating the land. Thus Friedrich's eccentric world is eliminated to make way for a "normal" life. Ursula Naumann perceptively raises the question of whether, in terms of Hegelian aesthetics, this tale might indeed be Stifter's parable concerning the finiteness of the arts and of artistic endeavors per se.[46] Naumann sees correctly that this argument is only partially valid, since it is, after all, Stifter's mission to show in metaphorical terms in *all* of his works that it is man's natural inclination to cultivate the wastelands for the good of all.[47] Just how closely Stifter identifies with his artist/painter Friedrich Roderer he tells his wife Amalia with understatement:[48] "In the end I am but a Roderer myself."[49]

Like Friedrich Roderer, Stifter too had always wished to become a professionally recognized painter, although he realized his limitations from early on.[50] Thus, painting and sketching became a serious "pastime" to him, however similar to his descriptive imaginative prose, and, like his narratives, second in meaning only to religious reverence. Although Stifter much preferred to write about painting, his love for descriptive detail and realistic exactness is certainly characteristic of both of his art forms.[51] The reason for ranking writing above painting is perhaps best described by his summary statement, namely, that the "canvas" was like a "sieve . . . which could only capture the coarse; the refinements, the tender things, and the truth would sift through it."[52] Small wonder then that Stifter became the "painting narrator" (and the "narrating painter") in the Winckelmannian tradition: by idealizing and sublimating reality whenever and wherever possible.[53] Thus painting, as does imaginative literature, serves the educational ideal of humanizing mankind. Hence, painting for Stifter always stood in the service of a Schillerian "Aesthetic Education of Mankind."[54]

Fritz Novotny has affirmed the impossibility of associating Stifter with a particular "school" of painting. Seen historically, nineteenth-century German landscape painting developed from a preference for religious motifs, clearly showing that, following the Romantics, nineteenth-century painters intended to mimetically objectify their work, thus distancing themselves from romantic "portraitures" of subjective, predominantly Christian perceptions. Therefore, one can only identify Stifter as a "realistic" painter of landscapes and of natural objects devoid of religious motifs or symbols, however deep his religious reverence is. Through painting, but above all through poetically realistic literature, mankind could be educated to becoming aesthetic and thereby ethical again, that is to say, could harmonize again the real with the ideal, or so it would seem! Imaginative prose *and* painting could perhaps synthesize the ideal with the real and become instrumental in achieving a *Förderung humaner Bildung,* an "advancement of human education." After religion it is "art that appeases, ennobles and purifies the hearts of mankind."[55] Therefore, according to Stifter, "great poets and painters like to choose the simplest subjects. Spurred on by the abundance of one's inner richness, they know how to portray this inner quality so exquisitely with few strokes in most subtle forms."[56] The purpose of artistic creativity, regardless of the medium, is not only to educate mankind to become aesthetic, but also to harmonize the real with the ideal. If this is truly so, then one is puzzled by Stifter's contrastive pronouncement in *Nachkommenschaften,* where Friedrich

Roderer gives up painting to the point of destroying his work, perhaps realizing the impossibility of such a synthesis. And just as Friedrich Roderer destroys his canvass(es), so too did Stifter so often in despair. But is it not perhaps the realization of the artist's inability to resolve the conflict between the real and the ideal that also compelled Stifter to continue on as a poetic writer?

Fritz Novotny's extensive search and research about Stifter's oils, permanent colors, pencils, some charcoals, and a few watercolors have made it possible to positively identify ninety-nine pictures as his. The most productive years of Stifter's "serious pastime" began with his first attempts while a pupil at Kremsmünster and peaked in the year when he was appointed *Schulrat*, i.e. a time span from 1823 to 1850. His paintings and sketches after 1850 consisted for the most part of fragments and unfinished works, nine of which he conceived as symbolic landscapes:

1. "Die Verhangenheit. Römische Ruinen" (The Past. Roman Ruins)
2. "Die Heiterkeit. Griechische Tempeltrümmer" (Cheerfulness. Greek Temple Ruins)
3. "Die Sehnsucht. Mondstück" (Longing. A Moon)
4. "Die Bewegung. Strömendes Wasser" (Motion. Streaming Water), and so forth.

Stifter's extensive and minutely detailed diary on the nine symbolic landscapes, his "Tagebuch meiner Malerarbeit" (Diary of My Work on Painting) appeared in 1854, the same year his and Aprent's primer *Lesebuch zur Förderung humaner Bildung* was published. On the one hand it shows the importance he ascribed to the nine scapes, and, on the other, as Naumann suggests,[57] a feeling of inadequacy and frustration when painting. It is interesting to note in this connection Stifter's predilection for such subjects as cloud formations and skyscapes, for Hungarian *puszta*scapes, for stones and tree trunks (or stumps), and, above all, for ruins. His land- and skyscapes did not minimize his fascination for such seemingly trivial "objects" or "things" of nature that go unnoticed by most: a blade of grass, a snowflake, a leaf, a stone, a blossom. Both in his prose and in his paintings, Stifter conveys his deep affinity and love for "things" natural[58]—spiritually, ecologically, and ethologically. It is a deeply felt symbiotic relationship with anything and anyone natural,[59] which can only be conveyed descriptively and most certainly not "dramatically." Thus, dialogues become unnecessary or are sparse. The ruins of fortresses and temples in his pictures and narratives grandly express his restorative concerns—to "preserve" them from the transitoriness of all things.[60] This too is the mission of the artist.

Stifter's attraction for ruins expresses his keen sense for historical change;[61] his artistic and literary "paintings" of them are his outcry for the preservation of "things" of beauty and form. It is exactly this attitude that led him to accept the honorary position as "Conservator für Oberöster-reich" in 1853—the year of his *Bunte Steine*—in other words, as Conserver and Curator of historical art objects. The "k. k. Centralkommission zur Erhaltung und Erforschung der Kunst- und historischen Denkmale (The Royal Imperial Central Commission for the Preservation and Research of Artistic and Historical Monuments) found in Stifter a superb servant in its efforts to preserve and restore medieval, i.e., primarily Gothic art, which the Romantics had "rediscovered." As a conserver, restorer, and therefore as a *conveyor* of things beautiful, Stifter was especially effective in the restoration of the hand-carved High Altar of the church in the town of Kefermarkt near Linz.[62]

*

This critical overview concerned with Stifter's life, his works, and his thoughts became, of necessity, increasingly philosophical. The final part of this essay, then, intends to consider summarily those philosophical views of Stifter which have not received much emphasis here earlier. As we have seen, in the late fifties Stifter had become increasingly disheartened by numerous experiences;[63] the feeling of isolation grew. Horrified by the death of his "daughter," the noticeable failing of his physical and psychological condition in 1864, and finally the foreboding of his alienation from society that would not understand or support his humanitarian, restorative values, brought on increasing expressions of despair. Orthodox religion brought him no solace, only his writing. Stifter was only "religious" in the sense that his painting and writing stood in its service. He was "religious" in recognizing that mankind was a reflection of a divine force or spirit, naturally destined to carry out the plan of that divine will for mankind's common good.[64] His works, his essays, and his correspondence clearly make him the poet/priest of nineteenth-century German Realism.[65] Since reason and a free will are God's gifts to man, it becomes our (categorical) duty, in Stifter's view, "to develop reason and free will which are given us only in the form of sprouts; there is no other path to the happiness of mankind, because reason and free will are given only to man as his highest characteristics, and because they can be developed infinitely."[66] In conformity with eighteenth-century German Idealism, Stifter realizes that man's progress toward ethical perfection is constantly challenged and endangered by antagonistic forces, such as passion, animalistic-instinctive behavior, i.e., by irrationality, immodesty, and by selfishness.[67] In his *Studien* and even earlier novellas, and then in the original versions prior to their "refinements" for the *Bunte Steine*, the brash, subjective, and impassioned individuals predominated.[68] Many of these earlier figures transgressed against the cosmic law of harmony and order,[69] and in so doing succumbed to a life of sterility and isolation.[70] In posing the question of whether man is a victim of a blind and indiscriminate fate or whether his place in the harmonic constellation of the universe is attached to the "chain of causes and effects," Stifter sides with the Leibnizian view that man is "naturally" free to act ethically. In his philosophical preamble to *Abdias*, Stifter's identification with Leibniz' idealism is striking:

> . . . there is neither a fate as an ultimate absurdity of being, nor are we affected by single events; instead, a merry chain of flowers is fastened through the infinity of the universe and transmits its luster into our hearts—the chain of causes and effects—and into the head of man the most beautiful of these flowers was cast, reason, the eye of the soul. . . .[71]

Although *Abdias* carries perhaps the longest and most philosophical introductory passage, the plots of most other novellas and stories are prefaced as well, particularly so by minute and oftentimes lulling descriptions of landscapes long before the plot (or "action") is set into motion. To the Stifter-novice such passages can indeed be tiring, although they best convey Stifter's profound visual relationship to "things" in nature. Patient reading of such passages clearly brings to light a Leibnizian cosmos, grand and divine in its harmony, as if Stifter so consciously clings fast to such harmony out of an inherent fear it may ultimately be destroyed or vanish. Stifter's relationship to these *Dinge* or *Dinglichkeiten*, whether they are "things" in nature or those found at home, is analogous to his symbiotic kinship with the "Gentle Law" which is said to regulate all. Since these "things," since nature itself, *est un miroir vivant de l'univers*, i.e. a reflection of a divine order of "things," Stifter's protagonists often observe nature through telescopes, windows, and window frames,[72] such as segments of forests or the steppes (*Brigitta*), parts of mountainous deserts (*Abdias*); the skyscapes of his *Wolkenstudien* (cloud studies) are framed, and the descriptions of interior designs of structures and particularly of private rooms become minute. His protagonists are either symbiotically at one with these "things" or else, because of their "blind-ness," trespass against them. No matter how deep or shallow this symbiosis may be, elements of unforeseen, unpredictable, and potentially catastrophic forces always lurk in the background, as if this grand, divine, and fragile harmony of "things" is continually threatened. What Stifter then shows in all of his works, is the tenderness and frailty of this God-given harmony, the susceptibility of it to chaos. And when man trespasses and transgresses the "Gentle Law" of nature, chaos triumphs.[73] This dialectical and often paradoxical position of Stifter makes his narratives incredibly modern and, at times, truly Kafkaesque.[74] His frequent use of oxymora, particularly in nature descriptions, such as "white darkness," "white blackness," "horri-fying sublimity, frightening beauty," and "thunderous lightning" or a "destructive hailstorm" "crashes in" from a "clear blue" or "cheerful" sky. Such contrastive, even contradicting and paradoxical descriptions create "unsettling feelings" on the part of the reader. Such a stylistic technique leads to one's questioning whether nature and the universe are after all as harmonious and guided by a "Gentle Law" as Stifter would like to have us believe! Be that as it may: what makes his prose timeless is especially its educational import: to tend and to cultivate this fragile harmony for the "furtherance of mankind" (*Zur Förderung humaner Bildung*). In Stifter's words: "The higher the artist strives with his heart, . . . the more intensely will he experience the splendor of nature, be it landscape, be it man's soul."[75]

We have seen that Stifter's educational philosophy is based primarily on Herder's educational reforms,[76] and that it is closely linked to his anti-revolutionary political idealism. These ideas are expressed succinctly in a number of socio-political essays that appeared between 1848 and 1850: "Der Staat" (The State), "Rückkehr nach der Revolution" (Return after the Revolution), "Die oktroyierte Verfassung" (The Imposed Constitution), "Was ist Freiheit?" (What is Freedom)?, "Was ist Recht?" (What is Justice?), and others. But if one singled out Stifter's most definitive philosophical pronouncement it would unquestionably be the "Foreword" of 1852 to his *Bunte Steine* of 1853. Understating there with utmost modesty that his six novellas are merely "pastimes for young hearts," he underplays the stories' high poetic quality and their educational content by saying elsewhere, two years before his "Foreword":

> My books are not merely imaginative narrations (as such they have—most likely—very short-lived values); but as ethical revelations, as expressions of human dignity . . . they do have value, a value which will endure for a longer period of time . . . while being surrounded by miserable, frivolous writings.[77]

It is therefore not surprising Stifter divorced himself from all politically oriented imaginative literature such as the *littérature engagée* of *Junges Deutschland* (Young Germany); politics and imaginative literature are, according to Stifter, totally incompatible with each other:

> Young Germany I feared the most because I do not at all agree with its attitude of mixing questions pertaining to the day and feelings pertaining to the day with poetic literature, but my thoughts run contrary: that beauty has no other purpose than being beautiful and that politics should not be made in verse-form nor in declamations but instead through Political Science which should be studied and comprehended beforehand, and through time-conscious actions which should not be put on paper until later. . . .[78]

Let me conclude this critical overview with three evaluations which confirm Stifter's timeless impact on those who seek to understand him—as a poet, as a poet/priest, as an educator, as a "restorative" idealist in search of the preservation and furtherance of humanity.

Hugo von Hofmannsthal often expressed his identification with his countryman Stifter, perhaps best in *Österreich im Spiegel seiner Dichtung* (1918, Austria Reflected in its Imaginative Literature):

> Have a look at an individual such as Stifter: civil servant, pedagogue, relatively revered pedagogue. . . . I know of no stranger synthesis than this Stifterian piety, this *synthesis of the Christian with the Antique, actually a Christian attitude*

synthesized with an antique belief in the powers of nature.
. . . It is not mannerism, not affectation when coming
from a person whose imaginative powers and whose soul
are of such purity as are Stifter's. The innermost nature of
Stifter's character seems to be engaged with the simplest of
natural objects; he attaches them to his own character and
releases them again to nature. . . .[79]

It is not coincidental, then, that the Austrian *fin-de-siècle* poet Hugo von
Hofmannsthal (1874-1929), like Stifter in *Bunte Steine,* introduced his
own collection of eighteenth- and nineteenth-century prose texts, *his*
education-oriented anthology *Deutsche Erzähler* (German Narrators) of
1912 with an Introduction incredibly "Stifterian." Like Stifter, Hofmannsthal made his selection following "an urge that is inherent in every
human being and which becomes clearly manifest in children and people
of that old, pure age: that we are seized by that which is harmonious, that
we integrate with it or serve it, to make that which is rich even richer or
else, as the Scriptures express it, to give those who have even more."[80]
Hofmannsthal's anthology, like Stifter's *Bunte Steine,* consists of a "chain"
of prose selections. They bear the theme common to both authors—the
theme of universal "love."[81] As in Stifter's prose collection, as in his and
Aprent's *Lesebuch zur Förderung humaner Bildung* of 1854, Hofmannsthal's
selections are intended to present "a Germany which is not quite there
anymore"—a world contrastive to "our atmosphere"—which has become
a world, so Hofmannsthal in the "Introduction," "thick and full of
prejudices, which however are not honest as those of the ancients . . .;
everywhere discord, dissension, inner reservation, nervous disorders are the
last remnants." In Hofmannsthal's story selections, "love" is "everywhere,"
"but not only the love of man toward woman, of the youth toward the
maiden, but of the friend to the friend as well, of the child to his parents,
of mankind to God, the love of the lonely to a flower, to a plant, to an
animal, to a violin, to the landscape. . . ."[82]

A poet with the same sensitivity and complexity as Hofmannsthal and
Stifter, Rainer Maria Rilke (1875-1931), is equally awed: next to Petrarch,
only Kleist and Stifter assume canonized stature! In 1913 Rilke writes:

A pensive reader of Stifter . . . could easily perceive that
this poetic narrator had realized his innermost profession at

that very moment when he—during an unforgettable day—first sought to attract an extremely distant point of a landscape by means of a telescope and then—in a vision of utter dismay—experienced an escape of space, of clouds and of objects, experiencing fright at such abundance that his startled disposition during these seconds beheld a world, as did Danae perceive the creation of Zeus.[83]

I conclude this portrayal of Adalbert Stifter with an appraisal of a contemporary Austrian writer, Peter Rosei (born 1946), who speaks of his own, of Peter Handke's, Thomas Bernhard's, and of G. F. Jonke's far-reaching indebtedness to Stifter in his essay of 1976, "Versuch über Stifter und einige Schriftsteller der Gegenwart" (Concerning Stifter and Several Contemporary Writers). According to Rosei, Handke's, Jonke's and, to a lesser degree, Bernhard's, but especially his own affinity for detailed landscape depictions often evoke the perception of existential isolation once a person in their works becomes lodged or wedged between artificial, unnatural "things" or events. However, Rosei observes that his own conception of Stifter departs somewhat from Handke's, Bernhard's, and Jonke's, because to him Stifter is "not the restorer of truth, of goodness, of beauty, [because] he does not play with these things, he has no distance from them. *Stifter tries to live his credo but fails time and again.* . . . In stating this opinion, [Stifter] is close to Handke, [since] writing per se for Stifter is a sort of escapism."[84] What unites Rosei with Bernhard, Handke, and Jonke is the following:

> [Stifter's] landscape is the natural stage for the people who appear in it. This I established by observing Stifter's depictions of interiors. After all, Stifter makes use of his landscapes in the same fashion he observes the principles of interior spaces: *everything is calculated optically.* . . . No matter how vast the space he uses to describe nature and its things, his real interest is not focused on them but on mankind. *Stifter strives to verify fanatically* time and again *that man's soul is plain, grand and good,* thus his credo. *That which unites Stifter with certain contemporary literary trends far beyond any skilled procedural methods is a similar existential situation.* . . . *When studying Stifter's imaginative*

> *prose closely it is difficult to avoid feeling that the abyss is*
> *open under the naively and ideally described relations, that*
> *Stifter attempts desperately to bridge this abyss or else, even*
> *better: to conceal it altogether. . . .* I regard this procedure to
> be only *an attempt to master existence.*[85]

Other voices will follow. They will be those who, with Adalbert Stifter, persist in their attempt to master existence by seeking to discover, protect, and preserve this fragile Law of Humanity: the "Gentle Law."

Notes

1. See Adalbert Stifter, "Autobiographisches Fragment" (from about one year before his death), reprint in Kurt Gerhard Fischer, *Adalbert Stifter. Leben und Werk in Briefen und Dokumenten* (Frankfurt, 1962), pp. 678-682.

2. It is debatable which of the terms "stories," "novellas," or "small novels" applies best to Stifter's shorter prose. For the most part all of it would fall into the three sub-genres; the narratives are highly descriptive, often simultaneously intensely dramatic, and frequently portray a person's life from youth to old age.

3. For the most extensive studies of Stifter's painting, see Fritz Novotny, *Adalbert Stifter als Maler* (Vienna/Munich: Anton Schroll, 1979). See also Franz Baumer, *Adalbert Stifter als Zeichner und Maler. Ein Bilderbuch* (Passau: Verlag Passavia, 1979), which contains excellent reproductions.

4. Gustav Konrad, "Adalbert Stifter," speaks of Stifter's "escape into imaginative literature." Here and elsewhere I choose to translate the German word and concept of *Dichtung* as "imaginative prose" or "imaginative literature."

5. See *SW*, XVIII, p. 138; also in Ursula Naumann, *Adalbert Stifter.* (Stuttgart: Sammlung Metzler, 1978), p. 16. All Stifter quotations, unless noted otherwise, are taken from Adalbert Stifter, *Sämtliche Werke,* ed. August Sauer, et al. (Prague, 1904ff), noted consecutively here as *SW*. For the superb, as yet incomplete critical edition by Alfred Doppler and Wolfgang Frühwald, 1978, see *Select Bibliography.*

6. See note 2.

7. See *SW*. XVII, p. 38; letter of 22 February 1850.

8. Quoted from Urban Roedl, *Adalbert Stifter in Selbstzeugnissen* (Reinbek b. Hamburg: Rowohlt Tb., 1965), p. 150.

9. See Moriz Enzinger, *Adalbert Stifter im Urteil seiner Zeit* (Graz/Vienna/Cologne: Hermann Böhlaus Nachf., 1968), pp. 128-133.

10. The *Bayrische Wald* is part of the *Böhmer Wald*, the (south)western extension of the *Böhmer Wald*, i.e., approximately between Regensburg and Passau, the north of the Danube.

11. In countless narratives the theme and motif of the "animalistic" as a component of man's character is prevalent; example, Adalbert Stifter, "We all have an animalistic character trait just as much as we have a divine one. And if the animalistic trait is not aroused, so we would think it was non-existent and that only the divine character trait would prevail." From A.S., *Zuversicht* (Trust), in *Bunte Steine. Späte Erzählungen*, ed. Max Stift (Augsburg, 1960), p. 360.

12. Far too little critical attention has been paid to Stifter's anti-revolutionary, educational, and in that sense philosophical, essays in the *Wiener Bote*.

13. Stifter's educational philosophy as a legacy of Johann Gottfried Herder's, Wilhelm von Humboldt's, and others of the eighteenth century still has to be studied in depth.

14. "Vorwort" in *Lesebuch zur Förderung humaner Bildung* (Graz: Akademische Druck- und Verlagsanstalt, 1982), p.v. Reprint of the original edition of 1854 (Pest: Heckenast).

15. Only his three small excerpted passages in translation exist to date: Margaret Gump, *Adalbert Stifter* (New York: Twayne, 1974), p. 74; David Luke, editor and translator of *Limestone und Other Stories [Tourmaline and The Recluse]* (New York: Harcourt, Brace & World, 1968), pp. 22-23, "Introduction;" Martin & Erika Swales, *Adalbert Stifter. A Critical Study* (London/Sidney: Cambridge University Press, 1984), minute excerpts on pp. 30, 31, 32. I have translated the "Forewords" to *Bunte Steine* (Colorful Stories) in their entirety; forthcoming with an exegesis.

16. Stifter's and Aprent's one-volume anthology is divided into two parts: the first is entitled "Von Außen" (From the Outside), the second "Nach Innen" (To Within).

17. See Moriz Enzinger, *Adalbert Stifter im Urteil seiner Zeit*, especially beginning in the fifties.

18. Ibid., pp. 229-231.
19. Ibid.
20. See note 2.
21. See David Luke, editor and translator, note 22. For translations of *Abdias, Brigitta, Rock Crystal,* and *Indian Summer,* see *Select Bibliography.*
22. Only recently did this novel find a skillful translator in Wendell Frye, *Indian Summer* (New York/Bern/Frankfurt am Main: Lang, 1985).
23. Stifter called it "eine Erzählung" (a narrative) instead of a novel.
24. As does Gustav Konrad in his otherwise excellent critical essay, "Adalbert Stifter," in *Deutsche Dichter des 19. Jahrhunderts,* ed. Benno von Wiese (Berlin: Erich Schmidt, 1969), p. 378.
25. *SW,* XIX, p. 93.
26. See Moriz Enzinger, *Adalbert Stifter im Urteil seiner Zeit,* pp. 229-231.
27. Ibid., p. 290.
28. Ibid.
29. Friedrich Nietzsche, *Menschlich, Allzumenschliches,* vol. 2, no. 109, ed. Karl Schlechta (Munich: Carl Hanser, 1960); also in Moriz Enzinger, *Adalbert Stifter im Urteil seiner Zeit,* p. 367.
30. Most likely cirrhosis of the liver and/or liver cancer.
31. Note Stifter's numerous canvasses of the Wittinghausen ruins, especially "Die Ruine Wittinghausen I," painted between 1833 and 1835 (Fritz Novotny no. 22), and "Die Ruine Wittinghausen II" (Novotny no. 42) from about 1839. See Note 9.
32. Stifter took this information from Franz von Palacky's *Geschichte von Böhmen* which names Witiko as the oldest known ancestor of the Rosenbergers in the twelfth century.
33. A striking affinity exists between Stifter's political philosophy and Adam Müller's (Berlin 1779–Vienna 1829) "Political Romanticism." A. Müller edited with Heinrich von Kleist the journal for art and literature, *Phoebus.* He was acquainted with Friedrich Schlegel and Metternich, whom he accompanied to Paris in 1815. Since 1827 he was *Hofrat* in Vienna. As political and social scientist he conceptionalized an organic catholic and universal type of state as a godly institution.
34. *SW,* XIX (6 August 1861), p. 282.

35. Note the striking resemblance to the political theories of Charles Montesquieu (1748, *L'Esprit de lois*), of Johann Gottfried Herder (1774, *Auch eine Philosophie zur Geschichte der Bildung der Menschheit*), and of Friedrich Schiller!

36. With *Witiko,* Stifter's "Gentle Law" has become magnified to encompass all laws upon which human conduct is based.

37. Note the similarity in title to Herder's *Briefe zur Beförderung der Humanität* (1793-1797): Humanity as the purpose and mission of mankind!

38. Of Stifter's twelve essays here, five have become the best-known: "Der Tandelmarkt" (The Open Market); "Aussicht und Betrachtungen von der Spitze des St. Stephansturmes" (Views and Observations from the Spire of St. Stephen's Cathedral); "Leben und Haushalt dreier Wiener Studenten" (Life and Ways of Living of Three Viennese Students); "Wiener Salonszenen" (Scenes of the Viennese Salons); and the most "telling," "Ein Gang durch die Katakomben" (A Stroll through the Catacombs).

39. It is an established fact that the "Snow"-chapter in Thomas Mann's *Magic Mountain* (1924) was inspired by Stifter's blizzard-essay of 1767 in *Aus dem Bayrischen Walde.*

40. In XII of *SW.*

41. Stifter's autobiographical reminiscence of his unrequited love for "Fanny" Greipl (from about 1827 to about 1835) is at play here.

42. The confessional tone of Stifter's existential experiences as a writer becomes obvious here: by identifing himself with the "Obrist," but especially with Augustinus, he will never be able to cease writing "his" portfolio (metaphorically speaking), since his own life, filled with paradoxes and dreams of a humanity "restored," never became synthesized.

43. See *SW,* XX, 216, his "confession" of 28 August 1764.

44. In addition to the most definitive and extensive three-volume study by Sengle (ibid.), see also *Begriffsbestimmung des literarischen Biedermeier,* ed. Elfriede Neubuhr, *Wege der Forschung,* vol. cccxviii (Darmstadt: Wissenschaftliche Buchgesellschaft, 1974); *Begriffsbestimmung des literarischen Realismus,* ed. Richard Brinkmann, ibid., vol. ccxii (ibid., 1969) and Fritz Martini, *Deutsche Literatur im Bürgerlichen Realismus. 1848-1898* (Stuttgart: J.B. Metzler, 1962ff).

45. A comparative study on Stifter's indebtedness to Schiller's aesthetics

has yet to be written, with special attention given to *Der Nachsommer* and *Nachkommenschaften.*

46. Particularly here (and elsewhere) I remain indebted to Ursula Naumann's insights in her *Adalbert Stifter,* here p. 66. I add that the careful cultivation of wastelands for utilitarian purposes is already a central theme in *Brigitta* (1843).

47. Ibid.

48. Stifter's wife Amelia Mohaupt had absolutely no understanding nor any feeling for his work as a writer or as a painter.

49. *SW,* XX, p. 147; 20 October 1833.

50. Stifter never sought instruction in painting; his frustration in painting assumed tremendous proportions, leading to destruction upon destruction.

51. A comparative study on his narrative styles and his techniques in painting has yet to be written.

52. Translated from Ursula Naumann, *Adalbert Stifter,* p. 90.

53. See Johann Joachim Winckelmann (1717-1768), *Gedanken über die Nachahmung der griechischen Werke in der Malerei und Bildhauer-kunst* (1755), advocating the imitation of Greek sublimical beauty as descriptively expressed in Greek sculpture (and painting), a stylistic necessity applicable to literature as well. Only through idealized, sublimical beauty would mankind advance toward a true humanity.

54. Compare Stifter's concept of art with Schiller's *Über die ästhetische Erziehung des Menschen in einer Reihe von Briefen* (1795): "Duty" and "Inclination" as antagonistic opposites for Kant are for Schiller reconcilable through the arts: "There is no other way to make the sensual individual become rational than by first making him aesthetic."

55. *SW,* XIV, p. 48. For Fritz Novotny, see note 3.

56. Adalbert Stifter quoted from Ursula Naumann, *Stifter,* p. 93.

57. Ibid., p. 91.

58. The nouns "Ding," "Dinge," "Dinglichkeiten" are perhaps the ones most frequently found in Stifter's *oeuvre.*

59. I have shown elsewhere Stifter's deep symbiotic relationship with children and with animals (see *Select Bibliography*). The naive, the unspoiled and naturally trusting individuals, especially children and animals, experience the most harmonious interaction with nature.

60. I intend to pursue such aesthetic considerations elsewhere in a two-fold endeavor: to address Stifter's legacy to Johann Joachim Winckelmann and to compare Stifter's and Theodor Storm's (1817-1888) relationships of imaginative prose to pictures and other art objects.

61. For ruins in Stifter's prose, see especially *Abdias* (there the Roman ruins of North Africa), *Der Hochwald* (the destruction of Wittinghausen), *Der Nachsommer* (Wittinghausen constructed), and others. For ruins in paintings unquestionably attributed to Stifter, see "Friedberg und die Ruine Wittinghausen" (no. 13), "Klosterruine im Mondschein" (no. 14), "Friedberg und die Ruine Wittinghausen" (no. 15), "Die Ruine Wittinghausen" (no. 22), "Die Ruine Wittinghausen (no. 41), "Die Ruine Wittinghausen" (no. 42), "Römische Ruinen" (no. 69), "Griechische Tempelruinen: Die Heiterkeit" (no. 78), all in Fritz Novotny, *Adalbert Stifter als Maler.*

62. Kefermarkt: northeast of Linz; see Stifter's lecture "Über den geschnitzten Hochaltar in der Kirche zu Kefermarkt" in 1852, for a breathtaking section-photo of the carving, see Peter Becher, et al, eds. *Im Zeichen der Rose. Leben und Werk Adalbert Stifters* (Munich: Rieß-Druck, 1986), p. 49.

63. See Moriz Enzinger, *Adalbert Stifter im Urteil seiner Zeit.*

64. Note the striking similarity to Gotthold Ephraim Lessing's (1729-1781) grand historical, theological, and teleological vision and prophecy of the infallible "coming of humanity" in his *Die Erziehung des Menschengeschlechts* (1780, The Education of Mankind).

65. The poet as priest had his origins in eighteenth-century German Pietism, culminating there in the works of Friedrich Gottlieb Klopstock (1724-1803). "He" is then seen in Lessing, in Schiller, in Friedrich Hardenberg Novalis (1772-1801), and especially again in Stifter: in most humanistic-idealistic literature served to educate man toward ever higher levels of culture.

66. Adalbert Stifter, *Kleine Schriften* (Leipzig: Insel, 1940), p. 399.

67. See especially the final third of the "Foreword."

68. See also the first two versions of the *Mappe,* above.

69. Critics have noted the professed influence of Gottlieb Wilhelm Leibniz (1647-1716) on Stifter's idealistic philosophy, particularly Leibniz' concept of the animated, harmonious order of entelechies

he termed monads.

70. For example, in *Abdias* and the *Hagestolz* both protagonists fail to heed the laws of nature and thus live out their meager lives in loneliness.

71. Adalbert Stifter, from his preamble to *Abdias* (1843) in *Sämtliche Werke,* ed. H. Geiger, vol. 1 (Berlin/Darmstadt: Tempel, 1968), pp. 523 and 524.

72. The use of telescopes and windows to draw near, frame, and focus the unknown is a very frequent device found in all of Stifter's works.

73. See *Der Hochwald* (1841).

74. Max Brod's *Über Franz Kafka* (Fischer TB, April 1981) contains numerous references to Kafka's admiration for Stifter, especially to Stifter's *Studien,* to *Der Nachsommer,* and to the "Sanfte Gesetz" (pp. 46 and 330). According to Brod, Kafka especially admired Stifter's "search for a true, uncomplicated, spiritually guided existence." See also Naomi Ritter,"Stifter und Kafka: Berürungs- punkte," *VASILO,* Jg. 27, 1978, Folge 3/4, pp. 129-135.

75. *SW, XX,* p. 257.

76, See Sepp Domandl, *Adalbert Stifters Lesebuch und die geistigen Strömungen zur Jahrhundertmitte* (Linz: Oö Landesverlag, 1976), and Heidi Owren, *Herders Bildungsprogramm und seine Auswirkungen im 18. und 19. Jahrhundert* (Heidelberg: Carl Winter, 1985), especially pp. 197-215 on Stifter in particular.

77. *SW, XVII,* p. 38; letter of 22 February 1850, my translation.

78. Adalbert Stifter, 9 January 1845; quoted from Ursula Naumann, *Adalbert Stifter,* p. 16, my translation.

79. Hugo von Hofmannsthal, from Richard Exner, "Hugo von Hof- mannsthal zu Adalbert Stifter. Notizen und Entwürfe," *Adalbert Stifter. Studien und Interpretationen. Gedenkschrift zum 100. Todestage,* ed. Lothar Stiehm (Heidelberg: Lothar Stiehm, 1968), pp. 304-305. Italics and translation mine.

80. Hugo von Hofmannsthal, ed. *Deutsche Erzähler* (Wiesbaden: Insel, 1958 reprint), p. 5 from "Einleitung." First published 1912 by Insel in four volumes, Leipzig.

81. Ibid., pp 5-10.

82. Note the striking similarities here between Stifter's "Foreword" and Hofmannsthal's "Introduction," my translation.

83. Rainer Maria Rilke: quoted and translated from Joachim W. Storck, "Stifter und Rilke," in Lothar Stiehm, ed. *Adalbert Stifter Studien und Interpretationen*, p. 285, my translation.

84. See Peter Rosei's essay "Versuch über Stifter und einige Schriftsteller der Gegenwart," in *Literatur und Kritik* (April 1928), pp. 103-165, my translation. For the remainder of Rosei's assessment, pp. 161-167. All italics mine. Also see Erika Tunner, "Stifters Faszination auf österreichische Autoren der Gegenwart: Peter Handke, Peter Rosei, Jutta Schutting, Hermann Friedl, und Reinhold Aumaier," in *VASILO,* Jg. 36 (1987), Folge 3/4, pp. 57-70, and Alfred Doppler, "Die unaufhebbare Lebensspannung. Themen und Tendenzen bei Adalbert Stifter und Thomas Bernhard," ibid., pp. 19-29.

85. Rosei's original reads: "Ich sehe in meinem Vorgehen nur einen Versuch der Existenzbewältigung." Ibid., p. 166. Italics and translation mine.

Select Bibliography

I. Current Works by Stifter in German
"Autobiographisches Fragment." Reprint in Kurt Gerhard Fischer,
Adalbert Stifters Leben und Werk in Briefen und Dokumenten.
Frankfurt am Main, 1962.

Current in *Reclam*
Abdias, 3913.
Bergkristall, 3912.
Der beschriebene Tännling, 7548.
Brigitta, 3911.
Drei Schmiede ihres Schicksals, 9863.
Granit and "Vorrede" zu *Bunte Steine,* 7602 and 4195.
Der Hagestolz, 4194.
Der Hochwald, 3861.
Kalkstein, 9932.
Der Kondor; Das Heidedorf, 8990.
Die Mappe meines Urgroßvaters, 7963.
Nachkommenschaften, 7924.
Der Waldsteig, 3898.
Wien. Die Sonnenfinsternis, 8850.
Der Hagestolz. In: *Deutsche Erzähler.* Hugo von Hoffmansthal, ed. with
"Einleitung." Wiesbaden: Insel, 1912. 4 vols. Wiesbaden: Insel,
1958. 1 vol.
Brigitta; Erläuterungen und Dokumente, ed. Ulrich Dittmann. Reclam
8109. Stuttgart, 1970.
*Lesebuch zur Förderung humaner Bildung in Realschulen und in andern zu
weiterer Bildung vorbereitenden Mittelschulen.* Pest, 1854.
Reprint ed. Richard Pils. Graz, 1982.
Zur Psychologie der Thiere mit einem Nachwort von K.G. Fischer. Linz,
1963.

Collected Works
Gesammelte Werke, ed. Max Stefl. 6 vols. Leipzig 1939-1942. Wiesbaden,
1952.
Gesammelte Werke, eds. Michael Benedikt, Herbert Hornstein. 6 vols.
Bielefeld 1956/1957.

Gesammelte Werke, ed. Konrad Steffen. 14 vols. Basel/Stuttgart, 1962.
Sämtliche Werke, eds. August Sauer, et al. Prague 1904. Reichenberg 1927.
  Graz 1958/1960. Reprint: Hildesheim 1972.
Sämtliche Werke, ed. Hannsludwig Geiger. 3 vols. Darmstadt 1969.
Werke und Briefe. Historisch-Kritische Gesamtausgabe, eds. Alfred Doppler
  and Wolfgang Frühwald. Stuttgart 1978.

Bibliographies and Sources of Material

"Die Bibliographie der Veröffentlichungen zum 100." Todestag. In:
  VASILO 18, 1969, Folge 1/2, pp. 52-71.
Werner Heck. *Das Werk Adalbert Stifters. 1840-1940. Versuch einer*
  Bibliographie. Vienna 1954.
Eduard Eisenmeir. *Adalbert Stifter-Bibliographie.* In: *Schriftenreihe des A.S.*
  Instituts. Vol. 21. Linz 1964.
_____. *Adalbert Stifter-Bibliographie* 1. Fortsetzung. *Schriftenreihe* vol.
  26. Linz 1971.
_____. *Adalbert Stifter-Bibliographie* 2. Fortsetzung. *Schriftenreihe* vol.
  31. Linz 1978.
Ursula Naumann. *Adalbert Stifter.* Sammlung Metzler. Stuttgart 1979.
Karl Privat. *Adalbert Stifter. Sein Leben in Selbstzeugnissen, Briefen und*
  Berichten. Berlin 1946.
W.A. Reichart and W.H. Grilk. "Stifters Werk in Amerika und England.
  Eine Bibliographie." *VASILO* 9, 1960, Folge 1/2, pp. 39-42.
Herbert Seidler. "Adalbert-Stifter-Forschung 1945-1970." In: *Zeitschrift für*
  deutsche Philologie 91, 1970.
_____. *Die Adalbert Stifter-Forschung der siebziger Jahre.* In: *VASILO,*
  Jg. 30. 1981, Folge 3/4, pp. 89-134.
Urban Roedl. "Bibliographie." In U.R. *Adalbert Stifter in Selbstzeugnissen*
  und Bilddokumenten. Reinbek b. Hamburg: Rowohlt Tb.,
  1965.
Takashi Yoneda. "Stifters Werk in Japan. Eine Bibliographie." In:
  VASILO 12, 1963, pp. 64-66.

II. Works by Stifter in English

Abdias. Translated by N.C. Wormleighton and H. Mayer. In : *German*
  Narrative Prose, ed. E.J. Engel. Vol. 1. London 1965.
Brigitta. Translated by Edward Fitzgerald. Rodale Press. 1957.
_____. Translated by Hermann Salinger. In: *19th Century German*

Tales. New York: Ungar, 1966.

Brigitta with *Abdias; Limestone;* and *The Forest Path.* Translated by Helen Watanabe-O'Kelly. London: Angel Books, 1990. Now also in Penguin Books, London/New York, 1990.

Indian Summer. Translated by Wendell Frye. New York: Peter Lang, 1985.

Limestone and Other Stories (Tourmaline; The Recluse). Translation and Introduction by David Luke. New York: Harcourt, Brace & World, 1968.

Rock Crystal; A Christmas Tale. Translated by Elizabeth Mayer and Marianne Moore. Pantheon Books, 1945. Revised 1965.

_____. Translated by Lee M. Hollander. In *The German Classics of the Nineteenth and Twentieth Centuries. Masterpieces of German Literature Translated into English,* ed. Kuno Francke, vol. 8. Albany, NY, 1914.

III. Secondary Works on Stifter in English

Andrews, John S. "The Reception of Stifter in Nineteenth-Century Britain." In: *Modern Language Review,* 53 (1958), 537-544.

Blackall, Eric A. *Adalbert Stifter. A Critical Study.* Cambridge, 1948.

Branscombe, Peter. "Some Reflections on the Use of Dialogue in Stifter's Stories." In: *Adalbert Stifter Heute,* eds. Johann Lachinger, et al. Linz (1985), 12-24.

Bruford, Walter H. "Adalbert Stifter: 'Der Nachsommer.'" In: W.H.B., *The German Tradition of Self-Education. 'Bildung' from Humboldt to Thomas Mann.* London (1975), 128-146.

Gillespie, Gerald. "Space and Time Seen through Stifter's Telescope." In: *German Quarterly* 37 (1964), 120-130.

Gump, Margaret. *Adalbert Stifter.* New York: Twayne, 1974.

Klarner, Gudrun. *Pedagogic Design and Literary Form in the Work of Adalbert Stifter.* Frankfurt am Main/Bern/New York, 1986.

Mason, Eve. "Stifter's 'Turmalin': A Reconsideration." In: *Modern Language Review,* 72 (1977), 348-358.

Oertel-Sjögren, Christine. *The Marble Statue as Idea. Collected Essays on Adalbert Stifter's 'Der Nachsommer.'* Chapel Hill, 1972.

Pascal, Roy. "Adalbert Stifter. 'Indian Summer.'" In: R.P. *The German Novel. Studies.* Manchester (1956), 52-75.

Schoolfield, George. "The Churchmen in Stifter's 'Witiko.'" In: *Monats-*

hefte 43/6. Wisconsin (1951), 285-293.

Stern, Josef Peter, "Propitiations: Adalbert Stifter." In: J.P.S. *Reinterpreta-tions. Seven Studies in Nineteenth-Century German Literature.* London (1964), 239-300.

————. "Stifter's Fiction. 'Erhebung' without Motion." In: *Novel. A Forum on Fiction*, vol. 1. Province (1968), 239-250. Reprinted in *Idylles and Realities. Studies in Nineteenth-Century Literature.* London (1971), 97-122.

Stillmark, Alexander. "Stifter and Wordsworth. Observations on Some Affinities in Creative Imagination." In: *Adalbert Stifter Heute,* eds. Hohann, Lachinger, et al. Linz (1985), 25-36.

————. "Stifter contra Hebbel. An Examination of the Sources of Their Disagreement." In: *German Life and Letters*, vol. ?, (1967), 21-22; (1968), 93-107.

————. "Stifter's Early Portraits of the Artist. Stages in the Growth of an Aesthetic." In: *Forum of Modern Language Studies* 11 (1975), 142-164.

————. *Stifter's Symbolism of Beauty. The Significance of the Flower in His Works.* In: *Oxford German Studies* (1971/1972), 74-92.

Stopp, Frederick J. "The Symbolism of Stifter's 'Kalkstein.'" In: *German Life and Letters* (1953/1954), 116-125.

Struc, Roman. "The Threat of Chaos. Stifter's 'Bergkristall' and Thomas Mann's 'Schnee.'" In: *Modern Language Review* 24 (1963), 323-332.

Swales, Erika. "The Doubly Woven Text: Reflections on Stifter's Narrative Mode." In: *Adalbert Stifter Heute.*

———— and Martin Swales. *Adalbert Stifter. A Critical Study.* Cambridge, 1984.

Whiton, John. "Symbols of Social Revival on Stifter's 'Bergkristall.'" In: *Germanic Review* 47 (1972), 259-280.

IV. Major Studies on Stifter in German

Adalbert Stifter-Institut des Landes Oberösterreich. Vierteljahresschrift. In: *VASILO.* Linz, 1952.

Aspetsberger, Friedbert. "Die Aufschreibung des Lebens. Zu Stifters 'Mappe.'" In: *VASILO* 27, 1978. Folge 1/2 (1978), 11-38.

Bandet, Jean-Louis. *Adalbert Stifter. Introduction à la Lecture de ses Nouvelles.* Université de Haute-Bretagne, 1974.

Bertram, Ernst. *Studien zu Adalbert Stifters Novellentechnik.* Dortmund, 1907, 1966.

Böhler, Michael. *Formen und Wandlungen des Schönen. Untersuchungen zum Schönheitsbegriff Adalbert Stifters.* Bern, 1967.

Dehn, Wilhelm. *Ding und Vernunft. Zur Interpretation von Adalbert Stifters Dichtung.* Bonn, 1969.

Domandl, Sepp. "Die Idee des Schicksals bei Adalbert Stifter." In: *VASILO* 23. 1974. Folge 3/4, pp. 81-99.

Doppler, Alfred. "Adalbert Stifters Verhältnis zur Geschichte." In: *Stifter-Symposion.* Linz (1978), 64-69.

Enzinger, Moriz. *Adalbert Stifter im Urteil seiner Zeit.* Vienna/Graz/Cologne: Hermann Böhlaus Nachf., 1968.

_____. *Gesammelte Aufsätze zu Adalbert Stifter.* Vienna, 1967.

Fischer, K.G. *Adalbert Stifter. Psychologische Beiträge zur Biographie.* Linz, 1961.

_____. *Die Pädagogik des Menschenmöglichen. Adalbert Stifter.* Linz, 1962.

Hertling, Gunter H. "Adalbert Stifters Jagdallegorie 'Der beschriebene Tännling': Schande durch Schändung." In: *VASILO* 29, 1980, Folge 1/2, pp. 41-46.

_____. "Adalbert Stifters zeitlose Botschaft: Obadja-Abdias." In: *VASILO* 25, 1976, Folge 3/4, pp. 117-129.

Irmscher, Hans Dietrich. *Adalbert Stifter. Wirklichkeitserfahrung und gegenständliche Darstellung.* Munich, 1971.

Konrad, Gustav. "Adalbert Stifter." In *Deutsche Dichter des 19. Jahrhunderts,* ed. Benno von Wiese. Berlin: Erich Schmidt Verlag, 1969, pp. 336-386.

Lange, Viktor "Stifter. 'Der Nachsommmer.'" In: *Der Deutsche Roman. Vom Barock bis zur Gegenwart,* ed. Benno von Wiese. Vol. II. Düsseldorf: August Bagel Verlag, 1963, pp. 34-75.

Lunding, Erik. *Adalbert Stifter. Mit einem Anhang über Kierkegaard und die existentielle Literaturwissenschaft.* Copenhagen, 1946.

Martini, Fritz. *Deutsche Literatur im Bürgerlichen Realismus. 1848-1895.* Third edition. Stuttgart: Metzler, 1974, pp. 499-566.

Müller, Joachim. *Adalbert Stifter. Weltbild und Dichtung.* Halle, 1956.

Naumann, Ursula. *Adalbert Stifter.* In: *Sammlung Metzler* 186. Stuttgart, 1979.

Novotny, Fritz. *Adalbert Stifter als Maler.* Fourth edition. Vienna/Munich:

Anton Schroll, 1979.

Roedl, Urban. *Adalbert Stifter in Selbstzeugnissen und Bilddokumenten.* In: Rowohlts Monographien. Reinbek bei Hamburg, 1965.

Seidler, Herbert. "Adalbert-Stifter-Forschung 1945-1970." In: *Zeitschrift für deutsche Philologie* 91, 1, 2 (1972), 113-157, 252-284.

_____. "Die Adalbert-Stifter-Forschung der Siebziger Jahre," *VASILO* vol. 30, nos. 3/4 (1981), pp. 89-134.

_____. "Adalbert Stifters späte Erzählkunst im Rahmen des bürgerlichen Realismus." In: *Stifter Symposion,* Linz (1978), pp. 44-47.

Selge, Martin. *Adalbert Stifter. Poesie aus dem Geist der Naturwissenschaft.* Stuttgart, 1976.

Sengle, Friedrich. *Biedermeierzeit. Deutsche Literatur im Spannungsfeld zwischen Restauration und Revolution.* 3 vols. Stuttgart: Metzler. 1971-1980. Especially vol. 3, pp. 952-1019.

Steffen, Konrad. *Adalbert Stifter. Deutungen.* Basel/Stuttgart, 1955.

Stopp, Frederick. "Die Symbolik in Stifters 'Bunten Steinen.'" In: *Deutsche Vierteljahresschrift* 28 (1954), 165-193.

Zoldester, Philip H. *Adalbert Stifters Weltanschauung.* Bern, 1970.

Index